Lecture Notes in Artificial Intelli

Subseries of Lecture Notes in Computer Scie

Edited by J. G. Carbonell and J. Siekmann

T0250570

Lecture Notes in Computer Science

Edited by G. Goos, J. Hartmanis, and J. van Leeuwen

Springer
Berlin
Heidelberg
New York
Barcelona
Hong Kong
London
Milan
Paris
Tokyo

Petr Sojka   Ivan Kopeček
Karel Pala (Eds.)

Text, Speech and Dialogue

5th International Conference, TSD 2002
Brno, Czech Republic, September 9-12, 2002
Proceedings

Springer

Series Editors

Jaime G. Carbonell, Carnegie Mellon University, Pittsburgh, PA, USA
Jörg Siekmann, University of Saarland, Saarbrücken, Germany

Volume Editors

Petr Sojka
Masaryk University, Faculty of Informatics
Department of Programming Systems and Communication
Botanická 68a, 602 00 Brno, Czech Republic
E-mail: sojka@informatics.muni.cz

Ivan Kopeček
Karel Pala
Masaryk University, Faculty of Informatics
Department of Information Technologies
Botanická 68a, 602 00 Brno, Czech Republic
E-mail: {kopecek,pala}@informatics.muni.cz

Cataloging-in-Publication Data applied for

Die Deutsche Bibliothek - CIP-Einheitsaufnahme

Text, speech and dialogue : 5th international conference ; proceedings /
TSD 2002, Brno, Czech Republic, September 9 - 12, 2002. Petr Sojka ... (ed.). -
Berlin ; Heidelberg ; New York ; Barcelona ; Hong Kong ; London ; Milan ;
Paris ; Tokyo : Springer, 2002
  (Lecture notes in computer science ; Vol. 2448 : Lecture notes in
artificial intelligence)
  ISBN 3-540-44129-8

CR Subject Classification (1998): I.2.7, H.3, H.4, I.7

ISSN 0302-9743
ISBN 3-540-44129-8 Springer-Verlag Berlin Heidelberg New York

Springer-Verlag Berlin Heidelberg New York
a member of BertelsmannSpringer Science+Business Media GmbH

http://www.springer.de

© Springer-Verlag Berlin Heidelberg 2002

Typesetting: Camera-ready by Petr Sojka from source files by respective authors,
data conversion by Petr Sojka and PTP-Berlin, Stefan Sossna e.K.
Printed on acid-free paper   SPIN: 10871089   06/3142   5 4 3 2 1 0

Preface

The Text, Speech and Dialogue (TSD) Conference 2002, it should be noticed, is now being held for the fifth time and we are pleased to observe that in its short history it has turned out to be an international forum successfully intertwining the basic fields of NLP. It is our strong hope that the conference contributes to a better understanding between researchers from the various areas and promotes more intensive mutual cooperation. So far the communication between man and computers has displayed a one-way nature, humans have to know how the machines work and only then can they "understand" them. The opposite, however, is still quite far from being real, our understanding of how our "user-friendly" computers can understand us humans is not deep enough yet. A lot of work has to be done both in the near and distant future. Let TSD 2002 be a modest contribution to this goal.

The conference also serves well in its second purpose: to facilitate researchers meeting in the NLP field from Western and Eastern Europe. Moreover, many participants now come from other parts of the world, thus making TSD a real crossroads for researchers in the NLP area. This volume contains the proceedings of this conference held in Brno, September 9–12, 2002. We were honored to have as keynote speakers James Pustejovsky from Brandeis University, and Ronald Cole from the University of Colorado.

We would like to thank all the Program Committee members and external reviewers for their conscientious and diligent reviewing work. This year we had a total of 66 accepted papers out of 134 submitted, altogether contributed by 182 authors. It can be seen that this time the competition was quite tough. We thank all of the authors for their high-quality contributions. Generous thanks are due to all the members of the Organizing Committee for their tireless efforts in organizing the conference. We deeply appreciate the help and cooperation of the Chair of the Program Committee, Hynek Hermansky. We would like also to express our sincere thanks to Dagmar Janoušková and Dana Komárková whose dedicated help contributed substantially to the preparation of the conference, and to Petr Sojka for his TEXpertise which resulted in the nice volume with a subject index which you are holding in your hands just now. We hope that you will be inspired by the conference and the proceedings, and that the program meets your expectations.

July 2002

Ivan Kopeček, Karel Pala
Chairs of the Organizing Committee, TSD 2002

Organization

TSD 2002 was organized by the Faculty of Informatics, Masaryk University, in cooperation with the Faculty of Applied Sciences, University of West Bohemia in Plzeň. The conference webpage is located at www.fi.muni.cz/tsd2002/

Program Committee

Jelinek, Frederick (USA), *general chair*
Hermansky, Hynek (USA), *executive chair*
Eneko, Agirre, (Spain)
Baudoin, Geneviève (France)
Ferencz, Attila (Romania)
Hajičová, Eva (Czech Republic)
Hlaváčová, Jaroslava (Czech Republic)
Hovy, Eduard (USA)
Kopeček, Ivan (Czech Republic)
Krauwer, Steven (The Netherlands)
Krishnamurthy, Ramesh (UK)
Matoušek, Václav (Czech Republic)
Nöth, Elmar (Germany)
Oliva, Karel (Czech Republic)
Pala, Karel (Czech Republic)
Pavesić, Nikola (Slovenia)
Petkevič, Vladimír (Czech Republic)
Psutka, Josef (Czech Republic)
Rothkrantz, Leon (The Netherlands)
Schukat-Talamazzini, E. Günter (Germany)
Skrelin, Pavel (Russia)
Vintsiuk, Taras (Ukraine)
Wilks, Yorick (UK)

Organizing Committee

Robert Batůšek, Pavel Cenek, Jan Černocký, Pavel Gaura, Aleš Horák, Dagmar Janoušková, Dana Komárková (Secretary), Ivan Kopeček (Co-chair), Karel Pala (Co-chair), Martin Povolný, Pavel Smrž, Petr Sojka (Proceedings), Marek Veber

Supported by:

International Speech Communication Association

Table of Contents

II Speech

III Dialogue

Part I

Text

"**Text**: a book or other written or printed work, regarded in terms of its content rather than its physical form: *a text which explores pain and grief.*"
NODE (New, Oxford Dictionary of English), Oxford, OUP, 1998, page 1998, meaning 1.

Part I

Text

A Common Solution for Tokenization
and Part-of-Speech Tagging*
One-Pass Viterbi Algorithm vs. Iterative Approaches

Jorge Graña, Miguel A. Alonso, and Manuel Vilares

Departamento de Computación
Universidad de La Coruña, Campus de Elviña s/n
15071 - La Coruña, Spain
E-mail: grana@dc.fi.udc.es, alonso@dc.fi.udc.es, vilares@dc.fi.udc.es

Abstract. Current taggers assume that input texts are already tokenized, i.e. correctly segmented in *tokens* or high level information units that identify each individual component of the texts. This working hypothesis is unrealistic, due to the heterogeneous nature of the application texts and their sources. The greatest troubles arise when this segmentation is ambiguous. The choice of the correct segmentation alternative depends on the context, which is precisely what taggers study.

In this work, we develop a tagger able not only to decide the tag to be assigned to every token, but also to decide whether some of them form or not the same term, according to different segmentation alternatives. For this task, we design an extension of the Viterbi algorithm able to evaluate streams of tokens of different lengths over the same structure. We also compare its time and space complexities with those of the classic and iterative versions of the algorithm.

1 Introduction

Some languages, like Galician or Spanish, show complex phenomena that we have to handle before tagging. Among other tasks, the segmentation process is responsible for identifying information units such as sentences or words. In the case of words, for instance, the problem is that the spelling of a word does not always coincide with the linguistic concept. Therefore, we have two options:

1. The simpler approaches just consider "spelled words" and extend the tags in order to represent relevant phenomena. For instance, the Spanish word reconocerse (*to recognize oneself*) could be tagged as V+Pro even when it is formed by a verb and an enclitic pronoun, and the words of the Spanish expression a pesar de (*in spite of*) would be respectively tagged as P13, P23 and P33 even when they constitute only one

---

* This work has been partially supported by the Spanish Government (under the projects TIC2000-0370-C02-01 and HP2001-0044), and by the Galician Government (under the project PGIDT01PXI10506PN).

term[1]. However, this approach is not valid for Galician because its great morphological complexity would produce an excessive growth of the tag set, and the process of building reference texts containing all those tags in a significantly representative number of situations would be an extremely hard task.

2. Another solution is not to extend the basic tag set. As an advantage, the complexity of the tagging process is not affected by a high number of tags. As a drawback, this approach makes the tasks of the tokenizer more complex. Now, it not only has to identify "spelled words", but often also has either to split one word into several words, or join several words in only one.

In our work, we have chosen the second option. The greatest troubles arise when this segmentation is ambiguous. For instance, the words in the Spanish expression sin embargo will normally be tagged together as a conjunction (*however*), but in some context they could be a sequence of a preposition and a noun (*without seizure*). In the same way, the Galician word polo can be a noun (*chicken*), or the contraction of the preposition por and the article o (*by the*), or even the verbal form pos with the enclitic pronoun o (*put it*).

In this way, the preprocessor should only perform the detection and pretagging of alternatives. The choice of the correct one depends on the context, which is precisely what is studied by the tagger. In consequence, the aim of the present work is to develop a tagger able not only to decide the tag to be assigned to every token, but also to decide whether some of them form or not the same term, and assign the appropriate number of tags on the basis of the alternatives provided by the preprocessor. For this task, we extend the Viterbi algorithm in order to evaluate streams of tokens of different lengths over the same structure. Finally, we will perform an intuitive study of performances by comparing time and space complexities of the new algorithm with those of the classic and iterative versions.

2 Viterbi-L: The Viterbi Algorithm on Lattices

2.1 Why Lattices?

In the context of part-of-speech tagging with Hidden Markov Models (HMMs), the classic version of the Viterbi algorithm [5] is applied on trellises, where the first row contains the words of the sentence to be tagged, and the possible tags appear in columns below the words. However, let us consider, for instance, a sentence in which the expression sin embargo appears. As we can see in Figure 1, problems arise when we try to situate the tag C because, in both options, the tag should apply to the whole expression, and hence the paths marked with dashed lines should not be allowed, and the ones marked with thick lines should be allowed.

We can represent the kind of ambiguous segmentations described above more comfortably by using lattices. In these structures, the arcs that conform the paths have their origin and target points in the gaps between words. The labels of these arcs contain the tags, as is shown in Figure 2, where we can see that it is even possible to represent overlapped dependencies.

---

[1] To simplify, in this work, we use Adj for adjective, Adv for adverb, C for conjunction, Det for determiner, P for preposition, Pro for pronoun, S for substantive, and V for verb. The tags that appear in real life come from projects GALENA (*Generation of Natural Language Analyzers*) and CORGA (*Reference Corpus of Current Galician*). See http://coleweb.dc.fi.udc.es for more information on both projects.

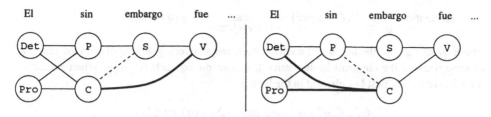

Fig. 1. Trellises cannot represent ambiguous segmentations.

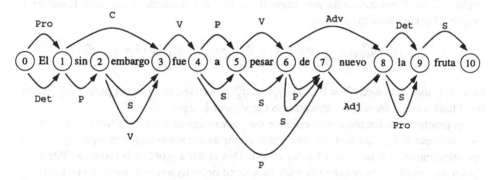

Fig. 2. Ambiguous segmentations represented on a lattice.

For the purposes of a later discussion, we indicate that this lattice contains 20 arcs, with which we can build 234 possible paths. The lengths of these paths are 7, 8, 9 or 10 tokens. The correct tagging is the one formed by the 8 arcs drawn in the upper part of the lattice, and corresponds to the following sense: *He however went to weigh again the fruit* (literal translation).

2.2 The Viterbi-L Equations

The equations of the Viterbi algorithm can be adapted to process a language model operating on a lattice as follows [1]. Instead of the words, the gaps between the words are enumerated (see Figure 2), and an arc between two gaps can span one or more words, such that an arc is represented by a triple (t, t', q), starting at time t, ending at time t' and representing state q. We introduce accumulators $\Delta_{t,t'}(q)$ that collect the maximum probability of state q covering words from position t to t'. We use $\delta_{i,j}(q)$ to denote the probability of the derivation emitted by state q having a terminal yield that spans positions i to j.

- Initialization: $\Delta_{0,t}(q) = P(q|q_s)\, \delta_{0,t}(q)$.
- Recursion:

$$\Delta_{t,t'}(q) = \max_{(t'',t,q') \in \text{Lattice}} \Delta_{t'',t}(q')\, P(q|q')\, \delta_{t,t'}(q) \quad \text{for } 1 \leq t < T \quad (1)$$

– Termination: $\displaystyle\max_{Q\in\mathcal{Q}^*} P(Q, \text{Lattice}) = \max_{(t,T,q)\in\text{Lattice}} \Delta_{t,T}(q)\, P(q_e|q).$

where q_s and q_e are the initial and ending states, respectively. Additionally, it is necessary to keep track of the elements in the lattice that maximized each $\Delta_{t,t'}(q)$. When reaching time T, we get the best last element in the lattice

$$(t_1^m, T, q_1^m) = \arg\max_{(t,T,q)\in\text{Lattice}} \Delta_{t,T}(q)\, P(q_e|q)$$

Setting $t_0^m = T$, we collect the arguments $(t'', t, q') \in$ Lattice that maximized Equation 1 by going backwards in time:

$$(t_{i+1}^m, t_i^m, q_{i+1}^m) = \arg\max_{(t'',t_i^m,q')\in\text{Lattice}} \Delta_{t'',t_i^m}(q')\, P(q_i^m|q')\, \delta_{t_i^m,t_{i-1}^m}(q_i^m)$$

for $i \geq 1$, until we reach $t_k^m = 0$. Now, $q_1^m \ldots q_k^m$ is the best sequence of phrase hypothesis (read backwards). We will call this process the Viterbi-L algorithm.

In practice, our intention is to estimate the parameters of our HMM from tagged texts, and use linear interpolation of uni-, bi-, and trigrams as our smoothing technique [3], i.e. our operating model will be a second order HMM. This is not a problem because the Viterbi-L algorithm described above can work with the second order hypothesis simply by considering pairs of tags (or states) as labels of the arcs, instead of only one tag (or state).

2.3   Complexity of the Viterbi-L Algorithm

Intuitively, we can consider the space complexity as the number of probability accumulators that we have to store during execution. In this version, we have one accumulator per arc. For time complexity, we consider the number of operations that we have to perform. This is, for a given arc, the number of arcs reaching the origin point of the arc under consideration. For instance, in order to pass Viterbi-L on the lattice of Figure 2, we need 20 accumulators and 36 operations.

However, we have to make the following reflection. With this simple version of the algorithm, the shortest paths have priority because they involve a smaller number of multiplications and hence they obtain a better cumulative probability. This is a problem, since the shortest paths do not always correspond to correct interpretations.

To avoid this problem, we could consider the individual evaluation of lattices with paths of the same length, and their subsequent comparison. It would therefore also be necessary to define an objective criterion for that comparison. If the tagging paradigm used is the framework of the HMMs, as is our case, a consistent criterion is the comparison of the normalization of the cumulative probabilities. Let us call p_i the cumulative probability of the best path in a lattice with paths of length i tokens. In the case of Figure 2, we would have p_7, p_8, p_9 and p_{10}. These values are not directly comparable, but if we use logarithmic probabilities, we can obtain normalized values by dividing them by the number of tokens. In this case, $p_7/7$, $p_8/8$, $p_9/9$ and $p_{10}/10$ are now comparable, and we can select the best path from the best lattice as the most probable interpretation. One reason to support the use of HMMs is that in other tagging paradigms the criteria for comparison may not be so easy to identify.

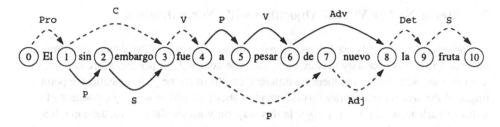

Fig. 3. A lattice with conflictive paths.

However, the number of different lattices to evaluate is not always the number of different lengths for the paths. For instance, we can see in Figure 3 how two paths of the same length (the one that only uses the upper arcs of the lattice, and the one that uses lower arcs when available, both of 8 tokens) can produce another path with different length (the one of 7 tokens marked with dashed arcs). Therefore, we could need more than one lattice to represent the paths of the same length without conflicts. In the case of Figure 2, although we have 4 possible lengths for the paths (7, 8, 9 or 10 tokens), we need a total of 6 lattices, which come from the mutual exclusion of the different alternatives of each ambiguous segmentation. This analysis is shown in the decision tree of Figure 4. To save space, we have not drawn the corresponding lattices, but for each of them we indicate: the number of possible paths, the length of those paths in tokens, the number of arcs in the lattice, and the number of operations needed to pass Viterbi-L on it. Therefore, by looking at the total numbers involved in this set of lattices, we can deduce that the real space and time complexities of the algorithm are 82 accumulators and 119 operations.

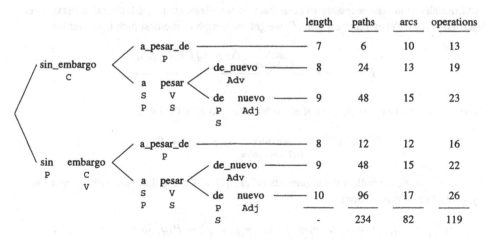

Fig. 4. Decision tree to avoid conflictive paths.

3   Viterbi-N: The Viterbi Algorithm with Normalization

Our proposal is to use only one lattice, and perform only one pass of the Viterbi algorithm. In order to do so, it is necessary to store more than one accumulator per arc. More exactly, we keep as many accumulators as there are different lengths of all the paths reaching the point of origin of the arc. We incorporate this information about lengths in a third component of the index of each accumulator: $\Delta_{t,t',l}(q)$. In this way, only accumulators with the same length l are compared in the maximization operations to obtain the corresponding $\Delta_{t',t'',l+1}(q')$. When reaching the final instant, we will have obtained as many accumulators as there are different lengths, allowing us to normalize their corresponding best paths according to those lengths before selecting the most probable interpretation. We will call this process the Viterbi-N algorithm.

3.1   The Viterbi-N Equations

Assuming the use of logarithmic probabilities to speed up the calculations and avoid problems of precision that arise in products with factors less than 1, we replace those products by sums and adapt the equations as follows:

- Initialization: $\Delta_{0,t,1}(q) = P(q|q_s) + \delta_{0,t}(q)$.
- Recursion:

$$\Delta_{t,t',l}(q) = \max_{(t'',t,q')\in\text{Lattice}} \Delta_{t'',t,l-1}(q') + P(q|q') + \delta_{t,t'}(q) \quad \text{for } 1 \le t < T \quad (2)$$

- Termination: $\displaystyle\max_{Q\in Q^*} P(Q,\text{Lattice}) = \max_l \frac{\displaystyle\max_{(t,T,q)\in\text{Lattice}} \Delta_{t,T,l}(q) + P(q_e|q)}{l}$.

Additionally, it is also necessary to keep track of the elements in the lattice that maximized each $\Delta_{t,t',l}(q)$. When reaching time T, we get the length of the best path in the lattice

$$L = \arg\max_l \frac{\displaystyle\max_{(t,T,q)\in\text{Lattice}} \Delta_{t,T,l}(q) + P(q_e|q)}{l}$$

Next, we get the best last element of all paths of length L in the lattice

$$(t_1^m, T, q_1^m) = \arg\max_{(t,T,q)\in\text{Lattice}} \Delta_{t,T,L}(q) + P(q_e|q)$$

Setting $t_0^m = T$, we collect the arguments $(t'', t, q') \in$ Lattice that maximized Equation 2 by going backwards in time:

$$(t_{i+1}^m, t_i^m, q_{i+1}^m) = \arg\max_{(t'',t_i^m,q')\in\text{Lattice}} \Delta_{t'',t_i^m,L-i}(q') + P(q_i^m|q') + \delta_{t_i^m,t_{i-1}^m}(q_i^m)$$

for $i \ge 1$, until we reach $t_k^m = 0$. Now, $q_1^m \ldots q_k^m$ is the best sequence of phrase hypothesis (read backwards).

3.2   Viterbi-N vs. Viterbi-L

By using intuition again, we can also consider the space complexity of the Viterbi-N algorithm as the number of accumulators, and the time complexity as the number of operations to perform. In this case, for space complexity, we can have more than one accumulator per arc, as has been explained above. And for time complexity, we calculate, for each arc, the sum of the number of accumulators of the arcs reaching its point of origin. In order to pass Viterbi-N on the lattice of Figure 2, we need only 44 accumulators (instead of the 82 needed by Viterbi-L) and 73 operations (instead of 119). Furthermore, we also avoid the analysis of conflictive paths and their distribution in several lattices.

4   Viterbi-I: The Iterative Viterbi Algorithm

To find the best normalized path in a lattice is a problem that has already been studied [4]. In that work, the authors prove the correctness of the following iterative algorithm.

4.1   The Viterbi-I Equations

We have the following available elements: L, a set of possible sentences in a lattice, where any sentence S has $|S|$ tokens; a cost function C that associates a real number $C(S)$ to any sentence S; and an algorithm $\mathcal{A}(L, C, \beta)$ that permits us to find $\arg\max_{S \in L} C(S) - \beta|S|$ for any real number β.

The algorithm $\mathcal{I}(\mathcal{A}, L, C)$ extracts the solution of $\arg\max_{S \in L} \bar{C}(S)$, where $\bar{C}(S) = C(S)/|S|$:

- Initialization: $\bar{C}(S_{-1}) = 0$.
- Recursion: We calculate $S_i = \arg\max_{S \in L} C(S) - \bar{C}(S_{i-1})|S|$ by using the algorithm $\mathcal{A}(L, C, \bar{C}(S_{i-1}))$.
- Termination: We stop iterations when $|S_i| = |S_{i-1}|$. Now, S_i is the solution.

4.2   Viterbi-I vs. Viterbi-N

The cost function C involves the usual transitions and emission probabilities, and can be applied in the frame of algorithm $\mathcal{A}$ by a technique similar to the Viterbi process. Hence the name Viterbi-I algorithm. This means that to every iteration of the algorithm we can attach the smallest space and time complexities that we found for lattices, i.e. 20 accumulators and 36 operations in the case of Figure 2. However, at least two iterations are needed to reach a solution (which implies multiplying the cited time complexity at least by 2), and it is not possible to guarantee that two iterations will be enough in all cases.

The average number of iterations in the context of part-of-speech tagging should be investigated further. But even though this number is close to 2, the Viterbi-N algorithm will always provide a solution with only one pass over the corresponding lattice, with a space complexity approximately the double of the number of arcs, which is not critical in practice (44 vs. 20 accumulators, in the case of Figure 2), and with approximately the same time complexity as the minimum needed by Viterbi-I (73 vs. $36 \times 2 = 72$ operations).

5   Conclusion and Future Work

We have presented an extension of the Viterbi algorithm that allows us to analyze ambiguous segmentations in only one pass, and a discussion about intuitive complexities. It would of course be necessary to perform a formal study of theoretical complexities. This implies generalizing the number of nodes and arcs in the lattice. By doing this, we could see that the space complexity of our one-pass algorithm presents a cubic growth, while in the iterative case we would only appreciate an increment in the number of iterations. However, this is not a practical problem, since lattices with millions of interpretations do not correspond to real sentences. In fact, the guide example used in this work is somewhat artificial. It is possible to assume that real sentences will not present more than one or two ambiguous segmentations, the one-pass approach therefore being more suitable for part-of-speech tagging. Be that as it may, the most important future task is to apply these algorithms on large real data. We expect this general approach to work well, especially for Galician, where it is more frequent to find ambiguous segmentations.

References

1. Brants, T. (1999). Cascaded Markov models. In *Proc. of the Ninth Conference of the European Chapter of the Association for Computational Linguistics (EACL 99)*, Bergen, Norway, pp. 118–125.
2. Brants, T. (2000). TNT – A statistical part-of-speech tagger. In *Proc. of the Sixth Applied Natural Language Processing Conference (ANLP 2000)*, Seattle, WA.
3. Graña, J.; Chappelier, J.-C.; Vilares, M. (2001). Integrating external dictionaries into part-of-speech taggers. In *Proc. of the Euroconference on Recent Advances in Natural Language Processing (RANLP 2001)*, Tzigov Chark, Bulgaria, pp. 122–128.
4. Rozenknop, A.; Silaghi, M. (2001). Algorithme de décodage de treillis selon le critère du coût moyen pour la reconnaissance de la parole. In *Actes de la 8ème conférence sur le Traitement Automatique des Langues Naturelles (TALN 2001)*, Tours, France, pp. 391–396.
5. Viterbi, A.J. (1967). Error bounds for convolutional codes and an asymptotically optimal decoding algorithm. *IEEE Trans. Information Theory*, vol. IT-13 (April), pp. 260–269.

Rule Parser for Arabic Stemmer

Imad A. Al-Sughaiyer and Ibrahim A. Al-Kharashi

Computer and Electronics Research Institute
King Abdulaziz City for Science and Technology
P. O. Box 6086, Riyadh 11442, Saudi Arabia
E-mail: imad@kacst.edu.sa, kharashi@kacst.edu.sa

Abstract. Arabic language exhibits a complex but very regular morphological structure that greatly affects its automation. Current available morphological analysis techniques for the Arabic language are based on heavy computational processes and/or the need for large amount of associated data. Utilizing existed morphological techniques greatly degrade the efficiency of some natural language applications such as information retrieval system. This paper proposed a new Arabic morphological analysis technique. The technique is based on the pattern similarity of words derived from different roots. Unique patterns are extended and coded as rules that encode morphological characteristics. The technique does not require either complex computation or associated data yet adjustable to maintain enough accuracy. This technique utilizes a very simple parser to scan coded rules and decompose a given Arabic word into its morphological components.

1   Introduction

Morphological analysis techniques are computational processes that analyze natural words by considering their internal morphological structures. Stemming algorithms, on the other hand, are processes that gather all words sharing the same stem with some semantic relation. Stemming, as a term, is widely used by researchers dealing with languages with simple morphological systems while morphological analysis, as a term, is widely used by researchers in languages with complex morphological system such as Arabic and Hebrew. The main objective of the stemming algorithms and one objective of morphological analysis techniques is to remove all possible affixes and thus reduce the word to its stem [1,2].

The major difference between Arabic and most of other languages resides mainly on its complicated, very regular and rich morphological structure. Arabic language is derivational while most of other languages are concatenative. Most of Arabic words are generated based on root-pattern structure. Arabic word generation is highly affected by its morphological characteristics [3,4,5]. Stems are generated from roots using one or more patterns. Suffixes, prefixes, and infixes can be added to a stem to generate an Arabic word. A reverse process is used to analyze Arabic words. Schematic diagram for analysis and generation processes is shown in Figure 1.

Due to its non-concatenative nature, processing Arabic language is not an easy task. Tens or hundreds of words are generated using single root, few patterns and few affixes based on

P. Sojka, I. Kopeček, and K. Pala (Eds.): TSD 2002, LNAI 2448, pp. 11–18, 2002.
© Springer-Verlag Berlin Heidelberg 2002

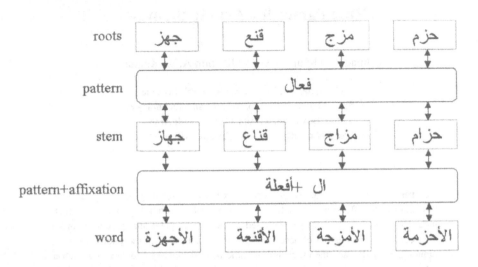

Fig. 1. Arabic system for generating/analyzing words.

root-pattern schemes. Also, Arabic has a high degree of ambiguity because of many reasons such as missing of vowels and similarity between affixation letters and stem or root letters.

Arabic morphological analysis techniques are classified into table lookup, linguistic and combinatorial approaches [3,6,7]. Table lookup approaches utilize huge list that stores all valid natural Arabic words along with their morphological decompositions. A given Arabic word is analyzed by accessing the list and retrieving information associated with that entry [8].

Linguistic approaches, on the other hand, simulate the behavior of a linguist by considering Arabic morphological system and deeply analyzing input Arabic words accordingly to their morphological components. In such approaches, prefix and suffix of a given word are removed by comparing leading and trailing characters with a list of known affixes. Remaining part is either accepted as the required stem or modified using deletion, addition, or substitution of internal letters to generate the valid stem. The resultant stem is transformed to Arabic root simply by filtering process using valid list of patterns. Most of the published works are mainly linguistic based [3,6,9,10,11,12,13,14,15,16,17,18].

Finally, in combinatorial approaches all combinations of letters of tested word are generated. Resulting combinations are compared against lists of Arabic valid roots. On a match, valid root, stem and patterns are extracted. Otherwise other combinations will be tested [7,19,20].

To analyze Arabic words, some researchers suggested to reach their roots [3] while others suggested analyzing them to their stems only [4,5]. Analyzing words to their roots is useful in linguistic processing, while analyzing words to their stems is preferred in some other applications such as information retrieval-based systems.

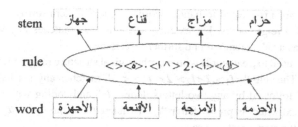

Fig. 2. Sample rule usage.

2 Rule-Based Arabic Stemmer

This section introduces a new approach that utilizes the apparent symmetry of generated natural Arabic words. In this approach, a unique regular expression-based rule is generated for group of similar Arabic words as shown in Figure 2. Regular expressions are compact patterns of characters or simple keyword searching sets of symbols used to match complex patterns in text strings.

Rules are used to describe the internal morphological structure of Arabic words and guide the decomposition process of a given word to its basic components i.e. stem, prefix and suffix. Rules are written from right to left to match script writing direction of Arabic language. Rule pattern may contain up to three distinct parts. The first and last parts describe affixation properties of the word while the middle part controls the stem extraction process. Pairs of angle brackets surround affixation parts. Absence of prefix or suffix in the rule patterns is sometimes denoted by empty angle brackets. This is necessary in order to distinguish them from an angle-bracketed part of the stem.

Rule complexity varies from very simple ones to very complicated rules that deal with complex morphological behaviors. Their syntax were generated after deep analysis of a randomly selected Arabic text and created with the following structure:

$$prefix\text{-part } stem\text{-part } suffix\text{-part}$$

where **prefix**-part represents attached prefix, if any, and can be drawn from a finite list of prefixes, **stem-part** represents stem structure and guide the process of extracting its original form and **suffix-part** represents attached suffix, if any, and can be drawn from a finite list of suffixes.

Rule patterns are constructed using the following conventions:

<str>　to match the string *str* and delete it if in the stem part or consider it as prefix/suffix if in the prefix/suffix part.

$<s_1\hat{\ }s_2>$　to substitute s_1 by s_2 in stem and suffix parts. This notation is also used for insertion $<\hat{\ }s_2>$.

< >　An empty bracketed string to indicate null prefix or suffix. This is necessary to distinguish the prefix/suffix from the start/end part of the stem part.

.n　to match n number of characters where n is an integer greater than one. Single letter is denoted by single dot. Matched characters are used to construct the stem.

Set of simple rules is created to handle words already in stem forms, isolated articles, proper names and foreign words. For example the rule ".4" matches any word with four letters and pass it as a valid stem with no further processing.

Other rules are used to treat words with morphological structure ranging from very simple to very complex. The rule "$<l_1>.2<l_2>.2<^l_3><>$" matches any six letters word with leading letter "l_1" followed by any two letters, letter "l_2" and ending with any two letters. The letter "l_1" is extracted as prefix, letter "l_2" is deleted and the letter "l_3" is inserted in order to complete the stem creation process.

In the following pattern "$<><l_1>.3<l_2^s_1><>$" the "$<l_2^s_1>$" part is used to substitute the letter "l_2" with the substring "s_1". Leading and ending empty bracketed parts denote the absence of both prefix and suffix. Table 1 lists few rules extracted from a list of about 1200 rules generated using the text collection.

Table 1. Sample Rules.

Applied Rule	Word	Resultant		
		Prefix	Stem	Suffix
3.	علی		علی	
<دية3.<ال>	النارية	ال	نار	ية
<>><دة>.<اٸ2.<أ><ال>	الأتربة	ال	تراب	
<اٸ<حو.حت><>	تموت		مات	
<ب><دة>	به	ب		ـه
<دة>.<ىٸوا>.<أ><ال><حو	والأفئدة	وال	فؤاد	
<>				
<دها.<أ>.<اٸ><>	أمالها		أمل	ها
<دية4.<ال>	السريرية	ال	سرير	ية
<ة8دات>3.<وللل>	وللمسرات	و	مسرة	ات
<دهم><اى>.<ي8ي>2.	وزرائهم		وزير	هم
<><أ>.<اٸ2.<دة><>	أجهزة		جهاز	
<حو>.2<ال>	الرموز	ال	رمز	
5.<ب>	بزراعة	ب	زراعة	
6.<ة>	متكاملة		متكامل	ة
<اٸ حو.<دي>.<حوس>	وسيقول	وس	قٸل	
<><دىٸية>2.<ال><حو	والرؤى	وال	رؤية	
<><دية8ٸ<دءٸ>2.<أ><>	أوعية		وعاء	

3   Rule Parser

A very simple rule parser was developed to perform the analysis to process and extract word morphological components. The parser is used to perform matching between input rule and a given Arabic word. The matching process is achieved when the parser successively analyze the input word and decompose it, according to the parsed rule, to its valid components.

The parser is divided into three distinct parts to treat prefix, suffix and stem. Extracting morphological parts of a given word is merely done by interpreting the corresponding part of the rule. Initially, the parser scans the suggested rule to identify boundaries of each part. The angle-bracketed substring at the beginning/end of the rule string distinguishes prefix/suffix parts. The remaining middle part of the rule is the stem part. Each part guides the parser during the process of extracting word morphological parts.

Prefix and suffix are extracted using simple string matching process between the beginning/end of the word and the string in the prefix/suffix part of the rule. Suffix may contain a code that affect extracted stem. Stem part is generated by sequential copying from the middle of the word with the possibility of going through insertion, deletion and/or substitution. A simplified pseudo code of the parser is shown in Listing 1.

A rule is said to be fired if it has the same length as the length of the processed word. A match is achieved if and only if a fired rule produces the correct prefix, stem and suffix. A given word should fire at least one rule and match only one rule.

```
Listing 1.
parser(word)
   for every rule
     if word length = rule length
       identify rule prefix boundaries
       identify rule stem boundaries
       identify rule suffix boundaries
       if rule prefix = word beginning
         copy word beginning to prefix
       else
         match fail
       end if
       while rule stem
         if dot
           copy n symbols from the
           word proper position to stem
         end if
         if angle-bracketed ^ expression
           copy to the stem with substitution
         end if
       end while
       if rule suffix = word end
         copy word end to suffix
         if ^ expression
           append to stem
         end if
       else
         match fail
       end if
       if empty rule AND empty word
         match succeed
```

```
        else
          match fail
        end if
      end if
    end for
  end parser.
```

4 Experiment

Rule generation process is performed by inspecting about 22,000 Arabic words. Words were extracted from 100 short Arabic articles collected randomly from the Internet. Extracted words were normalized by removing vowels, if any, and then stored in binary file in the same order as the original natural text. Since word order was preserved, it is very easy to deduce the contextual meaning of the word by listing few words before and few words after the current word. Each word in the file was manually investigated where stem, prefix and suffix were manually generated and stored in the same file. The stem in the work is defined as a singular, masculine and past tense Arabic word without affixes.

The first part of the experiment was designed to study rule growth in a natural text. In this part each word passed to the parser for analysis. The parser has access to list of accumulated rules. The parser tries to fire rules in sequence. On a match, the word structure will be updated with number of fired rules, the id of matched rule and its sequence. On a mismatch, a new rule should be created and appended to the rule list then parser will be executed again.

The growth of rules is shown in Figure 3. It shows very rapid growth at lower number of words and a tendency to be stabilized as more words introduced. The figure also shows number of generated rules for every thousand words. It clearly shows that number of generated rules decreases as number of words increases.

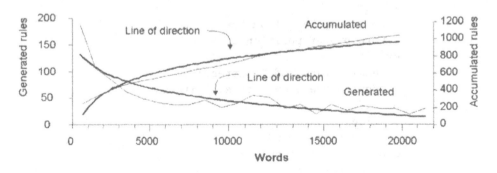

Fig. 3. Growth of generated rules.

Order of rule firing plays an important role in the efficiency of the stemmer. For a given word, it is desirable to fire less number of rules and to maintain firing order in such a way that first fired rule is the matched one. Figure 4 shows the firing behavior of the stemmer for the set of rules arranged according to their generation order. Despite the uncontrolled list of rules in terms of its order, the experiment revile promising behavior. For a given word that fires a set of rules, it is most likely that the first fired rule will achieve a match.

In order to optimize the stemmer performance the curve in Figure 4 should show a sharp drop. Although it is impractical to achieve such optimum state, it is possible to have certain rule ordering that produces the best performance for such rule set.

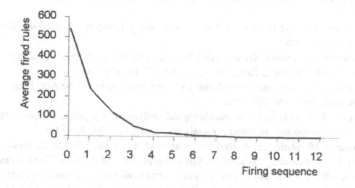

Fig. 4. Average number of fired rules per 1000 words.

5   Conclusion

Available Arabic morphological analysis techniques suffer from few problems including slowness in processing and the need for prepared data. This paper introduced a new Arabic stemmer that requires neither prepared lists nor extensive computations. This work showed the practicality, simplicity and expandability of the proposed stemmer.

Firing policies should thoroughly be studied to enhance the accuracy and correctness of the proposed system. Furthermore, coverage of the system should be increased by introducing more rules. Rule merging and cascaded firing are currently under investigation.

References

1. J. Lovins. Development of a stemming algorithm. Mechanical Translation and Computational Linguistics, No. 11, pages 22–31, March 1968.
2. J. Dawson. Suffix removal and word conflation. ALLC Bulletin, 2(3): 33–46, 1974.
3. N. Ali. Arabic Language and Computer. Ta'reeb,1988. (in Arabic).
4. A. Alsuwaynea. Information Retrieval in Arabic language. King Fahad National Library, 1995 (in Arabic).
5. M. Al-Atram. Effectiveness of Natural Language in Indexing and Retrieving Arabic Documents. KACST, AR-8–47. 1990. (in Arabic).
6. M. El-Affendi. An algebraic algorithm for Arabic morphological analysis. The Arabian Journal for Science and Engineering. 16(4B):605–611, Oct 1991.

7. S. Al-Fadaghi and F. Al-Anzi. A new algorithm to generate root-pattern forms. Proceedings of the 11th National Computer Conference, KFUPM, pages 391–400, March 1989.

8. W. Frakes and R. Baeza-Yates. Editors. Information Retrieval: Data Structures & Algorithms. Prentice Hall, 1992.

9. 9. B. Thalouth and A Al-Dannan. A comprehensive Arabic morphological analyzer/generator. IBM Kuwait Scientific Center, February 1987.

10. T. El-Sadany and M. Hashish. An Arabic morphological system. IBM Systems Journal, 28(4):600–612, 1989.

11. G. Kiraz. Computational analysis of Arabic morphology. Computer Laboratory, University of Cambridge, March 1995.

12. N. Hegazi and A. Elsharkawi. Natural Arabic language processing. Proceedings of the 9th National Computer Conference, Vol. 2, Pages (10-5-1)–(10-5-17), Riyadh. October 1986.

13. Y. Hlal. Morphology and syntax of the Arabic language. Proceedings of the Arab School of Science and Technology, pages 201–207, 1990.

14. M. Gheith and T. El-Sadany. Arabic morphological analyzer on a personal computer. Proceedings of the 1st KSU Symposium on Computer Arabization, pages 55–65, April 1987.

15. A. Aluthman. A Morphological Analyzer for Arabic. M. S. Thesis, KFUPM, Dhahran, 1990.

16. K. Beesley. Finite state morphological analysis and generation of Arabic at Xerox research: status and plans in 2001. 2001. http://www.elsnet.org/arabic2001/beesley.pdf.

17. M. Aref. Object-oriented approach for morphological analysis. Proceedings of the 15th National Computer Conference. pages 5–11, KFUPM, Dhahran 1997.

18. M. Albawab and M. Altabban. Morphological computer processing for Arabic. Arabian Journal for Sciences, No. 32, pages 6–13, 1998. (in Arabic).

19. R. Al-shalabi. Design and implementation of an Arabic morphological system to support natural language processing. Ph.D. Dissertation. Computer Science Department, Illinois Institute of Technology. Chicago, 1996.

20. M. El-Affindi. Performing Arabic morphological search on the internet: a sliding window approximate matching (SWAM) algorithm and its performance. Dept. of Computer Science. CCIS, KSU. Saudi Arabia.

Achieving an Almost Correct PoS-Tagged Corpus

Pavel Květoň[1] and Karel Oliva[2]

[1] Institute of Formal and Applied Linguistics,
Faculty of Mathematics and Physics, Charles University,
Malostranské nám. 25, CZ - 118 00 Praha 1 - Malá Strana, Czech Republic
E-mail: kveton@ufal.ms.mff.cuni.cz
[2] Austrian Research Institute for Artificial Intelligence (ÖFAI),
Schottengasse 3, A-1010 Wien, Austria
E-mail: karel@oefai.at

Abstract. After some theoretical discussion on the issue of representativity of a corpus, this paper presents a simple yet very efficient technique serving for (semi-) automatic detection of those positions in a part-of-speech tagged corpus where an error is to be suspected. The approach is based on the idea of learning and application of "invalid bigrams", i.e. on the search for pairs of adjacent tags which constitute an incorrect configuration in a text of a particular language (in English, e.g., the bigram ARTICLE - VERB). Further, the paper describes the generalization of the "invalid bigrams" into "extended invalid bigrams of length n", for any natural n, which provides a powerful tool for error detection in a corpus. The approach is illustrated by English, German and Czech examples.

1 Introduction

The quality of corpus annotation is certainly among the pressing problems in current corpus linguistics. This quality, however, is a many-faceted problem in itself, comprising both issues of a rather theoretical nature and also quite practical matters. In order to reflect this division (albeit only roughly and only within the area of part-of-speech tagging of written texts), this paper will have two layers.

In the first layer, we shall touch upon the predominantly theoretical problem of (grammatical) representativity. In the second layer, the applications of the theoretical ideas developed in the first layer will be discussed, in particular, we shall

- present some ideas concerning a method for achieving high-quality PoS tagging.
- demonstrate the practical results which were achieved when this method was applied on the NEGRA corpus ([1,2,6,7]) of German.

2 Issues of Representativity of a Corpus

The notion of (grammatical) representativity of a PoS-tagged corpus of a language can be understood in at least the following two ways:

P. Sojka, I. Kopeček, and K. Pala (Eds.): TSD 2002, LNAI 2448, pp. 19–26, 2002.
© Springer-Verlag Berlin Heidelberg 2002

- representativity wrt. the presence of a phenomenon (broadly defined) of this language;
- representativity wrt. the relative frequency of occurrences of a (broadly defined) phenomenon in this language.

From this it is easy to conclude that representativity (in this understanding) is dependent on what is taken to be a phenomenon. (i.e. dependent on what is to be represented – not a surprising conclusion in fact In order to expose the idea of representativity and its importance in some detail, let us consider the example of representativity as needed for a training corpus for a bigram-based statistical tagger[3]. In this case, the phenomena[4] whose presence and relative frequency are at stake are:

- bigrams, i.e. pairs [First,Second] of tags of words occurring in the corpus adjacently and in this order;
- unigrams, i.e. the individual tags.

The qualitative representativity wrt. to bigrams consists in this case of two co mplementary parts:

- the representativity wrt. the presence of all possible bigrams of the language in the corpus, which means that if any bigram [First,Second] is a bigram in a correct sentence of the language, then such a bigram occurs also in the corpus – we shall call this positive representativity,
- the representativity wrt. the absence of all invalid bigrams of the language in the corpus, which means that if any bigram [First,Second] is a bigram which cannot occur in a correct (i.e. grammatical) sentence of the language, then such a bigram does not occur in the corpus – this we shall call negative representativity.

If a corpus is both positively and negatively representative, then indeed it can be said to be a qualitatively representative corpus[5] In our particular example this means that a bigram occurs in a qualitatively representative (wrt. bigrams) corpus if and only if it is a possible bigram in the language (and from this it already follows that any unigram occurs in such a corpus if and only if it is a possible unigram[6]).

The requirement of quantitative representativity of a corpus wrt. bigrams can then be explained as the requirement that the frequency of any bigram and any unigram occurring in the corpus be "in exactly the right proportion" – i.e. in the proportion "as in the language performance" – to the frequency of occurrence of all other bigrams or unigrams, respectively.

---

[3] The case of a trigram-based tagger, more usual in practice, would be almost identical, but more lengthy. For the conciseness of argument, we limit the discussion to bigram-based taggers only, without loss of generality of argument towards general n-gram taggers.

[4] In an indeed broadly understood sense of the word "phenomenon" – of course a bigram is nothing that would be called a linguistic phenomenon (or at least not called a phenomenon in linguistics).

[5] The definitions of positive and negative representativity are obviously easily transferable to cases with other definitions of a phenomenon. Following this, the definition of qualitative representativity holds of course generally, not only in the particular case of corpus representative wrt. bigrams.

[6] This assertion holds only on condition that each sentence of the language is of length two (measured in words) or longer. Similarly, a corpus qualitatively representative wrt. trigrams is qualitatively representative wrt. bigrams and wrt. unigrams only on condition that each sentence is of length three at least, etc.

However, even when its basic idea is quite intuitive and natural, it is not entirely clear whether quantitative representativity can be formalized really rigorously. The main problem here is that what is at stake is measuring the occurrence of a bigram (or unigram, for that matter) within the full "language performance", understood as set of utterances of a language. This set, however, is infinite if considered theoretical ly (i.e. as set of all possible utterances in the language) and finite but practically unattainable if considered practically as a set of utterances in a language realized within a certain time span. Notwithstanding the theoretical problems, the frequencies are used in practice (e.g., for the purpose of training statistical taggers), and hence it is useful to have a look what they (the practical ones) really mean: in our example, it is the relative frequencies of the bigrams (and unigrams) in a particular (training or otherwise referential) corpus. However, nothing can be said as to whether this corpus is quantitatively representative or not in the original, intuitive sense.

3 Negative Representativity in Theory wrt. Bigrams

By quality we mean above all representativity wrt. the "phenomena" which the operation of the tagger is based on. (such as, e.g., bigrams or trigrams). In an ideal case this representativity would be a quantitative one. However, as shown above, the quantitative representativity is a problematic concept even in theory (let alone in practiced). For this reason, it seems more appropriate to strive (at least currently) for achieving a qualitatively representative corpus. In order to be able to achive this, we shall try to interpret the notion of bigram linguistically in this paragraph. The main aim of such an enterprise is to establish linguistic grounds for a corpus which is representative wrt. bigrams – and hence, to provide for means of creating such a corpus.

From a linguistic viewpoint, the pair of tags [First,Second] is a linguistically valid bigram in a certain natural language if and only if there exists a sentence (at least one) in this language which contains two adjacent words bearing the tags *First* and *Second*, respectively[7]. Such a sentence then can be assigned its (constituent) structure. This, in turn, means that for any valid bigram *[First,Second]* it is possible to find a level of granularity of the constituents such that this bigram is represented by a structural configuration where there occur two adjacent constituents *LC* (for "Left Constituent") and *RC* (for "Right Constituent"), such that LC immediately precedes RC and the last (rightmost) element of terminal yield of LC is First and the first (leftmost) element of the terminal yield is Second, cf. Figure 1, where also the common ancestor (not necessarily a direct ancestor!) of LC and RC is depicted (as AC, "Ancestor Constituent").

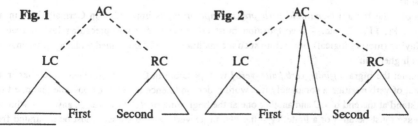

Fig. 1   AC   LC   RC   First   Second   **Fig. 2**   AC   LC   RC   First   Second

---

[7] As an example of a linguistically valid bigram of English, we can put forward, e.g., the pair *[finite_verb,adv]*. This bigram is valid because, e.g., the sentence *John walks slowly* is a correct sentence where the words *walks* and *slowly* bear the tags *finite_verb* and *adv*, respectively.

Correspondingly, the pair of tags *[First,Second]* is a linguistically invalid bigram in a certain natural language if and only if there exists no grammatically correct sentence in this language which contains two adjacent words bearing the tags *First* and *Second*, respectively. Seen from a structural perspective, *[First,Second]* is an invalid bigram if one or more of the following obtains:

1. the configuration from Figure 1 is impossible because in all constituents *LC*, *First* must necessarily be followed by some other lexical material[8];
2. the configuration from Figure 1 is impossible because in all constituents *RC*, *Second* must necessarily be preceded by some other lexical material[9];
3. the configuration from Figure 1 is impossible because *LC* and *RC* can never occur as adjacent sisters standing in this order – cf. Figure 2[10].

4 Negative Representativity in Practice

In practice, the invalid bigrams occur in tagged corpora for the following reasons:

- in a hand-tagged corpus, an "invalid bigram" results from (and unmistakeably signals) either an ill-formed text in the corpus body or a human error in tagging;
- in a corpus tagged by a statistical tagger, an "invalid bigram" may also result from an ill-formed source text, and further either from incorrect tagging of the training data (i.e. the error was seen as a "correct configuration" in the training data, and was learned by the tagger) or from the process of so-called "smoothing", i.e. of assignment of non-zero probabilities also to configurations (bigrams, in the case discussed) which were not seen in the training phase[11].

However, the above theoretical considerations can be turned straightforwardly into a practical method for finding and removing the invalid (i.e. ungrammatical) bigrams in a standing corpus, achieving thus a high-quality PoS-tagging. The starting point for implementing this idea will be the search for the set of all invalid bigrams. For a particular language with a particular tagset, the set of invalid bigrams can be obtained by a reasonable combination of simple empirical methods leaning on the language performance that can be obtained from a corpus with a careful competence-based ("linguistic") analysis of the language facts. For

---

[8] Example: the bigram *[article,verb]* is impossible in English since in any *LC* – NPs, PPs, Ss etc. – article must be followed by (at least) a noun/adjective/numeral before an *RC* (in this case a VP or S) can start.

[9] Example: the bigram *[separable_verb_prefix,postposition]* is impossible in German since in any *RC* – NPs, PPs, Ss etc. – a *postposition* must combine with some preceding lexical material displaying (morphological) case before such a constituent can be combined with any other material into a higher unit.

[10] Example: the bigram *[finite_verb,finite_verb]* is impossible in Czech even when Czech has in the respect of verb position a completely free word order, and hence it would be possible that one finite verb stand at the end of *LC* and another one at the beginning of *RC*; however, in any *AC* – which in this case must be an S or a finite VP – the two finite verbs / verb phrases must be separated from each other by at least a conjunction (coordinating or subordinating) and/or by a comma.

[11] This "smoothing" is necessary since – put very simply – otherwise configurations (bigrams) which were not seen during the learning phase cannot be processed if they occur in the text to be tagged.

the sake of easiness of explanation, let us make a provisional and in practice unrealistic assumption (which we shall correct immediately) that we have a qualitatively representative (wrt. bigrams) learning corpus of sentences of a certain language at our disposal[12]. Given such a (hypothetical) corpus, the next steps seem obvious and also easy to perform. First, all the bigrams in the corpus are to be collected to a set *VB* (valid bigrams), and then the complement of *VB* to the set of all bigrams (i.e. to the Carthesian product of the tagset) is to be computed; let this set be called *IB* (invalid bigrams). The idea is now that if any element of *IB* occurs in a PoS-tagged corpus whose correctness is to be checked, then the two adjacent corpus positions where this happened must contain an error (which then can be corrected). When implementing this approach to error detection, it is necessary to realize that learning the "invalid bigrams" is extremely sensible to the qualitative representativity of the learning corpus:

- the presence of an erroneous bigram in the set of *VB* causes that the respective error cannot be detected in the corpus whose correctness is to be checked (even a single occurrence of a bigram in the learning corpus means correctness of the bigram),
- the absence of a valid bigram from the *VB* set causes this bigram to occur in *IB*, and hence any of its occurrences in the checked corpus to be marked as a possible error (absence of a bigram in the learning corpus means incorrectness of the bigram).

However, the available corpora are neither error-free nor qualitatively representative. Therefore, in practice these deficiencies have to be compensated for by linguistic competence – by manual checking of the sets *VB* and *IB* obtained from the corpus.

5   Advanced Practice: "Stretching" the Invalid Bigrams

The "invalid bigrams" are a powerful tool for checking the correctness of a corpus, however, a tool which works on a very local scale only, and hence it is able to discover solely errors which are detectable as deviations from the set of possible pairs of adjacently standing tags. Thus, obviously, quite a number of errors remain undetected by such a strategy. As example of such as yet "undetectable" errors we might put forward:

- the configuration article - adverb - verb in English,
- the configuration separable verb prefix - comma - postposition in German,
- the configuration finite verb - noun - finite verb in Czech.

There are two interesting observations to be done at these examples.

First, these configurations are wrong but they cannot be detected as such by the application of invalid bigrams: *[article, adverb]* and *[adverb, verb]* are certainly valid bigrams for English, and the same holds for the bigrams *[separable_verb_prefix, comma]* and *[comma, postposition]* in German, and also for the bigrams *[finite_verb, noun]* and *[noun, finite_verb]* in Czech.

Second, and more importantly, the linguistic argumentation why such configurations are erroneous is in fact the same as it was in the examples in Section 2:

---

[12] Note that we do not presuppose that the corpus is error-free – it might well contain tagging errors (and possibly other errors, e.g., ungrammaticalities in the input), only that none of them must cause an "invalid bigram" to occur in the corpus.

- the English example configuration article - verb can become correct only if a non-pronominal nominal element (noun, adjective or numeral) is inserted inbetween the two elements, but not by insertion of an adverb (and, for that matter, neither by insertion of a preposition, conjunction, pronoun, verb,...)[13];
- likewise, the German example cannot be put right without insertion of a nominal element;
- and the Czech example will not be corrected until a comma or a conjunction is inserted inbetween the two finite verbs – any other material does not count for this purpose.

The central observation hence is that the property of being an impossible configuration is often retained also after the components of the invalid bigram get separated by certain kind of material occurring inbetween them. In fact, the addition of any amount of such material cannot make the configuration in question grammatical until the "right" material is inserted. Turned into practice, this observation yields a powerful tool for error detection in a corpus already tagged. In particular, it is possible to generalize on the set of already known invalid bigrams as follows. For each invalid bigram *[First,Second]*, collect all trigrams of the form *[First,Middle,Second]* occurring in the tagged corpus, and put all the possible tags *Middle* into the set *Allowed_Inner_Tags*. Further, given the invalid bigram *[First,Second]* and the set *Allowed_Inner_Tags*, search for all tetragrams *[First,Middle_1,Middle_2,Second]*. In case one of the tags *Middle_1, Middle_2* occurs already in the set *Allowed_Inner_Tags*, no action is to be taken, sice the tetragram is linguistically licensed by the legality of the respective trigram, but in case the set *Allowed_Inner_Tags* contains neither of *Middle_1, Middle_2*, both the tags *Middle_1* and *Middle_2* are to be added into the set *Allowed_Inner_Tags*. The same action is then to be repeated for pentagrams, hexagrams, etc., until the maximal length of sentence in the learning corpus prevents further prolongation of the n-grams and the process terminates. At last, construct the set *Impossible_Inner_Tags* as the complement of *Allowed_Inner_Tags* relatively to the whole tagset. Now, any n-gram consisting of the tag *First*, of any number of tags from the set *Impossible_Inner_Tags* and finally from the tag *Second* is very likely to be an invalid n-gram in the language. The respective algorithm in a semi-formal coating looks like as follows:

```
forall invalid_bigram [First, Second]
{ n := 3;
   allowed_i_t := empty_set;
   while  n =< maximal_sentence_length_in_corpus
   do { find all inner-sentential n-grams
          [First, V1, V2, .., Vn-2, Second];
      for each n-gram found
      do if {V1, V2, .., Vn-2} n allowed_i_t = empty_set
         then allowed_i_t :=  allowed_i_t + {V1, V2, .., Vn-2};
      n := n + 1;
   };
   impossible_i_t([First, Second]) := tagset - allowed_i_t;
}
```

---

[13] This is not to say that by insertion of, e.g., a noun the configuration becomes necessarily correct – however, unless a nominal element is inserted, it remains necessarily incorrect.

As above, this empirical (performance-based) result has to be checked manually (through a human language competence) for correctness, since the performance results might be distorted by tagging errors or by lack of representativity of the corpus.

6   Results on NEGRA

By means of the error-detection technique described above, we were able to correct 2.661 errors in the NEGRA corpus. The prevailing part of these errors was indeed that of incorrect tagging (only less than 8 % were genuine ungrammaticalities in the source, about 26 % were errors in segmentation). The whole resulted in changes on 3.774 lines of the corpus; the rectification of errors in segmentation resulted in reducing the number of corpus positions by over 700, from 355.096 to 354.354.

The paradoxical fact is, however, that the experience with research described above suggests strongly that large and simultaneously highly correct training data needed for statistical tagging cannot be achieved without using algorithms based on a good portion highly refined linguistic expertise.

7   Conclusions

The main contribution of this paper lies in the presentation of a method for detecting errors in part-of-speech tagged corpus which is both quite powerful (as to coverage of errors) and easy to apply, and hence it offers a relatively low-cost means for achieving high-quality PoS-tagged corpora. The main advantage is that the approach described is based on focussed search for errors of a specific type on particular "suspect' spots in the corpus, which makes it possible to detect errors even in a very large corpus where manual checking would not be feasible (at least in practice), since it requires passing through the whole of the text and paying attention to all kinds of possible violations.

The approach is also a very rewarding as to the possibilities of other applications it brings along with: in particular, it should not pass unnoticed that the set of invalid bigrams is a powerful tool not only for error detection in corpora already tagged, but also for avoiding errors in tagging raw texts, since an invalid bigram should never be used in – and hence never come into being as a result of – tagging a raw corpus (which, e.g., for a trigram-based tagger means that any trigram [first,second,third] containing an invalid bigram – i.e. if [first,second] or [second,third] are invalid bigrams – should be assigned probability 0 (zero), and this also after smoothing or any similar actions are preformed). Another merit of the method worth mentioning is that it allows not for detecting errors only, but also for detecting inconsistencies in hand-tagging (i.e. differences in application of a given tagging scheme by different human annotators and/or in different time), and even inconsistencies in the tagging guidelines.

A particular issue is further the area of detecting and tagging idioms/collocations, in the case when these take a form deviating from the rules of standard syntax (i.e. they are detected as "suspect spots").

For details on all these points, including the particular problems encountered in NEGRA, cf. Květoň and Oliva (in prep.).

Acknowledgement. The quality of this paper profited immensely from comments supplied to us by Detmar Meurers. The work itself has been sponsored by the Fonds zur Förderung der wissenschaftlichen Forschung (FWF), Grant No. P12920. The Austrian Research Institute for Artificial Intelligence (ÖFAI) is supported by the Austrian Federal Ministry of Education, Science and Culture.

References

1. NEGRA: http://www.coli.uni-sb.de/sfb378/negra-corpus.
2. Brants T.: TnT – A Statistical Part-of-Speech tagger, In: Proceedings of the 6th Applied Natural Language Processing Conference, Seattle (2000).
3. Hirakawa H., K. Ono and Y. Yoshimura: Automatic refinement of a PoS tagger using a reliable parser and plain text corpora, In: Proceedings of the 18th Coling conference, Saarbrücken (2000).
4. Květoň P. and K. Oliva (in prep.) Correcting the NEGRA Corpus: Methods, Results, Implications, ÖFAI Technical Report (in prep.).
5. Oliva K.: The possibilities of automatic detection/correction of errors in tagged corpora: a pilot study on a German corpus, In: 4th International conference Text, Speech and Dialogue, TSD 2001, Lecture Notes in Artificial Intelligence 2166, Springer, Berlin (2001).
6. Schiller A., S. Teufel, C. Stöckert and C. Thielen: Guidelines für das Tagging deutscher Textcorpora, University of Stuttgart / University of Tübingen (1999).
7. Skut W., B. Krenn, T. Brants and H. Uszkoreit: An annotation scheme for free word order languages, In: Proceedings of the 3rd Applied Natural Language Processing Conference, Washington D.C. (1997).

Evaluation of a Japanese Sentence Compression Method Based on Phrase Significance and Inter-Phrase Dependency

Rei Oguro, Hiromi Sekiya, Yuhei Morooka,
Kazuyuki Takagi, and Kazuhiko Ozeki

The University of Electro-Communications, Chofu, Tokyo 182–8585, Japan
E-mail: rei@ice.uec.ac.jp, sekiya@ice.uec.ac.jp, m_yuu@ice.uec.ac.jp,
takagi@ice.uec.ac.jp, ozeki@ice.uec.ac.jp

Abstract. Sentence compression is a method of text summarisation, where each sentence in a text is shortened in such a way as to retain the original information and grammatical correctness as much as possible. In a previous paper, we formulated the problem of sentence compression as an optimisation problem of extracting a subsequence of phrases from the original sentence that maximises the sum of topical importance and grammatical correctness. Based on this formulation an efficient sentence compression algorithm was derived. This paper reports a result of subjective evaluation for the quality of sentences compressed by using the algorithm.

1 Introduction

Text summarisation is an important area in natural language processing, rapidly growing in recent years [1,2]. To generate an ideal summary, it will be necessary to understand the whole text, and then reconstruct it in a shorter form. Because of technical difficulty to implement this idea, most text summarisation methods reported so far are instead based on the idea of extracting important parts from the original text. Extraction-based text summarisation methods are classified into the following two broad classes depending on the extraction unit chosen. Hybrid methods will also be possible.

1) Extraction of significant sentences from a text to make a shorter text.
2) Extraction of significant words or phrases from a sentence to make a shorter sentence.

This paper is concerned with the latter method, which is referred to as *sentence compression*, or *sentence compaction* [3,4,5,6].

In sentence compression, it is important to retain not only original information but also grammatical correctness as much as possible. In a previous paper [4], we formulated the problem of Japanese sentence compression as a problem of extracting a sequence of phrases from the original sentence that maximises the sum of topical importance and grammatical correctness. This problem can be solved efficiently based on DP-based algorithm. In this formulation, the topical importance is defined on the basis of significance of each phrase, and the grammatical correctness on the basis of dependency strength between phrases. Therefore, in order to get the algorithm to actually work, it is necessary to give phrase significance and dependency strength as *system parameters*. Also, optimum weights for the topical

P. Sojka, I. Kopeček, and K. Pala (Eds.): TSD 2002, LNAI 2448, pp. 27–32, 2002.

importance and the grammatical correctness need to be given. In the following, methods of determining those system parameters are described. Then, a subjective evaluation result for the performance of the method, together with that for human performance, is presented.

2 Overview of Sentence Compression Method

A Japanese sentence is a sequence of phrases, where a phrase is a syntactic unit called *bunsetsu* in Japanese, consisting of at least one content word followed by (possibly zero) function words such as particles and auxiliary verbs. From a dependency grammatical point of view, the syntactic structure of a Japanese sentence is determined by specifying which phrase modifies which phrase. In other words, the syntactic structure of a phrase sequence $v_0 v_1 \cdots v_{l-1}$ can be represented by a mapping

$$s : \{0, 1, \ldots, l - 2\} \to \{1, 2, \ldots, l - 1\},$$

which indicates that $v_{s(m)}$ is the phrase modified by v_m. For a normal Japanese sentence, this mapping must satisfy

a) $m < s(m)$ $(\forall m \in \{0, 1, \ldots, l - 2\})$,
b) if $m < n$ then $[s(m) \leq n$ or $s(n) \leq s(m)]$ $(\forall m, n \in \{0, 1, \ldots, l - 2\})$.

A mapping satisfying the conditions a) and b) is referred to as a *dependency structure* on a phrase sequence $v_0 v_1 \cdots v_{l-1}$.

Now let $w_0 w_1 \cdots w_{M-1}$ be a sentence to be compressed. The sentence compression problem is formulated as a problem of extracting a *good* subsequence $w_{k_0} w_{k_1} \cdots w_{k_{N-1}}$ of length N $(N < M)$ from the sentence. Let $p(w_n, w_m)$ be a function that represents the strength of inter-phrase dependency between w_n and w_m, or the degree of validity for w_n to modify w_m. Then the grammatical correctness of $w_{k_0} w_{k_1} \cdots w_{k_{N-1}}$ can be measured by $\max_s \sum_{n=0}^{N-2} p(w_{k_n}, w_{s(k_n)})$, where s runs over all the dependency structures on the phrase sequence. Let $q(w_n)$ be another function to represent the significance of w_n. Then the topical importance of the phrase sequence can be measured by $\sum_{n=0}^{N-1} q(w_{k_n})$. The total goodness of the phrase sequence $w_{k_0} w_{k_1} \cdots w_{k_{N-1}}$ is then defined as a weighted sum of the grammatical correctness and the topical importance [4]:

$$
\begin{aligned}
& g(k_0, k_1, \ldots, k_{N-1}) \\
& \overset{\triangle}{=} \begin{cases} q(w_{k_0}), & \text{if } N = 1; \\ \alpha\{\max_s \sum_{n=0}^{N-2} p(w_{k_n}, w_{s(k_n)})\} + (1 - \alpha)\{\sum_{n=0}^{N-1} q(w_{k_n})\}, & \text{otherwise,} \end{cases}
\end{aligned}
$$

where s runs over all the dependency structures on the subsequence of phrases, and α is a parameter to control the weights for the grammatical correctness and the topical importance. An efficient algorithm that maximises $g(k_0, k_1, \ldots, k_{N-1})$ has been reported [4].

3 Corpus and Subjects

Kyoto University Text Corpus [7] was used as language material. This corpus contains 38383 sentences selected from Mainichi Shinbun (Mainichi Newspaper), January $\sim$ December,

1995. Each sentence is given labels for word and phrase boundary, part-of-speech, as well as dependency structure. From this corpus, various sets of sentences were created for system parameter determination and for final evaluation as shown in Table 1. Table 2 shows subject groups employed for determination of system parameters and for final evaluation.

Table 1. Sentence sets.

Set	#Sentences	Remarks
A	34848	Estimation of dependency strength.
B	200	Estimation of phrase significance. $B \cap A = \phi$.
C	20	Estimation of α. $C \subset B$.
D	200	Final evaluation. $D \cap A = \phi$, $D \cap B = \phi$.

Table 2. Subject groups.

Group	#Subjects	Remarks
X	13	Estimation of phrase significance.
Y	3	Estimation of α. $Y \subset X$.
Z	1	Generation of compressed sentences by human. $Z \subset Y$.
W	5	Final evaluation. $\#(W \cap X) = 2$. $Z \cap W = \phi$.

4 Determination of System Parameters

4.1 Inter-phrase Dependency Strength

Inter-phrase dependency strength was defined on the basis of a morphological *dependency rule* and statistics for dependency distance [8]. Modifying phrases were classified into 219 classes according to the phrase-final word, while modified phrases were classified into 118 classes according to the left-most content word. First, a dependency rule $B(C_k, C_u)$ for modifying phrase class C_k and modified phrase class C_u was defined using Set A in Table 1 as follows:

$$B(C_k, C_u) \triangleq \begin{cases} T, \text{ if there is a phrase in } C_k \text{ that modifies a phrase in } C_u; \\ F, \text{ otherwise.} \end{cases}$$

Also, the relative frequency $P(x, y)$ of dependency distance between phrases x and y, given the class to which x belongs as well as sentence-final/ non-final distinction for y, was calculated on Set A [8]. Based on the functions $B(C_k, C_u)$ and $P(x, y)$, the inter-phrase dependency strength was defined as

$$p(x, y) \triangleq \begin{cases} \log P(x, y), \text{ if } B(C_k, C_u) = T; \\ -\infty, \quad\quad\quad \text{ if } B(C_k, C_u) = F, \end{cases}$$

where C_k and C_u are classes to which x and y belong, respectively.

4.2 Phrase Significance

In order to estimate the phrase significance, a preliminary experiment was conducted in which the sentences in Set B were compressed by the subjects in Group X. They were asked to compress each sentence at each of 5 compression rates: 80 %, 65 %, 50 %, 35 %, and 20 %, where the compression rate means the ratio of the number of phrases in the compressed sentence to the number of phrases in the original sentence. The result was analysed statistically. First, phrases were classified into 13 classes according to the part-of-speech of the main content word, and also to the phrase-final function word when the main content word is a noun. Then the remaining rate of each phrase class at each compression rate was computed to define the phrase significance as follows:

1. Count the frequency $C(i)$ of phrases in the class i in the original sentences.
2. Count the frequency $C(i, k)$ of phrases in the class i in the compressed sentences at kth compression rate.
3. Compute the remaining rate of the class i: $R(i, k) = C(i, k)/C(i)$.
4. Normalise the distribution of $R(i, k)$: $F(i, k) = R(i, k)/\sum_i R(i, k)$.
5. Average the distribution over the steps of compression rate:
   $F(i) = (\sum_k F(i, k))/K$, where $K(= 5)$ is the number of steps of compression rate.
6. Define the significance $q(i)$ of the phrase class i as $q(i) = \log F(i)$.

4.3 Parameter α

Another preliminary experiment was carried out to determine the optimum value of the parameter α. By using the phrase significance and the inter-phrase dependency strength obtained as in the previous subsections, automatic sentence compression was carried out for the sentences in Set C. Sentence compression was done at each of 5 compression rates with values of α varying in step of 0.1, and the total impression of each compressed sentence was evaluated with a score 1 (poor) $\sim$ 6 (good) by the subjects in Group Y. Table 3 shows the mean score per compressed sentence as a function of α. Thus, $\alpha = 0.5$ was found to give the best mean subjective score.

Table 3. Mean score as a function of α.

Value of α	0.1	0.2	0.3	0.4	0.5	0.6	0.7	0.8	0.9
Mean Score	3.33	3.34	3.37	3.23	3.40	3.27	3.24	3.19	3.14

5   Sentence Compression Experiments

The Set D was used in the final sentence compression experiment. The distribution of sentence length in Set D, measured in the number of phrases, was as follows: 66 sentences of length 7 (short), 68 sentences of length 13 $\sim$ 14 (middle), and 66 sentences of length 18 $\sim$ 50 (long). The phrase significance, the dependency strength, and the value of α were set at values determined in the prelimimary experiments. Sentence compression was done at each of 5 compression rates. For comparison, sentence compression was also conducted by the subject in Group Z (only one subject) for the same sentence set. Furthermore, a random compression experiment was carried out. Thus, 15 compressed sentences (3 ways of compression multiplied by 5 steps of compression rate) were generated for each original sentence.

6   Subjective Evaluation

The total impression of each compressed sentence, taking both retention of the original information and grammatical correctness into account, was evaluated with a score 1 (poor) $\sim$ 6 (good) by the subjects in Group W according to an evaluation manual. They were presented the original sentence, and then the 15 compressed sentences in random order. They were not told how those compressed sentences were generated, and given enough time for evaluation. This process was repeated for the 200 sentences in Set D. Scores were averaged over the compressed sentences at each compression rate for each subject. Then, those scores were further averaged and standard deviation was calculated over the subjects at each compression rate as shown in Table 4.

Table 4. Mean score and standard deviation over the subjects.

	Compression Rate (%)				
	80	65	50	35	20
System	4.56±0.36	3.81±0.16	3.42±0.12	3.20±0.12	3.01±0.10
Human	5.08±0.45	4.39±0.29	4.01±0.26	3.58±0.24	3.17±0.17
Random	4.30±0.32	3.40±0.09	3.00±0.14	2.75±0.22	2.55±0.28

It is seen in Table 4 that human compression outperforms both compression by the system and random compression. Compression by the system performs significantly better than random compression, evaluated just between human compression and random compression at each compression rate, as expected. Thus, if we accept an average score of 3.8, for example, a compression rate of 65 % is allowed for compression by the system, 50 % for human compression, and 80 % for random compression.

Table 5. Evaluation score by Subject 1 and Subject 5.

Subject 1	Compression Rate (%)				
	80	65	50	35	20
System	4.79	3.67	3.24	3.02	2.89
Human	5.43	4.23	3.72	3.22	2.91
Random	4.47	3.24	2.81	2.52	2.25

Subject 5	Compression Rate (%)				
	80	65	50	35	20
System	3.86	3.58	3.48	3.39	3.15
Human	4.22	3.92	3.67	3.42	3.40
Random	3.68	3.40	3.12	3.09	2.95

The standard deviations in Table 4 show that there are considerable variations among the scores by different subjects. Although the evaluation score naturally goes down as sentences are compressed more, the degree of declination depends greatly on the subject. Table 5 shows examples of scores by 2 subjects having considerably different tendency. Subject 1 gives high scores for 80 % compression rate cases, but the scores rapidly go down as the compression rate becomes smaller. On the other hand, Subject 5 evaluates compressed sentences rather in a flat manner: he does not give very high scores for 80 % compression rate cases, nor does he give very low scores for 20 % compression rate cases. To reduce this kind of variability among subjects, improvement on the evaluation method might be necessary.

7   Conclusion

Based on an algorithm previously proposed, a Japanese sentence compression experiment was conducted. The result of subjective evaluation showed that sentence compression using the algorithm is significantly better than random compression, though not reaching the human performance. Our future work includes

1) Improvement on the definitions of the phrase significance and the dependency strength.
2) Separate evaluation for information retention and grammatical correctness.
3) Employment of more subjects to generate human-compressed sentences.

References

1. Okumura, M., Nanba, H.: Automated text summarization: A survey. Journal of Natural Language Processing 6(6)(1999) 1–26.
2. Wakao, T., Ehara, T., Shirai, K.: Summarization methods used for captions in TV news programs. Technical Report of Information Processing Society of Japan, 97-NL-122-13 (1997) 83–89.
3. Mikami, M., Masuyama, S., Nakagawa, S.: A Summarization method by reducing redundancy of each sentence for making captions for newscasting. Journal of Natural Language Processing 6(6) (1999) 65–81.
4. Oguro, R., Ozeki, K., Zhang, Y., Takagi, K.: An efficient algorithm for Japanese sentence compaction based on phrase importance and inter-phrase dependency. Proc. TSD 2000 (LNAI 1902) (2000) 103–108.
5. Knight, K., Marcu, D.: Statistics-based summarization – Step one: Sentence compression. AAAI/IAAI 2000 Proceedings (2000) 703–710.
6. Hori, C., Furui, S.: Advances in automatic speech summarization. Proc. EuroSpeech 2001 3 (2001) 1771–1774.
7. Kyoto University Text Corpus Version 2.0 (1998).
   http://pine.kuee.kyoto-u.ac.jp/nl-resource/corpus.html.
8. Zhang, Y., Ozeki, K.: Dependency analysis of Japanese sentences using the statistical property of dependency distance between phrases. Journal of Natural Language Processing 4(2) (1997) 3–19.

User Query Understanding by the InBASE System as a Source for a Multilingual NL Generation Module
First Step

Michael V. Boldasov[1], Elena G. Sokolova[2], and Michael G. Malkovsky[1]

[1] Moscow State University (MSU),
Computational Mathematic and Cybernetic department,
Moscow, Russia,
E-mail: malk@cs.msu.su

[2] Russian Research Institute for Artificial Intelligence (RRIAI),
Moscow, Russia,
E-mail: sokolova@aha.ru

Abstract. In the paper we discuss the NL generation module of InBASE system – the system for understanding of NL queries to data bases. This module generates a new NL-query from the internal InBASE representation of user query. During the planning phase a linearly positioned query representation is constructed. The positions first bear conceptual information, to be followed by syntactic information. The realization phase deals with NL means to express the concepts (objects, attributes, values, relations between objects and attributes). The NL generation module is conceived as the first step from a one way question – answering system which is the present state of InBASE, to a larger-scale information system capable of communicating with the user in various areas.

1 Introduction

Our first goal is practical – to construct a natural language generation (NLG) module for a commercially oriented InBASE system[3] which is used for NL queries understanding and information delivery in the form of DB fragments. Problems can arise from misunderstanding of the user query by the system, so that irrelevant information can be delivered and the user will never learn about it. The most general way to resolve these problems is to construct an NLG module generating an NL query from the internal query representation. The system generates a rephrased query and the user can control the correctness of the query understanding. The rephrased query can be also shown together with the fragment of DB to explain how the structure of the data was delivered. On the other hand, new generation facilities will be a step to an interactive mode for the InBASE system.

To date, some question – answering systems are already available in the Internet, for example, START[4], which answers questions about USA geography. START and other

---

[3] http://www.inbase.artint.ru/nl/nllist-eng.asp
[4] http://www.ai.mit.edu/projects/infolab/ailab.html

P. Sojka, I. Kopeček, and K. Pala (Eds.): TSD 2002, LNAI 2448, pp. 33–40, 2002.
© Springer-Verlag Berlin Heidelberg 2002

Internet systems are monothematic. The InBASE system is multithematic. It is oriented at the register of database queries and can be customized to any thematic area [1]. This makes it robust and well thought over, and demands as much from the generation module. We are thus constrained in inventing the system's responses.

The second goal of the investigation is theoretical. The methods of NLG are not discussed in relation to practical Internet systems like the cited START system. Rather they are investigated in research projects like DRAFTER [4], GhostWriter [5], AGILE [3]. DRAFTER and GhostWriter were aimed to generate formal representations oriented to the NL communication from specifications designed for computer processing. In the contrary, the aim of AGILE project was the generation of NL software instructions from formal representations oriented to NL communication. Software instructions were created by the user in automated mode. Instructions were generated in three Slavic languages – Bulgarian, Czech and Russian. Also, the English-language resources could be involved. Theoretically speaking we can think of the Russian resources from AGILE system as means to generate user queries. But there arise two problems: the first one is that the Russian resources are manageable in the KPML environment [8], which is a powerful research system based on systemic functional grammar (SFG) [7]. But it is too large to be used in the commercially oriented InBASE system. The second is the fact that, unlike AGILE, our generation module integrates two functions of the above types of systems mentioned before. On the one hand its source data are the specifications oriented to computer processing (Q representation of user query – an XML based SQL-like InBASE internal OQL representation). On the other hand it produces the NL queries. So, NL communication-oriented representation must be created as intermediate one for an NL query realization.

In Section 2 we consider the source Q-representation of a user query emphasizing its knowledge nature in contrast to AGILE-like systems. Then we consider generation in InBASE system as a process divided into the following phases: interpretation of Q-representation in the form convenient for further generation process – planning, Section 3; associating of Q-representation items with generator vocabulary items, Section 4; grammatical realization of relations between lexicalized domain model (DM) concepts in Q-representation Section 5.

2   Source Representation

Generation systems often follow the descriptive logic paradigm. Some of them, including KPML and AGILE systems, are based on the KL-ONE [6] tradition. Accordingly, the source knowledge base is presented in two parts: one being Terms box (T-box) which contains the hierarchy of concepts for DM and the other consisting of multiple expressions which are constructed from the DM – Assertion box (A-box). So they are named entities with the features defined in T-box. Normally, in multilingual generation systems language independence of source representations is declared. But in fact it is usually not so. For example, in the AGILE system the T-box is based on two ontologies – the domain ontology of things and Upper Model [2] – a language specific ontology of things and processes (UM). The core of the T-box structure is UM. For example, the process OPEN (*to open*) is classified in the UM as DIRECTED-ACTION. Additionally the roles Actor and Actee link the process with its participants – USER (*user*), and SCREAN-OBJECT (for example, *a dialogue box*).

So we can construct a configuration and realize it in Russian: *Pol'zovatel'* (Actor) *otkryvaet dialogovoe okno* (Actee) and in English: *The user* (Actor) *opens the dialogue box* (Actee). Language specifity is clear from the grammar nature of the type DIRECTED-ACTION.

The Q-representation is not semantic, rather a knowledge representation. It comprises not abstract semantic notions like DIRECTED-ACTION, but exact notions from object domain model (ODM) which is closer to naive human mentality than the DB structure [1]. ODM consists of objects and attributes related to the attributes and values of DB.

ODM can also be augmented by some notions of the DB access register which are present in the Dictionary of the InBASE system. These are operations and logical links used in Q language – *not, count, asc.*, and some others. So, augmented ODM can be seen as T-box for our generation system.

We consider Q-representations as A-boxes in our module. The illustrative part of the Q-representation for a query is presented in Figure 1. Below we will speak of it as of Q representation, skipping the technical details. The example shows that, if the ODM is multiobjective the elements of Q representation can form multilink chains – accessors. Figure 1 shows Q-representation for a query to a DB about selling cars. The accessor in the SELECT part declares the Cost to be a car attribute as an Offer – the thing that you can buy, and that is related to the object Model. The accessor in the WHERE part declares the object Model which acquires the attribute Company through of the object Mark.

```
Q result=
    'SELECT avg(Model.Offer.Cost)
    FROM Model
    WHERE ((Model.Mark.Company.Company LIKE '\%LADA\%')))'
```

Fig. 1. The Q-representation for the user query: *Average cost of LADA?*

3   Planning the NL-Oriented Representation

The aim of planning is to represent the content in an NL communication oriented form. First of all this implies fragmentation equivalent to clauses.

We have investigated NL forms of user queries. Most of them consist of single interrogative or imperative sentences or of a noun group. The latter is the most frequent form in Russian. In Figure 2 three variants of a query realization are presented. The list can be continued by style variations – synonyms, slang elements, ellipsis.

Workers without high school education.
Who has no secondary education?
List the workers who has no high school education!

Fig. 2. Query variations.

At the first step we consider the planning and realization of a noun group form. Q-representation matches the form very naturally since it is a description of an object – the object of the user's interest.

The second task of the planning process is to make query Q representation closer to human view of its content. In our case, during the analysis and interpretation some information which was not presented in the NL query is added automatically by the analyzer. This information includes: a) default attributes in SELECT part, for example, the query *"who belongs to the staff"*, is interpreted by the system as delivering general information about the object *"employee"*, i.e. Name, Surname and Position attributes of Employee object; b) some information is added by the system in concrete situations. For example, in the Q representation in Figure 3 the WHERE part is augmented in comparison to the NL form due to the fact that a person having no secondary education neither has higher education, so only persons with lower education must be listed. Also in the SELECT part the fourth accessor Employee.Education is added from the WHERE part in order the Education attribute could be delivered to the user. But it is is redundant for the NL form.

```
SELECT Employee.Surname, Employee.Name, Employee.Position,
Employee.Education FROM Employee WHERE
(Employee.Education<>'secondary') AND
    (Employee.Education<>'BA') AND
    (Employee.Education<>'MS')
```

Fig. 3. Q-representation for the query shown in Figure 2.

4 Vocabulary

To ensure the wording of Q-representation elements we need the vocabulary that associates them with lexical items. There is a vocabulary of the InBASE understanding module that includes names of the ODM concepts and other lexemes, used in the analysis, as typed items having a number of features. The type of a lexical item defines its features, as well as its semantic role in a query. They are Object, Conjunction (comma, co-ordinate conjunction), Value, Unit (*litre, dollar,...*), Relation (*equal, less,...*), Functor (actions with the Q-representation elements, for example, *count, sum,...*) etc. The lexical item types belong to the knowledge concepts layer that communicates directly with language semantics [7], but is not language-based. The vocabulary of the InBASE understanding module supplies ODM with lexical information and extends it by typical attributes' values, functors and relations.

The generation process is not reverse to the understanding process. The attempt to use the understanding module vocabulary directly for generation will face with a number of difficulties. Let us explain it by the following example. Below are lexical items extracted from the vocabulary, associated with the Object *Employee* of "employee" ODM: *Employee* → *anybod, each, employee, everybod, individual, member, official, people, person, personnel, staff, who, worker, collaborator, colleague, specialist, guy.*

One ODM concept can be associated with many lexical items. Some of these variants can be used in the generation process for style management. For example, *Employee* → *employee* (literary style), *Employee* → *guy* (colloquial style). There are words that have no association to ODM items, such as *anybod, each, everybod* etc. In some cases we can only find interrogative pronouns associated with an ODM item, and so have no lexical realization for the generator.

Thus, we need to build a separate generator vocabulary. We can develop it apart from the understanding module vocabulary or adapt it from the latter by importing items to the new generator vocabulary. For the first step the latter variant was chosen, but generally we should maintain a new multilingual generation module vocabulary.

Generator vocabulary items are of one of four types:

- NL-Object – is the language equivalent of the ODM item. Features:
  - ODM item ID,
  - Language features and preferred flag.
- NL-Value – is the language equivalent of the ODM item value. Features:
  - Search pattern in Where section of Q-representation,
  - ODM attribute item ID,
  - Language features and preferred flag.
- Operation – is the language equivalent of operator (*LIKE*, =, >, <, ≥, ≤, <>) from Where section of Q-representation. Attributes:
  - Operator ID,
  - ODM attribute item ID,
  - Language features and preferred flag.
- Action – is the language equivalent of functor (*count, sum, avg, max, min*) from Select section of Q-representation. Attributes:
  - Functor ID,
  - ODM attribute item ID, with which the respective functor is used,
  - Language features and preferred flag.

Every generator vocabulary item has a link to Q-representation or to ODM item referred to by Q-representation. However because of the preferred flag present in every item the reference from Q-representation to the generator vocabulary is unique.

Select:N,Def		From-object:N,Pl		Where:Def
Ru:	En:	Ru:	En:	*see the next table*
Case=Nom		SEMANTIC LINK		
"цена"	*"the cost"*	attribute-object		
		Case=Gen	Pr="of"	
		"машин"	*"of cars"*	

Fig. 4. Preselects of three Q-query parts, "attribute-object" relation.

SEMANTIC LINK		SYNTACTIC LINK	
Ru:	En:	Ru	En
comitative		**attributive clause**	
Where:N,Sg		Where:V,Active participle	
Case=Instr Pr="с"	Pr="with"		
с ценой [.] со стоимостью [.]	with the price of with the cost of	весящие [.]	weighing [.]
transitive		**have attributive clause**	
Where:N,Sg		HAVE,Where:N,Sg	
Case=Dative Pr="по"	Pr="at"	Case=Acc	
по цене [.] *по стоимости [.]	at the price of [.] at the cost of [.]	имеющие цену [.]	having the price [.]
mediative		**relative clause**	
Where:N,Sg	*	Where:V,Present tense, 3p Ghost participant:From-object,Nom	
Case=Instr			
*ценой [.] стоимостью [.]		которые весят [.]	that weighs [.]
qualitative		**have relative clause**	
Where:N,Sg	*	HAVE,Where:N,Sg Ghost participant:From-object,Nom	
Case=Gen		Case=Acc	
завода [.] *цены [.]		которые имеют цену [.]	that have the price [.]
		be relative clause	
		BE,Where:N,Sg	*
		Case=Nom Pr="v"	
		у которых цена - [.]	
		inv be relative clause	
		Where:N,Sg Ghost participant:From-object,Nom	
		Case=Nom	
		цена которых - [.]	the price of which is [.]

Left side row labels: Prepositional group (comitative, transitive), Nominal group (mediative, qualitative); right side label: Clause.

Fig. 5. "Object-attribute" relation.

5 Grammatical Realization

Most NLG systems deal with semantic representations of text propositions, using semantic relations, as intermediate representation between domain representation and NL-text. For example, in the AGILE system the semantic representation is presented in terms of SPL (Sentence Plan Language) – the formalism of the KPML environment. We begin the development of the InBASE generator with the Q-representation and retain its concepts in the text plan. We consider relations between the parts of Q-representation in the context of NL communication as generalized semantic links thinking about the realization of the "attribute-object" relation in the SELECT-FROM construction, and "object-attribute" relation in the

FROM-WHERE construction. The generated text unlike the user query, has a regular form. The principles we follow are: all Values must be presented explicitly with their Attributes, and all the relations between elements must be expressed by grammatical means. In Figures 4, 5 we present our fragment of grammar in the form of a table. It can be likened to the network in SFG tradition based on UM notions: it has semantic relations, choices, and we can think of creating choosers. The principle difference between the SFG grammar network and our grammar fragment presented in Figures 4, 5 is that our grammar is syntagmatic (it describes what grammar means are available to express concrete object configuration) unlike SFG's one which is paradigmatic (it describes the organization of language means). So our choosers must also include the syntactic motivations for the realization.

In the figures semantic and syntactic relations are presented in bold. Generalized semantic relation "attribute-object" (Figure 4) is presented and regularly expressed by a genitive construction (an equivalent of "of-phrase" in English). The "object-attribute" (Figure 5) relation is realized differently according to the object's semantics. It is shown by semantic relations that we took from [9].

The "object-attribute" relation also can be expressed in a subordinate proposition with syntactic motivation for realization. Proposition is represented as a relative clause with "ghost participant" from the main part expressed by a relative pronoun, or as an attributive clause with the predicate expressed by a participle form. The clause is centered around the predicate. We distinguish the realization possibilities for the chain of three elements: Object – Attribute – Value. There are three variants of their NL-realization: realization of the Attribute as a verb (*kotoryj stoit 10$ – "which costs 10$"*), addition of the HAVE verb between the Object and the Attribute with the Value adjoined to the Attribute (*kotoryj imeet tsenu 10$ – "which has price 10$"*), addition of the BE verb between the Attribute and the Value (*tsena kotorogo (est') 10$ – "price of-which is 10$"*). The possibilities are presented in Figure 5.

All the elements of the table are pairs Attribute – Value of the WHERE that must be organized into coordinated strings in NL query. As it is shown in Figure 5, WHERE part allows various means for realization. So Choosers should realize rules like "SEMANTIC realization first, SYNTACTIC – after". For example, *a man with a stick that has a hat* rather than *a man that has a stick with a hat*. Also the grammar should realize a semantic ordering rule for postmodifiers as it is formulated for premodifiers in the nominal group in [7]. The ordering rule can be described like "determiner first, quality after".

6 Conclusion

We describe the common principles of an NLG module designed for the commercially oriented multithematic system InBASE, which is used in e-commerce for NL access to Internet data stored for shops and catalogs of different areas: minicomputers, radiophones, furniture, goods for children and some others.

Developing the generator system we acquire an experimental base to pose and resolve some NLG tasks like postmodifier's realization. On the other hand, our module constitutes an environment for contrastive analysis of languages since we have user NL query as the source data for the InBASE system and its language independent Q-representation as far as a rephrased query (in the same or another NL) as the generator's output. The generator interface is being developed under J++ platform and is planned as a COM-Interface like other components of the InBASE system. The morphology stage was realized using external Morph Generator "Lemmatizer" COM-Interface.

References

1. Zhigalov, V.A., Sokolova, E.G.: InBASE Technology: Constructing Natural Language Interface with Databases. (in Russian) Computational Linguistics and Its Applications International Workshop Proceedings, Vol. 2., Dialogue, Aksakovo, (2001) 123–135.
2. Bateman, J., Renate, H., Fabio, R.: The Generalized Upper Model 2.0. GMD-IPSI Technical Report. http://www.darmstadt.gmd.de/publish/komet/gen-um/newUM.html (1996).
3. Kruijff, G-J., Bateman, J., Dochev, D., Hana, J., Kruijff-Korbayova, I., Skoumalova, H., Sharoff, S., Sokolova, E., Staykova, K., Teich, E.: Multilinguality in a Text Generation System for Three Slavic Languages. Proc. COLING-2000, Luxemburg, (August, 2000).
4. Paris, C., Vander, Linden K., Fischer, M., Hartley, A., Pemberton, L., Power, R., Scott, D.: A support tool for writing multilingual instructions. Proc. IJCAI '95. Montreal, August 20–25 (1995) 1398–1404.
5. Reiter, E., Mellish, C., Levine, J.: Automatic generation of technical documentation. Applied Artificial Intelligence, Vol. 9, no. 3 (1995).
6. Woods, W.A., Schmolze, J.G.: The KL-ONE Family. In: Computers and Mathematics with Applications: 23:2–5, (1992) 133–178.
7. Halliday, M.A.K.: An Introduction to Functional Grammar. London, Edward Arnold, (1985).
8. Bateman, J.A.: Enabling technology for multilingal natural language generation: the KPML development environment. Natural Language Engineering, 3 (1), (1997) 15–55.
9. Zolotova, G.A.: Syntactic dictionary. Repertory of the element units for Russian syntax. (in Russian) Nauka, Moscow, (1988).

The Role of WSD
for Multilingual Natural Language Applications

Andrés Montoyo, Rafael Romero, Sonia Vázquez, Carmen Calle, Susana Soler

Grupo de investigación del Procesamiento del Lenguaje y Sistemas de Información.
Departamento de Lenguajes y Sistemas Informáticos. Universidad de Alicante. Spain
E-mail: montoyo@dsli.ua.es, romero@dsli.ua.es, susana@dsli.ua.es

Abstract. Nowadays, the need of advanced free text filtering in multilingual environment is increasing. Therefore, when searching for specific keywords in multilingual
information space, it is desirable to eliminate occurrences where the word or words
of each language are used in an inappropriate sense. This task could be exploited
in internet browsers, and resource discovery systems, relational databases containing free text fields, electronic document management systems, data warehouse and
data mining systems, etc. In order to resolve this problem in this paper we present a
Word Sense Disambiguation interface, which it returns the words senses in different
languages and it could be employed for multilingual natural language applications.
This interface resolve lexical ambiguity of nouns and verbs in some European languages (English, Spanish) input texts, using the taxonomy of the EuroWordNet lexical
knowledge database, and returning a multilingual output of the words senses (English,
Spanish, Catalan and Basque). In addition to the relations in WordNet 1.5, EuroWord-
Net includes cross-language and cross-category relations, which are directly useful for
multilingual Word Sense Disambiguation. This interface has been implemented using
programming language C++ and providing a visual framework.

1 Introduction and Motivation

The development and convergence of computing, telecommunications and multilingual
information systems has already led to a revolution in the way that we work, communicate
with each other in different countries and different languages, buy goods and use services,
and even in the way we entertain and educate ourselves. The revolution continues and one
of its results is that large volumes of multilingual information will increasingly be held
in a form which is more natural for users than the data presentation formats typical of
computer systems of the past. Natural Language Processing (NLP) is crucial in solving these
problems and language technologies will make an indispensable contribution to the success
of the information systems. Designing a system for NLP requires abundant knowledge on
language structure, morphology, syntax, semantics and pragmatic nuances. Morphological
knowledge provides the tools for building words, while syntactic knowledge combines words
to form sentences. Semantic knowledge provides the meaning of a given word, and pragmatic
knowledge helps us to interpret the complete sentence in its true context. All of these
different linguistic knowledge forms, however, have a common associated problem, their
many ambiguities, which is difficult to resolve. One of the main objectives in designing any

P. Sojka, I. Kopeček, and K. Pala (Eds.): TSD 2002, LNAI 2448, pp. 41–48, 2002.
© Springer-Verlag Berlin Heidelberg 2002

NLP system, therefore, is the resolution of ambiguity. Furthermore, each type of ambiguity, whether it be structural, lexical, quantifying, contextual or referential, requires its specific resolution procedure. This paper is motivated by two reasons. First, we concentrate on the design and implementation of an interface to resolve the lexical ambiguity that arises when a given word has several different meanings. This specific task is commonly referred to as Word Sense Disambiguation (WSD) [2]. In general terms, WSD involves assigning a definition to a given word, in either a text or a discourse, that endows it with a meaning that distinguishes it from all of the other possible meanings that the word might have in other contexts. Second, the WSD interface we propose in this paper, will allow a tool to disambiguate the content words of different languages by matching the context in which they appear with information from an external knowledge source (knowledge-driven WSD). This tool will also provide support across different languages converting the words senses from one language into other languages. It will also could be used as a basic resource for supporting other multilingual natural language applications, such as Machine Translation (MT), Question Answering, Information Retrieval (IR), hypertext navigation, etc. In order to accomplish these tasks, we use the following two different WSD methods for disambiguating nouns and verbs of texts: Specification Marks Method [6,7] for nouns and Semantic Similarity [11] for verbs. Both methods use EuroWordNet [13] as it combines the features of both dictionaries and thesauruses, and also includes other links among words by means of several semantic relations, (Hyponymy, hypernymy, meronymy, etc.). In other words, EuroWordNet provides definitions for the different senses that a given word might have (as a dictionary does) and defines groups of synonymous words by means of "Synsets", which represent distinct lexical concepts, and organizes them into a conceptual hierarchy (as a thesaurus does). EuroWordNet also contains multilingual relations from each monolingual wordnet (Spanish, Catalan, etc.) to English (WordNet 1.5 [5]). The organization of this paper is as follows: after this introduction, in Section 2 we describe the architecture employed in developing the multilingual natural language interface. In Section 3, we describe the two WSD methods used and its application. In Section 4, we describe the WSD interface which allows the disambiguation of words from one language into other languages. And finally, discussions, conclusions and an outline of further lines of research are shown.

2   Architecture Employed

In this section we describe, in detail, the architecture employed in developing the WSD interface for multilingual natural language applications. Figure 1 illustrates this architecture.

The input text (Spanish or English) that is to be disambiguated come from different files and are passed through a preprocessing stage. If the input text is Spanish, the first step in preprocessing consist of using a Spanish part-of-speech (PoS) tagger [10] to automatically assign lexical tags to the text. Next, a Spanish SUPP Partial Parser [1] is used to extract constituents like noun phrase (NP), prepositional phrase (PP) and verbal chunks. This parser also includes some heuristics to provide functional categories, such as subject and object. A grammar (SUG) for Spanish that recognizes every syntactic constituent (NP, PP, verbal chunks) is first defined. Our process, however, only uses the NP to disambiguate the nouns of a sentence and the verbal chunk with its functional category to disambiguate the verbs. This grammar is automatically translated into Prolog clauses. The translator will provide a

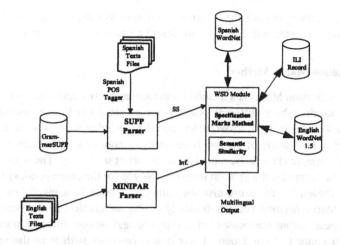

Fig. 1. Architecture.

Prolog program that can parse sentences. The program will return structure (SS) for each parsed sentence. This SS stores the syntactic, morphological and semantic information of the NP and verbal chunks constituents. After a sentence has been parsed, its SS will be the input for the WSD module. If the input text is English, the first step in preprocessing consist of using MINIPAR parser [3] to extract the same constituents as in Spanish process. After a sentence has been parsed, this information will be the input for the WSD module. The WSD module is composed of two different WSD methods: Specification Marks Method for disambiguating nouns and Semantic Similarity for disambiguating verbs. This module will consult the EuroWordNet knowledge database for nouns and verbs that appear in the context, returning all of their possible senses. The WSD module will then select the correct method for disambiguating the nouns or verbs and after these methods will be applied a multilingual output will be returned, in which the words have the correct sense assigned. We should like to emphasize that this resolution skill allows us to produce modular NLP systems in which the grammatical rules, the knowledge base (EuroWordNet), the parsing scheme and the WSD module are all quite independent of one other.

3 Word Sense Disambiguation Modules

The Word sense disambiguation module employed in this paper is composed of two different WSD methods. This two method are Specification Marks Method for disambiguating nouns and Semantic Similarity Method for disambiguating verbs. We should like to clarify, these two methods employ EuroWordnet for disambiguating the words senses. EuroWordNet lexical database consists on a WordNet like database for each of the language covered, linked through a common interlingual index. Then, if we map a word in Spanish against its corresponding synset in the Spanish WordNet, we can obtain its Interlingual Index (ILI) record number. This number is the language neutral semantic representation of the Spanish word. Mapping all the words into their corresponding synsets will provide us with the Spanish and English words senses. In this section, we describe each one of this method.

3.1 Specification Marks Method

WSD with Specification Marks is a method for the automatic resolution of lexical ambiguity of groups of words, whose different possible senses are related. The disambiguation is resolved with the use of the EuroWordNet lexical knowledge base. The method requires the knowledge of how many of the words are grouped around a specification mark, which is similar to a semantic class in the monolingual WordNet taxonomy. The word-sense in the sub-hierarchy that contains the greatest number of words for the corresponding specification mark will be chosen for the sense-disambiguating of a noun in a given group of words. Specification Marks Method consists basically of the automatic sense disambiguating of nouns that appear within the context of a sentence and whose different possible senses are related. Its context is the group of words that co-occur with it in the sentence and their relationship to the noun to be disambiguated. The input for the WSD algorithm will be the group of words $W = \{w_1, w_2, \ldots, w_n\}$. Each word w_i is sought in monolingual WordNet, each one has an associated set $S_i = \{S_{i1}, S_{i2}, \ldots, S_{in}\}$ of possible senses. Furthermore, each sense has a set of concepts in the IS-A taxonomy (hypernym/hyponym relations). First, the concept that is common to all the senses of all the words that form the context is sought. We call this concept the Initial Specification Mark (ISM), and if it does not immediately resolve the ambiguity of the word, we descend from one level to another through monolingual WordNet hierarchy, assigning new Specification Marks. The number of concepts that contain the sub-hierarchy will then be counted for each Specification Mark. The sense that corresponds to the Specification Mark with highest number of words will then be chosen as the sense disambiguation of the noun in question, within its given context. We should like to point out that after having evaluated the method, we subsequently discovered that it could be improved with a set of heuristics, providing even better results in disambiguation. The set of heuristics are Heuristic of Hypernym, Heuristic of Definition, Heuristic of Common Specification Mark, Heuristic of Gloss Hypernym, Heuristic of Hyponym and Heuristic of Gloss Hyponym. Detailed explanation of the method can be found in [6,7,8], while its application to NLP tasks are addressed in [9].

3.2 Semantic Similarity Method

The method of WSD proposed in this paper is based on knowledge and consists basically of sense-disambiguating of the verb that appear in an Spanish or English sentence. A simple sentence or question can usually be briefly described by an action and an object [4]. For example the main idea from the sentence "He eats bananas" can be described by the action-object pair "eat-banana". Our method determine which senses of these two words are more similar between themselves. For this task we use the concept of semantic similarity [12] between nouns based on EuroWordNet hierarchy. In EuroWordNet, the gloss of a verb synset provides a noun-context for that verb, i.e. the possible nouns occurring in the context of that particular verb [4]. The glosses are used here in the same way a corpus is used. Our method takes into consideration the verb-noun pair extracted from the sentence. This verb-noun pair is the input for the algorithm. The output will be the sense tagged verb-noun pair, so we assign the sense of the verb. The algorithm is described as follows:

Step 1. Determine all the possible senses for the verb and the noun by using WordNet. Let us denote them by $< v_1, v_2, \ldots, v_k >$ and $< n_1, n_2, \ldots, n_m >$.

Step 2. For each sense of verb v_h and all senses of noun $< n_1, n_2, \ldots, n_m >$:

2.1. Extract all the glosses from the sub-hierarchy including v_h. The sub-hierarchy including a verb v_h is determined as follows: consider the hypernym h_h of the verb v_h and consider the hierarchy having h_h as top [4].

2.2. Determine the nouns from these glosses. These constitute the noun-context of the verb. Determine all the possible senses for all these nouns. Let us denote them by $< x_1, x_2, \ldots, x_n >$.

2.3. Then we obtain the similarity matrix (Sm) using the semantic similarity, where each element is defined as Formula 1:

$$Sm(i, j) = sim(x_i, n_j) \tag{1}$$

For determining the semantic similarity $sim(x_i, n_j)$ between each sense of the nouns extracted from the gloss of verb and each sense of the input noun, we use the Formula 2 and 3:

$$sim(x_i, n_j) = 1 - sd(x_i, n_j)^2 \tag{2}$$

$$sd(x_i, n_j) = \frac{1}{2} \cdot \left(\frac{D1 - D}{D1} + \frac{D2 - D}{D2} \right) \tag{3}$$

where $sim(x_i, n_j)$ is the semantic similarity between two concepts defined by their WordNet synsets x_i and n_j; $sd(x_i, n_j)$ is the semantic distance for nouns. $D1$ is the depth of synset x_i, $D2$ is the depth of synset n_j, and D is the depth of their nearest common ancestor in the monolingual WordNet hierarchy.

2.4. Determine the total similarity between the sense h of verb (v_h) and all the senses of input noun $< n_1, n_2, \ldots, n_m >$. For each n_j: $Ts(h, j) = \sum_{i=1}^{n} sim(x_i, n_j)$ where n is the number of nouns extracted from the gloss of the sense h of the verb.

Step 3. To resume all similarity matrixes (Sm) obtained in Step 2 for each sense of verb, we make now the total similarity matrix (Tsm) composed by total similarity (Ts) for each sense of verb and each sense of noun. Each element of this matrix is defined as follows: $Tsm(i, j) = Ts(i, j)$.

Step 4. The most similar sense combination scores the highest value in the total similarity matrix (Tsm). So the output of the algorithm is the pair verb-noun $(v_i - n_j)$ that contains this value in the matrix. Therefore the sense of the verb is chosen and given as the solution.

4   Multilingual Natural Language Interface

In order to resolve the lexical ambiguity in Spanish and English texts it is necessary the creation of an interface to disambiguate the words senses that appear in the context of a sentence. This interface is made up of a set of computer programs that do all the processing to assign ultimately the correct sense to the Spanish and English words. First, users introduce a Spanish or English sentence in the WSD interface. This sentence is sent to the parser for starting the analysis process. After, a process checks the information returned by the parser and endows it the appropriate structure for their handling for the WSD module and insert it in a file. This file is the input data to the WSD process that carries out the disambiguation of the text based in Specification Marks and Semantic similarity methods and using the lexical database EuroWordNet. Finally, when the WSD process concludes another process formats the information disambiguated and this information is sent to the interface in order to show it to the user. This interface is illustrate in the Figure 2.

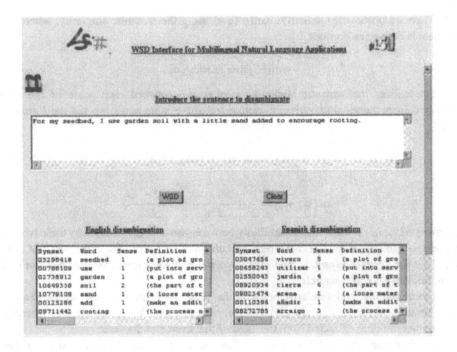

Fig. 2. WSD Interface.

The user interface offers the operations followed:

Run WSD process. The command button WSD allows one to run the lexical ambiguity methods (Specification Marks and Semantic Similarity) from the input sentence and the words senses is returned in Spanish and English languages.

Clear Process. The user clicks on this command button to delete the information that appears in both text windows.

Sometimes one or more words cannot be disambiguated, then this kind of words is shown in both texts window below command buttons preceded by the symbol asterisk (*). In this case it is shown all the possible senses of the word.

5 Discussions and Conclusions

This paper presents a WSD interface, which it could be very useful for multilingual natural language applications, because it returns the words senses in different languages. This interface use the taxonomy of EuroWordNet lexical knowledge database to resolve lexical ambiguity of nouns and verbs in Spanish and English input texts. WSD module uses two different WSD methods for disambiguating the nouns and verbs of the texts: Specification Marks Method for nouns and Semantic Similarity for verbs, respectively. The University of Alicante system presented at Senseval-2 workshop joins these two methods in the WSD task. Specification Marks for nouns, and Semantic Similarity for verbs had been used in order to process the test data of English lexical sample task and Spanish lexical sample task. The system obtains a successful score when comparing with the evaluation results of other unsupervised systems. A relevant consequence of the application of this interface is that provide support across different languages converting the words senses from one language into other languages. Besides, it will also could be used as a basic resource for supporting other natural language applications, such as Machine Translation (MT), Question Answering, Information Retrieval (IR). For example, an interesting possibility is to use this multilingual interface to improve cross languages information retrieval systems.

References

1. A. Ferrández, M. Palomar, and L. Moreno. Slot Unification Grammar. In *Proceedings of the Joint Conference on Declarative Programming. APPIA-GULP-PRODE*, pages 523–532, Grado, Italy, 1997.

2. N. Ide and J. Veronis. Introduction to the Special Issue on Word Sense Disambiguation: The State of the Art. *Computational Linguistics*, 24(1):1–40, 1998.

3. D. Lin. Dependency-based Evaluation of MINIPAR. In *Workshop on the Evaluation of Parsing Systems*, Granada, Spain, 1998.

4. Rada Mihalcea and Dan Moldovan. A Method for word sense disambiguation of unrestricted text. In *Proceedings of the 37th Annual Meeting of the Association for Computational Linguistic*, pages 152–158, Maryland, Usa, 1999.

5. G. Miller, R. Beckwith, C. Fellbaum, D. Gross, and K. Miller. WordNet: An on-line lexical database. *International journal of lexicography*, 3(4):235–244, 1990.

6. Andrés Montoyo and Manuel Palomar. Word Sense Disambiguation with Specification Marks in Unrestricted Texts. In *Proceedings of 11th International Workshop on Database and Expert Systems Applications (DEXA 2000). 11th International Workshop on Database and Expert Systems Applications*, pages 103–107, Greenwich, London, UK, September 2000. IEEE Computer Society.

7. Andrés Montoyo and Manuel Palomar. WSD Algorithm Applied to a NLP System . In Mokrane Bouzeghoub, Zoubida Kedad, and Elisabeth Métais, editors, *Proceedings of 5th International conference on Applications of Natural Language to Information Systems (NLDB-2000). Natural Language Processing and Information Systems*, Lecture Notes in Computer Science, pages 54–65, Versailles, France, June 2000. Springer-Verlag.

8. Andrés Montoyo and Manuel Palomar. Specification Marks for Word Sense Disambiguation: New Development. In A. Gelbukh, editor, *Proceedings of 2nd International conference on Intelligent Text Processing and Computational Linguistics (CICLing-2001). Computational Linguistics and Intelligent Text Processing*, Lecture Notes in Computer Science, pages 182–191, Mexico City, February 2001. Springer-Verlag.

9. M. Palomar, M. Saiz-Noeda, R. Muñoz, A. Suárez, P. Martínez-Barco, and A. Montoyo. PHORA: A NLP aystem for Spanish. In A. Gelbukh, editor, *Proceedings of 2nd International conference on Intelligent Text Processing and Computational Linguistics (CICLing-2001)*. *Computational Linguistics and Intelligent Text Processing*, Lecture Notes in Computer Science, pages 126–139, Mexico City, February 2001. Springer-Verlag.

10. F. Pla. *Etiquetado Léxico y Análisis Sintáctico Superficial basado en Modelos Estadísticos*. Tesis doctoral, Departamento de Sistemas Informáticos y Computación. Universidad de Politécnica de Valencia, Septiembre 2000.

11. Susana Soler and Andrés Montoyo. A Proposal for WSD using Semantic Similarity. In A. Gelbukh, editor, *Proceedings of Third International conference on Intelligent Text Processing and Computational Linguistics (CICLing-2002)*. *Computational Linguistics and Intelligent Text Processing*, Lecture Notes in Computer Science, pages 165–167, Mexico City, February 2002. Springer-Verlag.

12. J. Stetina, S. Kurohashi, and M. Nagao. General word sense disambiguation method based on full sentencial context. In *Proceedings of Usage of WordNet in Natural Language Processing. COLING-ACL Workshop*, Montreal, Canada, 1998.

13. P. Vossen. EuroWordNet: Building a Multilingual Database with WordNets for European Languages. *The ELRA Newsletter*, 3(1), 1998.

Gibbsian Context-Free Grammar for Parsing

Antoine Rozenknop

Swiss Federal Institute of Technology, I&C-IIF-LIA, CH-1015 Lausanne, Switzerland,
E-mail: Antoine.rozenknop@epfl.ch

Abstract. Probabilistic Context-Free Grammars can be used for speech recognition or syntactic analysis thanks to especially efficient algorithms. In this paper, we propose an instantiation of such a grammar, which mathematical properties are intuitively more suitable for those tasks than SCFG's (Stochastic CFG), without requiring specific analysis algorithms. Results on the Susanne text show that up to 33 % of analysis errors made by a SCFG can be avoided with this model.

1 Motivations

Stochastic Context-Free Grammars (SCFGs) are far from being up-to-date models for the desciption of natural languages, but they still remain interesting models for Parsing and Speech Recognition [4], thanks to particularly efficient algorithms they provide for those tasks [6,11,2]. They can also be used as computational representations of richer grammars, such as Polynomial Tree Substitution Grammars [3].

However, their mathematical properties seem somewhat strange and lower the quality of the results they provide when used for such tasks [10].

This article describes a new probabilisation of Context-Free Grammars, which essentially is a non-generative variation of the SCFGs, and which will be denoted as GCFG (for "Gibbsian CFG"). In this model, each context-free rule of the CFG is mapped to a "potential" instead of a probability, and the learning criteria is turned to fit the analysis task instead of a generative task. This model should have a better parsing behaviour while taking benefit of the efficiency of SCFGs parsing algorithms.

In the remaining of this paper, an example of a non-intuitive behaviour of SCFGs is shown in Section 2, the GCFG model is described, along with a learning algorithm, in Section 3, SCFGs and GCFGs are experimentally compared in Section 4, and conclusions are given in Section 5.

2 Non-intuitive Behaviour of a SCFG

This example is extracted from M. Johnson's study [7], and illustrates a seemingly paradoxal behaviour of SCFGs. Suppose we have a treebank $\widetilde{\mathcal{T}}_1$ with two trees (A) et (B) (Figure 1), where (A) appears with relative frequency f. An SCFG is trained on this corpus with the usual method, which consists in assigning to the rules probabilities proportionnal to their frequency in the corpus. Rules probabilities $(\hat{P}_1)$ obtained from this corpus are as follows:

P. Sojka, I. Kopeček, and K. Pala (Eds.): TSD 2002, LNAI 2448, pp. 49–56, 2002.

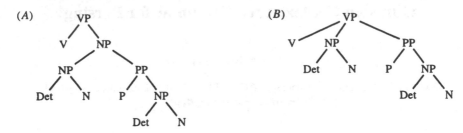

Fig. 1. Training corpus $\tilde{\tau}_1$. This corpus contains the tree (A) with relative frequency f, and (B) with r.f. $(1 - f)$.

$\hat{P}_1 (VP \to V\ NP) = f$, $\hat{P}_1 (VP \to V\ NP\ PP) = 1 - f$, $\hat{P}_1 (NP \to Det\ N) = 2/(\varrho + f)$ and $\hat{P}_1 (NP \to NP\ PP) = f/(\varrho + f)$. Thus, the probabilities of producing (A) and (B) with the resulting model are: $\hat{P}_1 (A) = 4f^2/(\varrho + f)^3$ and $\hat{P}_1 (B) = 4(1 - f)/(2 + f)^2$. The estimated relative frequency of (A) among trees parsing V Det N P Det N is: $\hat{f}_1 = \hat{P}_1 (A) / (\hat{P}_1 (A) + \hat{P}_1 (B)) = f^2/(\varrho - f)$. Ideally, $\hat{f}_1$ should be close to the observed relative frequency f. Figure 2 shows $\hat{f}_1$ as a function of f; as can be seen, $\hat{f}_1$ and f can differ substantially. For instance, if $f = 0.75$, $\hat{f}_1 = 0.45$, i.e. even if (A) appears three times as often as (B) in the training corpus, V Det N P Det N will be parsed as (B).

M. Johnson suspects that this behaviour is due to the non-systematicity of the structures in the training corpus: in tree (A), $(NP \Rightarrow {}^* Det\ N\ PP)$ follows Chomsky's Adjonctive Form, whereas $(VP \Rightarrow {}^* V\ NP\ PP)$ has a flat structure in (B). To test this hypothesis, the corpus is modified, either by flattening $(NP \Rightarrow {}^* Det\ N\ PP)$ in (A) (i.e. representing the structure by the unique rule NP $\to$ Det N PP), or by replacing $(VP \to V\ NP\ PP)$ in (B) with $(VP \to VP\ PP)$ and $(VP \to V\ NP)$. Each of the two modified corpora thus obtained are used to train an SCFG, and the estimated relative frequency of the first tree as a function of its observed frequency is respectively: $\hat{f}_2 = (f^2 - 2f)/(2f^2 - f - 2)$, and $\hat{f}_3 = f^2/(\varrho - 3f + 2f^2)$. Those estimated frequencies are closer to f than $\hat{f}_1$, but remain lower, as illustrated by Figure 2. In each case, when the observed frequency of the NP-attachment of PP is 0.6, the computed model will affect a higher score to the VP-attachment of PP.

3   Gibbsian Context-Free Grammar (GCFG)

We now describe the GCFG model, which is strongly inspired from SCFGs. The grammar is composed of a set of N_r rewriting rules $X \to Y_1 \ldots Y_{|r|}$, N_s terminal and non-terminal symbols, terminal symbols only appearing in right parts of rules. Moreover, each rule r_i is associated with a potential value λ_i (instead of a probability as in SCFGs).

3.1   Potential of a Tree and Conditional Probability

As opposed to a SCFG, this model is not generative. One thus does not seek to define the probability of producing a tree with this model. On the other hand, one defines the **potential of an analysis tree** x as the sum of the potentials of the rules which constitute it. It is thus

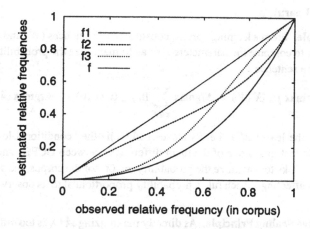

Fig. 2. Estimated relative frequencies of NP-attachment of the PP group, as a function of its observed relative frequency in the different training corpora.

the scalar product $\lambda \cdot f(x)$ of two vectors of size N_r (the number of context-free rules), component i of λ being the potential λ_i of rule r_i, and component i of $f(x)$ being the number of occurrences f_i of the rule r_i in the tree x.

One defines moreover the probability of an analysis tree x conditionally to its leaves $w = (w_1 \ldots w_n)$ (i.e. w stands for the analysed sentence) with the formula:

$$p(x \mid w) = \frac{e^{\lambda \cdot f(x)}}{\sum_{y \Rightarrow^* w} e^{\lambda \cdot f(y)}},$$

where $\sum_{y \Rightarrow^* w}$ is the sum over all trees y of the grammar which leaves are w.

3.2 Syntactic Analysis with a GCFG

The syntactic analysis of a sentence w consists in finding the tree $\bar{x}$ with the highest potential among possible analysis trees. As stated by the previous formula, this is equivalent to finding the tree with the highest conditional probability:

$$\bar{x} = \operatorname*{Argmax}_{x \Rightarrow^* w} \lambda \cdot f(x) = \operatorname*{Argmax}_{x \Rightarrow^* w} p_\lambda(x \mid w) = \operatorname*{Argmax}_{x \Rightarrow^* w} \prod_{r_i \in x} e^{\lambda_i f_i(x)}$$

The last expression shows how close this model is to a SCFG, where the solution of the syntactic analysis is: $\bar{x} = \operatorname*{Argmax}_{x \Rightarrow^* w} p(x) = \operatorname*{Argmax}_{x \Rightarrow^* w} \prod_{r_i \in x} p(r_i)^{f_i(x)}$

GCFGs thus do not require the development of specific analysis algorithms: one can use as is any SCFG's algorithm, provided it does not make use of the condition $p(r_i) \leq 1$. In particular, $A*$-algorithms use this condition by making the assumption that the score monotonically decreases with the length of the hypotheses, and cannot be used here. A bottom-up chart parser, described in [2], has been used for our tests, by simply replacing the rule probabilities $p(r_i)$ with e^{λ_i}.

3.3   Parameter Learning

Learning Principle. From a learning corpus, constituted of sentences (W) and their analysis trees (X), we seek to compute the parameters λ so as to maximize the probability of the trees conditionally to the sentences:

$$\bar{\lambda} = \underset{\lambda}{\text{Argmax}}\, p_\lambda\,(X\,|W) = \underset{\lambda}{\text{Argmax}}\sum_{x \in X} \ln p_\lambda\,(x\,|w\,(x)\,) = \underset{\lambda}{\text{Argmax}}\,\mathcal{A}\,(\lambda)$$

(by writing $w\,(x)$ the leaves of x, i.e. its leaves.) $\mathcal{A}\,(\lambda)$ is the "conditional log-likelihood" of the corpus; note that this is one of the main differences between GCFGs and SCFGs, for which one usually seeks to maximize the probability $p_\lambda\,(X)$ of the corpus, the solution being easily obtained by affecting to each rule a probability proportionnal to its observed frequency.

Improved Iterative Scaling Principle. As directly maximizing $\mathcal{A}\,(\lambda)$ is too difficult, we start from an initial model λ_0 (the choice of this initial model can be crucial, but is not discussed here), and iteratively improve it. A step of iteration consists in passing from a model λ to a model λ', by trying to maximize $\mathcal{D}_\lambda\,(X) = \mathcal{A}\,(X) - \mathcal{A}\,(\lambda) = \sum_{x \in X} \ln \frac{p_{\lambda'}\,(x|w\,(x)\,)}{p_\lambda\,(x|w\,(x)\,)}$. As this maximization is again untractable, a step of IIS will maximize the intermediary function $\mathcal{B}_\lambda\,(X)$ which is a minorant of $\mathcal{D}_\lambda\,(X)$:

$$\mathcal{B}_\lambda\,(X) = \sum_{x \in X}(X - \lambda)\cdot f\,(x) - \sum_{x \in X}\sum_{y \to w\,(x)} p_\lambda\,(y\,|w\,(x)\,)\sum_i \frac{f_i\,(y)}{f^\#\,(y)}e^{\,(X - \lambda_i)f^\#\,(y)} + |X|$$

where $f^\#\,(y) = \sum_i f_i\,(y)$ is the number of rules appearing in a tree y. Details about the mathematical derivations of $\mathcal{B}_\lambda\,(X)$ from $\mathcal{D}_\lambda\,(X)$ are well explained in [1,9,8].

Maximizing $\mathcal{B}_\lambda\,(X)$ is done by finding the point where its partial derivatives are null, i.e. by solving for each rule r_i:

$$0 = -\sum_{x \in X} f_i\,(x) + \sum_{x \in X}\sum_{y \to w\,(x)} p_\lambda\,(y\,|w\,(x)\,)f_i\,(y)\,e^{\,(\lambda'_i - \lambda_i)f^\#\,(y)} \tag{1}$$

Due to the convexity of the polynoms involved in these equations, their solutions can easily be computed with a Newton's method.

Inside-Outside Algorithm. The first term of the polynom, $-\sum_{x \in X} f_i\,(x)$, is trivially obtained as the frequency of r_i in the training corpus. But the other coefficients are far more complex to compute: the term $\sum_{y \Rightarrow^* w}\,\dots$ requires a summation over all possible analyses of w, which can be an exponential problem. This step is sometimes approximatively solved by sampling methods [9]. Here, we can happily factorize the computation by using an Inside-Outside algorithm, as shown by the following manipulations.

Let us rewrite the third sum of (1):

$$S_{w,\lambda}\,(\alpha) = \sum_{y \to w} p_\lambda\,(y\,|w\,)f_i\,(y)\,\alpha^{f^\#\,(y)} = \Big(\sum_{y \to w} e^{\lambda\cdot f\,(x)}\Big)^{-1}\sum_{y \to w} e^{\lambda\cdot f\,(y)}f_i\,(y)\,\alpha^{f^\#\,(y)}$$

$$= Z_{\lambda,w}^{-1}\sum_{1 \le j \le k \le |w|\,|\,y \Rightarrow^* w}\sum V\,(y)C\,(y,[j,r_i,k])$$

where $C(y, [j, r_i, k])$ is the number of occurrences of r_i in y at position (j, k) (i.e. when r_i dominates $w_j \ldots w_k$ in y), where $V(y) = e^{\lambda \cdot f(y)} \alpha f^*(y) = \prod_{r_i \in y} (f_i \alpha)^{f_i(y)}$ is the product of the polynoms $P_i(\alpha) = (\lambda_i \alpha)$ associated with the rules r_i that constitute y, and $Z_{\lambda,w} = \sum_{y \Rightarrow^* w} e^{\lambda \cdot f(x)}$.

Following [5] (pp.26–57) $\sum_{y \Rightarrow^* w} V(y)C(y, [j, r_i, k])$ can then be computed for each r_i, j and k with an Inside-Outside algorithm, which we can sketch by:

– For each triplet (j, r_i, k), compute $inside_r[j, r_i, k]$ as the sum of the values $V(y)$ of trees y which top rule is r_i, and which leaves are $w_j \ldots w_k$.
– For each triplet (j, A, k), compute $outside[j, A, k]$, as the sum of the values $V(y)$ of trees y which leaves are $w_1 \ldots w_{j-1} A w_{k+1} \ldots w_n$.
– Noting $G(r_i)$ the left-side symbol of r_i, the result is obtained with:

$$\sum_{y \Rightarrow^* w} V(y)C(y, [j, r_i, k]) = inside_r[j, r_i, k] * outside[j, G(r_i), k].$$

Improved Iterative Scaling Algorithm. Finally, the training algorithm can be summed up as follows:

```
Define an initial model λ'
Repeat:
    λ ← λ'.
    /* from λ to λ' */
    Initialize to zero the polynoms Sʳ(α) associated with rules r.
    For each example x of the learning corpus:
        Analyze w(x) with the Inside-Outside algorithm.
        Compute Z_{λ,w(x)} as the sum of the coefficients of the polynom
        ∑_r inside_r[1,r,n].
        Foe each element [j,r,k] of the Inside-Outside chart
            Sʳ(α) := Sʳ(α) + Z⁻¹_{λ,w(x)} ∑_{y⇒*w} V(y)C(y, [j,r_i,k])
                   (= Sʳ(α) + Z⁻¹_{λ,w(x)} inside_r[j,r,k] * outside[j,G(r) k])
        Foe each rule r_i of the CFG:
            Solve: Sʳⁱ(α₀) = -sum_{x∈X} f_i(x)
            Compute the model parameter λ' with: λ'_i = λ_i + log α₀
until convergence of criterium A(λ)
```

4 Experimental Results

The GCFG model has been tested on a SUSANNE-derived corpus, containing 4292 trees, 1920 non-terminal symbols, 11935 terminal symbols, 17669 rules. Some unary rules were manually removed so as to obtain a non-looping grammar.

The first test consists of learning the model from the complete corpus, parsing the sentences of the corpus with the obtained parameters, and comparing the resulting trees with the reference trees. Results are grouped under the label $Test = Learn$ in Figure 3. Column Tx(Par) represents the rate of sentences receiving a parse, and among them Tx(Cor) represents the rate of those which parse is the correct one. Precision and Recall rates (columns Pre et Rec) are obtained by considering the sequence of parse trees $\tilde{\tau}$ as a set $E(\tilde{\tau})$ of triplets $< g, N, d >$, where N is a non-terminal symbol, and g et d are the positions in the corpus of the first and last words dominated by N. When comparing with the reference trees $\tilde{T}'$, la precision and recall are computed as:

$$Tx\,(Pre)\,\tilde{T}) = \frac{|E\,(\tilde{T}) \cap E\,(\tilde{T}')|}{|E\,(\tilde{T})|}\,, \quad Tx\,(Rap)\,\tilde{T}) = \frac{|E\,(\tilde{T}) \cap E\,(\tilde{T}')|}{|E\,(\tilde{T}')|}$$

In the second experiment, the training process takes place on 9 tenth of the corpus, and the test is performed on the remaining part. In order to cope with the very low coverage of the grammar, the split has been performed so that each rule appearing in the test part appears at least 9 times in the training part of the corpus. The grammar has been simplified in order to make parsing ambiguous enough for the statistics to be useful.

The SCFG model was tested on the same corpora, and we give the *diminution of Error-Rates* that GCFG provide in comparison. These values are computed as: $1 - \frac{1-Tx[GCFG]}{1-Tx[SCFG]}$.

| | | Test = Learn | | | Test $\neq$ Learn | | | |
| | | Lexicalized corpus | | | Simplified corpus | | | |
Model	Tx(Par)	Tx(Cor)	Pre	Rec	Tx(Par)	Tx(Cor)	Pre	Rec
SCFG	1	0.788	0.989	0.988	1	0.860	0.983	0.982
GCFG	1	0.860	0.994	0.994	1	0.866	0.984	0.982
Diminution of Error-Rate		33 %	48 %	49 %		4.1 %	4.5 %	5.6 %

Fig. 3. Compared results of SCFGs and GCFGs, for a parsing task.

4.1 Discussion

The example of Section 2 shows that a SCFG which parameters are learned from a treebank can exhibit an unexpected behaviour, affecting higher probabilities to seldom forms. On the same example, a GCFG conforms to intuition, i.e. the estimated and observed frequencies of (A) are the same (which we do not demonstrate here). This difference is mainly explained by the difference between their learning criteria: SCFGs are usually considered as generative models, and their learning stage maximizes the probability of generating the corpus with an underlying stochastic process starting from the root of a tree. Their learning criterium thus is [1]: $p_\lambda\,(X)$. Such a model makes the assumption that language is generated by a grammatical process.

On the contrary, GCFGs are designed as analysis models, and their learning criterium is $p_\lambda\,(X\,|W)$, which intuitively corresponds to the probability of generating the corpus from its leaves. If possible, this criterium is maximized when the estimated frequencies of trees of same leaves are proportional to their frequency in the corpus. As there are enough parameters to reach this result in the example, this explains the perfect adequation of the observed and estimated frequencies.

---

[1] cf. Section 3 for notations

Section 2 also relates the fact that representing the structures (NP ⇒ * Det N PP) and (VP ⇒ * V NP PP) in a similar way in the corpus (i.e. either both flattened or both under Chomsky's Adjonctive Form) enhances the performance of the trained SCFGs. Nothing comparable can be observed for GCFGs, which behave in the same way in every case. However, tests with more realistic corpora [7] show that only the flattening scheme really enhances the performance of SCFGs. M. Johnson suspects the reason is linked to the weakening of independance assumptions of CF grammars this flattening scheme induces. It should be interesting to measure in the same way the impact of this flattening operation on a GCFG, for which independance assumption are not so strong: the potential of a rule is computed in comparison with all rules of the grammar, and not only with the rules that share the same head, as in SCFGs.

GCFGs perform well in self-test (*Test* = *Learn* column of Figure 3): with the same number of parameters as a SCFG trained in the same conditions, the number of incorrect parses is multiplied by $2/3$, and the label precision and recall error rates are multiplied by $1/2$: GCFGs "stick" undoubtedly better to learning data than SCFGs.

In the generalisation scheme (*Test* = *Learn* column), most of our experiments show no significant improvement when using GCFGs, due to the very low coverage of the underlying CFG: only 6 % of test sentences are parsed by this CFG (26 sentences out of 429). Moreover, the number of context-free rules (17669) is huge as compared to the size of the learning corpus (4292 − 429 trees), and the computed parameters are likely to be insignificant for generalization. However, when we simplify the grammar, so as to insure meaningful statistics on the corpus, GCFGs perform slightly better than SCFGs (see Figure 3).

5 Conclusion

This contribution presents a valuation method for Context-Free Grammars, which differs from SCFGs by its training criterium, suited to a parsing task, and by the relaxation of stochastic constraints ($p_i \leq 1$, et $\sum p = 1$) imposed to the parameters of a SCFG. The resulting grammars (GCFG) having essentially the same form as SCFGs, we are provided with standard efficient parsing algorithms that can be used without modification. We have also detailed an algorithm for training the GCFG model within a reasonnable time.

Experimental studies show that GCFG parameters better stick to training data and intuition than SCFG ones. This is also true when parsing unseen sentences, provided that the grammar has a sufficient coverage, and that the corpus is big enough to compute meaningful statistics, which can be the main issue for using such models in real life applications.

Other applications of the exposed principle are foreseen, such as its adaptation to Polynomial Tree Substitution Grammars [3], We also plan to adapt GCFGs to deal with a Speech Recognition task, by changing its learning criterium.

References

1. Adam Berger. Convexity, maximum likelihood and all that.
2. J.-C. Chappelier and M. Rajman. A generalized CYK algorithm for parsing stochastic CFG. In *Proc. of 1st Workshop on Tabulation in Parsing and Deduction (TAPD'98)*, pp. 133–137, Paris (France), Apr 1998.

3. J.-C. Chappelier and M. Rajman. Grammaire à substitution d'arbre de complexité polynomiale: un cadre efficace pour dop. In *Actes de la 8ème conférence sur le Traitement Automatique des Langues Naturelles (TALN 2001)*, volume 1, pp. 133–142, 2001.

4. J.-C. Chappelier, M. Rajman, R. Aragüés, and A. Rozenknop. Lattice parsing for speech recognition. In *Proc. of 6ème conférence sur le Traitement Automatique du Langage Naturel (TALN '99)*, pp. 95–104, Cargèse (France), Jul 1999.

5. Joshua T. Goodman. *Parsing Inside-Out*. Ph.D. thesis, Harvard University, Cambridge, Massachusetts, May 1998.

6. F. Jelinek, J. D. Lafferty, and R. L. Mercer. Basic methods of probabilistic context-free grammars. In P. Laface and R. De Mori, editors, *Speech Recognition and Understanding: Recent Advances, Trends and Applications*, volume 75 of *F: Computer and System Science*. Springer, 1992.

7. Mark Johnson. Pcfg models of linguistic tree representations. *Computational Linguistics*, 24(4):613–632, December 1998.

8. John Lafferty. Gibbs-Markov models. In *Computing Science and Statistics*, volume 27, pp. 370–377, 1996.

9. Stephen Della Pietra, Vincent J. Della Pietra, and John D. Lafferty. Inducing features of random fields. *IEEE Transactions on Pattern Analysis and Machine Intelligence*, 19(4):380–393, 1997.

10. Antoine Rozenknop and Marius-Calin Silaghi. Algorithme de décodage de treillis selon le critère du coût moyen pour la reconnaissance de la parole. In *Actes de la 8ème conférence sur le Traitement Automatique des Langues Naturelles (TALN 2001)*, number 1, pp. 391–396, Tours, juillet 2001. Association pour le Traitement Automatique des Langues.

11. A. Stolcke. An efficient probabilistic context-free parsing algorithm that computes prefix probabilities. *Computational Linguistics*, 21(2):165–201, 1995.

Cross-Language Access to Recorded Speech in the MALACH Project

Douglas W. Oard[1], Dina Demner-Fushman[1], Jan Hajič[2], Bhuvana Ramabhadran[3], Samuel Gustman[4], William J. Byrne[5], Dagobert Soergel[1], Bonnie Dorr[1], Philip Resnik[1], and Michael Picheny[3]

[1] University of Maryland, College Park, MD 20742 USA,
E-mail: oard@umiacs.umd.edu, demner@umiacs.umd.edu, bonnie@umiacs.umd.edu, resnik@umiacs.umd.edu, ds52@umail.umd.edu
[2] Charles University, CZ-11800 Praha 1, Czech Republic
E-mail: hajic@ufal.ms.mff.cuni.cz
[3] IBM T. J. Watson Research Center, Yorktown Heights, NY 10598 USA E-mail: bhuvana@us.ibm.com, picheny@us.ibm.com
[4] Survivors of the Shoah Visual History Foundation, Los Angeles, CA 90078 USA
E-mail: sam@vhf.org
[5] Johns Hopkins University, Baltimore, MD 21218 USA,
E-mail: byrne@jhu.edu

Abstract. The MALACH project seeks to help users find information in a vast multilingual collections of untranscribed oral history interviews. This paper introduces the goals of the project and focuses on supporting access by users who are unfamiliar with the interview language. It begins with a review of the state of the art in cross-language speech retrieval; approaches that will be investigated in the project are then described. Czech was selected as the first non-English language to be supported, so results of an initial experiment with Czech/English cross-language retrieval are reported.

1 Introduction

Digital archives of recorded speech are emerging as an important way of capturing the human experience. Before such archives can be used efficiently, however, their contents must be described in a way that supports access to the information that they contain. Our ability to collect and store digitized speech now greatly outstrips our ability to manually describe what we have collected, but present automated technologies for search and exploration in spoken materials still have sharply limited capabilities. The MALACH (Multilingual Access to Large Spoken Archives) project is working with what we believe is the world's largest coherent archive of video oral histories to apply emerging speech recognition and natural language processing technologies to this important problem. In this paper we identify the research issues raised by the project, with particular emphasis on those related to handling Eastern European languages, describe the approach that we plan to take to explore these issues, and present the results of an initial cross-language retrieval experiment between Czech and English.

P. Sojka, I. Kopeček, and K. Pala (Eds.): TSD 2002, LNAI 2448, pp. 57–64, 2002.

2   The MALACH Project

MALACH is a five-year project that brings together the Survivors of the Shoah Visual History Foundation (VHF), the University of Maryland, the IBM T.J. Watson Research Center, Johns Hopkins University, Charles University and the University of West Bohemia to (1) advance the state of the art in speech recognition to handle spontaneous, emotional, heavily accented, and elderly speech in multiple languages with uncued language switching, (2) develop automated techniques for the generation of metadata in multiple languages to support information access, and (3) advance the state of the art in information retrieval to provide efficient search, indexing and retrieval of recorded interviews.

In 1994, after releasing the film *Schindler's List*, Steven Spielberg was approached by many survivors to listen to their stories of the Holocaust. Spielberg decided to start the VHF so that as many survivors as possible could tell their stories so that they could be used to teach about the horrors of intolerance. Today, the VHF has collected almost 52,000 testimonies (116,000 hours of video) in 32 languages. Five copies of each testimony exist, including an MPEG-1 3 Mb/s version for digital distribution. The entire digitized archive occupies 180 terabytes of storage. During the collection of each testimony, a forty page survey in the survivor or witnesses native language was taken. These surveys have been entered into the digital library and form an initial catalog for searching through the subject matter in each interview. Working with information scientists and historians, a cataloging system for indexing the content of each testimony has been created. Today, thirty catalogers work with this system to manually assign metadata from a thesaurus tailored for this purpose to portions of each video at a rate of about 1,000 hours per month.

Our preliminary experiments with three different speaker-independent English speech recognition systems trained with very different material (broadcast news, dictation and telephone conversations) resulted in remarkably similar word error rates (nearly 60 %) on the VHF collection. Conventional adaptation techniques improved the performance significantly, bringing the word error rate down to around 33 % for fluent speakers and 46 % for heavily accented and disfluent speakers (which are common in the collection). Moreover, approximately 15 % of the words were outside the vocabulary on which the recognizer was trained, so these domain-specific terms, many of which are named entities, will require special handling. Although the ultimate goal of speech recognition research is to produce readable transcripts, our more limited immediate goal in this project is to produce transcripts that are adequate to support metadata creation and information retrieval (see [7] for a description of the issues involved). The huge size of the collection makes it a unique resource for exploring the effect of corpus size on the word error rate reduction that can be achieved through long-term adaptation, and the presence of so many languages makes it an unmatched resource for exploring the potential of bootstrapping speech recognition systems in less frequently spoken languages for which sharply limited quantities of annotated training data might be available.

The linear nature of recorded speech poses unique problems for information access that we plan to investigate. The linguistic diversity of the collection adds additional challenges, both because we want to support queries in the same language as the materials (and must therefore support many languages) and because we think it will be valuable to provide access to interviews that were not conducted in the language in which the query was posed. We have described the other issues in detail elsewhere (see [4]), so for the remainder of this paper we focus on supporting cross-language access to spoken word collections.

3 Cross-Language Access to Recorded Speech

Cross-language access to recorded speech poses three challenges: (1) automatically searching the collection using queries that may be expressed in a language different from that used by the speaker, (2) manually selecting portions of the top-ranked recordings that satisfy the searcher's information need, and (3) making use of the selected parts of those recordings. We believe that the first two problems are tractable within the scope of this project, and we ultimately hope that our results will be applied synergistically with ongoing research efforts in speech-to-speech translation for an overview of recent research on this topic). Present speech-to-speech translation systems achieve robust performance only in limited domains, however, so we expect that in the near term cross-language use of materials that are found using the technology that we are building will be achieved through collaboration between a subject matter expert (who may lack needed language skills) and an assistant who is fluent in the spoken language. In the remainder of this section we therefore address each of the first two challenges in turn.

Cross-language text retrieval and monolingual speech retrieval are both well-researched problems (see [9] for a survey of the first and [1] for a survey of the second), and these two challenges have been explored together using the Topic Detection and Tracking (TDT) collections. All of the work to date on speech retrieval – both monolingual and cross-language – has focused on broadcast news, one of the more tractable applications for speech recognition technology. The conversational, emotional, and accented speech in the VHF collection pose substantial challenges to presently available speech recognition techniques, and addressing those challenges is a principal focus of the MALACH project. In a related project, we are developing inexpensive techniques for extending cross-language retrieval capabilities to new language pairs, and as speech recognition techniques that are tuned to the characteristics of the VHF collection are developed we will begin to explore the potential of automated cross-language search techniques for this application. We expect that techniques we have used with the TDT collection such as document expansion based on blind relevance feedback [6] and phonetic transliteration rules learned from examples [8] will be useful, and what we learn about the unique characteristics of oral history interviews in our monolingual experiments may help us to see additional opportunities to improve cross-language search capabilities.

The availability of manually-assigned thesaurus descriptors offers a complementary basis for cross-language searching. Thesaurus-based searching can be quite effective if the searcher is familiar with the structure of the thesaurus, so one option is to arrange for the assistance of a specially trained search intermediary. Automated text classification can also be used to help users find thesaurus terms that are associated with natural language (free text) queries (see [3] for an example of how this can be done). The VHF collection provides an unmatched source of data for training automatic text classification algorithms, with nearly 200,000 training examples in which a three-sentence English summary of a topically-coherent interview segment is associated with one or more thesaurus descriptors. In another project, we are exploring the extension of similar capabilities to new languages by annotating the English half of a parallel (translation-equivalent) corpus, projecting the annotations to the other language, and then training a new classifier using the projected annotations (see [11] for a description of how this idea has been applied to related problems). In order to apply this idea to our classification task, we will need to assemble a large collection of topically appropriate parallel texts and we will need to develop classification algorithms that are relatively insensitive to the types of divergences that we observe between languages (e.g., head switching). Translation of documents about the Holocaust is a common practice, so we expect to be able to meet the first requirement for at least some language pairs, and we expect that the second task will benefit from the results of an investigation of translation divergence that we are presently undertaking (see [2] for some early results from that work). We therefore expect to be able to provide some useful degree of mapping between free text search terms and controlled vocabulary thesaurus descriptors, even before thesaurus term translations are available.

Cross-language document selection has only recently received attention from researchers. In the first multi-site evaluation effort of interactive cross-language retrieval from a collection of text, the Cross-Language Evaluation Forum's interactive track (iCLEF) [10], Lòpez-Ostenero, et al. found that translated key phrases could be used as a basis for selection as effectively as full (but sometimes disfluent) machine translations. Merlino and Maybury found that similar phrase-based summaries were also helpful for interactive monolingual retrieval from multimedia (audio and video) collections. The manually assigned thesaurus descriptors in the VHF collection provide an excellent starting point for extending these techniques to support interactive cross-language selection of recorded speech. The present thesaurus contains only English vocabulary, but the relatively compact and specialized vocabulary used in the thesaurus facilitates translation. Moreover, the concept relationships that the thesaurus encodes offer an additional source of evidence to guide automatic or semiautomatic disambiguation algorithms. We also plan to leverage the human-assigned descriptors in the VHF collection to explore the degree to which we can provide similar support for document selection using automatic text classification techniques based on annotation projection through parallel corpora.

4   Searching Czech Documents with English Queries

Czech will be the first non-English language for which we plan to develop speech recognition techniques that are tuned to the VHF collection. We are not aware of any prior work on Czech/English cross-language information retrieval, so we have conducted a preliminary experiment to begin to explore the issues involved in supporting automatic search between Czech and English.

For our experiments, we used an information retrieval test collection from the Cross-Language Evaluation Forum (CLEF 2000). The collection contains 113,000 English news stories from the Los Angeles Times (about 435 MB of text), 33 English topic descriptions,[6] and binary (yes-no) relevance judgments for topic-document pairs.[7] The title and description

---

[6] The CLEF 2000 collection contains 40 topics, but no relevant English documents are known for topics 2, 6, 8, 23, 25, 27, and 35, so they were excluded.

[7] The set of relevance judgments is incomplete, but the pooled assessment methodology generally results in reliable comparisons between alternative conditions.

fields of the 33 topic descriptions were translated from English into Czech by a native speaker of Czech in a way that they felt represented a natural style of expression for a statement of an information need in that language. In CLEF topic descriptions, the title field is typically crafted in a manner similar to typical Web queries (2–3 content-bearing terms), while the description fields are typical of what a searcher might initially say to an intermediary such as a librarian that might help with their search (1–2 sentences).

We obtained translation knowledge for our automated cross-language search system from two sources. (1) We submitted each word in the Czech queries (and their lemmas, obtained as described below) to the PC Translator V98 (for MS Windows) Czech-English machine readable bilingual dictionary (http://www.langsoft.cz/) and aligned the results to create a bilingual term list. The dictionary contained only Czech lemmas, and translations were found in this way for 213 of the 291 unique words that appear in the queries. (2) We obtained 800 additional English-Czech lemma pairs from the freely available Ergane translation tool (http://download.travlang.com/Ergane). These term pairs are not query-specific – we used every term pair that Ergane provides. We merged these two resources to form a single bilingual term list for use in subsequent processing.

We used a simple translation process for automatic word-by-word query-translation, in which the following processing stages were tried in order: (1) Look up the lemma in the Czech side of the bilingual term list (we used a morphological analyzer distributed with the Prague Dependency Treebank to lemmatize Czech words [5]), and (2) if the lemma is not found, strip diacritic marks from the characters in the word to obtain a 7-bit ASCII representation of the word that might be a correct transliteration. We also tried a variant of the third stage in which certain obvious transliteration corrections were made manually (afrika to africa, rusku to russia) as a way of exploring the potential effect on retrieval if we were to develop a more sophisticated automatic transliteration algorithm.

We used the InQuery text retrieval system with the default English stemmer (kstem) enabled for both document and query processing. Structured queries were formed by including alternate translations for a single query term in InQuery's #syn operator, which has the effect of computing a single term weight for the aggregate set of translations by first aggregating the term frequency (aboutness) and document frequency (term specificity) evidence separately and then computing the term weight on the aggregated statistics. This approach has been shown to outperform techniques based on aggregating term weights in a broad range of language pairs (when translation probabilities are not known). We used trec_eval to compute the uninterpolated average precision for each query, and we report the mean (over 33 queries) of those values as a single-figure measure of retrieval effectiveness.

Table 1 shows the results for title-only and title+description queries. The "Monolingual" results establish an upper baseline, obtained by forming queries using the English topic descriptions that had served as the basis for the Czech translations that are used in the remainder of the runs. The Dictionary-based Query Translation (DQT) runs were created as described above, with the "DQT + Names" run showing the effect of manually correcting the transliteration of some names (also described above). The "No Translation" runs establish a lower baseline, obtained by using the Czech queries to search the English document collection without benefit of any translation.

These results are typical of initial experiments in new language pairs, for which it is common to obtain between 40 % and 60 % of monolingual retrieval effectiveness when

Table 1. Mean uninterpolated average precision, title queries.

	Title	Title+Desc
Monolingual	0.3279	0.4008
DQT	0.1826	0.1705
DQT + Names	0.1882	0.1996
No Translation	0.0285	0.0258

simple word-by-word dictionary-based techniques are used. Better results can typically be obtained if pre-translation and/or post-translation query expansion is performed using well-tuned blind relevance feedback, and incorporation of translation probabilities and making greater use of context (e.g., by translating phrases in preference to single words) can also be helpful. These early results are, however, sufficient to serve as a basis for some further investigation into the unique characteristics of Czech. We therefore performed a query-by-query failure analysis, using the plots in Figure 1 to identify the topics for which the spread between the DQT and Monolingual runs was relatively large. We then examined the topic descriptions and the translated queries in an effort to identify a plausible cause for this effect. Through this process, we made the following observations:

Topic 7. All terms were translated, but soccer was expanded to soccer and football. This could have an adverse effect on precision when searching newspaper stories from the United States.

Topic 12. The query term "Solar Temple" (a named entity) had solar replaced by sun, sunshine, etc., and English stemming failed to discover the relationship between these words and solar.

Topic 19. The query term "Gulf War Syndrome" resulted in many synonyms for gulf and syndrome, and war was lost in the translation process.

Topic 24. The query term "World Trade Organization" resulted in loss of world and replacement of trade with business, commercial, mercantile, etc., none of which were conflated by the English stemmer with trade.

Topic 30. The named entity Nice (a city in France) was transliterated as niche (an English word with an unrelated meaning).

Topic 32. Several query terms were lost in the translation process.

The same analysis produced similar results on title+description queries. Word-by-word dictionary-based cross-language retrieval techniques are known to be vulnerable to mishandling phrases and named entities, so these results do not point to any unusual characteristics that are unique to the Czech/English language pair. We therefore expect that techniques that we have used previously in other language pairs to boost cross-language retrieval effectiveness and to integrate translation with speech recognition are likely to achieve similar results in Czech.

5   Conclusion

The collection that we are working with contains tens of thousands of hours of speech in Eastern European languages, so we have a keen interest in collaboration with members of the

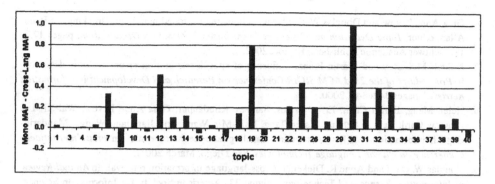

Fig. 1. Uninterpolated average precision by topic, title queries.

research communities that have come together for the Text, Speech and Dialogue conference. We see significant opportunities for synergy with those working on speech recognition, spoken language identification, natural language processing, text classification, machine translation and information retrieval, with the MALACH project providing an unmatched environment in which to demonstrate how these technologies can be integrated to produce compelling applications. The potential impact of such joint efforts could extend far beyond this one project, however. It is our hope that the technologies we develop will also be used in the service of additional efforts to preserve our memory, and to give an enduring voice to those who have built the world in which our children and grandchildren will live.

Acknowledgments

The authors would like to thank Ivona Kučerová for translating the queries and Jan Curin for help with PC Translator. This work has been supported in part by NSF grant IIS-0122466 and DARPA cooperative agreement N660010028910.

References

1. James Allan. Perspectives on information retrieval and speech. In Anni R. Coden, Eric W. Brown, and Savitha Srinivasan, editors, *Information Retrieval Techniques for Speech Applications*, pages 1–10. Springer, 2002. Lecture Notes in Computer Science 2273.
2. Bonnie J. Dorr, Lisa Pearl, Rebecca Hwa, and Nizar Habash. Improved word-level alignment: Injecting knowledge about MT divergences. Technical Report CS-TR-4333, University of Maryland, Institute for Advanced Computer Studies, 2002.
3. Frederic C. Gey, Michael Buckland, Aitao Chen, and Ray Larson. Entry vocabulary – a technology to enhance digital search. In *First International Conference on Human Language Technologies*, 2001.
4. Samuel Gustman, Dagobert Soergel, Douglas Oard, William Byrne, Michael Picheny, Bhuvana Ramadhadran, and Douglas Greenberg. Supporting access to large digital oral history archives. In *The Second Joint Digital Libraries*, June 2002. to appear.
5. Jan Hajič, Eva Hajičová, Petr Pajas, Jarmila Panevová, Petr Sgall, and Barbora Vidová-Hladká. Prague dependency treebank 1.0, 2001. LDC2001T10.

6. Gina-Anne Levow and Douglas W. Oard. Signal boosting for translingual topic tracking. In James Allan, editor, *Topic Detection and Tracking: Event-based Information Organization*, pages 175–195. Kluwer Academic Publishers, Boston, 2002.

7. J. Scott McCarley and Martin Franz. Influence of speech recognition errors on topic detection. In *Proceedings of the 23rd ACM SIGIR Conference on Research and Development in Information Retrieval*, pages 342–344, 2000.

8. Helen Meng, Berlin Chen, Erika Grams, Sanjeev Khudanpur, Gina-Anne Levow, Wai-Kit Lo, Douglas Oard, Patrick Schone, Karen Tang, Hsin-Min Wang, and Jianqiang Wang. Mandarin-English information (MEI): Investigating translingual speech retrieval. In *First International Conference on Human Language Technologies*, San Diego, March 2001.

9. Douglas W. Oard and Anne R. Diekema. Cross-language information retrieval. In *Annual Review of Information Science and Technology*, volume 33. American Society for Information Science, 1998.

10. Douglas W. Oard and Julio Gonzalo. The CLEF 2001 interactive track. In Carol Peters, editor, *Proceedings of the Second Cross-Language Evaluation Forum*. 2002.

11. D. Yarowsky, G. Nagi, and R. Wicentowski. Inducing multilingual text analysis tools via robust projection across aligned corpora. In *First International Conference on Human Language Technologies*, 2001.

Using Salient Words to Perform Categorization of Web Sites*

Marek Trabalka and Mária Bieliková

Department of Computer Science and Engineering
Slovak University of Technology
Ilkovičova 3, 812 19 Bratislava, Slovakia
E-mail: trabalka@webinventia.sk, bielik@elf.stuba.sk
WWW: http://www.dcs.elf.stuba.sk/~bielik

Abstract. In this paper we focus on web sites categorization. We compare some quantitative characteristics of existing web directories, analyze the vocabulary used in descriptions of the web sites in Yahoo web directory and propose an approach to automatically categorize web sites. Our approach is based on the novel concept of salient words. Two realizations of the proposed concept are experimentally evaluated. The former uses words typical for just one category, while the latter uses words typical for several categories. Results show that there is a limitation of using single vocabulary based method to properly categorize highly heterogeneous spaces as the World Wide Web.

1 Introduction

Huge amount of web sites existing nowadays evolves a special type of web sites used for reference purpose – web directories. Web directories include links to other web sites together with a short description of their content. Web sites descriptions and corresponding links are stored in a hierarchy of categories. Hierarchies are usually defined by human maintainers. Usually only incremental additions are performed. Existing structure is rewritten very rarely.

Usefulness of web directories is similar to the Yellow pages. When a user is looking for an information or service, he simply browses through relevant categories in order to find matching web sites. However, manual creation and maintenance of the directory is quite expensive.

The aim of this paper is to present an approach to perform addition of new web sites into existing categorization automatically. We use results from the vocabulary analysis of established categorization hierarchy. The analysis is based on the novel concept of *salient words*, which is experimentally evaluated within a real collection of web sites.

There exist significant amount of work related to the categorization of documents. Many authors use for evaluation non-web texts like the Reuters corpus, medical OHSUMED collection or patent corpuses [11,5,9]. In fact, these collections are incomparable to a web site collection. Web site collections are extremely diverse in means of topic diversity, length of documents and variability of documents quality.

---

* This work was partially supported by Slovak Science Grant Agency, grant No. G1/7611/20.

P. Sojka, I. Kopeček, and K. Pala (Eds.): TSD 2002, LNAI 2448, pp. 65–72, 2002.

In a past five years interest in web categorization of web documents rapidly grows. Most of existing approaches use existing web directories as a source of training and testing data [4]. Some authors just apply standard classification techniques to flattened categories [3]. Koller and Sahami [6] present an improvement of categorization speed and accuracy by utilizing hierarchical topic structure. They proposed small independent classifiers for every category instead of one large classifier for the whole topic set. Unfortunately, evaluations were done only on quite limited hierarchy of topics [2,6]. We performed broader analysis in order to find limitations of simple vocabulary analysis for detailed categorization.

The rest of the paper is organized as follows. In Section 2 we analyze structural characteristics of web directories. The analysis provides basis for proposed method of vocabulary analysis (Section 3). The concept of salient words is realized using words typical for one category and using words typical for several categories. In Section 4 we provide results of experimental evaluation. The paper concludes with summary and possible directions of research.

2   Structural Characteristics of Web Directories

At the present time there exist many web directories. Some of them are global; some of them are limited to some extent. There are various local web directories with respect to the country or language used. Also various thematic web directories exist that try to map more in-depth some particular field of interest.

Structural characteristics of local web directories are in most cases similar to global ones. Table 1 gives a comparison of two global directories and three local Slovak web directories.

Table 1. Comparison of web directories.

Site	Yahoo	DMOZ	Zoznam	Atlas	SZM
Language	English	English and others	Slovak	Slovak	Slovak
All categories	372 343	397 504	864	1 213	372
Top level categories	14	21	14	12	14
Second level categories	353	539	249	280	169
Third level categories	3 789	6 199	424	622	170
Depth of hierarchy	16	14	5	5	6
Average length of category title	14.05	12.03	16.01	15.43	12.84
Total number of sites	1 656 429	2 912 282	22 266	20 314	11 256
Average number under category	8.85	8.60	26.16	17.85	34.42
Average length of site title	22.37	23.20	18.71	16.77	21.26
Average length of site description	67.55	96.21	72.42	111.22	69.43

We use Yahoo and DMOZ global web directories. *Yahoo* (www.yahoo.com) is the best-known commercial web directory existing since 1995. *DMOZ – Open Directory Project* (www.dmoz.com) is a non-commercial web directory updated by volunteers. *Zoznam* (www.zoznam.sk), *Atlas* (www.atlas.sk) and *Superzoznam* (www.szm.sk) are the three most popular Slovak web directories.

Web directories are generally quite similar each to other. They have many categories in common and also their look and feel is the same. The main difference between local and global web directories is in the number of covered web sites that affects also size of the hierarchy of categories. We explored also other web directories and found out that they share almost the same characteristics. The number of top-level categories is usually between 10 and 16; typical number of subcategories is between 2 and 30. Lengths of titles are also very similar in average. The only difference is sometimes in the length of site descriptions where some directories limit the maximum length.

3   Analysis of Vocabulary and Categorization

Existing web directories are the great source of information for training categorization. Most of them are manually checked and therefore their quality is high. Furthermore, they contain large amount of information that could be used to acquire explicit knowledge about the categories and also about the whole domain.

There is a strong correspondence between a category and the vocabulary used in web sites assigned to the category. We consider the following text categorization assumption: *it is possible to correctly assign a web site into the category only by means of its textual information*. In a real life this assumption is not always the truth, indeed. There exist web sites containing most of their content in images or other non-textual kind of presentation that prohibits categorization by analyzing only the text. Analysis of images is beyond the scope of our research, we assume that such information can be converted to the text.

The web directory covers internal information – stored directly in the web directory (URLs, site descriptions and title) and external information – the web sites themselves referred by URLs. We use only the internal information to build representative texts. Of course when categorizing a new web site into the hierarchy we have to deal with its content as the only available information. It is obvious that using also external data, i.e. the content itself, provides more valuable data. On the other hand, such approach would require more computing resources.

Text categorization assumption implies the possibility to create a classifier able to correctly classify web sites by examining their textual contents. It is necessary to have a model of every category to compare the web sites with. There were proposed various models in information retrieval community to deal with a document clustering that could be applied in our case as well (for review see [9]). Commonly used is the Vector Space Model proposed by Salton in SMART project [8]. In this model a feature vector represents every document, query or group of documents. Usually, features are words or stems, and their values in the vector correspond with the number of occurrences in the object. Similarity of objects is computed by cosine of angle between these two vectors:

$$r = \frac{\sum_{i=1}^{n} q_i d_i}{\sqrt{\sum_{i=1}^{n} q_i^2 \sum_{i=1}^{n} p_i^2}} = \frac{Q, D}{||Q||\,||D||} = \cos\theta$$

This method has several advantages, including easy implementation. Its main disadvantage is high computational cost due to high dimensionality of vectors. When words or their stems are used as features the vector could have dimensionality of tens or even hundreds of thousands that significantly slows down the comparison process.

Many approaches to improve this method focus primarily on dimensionality reduction of the feature vector [6]. Dimensionality reduction can be achieved by selection of the most useful words. (e.g., the words able to distinguish between categories). Figure 1 depicts the difference between common word *'and'* and a category specific word *'newspaper'*. The figure displays how differ relative occurrences of these two words in documents within top-level categories. General terms have similar relative occurrences in all categories while category specific words are often used in one or few categories and in others are quite rare.

Our approach is to explicitly find the words significant for a category distinction within neighboring categories. Such words are identified for every category and its respective direct subcategories because a word able to distinguish between subcategories of one category may have similar occurrences between subcategories of another category. We call such words *salient words*.

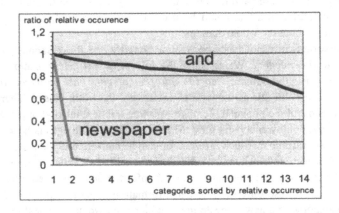

Fig. 1. Occurrence of common word and category specific word.

3.1 Categorization Using Words Typical for One Category

When human roughly analyses topic of a text he often relies on salient words – terms typical for the topic. Brief view on the article vocabulary without in-depth semantic analysis is often sufficient for human to distinguish the topics.

Similarly to human approach, we suggest a concept of salient words to be applied in automatic classification of web documents. Main idea is to use for categorization only the words typical for a particular category. This leads to a significant reduction of computation costs during the categorization. Together with hierarchical analysis it makes the processing fast and efficient.

The method of identifying salient words consists of the following steps performed for every category (including root category):

1. Collect words used in the category with a number of occurrences above defined threshold (to refuse rare words).
2. Perform steps 2a – 2c for every collected word:

(a) Compute the relative occurrence of the word w for every subcategory c, i.e. the number of word's occurrences divided by occurrences of all words within the subcategory.

(b) Compute the sum of the relative occurrences within direct subcategories $sum_{c,w}$.

(c) Find the maximum of relative occurrences within direct subcategories $max_{c,w}$.

(d) If $max_{c,w} \geq sum_{c,w} \times salient\_const$, mark the word as a salient for the subcategory with the highest $max_{c,w}$. Remember the strength of this word for a category distinction as $strength_{c,w} = max_{c,w}/sum_{c,w}$. The $salient\_const$ constant is a tunable parameter usually between 0.5 and 1. The higher the constant is the less number of salient words we acquire.

Text categorization is performed by traversing through the hierarchy looking for the best matching category. The process starts by computing the relative occurrence for all words in given text. Next, for the root category the following steps are performed:

1. Find all direct subcategories of the category; terminate if there are no subcategories.
2. Compute similarity between every subcategory and a given text as
$$similarity_c = \sum\nolimits_{i=salient\_word} strength_{c,j} \times relocc_i$$
where $relocc_i$ is the relative occurrence of the word i within given text.
3. Find the maximum of similarities max_{sim}. If $max_{sim} < similarity_{bias}$, terminate. If it is above the bias, append the subcategory with the max_{sim} in the resultant stack and perform recursively these steps for the subcategory.

3.2   Categorization Using Words Typical for Several Categories

Actually, there exist many significant words that are not typical just for one category but for two or more categories. If the presence of a word could eliminate at least few categories we call such word *separable*. Separable words include also salient words.

We collect separable words for every category. Separable words are related to a parent category. They are used to distinguish between direct subcategories of the category. The feature vectors for sibling categories and the list of words used in the feature vector are kept.

The method of identification separable words consists of the following steps performed on every category (including root category):

1. Collect words used in the category with the number of occurrences above defined threshold.
2. For every collected word compute its relative occurrences for every subcategory. If at least for one category value exceeds $separable_{bias}$, insert the word into the list of separable words for the category. For every subcategory insert the number of occurrences of this word into the feature vector of the subcategory.

For a given text of a web site the category tree is traversed and at each step the closest category feature vector is selected. The process starts by computing the number of occurence for all words in the given text. Next, for the root category the following steps are performed:

1. Find all direct subcategories of the category; terminate if there are no subcategories.

2. Prepare text feature vector as a list of occurrences of separable words for the examined category.

3. For every subcategory compute similarity between the subcategory feature vector and the text feature vector as

$$similarity_c = \frac{\sum_{i=1}^{n} cat_i \times doc_i}{\sqrt{\sum_{i=1}^{n} cat_i^2 \sum_{i=1}^{n} doc_i^2}}$$

where cat_i, resp. doc_i is the number of occurrences of i-th separable word in the processed category, resp. the text of the document.

4. Find maximum of similarities max_{sim}. If $max_{sim} < similarity_{bias}$, terminate. If max_{sim} is above the bias, append the subcategory with max_{sim} in the resultant stack and perform recursively these steps for the subcategory.

4   Experimental Evaluation

We implemented proposed methods of web sites categorization and made several improvements and optimizations. Firstly, to improve both, speed and recall we employ stemming of words using the Porter's suffix removal algorithm [2].

To reduce number of different words to be analyzed we use approximately 500 stop words that were removed from all processed texts. We also removed stems with a rare occurrence in the whole web directory (bellow the threshold of 10 occurrences in our experiments). This decreased the number of stems from 299 470 to 29 201. We used the vocabulary of titles and short descriptions of web sites to acquire significant words. Analyzed Yahoo web directory contained almost 400 000 categories. Most of them contained only a few sites and therefore did not provide enough text for training. For the evaluation we selected only categories that contained at least 1 000 sites (including their subcategories). For acquired 978 categories we built the vocabulary from descriptions of sites registered within these categories and their subcategories.

We randomly selected web sites registered within the Yahoo and downloaded their contents up to 100 kB. Many researchers analyze only web site's first page directly referred by registered URL [5,3] or snippets returned by the search engine [2]. We decided to download larger portion of the web site in order to analyze whether increased amount of data will improve quality of the analysis. We experimented with two sets of the web sites. Smaller set A contains 369 web sites with more than 100 kB of text per site while the larger set B contains 1277 web sites with at least 10 kB of text per site.

We used the set A to analyze the impact of the size of analyzed portion of the web site on quality of results. We compared the results based on a starting page, first 1 kB of text, first 10 kB of text and first 100 kB of text. Table 2 shows the results of analysis using words typical for one category. We obtained the best results for 10 kB portion of a web site. It also proves our hypothesis that using only the first page for categorization is not always sufficient.

Then we used 10 kB parts of more than 1 000 web sites to analyze overall quality of proposed approach and dependence of estimation with respect to the appropriate category. Table 3 shows that there are significant differences between the categories. In-depth analysis of the most erroneous categories shows that many invalid top-level assignments were to Business & Economy and Computers & Internet categories.

Table 2. Analysis of web pages with different size.

Correctly estimated levels of categories	First page	1 kB	10 kB	100 kB
0 levels	55%	46%	42%	43%
1 level	11%	8%	8%	9%
2 levels	16%	17%	19%	18%
3 levels	9%	11%	10%	13%
4 levels	6%	11%	13%	10%
5 levels	1%	3%	2%	2%
6 levels	0%	1%	2%	1%

Table 3. Categorization of web sites according different categories.

Correctly estimated levels of categories	Overall	Arts	Regional	Business	Computers	Entertainment
0 levels	44%	68%	47%	45%	26%	19%
1 level	10%	3%	2%	14%	31%	11%
2 levels	18%	4%	15%	22%	19%	22%
3 levels	10%	9%	16%	5%	20%	20%
4 levels	9%	5%	7%	5%	1%	18%

5 Conclusion

In this paper we described two methods for categorization of web sites based on analysis of salient words. We use short descriptions of web sites in a web directory to select words useful to distinguish categories. Categorization process uses category tree to limit the number of necessary comparisons and speed up the processing. We evaluate success of categorization by comparing estimated and actual categories of the web site within web directory. We also show how size of downloaded portion of a web site affects the result of categorization and present the difference in success within different top-level categories.

In the further research we would like to compare results of our methods when trained on full texts of web sites rather than their short descriptions in the web directory. We also plan to extend the amount of evaluated web sites in order to gain more precise results.

References

1. Brin, S., Page, L.:The Anatomy of a Large-Scale Hypertextual Web Search Engine (1998).
2. Dumais, S., Chen, H.: Hierarchical Classification of Web Content. In: Proc. of 23rd Int. ACM Conf. on Research and Development in Information Retrieval (SIGIR), Athens, Greece (2000) 256–263.
3. Mase, H.: Experiments on Automatic Web Page Categorization for IR system. Technical report, Standford University (1998).
4. Mladenic, D.: Turning Yahoo into an Automatic Web-Page Classifier. In: Proceedings of ECAI - European Conference on Artificial Intelligence (1998).
5. Karypis, G., Han, E.: Fast Supervised Dimensionality Reduction Algorithm with Applications to Document Categorization & Retrieval (2000).

6. Koller, D. and Sahami, M., Hierarchically classifying documents using very few words, in International Conference on Machine Learning (ICML) (1997) 170–178.
7. Porter, M. F.: An Algorithm for Suffix Stripping. Program, 14 (3) (1980) 130–137.
8. Salton, G.: A New Comparison Between Conventional Indexing (MEDLARS) and Automatic Text Processing (SMART). In: Journal of the American Society for Information Science 23 (2) (1972) 75–84.
9. Trabalka, M.: Document Retrieval. A Written Part of Ph.D. Examination. Slovak University of Technology (2001).
10. Wang, K., Zhou, S., He, Y.: Hierarchical Classification of Real Life Documents. First SIAM International Conference on Data Mining (2001).
11. Yang, Y., Pedersen, J. O.: A Comparative Study on Feature Selection in Text Categorization. In: Proc. of 14th Int. Conf. on Machine Learning (1997).

Discourse-Semantic Analysis of Hungarian Sign Language

Gábor Alberti[1] and Helga M. Szabó[2]

[1] University of Pécs
E-mail: albi@btk.pte.hu
[2] National Association of the Deaf, Hungary
E-mail: szabo.helga@gszi.bme.hu

Abstract. A text in Hungarian Sign Language is analyzed in this paper.[3] The discourse-semantic framework we use is a generalized version of van Eijck-Kamp's DRT [1], called Lifelong DRT, where the crucial innovation is regarding the interpreter's information state containing the mutual background knowledge shared by "speaker" and interpreter as a gigantic "lifelong" DRS where all pieces of the interpreter's lexical, cultural/encyclopedic and interpersonal knowledge are accessible whose mobilization the exhaustive interpretation of the given text requires.

1 Introduction

A text in Hungarian Sign Language (HSL), which is performed by a deaf person with this language as his mother tongue, is analyzed in this paper. The discourse-semantic framework we use is Lifelong DRT [2,3], where the crucial innovation, which plays a decisive role in the analysis of (typically "ballad-like") texts in sign languages, is regarding the interpreter's information state (IIS) containing the mutual background knowledge shared by "speaker" and interpreter as a gigantic "lifelong" DRS (discourse representation structure) where all pieces of the interpreter's lexical, cultural/encyclopedic and interpersonal knowledge are accessible whose mobilization the exhaustive interpretation of the given text requires.

What makes sign languages seem to "ballad-like" relative to oral languages is, among other factors, the absence of affixation.[4] Let us consider S1 in Figure 1 below, which shows the sequence of signs that can be considered to be the first unit (sentence) of the text to be analyzed. It is written as an underspecified proto-DRS where pairwise strictly different temporary referents occupy argument positions of predicates.

In our approach the problem of interpretation is formulated as follows: how can a complete (and adequate) DRS, like the one in DRS1-1 in Figure 1, be derived from the proto-DRS expressing the immediate semantic contribution of a certain group of signs on the basis of the (almost unknown) grammar of the Hungarian Sign Language?

The main part of the task of calculation consists of the unification of temporary referents and their identification with "old" referents or "new" ones in the discourse

[3] Special thanks are due to OTKA (T-035046) and SzPÖ (Alberti) for their financial support. We are also grateful to Péter Mongyi for his comments on his video recording, which we have analyzed.

[4] Many constructions in several oral languages lack affixation as well, so what we reveal in connection with sign languages is considered to be true in these cases too.

P. Sojka, I. Kopeček, and K. Pala (Eds.): TSD 2002, LNAI 2448, pp. 73–80, 2002.
© Springer-Verlag Berlin Heidelberg 2002

S1: bus x1 ∧ get-on x2 x3 ∧ black x4 ∧ boy x5
DRS1-1: r1 ∧ bus r1 ∧ get-on[e1] r2 r1 ∧ time
e1 t1 ∧ place e1 l1 ∧ black r2 ∧ boy r2 ∧ r2
S2: start-from x1 x2 ∧ catch-at x3 x6 ∧ above
x6 x3 ∧ catch-at x4 x7 ∧ above x7 x4 ∧
catch-at x5 x8 ∧ above x8 x5 ∧ chew-gum x9
DRS1-2: ... ∧ start-from[e2] r2 l1 ∧ time e2 t2
∧ t1<t2 ∧ move-forwards[s1] r2 ∧ time-int s1 t3
∧ catch-at[e3] r2 r3 ∧ time e3 t4 ∧ t2<t4 ∧
t4⊂t3 ∧ place e3 l2 ∧ above r3 r2 ∧
catch-at[e4] r2 r4 ∧ time e4 t5 ∧ t4<t5 ∧ t5⊂t3
∧ place e4 l3 ∧ above r4 r2 ∧ catch-at[e5] r2 r5
∧ time e5 t6 ∧ t5<t6 ∧ t6 ⊂ t3 ∧ place e5 l4 ∧
above r5 r2 ∧ handstrap r3 ∧ handstrap r4 ∧
handstrap r5 ∧ chew-gum[s2] r2 ∧ time-int s2 t4
∧ overlap t3 t4
S3: chew-gum x1
DRS1-3: ... ∧ chew-gum[s2] r2 ∧ time-int s2 t4
∧ overlap t3 t4
S4: catch-at x3 x6 ∧ above x6 x3 ∧ catch-at
x4 x7 ∧ above x7 x4 ∧ catch-at x5 x8 ∧ above
x8 x5 ∧ look-for x9 x10 ∧ lower x10 x9 ∧ seat
x11 ∧ catch-at x12 x13 ∧ above x13 x12 ∧ find
x14 x15 ∧ there x16
DRS1-4: ... ∧ look-for [s2] r2 r6 ∧ time-int s2
t5 ∧ overlap t5 t2 ∧ seat r6 ∧ lower r6 r2 ∧ find
[e6] r2 r7 ∧ seat r7 ∧ time e6 t6 end-point t6 t5
∧ place e6 l5 ∧ catch-at [e7] r2 r9 ∧ time e7 t7
∧ overlap t7 t6 ∧ place e7 l6 ∧ overlap l5 l6
S5: old x1 ∧ lady x2 ∧ be-afraid x3 look-up x4
x5 ∧ draw-away x6
DRS1-5: ... there-is [s3] l5 r 10 ∧ old r 10 lady
r10 ∧ be-afraid r10 ∧ look-up r10 r2 ∧ sit r 10 ∧
draw-away r10
S6: sit-down x1 x2 ∧ tough x3
DRS1-6: ... sit-down [e8] r2 r7 ∧ time e8 t8 ∧
t6 < t8 ∧ tough e8
S7: two-persons-next-to-each-other x1 x2
DRS1-7: ... two-persons-sit-next-to-each-other
[s4] r2 r10 ∧ time-int s4 t9 ∧ starting-point t9 t8
S8: cross-legs x1 ∧ look-at x2 x3 ∧ chew-gum
x4 ∧ provocative x5
DRS1-8: ... ∧ cross-legs r2 ∧ look-at [e8] r2
r10 ∧ chew-gum r2 ∧ provocative e8
S9: look-at x1 x2
DRS1-9: ... look-at [e9] r2 r10 ∧ time e9 t 10
S10: old x1 ∧ lady x2 ∧ mutter x3 ∧
look-at x4 x5
DRS1-10: ... ∧ mutter [s5] r10 ∧ time-
int s5 t11 ∧ look-at[e10] r10 r2 ∧ time e10 t12 ∧
t10<t12 ∧ starting-point t12 s5
S11: ... disgusting x1 ∧ dirty x2 ∧ smelly x3 ∧
company x4 ∧ work x5 ∧ not x6 ∧ lazy x7 ∧
terrible x8

DRS1-11: ...∧ disgusting[s6] r12 ∧ dirty[s6] r12 ∧
smelly[s6] r12 ∧ company r11 ∧ member r2 r11 ∧
representative r12 r11 ∧
black r12 ∧ work[s7] r12 ∧ lazy[s8] r12 ∧
terrible[s8] r' (?) wrl(s6) = w1, wrl(s7) = w2
S12: mutter x1
DRS1-12: ... ∧ mutter[s9] r10 ∧ s5≡s9 ∧ time-
int s9 t13
S13: look-at x1 x2 ∧ interesting x3
DRS1-13: ... ∧ look-at[e11] r2 r10 ∧ time e11 t14 ∧
endpoint t14 s9 ∧ interesting[s10] r13 ∧ is-somebody's-
opinion-about r10 r12 r13; wrl(s10) = w4
S14: sudden x5 ∧ get-on x1 x2 ∧ checkman x6 ∧
approach x3 x4
DRS1-14: ... get-on [e12] r14 r1 ∧ time e12 t15 ∧ t14
< t 15 ∧ approach r14 r 10 ∧ checkman r14 ∧ approach
[s11] r14 l6 ∧ time-int s11 t 16 ∧ starting-point t16 t 15
S15: grasp x1 x2
DRS1-15: ... grasp [s12] r10 r15
S16: old x1 ∧ lady x2 ∧ grasp x3 x4
DRS1-16: ... grasp [s12] r10 r15
S17: ticket x1
DRS1-17: ... ticket [s13] r15
S18: oops!
DRS1-18: ... invent [e13] r2r16
S19: reach-out-for x1 x2 ∧ snach-out x3 x4 x5 ∧
swallow x6 x7
DRS1-19: ... reach-out-for [e14] r2 r15 ∧ snach-out
[e15] r2 r15 r10 ∧ swallow [e16] r2 r15 ∧ time e16 t 17
∧ t17=n
S20: all-over x1
DRS1-20: ... come-to-nothing [e17] r15
S21: old x1 ∧ lady x2 ∧ dumbfounded-with-surprise x3
DRS1-21: ... dumbfounded-with-surprise [s14] r10
S22: come-to x1 ∧ inspector x2
DRS1-22: ... come-to [e18] r14
S23: black x1 ∧ show-season-ticket x2
DRS1-23: ... show-season-ticket [e19] r2
S24: he x1 ∧ eat x2 x3
DRS1-24: ... eat [e20] r2 r15 ∧ time e20 t17
S25: he x1
DRS1-25: r17 ∧ eat [e20] r17 r15 ∧ identical [s15] r17
r2
S26: ... ticket x1 ∧ my x2 ∧ eat x3 x4 ∧ he x5
DRS1-26: eat [e20] r2 r15 ∧ have r10 r15
S27: ... inspector x1 ∧ incredulous x2 ∧ impose-a-fine
x3 x4
DRS1-27: incredulous [s16] r14 ∧ time t18 ∧ impose-
a-fine [e21] r14 r10 ∧ time-int t19 ∧ overlap t18 t19
S28: ... wry x1 ∧ swallow x2 x3 ∧ pay x4 x5 x6
DRS1-28: ... wry [s17] r10 ∧ time-int t20 ∧ "swallow-
the-bitter-pill" [e22] r10 r18 ∧ time-int t21 ∧ overlap
t20 t21 ∧ angry r18 e21 ∧ pay r10 r19 r14 ∧ penalty r19
r18 ∧ steal-a-ride [s18] r10 r1

Fig. 1. The relevant steps of the analysis.

(x1=x3=r1, x2=x4=x5=r2), and the introduction of eventuality referents (e1) and temporal (t1) and spatial (l1) reference-points. The grammar (to be revealed) manifests itself in factors such as order of signs, (partial) overlap of their performance, characteristic points of the space used by the "speaker", special features of face and body, and iteration of signs. The creation of the full discourse-semantic interpretation, however, straightforwardly requires, from the interpreter, a huge amount of background information concerning lexical and cultural/encyclopedic meanings, interpersonal knowledge and discourse-construction strategies (incl. the simultaneous application of alternative "worlds" in the discourse); that is what LDRT is intended to supply.

In the example mentioned above, the immediate information at the interpreter's disposal is that a bus and a boy are referred to, and something is black, and there is a "getting-on" eventuality. The partial overlap between the performance of the signs of *black* and *boy* is undoubtedly intended to show that it is the boy that is black (and not the bus). The story-telling situation suggests that the bus and the boy are new referents (which are not likely to be identified with entities well-known to the interpreter). Finally, the interpreter's lexical and/or encyclopedic knowledge makes it unambiguous that the boy gets on the bus (and not *vice versa*). The interpreter's cultural knowledge concerning Hungarian public buses will be required later: it should be known that there are handstraps and double seats in these buses, and sometimes an inspector gets on the bus to check tickets.

2 A Lifelong Model of (Dynamically Changing) IIS

DRT (e.g. [1,4,5]) is a successful attempt to extend the sentence-level Montagovian model-theoretic semantics, which had not only failed to exceed this level but had also been unsuccessful in the treatment of certain types of anaphoric relations, to the discourse level. Its essence lies in the discovery that the failure of the immediate interpretation of sentences in the static Montagovian world model is to be attributed to the fact that the discourse under interpretation is permanently becoming part of the world in which it is being interpreted; thus a level of discourse representation *must* be inserted in between the language to be interpreted and the world model serving as the context of interpretation. This *dynamic perspective* of DRT can be captured by regarding the content of DRSs as a "(partial) function mapping information states to information states" [6].

Nevertheless, the picture of IIS in dynamic theories is oversimplified and in certain areas simply counter-intuitive: practically (total) models are used as information states. In this approach atomic statements (e.g. 'Pat got on a bus') are to be held as *tests*, which means that an assertion heard is supposed to be either corroborated or rejected. The typical case is excluded: to regard an assertion as a new piece of information for the interpreter. (Another basic problem of DRT – the one concerning the compositional transition between syntax and DRS – is discussed in [2,7].) Interpreters, counter to the oversimplified picture sketched above, practically always have a partial knowledge. And nothing else than DRS serves the purpose of representing partial knowledge...

The interpreter's permanently changing information state can be defined by simultaneous recursion ([3] provides the formal definition; here we try to capture its essence). This definition is practically a generalization of the (simultaneously recursive) definition of DRSs given in [1]; or this original definition may be regarded as one suitable for discourses with an empty mutual background knowledge shared by speaker and interpreter. This stipulation on background knowledge may often serve (or have served so far) as a useful working hypothesis – especially when DRT is compared to the Montagovian semantics – but it is undoubtedly far from being a realistic picture of discourses. It is high time, hence, to turn to the general situation; and we claim [2,3] that this turn also serves as a key to the solution of a wide range of classical formal-semantic puzzles (as to the creation (or retrieval?) of referents for pronouns and definite descriptions in universal and belief contexts and in other special cases).

First of all, three infinite sets of *pegs*[5] should be assumed to be at the interpreter's disposal: those of *referents* (R), *predicate names* (P) and *worlds* (W). The inner structure of these sets and the rich system of connections among them are due to six (partial) functions/relations. The *extension of predicates* is a partial function $ext : P \rightarrow Pow(R^*)$ from predicates to the powerset of referent sequences (* denotes the Kleene star). Another partial function $ref : R \rightarrow Pow(P \times R^*)$ (*referent function*) assigns each referent in its domain a set of sequences consisting of a predicate name and referents; an element of $Pow(P \times R^*)$ is essentially a basic kind of DRS so members of the domain of function ref serve as *eventuality referents*. Relation prc (*precedes* or <) is a partial ordering in $W \times W$ with a least element, denoted by v (the *basic world*). Operation $wrl : (P \cup R) \rightarrow W$ is also a partial function (*world function*); it assigns a predicate name or a referent to a world. There is a *cursor*, a partial function $cur :\{W, R\} \rightarrow W \cup R^*$, which chooses an *active* world (cur(W)) and a sequence of referents playing distinguished roles in different respects in the current state of the interpreter's (permanently changing) information state: $cur(R) =< cur_{temporal}(R), cur_{spatial}(R), cur_{topic}(R), > \ldots$. There is also a *meaning function*: a partial function $mea : P \rightarrow Pow(P \times R^*)$. It maps a predicate name to a DRS (meaning postulates).

The starting-point of the simultaneously recursive definition of IIS as a sextuple < *ext, ref, prc, wrl, cur, mea* > is fixing a one-member base: $< \emptyset, \emptyset, \emptyset, \emptyset,$ $cur(W) = v, \emptyset >$. Seven kinds of recursive steps are proposed in [3]; their names are intended to refer to their operation: *expansion (of extensions) of predicates* (EXP), *introduction of a new predicate* (INP), *cursor move* (CUM), *introduction of a new referent into the active world* (IREA) and *a new world* (IREN), *referent assignment to a (generalized) DRS* (RED), *specification of an associated DRS* (SPED). Observe the first four components of IIS (the LDRS) define a DRS: the usual box structure corresponds to the tree of worlds, and the function wrl is responsible for linking referents to boxes. The recursive steps are to capture different linguistic (and extralinguistic) ways of gathering information at the interpreter's disposal, and further members can be proposed, of course. Kálmán's [8] example, where IIS after working up (a) contains no referent for a priest/dog, illustrates the apparatus: (a) *Joe got married yesterday.* (b) ... *THE PRIEST spoke harshly.* / (c) ...???*THE DOG barked loudly.* SPED enables us to create the priest's referent, by applying it to the pair of *associated* DRSs: 〈 "x gets married," "y organizes x's marriage, y is a priest"〉. (c) can also serve as a continuation of (a); he source of "mediating" information differs (*interpersonal* knowledge (a+c) / *cultural/enyclopedic.* knowledge (a+b), whilst *logical consequences* can also be used elsewhere). All information types are assumed to be stored in IIS in similar format and, hence, are accessible while processing a discourse. In this way several phenomena are accounted

---

[5] They are 'pegs' in the sense that before use they contain no information, they are only carriers of information.

for where referents should be "produced" (while the interpreter *commits* herself to a whole "story" [8]). This facility will prove to be useful in interpreting texts in (H)SL.

3   The Story of the Eaten Bus Ticket

The brief story in English: *A black boy got on the bus. He went forwards clutching the handstraps above and chewing a bubble gum. He was looking for a seat. Finally he found one side of a double seat beside an old lady. He sat down and crossed his legs. She glanced at the boy frightened and drew a bit away. Then she started to mumble: "They are a disgusting, dirty, stinking company. They don't like working they are lazy. It is terrible!" The boy looked at the lady taking interest, but he left it unanswered. Suddenly an inspector got on the bus at the front door and neared more and more. The old lady was clasping her ticket in the hand she was going to show it to the inspector. The boy driven by a sudden brainwave snatched the ticket out of the lady's hand and swallowed it. She was dumbfounded with surprise. The inspector came to them. The boy showed his season ticket with a bored face while the lady started to complain screaming: "He has eaten (my ticket)! He has eaten it!" The inspector didn't believe this explanation and imposed her a fine. She swallowed the bitter pill and paid the penalty.*

Analyzing this story the predicates were described sign by sign, and the elements have received their referents considering the syntactic and discursive rules of HSL. A large number of constructions typical of sign language discourses could be found.

A characteristic feature of sign languages is *the spatial index* on which the whole pronoun system is based [9,10]. The signing space can be distributed into four big sections (I - you - (s)he(1) - (s)he(2)), and these four ones can be cut into smaller ones. At the first mentioning of a character a spatial point is to be assigned to her / him and this index from that moment on works in an anaphoric way. Later when we want to refer back to a character we just have to activate her index pointing to it or changing the movement and orientation component of the inflecting verbs (e.g. [11,12,13]). Our partner can find the proper character and so the continuity of signing and interpreting narratives is ensured. We could bring our characters into action by means of pronoun copy [14]; sign languages use this grammatical tool both in clauses and on verb finals if the relation between the character and her pronoun (index) or the subject of the proposition seems to grow dim.

The mode of reference depends on the *signing style* too [15]. In *narrative style* the signer stays neutral, he points to the spatial indices and/or (s)he adjusts inflectional verbs to these indices. In *participant style*, the trunk of the signer "turns" into the space, he puts on the mimic and non-verbal behavior of the characters alternating [15]. The story analyzed here represents the latter style: the informant narrated an interesting anecdote in an informal style. During the narration it was always clear which character was mentioned. The old lady was sitting on the left side, the boy on the right side of the double seat; the signer turned his trunk and changed the orientation component of signs. Both passengers were sitting, so their spatial indices were a little bit lower than the index of the inspector, who was standing and walking. The signer changed the perspective by raising or lowering his look. In this story, the behavior of the characters was also strongly different: there was mentioned a tough boy chewing a bubble gum all the time, a shy old lady and a rigorous inspector. In compliance with this, the signer used very different facial expressions: the lady always looked at the boy scared and with aversion, the boy looked at the lady smiling but calm and moving his jaw unceasingly. In S15, e.g., the agent (the old lady) of the predicate ('clutch ticket in the hand') can be interpreted only by the position of the signer's trunk and by his mimic. And at the last sentence of the narration the signer finished changing roles and turning his look and body, he looked forward, straight in the face of the interpreter (in the camera), indicating that the story comes to an end, this is the conclusion. It is similar to the stress and intonation of spoken languages in parallel cases.

From the point of view of discursive dramaturgy, *verb signs* are divided into two groups depending on their *morphological structure* (and meaning) [19]. Verbs articulated ("bounded") on the body have only one standard constructing way where the character can be joined to the action only with pointing to his spatial index: MUMBLE, CHEW(ING)-GUM, GULP(-DOWN) (cited from the story). While verbs articulated on an arbitrary point of the space can incorporate the spatial index of the character(s) flexibly and so morphological features of the given lexical item are modified: LOOK-AT, GET-INTO, NEAR-TO. In this case the direction of the motional component accommodates to the situation. The perspective is equal to the standpoint of the signer who describes actions and characters' position.

A special subclass of pronouns, called proforms (e.g. [20]), can express certain aspects of meaning of characters. These proforms are articulated structurally without restriction in the space, so they can be moved to an arbitrary spatial index. A few examples from the story are TWO-PERSONS-SITTING-NEXT-TO-EACH-OTHER, SOMEONE-GET-INTO, OPPOSITE-TO-ME. Due to this flexibility of the pronoun and verb system of sign languages, the signer can also move the spatial index of characters without losing the relation between the old and the new ones. The boy, for instance, got on the bus at the rear, he went forwards, and then he sat down next to the old lady; the inspector got on at the front of the bus, then he approached to the boy and the lady, etc.

Now we would like to demonstrate two areas of discourse-building where the (L)DRT technique enables us to express (and reveal) slight details of the meaning of texts. The first area, which will be illustrated with the embedding of the proto-DRS belonging to S2 (the second sentence) into the LDRS, is that of *the temporal and spatial organization of discourses*. Just after interpreting S1 (which is about a boy's getting on a bus), a certain temporal reference-point and a certain spatial reference-point are at the interpreter's disposal: t1 and l1 in our analysis. It follows from general principles of discourse building [5] that they serve as the (temporal and spatial) starting-points of the boy's movement inside the bus. This movement can also be assigned a temporal referent but one of the interval type – denoted by t3 in our analysis. The signer shows three times that the boy catches at a handstrap (for standing people); they are not mentioned but can be "introduced" due the interpreter's cultural knowledge. The three actions are instantaneous ones with point-like temporal referents, which, at least according to the simplest possible discourse-building strategy, are inside interval t3. The permanent activity of chewing a bubble gum is also mentioned. The interval-type temporal referent belonging to this activity is denoted by t4. What is sure at this point is only that time-intervals t3 and t4 are in an overlapping relation; it turns out later that t3 is a part of t4.

Sentence 10, where the old lady's muttering is mentioned, requires a special step in the interpretation. To perform this step a sophisticated apparatus of LDRT is needed: namely the *introduction of a new (fictive) world*, which can be regarded as the old lady's beliefs and prejudices. The reference to a *company* in S11 makes it unambiguous that the interpretation of this sentence (its embedding into the temporary discourse representation) requires the application of a rare technique: the predicates *disgusting, dirty* etc. concern a new referent, r12, which has something to do with the boy's referent r2 but they are not the same. Referent r12 is to be regarded as the prototypical representative of a characteristic group, that r2 belongs to (in the lady's world of beliefs).

4 Conclusion

We do *not* claim that either the theoretical elaboration of LDRT and GASG is ready or the grammar and the information structure of the sign language has been revealed. What we claim is that GASG, due to its *total lexicalism*, enables us to separate a level of analysis where the underspecified meanings of performed signs can be represented (S1, ..., S28 in Figure 1), and then LDRT, due to the homogeneous treatment of information of different sources / types, enables us to "create" the rich system of connections among these meanings and their embedding in discourse (DRS1-28) – making the first steps towards the precise revelation of the special grammar and discourse building strategies of HSL, as well as the nature of UG the family of whose realizations sign languages also belong to.

References

1. van Eijck, J., H. Kamp: Representing discourse in context. In: van Benthem, J., A. ter Meulen (Eds.): Handbook of Logic and Language. Elsevier, Amst. & MIT Press, Cambridge, Mass. (1997).
2. Alberti, G.: Generative Argument Structure Grammar: A Strictly Compositional Syntax for DRS-Type Representations. Acta Linguistica Hungarica 46 (1999) 3–68.
3. Alberti, G.: Lifelong Discourse Representation Structures. Gothenburg Papers in Computational Linguistics 00-5 (2000) 13–20.
4. Kamp, H.: A theory of truth and semantic representation. In: Groenendijk, J., T. Janssen, M. Stokhof (Eds.): Formal methods in the study of language. Amsterdam, Math. Centre. (1981).
5. Kamp, H., U. Reyle: From Discourse to Logic. Kluwer Academic Publ. (1993).
6. Zeevat, H.: Aspects of Discourse Semantics and Unif. Gr. Ph.D., U. Amsterdam (1991).
7. Alberti, G., K. Balogh, J. Kleiber: GeLexi Project: Prolog Implementation of a Totally Lexicalist Grammar. To appear in ILLC, Amsterdam (2002).
8. Kálmán, L.: Deferred information: the semantics of commitment. In L. Kálmán and L. Pólos (Eds.): Papers from the 2nd Symp. on Logic and Language. Akadémiai, Bp. (1990) 125–157.
9. Berenz, N., L. F. Brito: Pronouns in BCSL an ASL. In [16], (1990) 26–36.
10. Bergman, B.: Grammaticalization of Location. In [16], (1990) 37–56.
11. Ahlgren, I., B. Bergman: Preliminaries on Narrative Discourse in Swedish Sign Language. In [17], (1990) 257–263.
12. Bos, H.: Person and Location Marking in Sign Language of the Netherlands: Some Implication of a Spatially Expressed Syntactic System. In [17], (1995) 231–246.
13. Meir, I.: Explaining Backwards Verbs in ISL: Syntactic-Semantic Interaction. In [18], (1995) 105–119.
14. Bos, H.: Pronoun Copy in Sign Language of the Netherlands. In [18], (1995) 121–147.
15. Boyes-Braem, P.: Zitat und Zitieren in der Gebärdensprachen der Gehörlosen. In Zeitschrift für Semiotik 14/1–2 (1992) 79–109.

16. Edmondson, W. H., F. Karlson (Eds.): Papers from the Fourth International Symposium on Sign Language Research. Hamburg: Signum Press (1990).
17. Prillwitz, S., T. Vollhaber (Eds.): Current Trends in European Sign Language Research. Hamburg: Signum Press (1990).
18. Bos, H., T. Schermer (Eds.): Sign Language Research 1994. Hamburg: Signum (1995).
19. Szabó, M. H.: Lokalitás, perspektíva és akcióminõség a jelnyelvekben [Localization, Perspective and Actions Art in Sign Languages]. In: Nyelvtudományi Közlemények 96. (1998–1999) 232–246.
20. Bellugi, U., E. S. Klima (1991) Eigenschaften räumlich-visueller Sprachen. In [17], 134–166.

Dependency Analyser Configurable by Measures

Tomáš Holan*

Department of Software and Computer Science Education, Faculty of Mathematics and Physics,
Charles University, Prague, Czech Republic,
E-mail: holan@ksvi.ms.mff.cuni.cz

Abstract. In this paper we present a dependency analyser able to compute syntax recognition and analysis according to dependency grammars. The analyser is able to deal with nonprojective constructions, it has means to express the level of word-order freedom and its limitations. The level of word-order freedom and the level of robustness (correctness) of sentences can be specified as parameters of the analysis. Data specification language and grammar definition language are also presented.

1 Introduction

Syntactic analysis is a part of many tasks of computational linguistics such as e.g. machine translation, natural-language communication, grammar-checking or full-text search.

One of the big problems of syntax analysis of natural languages is a complexity of the computation and a high number of results caused by ambiguity of natural language words and/or ambiguity of syntax. This complexity grows even more if we want to use some form of relaxation of language and to allow for an analysis of sentences containing some errors.

The methods used to solve the problem of complexity are disambiguation, pruning or heuristics that more or less help to find the "correct" tree/derivation for the sentence.

In our case where analysis is used as part of a grammar-checker or as a testing/debugging tool supporting work on the grammar of natural language, these methods are not acceptable because we need to get *all* trees/derivations of the sentence that can be found.

So we use other means to decrease time and space complexity of analysis.

The means are measures of word-order complexity ((non)projectivity), measures of robustness (number of errors allowed) and the analyser computing syntax analysis limited by the given values of those measures.

2 Definitions

We will introduce the concepts of D- and DR-trees, measures of (non)projectivity, D-grammars and grammars with errors. We will proceed in a rather informal way; exact definitions can be found e.g. in [12].

---

* This work was supported by the grant of the Grant Agency of the Czech Republic No. 201/02/1456.

P. Sojka, I. Kopeček, and K. Pala (Eds.): TSD 2002, LNAI 2448, pp. 81–88, 2002.

2.1 Trees, Measures

Dependency structure of the sentence is expressed by a *dependency tree (D-tree)*, where the edges oriented from leaves to the root show dependencies between the words. Each node contains as its elements *symbol, horizontal index* (serial number of the word in the sentence), *vertical index* (level, distance from the node to the root) and *dominancy index* (horizontal index of the node this node depends on).

So as to demonstrate the order of reduction or the order of creation of dependencies we use a *DR-tree* (delete-rewrite-tree), where each vertical edge marks the rewriting of the dominant symbol and each oblique edge corresponds to the deletion of the dependent symbol during the reduction.

D-trees and DR-trees are related by the concept of *contraction*. We say that the D-tree T is the *contraction of the DR-tree TT* if oblique edges join the same pairs of horizontal positions inside the sentence (corresponding nodes have the same value of the dominancy index).

For both D-trees and DR-trees we can define a $Cov(u, T)$ — *coverage of a node u in the tree T* as a set of all *horizontal indices* of all the nodes from which a path (bottom up, including empty path) leads to u.

If $Cov(u, T) = \{i_1, i_2, \ldots, i_m\}, i_1 < i_2 < \cdots < i_{m-1} < i_m$, we say that the pair (i_j, i_{j+1}) forms a *gap* in $Cov(u, T)$, iff $i_{j+1} - i_j > 1$.

The measure $dNg(u, T)$ is defined as a number of gaps in the $Cov(u, T)$; $dNg(T)$ denotes the maximum of $dNg(u, T)$ for all the nodes u of the tree T. The value $dNg(T)$ is called the *measure of nonprojectivity of the dependecy tree T*; we say that the dependency tree T is *projective* if $dNg(T) = 0$, otherwise we say that the tree T is *nonprojective*.

This definition of (non)projectivity provides us with the same dividing line between the sets of projective and non-projective trees as other definitions based e.g. on the crossing of edges (see [1,2]) but this definition is easy to evaluate during the process of the bottom-up analysis.

Similarly, we define $Ng(u, T)$ as a number of gaps in the coverage of the node u of the DR-tree and $Ng(T)$ as the *measure of nonprojectivity of the DR-tree T*. We say that DR-tree T is *projective* iff $Ng(T) = 0$.

2.2 Dependency Grammars

In [9] we have introduced a class of formal grammars called *Robust Free-Order Dependency Grammars (RFODG's)* as a formal foundation for the development of a grammar-checker for Czech which is a natural language with a considerable degree of word-order freedom. In this text we will call these grammars simply *dependency grammars (DG)*.

Dependency grammar (D-grammar) is a quadruple $G = (T, N, S_t, P)$ where T is the set of terminals, N is the set of nonterminals, $S_t \subseteq (T \cup N)$ is the set of starting symbols and P is the set of rewriting rules of two forms: $A \rightarrow_X BC$ and $A \rightarrow B$, where $A, B, C \in (T \cup N)$ and $X \in \{L, R\}$. The letters L (R) in the subscripts of the rules mean that the first (second) symbol on the right-hand side of the rule is considered *dominant*, and the other *dependent*. If a rule has only one symbol on its right-hand side, we consider the symbol to be *dominant*.

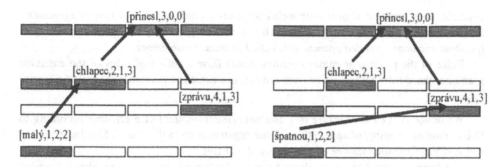

Fig. 1. Examples of projective ($dNg = 0$) and non-projective ($dNg = 1$) D-trees with marked coverages of their nodes.

The rule has the following interpretation (for the reduction): The dependent symbol is deleted (if there is one on the right-hand side of the rule) and the dominant one is rewritten (replaced) by the symbol standing on the left-hand side of the rule. The rules $A \to_L BC$, $A \to_R BC$ can be used for a reduction of a sentence (sentential form) w for any of the occurrences of the symbols B, C in w, where B precedes (*not necessarily immediately*) C in w. During the reduction, the rule $A \to B$ can rewrite any occurrence of B in w.

We say that a DR-tree T is a DR-tree according to dependency grammar G if the symbol of the root node belongs to the set of starting symbols of the grammar G and for every non-terminal node it is possible to find a rule of the grammar G describing a relation between the node and its daughters (dominant-vertical edge, dependent-oblique edge, order of daughters (left-right)). In the case of the DR-tree according to any dependency grammar we can talk about a *rule assigned to the edge*.

We can refine the generative power of the D-grammars by introducing the *local limitations of non-projectivity*:

The *set of limitations of non-projectivity of symbols* is a set $Cs = \{[A, i] | A \in (N \cup T), i \geq 0\}$. The pair $G_{Cs} = (G, Cs)$ is called *1-DG grammar*. We say that DR-tree T is a *DR-tree according to 1-DG* (G, Cs) iff it is a DR-tree according to the D-grammar G and for every node u of T it holds that if A is the symbol contained in the node u and if $[A, x] \in Cs$, then $Ng(u, T) \leq x$.

1-DG grammars can describe all context-free languages without empty words and also some context-sensitive languages, e.g. language $\{a^n b^n c^n | n > 0\}$.

2.3 Grammars with Errors

In order to search for syntactic errors we can use a single grammar to recognize correct sentences and to mark the other sentences as incorrect. We think that it is necessary to make the difference between errors in the sentence and errors in (or insufficiency of) the grammar. Therefore we use two grammars, *positive grammar* and *extended grammar*, to classify sentences into three classes: *correct sentences*, i.e. those recognized by the positive grammar, *incorrect sentences*, i.e. those recognized by the extended grammar only (for example, the sentence contains some well-known errors such as the violation of agreement) and *unclassified sentences*, i.e. those which are not recognized by any grammar. The pair *(positive grammar, extended grammar)* is called *grammar with errors*.

Rules of the positive grammar *(positive rules)* form a subset of rules of the extended grammar, those rules which are present only in the extended grammar are called *negative rules*.

We define $Ne(T)$ as *measure of robustness (incorrectness)* of a DR-tree according to D-grammar as a number of applications of the negative rules in the tree T. Similarly, we can define $dNe(T)$ as the measure of robustness of a D-tree T.

The formalism used by our analyser for the definition of the grammar makes it possible to describe positive and extended grammars by one grammar by placing the "error rule" tag into the rule; this is used mostly in case some constraints are (not) fulfilled.

3   The Analyser

There are many well-known dependency analysers and formalisms for expressing dependency grammars, see e.g. [4,5,7]. They are appropriate for various languages (primarily English) and for various purposes.

Our approach differs from these formalisms in the way of expressing rules, in dealing with erroneous and nonprojective sentences and especially in the possibilities of expressing limitations of analysis by measures.

The entire tool consists of the following three parts: *data (sentence) specification language, grammar definition language* and *configurable analyser*.

3.1   Data (Sentence) Specification Language

This language is used for the specification of the input data — morphologically and lexically processed sentences of natural language. Words can have only simple attributes except for one complex attribute for a valency frame. The language also allows for an efficient way of the notation of morphological and lexical ambiguity.

The following example shows the (simplified) specification of the Czech word "květiny" (flowers) in this language.

```
kvetiny
LEXF: kvetina
WCL: noun
SYNTCL: noun
GENDER: fem
?
    NUM: pl
    CASE: ? voc , acc , nom !
,
    NUM: sg
    CASE: gen
!
END
```

This example illustrates the usage of the branching on the level of the whole sets of attributes (branching after the GENDER attribute) and also branching on the level of values (values of the CASE attribute). The entire specification corresponds to four unambiguous definitions. The question mark always denotes the place where the branching begins, commas separate the alternatives and the exclamation mark denotes the end of branching. The branchings can be nested; the resulting set of the descriptions is the set of all possible combinations (Cartesian product).

3.2 Grammar Definition Language

This language serves for the definition of grammars with errors. Meta-rules of a grammar are described as sequences of commands checking the conditions of the applicability of the meta-rule and forming the instance of the meta-rule for the given right-hand side symbols. The variables used in the meta-rule are: X for the left-hand side symbol of the rule, A,B for the first and second right-hand side symbol of the rule and P as a temporary variable for an element of the frameset.

The head of the meta-rule can contain attributes declaring the limitation of the meta-rule to the projective use only (PROJECTIVE), the limitation of non-projectivity of the meta-rule to the closest dominant symbol (CLOSEST), or negative-only meta-rules (NEGATIVE).

Commands forming the meta-rules are as follows:

- *hard-condition* declaring the value of the attribute needed for the application of the meta-rule, e.g.
  A.SYNTCL=noun.
- *soft-condition* declaring the value of the attribute needed for the application of the positive meta-rule and the name of the error in case the condition was violated, e.g.
  A.CASE ? B.CASE CaseDisagreement.
- *initialization* declaring which of symbols *A*, *B* will be dominant and initializing the dominant symbol which may be rewritten (left-hand side of the rule), e.g.
  X := B.
- *assignment* setting the value of the attribute of the (rewritten) dominant symbol (left-hand side of the rule), e.g.
  X.HasRightGenitive := yes.
- *selection from the frameset* selects one element from the specified frameset and puts it into the variable P, and then the rest of the rule is processed separately for all elements of the frameset, e.g.
  P in A.FRAMESET.
- *deletion from the frameset* deletes a selected element from the specified frameset, e.g.
  DELETE P from A.FRAMESET.
- *other statements* – OK (successful termination), FAIL (unsuccessful termination), ERROR name (error sign is set).
- *conditional statement* if-then-else-endif allowing the branching of the meta-rule, e.g.

```
        IF A.SYNTCL=noun THEN X.a := n
                    ELSE
```

```
        IF  A.SYNTCL=pronoun THEN X.a := p
                             ELSE FAIL
        ENDIF
    ENDIF
```

The following example presents the simplified definition of the meta-rule for adjoining the adjective as the left congruent attribute to the noun:

```
METARULE LeftCongruentAttribute
    A.SYNTCL=adj
    B.SYNTCL=noun
    A.GENDER ? B.GENDER GenderDisagreement
    A.CASE   ? B.CASE   CaseDisagreement
    A.NUMBER ? B.NUMBER NumberDisagreement
    X:=B
    OK
END_METARULE
```

If the interpretation of the meta-rule succeeds and all soft-conditions were met then we get the rule of the positive grammar. If any of the soft conditions is not true then the interpretation of the meta-rule continues but the resulting rule will be the negative rule of the extended grammar with the appropriate error code.

The set of attributes and the set of values are not fixed, the author of the grammar can use her/his own attributes and values. The dictionaries of attributes and values are created during the loading of the grammar and the input sentences.

3.3 Configurable Analyser

This analyser provides the computation of all the DR-trees and D-trees for a given sentence according to the given grammar fulfilling the limitations of the Ng, dNg and Ne measures. The results are presented on different levels, from the list of items of parsing to the sets of DR-trees or D-trees.

The output is represented as a list of DR-trees and their shapes and a list of D-trees and their shapes. These lists are interpreted by the TreeView program.

The analyser is based on the bottom-up parsing: it works with items representing the (sub)trees. An item contains the symbol and the horizontal position of the root of the subtree, its coverage and references to daughter items. The analyser tries to combine the two items, i.e. it checks disjunctivity of their coverages, computes their union as the coverage of a new item, checks whether it fulfils the given restrictions of nonprojectivity (Ng measure) and of robustness (Ne measure), then it tries to interpret the meta-rules on the symbols in the roots of the items (by horizontal indices left (A) and right (B)), and if the meta-rule succeeds (OK) then it creates a new item.

For every new item created the analyser checks whether there already exists an item with the same symbol, horizontal position of the root and coverage. If it exists then the new item is marked as *duplex item* and it will not be used for the creation of the new items. Duplex items are used later to find all the trees for the given sentence.

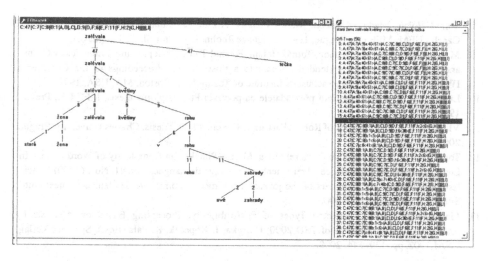

Fig. 2. Example of the output as displayed by TreeView. It shows the tree selected from the list of all the trees (the window on the right-hand side).

4 Conclusion

The main objective of this contribution was to present a dependency analyser configurable by measures.

This analyser can analyse non-projective sentences, it can deal with errors (extended grammar), it can use global limits of non-projectivity and correctness given as parameters of analysis. It can also use local limits of non-projectivity of single meta-rules, it computes the full set of trees without pruning because it is needed during the testing of the grammar.

The analyser was used for the pilot implementation of the grammar-checker [8] as a base of the robust analyser of Czech [11] and of the machine-aided translation tool [10], and also as a testing tool for the research of prepositional phrases in Czech [13].

References

1. Jürgen Kunze: Die Auslassbarkeit von Saltzteilen bei koordinativen Verbindungen im Deutschen. Akademie-Verlag-Berlin, 1972.
2. Ladislav Nebeský: A Projectivity Theorem. In: Prague Studies in Mathematical Linguistics (3), Academia, Prague 1972, pp. 165–169.
3. Alexej V. Gladkij: Formalnyje gramatiki i jaziki. Nauka, Moskva, 1973.
4. Martin Kay: Functional Unification Grammar: A formalism for machine translation.. In: Proceedings of the 10th International Conference on Computational Linguistics, Stanford University, California, 1984, pp.75–78.
5. Nicholas J. Haddock, Ewan Klein, Glyn Morrill: Categorial Grammar, Unification Grammar and Parsing. Edinburgh University Centre for Cognitive Science, Edinburgh 1987.
6. Igor A. Mel'čuk: Dependency Syntax: Theory and Practice. State University of New York Press, 1988.
7. Carl J. Pollard, Ivan A. Sag: Head-driven Phrase Structure Grammar. University of Chicago Press, Chicago 1994.

8. Tomáš Holan, Vladislav Kuboň, Martin Plátek: An Implementation of Syntactic Analysis of Czech. ÚFAL MFF UK, Prague, 1996, Language Technologies for Slavic Languages.
9. Martin Plátek, Vladislav Kuboň, Tomáš Holan: Formal Tools for Separating Syntactically Correct and Incorrect Structures (extended abstract to a poster). In: Proceedings of the Conference IWPT'97, pp. 247–248, Massachusetts Institute of Technology, Boston, MA, USA, 1997.
10. Libor Lisý: Pracovní prostředí překladatele na počítači PC. Diploma thesis, MFF UK, Prague, 1998.
11. Vladislav Kuboň: Problems of Robust Parsing of Czech. Ph.D. Thesis, Charles University, Prague, 2001.
12. Tomáš Holan, Vladislav Kuboň, Karel Oliva, Martin Plátek: On Complexity of Word Order. In: Les grammaires de dépendance - Traitement automatique des langues Vol. 41, No 1 (2000) (special issue on dependency grammars of the journal Traitement automatique des langues, guest editor Sylvain Kahane), pp. 273–300.
13. Markéta Straňáková: Selected Types of Pg-Ambiguity: Processing Based on Analysis by Reduction. In: Proceedings of TSD 2000, P. Sojka, I. Kopeček, K. Pala (Eds.), Springer Verlag, LNAI 1902, pp. 139–144, 2000.

The Generation and Use of Layer Information in Multilayered Extended Semantic Networks

Sven Hartrumpf and Hermann Helbig

University of Hagen, Applied Computer Science VII
Intelligent Information and Communication Systems, 58084 Hagen, Germany
E-mail: sven.hartrumpf@fernuni-hagen.de, hermann.helbig@fernuni-hagen.de

Abstract. The paradigm of Multilayered Extended Semantic Networks (MultiNet) is one of the most thoroughly described knowledge representantion systems along the line of semantic networks. The conceptual representation of MultiNet is characterized by embedding its nodes into a multidimensional space of layer attributes. These layer attributes play an important part during the syntactico-semantic analysis of natural language texts and during the inferential answer finding in question answering systems. The paper demonstrates the automatic generation of complex layer information for conceptual nodes and their use in the assimilation of knowledge pieces into a larger knowledge base.

1 Introduction

The paradigm of Multilayered Extended Semantic Networks (MultiNet) lies in the tradition of Semantic Networks (SN), which go back to Quillian [12] and are especially appropriate for the semantic representation of natural language information. Their main characteristic consists in the fact that concepts are represented as nodes of the SN and relations between them as arcs between these nodes. There can roughly be discerned two lines of development: On the one hand, we have the SN which are closely connected to logic and lean on a model-theoretic extensional semantics (prominent representatives are KL-ONE [2] and its successors, e.g. [1,11]). On the other hand, there are more cognitively oriented knowledge representation systems like MultiNet introduced in [4] and comprehensively documented in [5], which deny the possibility of a fully extensional interpretation of most (if not all) concepts and semantic primitives. Instead they prefer an operational or use-theoretic foundation of the semantics of the representational means. MultiNet and its representational means have been designed to fulfill, among others, the following criteria:

• Universality: They are applicable in every domain of application.

• Cognitive adequacy: They put the concept into the center of the semantic representation where every concept has a unique representative.

• Homogeneity: They can be used to describe the semantics of lexemes as well as the semantics of sentences or texts.

• Interoperability: They are the carriers of all NLP (natural language processing) tasks (be it lexical search, analysis, logical answer finding, or answer generation).

P. Sojka, I. Kopeček, and K. Pala (Eds.): TSD 2002, LNAI 2448, pp. 89–98, 2002.

In comparison with other knowledge representation systems, MultiNet (in the first stage) does not allow a concept to play the part of·a relation (as it is the case with KL-ONE).[1] From MultiNet's point of view, the logically oriented knowledge representation formalisms, like DRT [8], are - among other drawbacks - cognitively not adequate because of the lacking concept-centeredness. Furthermore, they are leaning on an extensional interpretation of the logical constructs, which cannot be upheld for many concepts.

One of the important features of MultiNet is the rich inner structure of the semantic representatives of concepts, which is expressed by the embedding of the nodes of the semantic network into a multidimensional space of attributes and their values. The use and processing of these so-called layer attributes is the main topic of this paper.

2   The MultiNet Paradigm

To explain the layer information, we have to deal briefly with the main features of Multi-Net (see Figure 1). Concepts are represented in MultiNet by nodes, and relations between concepts are represented as arcs between these nodes. MultiNet has several distinguishing features, the most important of them are:

• The nodes have a well-defined inner structure given by their embedding into certain layers of the network (see Section 3).

• Every node is classified according to a predefined conceptual ontology forming a hierarchy of sorts (see Appendix A).[2]

• Every arc is labeled by a member of a fixed set of relations and functions, which belong to a metalanguage with regard to the conceptual level. The relations are exemplarily described in Appendix B and fully specified by [5].

• The whole knowledge about a certain concept C represented by node N_C is divided into three parts (see Figure 1):

Part K: This part comprises all arcs connected to N_C that represent categorical knowledge about C. Knowledge which is marked by the feature value [K-TYPE *categ*] is valid without any exceptions and is connected with monotonic methods of reasoning; e.g. "*Every car has a motor*" is categorical knowledge with respect to the concept "car".

Part D: The prototypical knowledge, which has to be considered as a collection of default assumptions about C. It is characterized by the value [K-TYPE *proto*] and is connected with methods of nonmonotonic reasoning. Example: "*A car (typically) has an air bag.*"

Part S: Arcs of the SN starting or ending in a node N_C that have no influence on the basic meaning of C constitute the situational knowledge about C. They indicate the participation of concept C in certain situations (attribute-value [K-TYPE *situa*]). Example: "*Peter's car had been destroyed in an accident.*"

• MultiNet distinguishes an **intensional layer** from a **preextensional layer** where the latter is partially modeling the extension of the first.

• The relations and functions labeling the arcs at the concept level are themselves nodes at a

---

[1] Even the meaning of words like "*father*" are primarily represented as nodes (not relations) in Multi-Net. Only at a second stage they have an inner relational structure.

[2] Also disjunctions of sorts are allowed as characterizations of conceptual nodes to deal with underspecifications, vagueness, and semantic families.

meta level. They are interconnected by means of axiomatic rules (meaning postulates) which are the foundation for the inference processes working over a MultiNet knowledge base.

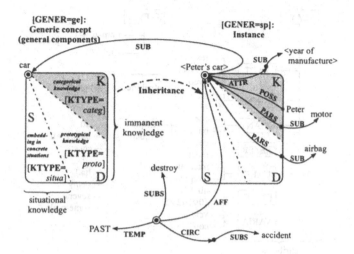

Fig. 1. The representation of concepts in MultiNet.

MultiNet has been used and is being used as a meaning representation formalism in several projects, e.g. [9]. Another important application is its use as an interlingua for representing the semantic structure of user queries in natural language interfaces to information providers in the Internet and to dedicated databases [6,10].

3   The Layered Structure of MultiNet

Nodes and arcs of MultiNet are characterized by so-called layer attributes. The layer specifications for arcs are comprised into the attribute K-TYPE and for nodes into the attribute LAY (see Figure 2). The specifications for the attribute LAY are organized along several dimensions which can itself be described by special attributes having their own values[3]:

● FACT: The **facticity** of an entity, i.e. whether it is really existing (value *real*), not existing (value *nonreal*), or only hypothetically assumed (value *hypo*). Example: "*Peter* [FACT *real*] *believed that (he was flying)* [FACT *hypo*]*.*"

● GENER: The **degree of generality** indicates whether a conceptual entity is generic (value *ge*) or specific (value *sp*). Examples: "*The crocodile* [GENER *ge*] *is a dangerous animal.*" vs. "*This crocodile* [GENER *sp*] *is a dangerous animal.*"

● QUANT: The intensional aspect of **quantification** specifies whether the concept is a singleton (value *one*) or a multitude (value *mult*) with the subtypes *fquant* and *nfquant* for fuzzy respective non-fuzzy quantifiers.

---

[3] For situational concepts, only the layer attributes FACT and GENER are relevant.

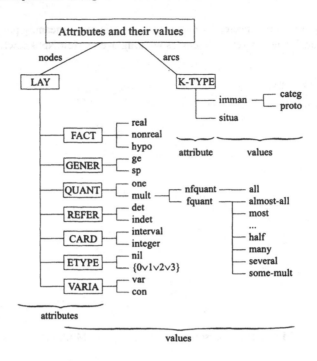

Fig. 2. The multidimensional space of layer attributes.

• REFER: The **determination of reference**, i.e. whether there is a determined object of reference (value *det*) or not (value *indet*). This type of characteristic plays an important part in text processing, especially for reference resolution (see Section 5). Example: *"The boy [REFER det] saw a crocodile [REFER indet]."*

• CARD: The **cardinality** characterizes a multitude at the preextensional level. Such cardinalities can be useful for the disambiguation of coreferences. Example: *"(A group of six thieves)ⱼ [CARD 1] stole (many cars)ᵢ. Six of (them [CARD (7, _)])ᵢ were found by the police."*

• ETYPE: The **type of extensionality** of an entity with values: *nil* – no extension, 0 – individual which is no set (e.g. ⟨Napoleon I⟩), 1 – entity with a set of elements from type [ETYPE 0] as extension (e.g. ⟨many bears⟩, ⟨the crew⟩), etc.

• VARIA: The **variability** describes whether an object is conceptually varying (value *var*) or not (value *con*). Example: *"This teacher [VARIA con] likes (every student) [VARIA var]."*

4 Automatic Generation of Layer Information

Layer information for nodes in semantic network representations of natural language sentences can be automatically generated by a parser. Based on lexicalized layer information and grammatical layer knowledge, it produces pairs of layer attributes and values, which can be partially underspecified or hypothetical.

$$\begin{bmatrix} \text{QUANT mult}^M \\ \text{VARIA con} \end{bmatrix}$$
(a) *die* (the) [pl.]

$$\begin{bmatrix} \text{QUANT one} \\ \text{REFER indet} \\ \text{CARD 1} \end{bmatrix}$$
(b) *ein* (a/an)

$$\begin{bmatrix} \text{QUANT all} \\ \text{REFER det} \\ \text{VARIA con} \end{bmatrix}$$
(c) *alle* (all)

$$\begin{bmatrix} \text{QUANT many}^M \end{bmatrix}$$
(d) *viele* (many)

$$\begin{bmatrix} \text{QUANT nfquant} \\ \text{CARD 4} \end{bmatrix}$$
(e) *vier* (four)

$$\begin{bmatrix} \text{CARD 1}^M \\ \text{ETYPE 0}^M \end{bmatrix}$$
(f) *Buch* (book)

$$\begin{bmatrix} \text{QUANT mult}^M \\ \text{CARD } (2,\_)^M \\ \text{ETYPE 1}^M \end{bmatrix}$$
(g) *Bücher* (books)

$$\begin{bmatrix} \text{GENER sp}^P \\ \text{QUANT one} \\ \text{REFER indet} \\ \text{CARD 1} \\ \text{ETYPE 0} \end{bmatrix} = \text{(b)} \sqcup \text{(f)}$$
(h) *ein Buch* (a book)

$$\begin{bmatrix} \text{QUANT many} \\ \text{CARD } (2,\_)^M \\ \text{ETYPE 1} \end{bmatrix} = \text{(d)} \sqcup \text{(g)}$$
(i) *viele Bücher* (many books)

$$\begin{bmatrix} \text{GENER sp}^P \\ \text{QUANT nfquant} \\ \text{REFER det}^P \\ \text{CARD 4} \\ \text{ETYPE 1} \\ \text{VARIA con} \end{bmatrix} = \text{(a)} \sqcup \text{(e)} \sqcup \text{(g)}$$
(j) *die vier Bücher* (the four books)

$$\begin{bmatrix} \text{GENER sp}^P \\ \text{QUANT all} \\ \text{REFER det} \\ \text{CARD 4} \\ \text{ETYPE 1} \\ \text{VARIA con} \end{bmatrix} = \text{(c)} \sqcup \text{(e)} \sqcup \text{(g)}$$
(k) *alle vier Bücher* (all four books)

$\perp = \text{(d)} \sqcup \text{(e)}$

(l) (*) *viele vier Bücher* (many four books)

Legend

(*)	ungrammatical expression	M	source: morphological analysis
$\perp$	contradiction (unification failure)	P	source: syntactic analysis (parser)

Fig. 3. Layer features for words and noun phrases.

The parsing process for a single sentence is intended to provide a solid base for the treatment of whole texts. When going from the sentence level to the text level, some layer attribute values must be refined or revised because some layer effects can be worked out and fully specified on the text level only.

The generation of layer information can therefore be seen in three steps: The initial information for individual words is provided by the lexicon, the parser adds information based on syntax and semantics of individual sentences, while the final set of layer information is achieved when combining sentence representations by means of text assimilation. (The last step is described in Section 5.)

The lexicon contains lexicalized layer values for determiners (articles, demonstrative determiners, quantifiers, etc.), pronouns, nouns, and complement descriptions of verbs. Some partial feature structures for lexical entries are shown in Figure 3, (a)-(g).[4]

The German parser (see [7]) installs a **layer agreement principle** inside noun phrases (NPs) by applying a unification operator $\sqcup$ to the elementary constituents of the NP so that the LAY feature of a complex NP will be obtained by this unification operation. Some results produced by the parser are shown in Figure 3, (h)-(l). The last example is ungrammatical. This can be formally explained by the layer agreement principle because the unification of

---

[4] As shown in the examples, quantifiers give rise to specific layer features. A quantifier like "*every*" may additionally introduce a dependency relation DPND from other network nodes to the quantified node as a lean representation of skolemizations.

the QUANT values *many* of (c) and *nfquant* of (d) fails (see Figure 2). In some cases, the parser may add defaults to the pure unification results (mark P in Figure 3).

To summarize, the layer feature system introduced to represent natural language semantics adequately with intensional and preextensional features allows to derive elegantly the layer information of complex NPs from lexicalized and grammaticalized layer information.

5 Layer Information and Knowledge Assimilation

The information contained in layer specifications plays an important part during the assimilation of knowledge and especially for resolving references. To explain this process, let us consider the following sentences:

(S1) *"The firm TRAVEL-X bought a new computer."*
(S2) *"Its hard disk had to be repaired."*

Without the help of background knowledge the reference of the word *"Its"* can not be properly resolved. First, one has to know that a computer has a hard disk, which is shown together with the semantic structure of (S1) in Figure 4(a).[5]

The fact that the relation (harddisk.1.1 PARS computer.1.1) belongs to the immanent knowledge is represented in the pop-up menu on the right side of Figure 4(a), where the value *imman* of the attribute K-TYPE is shown for both arguments of this relation. The node initiating a search for an antecedent is the semantic representative $c14$ for *"Its"* of sentence (S2), see Figure 4(b). This node bears the attribute value [REFER *det*], which is starting an inference process for the reference resolution.

To find the antecedent for $c14$, the assimilation process sets up a query:

(A-Q)   (X SUB harddisk.1.1) $\wedge$ (X PARS ??)

meaning *"Which object ?? has a hard disk as its part X?"*. X and ?? are variables, where the latter is denoting the focus of the question. Having answered this question by an appropriate inference technique [5], the nodes found for X and ?? in the background knowledge have to be identified with $c15$ and $c14$, respectively (stating that $c15$ has to be repaired and $c15$ (substituted for X) is the hard disk of $c14$).

To answer query (A-Q), further background knowledge is needed. In addition to the fact that a computer has a hard disk (i.e. (harddisk.1.1 PARS computer.1.1)), a piece of knowledge has to be provided that describes the inheritance of the part-whole-relationship in a SUB hierarchy:

(Ax1) (d1 SUB d2) $\wedge$ (d3 PARS d2) $\rightarrow$ $\exists$ d4 [(d4 SUB d3) $\wedge$ (d4 PARS d1)]

Applying this axiom to the knowledge represented in Figure 4(a) and instantiating the variables d1, d2, and d3 with $c13$, computer.1.1, and harddisk.1.1, respectively, one can deduce that there exists an object sk13=sk($c13$, computer.1.1, harddisk.1.1) which is a hard disk and also a part of $c13$.[6]

---

[5] The semantic network has been constructed by means of the workbench Multi-Net-WR [3] and the natural language analysis system NatLink.

[6] The Skolem term sk13=sk($c13$, computer.1.1, harddisk.1.1) indicates that the newly inferred object denoted by this term depends on the arguments of the Skolem function sk representing variable d4 from axiom (Ax1).

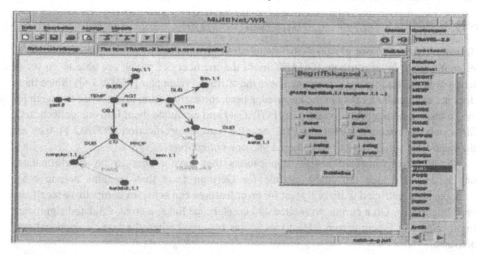

(a) Semantic representation of (S1) with a small piece of background knowledge

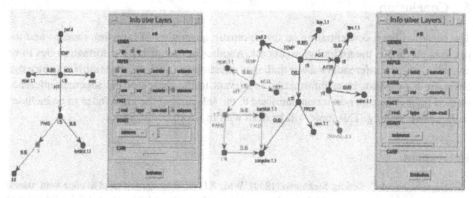

(b) Semantic representation of (S2)   (c) Result of the assimilation of the knowledge parts
                                          shown in Figure 4(a) and 4(b)

Fig. 4. Semantic representations during text assimilation for (S1) and (S2).

It is easy to see that the assimilation query (A-Q) can be answered on the basis of this
knowledge by the substitution $\sigma = \{c13/??, sk13/X\}$. Since on the one hand X and ?? in the
assimilation query (A-Q) stand for c15 and c14 in Figure 4(b), respectively, and on the other
hand c13 has been substituted for ?? and the inferred object sk13 has been substituted for X,
c15 must finally be identified with sk13 and c14 with c13 in the assimilation process. Putting
all results together, one gets the integrated network shown in Figure 4(c).

The layer information is important for resolving so-called cumulative references. They
are characterized by the fact that the phrase initiating the search for an antecedent has the
features of a plural NP, but there are no collections explicitly represented in the knowledge
base accumulated so far. Example:

(S3) "*Peter [QUANT one] met Paul [QUANT one] in the zoo.*"

(S4) *"Together they [REFER det, QUANT mult] went to the aquarium."*

To resolve the reference of *"they"* the assimilation process has to search for a collection C of entities with layer attribute [QUANT *mult*] the members of which are able to go (or in terms of MultiNet features[7]: they must have the attribute-value pair [POTAG +]). Since there does not exist such an entity in the knowledge base, the assimilation process has to search for single entities with attribute-value pair [POTAG +] and cumulate them into one collection C. Since only the concepts Peter and Paul bear the feature specification [POTAG +], they are the candidates which have to be gathered into one collection C.

We have implemented several applications that have access to layer information; one is a coreference resolution module for German texts that contains among other components a restricted unifiability test for layer features and achieves competitive recall and precision results. On a corpus with circa 480 coreference links, a cross-validated significant improvement in F-score from 69 % to 74 % was observed when the layer component was activated.

6 Conclusion

The paper has been concentrating on the automatic generation of layer information and the part it is playing in the assimilation process. Another impact of layer information lies in its crucial role for the inferential answer finding in question-answering over MultiNet knowledge bases. In this context, layer information is relevant to the choice of the adequate inference method (monotonic vs. non-monotonic) and to the selection of the knowledge to be included in the answer finding. This topic will be dealt with in a forthcoming paper.

References

1. Allgayer, J. and C. Reddig-Siekmann (1990). What KL-ONE lookalikes need to cope with natural language – scope and aspect of plural noun phrases. In *Sorts and Types in Artificial Intelligence* (edited by K. H. Bläsius, U. Hedtstück, and C.-R. Rollinger), pp. 240–285. Springer, Berlin, Germany.
2. Brachman, R. J. (1978). Structured inheritance networks. Technical Report No. 3742, Bolt Beranek & Newman, Cambridge, Massachusetts.
3. Gnörlich, C. (2000). MultiNet/WR: A Knowledge Engineering Toolkit for Natural Language Information. Technical Report 278, FernUniversität Hagen, Germany.
4. Helbig, H. (1997). Der MESNET Primer – Die Darstellungsmittel der Mehrschichtigen Erweiterten Semantischen Netze. FernUniversität Hagen, Germany.
5. Helbig, H. (2001). *Die semantische Struktur natürlicher Sprache: Wissensrepräsentation mit MultiNet.* Springer, Berlin.
6. Helbig, H., C. Gnörlich, and J. Leveling (2000). Natürlichsprachlicher Zugang zu Informationsanbietern im Internet und zu lokalen Datenbanken. In *Sprachtechnologie für eine dynamische Wirtschaft im Medienzeitalter* (edited by K.-D. Schmitz), pp. 79–94. TermNet, Wien.
7. Helbig, H. and S. Hartrumpf (1997). Word class functions for syntactic-semantic analysis. In *Proceedings of the 2nd International Conference on Recent Advances in Natural Language Processing (RANLP'97)*, pp. 312–317. Tzigov Chark, Bulgaria.

---

[7] Semantic features like "potential agent" [POTAG ±], "animate" [ANIMATE ±] are used to specify the selectional restrictions of concepts opening valencies.

8. Kamp, H. and U. Reyle (1993). *From Discourse to Logic: Introduction to Modeltheoretic Semantics of Natural Language, Formal Logic and Discourse Representation Theory.* Number 42 in Studies in Linguistics and Philosophy. Kluwer, Dordrecht.

9. Knoll, A., C. Altenschmidt, J. Biskup, H.-M. Blüthgen, I. Glöckner, S. Hartrumpf, H. Helbig, C. Henning, Y. Karabulut, R. Lüling, B. Monien, T. Noll, and N. Sensen (1998). An integrated approach to semantic evaluation and content-based retrieval of multimedia documents. In *Proceedings of the 2nd European Conference on Digital Libraries (ECDL '98)* (edited by C. Nikolaou and C. Stephanidis), number 1513 in Lecture Notes in Computer Science, pp. 409–428. Springer, Berlin.

10. Leveling, J. and H. Helbig (2002). A robust natural language interface for access to bibliographic databases. In *Proceedings of the 6th World Multiconference on Systemics, Cybernetics and Informatics (SCI 2002).* International Institute of Informatics and Systemics (IIIS), Orlando, Florida.

11. Peltason, C. (1991). The BACK system – An overview. *SIGART Bulletin*, 2(3):114–119.

12. Quillian, M. R. (1968). Semantic memory. In *Semantic Information Processing* (edited by M. Minsky), pp. 227–270. MIT Press, Cambridge, Massachusetts.

Appendix A: Detail from the Hierarchy of MultiNet Sorts

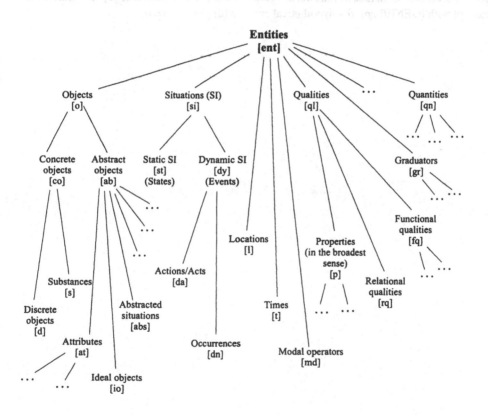

Appendix B: Description of Relations Used in This Paper

Relation	Signature	Short Description
AFF	$[si \cup abs] \times [o \cup st]$	C-Role – Affected object
AGT	$[si \cup abs] \times o$	C-Role – Agent
ATTR	$[o \cup l \cup t] \times at$	Specification of an attribute
CIRC	$si \times [ab \cup si]$	Relation between situation and circumstance
MODL	$\tilde{si} \times md$	Relation specifying a restricting modality
OBJ	$si \times [o \cup si]$	C-Role – Neutral object
PARS	$[co \times co] \cup [io \times io] \cup$ $[t \times t] \cup [l \times l]$	Part-whole relationship
POSS	$o \times o$	Relation between possessor and possession
PROP	$o \times p$	Relation between object and property
SUB	$[o \setminus abs] \times [\overline{o} \setminus \overline{abs}]$	Relation of conceptual subordination (for objects)
SUBS	$[si \cup abs] \times [\overline{si} \cup \overline{abs}]$	Relation of conceptual subordination (for situations)
TEMP	$[si \cup t \cup o] \times [t \cup si \cup abs]$	Temporal embedding of a situation
VAL	$at \times [o \cup qn \cup p \cup fe \cup t]$	Relation between attribute and its value

Sort symbols can be marked as follows: $\overline{o}$ – generic concept with [GENER *ge*]; $\dot{o}$ – individual concept with [GENER *sp*]; $\tilde{o}$ – hypothetical entity with [FACT *hypo*].

Filtering of Large Numbers of Unstructured Text Documents by the Developed Tool TEA

Jan Žižka[1] and Aleš Bourek[2]

[1] Department of Information Technologies, Faculty of Informatics,
Masaryk University in Brno, Botanická 68a, 602 00 Brno, Czech Republic
E-mail: `zizka@informatics.muni.cz`
[2] Department of Biophysics, Faculty of Medicine,
Masaryk University in Brno, Joštova 10, 662 43 Brno, Czech Republic
E-mail: `bourek@med.muni.cz`

Abstract. This paper describes a text-document-filtering software tool TEA (TExt Analyzer), which was originally developed for physicians to support selections of large numbers of unstructured medical text documents obtained from available Internet services. TEA learns interesting and relevant documents for *individual* users basically by the naïve Bayes algorithm. Moreover, TEA provides a number of additional functions that can improve its classification accuracy, allow more specific document selection for individual users, and enable users to work with dictionaries generated from analyzed documents. The learning process of TEA is based on a set of labeled positive and negative examples of text documents, which obtain their labels from users interested in documents of certain, usually very specific topics.

1 Introduction

Users, like physicians, of modern data-processing technologies mostly expect obtaining very specific information and knowledge from extensive resources provided, for example, by the Internet. Unfortunately, in too many cases the resources provide a lot of very raw data retrieved using only a set of key-words. Such a situation is still unsatisfactory because it is often impossible to manually separate hundreds or thousands of documents within a reasonable time. On the other hand, the users can employ computers and special software for the processing of rather raw data to obtain the requested information. One possibility is to use computers for learning which text documents are relevant for a specific user if this user can provide his or her parameters describing the area of interest. The text-filtering tool TEA (TExt Analyzer), described in the following sections, supports its users in separating unstructured text documents into two classes, *interesting* and *uninteresting*. TEA disposes of the basic functions *learning* and *classification*; moreover, it contains many additional functions which improve the final result – text documents that are mostly relevant and interesting for the users' specific needs. This approach is very important also in medicine because there is very often a huge number of documents, however, physicians usually need only a fragment covering their actual requirements. In addition, physicians as well as other users also deeply need to manage a lot of unstructured text materials which include great numbers of mutual

P. Sojka, I. Kopeček, and K. Pala (Eds.): TSD 2002, LNAI 2448, pp. 99–106, 2002.
© Springer-Verlag Berlin Heidelberg 2002

links. Preprocessing of huge numbers of text documents, which are accessible via different electronic archives distributed in the Internet, is generally inescapable, e.g., because of more than 10,000 medical documents published per day. On the other hand, text-document filtering can reveal that within a certain time interval, publication numbers of certain topics rapidly decrease, or specific new terms start to arise. Potential users of this kind of filtering software would also require *individual* adaptation of such tools (unlike the common WWW searching tools and browsers) for their specific needs. The described tool TEA has been developed and implemented for the operating system Windows, using the graphical user interface as illustrated in Figure 1.

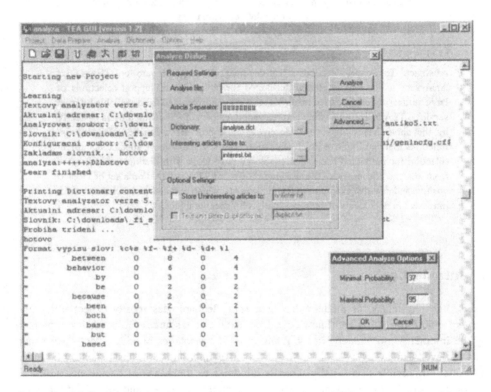

Fig. 1. The GUI (graphical user interface) of the text analyzer TEA – an example of the text analysis preparation.

2   The Essential Functions – Learning and Classification

The text-document classification tool TEA learns to recognize a user's interesting and uninteresting documents by the *naïve Bayes algorithm*. For its learning, TEA needs user-labeled sets of training examples, i.e., training text documents. Each example has a label – provided by a user before starting the learning process – as a mark of belonging either in a group of interesting or uninteresting documents. In other words, the learning process uses positive (interesting, relevant) and negative (uninteresting, irrelevant) examples of text documents, according to an individual user's requirements. Different users can naturally mark the same text documents differently if they need it.

TEA manipulates with the text documents as with sequences of words (or character strings), where these words are separated by the standard white space and punctuation marks and signs. In addition, all upper-case letters are converted into their lower-case equivalents. The separated individual words are then used as *distinct words* and are stored – together with their frequencies in all the training documents – into the dictionary.

To avoid a very long time of computation, the naïve Bayes algorithm assumes that positions of words are independent. Despite the fact that this assumption is not quite correct, results with (and not only) text documents are practically acceptable, which is described, e.g. in [4]. Thus, the frequencies of the distinct words are used for computing degrees to which a text document belongs to the interesting $(+)$ or uninteresting $(-)$ class. Let $Degree(+/-)$ stands for a degree of belonging to the $(+)$ or $(-)$ class, N_{all} stands for the total number of documents in both classes, $N_{(+/-)}$ stands for the number of documents in the $(+)$ or $(-)$ class, and $P(w_i|+/-)$ stands for the relative frequency of a word w_i in the $(+)$ or $(-)$ class (actually, *a posteriori probability*). Then, for n being the number of words in a classified text document, the belonging degree is given by the following equation (the degrees for $(+)$ and $(-)$ are computed separately):

$$Degree(+/-) = \frac{N_{(+/-)}}{N_{all}} \prod_{i=1}^{n} P(w_i|+/-)$$

After computing the degree, a classified document obtains the class $(+)$ or $(-)$ that corresponds to a greater degree value.

3 Classification Results of TEA

The implemented system TEA was tested using the cross-validation method and – at the present time – is used by physicians in the area of medical text documents obtained in huge numbers by various Internet tools and browsers. Among resources of text documents were, for example, on-line medical databases provided by the National Library of Medicine, many fulltext databases accessible to academics and professional health-care providers (Biological Abstracts, Zoological Record – database of BIOSIS comp., DL ACM – digital library of ACM, EIFL Direct – most important fulltext databases of EBSCO, LINK – scientific journals of Springer-Verlag, Web of Science – journals bibliography/citation DB, MEDLINE, etc.). During the processing of text documents, users of the initial TEA tool suggested and needed additional functions, which gradually extended possibilities of TEA and contributed to higher accuracies of classifications. The main goal of the users has always been to eliminate many uninteresting and irrelevant documents obtained from the Internet using mainly browsers and key-words because in too many cases there were so many documents that users did not have time enough to read them and to select only what was necessary.

The original tests, which used real data from the MEDLINE source, are published in [7,8]. The document set contained 701 interesting and 1,109 uninteresting documents with

12,631 different word forms. Classification accuracies were between 73–94 %, depending on different approaches: lower accuracy could be expected for sets of very similar documents (like, e.g., a very narrow medical branch), while higher accuracies were obtained for sets with more different document contains (e.g., documents from a medical branch with more aspects). Later, after the initial tests of the TEA's core, the experiments used much more text documents from different resources, and users could apply new additional functions as excluding certain words, setting up minimum and maximum occurrence of words, and so like. With this extended additional support, the TEA analyzer is now able to filter the retrieved material consistently with the average accuracy usually better than 85 %. The experiments with large and different data sets provided accuracies from 70 % up to 97 %.

The other group of extensive testing was performed using publicly accessible Internet newsgroups from 20 topics (*alt.atheism, comp.graphics, comp.os.ms-windows.misc, comp.sys.ibm.pc.hardware, comp.sys.mac.hardware, comp.windows.x, misc.forsale, rec.-autos, rec.motorcycles, rec.sport.baseball, rec.sport.hockey, sci.crypt, sci.electronics, sci.-med, sci.space, soc.religion.christian, talk.politics.guns, talk.politics.mideast, talk.politics.-misc*, and *talk.religion.misc*). The number of unstructured text documents was around 20,000 articles with 1,000 articles per class. The task of the TEA analyzer was based on the classification of text documents using 20 classes (20 more or less different newsgroup topics). The number of distinct words in all the original documents was 119,717. In this case, the classification accuracy was between 86 % and 89 %. The TEA's functionality for these 20 classes was almost the same as for the purely medical set of text documents mentioned above. The data of the newsgroups above mentioned can be found at [3].

According to the extensive experiments, the classification accuracy depends on several points. Higher numbers of training documents typically provide better accuracy. In addition, the number of training positive and negative documents should be as close as possible, e.g., 40 %:60 %, or even better, approximately 50 %:50 %. It is naturally not possible to obtain always the ideal data in practice, however, users very often prefer the help of the tool even in less advantageous situations, mainly if the number of the classified documents is very high (e.g., hundreds or thousands). Another important point is the possibility to exclude common words (typically the first 100 most common words for English) as well as certain words defined by a user. Such an exclusion improved the classification accuracies by 0.5 % to 5 %. On the other hand, the experiments also have revealed that the naïve Bayes algorithm becomes less effective for sets of data where positive and negative examples are very similar – however, in this case it is also often rather difficult for humans to unambiguously decide whether a text document belongs to the positive or negative class. Therefore, users can expect higher classification accuracies for large data sets containing more different documents within a certain area of interest or within different areas.

Descriptions of various problems and approaches of the naïve Bayes algorithm used for the text classification can be found, for example, in [5,6] and many others.

4   Additional Functions Supported by TEA

The current version of the TEA tool includes the naïve Bayes algorithm as its basic function for the learning and classification purposes. As the main result of learning, there is a dictionary containing words from documents together with computed probabilities of each word occurrence both in positive and negative text-document classes. In addition of learning, TEA enables its users to print the dictionary, to modify its contents in various ways, and to use the potentially modified dictionary subsequently as a basis for analyses of new documents. Another TEA's important function is the possibility to set up different restrictions for the learning and analyzing data to improve the classification results.

The additional functions supported by the TEA program can be divided into several groups:

- the system configuration,
- the program control functions,
- the users' projects (scripts as plans of actions) for running and controlling,
- the support of works with files and folders (directories),
- the setting up input and output files,
- the learning and analysis functions, and
- the work with words and dictionaries.

A brief, not complete description of the functions is provided in the following subsections. All the mentioned functions have more details and parameters as well as error messages, if necessary. The following description covers only the basic properties.

4.1   The System Configuration

The program TEA is designed and implemented to enable the work in an arbitrary language (provided that a certain language support was created). To select a communication language, for example, for error messages, there is a command *language:file*, where *file* defines a file containing messages. Moreover, the command *charset:file* can be used for changing a character set for a specified language (without this definition, the English alphabet characters are only used). The command *settings* displays the set up configuration. Finally, *free:configuration* cancels one of the configuration parameters; *free* without a specification simply sets up the program initial, default configuration.

4.2   The Program Control Functions

To finish the program run, the *exit* command is used; *help* supports displaying *Help* of the program. The command *print:message* displays a requisite *message* while *nprint:message* displays *message* with a new line.

4.3   The Users' Projects for Running and Controlling

The users' projects are actually scripts supporting repeated types of works, i.e., repeated sequences of commands. TEA uses *interpret:file* for running a project *file*. Without *file*, an interactive command line is started, so a user can combine both scripts and interactive commands. If a user wants to display script commands, he or she can turn on/off the activation by *say:on-off*.

4.4 The Support of Works with Files and Folders

The system TEA allows displaying of a current folder by *ls:mask*, for example, *ls:*.txt* displays all files having the *txt* extension. The command *cd:folder* changes a current *folder*, and *more:file* displays a requested *file*.

4.5 The Setting Up Input and Output Files

A dictionary is set up by *dictionary:file*; if the file does not exist, it is created. The functions of learning or analysis use a file defined by *input:file*. TEA also needs a configuration system containing string definitions of beginnings of interesting texts (the positive marking string starts with the character +, e.g., *+abc*) as well as uninteresting texts (the negative marking string starts with the character − , e.g., *− abc*). In addition, if interesting texts within a file have as their marks numbers, digits can be replaced by the character #, e.g., interesting text units having eight-digit numbers are represented in the configuration file as *+########*. If a user wants to add his or her comments into the text units, it is possible to define a beginning string of comments by *estring*, e.g., if a comment should start with *XXX*, then *eXXX*. The command *posfile:file* sets up an output file for interesting texts. To avoid a relatively frequent problem with duplicate or multiple text units (typically obtained from the Internet), a user can employ the command *test-file:file*; in addition, *dupfile:file* defines an output file for duplicates or multiplicities.

4.6 The Learning and Analysis Functions

The system TEA starts learning by *input:file* and *learn* or simply *learn:file*. After its learning, TEA can classify new texts by *analyse:file* or just *analyse* provided that a file was defined earlier. Interesting documents obtain probabilities higher than 50 %, up to 100 %. However, if a user wants to change the default value 50 %, the command *mipst:number* is available, e.g., from 75 % up to 100 %: *mipst:75*. On the other hand, if there are text units having suspicious, too high values, e.g., 98 %, a user can exclude such units by *mapst:number*, e.g., *mapst:98* in our case.

4.7 The Work with Words and Dictionaries

Users very often need to influence importance of certain words defined by the human approach because machines are still not so intelligent. During a normal work, TEA stores words − found in the testing data − with certain information. Each word is classified as, e.g., interesting, uninteresting, etc., using a scale *0, +, − , =, 1, 2, 3, 4, 5, 6, 7, 8, 9, n*. Generally, a word has the implicit classification =; if TEA during its analysis of a new text document (not included in the training set) finds an unknown word, it assigns *n* (as *unknown*) to it. In addition, a user can assign any item from the scale to a word; *0* means a word is not interesting at all, + means a positive key-word, − a negative key-word, = a word without any restriction. The other scale items can be used according to the user's meaning, if necessary. For example, in this way, the user can exclude common words (like *a, an, the, this, of, at, in, ...*) to improve TEA's classification. In addition, there is also an often used function that dynamically eliminates uninteresting words. Users can activate this function by *minpos:number*, *minsum:number*, and/or *masum:number*, which influences a needed ratio of words in positive and negative documents; therefore, depending of defined ratios, some words can be ignored. For example, *minsum:5* means that all words occurring less than five times in the testing data are ignored. Similarly, *masum:100* ignores words occurring more than 100 times (to avoid too frequent words). On the other hand, *minpos:0.4* says that a word occurring, for example, 45 times in interesting documents and 55 times in uninteresting documents will be ignored because $45/(45 + 55) = 0.45 > 0.4$.

The command *info* provides information about a current dictionary, and *show:dictionary: file* displays (or stores, if the *file* parameter is used) a dictionary as a text file. To retrieve a text file as a dictionary, the command *compile:file* is used. Sorting a dictionary is a task of *sort:asc* or *sort:desc* in the ascending or descending order, respectively. The command *cp:file* creates a copy of a dictionary; *file* is a name of the copy. Adding explicitly a new word is supported by *add:word*, where the classification is supposed to be =, otherwise the command *current:classification* can change the standard classification. If two dictionaries should be joined, the command *join:file* enables this function, where the *file* dictionary joins a current one.

5   Conclusions

As the popularity of the World Wide Web and other Internet services continues to increase, there is a growing need to develop tools and techniques that would help improve their overall usefulness. The all the time growing taking advantage of the Internet services among physicians indicates that this (and surely not only this) kind of users need efficient personal tools to enable PCs to boost user-creative thinking in areas requiring manipulation of vast amounts of textual information. Such a tendency has clearly been demonstrated in practice: the case of Czech Standards of Efficient Medical Care [1] and in tracking infertility treatment trends [2].

Experiments with a lot of real medical text-data verified the application of the naïve Bayes algorithm to be a useful method supporting results obtained from the Internet, especially when it was inevitable to process large numbers of more or less different documents selected only by key-words. The additional functions, which enable users to modify the document classification, e.g., excluding certain words or documents, increase the classification accuracy and decrease substantially the number of irrelevant, uninteresting text documents. However, this modifications and their results mostly depend on specific users' needs and on particular types of text documents – what is advantageous for a certain user could be disadvantageous for another one, even if they would work with the same set of documents. Therefore, the additional functions support individual settings of searching parameters while the naïve Bayes algorithm is generally responsible for the filtering itself. This also means that the next advantage of using a tool as TEA is the possibility to exploit the same set of documents for different purposes, even for more users, depending on a specific parameterization of the TEA system during its run.

References

1. Bourek, A., Suchý, M., and Svoboda, P. (2000): Standards of Efficient Medical Care (SEMC). In: *Proceedings of the 7th International Conference on System Science in Health Care, "Sustainable structure for better health."* Lyon, ISSHC, 436–439.
2. Bourek, A., Žižka, J., Ventruba, P., and Frey, L. (2000): The Use of the Internet for Monitoring Trends in Assisted Reproduction and Reproductive Medicine. *Gynekolog, 5,* 220–223 (in Czech).
3. Lang, K. (1995): http://www.ai.mit.edu/people/jrennie/20Newsgroups.
4. Lewis, D. D. (1998): Naïve (Bayes) at Forty: The Independence Assumption in Information Retrieval. In: *Proceedings of the 10th European Conference on Machine Learning ECML '98.* Springer Verlag, Berlin Heidelberg New York, 4–15.
5. McCallum, A. and Nigam, K. (1998): A Comparison of Event Models for Naïve Bayes Text Classification. In: *Proceedings of the AAAI-98 Workshop on Learning for Text Categorization.* ICML/AAAI-98, Madison, Wisconsin, July 26–27, 1998.
6. Rennie, J. D. M. (2001): Improving Multi-Class Text Classification with Naïve Bayes. Master Thesis, Massachusetts Institute of Technology, 2001. 43 pp.
7. Žižka, J., Bourek, A., and Frey, L. (2000): TEA: A Text Analysis Tool for the Intelligent Text Document Filtering. In: *Text, Speech, and Dialogue.* Springer Verlag, Berlin Heidelberg New York, LNCS 1902, 151–156.
8. Žižka, J., Bourek, A. (2002): Automated Selection of Interesting Medical Text Documents. In: *Computational Linguistics and Intelligent Text Processing.* Springer Verlag, Berlin Heidelberg New York, LNCS 2276, 402–404.

Visualisation Techniques for Analysing Meaning

Dominic Widdows, Scott Cederberg, and Beate Dorow[*]

Center for the Study of Language and Information
Stanford University, California
E-mail: dwiddows@csli.stanford.edu, cederber@csli.stanford.edu,
beate@csli.stanford.edu
WWW: http://infomap.stanford.edu

Abstract. Many ways of dealing with large collections of linguistic information involve the general principle of mapping words, larger terms and documents into some sort of abstract space. Considerable effort has been devoted to applying such techniques for practical tasks such as information retrieval and word-sense disambiguation. However, the inherent structure of these spaces is often less well-understood.

Visualisation tools can help to uncover the relationships between meanings in this space, giving a clearer picture of the natural structure of linguistic information. We present a variety of tools for visualising word-meanings in vector spaces and graph models, derived from co-occurrence information and local syntactic analysis. Our techniques suggest new solutions to standard problems such as automatic management of lexical resources, which perform well under evaluation.

The tools presented in this paper are all available for public use on our website.

1 Introduction

Large text corpora are used for many purposes in computational linguistics and NLP. Dictionaries can be built and enriched automatically or semi-automatically using corpora [6]. Bilingual texts can be used to enrich multilingual dictionaries [4]. Word-sense disambiguation systems can benefit from analysing distributional clusters in large corpora [9]. Information retrieval systems are built from large document collections in order to organise and access the information therein [1].

These systems all share the following property. Information derived from the text is built into some mathematical or conceptual model, and it is the model rather than the text itself which is used to solve the problem in question. Partly due to the focus of traditional NLP tasks such as parsing, this point has often been overlooked. Tremendous effort has been devoted to understanding the way the text itself should be processed, based upon sound linguistic principles. However, the properties of the resulting models are often less well-understood: knowledge of formal logic remains much more part of a traditional linguist's training than knowledge of different kinds of mathematical spaces and models.

* This research was supported in part by the Research Collaboration between the NTT Communication Science Laboratories, Nippon Telegraph and Telephone Corporation and CSLI, Stanford University, and by EC/NSF grant IST-1999-11438 for the MUCHMORE project.

P. Sojka, I. Kopeček, and K. Pala (Eds.): TSD 2002, LNAI 2448, pp. 107–114, 2002.

This paper presents some simple techniques which help researchers and users to understand the spaces they are working with more clearly, using techniques for visualising information that have been developed by the CSLI Infomap project. Our methods are specifically designed to uncover the meanings of words and word groups. We focus on two main types of mathematical spaces: vector spaces and graphs.

Vector spaces are the underlying spaces in the theory of linear algebra [10]. Points in the space can be specified by giving co-ordinates which measure the amount to which certain features or axes contribute to the point. One typical use of vector spaces is for information retrieval, where the points are words and the 'features' are documents. Using documents which are translated into more than one language, vector spaces can be built which encode multilingual information.

A *graph* in this paper means a set of nodes and a collection of links between those nodes [2]. Undirected graphs have been used to describe semantic networks and directed acyclic graphs have been used to describe ontological hierarchies. Connected with both of these models is the idea that proximity in the model reflects semantic similarity between word meanings.

In this paper we will describe how to build examples of both of these types of model automatically from text-corpora, and describe the tools we have built to enable users to interact with and visualise the results.

2   Vector Spaces

In this section we describe ways in which words can be mapped into vector spaces in such a way that the similarity between two words can be measured. We describe this process for both monolingual and bilingual corpora. We then present a technique for visualising the structure of the resulting space by projecting onto the 2 most significant dimensions.

2.1   Building Vector Models from Corpora

First we review the standard processes whereby such a vector space can be built from monolingual documents. The first examples of such spaces were pioneered for Information Retrieval [7,1]. Counting the number of times each word occurs in each document gives a *term-document matrix*, where the i, j^{th} matrix entry records the number of times the word w_i occurs in the document d_j. The rows of this matrix can then be thought of as *word-vectors*. *Document vectors* are then generated by computing a (weighted) sum of the word-vectors of the words appearing in a given document. The dimension of this vector space (the number of co-ordinates given to each word) is therefore equal to the number of documents in the collection. Typically, such *term-document matrices* are extremely sparse. The information can be concentrated in a smaller number of dimensions using singular-value decomposition, projecting each word onto the n-dimensional subspace which gives the best least-squares approximation to the original data. This represents each word using the n most significant 'latent variables', and for this reason this process is called *latent semantic analysis* [3].

Such techniques are used in information retrieval to measure the similarity between words (or more general query statements) and documents, using a similarity measure such as the cosine of the angle between two vectors [1, p. 27]. A less-well known but natural corrolary is that this technique can be used to measure the similarity between pairs of terms. Term-term similarities of this sort can be used for the process of *automatic thesaurus generation* [1, Chapter 5].

A variant of the traditional term-document matrix was developed by [8] specifically for the purpose of measuring semantic similarity between words. Instead of using the documents as column labels for the matrix, semantically significant *content-bearing words* are used, and other words in the vocabulary are given a score each time they occur within a context window of (say) 15 words of one of these content-bearing words. Thus the vector of the word *football* is determined by the fact that it frequently appears near the words *sport* and *play*, etc. This method has been found to be well-suited for semantic tasks such as word-sense clustering and disambiguation.

To build a bilingual vector model, we proceed as follows. A corpus consisting of 9640 German abstracts from medical documents and their English translations (*ca* 1.5 million words) was obtained from the Springer Link information service.[1] We have also built a bilingual vector model from the parallel French/English Canadian Hansard corpus.[2]

Each German/English document pair was treated as a single 'compound document' for the purpose of recording term-term co-occurrence. After stopwords were removed [1, p. 167], the 1000 most frequent English words were selected as content-bearing words. (English words were chosen because semantically significant units are more often single words in English but parts of compounds in German, and because other parallel corpora are more likely to have English as one of the languages.)

English and German words were regarded as co-occurring with a particular content-bearing word if they occurred in the same document as the content-bearing word, or the translation of this document. This avoided the need for in-depth alignment of the corpus, a simplification which was made possible by the brevity of most of the documents (*ca* 150 words on average). (A bilingual corpus of many thousand short documents is naturally much better aligned than a corpus of fewer much longer documents.) This bilingual model can be used to represent translational relationships between words, and can therefore be used for the automatic creation and enrichment of multilingual dictionaries, achieving an accuracy of over 90 % in cases where the similarity score between translation pairs is high [11].

In this way, words in one or more languages are mapped into a single 1,000-dimensional vector space. Singular value decomposition (LSI) is used to reduce the number of dimensions to 100. Semantic similarity between English and German terms could then be computed using cosine similarity in this 100-dimensional bilingual vector space. This method was used to measure term-term similarity throughout.

2.2   Visualisation by Planar Projection

This 100 dimensional vector space still contains far too many words and too many dimensions to be visualised at once. To produce a meaningful diagram of results related to a particular word or query, we perform two extra steps. Firstly, we restrict attention to a given number

---

[1] http://link.springer.de/

[2] http://www.ldc.upenn.edu/Catalog/LDC95T20.html.
This model is currently under development and will be publicly available by the time of the TSD conference.

of closely related words (determined by cosine similarity of word vectors), selecting a "local context" of up to 100 words and their word vectors for deeper analysis. This is done by selecting those words which are most similar to a particular target word, using cosine similarity.

A second round of Latent Semantic Analysis is then performed on this restricted set, giving the most significant directions to describe this local data. The 2 most significant axes determine the plane which best represents the data. (This process can be regarded as a higher-dimensional analogue of finding the line of best-fit for a normal 2-dimensional graph.)

The resulting diagrams give an accurate summary of the contexts in which a word is used in a particular document collection. This is particularly effective for visualizing words in more than one language. Users submit a query statement consisting of any combination of words in English or German, and are then able to visualize the words most closely related to this query in a 2-dimensional plot of the latent semantic space. English words appear in red and German words appear in blue. An example output for the English query word "drug" is shown below. Such words are of special interest because the English word "drug" has two meanings which are represented by different words in German (*medikament* = prescription drug and *drogen* = narcotic). The 2-dimensional plot clearly distinguishes these two areas of meaning, with the English word "drug" being in between. Such techniques can enable users to recognize and understand translational ambiguities.

As well as the bilingual corpus, the system has been trained to work on several (larger) monolingual corpora. These models are clearly effective at gathering words into contexts-of-use.

3   Graph Models Built Using Local Syntactic Information

The vector methods above are good at collecting together words which appear in similar contexts. However, they fail to distinguish between words in different semantic classes. So *drug* does appear with the words *pharmaceutical* and *alcohol*, but also words like *illicit*, *trafficking* and the names of drug companies such as *glaxo*.

We demonstrate that these types can be successfully distinguished using part-of-speech information, by building a *semantic graph*. The model was built using the British National Corpus[3] which is automatically tagged for parts of speech.

Each noun in the corpus is taken to be a node in the graph. A link is placed between two nodes if they co-occur in lists, separated by the words *and, or* or a comma. For example, consider the following sentences from the BNC:

> But she began to gather their limbs together and put them in order, **head, body, arms** and **legs**.
>
> A possible reason is that it was difficult to get **arms** and **ammunition** to the right place, despite the virtual absence of border controls between Germany and its western neighbours.

Based upon these sentences, we place links between the *arms* node and the *head, body, legs* and *ammunition* nodes. Since lists are usually comprised of objects which are similar

---

[3] http://www.hcu.ox.ac.uk/BNC/

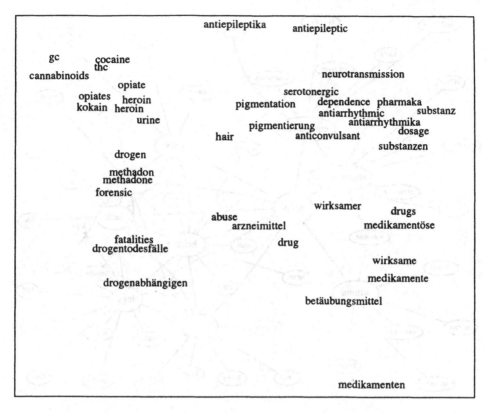

Fig. 1. Planar projection of the words similar to the English word *drug* in the bilingual Springer vector model.

in some way, these relationships have been used to extract groups of nouns with similar properties [5,6].

The links were weighted depending on the number of times the pair of nouns co-occurred. Various cutoff functions were used to determine how many times a relationship must be observed to be counted as a link in the graph. Using a simple rule-of-thumb such as "count two nodes as being linked if they co-occur more than ten times" proved unsatisfactory because of the bias it gives to more frequent words. A better-behaved option was to take the top *n* neighbours of each word, where *n* could be determined by the user. More detailed research should reveal optimal techniques for selecting the importance to assign to each link.

As an example, consider the portion of the graph showing the first and second order neighbours of the word *arms* (Figure 2). As well as being an interesting picture, diagrams such as this can be used for practical NLP tasks. Our extremely simple technique has proved to be extremely robust and successful. For example, using an incremental algorithm to add new nodes to clusters, the graph model achieved an accuracy of 82 % at a lexical acquisition task similar to that described by Roark and Charniak [6], whose accuracy is only 36 %. The overwhelming size of the British National Corpus will account for at least some of this gain.

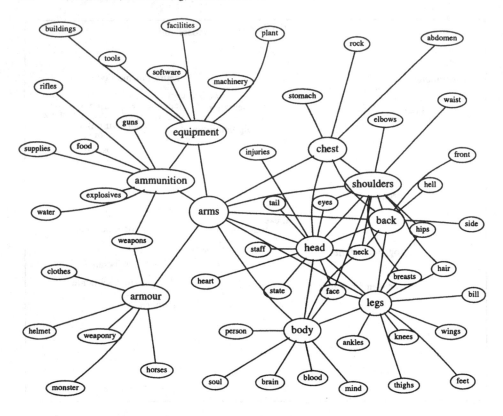

Fig. 2. Graph model centred on the word *arms*.

But the gain is also due to our increased understanding of the model we are using, enabled by our visualisation techniques.

The graph model can also be used for ambiguity recognition and resolution, a task which traditionally requires hand-labelled data. This process is both costly and inflexible. Defining what a 'word-sense' is a task that has traditionally been left to lexicographers, with the result that dictionaries omit senses that are relevant in a particular domain, and include senses that are not.

Suppose we want to know which senses of the word *arms* are frequently used in the BNC. Figure 2 can be used to give an empirical answer to this question. Removing the initial node *arms* from Figure 2 leaves two disconnected components, one about *arms* as in parts of the body and one about *arms* as in military equipment. Not only does the model recognise these senses as distinct, it also provides a technique for resolving the ambiguity. Since each sense is empirically derived, we can go back to our empirical observations and annotate them as belonging to one sense or the other. This can then be used as training data for a Bayesian classification. The potential of this system to both recognise *and* resolve ambiguity is currently under investigation. This insight would never have arisen in the first place without the visualisation techniques we have developed.

4 Conclusion

Creating 2-dimensional representations of semantic spaces can provide an excellent means for people to gain a quick, intuitive understanding of how a model built from linguistic information really works. We have also used our visualisation techniques to suggest empirical answers to fundamental challenges in NLP, including results that have already stood up to stringent evaluation criteria.

Methods such as these provide an exciting new extension to the traditional role of corpus linguistics. Rather than deciding our linguistic questions in advance and then approaching corpus material as a statistical resource to provide evidence for our hypotheses, our methods encourage us to observe word meanings with no prior agenda: to hear the corpus speak with its own voice. The tools we have developed enable humans to interpret this information: a tremendous asset when designing new ways to use empirical data in Natural Language Processing.

Demonstration

All of the tools described in this paper are publicly available at
<code>http://infomap.stanford.edu</code>
In particular, the bilingual vector model is accessible on
<code>http://infomap.stanford.edu/bilingual</code>
and the graph model on
<code>http://infomap.stanford.edu/graphs</code>.
The only software needed is a Java-enabled web browser.

References

1. Ricardo Beaza-Yates and Berthier Ribiero-Neto. *Modern Information Retrieval.* Addison Wesley / ACM press, 1999.
2. Béla Bollobás. *Modern Graph Theory.* Number 184 in Graduate texts in Mathematics. Springer-Verlag, 1998.
3. Scott Deerwester, Susan Dumais, George Furnas, Thomas Landauer, and Richard Harshman. Indexing by latent semantic analysis. *Journal of the American society for information science,* 41(6):391–407, 1990.
4. I. Dan Melamed. Automatic construction of clean broad-coverage translation lexicons. In: *2nd Conference of the Association for Machine Translation in the Americas,* Montreal, Canada, 1996.
5. Ellen Riloff and Jessica Shepherd. A corpus-based approach for building semantic lexicons. In Claire Cardie and Ralph Weischedel, editors, *Proceedings of the Second Conference on Empirical Methods in Natural Language Processing,* pages 117–124. Association for Computational Linguistics, Somerset, New Jersey, 1997.
6. Brian Roark and Eugene Charniak. Noun-phrase co-occurence statistics for semi-automatic semantic lexicon construction. In: *COLING-ACL,* pages 1110–1116, 1998.
7. Gerard Salton and Michael McGill. *Introduction to modern information retrieval.* McGraw-Hill, New York, NY, 1983.
8. Hinrich Schütze. *Ambiguity resolution in language learning.* CSLI publications, Stanford CA, 1997.

9. Hinrich Schütze. Automatic word sense discrimination. *Computational Linguistics*, 24(1):97–124, 1998.
10. Robert J. Vallejo. *Linear algebra: an introduction to abstract mathematics*. Undergraduate texts in mathematics. Springer-Verlag, 1993.
11. Dominic Widdows, Beate Dorow, and Chiu-Ki Chan. Using parallel corpora to enrich multilingual lexical resources. In: *To appear in the Third International Conference on Language Resources and Evaluation*. ELRA, 2002.

Statistical Part-of-Speech Tagging for Classical Chinese

Liang Huang[1], Yinan Peng[1], Huan Wang[2], and Zhenyu Wu[1]

[1] Department of Computer Science, Shanghai Jiaotong University
No. 1954 Huashan Road, Shanghai
P.R. China 200030
[2] Department of Chinese Literature and Linguistics, East China Normal University
No. 3663 North Zhongshan Road, Shanghai
P.R. China 200062

Abstract. Classical Chinese is essentially different from Modern Chinese, in both syntax and morphology. While there has recently been a number of works on part-of-speech (PoS) tagging for Modern Chinese, the PoS tagging for Classical Chinese is largely neglected. To the best of our knowledge, this is the first work in the area. Fortunately however, in terms of tagging, Classical Chinese is easier than Modern Chinese in that most Classical Chinese words are single-character-formed, thus no segmentation is needed. So in this paper, we will propose and analyze a simple statistical approach for PoS tagging of Classical Chinese. We first designed a tagset for Classical Chinese that is later shown to be accurate and efficient. Then we apply the hidden Markov model (HMM) Viterbi algorithm and made several improvements, such as sparse data problem handling and unknown word guessing, both designed particularly for Classical Chinese. As the training set grows larger, the accuracies for bigram and trigram increase to 94.9 % and 97.6 %, respectively. The contribution of our work also lies in proposing and solving some previously unseen problems in processing Classical Chinese.

1   Introduction

Part-of-speech tagging is fundamental in natural language processing. It selects the most likely sequence of syntactic categories (part-of-speech) for the words in a sentence, and passes its output to the next processing level, usually a syntactic parser. Over the last twenty years, the correctness of PoS tagging has increased dramatically on some famous English corpora such as the LOB corpus and the Brown corpus ([2,3]). And the PoS tagging for Chinese has also resulted in very high accuracies [8]. So in this section, we will first briefly summarize various approaches of PoS tagging, then point out the particularities of Chinese and Classical Chinese Processing, and finally gives the organization of the rest of the paper.

There are many machine learning approaches for automatic PoS tagging, and the most successful of them are rule-based methods and statistical methods. Typical rule based approaches [9] use contextual information to assign tags to ambiguous words. Average rule-based taggers have error rates substantially higher than the state-of-the-art statistical taggers [10]. But linguistically sound rules may also considerably outperform their statistical brethren. In [5], a transformation-based error-driven tagger was developed with contextual rules as patches, which greatly increases the accuracy.

P. Sojka, I. Kopeček, and K. Pala (Eds.): TSD 2002, LNAI 2448, pp. 115–122, 2002.
© Springer-Verlag Berlin Heidelberg 2002

Stochastic taggers [2,3,6,8,10] have obtained a higher degree of accuracy without performing any syntactic analysis of the input. There are many methods inside the statistical model, among which are the famous hidden Markov model (HMM) [2,3,8,10] and the maximum entropy approach [6].

The hidden Markov model is the most widely used model for PoS tagging. It originates from the Viterbi algorithm [1]. In this model, word-tag probabilities and n-gram probabilities (parameters in the hidden Markov model) are obtained from the training set, usually a manually annotated corpus.

Effective as it is, HMM also has a lot of drawbacks. The main limitations of HMM are sparse data problem (especially for higher order HMM) and unknown word guessing. A number of methods have been developed to solve these two problems [10,13,4,5]. The problem of sparse data set [8] or inadequate parameters emerges when we have to move from bigrams to trigrams, 4-grams and requires more co-occurrences of tags. In [10], a smoothing method is developed to solve it using interpolations of uni-, bi- and tri-grams. But this approach requires too much computation. In addition, previous works show that the accuracies for unknown words are substantially lower than those of known words [13,10]. In [4] and [5], guessing from suffixes is proposed, but it is not applicable to Chinese. And in [13], a supporting vector approach is presented, yet still too time-consuming.

In this paper, we will present simple-yet-effective methods to handle these 2 problems.

As we are tagging Classical Chinese texts, the particularities of the Chinese language must be carefully studied. Chinese is totally different from the Indo-European languages in its special grammar. And some features discussed above cannot be transplanted to the processing of Chinese directly.

The first obstacle one will meet in tagging Modern Chinese is word segmentation. Both Modern and Classical Chinese are written without spaces to separate between words. For example, consider the following phrase in Modern Chinese

江	泽	民	主	席
jiang	ze	min	zhu	xi

can be segmented in the following two ways:

江泽民 / 主席
jiang ze min / zhu xi
(in English, President Jiang Ze-Ming)

江泽 / 民主 / 席
jiang ze / min zhu / xi
(In English, rivers and ponds / democracy / seat)

Apparently, the second segmentation is nonsense. So a successful segmentation is the first step of PoS tagging [8], which made tagging for Chinese much more difficult than tagging European languages.

Although generally speaking Classical Chinese is even more difficult than Modern Chinese in its obsolete grammar patterns, we propose here that from the tagger's point of view, Classical Chinese is somewhat easier, because most words are written in the single-character (single-syllable) form, thus no word segmentation is required.

Another difficulty lies in the punctuations. Originally all Classical Chinese is written without any punctuation, and all the inputs to our program are manually punctuated. Fortunately however, most of the important Classical Chinese documents have already been manually punctuated in the 20th century, so our work is still right-to-use for applications.

Moreover, unknown word guessing is an area where methods for European languages are not applicable to Chinese Processing. In the literature of tagging European languages, a common approach using suffixes or surrounding context of unknown words is often applied [10,5]. But neither suffixes nor capitalization is extant in Chinese. Especially in Classical Chinese, a word is a single character, so no separation of word is possible. In Section 3 we will present our own approach for handling unknown words.

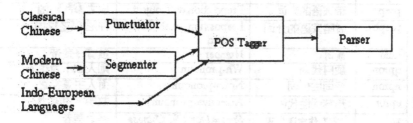

Fig. 1. The complete processing procedure of Modern/Classical Chinese by comparison to the Indo-European Languages.

The rest of the paper is organized as follows. In Section 2, we give a summary of lexical analysis of Classical Chinese and discuss the design the tagset. The dynamic-programming-based tagging algorithm and techniques are presented in Section 3. Our preliminary experimental results are evaluated in Section 4. In Section 5, we give a conclusion of the paper and briefly explore the future work.

2 Tagset Design

The design of tagset is very crucial to the accuracy and efficiency of the tagging algorithm, and this was largely neglected in the literature where many researchers use those famous corpora and their tagset as the standard test-beds. In this section, we will introduce our own tagset designed for Classical Chinese.

For the design, there is a tradeoff in the size of set. The sizes of tagsets in the literature vary from smaller than 20 to larger than 400. As Chinese grammar focus on the word-order rather than the morphological information, it is much more lexically ambiguous than languages with inflections such as Indo-European languages. In other words, contextual information contributes more to the part-of-speech tagging than lexical information. Taking this into account, we designed a tagset with special interest not only to the lexical categories, but also the categories of components a word may belong. For example, we discriminate adjectives into 4 subcategories like adjective as attributive (denoted as aa), etc. (See Figure 2). This discrimination turns out to be an important contributing factor of the tagging accuracy. (See Section 4). Note that we map punctuations into 2 sets: period and comma.

Table 1. Tagset for Classical Chinese

Tag	Meaning	English meaning	Examples
n	名词	Noun	楚人有直躬
aa	形容词作定语	Adjective as attributive	楚人有直躬
aw	形容词作谓语	Adjective as verbal phrase	被甲者少也
ab	形容词作表语	Adjective as predicate	仲尼以为孝
ad	副词	Adverb	必禁无用
vi	不跟宾语的动词	Verb without object	知者不惑
vt	跟宾语的动词	Verb with object	今兹文学
conj	连词	Conjunction	君子和而不同
yq	语气词	Exclamation	被甲者少也
prep	带宾语的介词	Preposition with object	应之以乱则凶
prepb	省略宾语的介词	Preposition with object omitted	仲尼以之为孝
num	数词	Number	虽有十黄帝
qpron	疑问代词	Wh-pronoun	则人孰不为也?
npron	名词性代词	Noun-pronoun	而人主兼礼之.
apron	形容词性代词	Adjective-pronoun	故明主用其力.
za	"之" 作定语后置标志	*Special for Old Chinese*	秦之美者
zj	"者" 作名词性词尾	*Special for Old Chinese*	秦之美者
zd	"之" 作 "的"	*Special for Old Chinese*	古之人不余欺.
fy	发语词	*Special for Old Chinese*	夫离法者罪.
period	终止性标点		。；？！
comma	停顿性标点		，、：

3 Tagging Algorithms and Features

Our tagging algorithm is based on HMM and the Viterbi Algorithm [1,11], which is Dynamic Programming in nature.

For the simplicity of programming and accuracy of tagging, we intentionally add a period tag before each sentence and assume that each sentence ends with a period. This method is better than the traditional loose end in other publications [10].

Trigram Model. For trigram model, the algorithm is still dynamic programming which takes 2 consecutive words as one phase, compared with the bigram model where phrases are single words. For the first word, as it is just after the first intentional period, it has fewer than 2 precedings, and for words just after any punctuation in the sentence, the same problem also occurs. So here we again add another intentional "dummy" head before the punctuations and intentional periods.

Unknown Word Handling. Recall that most methods used in unknown words guessing for European languages are not applicable to Chinese or Classical Chinese. So in this paper we present a simpler approach.

For any word that does not occur in the training set, we denote its word-tag probabilities to be the frequencies for word. For example, for an unknown word w, we have

$$\Pr(w|t_i) = freq(w) = \frac{f(w)}{N} \tag{1}$$

N is the total number of words in the training set

Though it violates the classical probability theory, experiments (see Section 4) indicate it quite effective, especially for trigram model. The underlying reason for its success is the independence of phases in Dynamic Programming.

Sparse Data Problem. Besides the unknown word handling, the problem of sparse data set is also difficult to handle. As stated before, the size of our corpus is very small, compared to well-established English corpora. So we need a technique to unknown sequences, i.e. unknown bigram pairs or trigram sequences. Rather than the complicated smoothing method in [10], we here present a simpler approach made of 2 steps:

Add a very small number, usually 10^{-60}, to all lexical probabilities. Obviously it will not affect the correct probabilities learned from the corpus. But by this addition, we enable the algorithm for guessing the most probable context sequence, when word-tag pairs sequence is not presented in the corpus. This is effective especially when context information is quite deterministic (provides enough hints) at certain positions.

In the dynamic programming, if still no possible sequence at certain position, then we use the lower-level n-gram, i.e., for bigram model, use lexical probabilities, and for trigram, use big ram's results. It is an expedient approach (a simplification of the standard smoothing method), yet still works quite well as experiments indicated.

4   Results

4.1   Corpora

The only established corpus of Classical Chinese is the Taiwan-Corpus [12]. But for the purpose of evaluating our own tagging algorithm and tagset, we constructed a small-sized corpus from the famous Classical Chinese documents such as *Lun Yu* and *Dao De Jing*, and some other classics.

Our selection criterion of texts is: omit those with proper nouns, very hard words, and grammatical exceptions. As these three assumptions actually hold for most, if not all, of Classical Chinese Documents, our corpus does reflect typical Classical Chinese. And finally we got a corpus of about 6000 words, among which 5500 words is used as the training set and 500 words used as the test set. We use the cross-validation technique to select the test set. It must be pointed out here that the average length of Classical Chinese sentences in our corpus is only 4–6 words long, much shorter than average English sentences. So the corpus contains about 1200 sentences.

4.2   Accuracies

We made the learning set enlarging slowly and test the performance (learning curves) of the tagset and the algorithm. As the training set grows larger, the result is show in the following figures. We not only test the overall accuracy, but also the known and unknown accuracy separately.

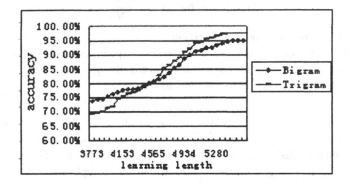

Fig. 2. Learning Curves for the overall accuracy: bigram model vs. trigrams model. The learning length increases from 3773 to 5500 tokens.

Figure 2 shows the learning curves of the taggers, i.e., the accuracy depending on the amount of training data. As learning set expanding, the accuracies of bigrams and trigrams increase from 73.9 % to 94.9 % and from 69.5 % to 97.6 %, respectively. At the beginning, when learning set is rather small, trigram accuracy is lower than that of bigram, due to the sparse data problem. And at the end, when contextual information is more abundant, trigram outperforms bigram significantly.

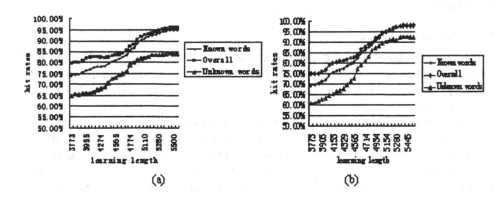

Fig. 3. Learning Curves of known words and unknown words. (a) Bigram model. (b) Trigram model. The percentage of unknown words decreases from 39.4 % at the beginning to 8 % at the end, almost linearly.

Figure 3 shows the learning curves of known and unknown words. Different from most PoS tagging works found in the literature where the accuracies for known words are very high even for very small corpora [11,10], our work shows that for tagging of Classical Chinese, the beginning accuracy for known words is rather low. This is because Classical Chinese is much more ambiguous in lexical categories than European languages. Our experiment shows that only 35.8 % words are not lexically ambiguous in Classical Chinese. Figure 3 shows the beginning accuracy for known words are only 79.7 % and 74.9 % for bigrams and trigrams, respectively.

Unknown word guessing is another successful part of our work. Figure 3 shows our guessing technique very effective. The beginning accuracy for bigrams and trigrams are 65.0 % and 60.9 %, respectively, about the same with state-of-the-art works in the literature [6,10,13]. But the learning curve for unknown words rises rapidly and at the end, the accuracies are 85.1 % and 93.2 %, a little higher than those previous works. The high accuracy of unknown words guessing of trigram model shows that our technique is especially effective when contextual information (hint) is quite deterministic at certain position.

5 Conclusion and Future Work

In this paper we have proposed and analyzed a simple corpus-based statistical method of part-of-speech tagging for Classical Chinese texts. The contribution of our paper lies primarily in the pioneering processing of Classical Chinese.

A special tagset is first presented for Classical Chinese. We then base our work on the hidden Markov model (HMM) model and the Viterbi algorithm. In addition, several features, such as sparse data problem handling are proposed and we also developed an unknown word guessing scheme especially for Chinese. We constructed a small-sized corpus from Classical Chinese classics and used the cross-validation technique to divide it into training set and test set. As the training set grows larger, the hit rate increases to 94.9 % for bigram and 97.6 % for trigram.

For future work, as stated before, the computational processing of Classical Chinese is just commencing. And our future work includes a top-down probabilistic context-free grammar (PCFG) parser for Classical Chinese. Another possible work is the sentence-punctuator. We think by a few changes in the HMM model will yield an effective dynamic-programming-based punctuator. Last but most important, we need larger corpora. The corpus used in our program is too small, and there are very few annotated Classical Chinese texts. So we may first construct a manually annotated medium-sized corpus for future study.

References

1. Viterbi, A.: Error bounds for convolution codes and an asymptotically optimal decoding algorithm. IEEE Trans. on Information Theory 13:260–269. 1967.
2. Leech, G. et al.: The Automatic Grammatical Tagging of the LOB Corpus, ICAME News, 7 (1983), pp. 13–33.
3. Merialdo, B.: Tagging Text with a Probabilistic Model, IEEE International Conference on Acoustics, Speech and Signal Processing (ICASSP), 1991, pp. 809–812.
4. Brill, E.: A simple rule-based part-of-speech tagger, In: Proceeding of the 3rd Conference on Applied Natural Language Processing (ACL), 1992, pp. 152–155.
5. Brill, E.: Transformation-Based Error-Driven Learning and Natural Language Processing: A Case Study in Part-of-Speech Tagging. Computational Linguistics, 21(4), 1995, pp. 543–565.

6. Ratnaparkhi, A. et al.: A Maximum Entropy Model for Part-of-Speech Tagging. In: Proceedings of Conference on Empirical Methods in Natural Language Processing(EMNLP-1), 1996, pp. 133–142.
7. Charniak, E. et al.: Equations for Part-of-Speech Tagging. In: Proceedings of the Eleventh National Conference on Artificial Intelligence (AAAI-93), 1993. pp. 784–789.
8. Lua, K.: Part of Speech Tagging of Chinese Sentences Using Genetic Algorithm, Proceedings of Conference on Chinese Computing, Singapore, Jun. 1996, pp. 45–49.
9. Hindle, D.: Acquiring disambiguation rules from text. In: Proceedings of 27th Annual Meeting of the Association for Computational Linguistics, 1989.
10. Brant, T.: TnT – A Statistical Part-of-Speech Tagger. In: Proceedings of the 6th Applied NLP Conference (ANLP-2000), 2000, pp. 224–231.
11. Allen, J.: Natural Language Understanding, The Benjamin/Cummings Publishing Company, Inc., 1995.
12. Wei, P. et al.: Historical Corpora for Synchronic and Diachronic Linguistics Studies, Pacific Neighborhood Consortium, 1997.
13. Nakagawa, T. et al.: Unknown Word Guessing and Part-of-Speech Tagging Using Support Vector Machines, Proceedings of the 6th Natural Language Processing Pacific Rim Symposium, 2001.

Spanish Natural Language Interface
for a Relational Database Querying System

Rodolfo A. Pazos Rangel [1], Alexander Gelbukh [2], J. Javier González Barbosa [3],
Erika Alarcón Ruiz [3], Alejandro Mendoza Mejía [3], and A. Patricia Domínguez Sánchez [3]

[1] Centro Nacional de Investigación y Desarrollo Tecnológico, Mexico,
E-mail: pazos@sd-cenidet.com.mx
[2] Computing Research Center (CIC), National Polytechnic Institute (IPN), Mexico,
E-mail: gelbukh@cic.ipn.mx   WWW: http://www.gelbukh.com/
[3] Instituto Tecnológico de Ciudad Madero, Mexico,
E-mail: jjgonzalezbarbosa@hotmail.com, erika_2k@hotmail.com,
amejia_jnm@hotmail.com, patricia5@infosel.net.mx

Abstract. The fast growth of Internet is creating a society where the demand on information storage, organization, access, and analysis services is continuously growing. This constantly increases the number of inexperienced users that need to access databases in a simple way. Together with the emergence of voice interfaces, such a situation foretells a promising future for database querying systems using natural language interfaces. We describe the architecture of a relational database querying system using a natural language (Spanish) interface, giving a brief explanation of the implementation of each of the constituent modules: lexical parser, syntax checker, and semantic analyzer.

1 Introduction

Providing simple access to database systems has become one of the problems of great interest for users and developers of database querying systems, especially since Internet became popular. Users are looking for systems that facilitate the use of databases, trying to reduce the time and effort required for learning how to use them [13]. To satisfy this demand, developers have designed and implemented friendlier interfaces. One of the most popular types of such interfaces is natural language interface (NLI).

Traditional natural language processing (NLP) has not yet provided database-querying systems with all the benefits that can be obtained from it (especially for the Spanish speaking community). Limited scope systems have been developed, mainly for a few languages such as English; some examples of these systems are California Restaurant Query, Expedia Hotels, GeoQuery [16], Hollywood [5], JobQuery [14], Masque/SQL [1], SQ-HAL [12], and SystemX [3].

Despite the long history of NLP and the numerous techniques developed, most of the work has been carried out for English; the situation with the Spanish language is far behind as compared with other major languages. This is especially worrisome, considering the spread and large population of the Spanish-speaking community in the world (390 million), and therefore the potential market for Spanish NLP tools.

P. Sojka, I. Kopeček, and K. Pala (Eds.): TSD 2002, LNAI 2448, pp. 123–130, 2002.
© Springer-Verlag Berlin Heidelberg 2002

Most of the NLP work done so far for Spanish is devoted to applications that have little or no relation with NLIs to databases (NLIDBs), for example: text interpretation [6], spelling correctors [11], and processing tools [7,9]. Only a few projects have dealt with NLIDBs, being the most important the following: GNBD [15], SISCO [10], and Sylvia-NLQ [4].

Most of NLIDB projects for Spanish have approached database querying from the AI perspective. Thus, they have focused mainly on deductive databases and overlooked the vast majority of existing database systems: relational databases, data warehouses, and object-oriented databases. The aim of the project described in this paper is to design and implement a relational database querying system with a natural language interface for the Spanish language.

The paper is organized as follows. First, the general architecture of the system is presented. Then, the implementation of the lexical parser, syntax checker, semantic analyzer, and the result presentation module is described. Then, domain customization issues are discussed. Finally, concluding remarks are given.

2   Architecture

The architecture of the querying system consists of two main modules: Database Query module and Domain Customization module – see Figure 1.

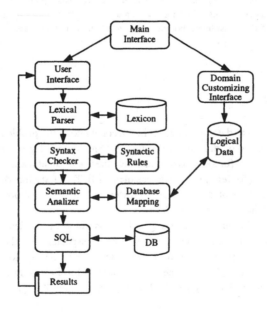

Fig. 1. System architecture.

The *Database Query module* is the main part of the system. The user types in its query through the user interface submodule. It is processed by the lexical parser, syntax checker, and semantic analyzer, which translate it in an SQL expression. The results of the SQL query are passed back to the user again through the user interface submodule.

The *Domain Customization module* is used to customize and maintain the data and dictionaries used by the NLP modules of the system. It interacts with the system administrator through the domain customization interface submodule.

A brief description of the implementation of the main components of the query module is presented below; the customization module is discussed later.

3 Lexical Parsing

Lexical parsing is in charge of reading the input sentence (query) and dividing it into words, which are minimal meaningful units also known as tokens. Then, it identifies the tokens in the lexical dictionary (lexicon) and retrieves the information about each token. Finally, it passes the tokens with the associated information on to the syntax checker and semantic analyzer.

The lexical parser interacts with the lexicon, which contains all the words that are expected to appear in user's queries. For each word, the dictionary includes its part of speech (noun, verb, article, etc.), gender, and number; the format of this dictionary is independent of the parser code. For this project, a database was used for storing each word, its type (part of speech) represented by an integer number according to Table 1, and subtype (the combination of gender and number, when applicable).

Table 1. Representation of the syntactic category.

Word	Type	Word	Type
Interrogative adjective	1	Preposition	8
Article	2	Conjunction	9
Noun	3	Pronoun	10
Adjective	4	Punctuation mark	11
Auxiliary verb	5	Relational operator	12
Verb	6	Error	*
Adverb	7		

4 Syntax Checker

Wrongly understood queries can cause incorrect and confusing results to be delivered to the user, which is potentially dangerous since the user may rely on them to make important decisions. Thus, of crucial importance for reliability of NLIs is verification that the query has the expected pattern that the system can understand correctly.

The syntax checker verifies that the queries have the expected structure. It checks the relationship among words according to their role in the sentence to make sure that the input sentence satisfies a predefined order or pattern.

For this purpose, the checker verifies if the string of tokens received from the lexical parser can be generated by the grammar. It informs the user if any syntactic error is detected and prevents the suspicious query from further processing.

After evaluation of existing types of syntax checkers, a state transition matrix approach [6] has been considered the most convenient because of the following reasons: the implementation of the algorithm is simple since it handles uniformly all the grammar rules; it permits to modify and add new rules to the grammar without having to change the algorithm code. The use of a state transition matrix permits the expansion of a grammar just by adding new states or syntactic categories to the matrix.

The grammar we currently use has the form of a simple bigram check: each word of the sentence is checked to be compatible with the immediately following word. Table 2 shows a fragment of the state transition matrix currently used for syntax checking. Of course, in the future a more sophisticated grammar can be implemented using the same program code but a different matrix.

Table 2. Fragment of the state transition matrix.

State	I.A. 1	Art. 2	Noun 3	Adj. 4	Aux.V. 5	V. 6	Adv. 7
0	1	*	*	*	*	6	*
1	*	*	3	*	5	6	*
2	*	*	3	*	*	*	*
3	*	*	3	4	5	6	7
4	*	*	*	*	5	6	*
5	*	2	*	*	*	6	*
6	*	2	3	*	*	*	7
7	*	*	*	4	*	*	7

* Error

Since each syntactic category is represented by an integer number, the interaction with the state transition matrix is realized through this number. Using the state transition matrix, the syntax checker determines if the first word of the sentence is an interrogative adverb or a verb (state 0, first line of the table); if so, the current state is updated and the next iteration is performed. For example, considering the following question:

$$\text{¿Cuántos créditos tiene Erika Alarcón?} \tag{1}$$

'How many units has Erika Alarcón?', the checker output is the following:

cuántos 'how many'	créditos 'units'	tiene 'has'	Erika Alarcón
1	3	6	3

If a syntactic error is found, i.e., the current word is not expected in the present state, the program will display a message indicating the error type and will stop the parsing process, since it will not be able to determine the next state to move into.

Additionally, the bigram method is used to verify the morphological compatibility of each pair of adjacent words. The lexical parser supplies with each input word its gender (feminine, masculine, neuter) and number (singular, plural, neuter); the value "neuter" is used when the gender is not defined (*estudiante* 'student') or not applicable (e.g., for adverbs), and similarly for the number. If two adjacent words have incompatible genders (feminine versus masculine) or numbers (singular versus plural), an error is reported.

5 Semantic Analyzer

Upon successful completion of syntax checking, the semantic analyzer extracts the meaning of the sentence and generates a logical structure. In this module, the sentence is analyzed again to identify the key words with which the system can interpret the query; in this way the analyzer obtains the meaning of the query.

This process is carried out using logical predicates [1] which constitutes the keystone of the semantic analyzer, since they permit to determine the words involved in the query for its successful execution. For this, each noun is looked up in a table where the logical predicates are stored. For example, consider the query (1) and the logical predicates shown in Table 3; the matching predicate for the question is *créditos* 'units', which needs a student *name* or *id number* as a parameter.

If a match occurs, the sentence is explored once more to obtain the data needed by the parameters of the logical predicate. When the parameter type is not explicit in the query, the analyzer looks for the parameter data in the database, in order to determine its type. This is done by finding the field name that corresponds to each of the possible parameters associated to the logical predicate.

Table 3. Fragment of the logical predicate information.

Predicate	Parameters	Predicate	Parameters
id number	name	créditos 'units'	name
especialidad 'major'	name	créditos 'units'	id number
especialidad 'major'	id number	promedio 'average mark'	name
nombre 'name'	id number	promedio 'average mark'	id number

In the example (1), the parameter data is *Erika Alarcón*. In this case the parameter type is determined by accessing first the word-to-field mapping information shown in Table 4, which indicates that the possible database fields associated to the parameter data are *STUD_ID* and *STUD_NAME*. Then the analyzer generates the following query to find *Erika Alarcón* in the field *STUD_NUM*:

```
select count(*) from STDATA where STUD_ID = 'ERIKA ALARCON'
```

In this case the database manager will not find a student whose *id number* is *Erika Alarcón*, and thus the analyzer will issue a similar query to check if there is any student with this name (using STUD_NAME instead of STUD_ID), which returns a positive answer.

Table 4. Fragment of lexicon words to database field mapping information.

Word	DB Field	Table	Database
id number	STUD_ID	STDATA	ACAD
major	STUD_MJR	STDATA	ACAD
name	STUD_NAME	STDATA	ACAD
units	STUD_UNITS	STDATA	ACAD
average mark	STUD_AVG	STDATA	ACAD

Each time a matching predicate is found and its corresponding parameter data is obtained, it is written in a structure called *logical data storage structure*. This structure holds the field names whose information is requested by the user, the database name, the table name, and the search conditions. The data structure for the example (Equation 1) is shown in Table 5. If no matching predicate is found, the system displays to the user a message asking for a reformulation of the query.

Table 5. Logical data storage structure.

Requested Data	Condition Parameter	Parameter Data	Table
STUD_UNITS	STUD_NAME	'ERIKA ALARCON'	STDATA

6   Results Module

The results module translates the natural language sentence into the target formal language. In this project, SQL (Structured Query Language) has been chosen as the target language for two reasons: (1) SQL is the most widely used query language for commercially available relational database engines and (2) this will enable the system to be used with many different databases.

This module accesses the logical data storage structure and extracts the field names whose data are requested and the search conditions. Using this information, the module constructs the SQL statement, which is executed with the selected database, and the result is presented to the user. The SQL query generated for the example (1) is:

```
select STUD_UNITS from STDATA where STUD_NAME = 'ERIKA ALARCON'
```

7   Domain Customization

This module was implemented in order to make the querying system independent of the underlying database, thus enabling the system to issue queries to different databases or tables without any need to modify the system software.

The domain customization module was implemented as a Java servlet so that it can be used over the Internet or intranet. This module provides an interface that permits the system administrator to establish a relationship between the words of the lexicon and the database fields, since the field names are usually abbreviated (e.g., word: *major*, field: STUD_MJR). Therefore, with this information the semantic analyzer will know which field corresponds to a given word in the query. Additionally, the system administrator can add words to the lexicon and define their syntactic category, gender, and number.

The domain customization module can only be used by an advanced user (administrator); otherwise, if an unauthorized person uses this module and enters erroneous data, the system could fail or generate incorrect results. To prevent this situation, access to this module is restricted by a password.

8 Final Remarks

Since 1997 our group has been implementing software tools that facilitate inexperienced users to query databases. One of these tools is a QBE (Query by Example) graphical interface [17] for querying relational databases via Internet. This interface allows simultaneous access to two or more databases and the formulation of queries that involve a combination of information from all open databases [8]. In order to facilitate the formulation of queries involving joins of two or more database tables, a new interface (EzQ) is being developed [2]. This new interface will permit users to formulate such queries even if they are not familiar with the concept of join (difficult to understand for users that are not information systems professionals).

A reflection about graphical interface limitations has revealed that it would be extremely difficult to further increase the ease of use of QBE interfaces to meet the needs of the majority of the Internet users, which are not information systems professionals. Therefore, in order to achieve this goal we considered necessary to include another technology: NLIs.

The work described in this paper constitutes the first step for providing the current system with an interface, as friendly as possible, that will involve both graphical and NLIs. Unlike most NLIDB projects for the Spanish language, we are approaching NLIDB issues from the information systems perspective.

Our current version of the Spanish grammar (syntax checker) handles 10 different simple and compound sentence patterns. The semantic analyzer has been tested with a specific domain (academic department database); however, it was implemented in such a way that it can be used for other domains just by changing the information supplied through the domain customization module.

Acknowledgements This work was done under partial support of CONACyT and SNI (Mexico) and RITOS-2 (CYTED).

References

1. Androutsopoulos, I.: Intefacing a Natural Language Front-End to a Relational Database. M.Sc. dissertation, Dept. of Artificial Intelligence, Univ. of Edinburgh; http://www.dai.ed.ac.uk/papers/documents/mt92103.html.

2. Carreón V., G.: Herramienta para Consultas EzQ para Multibases de Datos en Internet. M.Sc. dissertation (to be published), Computer Science Dept., National Center for Research and Technology Development (CENIDET), Cuernavaca, Mexico.

3. Cercone, N., P. McFetridge, F. Popowich, D. Fass, Ch. Groeneboer, G. Hall: The SystemX Natural Languaje Interface: Design, Implementation and Evaluation. Technical report, Centre for Systems Science, Simon Fraser University, British Columbia, Canada (1993); http://www.cs.sfu.ca/research/groups/NLL/4.html#4.1.

4. Computational Linguistics Laboratory: Project Sylvia-NQL; http://www.lllf.uam.es/proyectos/sylvia.html.

5. ELF Software: Hollywood Tutorial (1998); http://www.elf-software.com/Docs/Hollywood.htm.

6. Flores V., J.M., J.M. Matadamas H.: Sistema de Interpretación de Texto. In: Proc. 7th. International Congress on Computer Science Research, Technological Institute of Cd. Madero, Tampico, Mexico (2000) pp. 73–81.

7. González, J.C., J.M. Goñi, A.F. Nieto. ARIES: a ready for use platform for engineering Spanish-processing tools. In: Digest of the Second Language Engineering Convention, London, U.K. (1995) 219–226; http://wotan.mat.upm.es/~aries/papers.html.

8. May A., A., R.A. Pazos R., J. Pérez O., R. Ortega I.: Intermediario para acceso a multibases de datos en Internet. In: Proc. Simposio Español de Informática Distribuida, Univesity of Vigo, Ourense, Spain (2000) 259–267.

9. Monedero, J., J.C. González, J.M. Goñi, C.A. Iglesias, A.F. Nieto: Obtención automática de marcos de subcategorización verbal a partir de texto etiquetado: el sistema SOAMAS. In: Proc. XI Congreso de la Sociedad Española para el Procesamiento del Lenguaje Natural (SEPLN '95), Bilbao, Spain (1995) 241–254; http://wotan.mat.upm.es/~aries/papers.html.

10. Palomar, M., L. Moreno, A. Molina: SISCO: Sistema de interrogación en lenguaje natural a una base de datos geográfica. In: J. Procesamiento del Lenguaje Natural 14 (1993).

11. Rodríguez S., J. Carretero: Corrector ortográfico de libre distribución basado en reglas de derivación. In: Primer Encuentro del Grupo de Usuarios de TeX Hispanohablantes (EGUTH '99) (1999) 44–52; http://www.datsi.fi.upm.es/~coes/publications.html.

12. Ruwanpura, S.: SQ-HAL: Natural language to SQL translator; http://www.csse.monash.edu.au/hons/projects/2000/Supun.Ruwanpura.

13. Sethi, V.: Natural language interfaces to databases: MIS impact, and a survey of their use and importance. Technical report, Graduate School of Business, University of Pittsburgh, Pittsburgh, USA.

14. Thompson, C.A., R.J. Mooney, L.R. Tang: Learning to parse natural language database queries into logical form. In: Proc. ML-97 Workshop on Automata Induction, Grammatical Inference, and Language Acquisition, Nashville, USA (1997).

15. Validation and Business Applications Group: PASO - PC315 PROJECT, Generator of natural language databases interfaces; http://www.vai.dia.fi.upm.es/ing/projects/paso.htm.

16. Zelle, J.M., R.J. Mooney: Learning to parse database queries using inductive logic programming. In: Proc. Thirteenth National Conference on Aritificial Intelligence, Portland, USA (1996) 1050–1055.

17. Zloof M.M.: Query by Example: a database language. In: IBM Sys. Journal 16 No. 4 (1977) 137–152.

Word Sense vs. Word Domain Disambiguation: A Maximum Entropy Approach*

Armando Suárez and Manuel Palomar

Departamento de Lenguajes y Sistemas Informáticos
Universidad de Alicante
Alicante, Spain
E-mail: armando@dlsi.ua.es, mpalomar@dlsi.ua.es

Abstract. In this paper, a supervised learning system of word sense disambiguation is presented. It is based on *conditional maximum entropy models*. This system acquires the linguistic knowledge from an annotated corpus and this knowledge is represented in the form of features. The system were evaluated both using WordNet's senses and domains as the sets of classes of each word. Domain labels are obtained from the enrichment of WordNet with subject field codes which produces a polysemy reduction. Several types of features has been analyzed for a few words selected from the DSO corpus. Using the domain enrichment of WordNet, a 7 % of accuracy improvement is achieved.

1 Introduction

Word sense disambiguation (WSD) is an open research field in natural language processing (NLP). The task of WSD consists in assigning the correct sense to words using an electronic dictionary as the source of word definitions. This is a hard problem that is receiving a great deal of attention from the research community.

Currently, there are two main methodological approaches in this research area: *knowledge-based* methods and *corpus-based* methods. The former approach relies on previously acquired linguistic knowledge, and the latter uses techniques from statistics and machine learning to induce models of language usage from large samples of text [1]. These last methods can perform supervised or unsupervised learning. With supervised learning, the actual status (here, sense label) for each piece of data in the training example is known, whereas with unsupervised learning the classification of the data in the training example is not known [2].

At SENSEVAL-2 [3], researchers showed the latest contributions to WSD. Some supervised systems competed in the English lexical sample task. The Johns Hopkins University system combines, by means of a voting-based classifier, several WSD subsystems based on different methods: decision lists [4], cosine-based vector models, and two Bayesian classifiers. The Southern Methodist University system is an instance-based learning method but

---

* This paper has been partially supported by the Spanish Government (CICYT) under project number TIC2000-0664-C02-02.

P. Sojka, I. Kopeček, and K. Pala (Eds.): TSD 2002, LNAI 2448, pp. 131–137, 2002.

also uses word-word relation patterns obtained from WordNet and Semcor.LazyBoosting [5] is based on the AdaBoost.MH algorithm.

Pedersen [6] proposes a baseline methodology for WSD that relies on decision tree learning and Naïve Bayesian classifiers, using simple lexical features. Several systems combining different classifiers based on distinct sets of features competed at SENSEVAL-2, both in the English and Spanish lexical sample tasks.

This paper presents a system that implements a corpus-based method of WSD. The method used to perform the learning over a set of sense-disambiguated examples is that of maximum entropy models (ME) Linguistic information is represented in the form of feature vectors, which identify the occurrence of certain attributes that appear in contexts containing linguistic ambiguities. The context is the text surrounding an ambiguity that is relevant to the disambiguation process. The features used may be of a distinct nature: word collocations, part-of-speech labels, keywords, topic and domain information, grammatical relationships, and so on.

At SENSEVAL-2, the Stanford University implements several combinations of simple classifiers, and one of them makes use of conditional ME models. In [7] ME is used to perform semantic classification on machine translation tasks, but they also rely on another statistical training procedure to define word classes. In addition, we are aware of a few sites on the Internet which describe attempts to apply ME to WSD, but to our knowledge, these results have not yet been published.

Word Domain Disambiguation (WDD) is a variant of WSD where words in a text are tagged with a domain label in place of a sense label. On the one hand, labeling with such information causes a synsets clustering and then a polysemy reduction. Therefore, WDD must be more accurate than WSD. On the other hand, several researches argue that applications like Information Retrieval (IR) and Question Answering (QA) will be better improved with domain disambiguation than with sense disambiguation. An enrichment of WordNet is proposed using subject field codes [8]. At SENSEVAL-2, this enrichment were used by ITC-irst systems [9]. Another proposal using IPTC[1] subject codes can be seen in [10].

In the following discussion, the ME framework and the features implementation will be described. Then, the complete set of feature definitions used in this work will be detailed. Next, evaluation results using several combinations of these features for a few words will be shown. Finally, some conclusions will be presented, along with a brief discussion of work in progress and future work planned.

2   The Maximum Entropy Framework

ME modeling provides a framework for integrating information for classification from many heterogeneous information sources [2]. ME probability models have been successfully applied to some NLP tasks, such as part-of-speech (PoS) tagging or sentence boundary detection [11].

The WSD method used in this paper is based on conditional ME probability models. It has been implemented using a supervised learning method that consists of building word-

---

[1] The IPTC Subject Reference System has been developed to allow Information Providers access to a universal language independent coding system for indicating the subject content of news items. http://www.iptc.org

sense classifiers using a semantically tagged corpus. A classifier obtained by means of an ME technique consists of a set of parameters or coefficients which are estimated using an optimization procedure. Each coefficient is associated with one feature observed in the training data. The main purpose is to obtain the probability distribution that maximizes the entropy, that is, maximum ignorance is assumed and nothing apart from the training data is considered. Some advantages of using the ME framework are that even knowledge-poor features may be applied accurately; the ME framework thus allows a virtually unrestricted ability to represent problem-specific knowledge in the form of features [11].

Let us assume a set of contexts X and a set of classes C. The function $cl : X \rightarrow C$ chooses the class c with the highest conditional probability in the context x: $cl(x) = \arg\max_c p(c|x)$. Each feature is calculated by a function that is associated to a specific class c', and it takes the form of Equation 1, where $cp(x)$ is some observable characteristic in the context[2]. The conditional probability $p(c|x)$ is defined by Equation 2, where α_i is the parameter or weight of the feature i, K is the number of features defined, and $Z(x)$ is a constant to ensure that the sum of all conditional probabilities for this context is equal to 1.

$$f(x,c) = \begin{cases} 1 \text{ if } c' = c \text{ and } cp(x) = true \\ 0 \text{ otherwise} \end{cases} \tag{1}$$

$$p(c|x) = \frac{1}{Z(x)} \prod_{i=1}^{K} \alpha_i^{f_i(x,c)} \tag{2}$$

The implementation of the ME-based WSD system was done in C++ and features used to test its accuracy are described in the following section. A complete description of the system and some of the features mentioned in the following section can be found in [12].

A usual definition of features would substitute $CP(x)$ in Equation 1 with an expression like $info(x, i) = a$, where $info(x, i)$ informs of a property that can be found at position i in a context x, and a is a predefined value. For example, if we consider that 0 is the position of the word to be learned and that i is related to 0, then $word(x,-1)=$ "best" and $word(x,-1)=$ "big" could be used. In the following, we will refer to this type of features as "non-relaxed features".

Other expressions, such as $info(x, i) \in W_{(c',i)}$, may be substituted for the term $CP(x)$, as a way to reduce the number of possible features. In the expression above, $W_{(c',i)}$ is the set of attributes present in the learning examples at position i. For example, $word(x, -1) \in \{$ "best", "big"$\}$. So this kind of function reduces the number of features to one per each sense at position i. In the following, we will refer to this type of features as "relaxed features".

3 Evaluation

In this section we present the results of our evaluation. All nouns from the DSO sense-tagged English corpus [13] have been selected and evaluated. This corpus is structured in files containing tagged examples of several nouns and verbs. Tags correspond to senses in

---

[2] The ME approach is not limited to binary funtions, but the optimization procedure used for the estimation of the parameters, the *Generalized Iterative Scaling* procedure, uses this type of feature.

WordNet 1.5 [14]. In order to make use of WordNet Domains, tagged senses were mapped to WordNet 1.6 [15][3]. This corpus has been parsed using MiniPar [16].

- *Non-relaxed*
  - *0* **features**: ambiguous-word shape,
  - *s* **features**: words in positions ±1, ±2, ±3,
  - *p* **features**: PoS-tags of words in positions ±1, ±2, ±3,
  - *km* **features**: lemmas of nouns at any position in context, occurring at least *m*% times with a sense,
  - *r* **features**: grammatical relation of the ambiguous word,
  - *d* **features**: the word that the ambiguous word depends on,
  - *m* **features**: the ambiguous word belongs to a multi-word.
- *Relaxed*
  - *L* **features**: lemmas of content-words in positions ±1, ±2, ±3,
  - *W* **features**: content-words in positions ±1, ±2, ±3,
  - *S* **features**: words in positions ±1, ±2, ±3,
  - *B* **features**: lemmas of collocations in positions $(-2, -1)$, $(-1, +1)$, $(+1, +2)$,
  - *C* **features**: collocations in positions $(-2, -1)$, $(-1, +1)$, $(+1, +2)$,
  - *P* **features**: PoS-tags of words in positions ±1, ±2, ±3,
  - *D* **features**: the word that the ambiguous word depends on,
  - *M* **features**: the ambiguous word belongs to a multi-word, as identified by the parser.

Fig. 1. List of types of features.

The set of features defined for the training of the system is described in Figure 1. The majority of them depend on nearest words (for example, *s* or *L* types comprise all possible features defined by the words occurring at positions w_{-3}, w_{-2}, w_{-1}, w_{+1}, w_{+2}, w_{+3} related to the ambiguous word). Features are automatically defined as explained earlier and depend on the data in the training corpus. These features are based on words, collocations, part-of-speech (PoS) tags, and grammatical properties in the local context.

Table 1 shows the best results obtained for a sub-set of nouns using a 10-fold cross-validation evaluation method. Several feature combinations have been tested in order to find the best set for each selected word. The main goal was to compare best values of WDD (the left half of the table) and WSD (the right half) for each word.

In order to perform the ten tests on each word, some preprocessing of the corpus was done. For each word file in DSO, all senses were uniformly distributed in the ten folds (each fold contains one tenth of examples of each sense, except for the tenth fold, which contains the remaining examples). Those senses that had fewer than ten examples in the original corpus file were rejected and not processed; therefore, *Doms* (for "domains") and *Sens* (for "senses") columns show the number of classes effectively learned, *Features* the feature selection with the best result, *Ex* (for "examples") the number contexts, and *Accur* (for "accuracy") the number of correctly classified contexts divided by the total number of contexts. Column *MFS* is the accuracy obtained by most-frequent-sense classification.

---

[3] http://www.lsi.upc.es/~nlp/tools/mapping.html

Table 1. Example of best-feature-selection for WDD and WSD.

	Doms	Ex	Features	Accur	MFS	Sens	Features	Accur	MFS
action,N	4	1049	sprdm	59.35	46.75	5	OsprdmK10	52.69	46.75
activity,N	2	786	OsBCprdmK10	86.95	85.65	3	Osprdm	71.31	68.75
art,N	2	393	Most frequent	97.51	97.51	4	Osprdm	65.19	47.95
body,N	2	390	OLSsBCprdm	86.27	77.91	4	OLSsBCprdm	68.59	60.51
book,N	3	615	OsbcprdmK10	84.35	80.60	4	OsprdmK10	70.07	64.97
business,N	6	1483	OsbcprdmK10	64.97	50.30	7	OsBCprdmK10	64.15	50.30
case,N	3	1419	OsbcprdmK10	74.62	66.76	9	OsbcprdmK10	56.82	32.53
center,N	3	546	OLSsBCprdm	80.90	58.33	6	OsbcprdmK10	72.36	58.33
church,N	2	367	Osprdm	70.45	67.11	3	OsprdmK10	67.08	62.05
condition,N	2	624	OsbcprdmK10	87.88	84.59	3	OLSsBCprdm	83.38	79.63
course,N	4	337	OsBCprdmK10	78.85	49.36	5	OsBCprdmK10	72.14	42.32
interest,N	5	1476	OsprdmK10	71.79	45.86	6	OsprdmK10	70.87	45.86
line,N	14	1320	OLSsBCprdm	65.26	42.52	22	OsprdmK10	56.02	22.73
work,N	3	1419	OLSBCprdm	80.63	71.71	6	OsprdmK10	54.58	32.83

The data summarized in Table 1 reveal that all types of features, relaxed and non-relaxed ones, are useful. Nouns are better classified than verbs. Moreover, each word has its own best-feature-selection. If such strategy of selection is assumed, better values of accuracy are expected than applying the same types of features to all words. Obviously, these results are unreliable because train and test data overlap, but a toy test using SENSEVAL-2 data point to the usefulness of such information.

Table 2 shows the evaluation results for all nouns in DSO using several different sets of features. The first consequence of using domains instead synsets is the reduction of the number of classes (from an average of 4.8 senses to 3.5 domains per noun), and then the gain in accuracy of the method. Obviously, those words with the same number of domains than senses do not contribute to a gain in accuracy.

Table 2. Word domain and word sense disambiguation results.

Features	WDD	WSD	Diff
Most frequent	68.7	58.7	+9.98
LB	73.5	64.6	+8.94
SP	74.8	66.6	+8.20
OLB	75.4	67.1	+8.34
OSP	75.7	67.8	+7.96
sp	77.2	69.5	+7.70
Osp	77.7	70.2	+7.52
sprdm	78.1	70.6	+7.48
Osprdm	78.4	71.0	+7.37
OLSsBCprdm	78.6	71.0	+7.58
Osprdmk10	78.7	71.4	+7.26
OsBCprdmk10	78.7	71.4	+7.27
Osbcprdmk10	78.7	71.4	+7.33

As a direct consequence of the polysemy reduction, an average gain in accuracy of 7 % had been achieved. The DSO corpus has 121 nouns and 938 senses: 100 nouns reduce its polysemy to 629 subject field codes. Examining the last selections, there is not a great influence of adding more features to the training. In fact, using a 10-fold cross-validation paired Student's t-test [17] with a confidence value $t_{9,0.975} = 1.833$, BC features has no effect on accuracy (but they are worse than bc). The best feature selection ($0sbcprdmk10$), fails the significance test with the other four first ranked selections (with $sprdm$ succeeds) except for $0sBCprdmk10$ which is worse than it.

4 Conclusions

A WSD system based on maximum entropy conditional probability models has been presented. It is a supervised learning method that needs a corpus previously annotated with sense labels, or domain labels.

Several researches criticize the excessive polysemy of WordNet, specially for IR and QA applications, and propose a clustering of synsets to achieve more efficiency. WordNet Domains [8] is a proposal that assigns a subject field code to each synset reducing the polysemy degree, currently for nouns only. In order to evaluate the accuracy of the method when the set of classes is formed by domain labels instead of sense labels, all nouns were selected from the DSO corpus. A gain of a 7 % of accuracy of WDD against WSD were obtained.

Future research will incorporate domain information as an additional information source for the system in order to improve WSD and WDD. These attributes will be incorporated into the learning of the system in the same way that features were incorporated, as described above.

As we work to improve the ME method, we are also working to develop a cooperative strategy between several other methods as well, both knowledge-based and corpus-based.

References

1. Pedersen, T.: A decision tree of bigrams is an accurate predictor of word sense. In: Proceedings of the Second Annual Meeting of the North American Chapter of the Association for Computational Linguistics, Pittsburgh (2001) 79–86.
2. Manning, C.D., Schütze, H.: Foundations of Statistical Natural Language Processing. The MIT Press, Cambridge, Massachusetts (1999).
3. Preiss, J., Yarowsky, D., eds.: Proceedings of SENSEVAL-2. In Preiss, J., Yarowsky, D., eds.: Proceedings of the 2nd International Workshop on Evaluating Word Sense Disambiguation Systems, Toulouse, France, ACL-SIGLEX (2001).
4. Yarowsky, D.: Hierarchical decision lists for word sense disambiguation. Computers and the Humanities 34 (2000) 179–186.
5. Escudero, G., Màrquez, L., Rigau, G.: Boosting applied to word sense disambiguation. In: Proceedings of the 12th Conference on Machine Learning ECML2000, Barcelona, Spain (2000).
6. Pedersen, T.: A baseline methodology for word sense disambiguation. [18] 126–135.
7. García-Varea, I., Och, F.J., Ney, H., Casacuberta, F.: Refined lexicon models for statistical machine translation using a maximum entropy approach. In: Proceedings of 39th Annual Meeting of the Association for Computational Linguistics. (2001) 204–211.

8. Magnini, B., Strapparava, C.: Experiments in Word Domain Disambiguation for Parallel Texts. In: Proceedings of the ACL Workshop on Word Senses and Multilinguality, Hong Kong, China (2000).

9. Magnini, B., Strapparava, C., Pezzulo, G., Gliozzo, A.: Using Domain Information for Word Sense Disambiguation. [3] 111–114.

10. Montoyo, A., Palomar, M., Rigau, G.: WordNet Enrichment with Classification Systems. In Preiss, J., Yarowsky, D., eds.: Proceedings of NAACL Workshop WordNet and Other Lexical Resources: Applications, Extensions and Customizations, Pittsburgh, PA, USA (2001).

11. Ratnaparkhi, A.: Maximum Entropy Models for Natural Language Ambiguity Resolution. Ph.D. thesis, University of Pennsylvania (1998).

12. Suárez, A., Palomar, M.: Feature selection analysis for maximum entropy-based wsd. [18] 146–155.

13. Ng, H.T., Lee, H.B.: Integrating multiple knowledge sources to disambiguate word senses: An exemplar-based approach. In Joshi, A., Palmer, M., (Eds.): Proceedings of the Thirty-Fourth Annual Meeting of the Association for Computational Linguistics, San Francisco, Morgan Kaufmann Publishers (1996).

14. Miller, G.A., Beckwith, R., Fellbaum, C., Gross, D., Miller, K.J.: Five Papers on WordNet. Special Issue of the International journal of lexicography 3 (1993).

15. Daude, J., Padro, L., Rigau, G.: Mapping wordnets using structural information. In: Proceedings of the 38th Anual Meeting of the Association for Computational Linguistics (ACL 2000), Hong Kong (2000).

16. Lin, D.: Dependency-based evaluation of minipar. In: Proceedings of the Workshop on the Evaluation of Parsing Systems, First International Conference on Language Resources and Evaluation, Granada, Spain (1998).

17. Dietterich, T.G.: Approximate statistical test for comparing supervised classification learning algorithms. Neural Computation 10 (1998) 1895–1923.

18. Gelbukh, A.F.: Computational Linguistics and Intelligent Text Processing, Third International Conference, CICLing 2002, Mexico City, Mexico, February 17–23, 2002, Proceedings. In: Gelbukh, A.F., (Ed.): CICLing. Volume 2276 of Lecture Notes in Computer Science, Springer (2002).

Exploiting Thesauri and Hierarchical Categories in Cross-Language Information Retrieval*

Fatiha Sadat[1], Masatoshi Yoshikawa[1,2], and Shunsuke Uemura[1]

[1] Graduate School of Information Science, Nara Institute of Science and Technology (NAIST).
8916-5 Takayama, Ikoma, Nara 630-0101. Japan
[2] National Institute of Informatics (NII)
E-mail: fatia-s@is.aist-nara.ac.jp, yosikawa@is.aist-nara.ac.jp,
uemura@is.aist-nara.ac.jp

Abstract. As Internet resources become accessible worldwide, need to develop efficient methods for information retrieval across languages becomes primordial. In the present paper, we focus on query expansion techniques to improve the effectiveness of information retrieval. A combination to a dictionary-based translation and statistical-based disambiguation is indispensable to overcome translation's ambiguity. We propose a model, which uses multiple sources for query reformulation and expansion to select expansion terms and retrieve information needed by a user. Relevance feedback, thesaurus-based expansion, as well as a new feedback strategy, based on the extraction of domain keywords to expand user's query, are introduced and evaluated. We evaluated the effectiveness of the proposed combined method using an application of a French-English information retrieval.

1 Introduction

Cross-Language Information Retrieval (CLIR), consists of providing a query in one language and searching document collections in one or more languages.

In this paper, we focus on query expansion, which has been among the most important methods in overcoming the word mismatch problem in information retrieval. The proposed study is general across languages in information retrieval however; we have conducted experiments and evaluations on French and English languages. The rest of this paper is organized as follows: Section 2 gives an overview of translation and disambiguation approaches in CLIR. Query expansion techniques with different combinations are introduced in Section 3. Experiments and evaluations are discussed in Section 4. Section 5 concludes the paper.

2 Query Translation/Disambiguation in CLIR

In our approach, a term-by-term *translation* using bilingual machine-readable dictionary is performed after a simple *stemming* process of query terms to replace each term with its

---

* The present research study is supported in part by the Ministry of Education, Culture, Sports, Science and Technology of Japan, under grants 11480088, 12680417 and 12208032, and by the CREST program of the JST Corporation (Japan Science and Technology).

P. Sojka, I. Kopeček, and K. Pala (Eds.): TSD 2002, LNAI 2448, pp. 139–146, 2002.
© Springer-Verlag Berlin Heidelberg 2002

inflectional root and remove stop words and stop phrases. Missing words in the dictionary, which are essential for the correct interpretation of the query can be solved by an automatic *compensation* through a synonym dictionary related to that language or by an existing monolingual thesaurus. This case requires an extra step of looking up the query term in the synonym dictionary or thesaurus when missing words in the bilingual machine-readable dictionary, to find equivalent terms or synonyms of the concerned query term before translation. A disambiguation method [5,6] using *co-occurrence tendency* based on *log likelihood ratio* [2] is applied to filter and select best translations among candidates to create target queries and retrieve documents. An overview of the proposed information retrieval system is shown in Figure 1. Query expansion is completed using monolingual thesaurus, relevance feedback (interactive or automatic) or domain-based feedback.

3   Query Expansion in CLIR

Query expansion has proved its effectiveness in the performance of information retrieval [1,3]. In the present paper, we use an approach of combined automatic query expansion before and after translation with extraction and selection of expansion terms through the following techniques: Relevance feedback, with selection of best terms, domain-based feedback with extraction of domain keywords to add to the original query and thesaurus-based expansion with retrieval of synonyms from monolingual thesauri.

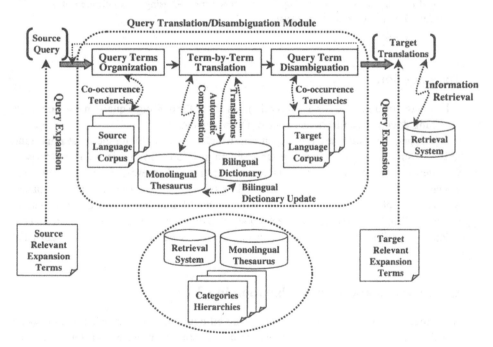

Fig. 1. Overview of the Proposed Information Retrieval System.

3.1 Relevance Feedback

A fixed number of term concepts will be extracted from the top retrieved documents and their co-occurrence in conjunction with original query terms are computed. However, any query expansion must be handled very carefully. Selecting any expansion term could be dangerous. Therefore, our selection is based on statistical co-occurrence tendency in conjunction with all terms of the original query, rather than with just one query term.

Assume that we have a query Q with n terms: $\{term_1 \ldots term_n\}$. A ranking factor based on the co-occurrence tendency between each term in the query and the expansion term candidate, is evaluated, as follows:

$$\text{Rank}(expterm) = \sum_{i=1}^{n} \text{co-occurrence}(term_i, expterm) \tag{1}$$

where, co-occurrence($term_i$, $expterm$) represents the co-occurrence tendency between a query term $term_i$ and an expansion term candidate $expterm$, and can be evaluated by any estimation such as log-likelihood ratio. Thus, all co-occurrence values were computed, summed for all query terms and an expansion candidate with the highest rank is selected as an expansion term for the concerned query.

3.2 Domain-Based Feedback

We introduce a domain-based feedback [6] as query reformulation strategy, which consists to extract domain keywords from a set of top retrieved documents using a standard relevance feedback to expand an original query set. Web directories such as Yahoo![3] or AltaVista[4] are human constructed and designed for human web browsing. They provide a hierarchical category scheme and documents are sorted into the given scheme. Our strategy relies on terms extraction using a standard relevance feedback with a condition that these terms represent a directory or category, which is denoted by a keyword describing its content and thus will be considered as a specific domain to collection of documents. Domain-based feedback's process is described as follows:

- Extract some terms or seed words using relevance feedback as well as a ranking strategy to select expansion terms, as explained in the previous section. This set is denoted by set_1.
- Collect domain keywords candidates, from categories and directories related to some hierarchical web directories such as: *Yahoo!*[1] or *AltaVista*[2] or *Open Directory*[5], which is denoted by set_2.
- Select a fixed number of domain keywords as seed words from set_1 but also a category candidate from set_2.

In case of large number of resulting domain keywords, a statistical process is applied to rank and select the best keywords. The resulting set of expansion keywords will be used to expand the original set of queries. This process may involve many keywords or just a subset of these keywords.

---

[3] http://www.yahoo.com/docs/pr
[4] http://www.altavista.com
[5] http://dmoz.org/

3.3 Thesaurus-Based Expansion

This approach is based on expanding a query with a fixed number of relevant terms from a structure derived from a lexical database. WordNet [9] for English queries and EuroWord-Net [10,11] for French queries could be seen as powerful tools to study lexical semantic resources and their language-specificity [8,11]. Our first suggestion is that synonyms of a query term can be used as expansion candidates. Following the research reported by Voorhees [9] on the use of lexical relations of WordNet for a query expansion, we can proceed by a simple look up to find synsets of a full query, otherwise we proceed by a term-by-term search in case of non-existence of a full query in the lexical database. An example is the term *computer*, which could be expanded with the following set of synonyms: {*data processor, electronic computer, information processing system, calculator, figurer, reckoner, estimator*}. Secondly, we suggest the use of statistical frequency in order to rank and select the expansion terms and thus avoid words that do not occur frequently with original terms such as the term *reckoner*, which will be removed from the synset list of the term *computer*. An appropriate weighting scheme will allow a smooth integration of these related terms by reducing their influence over the query [4]. Therefore, all terms retrieved from thesaurus will be given weight expressing their similarity to original query terms. The weighting scheme is based on the position of the expansion terms in the conceptual hierarchy of the original query term, also on the number of terms accompanying the expansion term in the same synset. Some strategies were proposed [4,9] for sense disambiguation and weight assignment to synonyms and other terms in a thesaurus. In the present study, weights assigned to any synonym of one synset would be related to an envelope of 0.5 dived by number of terms in the corresponding synset, which is proportional in the same synset. Following these assumptions, the expanded query with synonyms, would contain: {*computer, data processor, information processing system, calculator*}. The proposed weighting factor for retrieved expansion terms from synsets of a conceptual hierarchy related to the WordNet thesaurus, is described as following:

$$\text{Weight}(term, expterm_i) = \frac{\text{Sim}(term, expterm_i)}{2 \times M} \quad (2)$$

where M is the number of terms that belong to the same synset. $\text{Sim}(term, expterm_i)$ is the similarity between a *term* and an expansion candidate *expterm_i* and could be estimated by any similarity measure, such as the Cosine measure [7] as following:

$$\text{Sim}(term, expterm_i) = \frac{\sum_k v_{sk} v_{tk}}{\sqrt{\sum_k v_{sk}^2 \sum_k v_{tk}^2}} \quad (3)$$

where v_{sk} and v_{tk} are frequencies of *term* and *expterm_i* in a corpus, respectively.

Moreover, expanding a query with any of those weighted synonyms implies a careful selection and ranking, depending on the statistically most weighted terms in conjunction with all query terms not just one term query. For a query Q with k terms {*term_1, term_2, ..., term_k*}, weights values are computed for an expansion term candidate, summed for all query terms, if the expansion term appears in the related hierarchy and the highest weighted term is selected for query expansion, as follows:

$$\text{Weigth}(query, expterm) = \sum_{j=1}^{k} \text{Weight}(term_i, expterm) . \quad (4)$$

3.4 Combining Different Approaches

Following the research reported by Ballesteros and Croft [1] on the use of local feedback, adding terms that emphasize query concepts in the post and pre-translation phases improves precision and recall of information retrieval. This combined method is supposed to reduce the ambiguity by de-emphasizing irrelevant terms added by translation and will improve precision and recall of information retrieval. The new query Q_{new} can be defined as follows:

$$Q_{new} = Q_{orig} + \alpha_1 \sum_{bef} T_i + \alpha_2 \sum_{aft} T_j \quad (5)$$

where, Q_{orig} is an original query, $\sum_{bef} T_i$ and $\sum_{aft} T_j$ represent the added sets of terms before and after translation/disambiguation, consecutively. The two parameters α_1 and α_2, which represent the importance of each expansion strategy are given by human experimentally in the present research, but could be estimated using an Expectation-Maximization (EM) algorithm.

4 Experiments and Evaluation

Conducted experiments were completed on the proposed strategies for query translation disambiguation and expansion using an application of French-English information retrieval, i.e. French queries to retrieve English documents. Linguistic tools used in these experiments are described as follows:

- *Tipster volume 1 for TREC[6] test collection* was used for cross-language evaluation. Topics composed of fields <title> for title and <desc> for description, were considered in the conducted experiments. Key terms contained in these fields, which are averaged 5.7 terms by query are used to generate French and English source queries.
- *Hansard corpora* (Canadian Parliament Debates) are bilingual French-English parallel corpora, containing more than 100 million words of English text and their corresponding French translations. In this study, we have used Hansard as monolingual French/English corpora.
- *COLLINS[7] Series 100 French-English bilingual dictionary* was used to translate source queries. The bilingual dictionary includes 75.000 references and 110.000 translations, which seems to be plenty for research.
- *WordNet* [9] and *EuroWordNet* [11] are used as thesauri to query expansion and possible compensation, in case of limitation in *COLLINS* bilingual dictionary.

---

[6] http://trec.nist.gov/data.html
[7] Collins Series 100 Bilingual Dictionary

Table 1. Best results for different combinations of query translation/disambiguation and expansion using relevance feedback, domain-based feedback and thesaurus-based expansion.

Method	Mono_Eng	No_DIS	N_DIS	Feed.aft	Feed.bef_aft	Feed.bef_dom	Feed_wn
Avg. P	0.2628	0.2214	**0.2679**	0.2663	**0.2704**	**0.2725**	0.2518
%Mono	100	84.24	**101.94**	101.33	**102.89**	**103.69**	95.81

Feed.ewn	Feed.bef_ wn	Feed.ewn_ aft	Feed.ewn_ wn	Feed.dom_ dom	Feed.ewn_ wn	Feed.ewn_ wn_dom
0.2579	0.2571	0.2588	0.2540	0.2545	0.2608	**0.2741**
98.13	97.83	98.47	96.65	96.84	99.23	**104.29**

- *Porter*[8] *Stemmer* was used for the stemming part.
- *SMART*[9] information retrieval system, which has been used in many researches related to CLIR, would retrieve English documents.

4.1 Experiments and Results

Retrieval using original English queries is represented by *Mono_Eng*. *No_DIS* is the result of translation without disambiguation, i.e. selecting the first translation as target for each source query term. *N_DIS* refers to the translation and disambiguation method, also denoted by *trans-disambiguation*, in the rest of this paper. Query expansion techniques were represented by: *Feed.bef/Feed.aft* for relevance feedback before/after trans_disambiguation, respectively. *Feed.bef_aft* refers to combined relevance feedback, both before and after trans_disambiguation. Domain-based feedback was evaluated with *Feed.dom* after trans_disambiguation. Combined relevance and domain-based feedbacks was evaluated with *Feed.bef_dom*. WordNet-based expansion was evaluated using synsets of target translations with *Feed_wn*, as well EuroWordNet-based expansion using synsets of source queries with *Feed.ewn*. Combined thesauri-based expansion with relevance feedback was evaluated by *Feed.bef_wn* and *Feed.ewn_aft* methods. Combined thesauri-based expansion with domain-based feedback was evaluated by *Feed.dom_wn* and *Feed. ewn_dom* methods. Combined thesauri-based expansion was tested with *Feed.ewn_wn*. Finally, *Feed.ewn_wn_dom* represents combined thesauri with domain-based feedback. Results and performances of these methods are described in Table 1 using an average precision and a difference comparing to the monolingual counterpart, for experimental evaluations.

4.2 Discussion

The disambiguation method *N.DIS* showed a better improvement in terms of average precision, 101.94 % of the monolingual retrieval comparing to *No_DIS* or to monolingual

---

[8] http://www.tartarus.org/~martin/PorterStemmer/
[9] ftp://ftp.cs.cornell.edu/pub/smart

English retrieval. *Feed.aft* showed a good help to the average precision with 101.33 % of the monolingual counterpart. Combined relevance feedback techniques before and after trans_disambiguation *Feed.bef_aft* showed a better result with 102.89 % in average precision of the monolingual retrieval. This suggests that combined query expansion before and after trans_disambiguation helps to improve the effectiveness of information retrieval. Domain-based feedback showed a drop in term of average precision comparing to previous methods. However, combined with relevance feedback before and after trans_disambiguation, a greater result with 103.69 % in terms of average precision was deducted. Thesaurus-based expansion with WordNet *Feed_wn* or EuroWordNet *Feed.ewn* as well as different combinations to relevance feedback *Feed.bef_wn*, *Feed.ewn_aft* or domain-based feedback *Feed.dom_wn*, *Feed.ewn_dom* showed drops in average precision. Moreover, the combined thesauri-based expansion *Feed.ewn_wn* showed a drop in average precision. The best result was achieved by the combined thesauri-based expansion and domain-based feedback *Feed.ewn_wn_dom* with 104.29% of the monolingual counterpart, in term of average precision. This suggests that adding domain keywords to generalized thesauri improves the effectiveness of retrieval.

Thus, key techniques used in this successful method can be summarized as follows:

- A statistical disambiguation method based on co-occurrence tendency is crucial to avoid wrong sense disambiguation and select best target translations.
- Adding domain keywords to the original query and then selecting thesaurus word senses in order to avoid wrong sense disambiguation, is considered as an effective approach for information retrieval.
- Each type of query expansion has different characteristics and therefore their combinations could provide a valuable resource for the proposed system. The combined method showed a great improvement in term of average precision.

5   Conclusions and Future Works

Linguistics resources are readily available to achieve an efficient and effective query translation method in Cross-Language Information Retrieval. What we proposed and evaluated in this paper could be summarized as follows: First, a query disambiguation, which is considered as a valuable resource for query translation. Second, combined query expansion techniques before and after translation and disambiguation, using relevance feedback or domain-based feedback showed an effectiveness comparing to the following methods: monolingual retrieval, simple word-by-word dictionary translation or combined translation and disambiguation method. Third, combined thesauri-based expansion with domain-based feedback showed a great improvement for information retrieval.

Our ongoing work involves a deeper investigation on different relations of WordNet and EuroWordNet thesauri, exploiting multiple word senses beside the synonymy relation for query expansion in CLIR. An approach of learning from documents categorization or classification in order to extract relevant keywords for query expansion is another future research. Finally, our main interest is to find effective solutions to fulfill needs of information retrieval across languages.

References

1. Ballesteros, L. and Croft, W.B.: Phrasal Translation and Query Expansion Techniques for Cross-Language Information Retrieval. In: Proceedings of the 20th ACM SIGIR Conference (1997) pp. 84–91.
2. Dunning, T.: Accurate Methods for the Statistics of Surprise and Coincidence. Computational Linguistics, Vol. 19. No. 1 (1993) pp. 61–74.
3. Loupy, C., Bellot, P., El-Beze, M. and Marteau, P.-F.: Query Expansion and Classification of Retrieved Documents. In Proceedings of TREC-7. NIST Publication (1998).
4. Richardson, R., Smeaton, A.F.: Using WordNet in Knowledge-based Approach to Information Retrieval. In Proceedings BCS-IRSG Colloquium, CREWE (1995).
5. Sadat, F., Maeda, A., Yoshikawa, M. and Uemura, S.: Integrating Dictionary-based and Statistical-based Approaches in Cross-Language Information Retrieval. IPSJ SIG Notes, 2000-DBS-121/2000-FI-58 (2000) pp. 61–68.
6. Sadat, F., Maeda, A., Yoshikawa, M. and Uemura, S.: Query Expansion Techniques for the CLEF Bilingual Track. In: Proceedings of the CLEF 2001 Cross-Language System Evaluation Campaign (2001) pp. 99–104.
7. Salton, G. and McGill, M.: Introduction to Modern Information Retrieval. New York: McGraw-Hill (1983).
8. Yamabana, K., Muraki, K., Doi, S. and Kamei, S.: A Language Conversion Front-End for Cross-Linguistic Information Retrieval. In: Proceedings of SIGIR Workshop on Cross-Linguistic Information Retrieval, Zurich, Switzerland (1996).
9. Voorhees, M. E.: Query Expansion using Lexical-Semantic Relations. In: Proceedings of the 17th ACM SIGIR Conference (1994) pp. 61–69.
10. Vossen, P.: EuroWordNet, A Multilingual Database for Information Retrieval. In: Proceedings of the DELOS Workshop on CLIR, Zürich (1997).
11. Vossen, P.: EuroWordNet, A Multilingual Database with Lexical Semantic Networks. The Kluwer Academic Publishers (1998).

Valency Lexicon for Czech: From Verbs to Nouns

Markéta Lopatková, Veronika Řezníčková, and Zdeněk Žabokrtský*

Center for Computational Linguistics, Charles University (MFF),
Malostranské nám. 25, CZ-11800 Prague, Czech Republic
E-mail: stranak@ckl.mff.cuni.cz, rez@ckl.mff.cuni.cz,
zabokrtsky@ckl.mff.cuni.cz
WWW: http://ckl.mff.cuni.cz/

Abstract. Valency lexicon of Czech verbs has been intensively worked on for more than a year, and now we have at our disposal a detailed description of valency frames of several hundreds verbs. Presently, the challenge naturally arises, to use the existing lexicon for capturing valency of other word classes. In this paper, we focus on valency of nouns derived from verbs. We propose an algorithm for automatic prediction of valency frames of these nouns, and we test it on a sample of data.

1 Introduction

Valency Lexicon of Czech Verbs. (Only the basic features of our valency lexicon are mentioned here, see [5] for details). The lexicon contains a rich syntactic information based on Functional Generative Description (see [2] for references). Currently, the manual annotation of roughly 600 most frequent Czech verbs has been practically finished, the annotation of next 400 verbs is in progress.

The lexicon has the following structure: *(i)* There is a list of valency frames for each verb. Each verb has at least one valency frame (but usually more, which is typically caused by its polysemy). *(ii)* For each valency frame several attributes are specified: "pointer(s)" to EuroWordNet synset(s), semantic class (verba dicendi, verbs of motion etc.), synonymic expression(s), example sentence(s), lemma of its aspectual counterpart, and the sequence of frame slots are the most important ones. *(iii)* Each frame slot is associated with a functor (name of inner participant or free modifier), the type of relation (obligatory, optional, 'quasi-valency' or 'typical' modifier), and with its possible surface realization(s) (direct or prepositional case, infinitive, subordinating conjunction etc.).

Nominal Valency in Czech. In this paper, we discuss only nouns derived from verbs (non-deverbal nouns and their modifiers are studied e.g. in [7]). While describing valency frames of such nouns, J. Panevová differentiates (according to Kuryłowicz) two types of word-formative process: *syntactic derivation* (SD) and *lexical derivation* (LD). While in SD only syntactic function of derived word changes, in LD the lexical meaning of derived word is changed as well (see [4]). J. Panevová presumes the position of particular types of deverbal nouns on the virtual axis: nouns derived from verbs by SD ↔ nouns derived from verbs by

---
* The research reported on in this paper has been carried out under the projects GAČR 405/96/K214 and MŠMT LN00A063.

LD. While the most of nouns come at the either end of the axis, nouns that would be located "somewhere in the middle" exist as well (cf. [6]).

2   Verbal Frames versus Noun Frames

Morphological Means of Word-formative Process. The word-formative process is characterized by some typical suffixes with particular types of derivation: *(1)* Nouns derived by SD are produced especially by productive means, e.g. *-ní/-tí* (*létání* (flying)). *(2)* Nouns on the boundary between SD and LD are derived typically by non-productive means, e.g. with *-ba* (*stavba* (building)) or with zero suffix (*let* (flight)). *(3)* Nouns derived by LD belong for instance to: (i) actor names (derived from verbs by suffixes *-tel,-č* etc., e.g. *učitel* (teacher)), (ii) names denoting the place of action (derived by suffixes *-árna, -iště* etc., e.g. *umývárna* (washroom)) (iii) names denoting a tool (derived from verbs by suffixes *-dlo, -tko* etc., e.g. *ořezávátko* (a pencil sharpener).

Incorporated Role and its Deletion. Many deverbal nouns adopt all the functors of the "source" verb frame. We mark them PRED (they function similarly as the original "predicate"). On the other hand, there are nouns that take over a specific role from one of the participants or free modifiers of the source verb within the word-formative process (see [1]). The meaning of the noun itself occupies one valency slot of the original valency frame. Therefore the respective slot should be deleted when we try to transform the verbal frame into the frame of the noun. See Table 1 for the examples of incorporated participants.

Action vs. Substantival Usage. Besides the derivation by specific suffixes, especially the type of usage of a particular noun ("action usage" or "substantival usage", see Figure 2 (a)) determines the type of derivation. Thus the noun *psaní* (writing, a letter), derived from the verb *psát* (to write) can mean the action (*psaní dopisu Petrem trvalo asi 3 hodiny/*Writing a letter by Peter took him about three hours.), but also the result of this action - the letter (*Petrovo psaní leželo na stole/*Peter's letter lay on the table.). The noun *výhra* (a win) derived from the verb *vyhrát* (to win) can be used as an action noun (*Petrova výhra milionu šokovala celou rodinu/*Winning of one million crowns by Peter shocked the whole family.), but also again as a result of the action of winning – the amount of money (*Petrova výhra činila million korun/*Peter's win was one million crowns.). We will preferably study the nouns in the action usage, since they possess a richer valency behavior.

Change of Surface Realization. The process of nominalization of a verb is accompanied with a change of surface realization of particular members of the valency frame (cf. [3]). The possible transitions are depicted in Figure 2(b).

Table 1. Number of occurrences of selected incorporated roles in the handcrafted sample of nouns derived from 240 verbs (nouns with ending *-ní, -tí* are not counted in this table).

Role	#Occ.	Example noun and its frame
PRED	134	*hovor* ACT(2/pos) PAT(o+6) ADDR(s+7) (conversation with sb...)
ACT	61	*čtenář* PAT(2) (reader of st.)
PAT	9	*přínos* ACT(2/pos) BEN(pro+4) (sb's. contribution to st.)
EFF	6	*hra* ACT(2/pos) PAT(o+6) (sb's. play about st.)

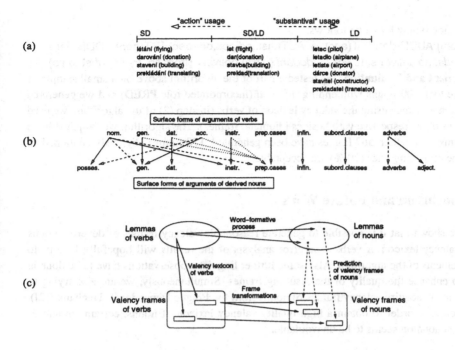

Fig. 1. (a) Distribution of nouns derived from verbs along the "derivational" axis. (b) Possible changes of surface realization (full arrows – the most typical transition, dashed arrows – lower frequency transitions, dotted arrows – really rare transitions). (c) The relation between verbs and nouns from the viewpoint of the valency predicting algorithm.

3 Prediction of Noun Frames

Algorithm for Frame Generating. We propose an algorithm that automatically generates valency frames of deverbal nouns. The algorithm consists of the following steps: *(1)* find the verb from which the noun is derived, *(2)* select the appropriate frame of the verb, *(3)* determine the incorporated role of the noun with respect to the verb, and delete the respective slot from the verbal frame (if necessary), *(4)* transform the surface realization of the remaining slots. (The situation is illustrated in Figure 2 (c): we emulate the valency lexicon of nouns (the dashed line) via traversing the picture in the anti-clockwise fashion.)

Several problems appeared during the implementation of the algorithm. First, it is not always clear, from which verb the noun was derived. Second, it is difficult to choose the appropriate frame. For instance, noun *odpověd'* is related to one frame of the verb *odpovídat* (to answer), while not to the second (to be responsible) nor to the third (to correspond). Third, the incorporated role can be only approximated using the primary meaning of suffixes (see paragraph Morphological means), but exceptions exist. As for the change of the surface realizations, we use (slightly modified) transformations of frames from [6] as well as our own rules that capture some more regularities in surface realization change we are aware of (however, this set of rules is still being developed). The resulting frame transformation

(verb→noun) may look like follows:
ACT(nom) ADDR(dat) PAT(acc) → ACT(instr,adjpos,od+gen) PAT(gen) ADDR(dat)
e.g., *dodat* (to deliver st to sb) → *dodání* ((sb's) delivery (from sb, by sb) of st to sb)
Experiment and Evaluation. We tested a part of the algorithm above on a small sample of data. We took 209 nouns with ending *-ní* or *-tí* (incorporated role PRED) and we generated their valency frames using the valency lexicon of verbs (in step (2) of the algorithm, we used all frames of the respective verb besides idiomatic frames). The algorithm was applicable on 197 nouns. Altogether, 567 frames have been generated. 170 frames obviously contained an error, the remaining ones (70 %) are acceptable.

4 Conclusion and Future Work

We have shown that it is possible to generate reasonable valency frames of deverbal nouns using valency lexicon of verbs. The error analysis of the results will hopefully lead us to improvements of the algorithm. Also some further linguistic observations have to be done in order to enhance the quality of the resulting frames. Simultaneously, we are also trying to automatically acquire valency frames of nouns from the Prague Dependency Treebank ([2]). In any case, in order to obtain a high-quality valency lexicon of nouns, certain amount of manual annotation seems to be unavoidable.

References

1. Dokulil, M.: Tvoření slov v češtině I. Teorie odvozování slov. (Word-formative process in Czech I. Theory of word-formation.) ČSAV, Praha (1962).
2. Hajičová E. et al.: The Current Status of the Prague Dependency Treebank. Proceedings of the 4th Internation Conference Text, Speech and Dialogue, LNAI 2166, Springer (2001).
3. Karlík, P., Nübler, N.: Poznámky k nominalizaci v češtině (Notes on nominalization in Czech). Slovo a slovesnost, 59, 105–112 (1998).
4. Kuryłowicz, J.: Dérivation lexicale et dérivation syntaxique. Bulletin de la Société linguistique de Paris, 37, 79–92 (1936).
5. Lopatková M., Žabokrtský Z.: Valency Dictionary of Czech Verbs: Complex Tectogrammatical Annotation. Proceedings of Third International Conference on Language Resources and Evaluation, Las Palmas, Spain (2002).
6. Panevová, J: Poznámky k valenci podstatých jmen (Notes on the valency of nouns). In: Hladká, Z., Karlík, P. (Eds.): Čeština – univerzália a specifika, Brno: MU, 173–180 (2000).
7. Piťha, P.: On the case frames of nouns. In: Prague Studies in Mathematical Linguistics, Vol. 7, Academia, Praha, 215–224 (1981).

Term Clustering Using a Corpus-Based Similarity Measure

Goran Nenadić, Irena Spasić, and Sophia Ananiadou

School of Sciences, University of Salford, UK
E-mail: G.Nenadic@salford.ac.uk, I.Spasic@salford.ac.uk,
S.Ananiadou@salford.ac.uk

Abstract. In this paper we present a method for the automatic term clustering. The method uses a hybrid similarity measure to cluster terms automatically extracted from a corpus by applying the C/NC-value method. The measure comprises contextual, functional and lexical similarity, and it is used to instantiate the cell values in a similarity matrix. The clustering algorithm uses either the nearest neighbour or the Ward's method to calculate the distance between clusters. The approach has been tested and evaluated in the domain of molecular biology and the results are presented.

1 Introduction

The identification of concepts, linguistically represented by domain specific terms [2], is a basic step in the automated acquisition of knowledge from textual documents. Textual documents describing new knowledge in an intensively expanding domain, such as molecular biology, are swamped by new terms representing newly identified/created concepts. This makes the automatic term extraction tools essential assets for efficient knowledge acquisition. However, automatic term extraction itself is not sufficient when it comes to structuring newly acquired knowledge. Namely, the extracted terms need to be associated with other extracted terms and the terms already stored in the existing knowledge-bases. The process of linking semantically similar terms together, called term clustering, irrefutably has a positive impact on improving information extraction, information retrieval, knowledge acquisition, and document categorisation..

In this paper, we present term clustering based on the automatic discovery of term similarities [6]. The similarity measure is corpus-dependent as we base similarities on the automatic extraction of lexical and syntactic patterns in which terms appear. This measure is fed into a clustering algorithm to link similar terms.

The paper is organised as follows. Section 2 gives an overview of the term similarity measure. The clustering approach is presented in Section 3, and the results of the experiments are presented in Section 4.

2 Term Similarity Measure

We introduce a hybrid similarity measure that combines three types of similarities: contextual, functional and lexical. In this section we provide a brief overview of the three measures.

P. Sojka, I. Kopeček, and K. Pala (Eds.): TSD 2002, LNAI 2448, pp. 151–154, 2002.

Our approach to *contextual similarity* is based on automatic pattern mining, which involves the identification of the most relevant lexico-syntactic patterns that describe contexts around the terms. *Context pattern* (CP) is a lexicalised regular expression that corresponds to left/right context of a term. Its basic constituents are the syntactical categories of the words that constitute a term context. However, other grammatical and lexical information (e.g. the lemmatised form of a simple/compound word) can also be used to additionally instantiate the CP constituents. Some of the CP constituents may be discarded if deemed impertinent to discriminate terms. In our experiments, we instantiated terms and verbs and removed adverbs and linking words from the CPs.

The relevance of an individual CP is determined according to a measure called CP-value. *CP-value* ranks CPs conforming to the following criteria: the frequency with which a CP occurs in a given corpus ($f(p)$), its length as the number of constituents ($|p|$), and the frequency with which it occurs as a part of other CPs ($|T_p|$, where T_p is a set of all CPs that contain p):

$$CP(p) = \begin{cases} \ln|p| \cdot f(p) & \text{, if } p \text{ is not nested} \\ \ln|p| \cdot \left(f(p) - \frac{1}{|T_p|} \sum_{b \in T_p} f(b) \right) & \text{, otherwise} \end{cases}$$

The higher the CP-value of a CP, the more relevant the CP is. Note that the relevant CPs are automatically identified. However, they are domain-specific as they rely solely on the information found in a domain specific corpus.

Contextual similarity between terms is measured by comparing the sets of CPs associated with them. Namely, if C_1 and C_2 are two sets of CPs associated with terms t_1 and t_2 respectively, then the contextual similarity between t_1 and t_2 is defined as follows:

$$CS(t_1, t_2) = \frac{2|C_1 \cap C_2|}{2|C_1 \cap C_2| + |C_1 \backslash C_2| + |C_2 \backslash C_1|}$$

In order to measure *functional similarity* between terms, we used several lexical patterns that indicate a high degree of correlation between terms. In each of these patterns terms are used concurrently within the same context. Some of these patterns have been previously used to discover hyponym relations between terms [3], and some describe coordination of terms. We base our approach on a hypothesis that the concurrent usage of terms within the same context indicates that the terms involved are highly correlated. Functional similarity between two terms equals 1 if the two terms appear concurrently in any one of the predefined lexical patterns, and 0 otherwise.

Lexical similarity between terms is based on the similarity between the words of which the terms consist. If two terms share the same head, it is likely that they share the same concept as an (in)direct hypernym (e.g. `progesterone receptor` and `estrogen receptor` are both receptors), and, therefore, can be regarded as being similar. Furthermore, if one of such terms has additional modifiers, then this may indicate concept specialisation (e.g. `orphan nuclear receptor` is a `nuclear receptor`), and again we use this fact to treat such terms as similar. Bearing this in mind, we base the definition of lexical similarity on sharing a head and/or modifier(s). Formally, if t_1 and t_2 are terms, H_1 and H_2 their heads, and M_1 and M_2 the sets of the stems of their modifiers, then the lexical similarity between t_1 and t_2 is calculated as follows:

$$LS(t_1, t_2) = \frac{1}{a+b} \left(a \cdot |H_1 \cap H_2| + b \cdot \frac{2|M_1 \cap M_2|}{2|M_1 \cap M_2| + |M_1 \backslash M_2| + |M_2 \backslash M_1|} \right)$$

where a and b are weights such that $a > b$, since we give higher priority to shared heads over shared modifiers.

Finally, the hybrid term similarity measure is defined as a linear combination of the three similarity measures described above:

$$S_{\alpha\beta\gamma}(t_1, t_2) = \alpha \cdot CS(t_1, t_2) + \beta \cdot FS(t_1, t_2) + \gamma \cdot LS(t_1, t_2) \tag{1}$$

The choice of the weights α, β and γ in formula (1) is not a trivial problem. Therefore, we applied a genetic algorithm approach in order to learn the weights automatically [6]. The resulting weights were $\alpha = 0.13$, $\beta = 0.06$, and $\gamma = 0.81$. The experiments described in Section 4 are based on these values.

3   Term Clustering

Term similarities, based on the hybrid measure, are used as a basis for establishing coherent term clusters, which link semantically similar terms together. Term similarities are fed into a similarity matrix. Each row in the matrix represents a similarity vector corresponding to a specific term. The distances between such vectors are used to establish clusters. We have used hierarchical clustering based on two different clustering methods: the nearest neighbour (NN) and the Ward's method.

The distance between two clusters in the NN method [1] is determined as the minimal distance between the members of the two respective clusters. The algorithm starts with a set of clusters each containing a single term. In each step, two clusters with the minimal distance are merged. On the other hand, the Ward's method [1] aims at minimising the increase in the sum of the distances between the members of a potential cluster. In other words, the method minimises the variance within a cluster. These two methods are opposed to each other in the sense that the NN method (also known as the single linkage method) tends to produce long chain-like clusters, since the clusters are 'chained' via their nearest members, while the Ward's method favours spherical clusters. In both cases, the resulting hierarchy (dendrogram) is subsequently decomposed into a set of clusters by cutting off the hierarchy at the certain depth and collecting the leaves corresponding to a sub-tree being cut off.

4   Experiments and Evaluation

Clustering techniques have been incorporated into the ATRACT workbench [5] and tested in the domain of molecular biology. The testing corpus contained 2082 abstracts retrieved from the MEDLINE database [4]. Clustering has been applied to a set of 174 top-ranked terms automatically extracted from the corpus using the C/NC-value method [2]. The resulting clusters have been evaluated by a domain expert, and the results, after discarding the singleton clusters, are given in Table 1. Although the distribution of clusters differed significantly for the two clustering methods, the overall precision did not significantly vary. However, the higher number of small clusters produced by the Ward's method is preferred, as the clusters are more coherent.

Table 1. Clustering results.

Cardinality of a cluster	Nearest neighbour			Ward's method		
	# of clusters	# of correct		# of clusters	# of correct	
		clusters	terms		clusters	terms
2	16	7 (44 %)	14	33	22 (67 %)	44
3	7	6 (86 %)	18	19	10 (53 %)	30
4	4	2 (50 %)	8	5	3 (60 %)	12
≥ 5	10	7 (70 %)	47	2	1 (50 %)	8
Total:	37	22 (59 %)	87 (63 %)	59	36 (61 %)	114 (71 %)

5   Conclusion

We have presented the results on term clustering using a hybrid term similarity measure. The measure is based on lexical and syntactical patterns automatically extracted from a corpus. The method achieves around 70 % precision in clustering semantically similar terms. It also proved to be consistent as similar terms shared most of their "friends" [6]. Since the initial results are promising, we plan to improve the results by further investigation into the clustering methods, the hybrid similarity measure and the size of corpus, since the measure is corpus-dependant.

References

1. Fasulo, D.: Analysis on Recent Work on Clustering Algorithms. Technical Report 01-03-02, University of Washington, Seattle (1999), p. 24.
2. Frantzi, K., Ananiadou, S., Mima, H.: Automatic Recognition of Multi-Word Terms. Int. J. on Digital Libraries 3/2 (2000), pp. 117–132.
3. Hearst, M.: Automatic Acquisition of Hyponyms From Large Text Corpora. Proc. of COLING 1992, Nantes, France (1992).
4. MEDLINE: National Library of Medicine. http://www.ncbi.nlm.nih.gov/PubMed/, (2002).
5. Mima, H., Ananiadou, S., Nenadić, G.: ATRACT Workbench: An Automatic Term Recognition and Clustering of Terms. In: Matoušek, V. et al. (Eds.): Text, Speech and Dialogue – TSD 2001. LNAI 2166. Springer Verlag (2001), pp. 126–133.
6. Spasić, I., Nenadić, G., Manios, K., Ananiadou, S.: Supervised Learning of Term Similarities. Proc. of IDEAL 2002, Manchester, UK (2002).

Word Sense Discrimination for Czech

Robert Král

Faculty of Informatics, Masaryk University, Brno
Botanická 68a, 602 00 Brno, Czech Republic
E-mail: rkral@fi.muni.cz

Abstract. This paper deals with the automatic discrimination of contexts of Czech ambiguous words. The Schütze's methodology was used, modified and transformed for the Czech language. This algorithm is based on vector space and clustering. The semantic discrimination could be understood as a subtask of word sense disambiguation. In this approach, the sense of word is defined as the cluster of contexts of ambiguous word. We show that Schütze's method is transportable into Czech. Our results are not as good as his because we have experimented with a highly ambiguous word.

1 Introduction

The problem of word sense disambiguation is defined usually as *the association of a given word in a text or discourse with a definition or meaning (sense) which is distinguishable from other meanings potentially attributable to that word* [3]. The solution consists of two steps: the summarizing of word senses and associating the correct meaning with the word occurrence. The area of wsd problem particularly covers the task of machine learning, information retrieval and text processing as well as others.

In this area many approaches have recently appeared: some of them are based on thesaurus (Wilks and Stevenson [9]), other take advantage of WordNet (Sussna [7]) or bilingual corpora (Brown [1]).

The sense definition and representation is one of the biggest problems in wsd. Schütze [6] proposed an approach which evades this question because he just diversifies and unites the contexts of a given word according to whether they are semantically similar or not. For this purpose he speaks about the context group discrimination based on clustering. The semantically similar contexts share a common cluster. Even if the contexts are not labelled by senses this labelling can be done if a correspondence between the senses and clusters exists. The sense discrimination is a subtask of the word sense disambiguation.

In this paper we would like to present an approach which is based on Schütze's research. His method has been simplified and applied to the Czech language.

In addition, we think that this approach could be applied not only to the word sense disambiguation but it could also be used for gaining comment examples for Czech WordNet synsets.

P. Sojka, I. Kopeček, and K. Pala (Eds.): TSD 2002, LNAI 2448, pp. 155–158, 2002.

2   Algorithm

Our task is to classify the contexts of an ambiguous word according to their semantic similarity. In the following text we shall cling to Schütze's terminology.

The algorithm begins with creating a vector space in which each context is represented by a vector. Then, all the context vectors are being grouped in a few clusters. Finally, each cluster represents one sense of a given ambiguous word.

The algorithm proceeds as follows:

1. A bigram matrix is constructed.
2. For each context its context vector is calculated.
3. The context vectors are grouped into clusters.

The *bigram matrix* is constructed so that in the left margin there are words called features and in the top margin there are words called dimensions. The number in each cell of the matrix expresses the number of times for which both words share the same context. The exploitation of bigram matrix overcomes the data sparseness problem since each word in the context is represented by a vector of few dimensions. As the features and dimensions we usually take lemmata of the most frequent and senseful nouns, adjectives and verbs in given contexts. Usually, the number of features is much higher than the number of dimensions.

Then, contexts are lemmatized by a morphological analyzer ajka [5]. At first, we compute a *word vector* for each word occuring in the given context. The word vector is obtained so that we consider all possible lemmata for the given word, select the corresponding rows in the bigram matrix and from the selected rows we compute an average value for each column. This way, we arrive at n-ary word vector (where n is the number of dimensions) for each occuring word. Finally, we get the resulting *context vector* by averaging all the word vectors.

Bigrams:	Atmosféra Atmosphere	Havárie Crash
rána/bang	0	4
ráno/morning	6	0
ozvat/resound	1	5
očekávat/expect	2	2

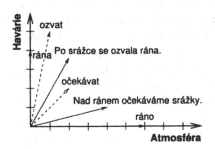

Fig. 1. Illustration example for two-dimensional vector space.

For example, let's assume an ambiguous word *srážka* and the bigram matrix shown in Figure 1. Then, for the sentence *Nad ránem očekáváme srážky/We expect some rainfalls before the morning*, which contains lemmata *ráno/morning*, *očekávat/expect*, we get the context vector $(4, 1)$ from the word vectors $(6, 0)$ for *ránem* and $(2, 2)$ for *očekáváme*. For the sentence *Po srážce se ozvala rána/A bang resounded after the crash*, which contains lemmata *ozvat/resound*, *ráno/mor-ning*, *rána/bang*, we get the context vector $(2, 3.5)$ from the word vectors $(1, 5)$ for *ozvala* and $(3, 2)$ for *rána (rána, ráno)*. Thus, the sentence is semantically close to the dimension *Havárie/Crash*.

The *clustering* of the context vectors into groups is the last stage of the algorithm. We chose the non-hierarchical clustering algorithm which is called k-means. In the beginning, k centroids in the vector space are selected. Then, each object (context vector) is assigned to the closest centroid. The clusters are created by vectors assigned to the same centroid. After that, the new centroids are calculated as a means of the cluster's members. This computation is repeated till the clusters are stabilized. The distance is measured by the angle between two vectors and describes the similarity of contexts.

The peculiarity of these clustering techniques is the initialization of centroids. They are usually selected at random. However, we could influence the cluster results with an appropriate initialization. In the task of gaining semantically similar contexts we could select centers so that they would correspond to the sense definition in a dictionary.

3   Experiment

We have tested the previous algorithm using the Czech National Corpus [2], or, to be more precise, using the two thousands contexts of the ambiguous word *srážka*. The contexts had the length of 20 positions or shorter if they overlapped the document border.

The bigram matrix had the dimensions of 300 rows (features) by 40 columns (dimensions). We decided to find four clusters ($k = 4$) because the word *srážka* has four basic meanings. The senses of the word *srážka* are *clash, discount, precipitation* and *collision* or *crash*. The centroids were initialized manually so that they corresponded to sense division. The settings could be done automatically from an electronic dictionary such as SSJČ [10] or EuroWordNet [8].

Table 1. The founded centroids in selected dimensions for *srážka*.

Cluster:	ozbrojený armed	daň tax	mzda wage	teplota temperature	oblačnost cloudiness	zahynout deaden	voják soldier	vlak train
1	0.07	0.01	0.01	0.01	0.00	0.02	0.04	0.01
2	0.01	0.16	0.20	0.01	0.00	0.01	0.01	0.00
3	0.02	0.01	0.01	0.12	0.08	0.01	0.01	0.00
4	0.03	0.01	0.01	0.01	0.00	0.08	0.02	0.04

The algorithm divided two thousand contexts into four groups. These contained 959, 288, 342 and 284 contexts. 127 contexts were not clustered because there was not enough context information within. The precision rate was that of 74 % and was measured for 200 contexts. Schütze claims the precision rate between 76 % and 83 % for a natural ambiguous word. But there is a distinction in the comparison because we have tried to disambiguate the highly ambiguous word.

4 Conclusions and Future Work

In this paper we have presented an approach that is based on the Schütze's research which uses the vector space and the clustering. We enrich his approach with the solution to more lemma variants in the context. By using the k-means clustering algorithm we attempt to show that there are many ways of initializing cluster centers. Considering that variability of algorithm, it is possible to change the number of senses and their definitions according to individuals neccesities. On the other hand, some simplification of the algorithm was done – we did not use the singular value decomposition and χ^2 test.

We have conducted small experiments with a highly ambiguous word. The advantage of gaining senses automatically was confirmed and it turned out to be neccessary to assess the words according to their discriminating potential (the log document frequency known from an information retrieval).

In the future work we would like to focus on enlarging the bigram matrix and testing the algorithm using more Czech lemmata. We hope it will be possible to incorporate this algorithm into the sophisticated WSD system used for the sense tagging of nouns in the corpus.

References

1. Brown, P. F. et al.: Word Sense Disambiguation using statistical methods, In Proc. of the 29th Annual Meeting, Berkeley, pp. 264–270, 1991.
2. Čermák F.: Czech National Corpus: Its Character, Goal and Background, In: Proc. of Workshop on TSD 1999, Springer, Pilsen, 1999.
3. Ide, N., Véronis, J.: Introduction to the Special Issue on Word Sense Disambiguation: The State of the Art, Computational Linguistics, Vol. 24, Num. 1, 1998.
4. Manning Ch.D., Schütze H.: Foundations of Statistical Natural Language Processing, The MIT Press, Cambridge, Massachusetts, 1999.
5. Sedláček R., Smrž P.: A New Czech Morphological Analyser ajka, In: Proceedings of the 4th Workshop on Text, Speech and Dialogue – TSD 2001, Berlin, 2001.
6. Schütze H.: Automatic Word Sense Discrimination, [3], p. 97–123.
7. Sussna M.: Word Sense Disambiguation for Free-text Indexing Using a Massive Semantic Network, Proc. of the 2nd International Conference on Information and Knowledge Management, Arlington, 1993.
8. Vossen, P., et al.: Set of Common Base Concepts in EuroWordNet-2, Final Report, 2D001, Amsterdam, October 1988.
9. Wilks Y., Stevenson M.: Sense Tagging: Semantic Tagging with a Lexicon, Proceedings of the SIGLEX Workshop on Tagging Text with Lexical Semantics: Why, What and How?, Washington, D.C., 1997.
10. Slovník spisovného jazyka českého (Dictionary of literary Czech), Academia, Praha, 1960, electronic version, Praha, Brno, 2000.

Tools for Semi-automatic Assignment of Czech Nouns to Declination Patterns

Dita Bartůšková and Radek Sedláček

Faculty of Informatics, Masaryk University Brno
Botanická 68a, 602 00 Brno, Czech Republic
E-mail: ydita@aurora.fi.muni.cz, rsedlac@fi.muni.cz

Abstract. In this paper, we present tools for semi-automatic assignment of Czech nouns to declination patterns. First, we explain the reasons for development of such tools and then we describe the structure of the system in detail. It is based on a decision tree that consists of questions and answers allowing to distinguish particular declination patterns. Finally, we provide basic statistic data that clarify the relation between the patterns we developed and the classical ones.

1 Introduction

One of the most time and money consuming phases in the process of the software development is its maintenance [10]. This holds true also in the case of programs occurring in the field of natural language processing. Moreover, in the systems that are based on various dictionaries or databases, there is one more complication, i.e. the maintenance of the stored data. Typical example of such a specialised database is a dictionary used by a morphological analyser (e.g. [1,6,8,9]). Dynamic actualisation (and the extension in particular) of the dictionary is important for increasing the number of successfully recognised word forms by the analyser in real texts. Furthermore, the correctness of this action (the assignment of new words to corresponding declination patterns) is crucial for further error-free processing. Due to this, the reason for automatising this process as much as possible is well-founded.

2 Structure of the System

The system we developed is based on interaction with an experienced user (usually an expert or a linguist) and the whole process of adding new words to particular declination patterns is a written answer-question dialogue. The hierarchical system of patterns based on distinctive features allows such an order of questions that leads to the precisely determined pattern. The aim of the system is to minimise the number of interactions, i.e. to minimise the number of questions that cannot be answered automatically by the system (e.g. on the base of the formal form of the new word), but they have to be answered by an expert.

We have implemented two program tools: a tool for user-friendly editing of the decision trees and an interpreter which can parse the trees and interacts with the user via answer-question dialogue. Indexing techniques and data structures [3,4] used in the implementation allow an efficient storage and retrieval of the data.

P. Sojka, I. Kopeček, and K. Pala (Eds.): TSD 2002, LNAI 2448, pp. 159–162, 2002.

2.1 Decision Tree

The basic part of the system is the pattern hierarchy, strictly speaking the structured set of questions reflecting the distinctive features of the particular patterns. We have elaborated the hierarchical system of declination patterns for Czech nouns, nevertheless the data structures and the formalism used for encoding questions and answers are applicable for other parts of speech as well.

To be precise, the hierarchy of questions is represented by a special form of an n-ary decision tree [2]. In the internal nodes, there are `answer-question` pairs where `answer` corresponds to the `question` stored in the predecessor. It is clear that in the root of the tree there is no answer and in the leaves there is no question. In the leaves, there are names of appropriate declination patterns instead of questions. We use the "?" character to distinguish questions from pattern names in the leaves. The following Figure 1 shows an example of a decision tree.

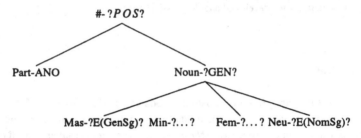

Fig. 1. Decision tree.

2.2 Interpreter

The interpreter parses a decision tree from its root. It asks the first question and waits for the answer (if it is not able to answer it itself). Once it gets the answer, it goes on to the successor in the tree dependent on the answered value. Then it asks the next question or determines the name of the pattern (if it is in the leaf).

Questions and answers are for the purpose of automatic processing encoded into a compact form, but it is still the possible to translate them into the user's natural language (e.g. "?E(GenSg)?" can stand for *What is the ending in genitive singular?* in the above Figure 1). Answers can be then viewed as values from a pre-defined domain. In fact, every question has its domain of possible answers and the user chooses the right one.

3 Declination Patterns

While creating the decision tree for declination patterns of Czech nouns, we bear in mind the following general principles:

1. Exceptions (or language phenomena) are dealt with as soon as possible, i.e. we try to eliminate them just at the beginning of the decision process. In most cases, exceptions are indicated automatically (e.g. foreign names, words with Latin endings etc.).
2. We try to keep the relation between the patterns we developed and the classical ones [5], however, there are some patterns in the system that fluctuate between two classical patterns.
3. Patterns that contain a certain type of vocalic alternations dependent on the type of the sounds of speech (e.g. consonant/vocal, hard/soft), are situated on the same level.
4. Answers that have to be answered by the user are dealt with in the later phases of the decision process; we use automatically answerable questions first.

For example, Figure 2 shows which word forms (in which cases) are distinctive of masculines inanimate with the appropriate ending in genitive singular.

```
-u      --> NomSg --> LocPl --> LocSg
                   --> LocSg --> LocPl
-u|a --> NomSg --> LocSg --> LocPl
                   --> LocPl
-a      --> NomSg
        --> LocSg --> LocPl
-e      --> NomSg --> LocPl
        --> LocSg --> LocPl
        --> NomSg
-\v{e}       --> NomSg
-e|u --> LocSg --> NomSg
-a|e --> LocSg
```

Fig. 2. Distinctive features of masculines inanimate.

We can see that the four questions are enough to determine the corresponding pattern. The relation to the classical patterns (cf. [7]), the number of exceptions and the maximum number of levels in the respective decision tree for all Czech nouns is provided in Table 1.

4 Conclusion

We have presented a tool that is used for semi-automatic assignment of new words to their respective declination patterns. The core of the presented system consists in a decision tree which encodes the distinctive features of particular patterns. At present, we have worked out a tree for Czech nouns, but our aim is to apply the same principle to other inflectional parts of speech, particularly to adjectives and verbs.

References

1. Jan Hajič. *Disambiguation of Rich Inflection (Computational Morphology of Czech).* Karolinum Press, Praha, 1st edition, 2001.

Table 1. Relation to classical patterns.

Masc. an.	#patt.	Masc. in.	#patt.	Femin.	#patt.	Neut.	#patt.
pán	44+28	hrad	49+14	žena	82+17	město	41+19
muž	22+2	les	15+1	růže	18+3	moře	5
předseda	15+3	stroj	17	píseň	9	kuře	7
soudce	2	hrad/les	14+1	kost	15	stavení	2
pán/muž	4	les/stroj	2	žena/růže	6+1	město/moře	3+1
		stroj/hrad	6	píseň/kost	18		
exceptions	6		3		2		8+3
ind./adj./pl.t.	2+8+5		2+1+28		1+4+29		7+4+11
total	141		153		205		111
levels	5		4		5		6

2. Peter Jackson. *Introduction to Expert Systems*. Addison Wesley Longman, Harlow, England, 3rd edition, 1999.
3. Donald E. Knuth. *The Art of Computer Programming: Fundamental Algorithms*, volume 1. Addison Wesley, 2nd edition, 1973.
4. Donald E. Knuth. *The Art of Computer Programming: Sorting and Searching*, volume 3. Addison Wesley, 2nd edition, 1973.
5. Miroslav Komárek. *Mluvnice češtiny II (Grammar of Czech)*. Academia, Praha, 1986. In Czech.
6. Wolfgang Lezius, Reinhard Rapp, and Manfred Wettler. A Freely Available Morphological Analyzer, Disambiguator and Context Sensitive Lemmatizer for German. In *Proceedings of the COLING-ACL*, 1998.
7. Klára Osolsobě. *Algorithmic Description of Czech Formal Morphology and Czech Machine Dictionary*. Ph.D. thesis, Faculty of Arts, Masaryk University Brno, 1996. In Czech.
8. Serdar Murat Oztaner. A Word Grammar of Turkish with Morphophonemic Rules. Master's thesis, Middle East Technical University, 1996.
9. Radek Sedláček and Pavel Smrž. A New Czech Morphological Analyser ajka. In: *Proceedings of TSD 2001*, pages 100–107, Berlin, 2001. Springer-Verlag.
10. Ian Sommerville. *Software Engineering*. Addison Wesley, Wokingham, 5th edition, 1996.

Part II

Speech

"**Speech**: the expression of or the ability to express thoughts and feelings by articulate sounds: *he was born deaf and without the power of speech*."
NODE (New, Oxford Dictionary of English), Oxford, OUP, 1998, page 1788, meaning 1.

Automatic Lexical Stress Assignment of Unknown Words for Highly Inflected Slovenian Language

Tomaž Šef, Maja Škrjanc, and Matjaž Gams

Institute Jožef Stefan, Department of Intelligent Systems,
Jamova 39, SI-1000 Ljubljana, Slovenia
E-mail: Tomaz.Sef@ijs.si, Maja.Skrjanc@ijs.si, Matjaz.Gams@ijs.si
WWW: http://ai.ijs.si

Abstract. This paper presents a two level lexical stress assignment model for out of vocabulary Slovenian words used in our text-to-speech system. First, each vowel (and consonant 'r') is determined, whether it is stressed or unstressed, and a type of lexical stress is assigned for every stressed vowel (and consonant 'r'). We applied a machine-learning technique (decision trees or boosted decision trees). Then, some corrections are made on the word level, according the number of stressed vowels and the length of the word. For data sets we used the MULTEXT-East Slovene Lexicon, which was supplemented with lexical stress marks. The accuracy achieved by decision trees significantly outperforms all previous results. However, the sizes of the trees indicate that the accentuation in the Slovenian language is a very complex problem and a simple solution in the form of relatively simple rules is not possible.

1 Introduction

Grapheme-to-phoneme conversion is an essential task in any text-to-speech system. It can be described as a function mapping the spelling form of words to a string of phonetic symbols representing the pronunciation of the word. A major interest of building rule based grapheme-to-phoneme transcription systems is to treat out of vocabulary words. Another applicability of storing rules is to reduce the memory amount required by the lexicon, which is of interest for hand-held devices such as palmtops, mobile phones, talking dictionaries, etc.

A lot of work has been done on data-oriented grapheme-to-phoneme conversion that was applied to English, and few other languages where extensive training databases exist [1]. Standard learning paradigms include error back-propagation in multilayered perceptron [2] and decision-tree learning [3,4]. Several studies have been published that demonstrates that memory-based learning approaches yield superior accuracy to both back-propagation and decision-tree learning [5].

Highly inflected languages are usually lacking for large databases that give the correspondence between the spelling and the pronunciation of all word-forms. For example, the authors [6] know of no database that gives orthography/phonology mappings for Russian inflected words. The pronunciation dictionaries almost exclusively list base forms. That is probably the main reason why data-oriented methods were not so popular and that only a few experiments were done for this group of languages. Another reason is that we usually need more than just the letter (vowel) within its local context to classify it, therefore all classical models fail on that problem.

P. Sojka, I. Kopeček, and K. Pala (Eds.): TSD 2002, LNAI 2448, pp. 165–172, 2002.

2 Motivation

It is well known that the correspondence between spelling and pronunciation can be rather complicated. Usually it involves stress assignment and letter-to-phone transcription. In Slovenian language, in contrast to some other languages, it is straightforward to convert the word into its phonetic representation, once the stress type and location are known. It can be done on the basis of less than 100 context-dependent letter-to-sound rules (composed by well-versed linguists) with the accuracy of over 99 %. A crucial problem is the determination of the lexical stress type and position. As lexical stress in the Slovenian language can be located almost arbitrarily on any syllable in the word, it is often assumed to be "unpredictable".

The vast majority of the work on Slovenian lexical analysis went into constructing the morphological analyser [7]. Since the Slovenian orthography is largely based on phonemic principle, the authors of dictionaries do not consider it necessary to give the complete transcriptions of lexical entries. In the only electronic version of Slovenian dictionary, a lexical entry is represented by the basic word-form with a mark for the lexical stress and tonemic accent, information regarding accentual inflectional type of the word, morphological information, eventual lists of exceptions and transcriptions of some parts of words. It is assumed that together with the very complex and extensive accentual schemes (presented as a free-form verbal descriptions that require formalization suitable for machine implementation), all the necessary information to predict the pronunciation of the basic word forms, their inflected forms and derivatives is given. The implemented algorithm has around 50,000 lines of a program code and together with the described dictionary allows correct accentuation of almost 300,000 lemmas. This represents several millions of different word forms. A morphological analyser, however, does not solve the problem of homographs with different stress placement and this problem requires stepping outside of the bounds of a separate word.

No dictionary can solve the "stress" problem for rare or newly created words. There exist some rules for Slovenian language, but the precision of those is not sufficient for good text-to-speech synthesis. Humans can (often) pronounce words reasonably even when they have never seen them before. It is that ability we wished to capture automatically in order to achieve better results. Therefore we introduce a two level model that applies the machine-learning methods for lexical stress prediction.

3 Methodology

We use a two level lexical stress assignment model for out of vocabulary Slovenian words. In the first level we applied the machine-learning model (Decision Trees (DT) or boosted DT) to predict the lexical stress on each vowel (and consonant 'r'). In the second level the lexical stress of the whole word is predicted according the number of stressed vowels and the length of the word. If the model (of the first level) predicts more than one stressed vowel, one of them is randomly chosen. If the prediction of the lexical stress of a whole word is false, then typically two incorrect lexical stresses had been made: one on the right syllable (which is not stressed) and the other on the syllable incorrectly predicted to be stressed.

For the first step we generated a domain, were examples were vowels and consonant 'r'. For each vowel (and consonant 'r') we trained a separate model (DT and boosted DT) on learning set and evaluate on the corresponding test set. The error was then calculated for the level of syllable and word.

Our goals were as follows: (1) to predict the lexical stress and (2) to see whether there exist some relatively simple rules for stress assignment. In our experiments we were focusing on accuracy of the models as well as on interpretability. Due to the measure of interpretability, the choice for DT method seems natural, since the tree models could be easily translated into rules.

4   Data

4.1   Data Acquisition and Preprocessing

The pronunciation dictionaries almost exclusively list base word forms. Therefore a new Slovenian machine-readable pronunciation dictionary was build. It provides phonetic transcriptions of approximately 600,000 isolated word-forms that correspond to 20,000 lemmas. It was build on the basis of the MULTEXT-East Slovene Lexicon [8]. This lexicon was supplemented with lexical stress marks. Complete phonetic transcriptions of rare words, that failed to get analysed by letter-to-sound rules, were also added. The majority of the work has been done automatically with morphological analyser [7]. The error was 0.2 percent. In slightly less than percent additional examination was recommended. Finally, the whole lexicon was reviewed by the expert.

For domain attributes we used 192,132 words. Multiplied instances of the same word-form with the same pronunciation, but with different morphological tags were removed. As the result we got 700,340 syllables (vowels). The corpus was divided in to training and test corpora. The training corpora include 140,821 words (513,309 vowels) and the test corpora include 51,311 words (51,311 vowels). The words (basic word forms, their inflected forms and derivatives) in the test corpora belong to different lemmas than the words in the training corpora. The entries in training and test corpora are thus not too similar. As unknown words are often the derivatives of the existing words in the pronunciation dictionary, the results obtained on the real data (unknown words in the text that is synthesized) would be probably even better than those presented in this paper. Another reason for that is the fact that unknown words are typically not the most common words and in general unknown words will have more standard pronunciations rather than idiosyncratic ones.

4.2   Data Description

The training and test corpora were divided by each vowel and consonant 'r'. Thus we got six separated learning problem. The number of examples in each set is shown in Table 1. The class distributions are almost the same in learning and test sets, except for letter 'r', where is a small variance.

Each example is described by 66 attributes including class, which represents type of lexical stress. Its values are 'Unstressed', 'Stressed-Wide', 'Stressed-Narrow', 'Un-stressed-Reduced_Vowel', and 'Stressed-Reduced_Vowel'. The factors that corresponds to remaining 65 attributes, are:

- the number of syllables within a word (1 attribute),

Table 1. Number of examples in learning and test sets.

	A	E	I	O	U	R
Learning examples	142041	119227	116486	100295	28104	7156
Test examples	50505	47169	41156	35513	9870	2818

- the position of the observed vowel (syllable) within a word (1 attribute),
- the presence of prefixes and suffixes in a word and the class they belong to (4 attributes),
- the type of wordforming affix (ending) (1 attribute), and
- the context of the observed vowel (grapheme type and grapheme name for three characters left and right from the vowel, two vowels left and right from the observed vowel) (58 attributes).

Self-organizing methods for word pronunciation start with the assumption that the information necessary to pronounce a word can be found entirely in the string of letters, composing the word. In Slovenian language placement of lexical stress also depends upon morphological category of the word. It is believed that the string of letters cannot be sufficient to predict placement of the stress. So, to pronounce words correctly we would need the access to the morphological class of a given word. A part of speech information is available in our TTS system with a standard PoS tagger even for unknown words but it is not too much reliable for the time being due to the lack of morphologically annotated corpuses (only around 100.000 words). Another reason that we did not include that information into our model (although that would be easy to implement) was a requirement to reduce the size of the lexicon for usage in the hand-held devices. Besides, some morphological information is included in the word-forming affix (ending) of the word and in present prefix and/or suffix of the word.

We achieved better results and more compact models if we represent the context of the observed vowel with the letter type (whether the letter is a vowel or consonant, a type of consonant, etc.) rather then letter itself. The letter itself is indicated in one of the attributes that describe separate letter types (for example, the attribute for a letter type 'vowel' can contain following values: 'a', 'e', 'i', 'o', 'u', '-' (not a vowel)). An example is presented in Figure 1.

5   Experiments

On the six domains, which correspond to five vowel and consonant 'r', we apply DT and boosted DT, as implemented in See5 system [10,11]. The evaluation was made on separated test sets.

The pruning parameter was minimum examples in leaves. We compare DT classifier with the boosted DT classifier for each value of pruning parameter, which varied between 2 and 1000 minimum examples in leaves. The results are presented in Table 2, Figure 2 and Figure 3. We can see that the lowest error was achieved by boosting and almost no pruning (minimum 2 examples in leaves).

As can be expected the machine-learning methods outperform the grammatical rules [9] (shown in Table 2). The error on the level of word of almost un-pruned boosted DT is reduced

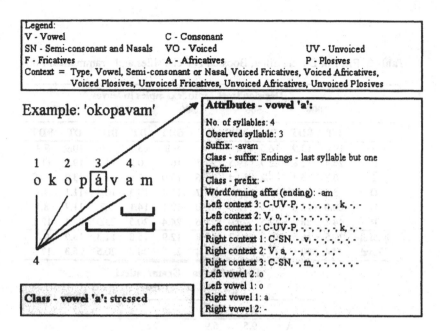

Fig. 1. Attributes for the third vowel ('o') of Slovenian word *"okopavam" (engl. "I earth up")*.

for 31.4 percent. We can also observe that even the error on a level of word on highly pruned trees is lower than error on grammatical rules. If we observe the error for each letter, in case of pruned trees (min. 1000 examples in leaves) the results of DT are slightly better, except for the letter 'r'. But the results of boosted DT, pruned with the same parameter, show noticeable improvement in accuracy (error was reduced for 5.4 to 10.6 percent). When we look at the accuracy for boosted DT with min. 2 examples in leave, the error reduction is 15.1 to 21.7 percent.

Another observation was that the DT error is similar to the error of boosted DT for all vowels. However, this is not the case for letter 'r'. During testing different pruning parameters we noticed an interesting anomaly for letter 'r'. Although the error increasing by pruning, it is slightly jumping up and down. If the pruning parameter was set to 400 min. examples in leaves, the error was lower (20.2 %) then if we varied this value between 300 and 500. This could be due to the fact, that this domain has significantly lower number of cases or that the distribution in testing set is slightly different then the distribution of the learning set. In other domains the error is monotony decreasing.

When we were reducing the pruning parameter we could see the accuracy is increasing, which means that pruning doesn't improve the accuracy. It could be due to many factors, such as anomalies in the data, missing information, provided by attributes, etc. With pruning DT the error increased the most for letter 'r'.

Regarding interpretability of the models, we could point out some of the characteristics of the DT: (1) they are very wide, (2) very deep, (3) the top nodes of the trees stays the same, when the trees are growing. Regarding (1) and (2) we can say, that the DT are very large and

Table 2. Error of DT classifier, Boosted DT classifier and grammatical rules.

| | Decision trees - min. examples in leaves | | | | | | | | | |
| | 1000 | | 500 | | 300 | | 150 | | 40 | |
	DT	BDT	DT	BDT	DT	BDT	DT	BDT	DT	BDT
A	19.6	13.9	16.5	10.6	16	9.8	13.7	8.6	10.9	7.1
E	24.4	21.8	22.9	19.5	22.3	16.8	20.2	14.3	19.1	11.6
I	20.3	16.4	19.2	14.4	17.6	13.0	15.9	11.4	13.9	10.5
O	15.3	13.4	15.4	12.3	13.7	11.4	13.3	10.3	11.1	9.1
U	20.0	12.8	18.3	12.8	18.0	12.1	14.1	9.7	11.7	8.1
R	44.1	28.2	27.5	23.0	28.6	24.4	20.5	23.9	22.1	13.1
Syllable	20.5	16.5	18.7	14.3	17.8	12.9	15.8	11.3	13.9	9.5
Word	37.4	30.1	34.2	26.0	32.4	23.5	28.8	20.5	25.3	17.3

| | Decision trees 2 | | Grammatical rules |
	DT	BDT	
A	9.5	6.9	22.8
E	16.1	11.7	29.4
I	11.3	9.5	22.7
O	10.0	8.4	24.0
U	10.6	7.8	22.9
R	14.2	11.9	33.6
Syllable	11.8	9.1	24.7
Word	21.5	16.5	47.9

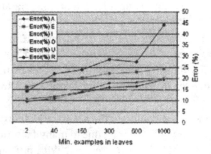 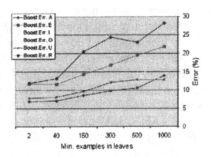

Fig. 2. DT error and Boosted DT error on different pruning parameters.

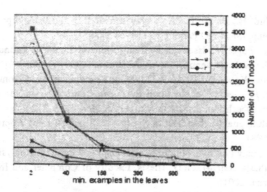

Fig. 3. Sizes of DT from Table 2.

hard to interpret, so with these attributes no simple rules can be extracted. The reason why the DT are so wide is in choice of attributes. Majority of attributes are discrete and have many values. For all vowels the structure of the trees is stable. The top nodes stay the same. The exception is again the letter 'r'.

6 Conclusion

In this paper we apply the machine learning technique – decision trees on data upgraded Slovenian dictionary in order to: (1) improve the accuracy of defining the lexical stress mark and (2) to establish whether exists some relatively simple rules for accentuation. The results show that both machine-learning techniques, DT and boosted DT, reduced error of grammatical rules for 26 to 31 percent on the level of word.

Based on our experiments we can conclude that for our data set pruning did not improve the performance. For all tested letters pruning actually increase the error for a couple of percent. We can notice difference in error behavior on letter 'r', which is slightly jumping up and down. Maybe the most interesting observation is considerable reduction of error in boosted DT. For instance the error on almost un-pruned DT was with boosting reduced for 16 to 27 percent.

Since DT have a large number of nodes and are also very wide, straightforward interpretation was not possible. The pruned trees were substantially smaller, but their error compared to the grammatical rules only slightly better. The size and structure of the trees indicates that simple or relatively simple rules for lexical stress assignment cannot be constructed on this set of attributes.

References

1. Daelemans, W. M. P., van den Bosch A. P. J.: Language-Independent Data-Oriented Grapheme-to-Phoneme Conversion. Progress in Speech Synthesis. Springer (1996) 77–89.
2. Sejnowski T. J., Rosenberg C. S.: Parallel networks that learn to pronounce English text. Complex Systems 1 (1987) 145–168.

3. Dietterich, T. G., Hild, H., Bakiri, G.: A comparison of ID3 and backpropagation for Eng-lish text-to-speech mapping. Machine Learning 19 (1995) 5–28.
4. Black, A., Lenzo K., Pagel V.: Issues in Building General Letter to Sound Rules. 3rd ESCA Workshop on Speech Synthesis, Jenolan Caves, Australia, (1998) 77–80.
5. Busser, B., Daelemans, W., van den Bosch A.: Machine Learning of Word Pronunciation: The Case Against Abstraction. Proceedings of the Sixth European Conference on Speech Communication and Technology (Eurospeech'99), Budapest, Hungary (1999) 2123–2126.
6. Sproat R. (ed.): Multilingual Text-to-Speech Synthesis: The Bell Labs Approach. Kluwer Academic Publishers (1998).
7. Šef, T.: Analiza besedila v postopku sinteze slovenskega govora (Text Analysis for the Slovenian Text-to-Speech Synthesis system). Ph.D. Thesis, Faculty of Computer and Information Science, University of Ljubljana (2001).
8. Erjavec T., Ide N.: The MULTEXT-East Corpus. First International Conference on Language Resources & Evaluation, Granada, Spain, (1998) 28–30.
9. Toporišič J.: Slovenska slovnica (Slovene Grammar), Založba Obzorja, Maribor (1984).
10. Quinlan J.R.: Induction of Decision Tress. Machine Learning 1 (1986) 81–106.
11. See5 system (http://www.rulequest.com/see5-info.html).

German and Czech Speech Synthesis Using HMM-Based Speech Segment Database*

Jindřich Matoušek[1], Daniel Tihelka[1], Josef Psutka[1], and Jana Hesová[2]

[1] University of West Bohemia, Department of Cybernetics,
Univerzitní 8, 306 14 Plzeň, Czech Republic
E-mail: jmatouse@kky.zcu.cz, dtihelka@kky.zcu.cz, psutka@kky.zcu.cz
[2] University of West Bohemia, Department of Applied Linguistics,
Riegrova 11, 306 14 Plzeň, Czech Republic
E-mail: jhesova@kaj.zcu.cz

Abstract. This paper presents an experimental German speech synthesis system. As in case of a Czech text-to-speech system ARTIC, statistical approach (using hidden Markov models) was employed to build a speech segment database. This approach was confirmed to be language independent and it was shown to be capable of designing a quality database that led to an intelligible synthetic speech of a high quality. Some experiments with clustering the similar speech contexts were performed to enhance the quality of the synthetic speech. Our results show the superiority of phoneme-level clustering to subphoneme-level one.

1 Introduction

This paper presents an experimental German speech synthesis system based on an automatically built speech unit database. In our previous work, such a system was successfully designed for the Czech language (see Figure 1) [2,3,4]. The synthetic speech of the Czech synthesizer sounds very intelligibly. This system can employ various concatenation-based speech synthesis techniques such as linear prediction (LP), PSOLA, Harmonic+Noise Model (HNM) or their combinations (e.g. LP-PSOLA). Being a concatenative speech synthesis system, there is a need to employ a speech segment database (SSD) during the synthesis process. This database was built in a fully automatic way using a statistical approach based on modeling and segmentation of speech by Hidden Markov models (HMMs). Our experience in such kind of speech modeling and the language independent nature of the statistical approach let us try to apply the same speech segment database construction method to another language. During centuries our country (and especially its western part) has been influenced by our German spoken neighbors, there are relatively many German loanwords in Czech language, so German was selected for the first experiments with our non-native speech synthesis.

The paper is organized as follows. Section 2 describes the main differences between Czech and German languages in view of speech synthesis. In Section 3 a detailed description

---

* This research was supported by the project no. MSM235200004 of the Ministry of Education of Czech Republic and the firm SpeechTech.

P. Sojka, I. Kopeček, and K. Pala (Eds.): TSD 2002, LNAI 2448, pp. 173–180, 2002.

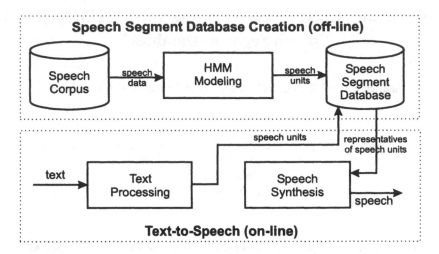

Fig. 1. A simplified scheme of a Czech TTS system which uses an automatically built speech segment database.

of the baseline German text-to-speech (TTS) system is given. Section 4 then presents our experiments with clustering similar speech contexts and shows the success of statistical approach to SSD modeling for the German language. Finally, Section 5 contains the conclusion and outlines our future work.

2   The Main Differences between Czech and German

This section is dedicated to the main differences between Czech and German languages. Since there are so many differences resulting from the diverse nature of these languages (Czech is a Slavic language, German is a Germanic one), we will limit ourselves to the most important ones in view of speech synthesis [10].

One of the most important differences are phonetic features and phonetic transcription of both languages. Phonetic forms of Czech words are very similar to their orthographic forms. This is a feature common to all Slavic languages. Relatively simple phonetic transcription rules can be employed to convert orthographic form (i.e. letters) to phonetic form (i.e. phonemes). On the other hand, the correlation between phonemes and letters is much more complicated in German. The phonetic transcription rules are then more complex and more difficult to describe (e.g. the same phoneme /f/ is pronounced in different letter contexts as in words *Film, Philosophie, vier*).

Due to very different nature of both languages there are many differences in their phonetic inventories, of course. In fact, German phonetic inventory is very large because there are many loanwords in German and the pronunciation of these non-German words introduces new phonemes to the German phonetic inventory. There are also relatively many loanwords in Czech but when pronouncing these non-Czech words foreign phonemes are replaced by "the most similar" Czech ones. German has more vowels (including e.g. schwa) than Czech. Both languages distinguish short and long vowels. However the pronunciation is rather different.

While most of German long vowels are closed and all short vowels open, all Czech vowels are pronounced rather in a neutral way. An example of different vowel systems is that Czech has just two vowels to pronounce the letters "e, é": short /e/ and long /e:/. In German there are five vowels to pronounce sounds similar to these two Czech vowels: /E, 9, e:, E:, 2:/ [5]. As for consonants, there are more consonantal phonemes in Czech language. Virtually, all German consonants except for /C/ and /pf/ are present in Czech language too. Czech consonants are influenced by the characteristic voiced/unvoiced much more than German in which the intensity of consonantal pronunciation has more distinguish feature. There are also aspirated consonants /p, t, k/ in word-initial position in German. On the other hand, no aspiration occurs in Czech. The German phonetic inventory used in our system is described in Section 3.1.

Some differences could be also found in prosodic features of both languages. Since prosody is ignored in the first version of our system, only the most distinct difference concerning stress will be mentioned. Contrast between stressed and unstressed syllables is more emphasized in German. German allows more reductions and elisions in unstressed positions. Stress is always on the first syllable in Czech. On the other hand, in German the stress is variable and is dependent on a word stem.

3   Baseline System

The baseline German speech synthesis system will be described in this section. The way the system was built was almost the same as in the case of a Czech TTS system ARTIC designed in our previous work [2,3,4].

3.1   Phonetic Inventory

When modeling or synthesizing speech the first step usually consists of defining the basic phonetic inventory of a language in focus. All speech units used in synthesis are then derived from this inventory. In our Czech TTS system 45 phonemes and significant allophones (including two kinds of pauses) were used [2]. The German phonetic inventory was defined in the extent of German SAMPA comprising 46 phonemes.

Some simplification was taken into account when defining the inventory. As mentioned in Section 2 there are relatively many loanwords in German. The pronunciation of these foreign words copies the pronunciation in the original language introducing new phonemes into German phonetic inventory (e.g. /æ/ in an English word Cat). If we respected this fact, the phonetic inventory would be augmented to include all phonemes possibly present in German pronunciations. To reduce the inventory size, domestic German phonemes were taken into account only. As in the case of Czech language the foreign phonemes were replaced by phonetically the most immediate German phonemes. From similar reasons nasalized vowels loaned from French (e.g. /õ/ in Fondue) are not supported by our phonetic inventory. Non-syllabic vowels and syllabic consonants are also ignored.

3.2   Speech Corpus

Speech corpus consists of important speech material needed to model speech units and to create speech segment database. In case of our Czech TTS the corpus comprised a large number of sentences described by their orthographic and phonetic forms, speech waveforms, glottal signals and parametric representations [2,3]. Glottal signals were measured by a device called electroglottograph and were used for the detection of the moments of principal excitation of vocal tract (usually the moments of glottal closure – so called pitch-marks) [4]. These pitch-marks are often used in contemporary standard speech synthesis techniques (e.g. PSOLA or some methods of harmonic synthesis). In [4] we experimented with speech corpus construction process and we found that a large number of carefully selected sentences spoken almost in a monotonous way and very precise pitch-mark detection are a need for a high-quality synthetic speech.

The German speech corpus was created under the same circumstances as the Czech one. The only exception was that no sentence selection was performed since limited amount of German text was available. About 6 000 German sentences were available in textual form. Some unsuitable sentences were excluded and all remaining 5 255 sentences were used. The comparison of Czech and German speech corpus is given in Table 1.

3.3 Speech Unit Modeling

The speech corpus is used as a basis for speech unit modeling. German speech units were modeled in the same way as the Czech ones, i.e. HTK system was used to model three-state left-to-right single-density crossword-triphone HMMs [2,3,8]. To make more robust models and to enable modeling triphones not present in the speech corpus, a clustering procedure is employed to tie similar triphones. This is very important for TTS synthesis since clustering ensures that an arbitrary triphone, i.e. arbitrary text, could be synthesized. In the baseline system the clustering was performed on model's state level. The more detailed information about modeling can be found in [2,3].

Table 1. A comparison of Czech and German speech corpora used for SSD construction. Number of clustered states is given for state-level clustering and number of triphones corresponds to model-level clustering.

	Czech	German
Number of sentences	5 000	5 255
Amount of speech data [min]	772	738
Number of phonemes	43	46
Number of clustered states	9 097	6 876
Number of triphones	6 258	4 687

3.4 Speech Segment Database

The resulting triphone HMMs were employed to segment the speech corpus into the basic speech units (in fact Viterbi search was realized to find the boundaries between these speech units in each sentence of the speech corpus). In the baseline system the basic speech unit represents a state of a crossword-triphone state-clustered HMM again. After segmenting there are many representatives (speech segments) of each speech unit in the speech corpus. The most representative segment of each unit is then selected and stored in the speech segment database. The same simple segment selection procedure as for Czech database was implemented [2,3]. These representative segments are used in the synthesis stage.

3.5 Text-to-Speech

In fully automatic TTS process an arbitrary input text is converted to the corresponding output speech. This is the case of the Czech TTS system ARTIC where phonetic transcription rules are applied to the input orthographic text producing a sequence of phonemes. This sequence is then converted to a sequence of speech units (in the baseline system these units are the clustered states) and finally a concatenative speech synthesis technique is employed to join the speech units in the resulting speech [2]. In fact all standard concatenative techniques can be used. A time domain synthesis method is implemented in the baseline system in the time of writing this paper. No text-to-prosody module has been implemented so far, so the synthetic speech exhibits constant prosodic features and sounds in monotone.

Once again, the German text-to-speech process copies the Czech one. However, there is one significant exception. Since the implementation of precise German phonetic rules is very difficult and exceeds our knowledge of German, a phonetic dictionary was created manually. This dictionary includes all words present in the speech corpus now and may be arbitrarily augmented to cover more and more words. The text is then firstly segmented into words, which are then looked up in the dictionary. Simple phonetic rules were also proposed to phonetically transcribe words not found in the dictionary. The form of phonetic rules is the same as for Czech [9]. Here is an example of such a rule for German:

$$i \rightarrow i : /\_ \langle e \rangle \ . \tag{1}$$

This rule is applied e.g. in a word *diese* [di:z@].

4   Clustering Issues

Several experiments were made as an extension of the baseline system. They concerned mainly the fluency and the overall quality of the synthetic speech. Since the number of resulting speech units strongly depends on the clustering procedure (see Section 3.3), the attention was focused on clustering issues. Various clustering thresholds also affect clustering results and they were already analyzed in [3]. In research described in this paper the phoneme/subphoneme level of clustering was examined.

Although the baseline system produces a very intelligible high-quality speech, some audible glitches can degrade the speech. These glitches appear at unit boundaries, especially in long sections of voiced speech. These problems can be possibly minimized by using a parametric domain synthesis technique which enables controlling spectral features of speech, i.e. spectral smoothing especially at unit boundaries. However, time domain has also some advantages like almost no signal processing, i.e minimum degradation of speech. When still staying in the time domain, reducing the number of concatenation points is an alternative solution. The basic speech unit used in the baseline system is so-called clustered state (or feneme [1,2]), which corresponds to a state of a state-clustered triphone HMM. On the signal level feneme represents a small subphoneme unit. It is a flexible unit that can effectively stand for an arbitrary speech context. However, concatenating such small units results in many concatenation points – possible discontinuity problems [7].

In our next research we tried to retain the same speech context quality modeling while reducing the number of concatenation points in synthesis. To do that, clustering was performed on model's level (in contrast to previous state-level modeling). The basic speech unit used was then the whole triphone (a phoneme-sized unit) and the number of concatenation points dramatically decreased to one point per phoneme. The same number of concatenation points is achieved also for diphones which are traditionally used in most of today's synthesis systems. Unlike diphones triphones take into account a context of both preceding and successive phonemes. The principles of these two different speech clustering processes are shown in Figure 2.

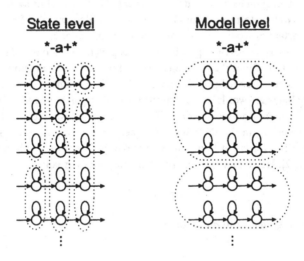

Fig. 2. An illustration of state-level (left) and model-level clustering (right) of all triphones derived from the phoneme /a/. Dotted lines show the examples of the resulting clusters.

Let us to compare both kinds of clustering from the synthesis point of view. As for speech recognition tree-based clustering on the state level was referred to outperform clustering on the model level [6]. As for speech synthesis our expectations came true. Indeed, the synthetic speech of a triphone-based synthesis system sounds more naturally and fluently and with less intrusive elements. It was evaluated to be better than synthetic speech of feneme-based system by the listeners. Spectral discontinuities can be easily identified when using fenemes (see Figure 3 for the differences). Indeed, it seems that triphone-based synthetic speech is superior to feneme-based one. However, some more detailed listening tests should be performed to be sure about it. Maybe some problems with triphone-based synthesis can appear when synthesizing a "very unknown" speech context – a triphone very different from speech data available in training speech corpus. Fenemes may model some rare contexts more precisely.

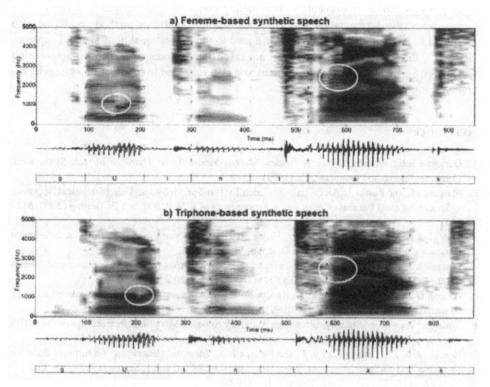

Fig. 3. A comparison of synthetic waveforms and spectrograms of a German sentence "*Guten Tag.*" when using fenemes (a) or triphones (b) as speech units. White ovals show the examples of a within-phoneme formant discontinuity typical for feneme-based synthesis. Dotted lines show phoneme boundaries in the synthetic speech.

5   Conclusion and Future Work

In this paper a new experimental German TTS system was presented. When building the system we took advantage of our experience with the Czech TTS system. The system uses automatically designed SSD. The synthetic speech is of a high quality and sounds very intelligibly. So, HMM-based approach to SSD construction implemented in [1,2,3] was shown to be language independent. Experiments with level of clustering were also performed and clustering on phoneme level was judged to outperform subphoneme-level clustering from the synthesis point of view. Samples of synthetic speech are available on http://artin.zcu.cz/projects/tts.

Since basic German synthesis system has been designed so far, there are many parts which could be improved. There is no doubt synthetic speech could be even better.

Phonetic dictionary should be augmented to cover more words and/or more precise phonetic transcription rules should be defined to describe the pronunciation of words out of dictionary more properly. Some experiments with modeling could be also realized to achieve more precise automatic segmentation and synthesis. Various synthesis methods could be also examined to find out the method that would lead to the highest quality of synthetic speech. Of course, there are two important parts not taken into account so far: text preprocessing and prosody generation. These issues should be also managed to have a TTS system of the highest quality.

References

1. Donovan R.E., Woodland P.C.: A Hidden Markov-Model-Based Trainable Speech Synthesizer. Computer Speech and Language, 13. (1999) 223–241.
2. Matoušek J., and Psutka J.: ARTIC: a New Czech Text-to-Speech System Using Statistical Approach to Speech Segment Database Construction. Proceedings of ICSLP2000, vol. IV. Beijing (2000) 612–615.
3. Matoušek J.: Text-to-Speech Synthesis Using Statistical Approach to Automatic Speech Segment Database Construction (in Czech). Ph.D. thesis, Pilsen (2001).
4. Matoušek J., Psutka J., and Krůta J.: On Building Speech Corpus for Concatenation-Based Speech Synthesis. Proceedings of Eurospeech2001, vol 3. AAlborg (2001) 2047–2050.
5. Gibbon D., Moore R., and Winski T.: Handbook of Standards and Resources for Spoken Language Systems. Mouton de Gruyter. Berlin (1997).
6. Young S.: Tree-Based State Tying for High Accuracy Acoustic Modelling. Proceedings of the ARPA Workshop on Human Language Technology. Plainsboro, New Jersey (1994) 307–312.
7. Hon H., Acero A., Huang X., Liu J., and Plumpe M.: Automatic Generation of Synthesis Units for Trainable Text-to-Speech Systems. Proceedings of ICASSP'98, vol. 1, Seattle (1998) 293–296.
8. Young S. et al.: The HTK Book. Entropic Inc. (1999).
9. Psutka J.: Communication with Computer by Speech (in Czech). Academia, Prague (1995).
10. Duden. Aussprachenwörterbuch (in German). Max Mangold, Duden-Verlag, vol. 6, Mannheim (1990).

Comparison and Combination of Confidence Measures

Georg Stemmer, Stefan Steidl, Elmar Nöth, Heinrich Niemann, and Anton Batliner

Universität Erlangen-Nürnberg, Lehrstuhl für Mustererkennung, Martensstrasse 3,
D-91058 Erlangen, Germany
E-mail: stemmer@informatik.uni-erlangen.de
WWW: http://www5.informatik.uni-erlangen.de

Abstract. A set of features for word-level confidence estimation is developed. The features should be easy to implement and should require no additional knowledge beyond the information which is available from the speech recognizer and the training data. We compare a number of features based on a common scoring method, the normalized cross entropy. We also study different ways to combine the features. An artificial neural network leads to the best performance, and a recognition rate of 76 % is achieved. The approach is extended not only to detect recognition errors but also to distinguish between insertion and substitution errors.

1 Introduction

Current speech recognizers are often extended by an additional module which computes a confidence measure for each recognized word. A confidence measure is an estimator of the correctness of the hypothesized word. If the confidence measure is accurate, it can be applied to various different tasks: For instance, a spoken dialogue system may ask the user for an additional confirmation if the confidence of a relevant word is very low. Other possible applications include unsupervised speaker adaption, where words with low confidence may be discarded for adaption, and the detection of out-of-vocabulary words. Confidence measures may also be used to repair speech recognition errors by an additional module. For certain applications, it may be important to extend the two class problem *correct* vs. *wrong* and to distinguish three different classes: *correct (cor)* *substitution (sub)* and *insertion (ins)*. A spoken dialogue system may simply ignore all inserted words, but ask back if there has been a substitution.

A great amount of different confidence measures can be found in the literature [1]. In the following, we will concentrate on confidence measures providing a word-level annotation, which seems to be most useful for a majority of applications. In order to compute confidence measures for a speech recognizer, a feature vector has to be calculated for each word hypothesis. From the features, the confidence of the word can be estimated by using the score of a suitable classifier. Decision trees and artificial neural networks (ANN) are often applied for this purpose.

The decision for a certain feature set for the confidence measure is often guided by two requirements: firstly, the features should be simple to implement and fast to compute, and secondly, the set should provide as much information about the confidence of a word as

P. Sojka, I. Kopeček, and K. Pala (Eds.): TSD 2002, LNAI 2448, pp. 181–188, 2002.
© Springer-Verlag Berlin Heidelberg 2002

possible. In this paper we compare a number of different features with respect to a common quality measure. We also evaluate the improvements which can be achieved by taking a combination of the features.

2   Quality of a Confidence Measure

For a fair comparison of different features we need to score the quality of the corresponding confidence measure. Several different methods have been described in the literature for this purpose. We decided to use two scoring methods. The first one is the Normalized Cross Entropy (NCE), which has been introduced by NIST. It is defined as the relative decrease in uncertainty brought by the confidence measure about the correctness of a word w

$$
\text{NCE} = \frac{H(X) + \frac{1}{N}\left(\sum_{w \in C_H} \log_2 P(c \mid w) + \sum_{w \in \mathcal{F}_H} \log_2(1 - P(c \mid w))\right)}{H(X)} \tag{1}
$$

where

$$
H(X) = -\left(p_c \log_2 p_c + (1 - p_c) \log_2(1 - p_c)\right).
$$

N is the number of words w which are taken into consideration, $P(c \mid w)$ is the confidence measure which estimates the probability that the word w is correct. p_c stands for the a-priori probability of the correctness of any word w. $\mathcal{F}_H$ is the set of words which are wrong and C_H contains the correct words. The NCE is always a value between zero and one. Only if the confidence measure performs worse than the a-priori classifier the result is negative. Please note that p_c in the normalization term is correlated to the performance of the recognizer. Several authors (e.g. [2]) mention that, despite of the normalization, the NCE depends on the error rate and therefore does not allow a fair comparison of confidence annotation across recognition systems. In the following, we will compute the NCE for confidence measures which estimate the probability of a word for being correct, being a substitution and being an insertion.

The second quality measure we used is simply the recognition rate of the confidence measure for the two class problem *correct* vs. *wrong* and also for the three class problem *cor*, *sub* or *ins*. We also compute the class-wise average of the recognition rates. Of course, the recognition rate is highly dependent on the error rate of the speech recognizer. Nevertheless, the recognition rate can give a good idea of the performance of a confidence measure in a real application. Closely related to the recognition rate are the values of precision and recall. If C_H contains the correct words, and $\mathcal{M}_c$ contains the words, which have been marked as *correct* by the confidence measure, then the precision of the class *correct* is defined as

$$
prc_c = \frac{|C_H \cap \mathcal{M}_c|}{|\mathcal{M}_c|} \tag{2}
$$

where $|\cdot|$ counts the number of elements in a set. Recall of the class *correct* is equivalent to the recognition rate:

$$
rec_c = \frac{|C_H \cap \mathcal{M}_c|}{|C_H|} \tag{3}
$$

3   Features for Confidence Measure Computation

3.1   Word-Based Features

Category of the word. Category-based confidence features are given by $P(c|cat(w))$, which is the probability that a word w which belongs to a category $cat(w)$ is correct. The probability is estimated from the training sample. We evaluate two different category systems, HANDCAT and POS, the corresponding features are WCHAND and WCPOS. HANDCAT contains about 160 categories, which have been derived manually. POS assigns one of 15 part-of-speech labels to each word of the vocabulary. The feature WCPOS can be extended by the part-of-speech labels of the left and right neighbors of w (feature WCPOS ± 1 and WCPOS ± 2 for two respective four neighbors). We also try to use simply the name of the part-of-speech label $cat(w)$ for confidence computation (feature WCPOSNAME).

Language model. In [3] it has been noted that a word w is more likely to be correct, if the score $P(w|\vec{v})$ of the language model for the word and its context $\vec{v}$ is high. In the following, $-\log P(w|\vec{v})$ is used as feature LSCORE for confidence estimation.

Word length. As long words are usually recognized better than short words [4], the length of a word may be a useful confidence feature. The length of a word hypothesis may be computed from the number of phones in the word (feature LPHONE) or its duration in frames (feature LFRAME).

Word frequency. If a word appears less frequently in the acoustic training data, the corresponding HMM may be trained worse. Therefore, we evaluate the feature WFREQ, which is the logarithm of the absolute frequency of the word in the data.

3.2   Features Based on the Acoustic Score

Similar to the feature LSCORE, the acoustic score $-\log P(O_{t_s}, .., O_{t_e}|w)$ for a word w and an observation sequence $O_{t_s}, .., O_{t_e}$ can be used as the feature ASCORE; t_s and t_e denote the start and end time of the word. A low acoustic score indicates that the word is misrecognized. We try to improve the results by applying some normalization. The feature MASCORE is the acoustic score divided by the duration of the word hypothesis:

$$MAScore(w) = \frac{AScore(w)}{t_e - t_s + 1} \tag{4}$$

Under adverse acoustic conditions, the overall score of all output densities $\mathcal{N}(O_t|\mu_k \Sigma_k)$ of the recognizer may be low. As a consequence an additional normalization factor PSCORE is introduced:

$$PScore(t_s, .., t_e) = \sum_{t=t_s}^{t_e} -\log \sum_k p_k \mathcal{N}(O_t|\mu_k \Sigma_k) \tag{5}$$

p_k stands for the a-priori probability of output density k and has to be estimated from the training data. The feature NASCORE takes PSCORE into account:

$$NAScore(w) = AScore(w) - PScore(t_s, .., t_e) \tag{6}$$

It is also possible to use PSCORE as a feature or to combine the two normalization methods (feature MNASCORE). The sum of the features PSCORE, ASCORE, MASCORE and NASCORE gives the new feature GSCORE.

3.3 Word Graph-Based Features

Beam width. The beam search algorithm increases the number of active states if the best path through the search space has a poor score. As the beam width bw_t depends on the current time frame t, we have to combine the values of bw_t for $t_s \leq t \leq t_e$ in order to derive a confidence feature for the word w. The feature MBEAM is the mean of bw_t in the interval $t_s \leq t \leq t_e$, SBEAM its standard deviation. MINBEAM is the minimum value of bw_t, while MAXBEAM corresponds to its maximum. The positions of the minimum and maximum, measured in percent of the interval length $t_e - t_s + 1$, give two additional features POSMINBEAM and POSMAXBEAM.

A-posteriori probability. The confidence in a word w, which covers the frames $t_s, .., t_e$ of an utterance $\vec{O}$ can be associated directly with its a-posteriori probability $P(w, t_s, t_e | \vec{O})$. The a-posteriori probability can be estimated from a word graph. As described in [5], all preceeding and succeeding contexts $\vec{w}_p$, $\vec{w}_s$ of the word w which can be found in the word graph have to be taken into consideration:

$$P(w, t_s, t_e \mid \vec{O}) = \sum_{\vec{w}_p} \sum_{\vec{w}_s} P(\vec{w}_p, w, \vec{w}_s \mid \vec{O})$$

$$= \frac{\sum_{\vec{w}_p} \sum_{\vec{w}_s} P(\vec{O} \mid \vec{w}_p, w, \vec{w}_s) \cdot P(\vec{w}_p, w, \vec{w}_s)}{P(\vec{O})} \tag{7}$$

where

$$P(\vec{O}) = \sum_{w} \sum_{\vec{w}_p} \sum_{\vec{w}_s} P(\vec{O} \mid \vec{w}_p, w, \vec{w}_s) \cdot P(\vec{w}_p, w, \vec{w}_s) \tag{8}$$

As a word graph usually contains several instances w_i of the word w which differ in $t_s(i)$ and $t_e(i)$ the confidence measure can be improved by summing up $P(w_i, t_s(i), t_e(i)|\vec{O})$ of all word hypotheses w_i which overlap in the time domain. The resulting feature will be denoted as APOSTERIORI.

4   Data

For our experiments we use a set of spontaneous dialogues between humans, which have been collected in the VERBMOBIL project [6]. In Table 1 the three subsets which are used to train the speech recognizer and to evaluate the confidence measures are shown.

5   Short Description of the Speech Recognizer

The speech recognizer used for the experiments is a speaker independent continuous speech recognizer. The recognition process is done in two steps. First, a beam search is applied,

Table 1. Subsets of the VERBMOBIL data which are used to evaluate the confidence measures.

subset	utterances	words
training of the speech recognizer	15647	358505
confidence measure evaluation	4938	103855
training of the classifier	3704	78125
test of the classifier	1234	25730

which generates a word graph. The beam search uses a bigram language model. In the second phase, the best matching word chain is determined from the word graph by an A^*-search, which rescores the graph with a 4-gram language model. Please refer to [7] for a more detailed description. The a-priori probabilities of the classes *cor*, *sub* and *ins* in the recognition result of the speech recognizer on the VERBMOBIL data are 0.646, 0.269 and 0.085. A confidence measure which would simply label every word as *correct* would have a recognition rate for the class *correct* of 64.6 % and a NCE of zero. The class-wise average of the recognition rates for *correct* and *wrong* would be 50 %.

6   Experimental Results

6.1   Comparison of the Features

For each of the individual features we train a decision tree classifier which has to assign the label *correct* or *wrong* to each word which has been hypothesized by the speech recognizer from the test data. We also measure the performance for the three classes *cor*, *sub*, *ins*. In Table 2 the NCE for all the features introduced in the previous section can be found. Please note, that the NCE in Eq. 1 is defined only for a two class problem. For the column *NCE(all)* the definition is extended for three class labels. In order to compute the NCE for only one of the classes *cor*, *sub* or *ins*, the other two classes are merged. The NCE of *cor*, *sub* or *ins* cannot be compared with each other, because the three classes differ w.r.t. the a-priori probability.

The results in Table 2 give a rank ordering of the confidence features. Despite some exceptions, like MNASCORE, SBEAM or POSMAXBEAM nearly every feature seems to contain useful information about the confidence of a word. The a-posteriori probability performs better than all other single features. The results indicate that feature combinations, like in GSCORE, improve results significantly. For WCPos we were able to get a better confidence annotation by incorporating the part-of-speech labels of the neighboring words.

6.2   Feature Combination

We combine all features into one feature vector for each word and classify it with a decision tree or an ANN. WCPOSNAME is not included because we did not want to code the name with several binary features. The ANN is a multilayer perceptron with two hidden layers and is trained with backpropagation. Each feature gets one input node, the number of output nodes corresponds to the number of classes (two or three). In Table 3, the NCE for all features is computed. In Table 4 the corresponding recognition rates are given. The ANN shows a

Table 2. Normalized Cross Entropy (NCE) for the individual features. Results are given for the two and the three class problem.

feature	correct vs. wrong NCE	cor vs. sub vs. ins			
		NCE (all)	NCE (cor)	NCE (sub)	NCE (ins)
WCHAND	0.018	0.081	0.018	0.047	0.171
WCPOSNAME	0.019	0.082	0.018	0.038	0.181
WCPOS	0.022	0.084	0.021	0.040	0.182
WCPOS ±1	0.057	0.121	0.054	0.061	0.246
WCPOS ±2	0.064	0.123	0.059	0.064	0.243
WFREQ	0.039	0.094	0.036	0.060	0.173
LSCORE	0.042	0.086	0.039	0.068	0.133
LPHONE	0.012	0.079	0.012	0.037	0.182
LFRAME	0.030	0.058	0.029	0.006	0.161
ASCORE	0.022	0.046	0.021	0.009	0.121
MASCORE	0.052	0.070	0.056	0.029	0.139
NASCORE	0.030	0.067	0.029	0.005	0.193
MNASCORE	0.003	0.039	0.005	0.016	0.097
PSCORE	0.029	0.063	0.028	0.004	0.183
GSCORE	0.089	0.123	0.095	0.073	0.211
MBEAM	0.024	0.039	0.025	0.040	0.043
SBEAM	0.012	0.043	0.013	0.007	0.123
MINBEAM	0.046	0.046	0.046	0.534	0.023
POSMINBEAM	0.020	0.034	0.019	0.005	0.085
MAXBEAM	0.017	0.049	0.016	0.023	0.112
POSMAXBEAM	0.008	0.007	0.007	0.002	0.012
all BEAM features	0.069	0.093	0.072	0.066	0.145
APOSTERIORI	0.126	0.100	0.113	0.135	0.001

Table 3. Normalized Cross Entropy (NCE) for all confidence features.

classifier	correct vs. wrong NCE	cor vs. sub vs. ins			
		NCE (all)	NCE (cor)	NCE (sub)	NCE (ins)
decision tree	0.236	0.248	0.237	0.211	0.275
neural network	0.241	0.253	0.239	0.217	0.293

slightly better recognition performance than the decision tree. We could further improve the results by taking the context of the current word into account: First, the confidence values are computed for the neighboring words. Next, these two numbers are used as two additional features for the confidence computation of the current word. The results can be found in Table 5. In Figure 1 the relation between precision and recall of the class *correct* is shown. Figure 1 also shows how precision and recall depend on the value of a threshold Θ, when all words w with $P(c|w) > \Theta$ are assigned to the class c.

Table 4. Recognition rates (RR) for the class *correct* and class-wise averaged recognition rates (avg) for two and three classes with all confidence features.

classifier		*correct* vs. *wrong*	*cor* vs. *sub* vs. *ins*
decision tree	RR	74.6 %	72.1 %
	avg.	71.4 %	59.9 %
neural network	RR	75.4 %	72.5 %
	avg.	72.9 %	62.1 %

Table 5. Recognition rates (RR) for the class *correct* and class-wise averaged recognition rates (avg) when the confidence of left and right neighbor is used.

	correct vs. *wrong*	*cor* vs. *sub* vs. *ins*
RR	76.1 %	72.8 %
avg.	73.0 %	63.7 %

7 Conclusion and Outlook

We compared a large number of features for confidence scoring. From all features the a-posteriori probability of a word achieves by far the best performance. However, the a-posteriori probability alone leads to a NCE of 0.126, which is only one half of the NCE that can be reached by the full set of features. Please note, that in order to determine the a-posteriori probability the complete word graph must be processed in forward and backward direction, which makes the feature computationally more time consuming than all other features. We tend to the conclusion that the decision for a certain classifier should not be overrated: The difference in recognition rate between the neural network and the decision tree could become even smaller if we put more effort in the initialization and optimization of the tree. We have shown that even for a low speech recognition accuracy, confidence measures can distinguish correct from wrong words with a reasonable performance. Even the three

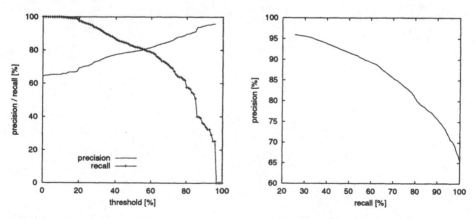

Fig. 1. Precision and recall for the class *correct* depending on a threshold Θ (left) and relation between precision and recall (right).

class problem seems to be solvable. In the future we want to investigate into the integration of the confidence scores into a spoken dialogue system and plan to evaluate whether the reliability of the confidence measure may be higher for semantically important words.

References

1. L. Chase: Error-Responsive Feedback Mechanisms for Speech Recognition. Ph.D. Thesis, Carnegie Mellon University (1997).
2. B. Mison and R. Gopinath: Robust Confidence Annotation and Rejection for Continuous Speech Recognition Proc. IEEE ICASSP (2001) Vol. 1.
3. E. Eide and H. Gish and P. Jeanrenaud and A. Mielke: Understanding and Improving Speech Recognition Performance through the Use of Diagnostic Tools. Proc. IEEE ICASSP (1995) Vol. 1, 221–224.
4. S. Cox and R. C. Rose: Confidence Measures for the SWITCHBOARD Database. Proc. IEEE ICASSP (1996) Vol. 1, 511–514.
5. F. Wessel and K. Macherey and R. Schlüter: Using Word Probabilities as Confidence Measures. Proc. IEEE ICASSP (1998) Vol. 1, 225–228.
6. W. Wahlster: Verbmobil: Foundations of Speech-to-Speech Translation. Springer (2000).
7. S. Steidl: Konfidenzbewertung von Worthypothesen. Student Thesis (in German), Chair for Pattern Recognition, University of Erlangen-Nürnberg (2001).

Strategies for Developing a Real-Time Continuous Speech Recognition System for Czech Language[*]

Jan Nouza

SpeechLab, Technical University of Liberec
Hálkova 6, 461 17 Liberec, Czech Republic
E-mail: jan.nouza@vslib.cz

Abstract. This paper presents a set of 'strategies' that enabled the development of a real-time continuous speech recognition system for Czech language. The optimization strategies include efficient computation of HMM probability densities, pruning schemes applied to HMM states, words and word hypotheses, a bigram compression technique as well as parallel implementation of the real recognition system. In a series of off-line speaker-independent tests done with 1,600 Czech sentences based on 7,033-word lexicon we got 65 % recognition rate. Several on-line tests proved that similar rates can be achieved under real conditions and with response time that is shorter than 1 second.

1 Introduction

In this paper we present our approach to developing a continuous speech recognition system that is capable of real-time operation with lexicons containing thousands of Czech words. The system is the result of a long-term research and was completely built in our lab. It inherited many features from its predecessor, a discrete-utterance recognition system [1], which found its main application field in telephony services [2].

The system is based on the one-pass strategy [3] that processes a speech signal in time-synchronous way by efficiently combining acoustic scores of word models with language model probabilities. The words are represented by HMMs (Hidden Markov Models) that are constructed from a small set of elementary phoneme HMMs. The language model employs bigram probabilities estimated from a large text corpus. The short response time (< 1 s) has been made possible by the optimization of the search procedure, efficient bigram handling due parallel multi-thread implementation. The latter can be exploited on a PC with the MS Windows NT/2000 operating system.

The paper is structured as follows. In the next section we summarize the basic principles of the one-pass Viterbi search with a special focus on those parts and equations that are subject of the optimization procedures mentioned later. The Section 3 gives some details on the acoustic and language model training. The proposed optimization strategies are presented in Section 4. Experimental results achieved in both off-line and on-line tests appear in Section 5, which is followed by conclusions.

---

[*] This work was supported by the Grant Agency of the Czech Republic (grant No. 102/02/0124) and project MSM 242200001. The author wants to thank Tomáš Nouza for his invaluable assistance in multi-thread programming.

P. Sojka, I. Kopeček, and K. Pala (Eds.): TSD 2002, LNAI 2448, pp. 189–196, 2002.

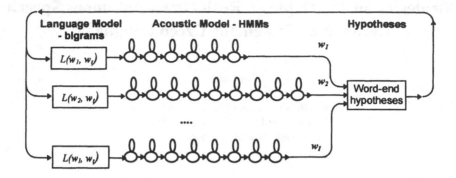

Fig. 1. Illustration of the one-pass speech recognition procedure as it is applied in the described system. It combines acoustic and language models to get the most likely hypotheses about the lexical content of the speech, within a computation optimized scheme.

2 Time-Synchronous Speech Decoding Procedure

The task we want to solve can be described in the following way: Let us have a speech signal, an utterance, parameterized into sequence $\vec{X}$ of T frame vectors $\vec{x}(1), \vec{x}(t) \ldots \vec{x}(T)$. The goal is to find its lexical content, i.e. sequence $\vec{W}$ of words $w_1, w_2 \ldots w_N$, with a priori unknown length N. We will do it by exploiting acoustic, phonetic, lexical and syntactic knowledge embedded in two statistic models, the acoustic one (AM) and the language one (LM). They allow us to search for the most probable sequence $\vec{W}$ given the $\vec{X}$ by maximizing log posterior probability $P(\vec{W}|\vec{X})$:

$$\ln P(\vec{W}|\vec{X}) = \max_{w,N} \left[\sum_{n=1}^{N} (A(w_n|\vec{x}(t_n) \ldots \vec{x}(t_{n+1} - 1)) + L(w_n, w_{n-1})) \right] \quad (1)$$

Equation 1 is presented in the way so that the sum of logarithmic contributions of the acoustic and language models are explicitly shown.

The first term in (1) is the contribution of the AM of word w_n, which has been aligned with the partial sequence of frame vectors $\vec{x}$ starting at time t_n. If we use the classic left-to-right HMM for the word AM, we can write:

$$A(w_n|\vec{x}(t_n) \ldots \vec{x}(t_{n+1} - 1)) = \max_{r,s} \left[\sum_{t=t_n}^{t_n 1} (\ln a_{rs} + \ln b_s(\vec{x}(t))) \right] \quad (2)$$

where a_{rs} is the probability of transition from previous state r to current state s and $b_s(\vec{x}(t))$ is the output probability of state s given frame vector $\vec{x}$ in time t.

The second term in (1) is the contribution of the LM. We employ a weighted bigram model:

$$L(w_n, w_m) = \ln g(w_n, w_m) \cdot C_{\text{LM}} + C_{\text{IP}} \quad (3)$$

where $g(w_n, w_m)$ is an estimate of the probability that in a sentence word w_n follows word w_m. Constant C_{LM} is a factor enhancing the contribution of the LM and C_{IP} is an insertion penalty. Optimal values for both the constants must be determined empirically on an evaluation database [6].

The well-known Viterbi algorithm searches for the solution of (1) by applying the dynamic programming method. It consists in time-synchronous evaluation of cumulative scores Q defined for each word w, its model state s and time t. Inside a word model the score is calculated according to Equation 4:

$$Q(t, s, w) = \max_r \left[Q(t - 1, r, w) + \ln a_{rs} + \ln b_s(\vec{x}(t)) \right] \tag{4}$$

and at word boundaries according to Equation 5:

$$Q(t, 0, w) = \max_v \left[Q(t - 1, S, v) + L(w, v) \right] \tag{5}$$

where the value in the initial (0-th) state of word w is determined as the best combination of the score in the final state S of previous word v and the corresponding bigram value. Word v maximizing the right side of (5) is stored as the best predecessor of w in time t.

In this way we get the most likely solution of (1) by finding the word sequence whose last word ends up in time T with the highest score:

$$\ln P(\vec{W}|\vec{X}) = \max_i Q(T, S, w_i) \tag{6}$$

After identifying the last word w_N through (6) we get the complete sequence $\vec{W}$ by tracking back the stored predecessors.

3   Acoustic and Language Models

In our system the acoustic model is based on the application of the Hidden Markov Model (HMM) technique. Three-state left-to-right continuous HMMs model spectral and temporal characteristics of 41 Czech phonemes and background noise [4]. Both context-independent (monophones) as well as context-dependent (triphones) models are available. However, due to the efficiency reasons discussed in the next section we give preference to the former ones. The models have been trained on the database containing about 20 hours of annotated speech recordings provided by almost 100 speakers. The recordings were sampled at 16 bit/8 kHz rate and pre-processed to get 26-feature frame vectors composed of 12 cepstral and 12 delta-cepstral coefficients complemented by delta energy and delta-delta energy. (The 2nd derivatives of the cepstrum were not included since their addition did not exhibit any further improvement of the recognition rate.)

Each word in the given lexicon is represented by concatenated phoneme models according to the phonetic transcription rules that are automatically applied during the lexicon generation [5]. Recently a single model per word is used, however, the system can handle multiple pronunciation variants as well.

The language model is based on word bigrams. They have been derived from a large corpus of printed text available in electronic form. The corpus is made mainly of newspaper articles but it includes also several novels. It contains 55,841,099 Czech words, with 856,288 distinct word forms. The total number of 18,458,806 different word pairs have been found in the corpus. These served as a base for estimating various types of smoothed bigram models and for optimizing the LM constants that occur in (3). The details are presented in the complementary paper [6]. The recent version of the real speech recognition system employs the bigram matrix smoothed according to the Witten-Bell discounting scheme, which yielded the best performance in a series of extensive evaluation tests.

4   Strategies Applied for Real-Time Processing

Even though the dynamic programming (DP) technique reduces significantly the complexity of the search task, the full evaluation of (4-6) in the whole three-dimensional space of w, s and t cannot be managed in real-time. Instead some heuristics and data manipulating tricks must be introduced. In the following subsections we describe those adopted in our system.

4.1   Acoustic Score Caching

The evaluation of the above mentioned DP equations seem to be quite simple, because they include mostly addition and maximization operations. The only CPU-power demanding part is the last term in (4). It represents the probability density function (pdf) defined as a mixture of multiple (8 – 32) gaussians in 26-dimensional space. However, since the evaluation of (4) is done synchronously with time, the pdf values computed for given frame vector $\vec{x}(t)$ can be stored in cache and reused whenever the same state s appears in another word (or even in the same word). This caching scheme is extremely efficient in case of monophones because there are only 41×3 different states to be matched with vector $\vec{x}(t)$. Thus, for example, in a 10 K word lexicon almost 99.94 % pdf calculations can be omitted and replaced by a much faster access to the cache. This is the main reason why we have built our system on the use of the monophones. Moreover, our choice has been justified by the fact that 32-mixture monophones yielded the same performance as the available 8-mixture triphones.

4.2   State and Word Pruning

During the search within the wst space many word hypotheses become unlikely. Due to the time-synchronous evaluation of (4–6) we can identify them according to their scores which are much lower compared with the currently best ones. Hence, at each time step we find the hypothesis with the best score Q_{best} and in the next time step we remove from the further consideration all HMM states s if:

$$Q(t - 1, s, w) < Q_{best}(t - 1) - C_{PT} \tag{7}$$

where C_{PT} is a state pruning threshold. Its value must be optimized to get the largest computation reduction with minimum lost of recognition accuracy [6].

Besides the above state pruning scheme we apply also a word pruning option. It is based on keeping track of the surviving states. We do it for each word by storing the highest index from all unpruned states. If there is no surviving state in the current word, that word is temporarily removed from the searched space.

4.3 Word-End Hypotheses Pruning

To start a word hypothesis for word w according to (5), the maximization over all predecessor words v should be done. For a lexicon with M items this means that at each time step the total number of $M \times M$ summations of word-end scores and bigrams should be performed. However, practical experiments showed that it was not necessary to consider all existing word-end hypotheses. Only a small number of the preceding words v – those with the highest scores – will play a dominant role in (5). Hence, at each time step t we order the word-end hypotheses according to their scores and keep just a short list of the best ones. If the list has C_{WE} ($C_{WE} \ll M$) members, we save a large portion of the computing load. Surprisingly, the C_{WE} can be set in range 5 – 20 even for large lexicons without any significant performance degradation. More details can be found again in the complementary paper [6].

4.4 Handling Bigrams

As the size of the application vocabulary increases, the memory space needed for storing the bigrams becomes prohibitively large. (For example, the full bigram matrix for a 10 K word task would occupy $10\,K \times 10\,K \times 4B = 400\,MB$.) However, it is well known, that the number of distinct bigram values is much smaller. In particular, there is a considerably large amount of values that are same, which is the result of the smoothing technique. The natural solution to this problem is to compress the bigram matrix and store its values in the way that allows for efficient access.

In our system the bigrams $g(w_r, w_p)$ are stored as vectors $h(w_p)$ that share the common previous word w_p:

$$[g(w_r, w_p)] = h(w_1), h(w_p), \ldots, h(w_M) \qquad (8)$$

The vectors $h(w_p)$ can be efficiently compressed because they contain smaller or larger groups of the same values. Moreover, we arrange the bigrams in the $h(w_p)$ not in the natural order (by index) but according to their values, from the higher to the lower ones. When evaluating the (5) we first initialize scores $Q(t, 0, w_r)$ by an appropriate default value and than we fill the scores using the ordered values taken from the vector $h(w_p)$. This arrangement together with the maximization principle embedded in (5) offers another computation saving. Thus only a small fraction from all the $C_{WE} \times M$ bigram combinations must be handled at each time step.

The reduction of memory requirements is even more significant. A bigram matrix for a typical 10 K word lexicon can be stored in the memory space smaller than 5 MB. Yet another reduction is possible if we allow the bigrams to be quantized and approximated by a limited set of values.

4.5 Parallel Processing

When speech recognition experiments are performed off-line, the signal is parametrized first and after that it is sent to the classifier. The same approach is often used also in on-line systems.

Modern computers and operation systems, however, enable the programmers to decompose complex tasks into separate subtasks that can run in parallel. The speech recognition task is quite suitable for such a decomposition. The most natural arrangement employs a three-level hierarchy. While the lowest level unit cares about the speech signal sampling, the middle level unit segments signal into frames and computes feature vectors, and the upper level unit focuses entirely on the classification procedure. The only critical issue is the correct synchronization of the units and the safe data transfer between them.

The demonstration version of our system employs the above parallel scheme. It runs on a PC with the Windows 2000 operating system, which gives support to multi-thread implementation. This allows the system to start the recognition procedure in the moment when speech is detected and finish it very soon after the end of the utterance is approved.

5 Performance Evaluation

The individual procedures and their parameters were evaluated mostly in off-line experiments. These consisted in batch-organized recognition tests performed on a large evaluation database. The database contains 1,600 utterances recorded by 40 people (23 men + 17 women) of various ages. The speakers were asked to read sentences that appeared on the PC screen. A common head-mounted microphone set was used for acquiring the signal. The recordings were done on different places (mostly at homes, in student rooms, occasionally in a computer lab.)

The sentences were drawn from newspaper articles on various topics: home and international news, sport events, culture articles, weather reports, etc. The 1,600 utterances represent 85 minutes of speech and contain 16,027 words (in average 10 per utterance). The lexicon was made of 7,033 different Czech words that covered all the sentences.

An initial series of experiments was aimed at establishing the optimal values of the search procedure parameters, namely the language model weighting factor C_{LM}, the word insertion penalty constant C_{IP}, the state pruning threshold C_{PT}, and the length of the hypotheses list C_{WE}. These experiments were part of the language model evaluation project and they are discussed in more details in paper [6]. Here we want to focus on the global performance assessment.

The measure we used for the system evaluation was the accuracy rate defined as:

$$Acc = \frac{N - S - I - D}{N} \times 100\% \qquad (9)$$

The accuracy – as opposed to the frequently used Correctness rate – is considered as the best measure representing the practical usage of a recognition system because it takes into account all kinds of errors, including the substitutions S, deletions D, insertions I, and relates them to the true number of words N in the correct transcription [7].

Table 1 summarizes some of the most relevant results and compares the impact of different acoustic and language models. The best-performing language model referred to as the WB was produced by the Witten-Bell smoothing technique applied on the independent training corpus mentioned in Section 3. The recognition times were measured on a PC (Athlon 1.3 GHz, 512 MB RAM).

The on-line tests could not be so extensive since it is more difficult to arrange them. Up to now, two people volunteered to participate in an experiment, in which the subject had to read 100 sentences directly to the PC using a common head-mounted microphone set. The text was

Table 1. Results from off-line speech recognition tests done with 1,600 Czech utterances.

Acoustic Model	Language Model	Accuracy [%]	Recog. Time per Sentence/Word [ms]
16-mixture HMM	zerogram, $C_{IP} = -35$	39.25	7,213/720
32-mixture HMM	zerogram, $C_{IP} = -35$	49.15	7,318/760
16-mixture HMM	WB, $C_{LM} = 6$, $C_{IP} = -6$	55.87	6,265/625
32-mixture HMM	WB, $C_{LM} = 6$, $C_{IP} = -6$	65.42	6,693/668

randomly drawn from the same list of 1,600 sentences. The system automatically detected the speech, did the classification, displayed the resulting word sequence and counted the errors according to (9). The response of the recognizer was really instantaneous. The output text appeared on the screen always in time shorter than 1 second after the speaker finished the utterance. This fast response was possible due to the parallel implementation of the speech processing and classification routines. For the results see Table 2.

Table 2. Online speech recognition tests (100 sentences per speaker, 7,033-word lexicon).

Speaker	Acoustic and Lang. Model	Accuracy [%]	Avg. Resp. Time [ms]
MJN	32-mixture HMM, WB	72.81	654
ZVS	32-mixture HMM, WB	66.23	583

6 Conclusions

In the paper we present several strategies that allowed us to implement one of the first continuous speech recognition systems applicable for the Czech language. So far the system has been tested on a middle-size lexicon with fairly promising results. We believe that the system capabilities could be extended for vocabularies containing tens of thousands words. Our future work is going to be focused on the improvements of the acoustic model (increasing the HMM training database, evaluating other features sets and testing different HMM arrangements) and on further development of the language model that should take into account some specific characteristic of Czech (inflections, case and gender agreement in noun and verbal phrases, etc.).

References

1. Nouza J.: A Czech Large Vocabulary Recognition System for Real-Time Applications. In: P. Sojka et al. (Eds.) Text, Speech and Dialogue: Proceedings of the Third International Workshop on Text, Speech, Dialogue. Springer-Verlag, Heidelberg, 2000, pp. 217–222.
2. Nouza J., Holada M.: A Voice-Operated Multi-Domain Telephone Information System. Proc. of 25th Int. Conference on Acoustics, Speech and Signal Processing (ICASSP2000), Istanbul, June 2000, vol. VI, pp. 3755–3758.

3. Ney H., Ortmanns S.: Dynamic Programming Search for Continuous Speech Recognition IEEE Signal Processing Magazine, Vol. 16, No. 5, Sept. 1999, pp. 64–83.
4. Nouza J., Psutka J., Uhlíř J.: Phonetic Alphabet for Speech Recognition of Czech. Radioengineering, Vol. 6, No. 4, Dec. 1997, pp. 16–20.
5. Nejedlová D., Volejník M.: Transkripce psaného českého textu do fonetické podoby (Phonetic transcription of printed Czech text). In: J. Nouza (Ed.), Počítačové zpracování řeči. Technical University of Liberec, 2001, pp. 10–22.
6. Nejedlová D.: Comparative Study on Bigram Language Models for Spoken Czech Recognition. In: Sojka P. et al. (Eds.): *Text, Speech and Dialogue*, Proceedings of the Fifth International Conference, Brno, Czech Republic, Septembe 9–12, 2002, pp. 197–204.
7. Huang X., Acero A., Hon H.-W.: Spoken Language Processing. A Guide to Theory, Algorithm and System Development. Prentice Hall. New Jersey 2001.

Comparative Study on Bigram Language Models for Spoken Czech Recognition *

Dana Nejedlová

SpeechLab, Technical University of Liberec,
Hálkova 6, 461 17 Liberec, Czech Republic
E-mail: dana.nejedlova@vslib.cz

Abstract. The article deals with the problem of continuous speech recognition of Czech language. The main goal of this study is to compare various kinds of bigram language models with respect to the accuracy and speed of speech recognition. The main types of bigram language models are described here as well as multiple parameters that affect the performance of a speech recognition system. A comparison with a zerogram model is also made. Different models and various parameter settings are compared by means of the accuracy rate in extensive experiments done with a large test database of 1,600 Czech sentences recorded by 40 speakers.

1 Introduction

Systems that recognize voice input in a form of isolated words or short discrete phrases have been available for Czech language for several years. Some perform well even for lexicons with thousands of words, and they have been already applied in public services [1]. The recognition of fluently spoken language is a much more challenging task. So far no usable system capable of doing this in Czech language has been brought to market. Its development is the main goal of the long-term research in our lab. Though some specific problems of Czech language make the task extremely difficult. Czech language has approximately 1 million word-forms, which is about 20 times more than in English. Such a large lexicon is a result of complex rules for inflection of Czech words. Many Czech words sound similarly having only different prefixes or suffixes. In comparison to English, the word order in Czech sentences is freer, which worsens the utility of language models. Nevertheless, this article shows that language models help substantially in the recognition of Czech. Experiments described in this article have been carried out with the use of the software system described in the complementary paper [2].

2 Test Speech Database

The people recorded for our both training and test databases were not professional speakers. In some cases it was hard even for a human to understand the complete sentence uttered by some of our speakers.

* This work has been supported by the Grant Agency of the Czech Republic (grant no. 102/02/0124) and through research goal project MSM 242200001.

P. Sojka, I. Kopeček, and K. Pala (Eds.): TSD 2002, LNAI 2448, pp. 197–204, 2002.

But even if the sentences had been uttered correctly, there would still have remained a space for some mistakes that could not be prevented. Those mistakes originate in words that have a different spelling but the same phonetic transcription. 1,600 test sentences contained 126 words of that kind having 44 different spelling word-forms. Our test speech database had 16,027 words having 7,033 different word-forms. It means that nearly 0.8 % of words could be messed up, if they had been classified only with the use of acoustic model by some perfect recognizer.

More details about our test (evaluation) speech database can be seen in [2].

3   The Role of Various Parameters in Speech Recognition System

3.1   Searching for the Optimal Parameter Settings

Our speech recognition system was controlled by several parameters whose optimal settings had to be searched for by making small perturbations of one of them, the rest staying constant, picking up the best value, and then making perturbations of another parameter. All these tuning experiments had to be done on a relatively large amount of the test data. We have used 800 sentences that were a subset of our test database, and our working vocabulary contained 3,622 words. If the database for finding the best settings had been smaller, the optimal settings of parameters found for it would have been far from optimal for the whole test database. We have used the following parameters to control the speech recognition:

1. acoustic model,
2. language model,
3. language model factor,
4. word insertion penalty,
5. number of word-end hypotheses,
6. prune threshold.

3.2   Acoustic Model

We have used either 16 or 32-mixture acoustic models trained on an independent speech database. Paper [2] describes the training speech database and compares the performances of the two types of acoustic models. 32-mixture model works more precisely at the expense of somewhat higher time consumption. All results shown in this article have been done using the 32-mixture acoustic model which we prefer to the 16-mixture one.

3.3   Language Model

Admissible values of the parameter specifying the language model can have the following effects:

1. using no language model (i.e. using a zerogram model),
2. using a dependent language model which has been made of the test data,
3. using some independent language model,
   (a) unsmoothed,

(b) smoothed,
- by adding one,
- by linear interpolation,
- by Witten-Bell discounting.

3.4 Language Model Factor and Word Insertion Penalty

Higher values of language model factor (C_{LM}) mean greater influence of language model on recognition. As it is shown below, the optimal value of this parameter was different for different language models.

Our recognition system has a tendency of preferring shorter words to longer ones. To suppress this phenomenon we have introduced the parameter called word insertion penalty (C_{IP}) that worsens each candidate word's score, which really had an improving effect on the accuracy of recognition. Similarly to the case of the language model factor mentioned previously, there is some optimal value of C_{IP} for each type of language model. We have used higher absolute values of C_{IP} with a negative sign for a greater word penalization. More details about C_{LM} and C_{IP} parameters are shown in paper [2].

3.5 Number of Word-End Hypotheses and Prune Threshold

The parameter that we denote as the number of word-end hypotheses (C_{WE}) influences the number of bigrams in language model that are examined while inter-word transitions are evaluated. The higher its value is the better is the performance of the recognizer, but when this value reaches a certain level, the performance is no longer better, only the time consumption rises. The role of the parameter called prune threshold or state pruning threshold (C_{PT}) is to reduce the number of words that are kept in memory as the most probable. From the practical point of view, the prune threshold parameter behaves the similar way as the number of word-end hypotheses.

For both C_{WE} and C_{PT} parameters it was necessary to choose optimal values assuring the highest possible performance without letting the time consumption soar too high. Figure 1 in Section 5 shows the results of changing the prune threshold or the number of word-end-hypotheses while all other parameters are constant. Mathematical details are in paper [2].

4 Language Models

4.1 N-Gram Language Models

When computing the probability of a given word sequence from sufficiently large amount of training text, we can see that this probability is very close to the probability of the same word sequence computed from some other amount of training text if these two training corpora share the same language characteristics. This property helps us to predict what word will follow if we know some sequence of preceding words in some utterance that has also the same language characteristics as the corpus from which we have derived the probability of the word sequence. This is the basic concept of n-gram language modeling. N-gram is a conditional probability that if we observe some sequence of $n - 1$ words w_1^{n-1} then some particular n-th word w_n will follow. It can be computed as the frequency of the word sequence w_1^n, also called w_1^n count and in further text denoted as $C(w_1^n)$, divided by the frequency of the word sequence w_1^{n-1}. N-gram language model is a collection of conditional probabilities for all n-word long sequences that can be composed of a given vocabulary. When $n = 2$, we speak about bigrams. In languages with some relatively small vocabulary like English also probabilities of word triples can be computed and these are called trigrams.

N-gram also called statistical language models are successfully employed in tasks where spontaneous speech is recognized because they are robust and flexible in comparison to rule-based models that use some strictly described grammar.

4.2 Maximum Likelihood Estimate

Maximum likelihood estimate (MLE) is the simplest possible n-gram model. It contains conditional probabilities for all possible n-grams as they appeared in the training data. Word sequences not present in the training corpus have their probabilities equal to 0. In a more formal way, the values in the model are computed according to the equation

$$P(w_n|w_1^{n-1}) = \frac{C(w_1^n)}{C(w_1^{n-1})}. \tag{1}$$

MLE model is the starting probability database from which all smoothed models can be derived. Our dependent language model was MLE of probabilities in our evaluation database the sentences of which were formed of 14,387 different word pairs. Source data for our independent language models were the 55,841,099-word corpus described in more details in [2]. From this corpus we have extracted all its word pairs that were formed of the 7,033-word vocabulary of our evaluation speech database. The result of this extraction was the database of 1,785,458 different word pairs. It means that non-zero bigrams covered 3.6 % of the matrix of all possible word pairs made of our working vocabulary. Albeit there are several software tools for n-gram language model smoothing available in the research community, we have developed our own ones.

4.3 Add-One Smoothing

Even in the relatively simple case of bigram model and some limited vocabulary there is no chance to collect so much meaningful texts written in a particular natural language so that the resulting MLE language model contains no zero probabilities. Even the biggest corpora ever collected give most of the probabilities in the MLE model equal to zero. On the other hand, nearly every written text or spoken utterance not present in the training corpus, from which MLE model has been created, contains some bigrams with non zero probabilities that have zero probabilities in the training corpus. Language models work better in speech recognition when they have all their probabilities equal to some number bigger than zero. The process of turning the MLE language model into some form with all probabilities above zero is called smoothing.

The simplest idea of smoothing is so-called add-one smoothing. All possible combinations of n-word sequences counts are incremented by one and MLE model is computed from the resulting data. The equation for add-one smoothing is

$$P(w_n|w_1^{n-1}) = \frac{C(w_1^n) + a}{C(w_1^{n-1}) + Va}, \tag{2}$$

where a is the constant added to all the counts (the model works better when we add less than one) and V is the number of words in vocabulary.

4.4 Witten-Bell Discounting

Witten-Bell discounting is introduced as Method C in [3]. Let $C(w_1^n)$ be the count of a particular sequence of n words, $C(w_1^{n-1})$ be the count of the first $n - 1$ word sequence (w_1^{n-1} is also called the history of w_1^n), $T(w_1^{n-1})$ be the number (not count) of all n-word sequences that begin with the same $n - 1$ word sequence, i.e. the number of all distinct word types that followed a particular $n - 1$ word sequence, and V be the size of vocabulary. Then the equations for Witten-Bell discounting are

$$P(w_n|w_1^{n-1}) = \frac{C(w_1^n)}{C(w_1^{n-1}) + T(w_1^{n-1})} \quad \text{if } C(w_1^n) > 0 \tag{3}$$

and

$$P(w_n|w_1^{n-1}) = \frac{T(w_1^{n-1})}{(V - T(w_1^{n-1})) \cdot (C(w_1^{n-1}) + T(w_1^{n-1}))} \quad \text{if } C(w_1^n) = 0. \tag{4}$$

Every smoothing method distributes some probability mass from the n-grams with probabilities above zero to all the n-grams not seen in the training corpus. Witten-Bell discounting does this separately for each group of n-grams that share the same $n - 1$ word history with the purpose to discount more probability mass from those n-gram groups that have relatively more ending words, i.e. that have relatively large $T(w_1^{n-1})$. This probability mass is then distributed among all the other possible words that have not followed the $n - 1$ word sequence in the training corpus. The reason for this strategy is that if some word sequence is followed by a relatively large number of word types in the training corpus then the probability that some other word types can follow it too is bigger.

4.5 Linear Interpolation Smoothing

Linear interpolation smoothing is published as deleted interpolation algorithm in [4]. Its idea is the following: If we have no examples of a particular word triple w_1^3 to help us to compute its trigram $P(w_3|w_1^2)$, we can estimate its probability by using the bigram probability $P(w_3|w_2)$, and if there is no occurrence of the word pair w_2^3 in the training corpus, we can look to the unigram $P(w_3)$. The method in which lower order n-grams are used for higher order n-grams estimation only if higher order n-grams have zero probability in the training corpus is called backoff. Its algorithm was introduced in [5]. The method in which lower order n-grams are always used for higher order n-grams estimation is called interpolation smoothing. Linear interpolation smoothing estimates the trigram probability $P(w_3|w_1^2)$ by adding together trigram, bigram, and unigram probabilities. Each of these is weighted by a linear weight λ

$$P(w_3|w_1^2) = \lambda_3 P(w_3|w_1^2) + \lambda_2 P(w_3|w_2) + \lambda_1 P(w_3) + \lambda_0/V \qquad (5)$$

and

$$\sum_i \lambda_i = 1. \qquad (6)$$

The last term λ_0/V in (5) represents uniform distribution of unigram probabilities (V is the size of vocabulary). The set of λ values is trained using a version of expectation-maximization (EM) algorithm which is also shown in [4]. The training corpus is divided into training and held-out data and the target λ values must minimize the cross entropy of smoothed models computed from both training and held-out corpora. Due to compression reasons explained in [2] we prefer language models that have large groups of the same probability values. Models smoothed by means of linear interpolation do not have this property. It can be seen in (5). N-grams that share the same history get different probabilities according to the frequencies of their ending words as well. In the initial phase of the search for the optimal parameter settings described in Section 3.1 we have found that linear interpolation models' performance is the second best after Witten-Bell discounting. Because of these reasons we have not implemented linear interpolation models for our whole evaluation database.

5   Experimental Results

Figure 1 illustrates the information given in Section 3.5 about the two parameters that are used for the reduction of a search tree in our recognizer.

Table 1 compares all language models tested on our 1,600-sentence evaluation database.

Table 1. The optimal parameter settings and the best accuracy achieved for different language models.

Language Model	Language Model Factor	Word Insertion Penalty	Number of Word-End Hypotheses	Prune Threshold	Accuracy
Zerogram	0	-42	1	130	48.63
Independent MLE	5	-12	10	130	47.52
Add-One Smoothing	5	-3	10	130	61.58
Witten-Bell	6	-5	10	130	65.48
Dependent MLE	2	-9	10	130	95.82

Accuracy values in Figure 1 and Table 1 are computed according to the standard definition – see for example [2].

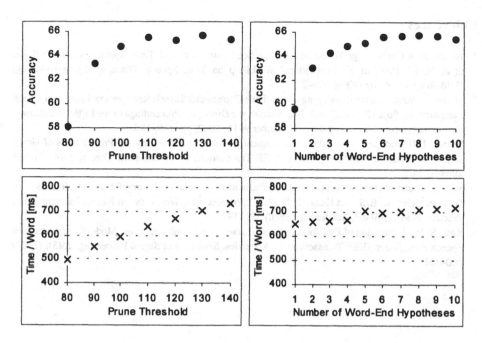

Fig. 1. When the value of prune threshold parameter increases, the accuracy of the recognition rises until it reaches some maximal point. The same rule applies for the case of the number of word-end hypotheses. Time measured on a PC (Athlon 1.3 GHz, 512 MB RAM) rises linearly in proportion to the both parameters.

6   Conclusion

In this paper we have applied several language models for the recognition of continuous speech in Czech. The results in Table 1 show that Witten-Bell discounting is the best independent bigram model used so far. An interesting demonstration of the necessity of language model smoothing is the fact that accuracy of unsmoothed independent MLE model is slightly worse than zerogram (i.e. when no language model is used). The result of dependent MLE model marks the upper bound of accuracy that can be possibly achieved. Another result shown in Table 1 is the fact that poor language models need greater penalization of each word insertion.

We have compared our language models also by means of their ability to be compressed for the operating memory savings reasons (details are in paper [2]). We are showing in Section 4.5 that linear interpolation model's compression feasibility is very low.

When using Witten-Bell language model and its best parameter setting (shown in Table 1) about 12 % of sentences were recognized with 100 % accuracy.

References

1. Nouza, J.: A Czech Large Vocabulary Recognition System for Real-Time Applications. In: P. Sojka et al. (Eds.): Proc. of 3rd International Workshop on Text, Speech, Dialogue, Springer-Verlag, Heidelberg, Germany (2000) 217–222.
2. Nouza, J.: Strategies for Developing a Real-Time Continuous Speech Recognition System for Czech Language. In: Sojka P. et al. (Eds.): *Text, Speech and Dialogue*, Proceedings of the Fifth International Conference, Brno, Czech Republic, September 9–12, 2002, pp. 189–196.
3. Witten, I. H. and Bell, T. C.: The Zero-Frequency Problem: Estimating the Probabilities of Novel Events in Adaptive Text Compression. IEEE Transactions on Information Theory, 37(4), (1991) 1085–1094.
4. Jelinek, F. and Mercer, R. L.: Interpolated Estimation on Markov Source Parameters from Sparse Data. In Gelsema, E. S. and Kanal, L. N. (Eds.), Proceedings, Workshop on Pattern Recognition in Practice. North Holland, Amsterdam (1980) 381–397.
5. Katz, S. M.: Estimation of Probabilities from Sparse Data for the Language Model Component of a Speech Recognizer. IEEE Transactions on Acoustics, Speech, and Signal Processing, 35(3), (1987) 400–401.

Integration of Speech Recognition and Automatic Lip-Reading

Pascal Wiggers, Leon J. M. Rothkrantz

Data and Knowledge Engineering
Delft University of Technology
Mekelweg 4, 2628 CD Delft, The Netherlands
E-mail: P.Wiggers@its.tudelft.nl, L.J.M.Rothkrantz@its.tudelft.nl

Abstract. At Delft University of Technology there is a project running on multimodal interfaces on the interaction of speech and lipreading. A large vocabulary speaker independent speech recognizer for the Dutch language was developed using Hidden Markov Toolkit and the Polyphone database of recorded Dutch speech. To make the system more noise robust audio cues provided by an automatic lip-reading technique were integrated in the system. In this paper we give an outline of both systems and present results of experiments.

1 Introduction

The topic of multimodal interfaces is attracting more and more attention in the research community. The focus is especially on the combination of automatic speech recognition with other modalities, either to improve recognition, as in the work done on audio-visual speech recognition by IBM [6,10] or the provide a natural human-computer interface as in the German SmartKom project [9].

At Delft University of Technology there is a project running on multimodal interfaces. Systems have now been developed for several modalities. An automatic speech recognizer has been build [1] using Hidden Markov Toolkit (HTK) and a automatic lip-reader has been developed [3]. In this paper we report about the interaction between these two modalities and present the speech recognizer and an integrated audio-visual recognizer. Experiments with these systems were conducted under noisy conditions to show that including the visual modality in a speech recognizer leads to more noise robustness.

2 Development of the Speech Recognizer

Although a number of well-performing speech recognition systems is now available, we lacked a system that could easily be altered or adapted to fit our specific needs. Therefore we decided to build our own system. The final system uses context dependent models, but as this system was build and refined incrementally, actually a whole set of recognizers has been created ranging from a simple monophone recognizer to a sophisticated multiple mixture triphone system. The system was developed using a variety of tools, programs and scripts. By

P. Sojka, I. Kopeček, and K. Pala (Eds.): TSD 2002, LNAI 2448, pp. 205–212, 2002.

far the largest set of tools and software libraries was taken from the Hidden Markov Toolkit [7]. Furthermore a number of programs was written that filled the gaps in the development process not covered by any of the tools. This includes a program for data selection, some tools for creating an initial acoustic model set and a tool for creating scripts for triphone clustering.

2.1 Data Preparation

The training and testing data for this project was taken from the Dutch Polyphone database [4]. This is a rather large corpus containing telephone speech from 5050 different speakers in 222075 speech files. The speakers were selected from all dialect regions in the Netherlands and the ratio between male and female speakers is almost fifty-fifty. The utterances contain all Dutch phonemes in as many phonetic contexts as the designers of the database could find.

To ensure well-trained models that can be used for recognizing speech recorded for example using a PC microphone only utterances that did not contain any background noise or disturbing hesitations were selected. Mouth noises, like smacking and loud breaths however were allowed. Nine items per speaker were used, all read sentences selected from newspaper articles. This resulted in a training set containing 22626 utterances. This system was created as a baseline system for further research on the subject of speech recognition within our group. In particular we wanted to build a continuous audio-visual speech recognition system. A problem with bimodal speech recognition experiments is however the lack of multi-modal databases containing both audio and visual information. Of the few databases available, like M2VTS [8], most contain only single words or digits and as a result they are not very well suited for the development of continuous speech processing systems. Therefore we recorded our own audio-visual data set. A number of respondents were asked to read prompts showed on the screen of a laptop in front of a digital video camera [2]. To be general purpose our prompt set includes isolated words, digit sequences, spelled words and phonetically rich sentences as well as commands from a telebanking application. Data from five of these subjects, male and female, was transcribed and used in the experiments described in this paper. A training set of approximately 500 utterances from all speakers and an independent test set containing 40 randomly chosen utterances from all speakers were formed.

The utterances in all data sets were encoded to Mel-frequency cepstral coefficient vectors. Each vector contains twelve cepstral coefficients with log energy and delta and acceleration coefficients added, all scaled around zero by subtracting the cepstral mean from all vectors. This resulted in 39 dimensional feature vectors. A sampling rate of 10 ms was used and each vector was calculated over a segment of 25 ms. The SAMPA set [4] was adopted as phoneme set for the recognizer. Three special purpose phonemes were added to model (optional) silence and mouthnoise. The resulting set contained 45 phones. For each of these phones a Hidden Markov Model was created. All models except the silence models share the same topology, which consisted of non-emitting start and end states and three emitting states using single Gaussian density functions. The states are connected in a left-to-right way, with self-loops and no skip transitions.

2.2 Training

As only unsegmented training data was available we initially set the mean and variance of all the Gaussians of all the models to the global mean and variance of the complete data set. These models were then trained iterative using embedded Baum-Welch re-estimation and Viterbi alignment. The short pause model, that is very susceptible to picking up vectors belonging to neighboring phones because of its optional nature, was added only after a few training cycles. The resulting single Gaussian monophone system was tested using a Viterbi decoder. An analysis tool, fully compatible with the standard US NIST scoring package, was used to calculate word recognition percentage and the word accuracy. In this test and in all other tests conducted during development the development test set was used. A backed-off bigram language model containing 1060 words was used in these tests. The first row of Table 1 shows the recognition results from the monophone system. To capture coarticulation effects word internal triphones were introduced. In total there were 8570 different triphones in the training data, but for many of these models there only was a single example in the training data making reliable estimates for these models difficult. To find the right balance between the number of models and their modeling accuracy data-driven state clustering was used to obtain a smaller set of generalized triphones. A system containing 2526 triphones provided a good balance between the number of parameters and the modeling accuracy. It contained less than one third of the original triphones and had at least three models per cluster and in most cases more. Each cluster had at least four examples in the training data. The transition matrices of the triphones that corresponded to the same monophone were tied. Models that ended up having their states in the same clusters and which had the same transition matrix were tied to obtain generalized triphones. To overcome the problem of unseen triphones, without resorting to knowledge based techniques, we introduced a technique that can be described as 'backed-off triphone approach'. In this approach the original monophone models augment the triphone model set. During recognition the word network is constructed by inserting the HMMs in the language model, triphone models are used whenever available, otherwise the corresponding monophone is used. This is implemented by tying all triphones that have no model of their own to the corresponding monophone. Essentially the monophones become generalized triphones. Of course they are less specialized than the other generalized triphones because they are trained on all corresponding triphones but the ones they represent, but being monophones they are general enough to cover the unseen triphones. For both the triphone model set and the monophone model set the number of Gaussian mixtures in the distribution functions was incremented to get more realistic distribution function. The results are shown in Table 1.

2.3 Evaluation Experiments

The final set of acoustic models consisted of the 17-mixture generalized triphone set and the 15-mixture monophone set. This system was tuned using the development test set. A grammar scale factor was used to regulate the relative influences of the language model and the acoustic model. These results presented so far were obtained on the test set that was used during the development process to tune several, to test the robustness of the system an evaluation test was performed using 100 sentences, each of which was spoken by a different person. The bigram language model used contained 5017 different words. The result is shown in Table 1. The experiment showed that the recognizer generalizes very well to speakers it was neither trained nor tuned on even when a large word network is used.

Table 1. Recognition results of ASR.

System	Percentage of words recognized	Word accuracy
monophone	38.34 %	-28.42 %
15-mixture monophone	56.81 %	15.51 %
17-mixture triphone	71.00 %	39.57 %
Development set	95.27 %	89.59 %
Evaluation set	93.55 %	88.76 %

3 Audio-Visual Speech Recognition

As is clear from Table 1 the recognizer performs well on relatively clean audio. But as with most speech recognizers performance degrades severely when background noise is involved (Figure 1). The visual modality is well known to contain some complementary information to the audio modality and, what is even more important in this context, it is not affected by any environmental noise. Thus, to get a more noise robust system the visual modality was taken into account by extending the speech feature vectors with features that were extracted using the lip-reading technique described in [3], resulting in a bimodal continuous speech recognizer. For these experiments the multi-modal data set we recorded was used. To get a baseline speech recognition system suited for comparison in these experiments the monophone system described above was adapted to the audio part of the data set by a number of re-estimation cycles. The results are shown in Table 2.

3.1 Feature Fusion

In feature fusion the feature vectors from both modalities are simply concatenated to generate a single vector on which a regular HMM based recognizer can then be trained. For this and subsequent experiments video features were extracted for all utterances of the multi-modal data set using the technique mentioned earlier. These features were then concatenated to the corresponding audio feature vectors. Because our data set is currently to small to train a robust bimodal recognizer from scratch, a different approach was taken. The multi-modal recognizer was created by extending the 39 dimensional distribution functions of the (unadapted) monophone speech recognizer to 50 dimensional distributions. The additional 11 means and variances of all states of all models were initialized with the global means and variances calculated over the entire video data set. Thus the audio part of the system was already reasonably trained and needed only some adaptation to the new data set, but the visual part could only be trained on the multi-modal data set. But as all models initially have the same parameters for their visual features the distribution of the feature vectors during Baum-Welch re-estimation will be guided by the speech features. This way a continuous multi-modal recognizer can be obtained in a few training cycles with a limited amount of training data. The speech part of the models ensures robustness while the video part may give valuable cues to differentiate between similar sounding phonemes. To train the video part of the system and adapt the audio part of the system, the combined models were re-estimated twice, using the bimodal training data. The models in this system thus received just as much training as the models in the adapted speech only system. The recognition results of this system are shown in Table 2.

3.2 Multi-stream Phoneme Models

The feature fusion system, although attractive because of its simplicity, was not able to improve upon the speech-only system. One of the problems with this approach is that is does not take into account the reliability of the separate streams. The audio stream is likely to be more reliable than the video stream in the setup described here, because of the clean audio and the well-trained speech part. The multi-stream HMM explicitly models the reliability of its streams. In its simplest form, the state synchronous multi-stream model, it uses separate distributions for its streams in each state.

$$b_j(o_t) = \prod_{s=1}^{2} N(o_t, \mu_{sj}, \Sigma_{sj})^{\gamma_s} \tag{1}$$

The observation likelihood of the state is the weighted product of the likelihoods of its stream components, as shown in formula 1, where the γ_s are the weights. A multi-stream recognizer was build using a similar approach as with the feature fusion model. The models from the baseline speech recognizer were used for the audio stream and the distributions in the video stream were initialize with the global mean and variance of the entire video data set. The system was re-estimated twice. Recognition experiments using different weighting schemes were performed, the results are shown in Table 2. The video and audio weights add up to two in all cases. By setting the weights so, as to put more emphasis on the audio stream this system is capable of doing a little better than the stand-alone speech recognizer. A shortcoming of this system is that it uses phones as basic units but from a lip-reading point of view it is hard to distinguish between certain phonemes, because of similar lip movements.

Table 2. Recognition results bimodal systems.

system	word rec. %	accuracy %
speech recognizer	84.24	83.82
feature fusion	83.69	78.61
phonemes; equal weights	83.69	78.61
phonemes; audio weight 1.2	84.43	79.41
phonemes; audio weight 1.4	84.22	78.88
visemes; audio weight: 0.9	84.76	80.48
visemes; audio weight: 1.0	85.56	80.28
visemes; audio weight: 1.1	85.92	82.09
visemes; audio weight: 1.2	85.03	80.75

3.3 Multi-stream Viseme Models

To solve the problem indicated above, it was decided to use visemes for the video stream. A viseme is basically a phoneme class; the following viseme classes were defined:

{sil, sp}, {E, E:}, {f, v, w}, {A, a}, {s, z}, {@}, {S, Z}, {p, b, m}
{O, Y, y, u, 2:, o:, 9, 9:, O:}, {g, k, x, n, N, r, j}, {t, d}, {I, e:}

The use of different units for the stream was realized by tying the distribution functions of corresponding states in the second stream for phonemes that are in the same phoneme class. The limited training data problem is also partially solved this way, because there is now more data per model in the second stream available. As with the previous systems this system was also re-estimated twice before recognition experiments were conducted. Table 2 shows the recognition results of a number of viseme systems with different weights. This system is capable of improving upon the speech recognizer even when both streams have equal weights.

4   Noise Robustness

In the experiments described in the previous section the improvements the bimodal system realized over the audio only system remain modest. This can be explained by the fact that both modalities encode similar information. If the video stream gives reason to belief that a plosive sound is uttered, and the speech recognizer has a hard time choosing between /p/ and /g/ then the bimodal system may correctly pick /p/. But if the speech recognizer already found that a /p/ was uttered then the additional information from the video data does not help much. Since relatively clean audio was used in the experiments described so far, the speech recognizer did not need the additional information from the lip-data, most of the time. But in a more noise environment the cues given by the video stream may be more valuable. To verify this hypothesis the multi-stream viseme system was tested using noisy data. This was done by adding different levels of white noise to the audio samples in the test set. The performance of the systems was measured for signal to noise ratios between 20 dB and -5 dB.

The performance of the speech-only system degrades rapidly under these conditions as can be seen in Figure 1. The multi-stream bimodal system with visemes is also shown. For low noise levels the multi-modal system performs slightly better than the speech recognizer, but as the noise level increases the bimodal system outperforms the unimodal system. At an SNR level of 5 dB the difference is 12 %. Recognition results for different SNR levels

From Figure 1 it can also be observed that the audio stream is no longer more reliable than the video stream. But is also proved hard to do better than the system with equal weights for both streams, by giving the video stream a higher weight. Our lip-reading technique seems to do especially well in discriminating between consonants (for example /f/ and /s/) therefore only the weighs of the consonant visemes were increased. Figure 1 also shows a system with consonant weights that were gradually increased as the noise level increased (up to a noise level of 0.8 dB, for higher levels the weights were decreased again). This system impressively outperformed all other systems.

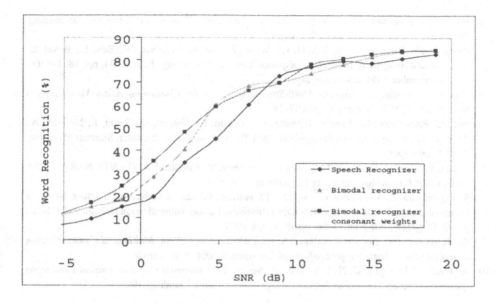

Fig. 1. Recognition results for different SNR levels.

5   Conclusion

In this paper we described the development of a large vocabulary speech recognizer for the Dutch language. The final system uses backed-off triphones that solve the problem of unseen triphones without the need for specific linguistic knowledge. The final system performs well, more than ninety percent of all words are recognized correctly. The recognizer can cope with noises like smacking or loud breathing and the system is speaker independent. It has been tested with vocabularies of more than 5000 words, the performance decreased only slightly in this case.

Our experiments with bimodal recognition showed that adding visual cues to our continuous speech recognizer results in better performance. This is especially the case in noisy environments. The best results so far were obtained by using a multi-stream Hidden Markov model with phoneme units for the speech stream and viseme units for the video stream. In the case of clean audio the speech stream dominates the performance of the system. In the case of noisy audio the relative performance of the system get better as the weights of the video stream are gradually increased according to the noise level. Improvements up to 16 % word recognition have been realized.

References

1. Wiggers, P, Wojdel J., Rothkrantz, L. *A Speech Recognizer for the Dutch Language*, In: Proceedings of Euromedia 2002, Modena, Italy.
2. Wojdel, J., Wiggers, P, Rotkrantz, L. *The Audio-Visual Corpus for Multimodal Speech Recognition in Dutch Language*, Submitted to ICSLP 2002, 2002.

3. Wojdel, J., Rothkrantz, L., *Using Aerial and Geometric Features in Automatic Lip-reading*, Proceedings of Eurospeech 2001, Scandinavia.
4. Damhuis M., Boogaart T., in 't Veld, C., Versteijlen, M.,W. Schelvis, W., Bos, L., Boves L., *Creation and Analysis of the Dutch Polyphone Corpus*, Proceedings ICSLP '94, pp. 1803–1806, 18–22 September 1994,Yokohama, Japan.
5. Dupont, S. Luettin J., *Using the Multi-Stream Approach for Continuous Audio Visual Speech Recognition*, IDIAP Research Report 97–14.
6. Neti, C. Potamianos, G., Luettin, J. Mattews I., Glotin, H., Vergyri, D., Sison, J., Mashari, A., Zhou, J., *Audio-Visual Speech Recognition*, IBM T.J. Watson Research Center, Summer Workshop 2000, Final Report.
7. Young, S., Kershaw, D., Odell, J., Ollason, D., Valtchev, V., Woodland, P., *The HTK Book (for HTK version 3.0)*, Cambridge University Engineering Department.
8. S. Pigeon and L. Vandendorpe, *The M2VTS multimodal face database*, in Lecture Notes in Computer Science: Audio- and Video- based Biometric Person Authentication (J. Bigun, G. Chollet and G. Borgefors, Eds.), vol. 1206, pp. 403–409, 1997.
9. Wolfgang Wahlster, Norbert Reithinger, Anselm Blocher: *SmartKom: Multimodal Communication with a Life-Like Character*, proceedings of Eurospeech 2001, Scandinavia.
10. A. Verma, T. Faruquie, C. Neti, S. Basu, A. Senior, *Late integration in audio-visual continuous speech recognition*, Automatic Speech Recognition and Understanding, 1999.

Utterance Verification Based on the Likelihood Distance to Alternative Paths

Gies Bouwman and Lou Boves

Department of Language and Speech, P.O. Box 9103,
6500 HD Nijmegen, The Netherlands
E-mail: G.Bouwman@let.kun.nl, L.Boves@let.kun.nl
WWW: http://lands.let.kun.nl/

Abstract. Utterance verification tries to reject incorrectly recognised utterances. For this purpose the probability of an error is often estimated by single confidence measure (CM). However, errors can have several different origins, and we argue that notion must be reflected in the design of the utterance verifier. In order to detect both in-vocabulary substitutions and out-of-vocabulary word errors, we compute CMs based on the log-likelihood distance to (1) the second best recognition result and to (2) the most likely free phone string.

Experiments in which different CMs were combined in different ways in the recognition of Dutch city names show that Confidence Error Rates [8] are reduced by 10 % by combining the CMs using a classification and regression tree instead of a linear combination with a decision threshold.

1 Introduction

The need for confidence measures in ASR no longer requires an explicit motivation. At the moment, we are exploring their use within the scope of the SMADA project [1], that investigates the practical implications of developing a system for nationwide directory assistance (DA). One of the subtasks is to recognise Dutch city names. Due to the high perplexity of the task, we face error rates exceeding 10 %. In order to enable a user-friendy dialogue in an automatic DA application, it is mandatory to automatically reject the least reliable recognition results. Another goal for which we need to identify utterances that were most probably misrecognised is automatic update of acoustic and language models based on speech that is recorded during the actual operation of the service.

Several studies (among others [2]) have analysed the origin of speech recognition errors. It is necessary to distinguish at least two different types of errors:

- the input speech is (partly) not modelled, for instance because it contains OOV words or word sequences that were not forseen in the grammar. As long as special measures, such as a garbage model, are not taken, "in domain" interpretation of those utterances is doomed to lead to one or more insertion errors.
- the input speech is modelled, but an alternative (incorrect) hypothesis happens to obtain a higher likelihood score. In this case a substitution error occurs.

P. Sojka, I. Kopeček, and K. Pala (Eds.): TSD 2002, LNAI 2448, pp. 213–220, 2002.

Of course, deletion errors can also occur. However, for the task under analysis, deletion errors are less important.

Because the causes of recognition errors can be many and varied, it would be surprising if a single indicator of the reliability of an output is sufficient to flag (virtually) all errors. Therefore, some investigators have attempted to combine multiple confidence measures [2,3,4,5]. Such combinations can take many different forms. In this paper we compare the power of a linear combination and a CART-like procedure.

In Section 2 we propose two measures to detect the two kinds of errors. We also describe our general system architecture and the material used to train and test the classifiers. In Section 3 we define the atomic confidence measures. We also outline two methods to combine these cues. Section 4 presents the results of our experiments, followed by a discussion of the results. Finally, Section 6 describes the main conclusions and perspectives for future work.

2   Method

2.1   Path Distance

The idea of our approach is that we compute two likelihood ratios. The first concerns the likelihoods of the best candidate and the runner-up in the N-best list.

$$\frac{P(X|W_1)}{P(X|W_2)} \tag{1}$$

If the quotient is much greater than 1, a substitution error with W_2 is unlikely, and the classification of X as W_1 is probably correct. Thus, the likelihood ratio of the two top hypotheses can serve as a measure to detect substitution errors.

However, incorrect classification may also be due to OOV speech. In that case the likelihood ratio between the first and second best hypotheses is not appropriate as confidence measure. For this reason, we also compute formula 2

$$\frac{P(X|W_1)}{P(X|W_{FPR})} \tag{2}$$

where W_{FPR} means the optimal phone string for the input speech, obtained with free phone recognition (FPR). Its likelihood score can serve as a normalisation coefficient for the likelihood of W_1. So when the word likelihood P(X | W_1) is higher than any other word, the free phoneme models may yield a much higher likelihood: relative to FPR, P(X | W_1) is small. In that case it is likely that an OOV word has been spoken.

In the following subsections we will elaborate on our general system architecture, our training and test material and some other elements of our design.

2.2   Architecture of the Utterance Verifier

We implemented our utterance verification method as a two-pass procedure. Figure 1 shows that in parallel to the recogniser generating an N-best city name list, the speech input is also decoded in terms of the optimal phone path. In the following steps, we compute four cues to decide whether the best solution is to be rejected or accepted:

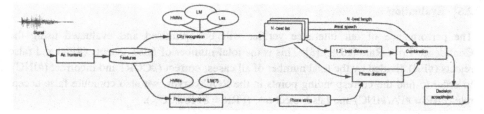

Fig. 1. System architecture.

1. the length of the original N-best list (> 0, ≤ N);
2. the number of frames assigned to other speech models than those of the recognised city name, like the garbage model or alternative city names;
3. the distance between the paths of the first and second best city name hypotheses;
4. the distance between the path of the best hypothesis and the path of phoneme recognition.

In the final step, we use either a linear combination (LC) or a classification and regression tree (CART) [6] to come to a decision. The linear combination combines the four measures into a one-dimensional confidence measure that allows one to reject (or accept) utterances based on some threshold value. The CART approach keeps the four dimensions separate; a rejection decision of a test case depends on the leaf node where that case is classified. We will return to this issue in Section 3.

2.3 Material and Models

Our material consists of the city name utterances of the DDAC2000 corpus [7]. Callers were prompted to say for which city they wanted a directory listing. The recordings were divided in a train, development and test set of 25 k, 11 k and 11.5 k utterances.

For the signal representation and ASR details we refer to [5]. The main characteristics of our ASR are that it is an HMM based system, with 2,369 city names in the lexicon and a bigram language model. The test set perplexity was 204.5.

2.4 Content Words

In our recognition experiments, the city names (or the expression 'I don't know') are the content words. These words convey the relevant information for the dialogue manager in this part of the interaction. Therefore, we evaluate recognition and verification only at that (semantic) level.

An implication of using N-grams (with discounting and backing-off strategies) is that recognition hypotheses may contain zero or multiple content words. The latter occur especially when lengthy OOV utterances are produced. In these cases, the first city name determines the value of the whole utterance and is passed on to the verification component; all other city names in the output are ignored.

2.5 Evaluation

The performance of our utterance verifier will be optimised and evaluated using the Confidence Error Rate (CER) [8]. This is the total number of false accepts (#FA) and false rejects (#FR) divided by the total number of all cases: correct (#COR) and incorrect (#INC). In order to find the corresponding points in the ROC curves, we also compute false accept rate (FAR = #FA/#INC) and false reject rate (FRR = #FR/#COR).

3 Implementation and Experiments

This section first describes the way the distance measures are computed, and the experiments to compare the different measures. Next, the implementation of the CART procedure is explained, and the way in which these implementations are compared.

3.1 Path Distance

First, we assume that the phone alignment of both paths is known. In other words, for each feature vector we have the information about which HMM unit was aligned against it. Doing this by forced segmentation, we are also able to obtain the corresponding acoustic log-likelihood scores. The absolute difference between two scores for the same time frame is a log-likelihood ratio (LLR) score at frame level, as displayed by formula 3.

$$LLR(x_t|S_t^b, S_t^a) = LL(x_t|S_t^b) \quad LL(x_t|S_t^a) \tag{3}$$

where S_t^b and S_t^a are the states of the best and alternative hypotheses aligned against x_t, the feature vector at time t. LL(x|S) is the log likelihood score of vector x as computed with S's pdf.

Next we combine the frame scores into a single score per content word. Formula 4 shows how we first take the average absolute LLR on phone level and next on word level.

$$\frac{1}{|W|} \sum_{\psi \in W} \left[\frac{1}{(\psi_e \quad \psi_s)} \sum_{t=\psi_s}^{\psi_e} abs \left(LLR(x_t|S_t^b, S_t^a) \right) \right] \tag{4}$$

where W is the content word we compute confidence for. $|W|$ denotes the number of phones in W. The index $\psi \in W$ runs over all phones of W with ψ_s and ψ_e being their respective start and end times.

In our experiments we used formula 4 to compute the distance between the recognised content word, i.e. the top candidate of the N-best list, and the runner up, if available. We refer to this distance as D_{rup}. At the same time, we compute the distance between the best content word and the optimal phone string resulting from free phone recognition, which we call D_{fpr} from now on.

3.2 The Role of Language Models

One of the assumptions we made is that the distance between first best and best FPR path says something about the credibility of the acoustic score. At this point the question arises whether to use a phone language model (LM) in the FPR. Using an LM can help to minimise phone error rate, but one may wonder if this is a goal to aim for. By ignoring prior knowledge we will truly maximise acoustic likelihood. For D_{rup} however, the language model scores are important and should probably not be ignored. After all, if two candidates have equal acoustic scores, but one is enforced by the language model, the a-posteriori probability of an error will be minimised by selecting the hypothesis with the best score including the LM. Summarising, in the distance ratio D_{fpr} the acoustic score ought to be sufficient, but in D_{rup} we should use both.

Experiment 1 In experiment 1 we investigate the role of LMs in the computation of the likelihood scores. There are four combinations (D_{fpr} with and without LM) x (D_{rup} with and without LM) and for each combination we computed the distance scores on a development and a test set. The distance between two paths is computed according to combination formula 4. The development set was used to train the coefficients of a linear combination function using LDA (for each of the four systems separately). With these functions we combined the distances of the test set and thus obtained a single confidence score for every utterance.

3.3 LC versus CART

Although LCs have the advantage of yielding a one-dimensional score, a linear separation may not be optimal in the face of multiple and unrelated causes of recognition errors. CART procedures have proven to be a very powerful alternative for LC in many speech recognition tasks. Therefore, we compare CART and LC for their power in distinguishing between correct and erroneous hypotheses at the output of our ASR system.

When training a CART, it is necessary to define an optimisation criterion for splitting a data set. Correctly recognised city names can thus be optimally separated from the incorrect ones. In our situation we shift a threshold over each of the four numerical confidence cues to classify the ASR output. The best threshold value according to either formula 5 or 6 is stored as the binary separator.

$$\hat{T} = \text{argmax}_T \left[1 - FAR(T) - FRR(T)^{1/\psi} \right] \tag{5}$$

$$\hat{T} = \text{argmax}_T \left[1 - FRR(T) - FAR(T)^{1/\psi} \right] \tag{6}$$

In words, these formulas express that the optimal threshold is at a value where false accept rate is optimised while false reject rate is close to its minimum or vice versa. The strictness of 'close' is controlled with exponent ψ, with typical values around 2.0.

Experiment 2 We estimate the parameters of the tree on the same development set as used in Experiment 1. The evaluation is of course on the test set. Since the CART approach yields only one optimal separation scheme, there is no straightforward way to generate an ROC curve. Therefore, we compare the performance of CART and LDA in terms of Confidence Error Rate.

4 Results

All verification results are based on a single run of our recogniser on the test set. Since previous reports, like [5], we have improved performance and currently 14.4% of the

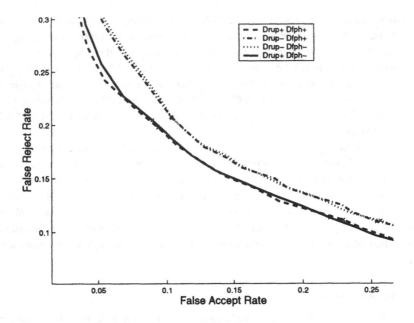

Fig. 2. ROC curves with and without language model contribution in the path distances.

utterances are incorrectly recognised. This percentage can be split up in different types of errors. 8.4 % of all recognition results contain a substitution error, while 4.2 % can be ascribed to the presence of OOV words (insertion errors). The remaining 1.8 % are deletion errors, that we consider as relatively harmless.

Figure 2 shows the ability to separate correct utterances from incorrect ones in terms of % False Accept and % False Reject. The +/- signs in the legend indicate whether LM scores are taken into account for the respective path distance. Table 1 shows the optimal CER values that correspond with these curves.

Table 1. CER, FAR and FRR when using the LM score (+lm) or disregarding it (-lm) in D_{rup} and D_{fpr}.

D_{rup}	D_{fpr}	%CER	%FAR	%FRR
-lm	+lm	11.2	51.3	4.4
-lm	-lm	11.4	53.0	4.4
+lm	+lm	10.5	54.2	3.1
+lm	-lm	10.5	54.1	3.2

The second experiment comprised building a CART. Its character cannot be illustrated by an ROC curve, because there is no threshold involved. After optimising the decision tree on our development set and classifying the test set, we measured the CER being 9.4 %. The corresponding FAR and FRR amounted to 31.3 % and 5.6 % respectively.

5 Discussion

When comparing the curves in Figure 2, we see that the two systems that take the language score distance into account for D_{rup}, have an ROC that is closer to the origin. This means that their ability to separate correct utterances from incorrect utterances is better. The CER values in rows 3 and 4 of Table 1 are significantly better than those in the first two rows (95 % confidence). At the same time we see that the use of a language model to optimise the free phone recognition makes no significant difference. Here we see a confirmation of our idea that minimising phone error rate is not a goal to aim for. However, this is no evidence that omitting the LM is beneficial.

When comparing the two confidence measure combination methods, it appears immediately that the classification tree method is better than the linear combinations. The relative improvement of CART when compared with the best result obtained with LC is about 10 %, which is significant. Although we did not perform a case-by-case analysis, this gives reason to believe that the problem of utterance verification is not optimally served by a one-dimensional confidence measure. Errors have diverse causes that can well be reflected in a multidimensional vector. The CART verifier has access to the vector components until the final decision moment.

We also examined the split parameters in our D-tree. It appeared that D_{rup} was in fact the most informative variable to split the population at the root node. The next split, down either of the branches, was based on D_{fpr}. The total number of nodes in the tree amounted to 8 and all four cues were used.

6 Conclusions

In this paper we proposed confidence scores on the basis of distances between the best and second best recognition hypotheses and between the best word and phone recognition results. In this way, we aimed to detect substitution and OOV errors. Reasoning that these two source processes are unrelated, we tested the hypothesis that a CART is a better combiner than a Linear Combination; the relative confidence error rate improvement of 10 % confirmed this assumption.

In future work we would like to include syllable-based measures that take lexical stress into account, like in the linear combinations we tested in [5]. Encouraged by the results of the present study, we believe that a CART may help to disclose more valuable information in specific parts of the complex space.

References

1. L. Boves, D. Jouvet, J. Sienel, R. de Mori, F. Béchet, L. Fissore, P. Laface ASR for Automatic Directory Assistance: the SMADA Project Proc. of ASR 2000, Paris (2000).
2. D. Charlet, G. Mercier, G. Jouvet: On Combining Confidence Measures for Improved Rejection of Incorrect Data. Proc. of EuroSpeech 2001. Aalborg (2001), pp. 2113–2116.

3. S. Kamppari, T. Hazen: Word and Phone Level Acoustic Confidence Scoring. Proc. of ICASSP 2000, Vol. III. Istanbul (2000), pp. 1799–1802.
4. T. Hazen, I. Bazzi: A Comparison and Combination of Methods for OOV Detection and Word Confidence Scoring. Proc. of ICASSP '01, Vol. I. Salt Lake City (2001), pp. 397–400.
5. G. Bouwman, L. Boves: Using Information on Lexical Stress for Utterance Verification. Proc. of ITRW on Prosody in ASRU. Red Bank (2001), pp. 29–34.
6. L. Breiman(ed) et al.: Classification and Regression Trees. Chapman & Hall. 1998.
7. J. Sturm, H. Kamperman, L. Boves, E. den Os: Impact of Speaking Style and Speaking Task on Acoustic Models Proc. of ICSLP 2000, Vol. I. Beijing (2000), pp. 361–364.
8. F. Wessel, K. Macherey, R. Schlüter: Using Word Probabilities as Confidence Measures. Proc. of ICASSP 1998, Vol. I. Seattle (1998), pp. 225–228.

Rejection Technique Based on the Mumble Model

Tomáš Bartoš and Luděk Müller

University of West Bohemia in Pilsen, Department of Cybernetics,
Univerzitní 8, 306 14 Plzeň, Czech Republic
E-mail: tbartos@kky.zcu.cz, muller@kky.zcu.cz

Abstract. In this paper a technique for detection and rejection of incorrectly recognized words is described. The speech recognition system we used is based on a speaker-independent continuous density Hidden Markov Model recognizer and so-called mumble model, which structure and function is also depicted. An improved rejection technique is presented in comparison with the heuristic rejection method that we previously used. The new method is fully statistically based. Therefore selection of features for training and classification, procedures for statistical models parameters estimation, and experimental results are reported. The improved rejection technique achieves approximately 12 % error rate in detection of incorrectly recognized words.

1 Introduction

Although a significant progress in speech recognition research has been done in last years the accuracy of current speech recognition systems is still not sufficient. Thus, one of the most important problems is to be sure if the recognized word (phrase) was correctly recognized. Often only one incorrectly recognized word can completely change the meaning of the whole sentence. In some cases even the opposite meaning of the really said utterance can be obtained. Thus some technique evaluating a confidence of recognized words is needed. This technique is usually called rejection technique because the low confident words determined by this technique are rejected as incorrectly recognized and subsequently some corrective action can be taken. In the following sections a new rejection technique in comparison with the previously one (presented in [3]) is described.

2 Speech Recognition System

The Speech Recognition (SR) system we used is based on a statistical approach to recognition. It incorporates a front-end, a language model (represented by a stochastic regular grammar) and a decoding block to find the best word sequence matching the incoming acoustic signal. The basic speech unit of the SR system is a triphone. Each triphone is represented by a 3-state left-to-right Hidden Markov Model (HMM) with a continuous output probability density function assigned to each state. Each density is expressed as a mixture of multivariate Gaussians with a diagonal covariance matrix. The Czech phonetic decision trees were used to tie states of Czech triphones.

P. Sojka, I. Kopeček, and K. Pala (Eds.): TSD 2002, LNAI 2448, pp. 221–228, 2002.

In order to determine the recognition confidence (i.e. decide if reject or do not reject the recognized word) the system is equipped with so-called Mumble Model (MM). The MM network and the HMMs recognition network are separated but work in parallel and each of them has its own output. Both outputs are time synchronized: the output in the time step t of the HMMs network corresponds to the output of the MM network in the same time step t. The outputs from both networks are network scores. The network score is a log-likelihood of such a surviving network state which likelihood is maximal in the time t. To obtain these scores we use a Viterbi search with beam pruning.

3   Mumble Model

The MM is constructed as a HMMs network. The network consists of parallel connected HMM branches. Each branch (HMM model) is 3-states left-to-right and represents one context-independent phone. The structure of the MM is shown in Figure 2. Indeed the probability of emission of an observation vector in a given state is evaluated as the maximal emission probability of all corresponding states of context-dependent triphones. Thus neither additional HMMs nor additional training is required. In addition, there is one backward loop with a transition probability that causes a various length of a phone sequence recognized by the MM network. While the higher value produces more insertions in recognized phone sequence, the smaller value induces more deletions.

This model can be used for two reasons. For rejection or for key-phrase (word) spotting. This paper refers only on using MM for the sake of the rejection technique. The MM implementation as a key-phrase filler model can be found in [3].

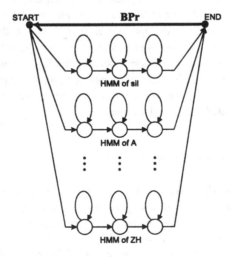

Fig. 1. Mumble model.

4   The Rejection Technique

Our rejection technique implementation idea consists in an assumption that MM network and HMMs recognition network scores differ more significantly for incorrectly recognized then for correctly recognized words. The network scores can be imagined as discrete time functions and thus it is possible to compute the difference between them in every time step because both scores are time synchronized.

The HMM recognition network (actually the mentioned decoder) assigns to each word utterance one vocabulary word that best matches the acoustic signal. This recognized word is represented by a sequence of triphones. The mumble model produces a sequence of context-independent phones regardless if they represent a vocabulary word or not. If on the input of the decoder is a word from the system vocabulary and this word is correctly recognized, then the phone sequences decoded by the HMM recognition network and by the MM network are nearly the same. In the case of incorrectly recognized word or out-of-vocabulary (OOV) word these sequences and also the scores will be more different.

4.1   The Previously Used Rejection Technique

In every time step the difference between the MM and the HMM network score is computed (networks are time synchronized). This difference is stored in a buffer B containing the last N computed score differences. Let us assume that M is such a constant that $0 < M < N$. In every time step $t > M$ the difference between the last buffer element $B[t]$ and the element $B[t-M]$ is computed and compared to a heuristically adjusted threshold. Note that we can use more than one threshold and thus more time intervals M (the use of 3 different M and 3 threshold is described in [3]). If the computed difference is higher than the threshold, then the recognized word is rejected. The equal error rate of this rejection technique was about 25 %.

4.2   The Improved Rejection Technique

The new rejection technique is not based on heuristically adjusted thresholds but it uses a statistical approach to find the optimal threshold values. The new method is based on the idea of firstly gathering a large collection of features and subsequently select the best informative feature set for the rejection classifier. The computation of differences between scores of MM and HMM networks remain unchanged. The more detail description of the new method is given in the next sections.

4.3   The Rejection and the Acceptation Models

The main goal is to identify words that were probably incorrectly recognized in order to have a chance to take some correcting action. The decision if an unknown word was correctly or incorrectly recognized can be expressed as a classification into two classes. Each class is represented by a set of words. The first set is the set of incorrectly recognized words and the second set contains only correctly recognized words. We should describe mathematically these sets in order to classify each recognized word into one of these two sets. Because we want to use a probability-based classifier we must find statistical models of these sets.

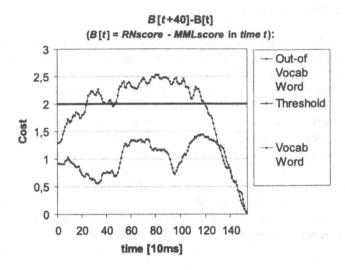

Fig. 2. The principle of the previously used method with heuristic thresholds.

We call them acceptation and rejection models. The acceptation model is trained on the set of correctly recognized words and the rejection model on the set of incorrectly recognized words.

Note, that there are two groups of incorrectly recognized words. The first one is a set of vocabulary words that were incorrectly recognized. The second group comprises OOV words. In summary the rejection model can be trained in three ways (on OOV set, on vocabulary words set, or on the both sets) and the error rate of the rejection technique slightly depends on the selected way.

4.4   Features Choice

Selection of features is based on the fact that the rise of variable $B(t)$ for a correctly recognized word is smaller then for the OOV word (or incorrectly recognized word). Generally, for a fixed value i the vector

$$M_i = B(t + i)   B(t), \quad t = 0, \ldots, T - i, \tag{1}$$

we can compute.

The vector M_i represents an increase of the difference between the MM score and the HMM score during the time interval i. We call these vectors M_i differential curves. Knowledge of this increasing is especially useful for detection of places where recognition errors probably occurred because these places are local maximums of the differential curves. Now we compute the M_i for a range of value i from 1 to 50 and draw the value of each vector M_i as a continuous curve i in time. The highest peaks of each M_i curve represent local maximums of recognition errors.

Several highest values (5–6) are used as features for the classifier responsible for the rejection decision. Figure 3 shows an example of curves for a different time interval i. a) is an example of differential curve between the MM and the HMM score for $i = 1$, in b) the same word-score for $i = 20$ is depicted.

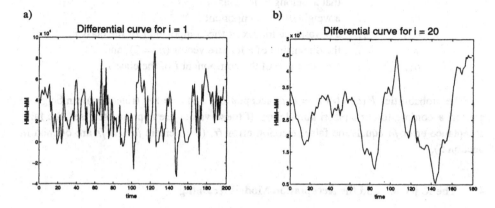

Fig. 3. An example of differential curves for $i = 1$ and $i = 20$.

4.5 Informative Feature Set Selection

There are many options which and how many features to chose. For example, for each differential curve with i from 1 to 50 we can take 5 or 6 highest peaks as useful classification features. In summary we get 250 or 300 features (5 or 6 peaks for each of 50 curves). Because the total number of features is too high and the classifier should work in real time we should reduce this enormous number of features (but without significant loss of information). For that reason we used two methods based on Karhunen-Loeve expansion [1,2].

The first method we used was the Kittler-Young (KY) method [1] and the second one the Fukunaga-Koontz (FK) method [2]. As a result we obtained a set containing only 2 (best informative) features.

4.6 Classification Criterion

Because we want to decide if the recognized word was recognized correctly or incorrectly the rejection classifier should classify into two classes – into the acceptation or into the rejection model. In addition, to further improve the decision criterion we used the Bayesian formula for the case of a uniform loss function:

$$g_r(x) = p(x|\omega_r) \cdot P(\omega_r), \quad r = \begin{cases} acc \ \text{(acceptation)} \\ rej \ \text{(rejection)} \end{cases} \tag{2}$$

$$p(x|\omega_r) = \sum_{i=1}^{3} \frac{c_i}{(2\pi)^{\frac{n}{2}}\sqrt{\det C_r}} \cdot \exp\left[-\frac{1}{2}(x - \mu_r)^T C_r^{-1}(x - \mu_r)\right], \tag{3}$$

where x ...   the 2-dimensional feature vector,

          r ...   the class identifier, $r \in \{acc, rej\}$,

          i ...   the mixture component index,

          $P(\omega_r)$ ...   a priori probability of occurrence of the class r

          $P(x|\omega_r)$ ...   a conditional probability of observation of the vector x given
                                that x belong to the class r,

          c_i ...   a weight of the component i,

          C_{ri} ...   a covariance matrix of the component i of the class r,

          n ...   the dimension of a feature vector ($n = 2$), and

          μ_{ri} ...   a mean value of the component i of the class r.

The probabilities $P(\omega_r)$ for $r = acc$ (acceptation) and $r = rej$ (rejection) can be given a priori according to our a priori knowledge. If these values are appropriately set, the false acceptance error fa equals the false rejection error fr, (both errors fa and fr are defined in Section 5).

4.7   The Rejection and the Acceptation Models Training

We assumed that the probability density functions of the both models (i.e. the acceptation model and the rejection model) have a form of a mixture of three continuous two-dimensional Gaussian distributions. For model parameters estimation the maximal a posteriori estimation method was used. This method leads to an expectation maximization (EM) algorithm. 15 parameters for each statistical model (3×2 mean values, 3×2 variance values, 3 weights) should be obtained. These parameters fully describe the models and thus the classifier.

If we denote:

          x_n nth sample represented by the nth feature vector,

          y a hidden variable (in case of Gaussian mixture the index
                     of the mixture component),

          λ a vector of model parameters (for each component - mean vector,
                     covariance matrix and component weight), and

          λ_0 initial values of vector parameters,

then the EM algorithm can be briefly explain as follows:

1.

$$\lambda = \lambda_0 \tag{4}$$

2.

$$Q(\lambda, \overline{\lambda}) = \sum_{n=1}^{N} \sum_{y} P(y|x_n, \lambda) \cdot \log p(x_n, y|\overline{\lambda}) \tag{5}$$

3.

$$\lambda^* = \arg\max_{\underline{\lambda}} Q(\lambda, \overline{\lambda}) \tag{6}$$

4.

$$\lambda = \lambda^* \tag{7}$$

5.   if $|\lambda - \lambda^*| > eps$ then return to 2.

The value eps is set up in advance before the algorithm starts. Its smaller value means a higher accuracy of estimated parameters. The algorithm finds only a local minimum, so the obtained parameters generally depend on the initial values λ_0.

5   Error-Rate Calculation

After the features selection/reduction, and models training trough the EM algorithm we obtained the resultant rejection classifier. In the classification stage for each recognized word the classification features are computed and the Bayes classifier is used to decide which model (i.e. acceptation or rejection) is more probable, i.e. if the spoken word was recognized correctly ($g_{acc}(x) > g_{rej}(x)$) or incorrectly ($g_{acc}(x) < g_{rej}(x)$).

FR - number of false rejected words

FA - number of false accepted words

TA - number of correctly accepted words

TR - number of correctly rejected words

Formulas for the false acceptance fa and the false rejection fr:

$fa = FA/(FA + TR) \cdot 100\%$

$fr = FR/(FR + TA) \cdot 100\%$

The equal error rate is defined for such a value of a priori probability

$$P_{acc}(x) = 1 \quad P_{rej}(x) \tag{8}$$

for which the false acceptance fa is equal to the false rejection fr.

6   Experimental Conditions and Experimental Results

The speech corpus comprises 380 speakers and 380 utterances (person names). Each utterance was spoken by a different speaker. The set of data was split into two subsets. The first subset contained 200 utterances and the second subset 180 utterances. The first subset was used for training statistical models (i.e. acceptation and rejection models), the second one as a test data for the rejection technique evaluation.

In Figure 4 the error-rates of the new rejection technique are given. Figure 4a) shows the result of the KY method and Figure 4b) the result of the FK method.

Conclusion

According to the new rejection method described above an approximately 12 % equal error rate was achieved. Nearly 9 from 10 incorrectly recognized words were detected. It is a significant improvement in comparison with our previous method based on a heuristically defined threshold. No significant difference between the KY and the FK method was observed (the difference of their equal error rates was about 1 %). It seems that the statistical approach is well suited for solving the rejection problem. The future direction should deal with a further improvement of our method e.g. new features choice, and speed and memory optimization.

228   T. Bartoš and L. Müller

a)   b)

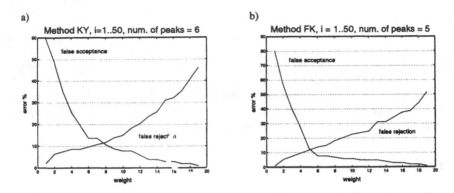

Fig. 4. Examples of error rates of the KY method (a) and the FK method (b).

Acknowledgment

This work was supported by the Ministry of Education of the Czech Republic project no.
MSM235200004.

References

1. Kittler, J., Young, P. C.: A New Approach to Feature Selection Based on the Karhunen Loeve
   Expansion. Pattern Recognition, 1973, n. 4, pp. 335–352.
2. Fukunaga, K., Koontz, W. L. G.: Application of the Karhunen Loeve Expansion to Feature
   Selection and Ordering. IEEE Trans. on Computers, C-19 (1970), n. 4, pp. 311–318.
3. Müller, L., Jurčíček F., Šmídl, L.: Rejection and Key-Phrase Spotting Techniques Using a Mumble
   Model in a Czech Telephone Dialogue System, Proceedings of the 6th International Conference on
   Spoken Language Processing ICSLP 2000, Beijing, China, 2000, pp. 134–137.

Efficient Noise Estimation and Its Application for Robust Speech Recognition*

Petr Motlíček[1,2] and Lukáš Burget[1,2]

[1] OGI School of Science & Engineering at Oregon Health & Science University
20000 NW Walker Road, Beaverton, OR, 97006, USA
[2] Faculty of Information Technology, Brno University of Technology
Božetěchova 2, Brno, 612 66, Czech Republic
E-mail: petr@asp.ogi.edu, lukas@asp.ogi.edu

Abstract. The investigation of some well known noise estimation techniques is presented. The estimated noise is applied in our noise suppression system that is generally used for speech recognition tasks. Moreover, the algorithms are developed to take part in front-end of Distributed Speech Recognition (DSR). Therefore we have proposed some modifications of noise estimation techniques that are quickly adaptable on varying noise and do not need so much information from past segments. We also minimized the algorithmic delay. The robustness of proposed algorithms were tested under several noisy conditions.

1 Introduction

The error rate of speech recognition systems increases dramatically in the presence of noise. It is therefore very convenient to use some noise reduction technique which can operate under adverse conditions. Often used speech enhancement systems based on spectral decomposition such as Wiener filtering or Spectral subtraction rely on an accurate estimation of the background noise energy as well as signal-to-noise ratio (SNR) in the various frequency bands.

A number of approaches were proposed to estimate the noise without the need for speech/pause detector. However the implementation of the front-end DSR system is limited by technical constraints, e.g. memory requirements, algorithmic delay, complexity. Since this limitation is given a-priori, we were supposed to come up with noise estimation algorithm that would satisfy the requirements and that would be the best for our noise suppression algorithm.

2 Experimental Setup

The noise suppression algorithms proposed for speech recognition system were tested on three SpeechDat - Car (SDC) databases used for Advanced DSR Front-End Evaluation:

---

* This research was supported by industrial grant from Qualcomm, DARPA N66001-00-2-8901/0006, and by the Grant Agency of Czech Republic under project no. 102/02/0124.

P. Sojka, I. Kopeček, and K. Pala (Eds.): TSD 2002, LNAI 2448, pp. 229–236, 2002.

Italian SDC [1], Spanish SDC [2], and Finish SDC. The recordings were taken from the close-talk microphone and from one of the hands-free microphones. Data were recorded at 16 kHz, but downsampled to 8 kHz. The databases contain various utterances of digits.

During experiments, the robustness was tested under three different training conditions. For each of these three conditions 70 % of the files were used for training, 30 % for testing.

- **Well-matched condition (wm):** All the files (close-talk and hands-free microphones) were used for training and testing.
- **Medium mis-matched condition (mm):** Only recordings made with the hands-free microphone were used for training and testing.
- **Highly mis-matched condition (hm):** For the training only close-talk microphone recordings were used, whereas for testing the hands-free files were taken.

3 Noise Suppression System

Many of noise suppression schemes exist. Practically all of them share the common goal of attempting to increase the signal-to-noise ratio (SNR). They differ in complexity and suitability for real-time processing. The noise suppression algorithm [3], which is being used in our feature extraction, has been derived from standard Spectral subtraction and Wiener filtering. The algorithm supposes that the noise and the speech signal are uncorrelated. Moreover we assume that their power spectral contributions are additive: $|X_k[n]|^2 = |Y_k[n]|^2 + |N_k[n]|^2$, where $|Y_k[n]|^2$ denotes the clean speech power spectrum at the given time n in the frequency subband k, and $|N_k[n]|^2$ is the noise power spectrum. The noise reduction algorithm can be viewed as a filtering operation where high SNR regions of the measured spectrum are attenuated less than low SNR regions. The mathematic description of our noise suppression filter is:

$$|H_k[n]|^2 = max\left(\frac{|X_k[n]|^2 \quad osub|N_k[n]|^2}{|X_k[n]|^2}, \beta\right)^2. \tag{1}$$

An oversubtraction factor $osub$ is a filter parameter which varies with time and is estimated from energy of signal and noise. While a large $osub$ essentially eliminates residual spectral peaks, it also affects quality of speech so that some of the low energy phonemes are suppressed. This drawback is reduced by dependency of $osub$ on SNR. Yet a spectral floor threshold β does not change with time and prevents the filter components from small values.

In order to alleviate the influence of musical noise, the filter transfer function $|H_k[n]|^2$ is smoothed in temporal domain, whereas the following smoothness in spectral domain showed itself to be very useful for low SNR as well as clean speech recognition.

4 Noise Estimation

As can be seen from Eq. 1, the noise suppression algorithm requires the accurate estimation of the noise power spectrum $|N_k[n]|^2$. This is however difficult in practical situations especially if the background noise is not stationary or SNR is low.

A commonly used method for noise spectrum estimation is to average over sections which do not contain speech, i. e. voice activity detector (VAD) is required to determine speech and non-speech sequences. It relies on the fact that there actually exists a sufficient amount of non-speech in the signal. Standard noise estimation methods without explicit VAD were tested in our feature extraction system.

4.1 Temporal Minima Tracking

The best estimation of noise in our experiments has been obtained with standard temporal minima tracking algorithm [4]. This algorithm is applied consequently on smoothed power spectrum:

$$P_{xk}[n] = \alpha P_{xk}[n-1] + (1 - \alpha)|X_k[n]|^2, \tag{2}$$

with forgetting factor α between $0.75 \ldots 0.8$. The algorithm is independently used on each spectral subband of $P_{xk}[n]$. The initial smoothing of power spectra slows down the rapid frame-to-frame movement. The estimated power spectrum of noise $P_{nk}[n]$ for k^{th} subband is found as a minimum of $P_{xk}[n]$ within a temporal window of D previous and current power sample:

$$P_{nk}[n] = min(P_{xk}[n-D] : P_{xk}[n]). \tag{3}$$

The processing window of D samples is at the beginning filled by first frame $P_{xk}[1]$. It reflects the assumption that the first frame of an utterance does not contain speech. The example of estimated noise $P_{nk}[n]$ is given in Figure 2 (lower panel). However the standard minima tracking algorithm causes problems of causality and large memory requirement. From many experiments we have observed that $P_{nk}[n]$ can be well estimated just from current and previous samples of $P_{xk}[n]$. But the necessity of large memory buffer makes this noise estimation technique not applicable for feature extraction part of DSR system.

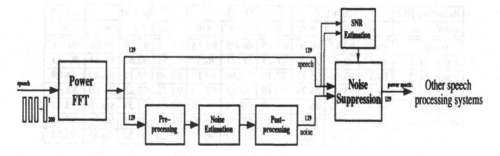

Fig. 1. Scheme of noise suppression system with noise estimation applied in Mel-scale filter bank domain.

The memory buffer size for minima tracking algorithm is given as D times r, where r denotes number of spectral subbands. In order to get sufficient estimation of $P_{nk}[n]$, D should not be smaller than 80. Usually r is 129. In [4], it is suggested to decompose one window of length D into W subwindows (for each spectral band independently), which brings some memory reduction but does not cause the system's degradation (*noise est. 2, 3, 4* in Table 1).

In our previous experiments we have observed some good properties of noise estimation algorithms when processing in spectral domain as well. Spectral domain processing is another possibility to reduce memory buffer for noise estimation. We may decrease the spectral resolution of $P_{xk}[n]$, estimate the noise and apply some kind of interpolation technique with spectral smoothing to get the initial number of spectral subbands *noise est. 6* in Table 1.

Another spectral processing we have tried in our experiments was to integrate the power spectra $|X_k[n]|^2$ into spectral bands applying the Mel filter bank. This operation can be viewed as a smoothing of power spectra in spectral domain. Then the noise estimation is done in this integrated spectrum. Number of spectral bands of initial power spectra $|X_k[n]|^2$ is 129 ($1 \ldots F_{sampling}/2$). After application of Mel filter bank, number of bands was reduced to 23. The estimated noise in Eq. 1 is however expected in power spectral domain (again 129 subbands). Hence we applied inverse projection from 23 spectral bands into 129 subbands of power spectra, which caused the additional smoothing. In order to keep the same energies in bands, standard Mel filter bank for direct projection was modified, so that the areas under particular triangular weighting functions were normalized to unity:

$$Mfb_{MOD_k}[i] = \frac{Mfb_k[i]}{\sum_{j=1}^{129} Mfb_k[j]}, \quad k \in 1 \ldots 23, i \in 1 \ldots 129. \tag{4}$$

The results obtained with noise estimated using previously described approaches are in Table 1.

Table 1. Speech recognition results for Italian, Finish and Spanish databases with noise estimation based on temporal minima tracking algorithm. The experiments' conditions are explained in Section 2. The detailed algorithm descriptions are in Table 3.

Accuracy [%]	Italian			Finish			Spanish			overall
conditions	hm	mm	wm	hm	mm	wm	hm	mm	wm	[%]
baseline	85.01	91.17	96.00	88.15	86.85	95.48	88.21	90.67	95.84	**91.81**
noise est. 1	86.77	92.77	96.90	91.17	88.92	96.67	92.51	92.85	96.43	**93.23**
noise est. 2	89.11	93.45	96.75	92.16	90.36	97.13	92.60	93.11	96.80	**93.89**
noise est. 3	89.21	93.41	96.74	92.19	90.22	97.13	92.72	93.22	96.60	**93.87**
noise est. 4	89.27	93.25	96.71	92.19	90.29	96.97	92.84	93.31	96.70	**93.83**
noise est. 5	88.24	92.53	96.59	92.12	88.17	96.97	91.94	93.55	96.86	**93.41**
noise est. 6	89.16	93.05	96.67	92.05	89.81	96.82	92.60	93.20	96.65	**93.71**

4.2   Noise Estimation Based on Filtering of Temporal Trajectories of Spectral Coefficients

Often used noise estimation algorithm, proposed in [5], which does not need information about speech/non-speech segments, has been tested in our experiments. Here each spectral subband is filtered by nonlinear estimator that might be perceived as an efficient implementation of temporal minima tracking in power spectral domain. This temporal processing also

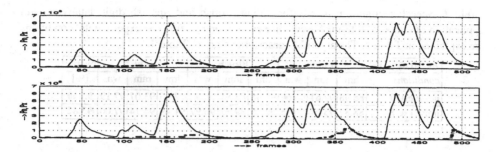

Fig. 2. Process of noise estimation in short-time power spectra (8th subband - related to 250 Hz). The solid lines represent the smoothed power spectra $P_{xk}[n]$, the dashed lines describe estimated $P_{nk}[n]$:
Upper panel: Filtering of spectral subbands in temporal domain.
Lower panel: Minima tracking in temporal domain.

requires a smoothed version of power spectrum $P_{xk}[n]$ pre-computed by Equation 2. The algorithm can be described as follows:

$$P_{nk}[n] = \gamma P_{nk}[n \quad 1] + \frac{1-\gamma}{1-\beta}(P_{xk}[n] - \beta P_{xk}[n-1]). \tag{5}$$

The minima tracking is ensured in this approach so that $P_{nk}[n] \leq P_{xk}[n]$, $\forall k, n$ as can be seen in Figure 2 (upper panel). Although this method does not bring any difficulties with memory size, the basic approach from [5] was not successful in our front-end system (*noise est. 7* in Table 2). That was mainly caused by high level of estimated noise in speech portions of processed sentences. Therefore we have experimented with implementation of some simple speech/pause detector. The used algorithm comes from [6] and is based on the evaluation of the SNRs in each spectral subband individually. We compute the relative ratio of noise energy to signal&noise energy NX for each subband:

$$NX_{relk}[n]) = \frac{NX_k[n] - NX_{mink}[n]}{NX_{maxk}[n] - NX_{mink}[n]}. \tag{6}$$

NX_{min} and NX_{max} are originally determined from the past (at least 400ms) which can cause memory complexity. Therefore we have used NX_{min}, NX_{max} fixed. For calculation of NX ratio, $P_{xk}[n]$ from Eq. 2 and $P_{nk}[n]$ from Eq. 5 were taken. For each spectral subband independently the speech is indicated, and $P_{nk}[n]$ is modified so that

$$P_{nk}[n] = \begin{cases} 0.4 P_{nk}[n] \; if \quad NX_{relk}[n] < thresh, \quad k \in 1 \ldots 129, \\ 1.1 P_{nk}[n] \qquad\qquad else \end{cases} \tag{7}$$

The threshold is in our case equal to 0.15. The example of estimated and later modified trajectory of $P_{nk}[n]$ is given in Figure 3.

Table 2. Speech recognition results for Italian, Finish and Spanish digit databases with application of temporal filtering based noise estimation system. The experiments' conditions are explained in Table 2. The algorithm descriptions are in Table 3.

Accuracy [%]	Italian			Finish			Spanish			overall
conditions	hm	mm	wm	hm	mm	wm	hm	mm	wm	[%]
noise est. 7	88.98	92.61	96.66	91.98	88.85	96.92	92.66	93.07	97.19	**93.60**
noise est. 8	88.87	93.57	96.65	92.69	89.67	96.97	91.49	94.74	97.00	**93.82**

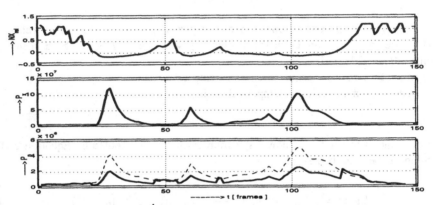

Fig. 3. Trajectories related to 15th spectral band (465 Hz).
Upper panel: $NX_{relk}[n]$ used for speech/pause detection.
Middle panel: Trajectory of $P_{xk}[n]$.
Lower panel: $P_{nk}[n]$ (dashed line) estimated using temporal filtering of $P_{xk}[n]$, and modified $P_{nk}[n]$ (solid line) by speech/pause detection.

5 Experimental Results

The whole proposed noise reduction algorithm is shown in Figure 1. At the beginning the power spectra $|X_k[n]|^2$ is computed using FFT algorithm. Then the input $|X_k[n]|^2$ is split into two branches. In the upper branch (Figure 1), the signal goes directly into noise suppression system.

In the lower branch, the noise estimation algorithm is applied.

The noise suppression algorithm is in our experiments only part of the feature extraction. The whole feature extraction system consists of several processing blocks, such as voice activity detection, mean and variance normalization or application of temporal filter in auditory spectrum. The experimented noise estimation algorithms have been tuned while the rest was kept constant so that we did not have to retrain any data-dependent algorithms.

The output features for speech recognizer were based on MFCCs. We have used the standard set of 23 triangular band filters with projection of output log-energies into 15 cosine basis. Table 1 contains the results with temporal minima tracking noise estimation technique, while Table 2 describes the results of experiments with noise estimation based filtering in temporal domain. The overall results of our experiments are obtained so that the **wm** conditions are weighted by 0.4, **mm** by 0.35, and **hm** by 0.25 over average of all databases.

Table 3. Description of noise estimation experiments (results mentioned in Table 1 and Table 2). Each algorithm contains the approximate size of processing memory buffer in floats.

baseline	Not used noise estimation and noise suppression algorithm at all.
noise est. 1	The average of the first 15 frames of each sentence used, (1x129 f).
noise est. 2	The whole temporal minima tracking alg. [4] in smoothed power spectra (129 spectr. bands), temporal window $D = 80$, (80x129 f).
noise est. 3	Derived from *noise est.* 2, decomposition of temporal window D into 10 subwindows, (10x129 f).
noise est. 4	Derived from *noise est.* 2, decomposition of temporal window D into 5 subwindows, (5x129 f).
noise est. 5	Derived from *noise est.* 2, addition of spectral smoothing using modified Mel-filter bank projection (23 critical banks), decomposition of temporal window D into 10 subwindows, (10x23 f).
noise est. 6	Derived from *noise est.* 2, decreasing the spectral resolution of initial $P_{xk}[n]$ by 2, decomposition of temporal window D into 5 subwindows, linear interpolation into 129 bands, (5x65 f).
noise est. 7	Appl. of standard temporal filter [5] (129 spectr. bands), (1x129 f).
noise est. 8	Derived from *noise est.* 7, speech/pause detector applied, (1x129 f).

6 Conclusions

Experimented noise estimation techniques for modified Wiener filter based noise suppression algorithm of feature extraction DSR system have been described. The standard temporal minima tracking noise estimation itself which is guaranteed to be very robust in our task does not satisfy the memory size limitation. Therefore we came up with modification in order to decrease this memory requirement. As can be seen from Table 1, the decomposition of one temporal window (applied for one spectral band) into several smaller ones does not bring almost any degradation. However such a memory reduction is not sufficient for our task. So we have experimented with algorithms estimating the noise from spectrum with reduced frequency resolution. Sufficient results were obtained with simple reduction of spectral resolution. The filtering of power spectra by modified Mel-filter bank seems to be applicable too.

On the other side, standard temporal filtering based noise estimation method did not work well. However its advantage is that there is no need for any memory buffer for algorithm processing. The results became interesting when we implemented simple speech/pause detector based on SNR estimation (Table 2). Its application for noise estimation based on minima tracking did not bring any improvement.

One of the goals of these experiments was to see if noise estimation techniques can be improved (better overall speech recognition) when doing additional spectral processing. Generally any other spectral processing algorithms, such as spectral smoothing or spectral resolution's reduction did not improve the noise estimation. The spectral processing seems to be good for clean speech (attenuate the noise suppression system's influence when clean speech is processed), but degrade robustness for noisy speech. However the complexity as well as memory size of such noise estimator is widely reduced. Very interesting fact is that spectral processing greatly increases the robustness of noise suppression algorithm when applied on its filter characteristics.

References

1. U. Knoblich. Description and Baseline Results for the Subset of the SpeechDat-Car Italian Database used for ETSI STQ Aurora WI008 Advanced DSR Front-End Evaluation, Alcatel, April 2000.
2. D. Macho. Spanish SDC-Aurora Database for ETSI STQ Aurora WI008 Advanced DSR Front-End Evaluation, Description and Baseline Results, UPC, November 2000.
3. QualComm-ICSI-OGI Aurora Advanced Front-End Proposal, Technical report, January 2002.
4. R. Martin. Spectral Subtraction Based on Minimum Statistics. In *Proc. of EUSIPCO '94*, Seventh European Signal Processing Conference, pp. 1182–1185, Edinburgh, Scotland, U. K., September 1994.
5. G. Doblinger. Computationally efficient speech enhancement by spectral minima tracking in subbands. In *EuroSpeech '95* - Proceedings of the 4th European Conference on Speech Technology and Communication, pp. 1513–1516, Madrid, Spain, September 1995.
6. E. C. Hirsch H. G., Noise estimation techniques for robust speech recognition. *Proc. ICASSP 1995* pp. 153–156, May 1995.

AlfaNum System for Speech Synthesis in Serbian Language

Milan Sečujski, Radovan Obradović, Darko Pekar, Ljubomir Jovanov, and Vlado Delić

Faculty of Engineering, University of Novi Sad, Yugoslavia
E-mail: secujski@uns.ns.ac.yu, tlk_delic@uns.ns.ac.yu

Abstract. This paper presents some basic criteria for conception of a concatenative text-to-speech synthesizer in Serbian language. The paper describes the prosody generator which was used and reflects upon several peculiarities of Serbian language which led to its adoption. Within the paper, the results of an experiment showing the influence of natural-sounding prosody on human speech recognition are discussed. The paper also describes criteria for on-line selection of appropriate segments from a large speech corpus, as well as criteria for off-line preparations of the speech database for synthesis.

1 Introduction

Being a very prospective speech technology, speech synthesis has been thoroughly studied at the University of Novi Sad, Yugoslavia, within the AlfaNum project, for several years. One of the main goals of this project is the design of a high-quality concatenation-based speech synthesizer for Serbian language. The first version of the AlfaNum synthesizer is based on TD-PSOLA algorithm, performed on segments selected on-line from a large speech database containing continuous speech, according to various criteria defined beforehand. This paper gives a detailed description of the AlfaNum synthesizer, including descriptions of a dictionary-based prosody generation module, and implementation of on-line selection of segments. Off-line preprocessing of the speech corpus which was necessary for implementation of TD-PSOLA algorithm is also described.

2 On Some Peculiarities of Serbian Language

In this paper we will discuss some peculiarities of Serbian language that are relevant for speech synthesis. There are several important aspects in speech synthesis where those peculiarities should be taken into account.

One of the most remarkable features of Serbian language is its most simple grapheme-to-phoneme conversion rule. Due to a radical language reform carried out in the 19th century, each letter today corresponds to exactly one sound. The exceptions to this rule are exceedingly rare and most of them can occur only at the boundaries between two words, where a voiced consonant can turn into its voiceless sibling if followed by a voiceless consonant and vice-versa, which makes detection of such exceptions trivial. Several phonemes have their allophones, but the only one that significantly affects speech intelligibility is the "velar n", a sound very similar to English n appearing in word such

P. Sojka, I. Kopeček, and K. Pala (Eds.): TSD 2002, LNAI 2448, pp. 237–244, 2002.

as 'song'. This allophone features only before velar stops, and is therefore quite simple to predict. Thus, the task of phonetization in Serbian speech synthesis is reduced to a trivial check, and solutions based on dictionaries and morphophonemic rules are not needed.

The task of a prosody generator is to ensure that the pronounced phrase sounds as naturally as possible. Generally, beside being more agreeable to a human listener, natural-sounding synthesized speech is easier to understand inasmuch as it is easier to perform lexical segmentation upon it, that is, to identify boundaries between words. In Serbian language, the importance of natural prosody is even more emphasized, since the location of stress within words is sometimes an essential feature of the meaning of that word. In order to confirm that natural prosody is of great importance for lexical segmentation and therefore for understanding, especially in adverse conditions, an experiment was conducted, which will be described later.

The five vowels of Serbian language can be stressed in four different ways each, according to pitch level during the stressed vowel itself, its relation to the pitch level of the next syllable, and duration of stressed syllable, which falls into two classes: long and short. Four different types of stress can thus be recognized as rise/long, rise/short, fall/long and fall/short, as shown in Figure 1. Depending on stress types, timbre of these vowels, as well as formant structure, can also vary. Due to difficulties in modifying vowel timbre without use of more computationally intensive parametric speech synthesis algorithms, and thus avoiding timbre mismatches that lower the quality of synthesized speech, the solution we adopted was defining classes of distinctive timbre variants of each vowel, and considering them as different vowels altogether. This is one of the criteria for on-line selection of segments which must be kept in mind. Another remarkable feature of Serbian language is characteristic of most other Slavic languages as well. Namely, the consonant R can serve as a vowel in case it is located between two other consonants. When pronounced as such, it is preceded by a vowel sound similar to one appearing in English word "burn". That sound is omitted in written Serbian language, but it is quite easy to reconstruct its position. All prosody modifications performed upon R serving as a vowel are actually performed on this vowel sound. All these facts must be taken into account not only when performing grapheme-to-phoneme conversion, but also when labeling the speech database.

3   The Speech Database

3.1   The Contents

The speech database contains approximately two hours of continuous speech, pronounced by a single female speaker. Having in mind possible applications of such a system, and the fact that concatenation of longer speech segments yields more intelligible speech, it was decided that the database should include phrases such as commonplace first and last names, addresses, names of companies, cities and countries, amounts of money, currencies, time and date phrases, weather reports, horoscope reports, typical phrases used in interactive voice-response systems, typical phrases used in e-mail messages etc. The database was recorded in laboratory conditions, and submitted to several off-line operations necessary for implementing TTS, such as labeling the database and its pitch-marking.

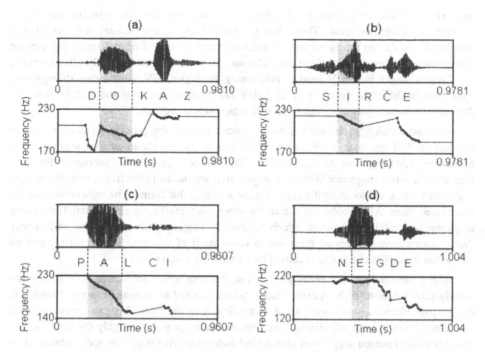

Fig. 1. Stress types in Serbian language and corresponding f_0 contours: (a) rise/long, (b) rise/short, (c) fall/long, (d) fall/short, as pronounced by the speaker involved in database recording.

3.2 Labeling and Pitch-Marking

The labeling of the database consists of placing boundaries between units belonging to a previously established set of units such as phonemes. It actually implies storing information about units in a separate database. The labeling of the AlfaNum speech database was predominantly phoneme based, although in some cases a better alternative was adopted, due to certain phonetic features of particular phones, as well as certain peculiarities of Serbian language. For instance, some classes of phones, such as plosives and affricates, were considered as pairs of semiphones (including occlusion and explosion in case of plosives and occlusion and friction in case of affricates). Vowels belonging to classes with significantly different timbres were considered as different vowels altogether, and therefore not interchangeable. Considering the way the phoneme R is pronounced in Serbian language (a periodical set of occlusions and explosions produced by the tongue oscillating against the hard palate), all of these occlusions and explosions were treated as distinct phonemes.

Labeling was performed automatically, using the AlfaNum continuous speech recognizer [6], and verified by a human expert. Verifying was based on signal waveform, its spectrogram and its auditory perception. The SpeechVis software, previously developed within the AlfaNum project, was used [7].

Implementing TD-PSOLA algorithm implies previous pitch-marking of the database, that is, detecting locations within phones most suitable for centering overlapping windows and extracting frames, in case a TTS algorithm which requires pitch-synchronous frame positioning should be used. Thus, during voiced frames, one marker per period was appointed, and during unvoiced frames, markers were appointed according to the average fundamental frequency throughout the database. In order to avoid audible effects caused by abrupt changes in V/UV marker positioning strategies, UV positioning strategy was somewhat modified in the vicinity of V/UV boundaries, and thus the rate with which distances between adjacent markers can vary was severely reduced.

As to positioning pitch markers within voiced frames, the process was carried out in two phases. To begin with, preliminary estimations of pitch contours of each segment were made using AMDF pitch-extraction method. Each of the segments was previously low pass filtered with cutoff frequency 900 Hz. The next step was locating the frame with the highest degree of voicing and locating the maximum peak within that frame. The initial pitch marker was placed there. Afterwards, the search for other pitch markers was conducted according to preliminary pitch estimations, which resulted in placing pitch markers in such a way that windows centered around them would cover most of the waveform's energy, and no significant distortion of the signal caused by windowing could occur.

Such a procedure is not entirely error-free, because low pass filtering can sometimes modify peak values to such an extent that peaks recognized as maximum in some segments do not coincide with peaks recognized as maximum in the rest. This can happen in case of voiced phones whose waveforms have two prominent peaks of roughly the same height. There is another reason why errors of this kind may occur. At the precise spot of boundaries between phones there is sometimes an irregularity in functioning of the glottis, leading to a discontinuity in positions of glotal impulses. If a phoneme-based pitch-marking is adopted, that is, if pitch-marking is performed independently within phones, and not within speech segments containing more than one phone, most of such errors are eliminated completely.

The database containing information about pitch markers is suitable for speech synthesis using any of the concatenation-based techniques, even in case of techniques that do not require explicit knowledge of pitch markers, since f_0 contours can be determined from pitch marker positions in a straightforward way.

4 Prosody Generation

Acoustic parameters such as f_0 contour were calculated in two steps. The first step consisted of analysing the sentence, word by word, in order to get information such as stress types and locations, part of speech classes and functions of particular words in the sentence. Grammatical information is essential for synthesis of natural-sounding prosody, since words in Serbian language can sometimes be stressed in different ways depending on their morphologic categories, and sometimes even have different meanings if stressed differently. In some cases even syntactic analysis does not help, and several interpretations of the same sentence, all of them grammatical, can be stressed in different ways and therefore yield different meanings. For human listeners there is no confusion, because they rely on contextual information.

4.1 The Dictionary

Since stress in Serbian language is fairly unpredictable, a dictionary-based solution was adopted. A special dictionary including information on stress configuration, part of speech class and morphologic categories for each word was created. Furthermore, since stress can vary along with inflections of the same word, and those variations are predictable only to a certain extent, it was necessary to include all word forms as separate entries in the dictionary. Several part of speech classes were identified as having regular behaviour when submitted to inflection and they were entered in the dictionary in a form which occupied little space, but was sufficient for correct determination of the stress of every inflected form. In such a way the dictionary containing more than one million entries (including inflected forms) occupied about 6.5 MB in plain text format.

Such a solution is not entirely error-free, since it does not include syntactic analysis, nor does it solve cases when syntactic ambiguities arise, and semantic analysis, however primitive, must be performed. It was decided to leave these two problems for later stages of the project. Syntactic analysis, when implemented, would rely on information from the dictionary, and semantic analysis will be limited to checking up collocations in the dictionary – that is, deciding in favour of words that typically occur in particular contexts related to other words, rather than in favour of words that do not. The information on collocations in Serbian language will be acquired through statistical analysis of very large textual databases, and entered into the dictionary along with other information.

Another problem that occurs is that some words may not be found in the dictionary. It can happen because of their rarity, because a nonstandard affix was used, but also frequently in case of foreign names, names of companies etc. In that case, strategies for determining the correct way of stressing must be defined. Strategies currently being developed within our projects include making analogies based on standard prefixes and suffixes and rhyming.

The graphical user-interface created for entering words in the dictionary is dialog-based and highly intuitive. The person entering the dictionary must be familiar with lexis of stress system in Serbian, and must be able to stress words properly. However, after a short introduction, even lay users of the TTS system are able to add words to the dictionary when needed.

4.2 F_0 Codebook

Using information from the dictionary, the system is able to reconstruct a particular stress configuration of a group of words which form a metrical unit. In this phase of the project, several f_0 contours are assigned to each metrical unit, depending on its position in the sentence (beginning, neutral, before comma, ending), and the resulting f_0 contour is smoothed in order to avoid audible pitch discontinuities and tilted towards the end of the sentence [1,3]. The curves were extracted from typical stress contexts. Such a method does not take into account syntactical information, but relies only on punctuation marks. However, results are still significantly better than in case of synthesizers with constant f_0, available in Serbian until now.

4.3 An Experimental Confirmation of the Influence of Prosody on Human Speech Recognition

Within this paper an experiment was conducted in order to show the influence of natural prosody on human speech recognition, that is, to show that listeners rely on prosody to a considerable extent, when required to reconstruct the syntactically and semantically correct sentence that they have heard.

To that purpose, the AlfaNum synthesizer was used to create 12 syntactically and semantically correct sentences, whose length did not exceed 8 words. Those sentences were intended for recognition by human listeners. Each of those sentences was created in three variants. The first variant had completely flat f_0 curve and equal durations of all vowels, which yielded metallic-sounding unnatural speech. The second variant had incorrect prosody features, based on wrong sentence accentuation, and the third had correct prosody features.

Considering that the intelligibility of all three variants was relatively high in normal conditions, the experiment was conducted in adverse conditions. Gaussian and impulse noise were introduced into synthesized sentences, and the experiment took place in the presence of intensive ambiental noise.

The experiment included 12 listeners, and each of them listened to 12 sentences – four sentences from the first group, four from the second and four from the third, in random order. Each of the listeners was required to repeat the sentence that they have heard, and in case of incorrect recognition, they were required to try again after hearing the sentence once more.

The results of the experiment are shown on Figure 2, and they clearly show the importance of natural prosody. Another important result of the experiment is that the sentences with wrong prosody features were harder to recognize than sentences with flat f_0 curve. This result also shows how much the listeners rely on prosody. When the f_0 curve is flat and all the vowels have the same durations, the listeners are aware that the prosody does not yield any information and concentrate their efforts on phoneme recognition and combining phonemes into meaningful words, and ultimately, into a meaningful sentence. When variations of f_0 and vowel durations are present, the listeners are under a wrong impression that the sentence is pronounced with a proper f_0 curve and try to spot meaningful words by the way they sound, but fail in most cases. Therefore, results are worse than in case there were no f_0 and duration variations at all.

5 Online Selection of Segments

Halfphones are considered as basic units which cannot be further segmented, but it is desirable to extract segments as large as possible, in order to preserve intelligibility. According to differences between existing and required values of parameters previously defined, each speech segment which can be extracted and used for synthesis is assigned target cost, and according to differences at the boundaries between two segments, each pair of segments which can be concatenated is assigned concatenation cost [2]. Target cost is the measure of dissimilarity between existing and required prosodic features of segments, including duration, f_0, energy and spectral mismatch. Concatenation cost is the measure of mismatch of the same features across unit boundaries. Various phoneme groups are treated in different fashion. Some types of phonemes, such as unvoiced plosives, are more suitable for

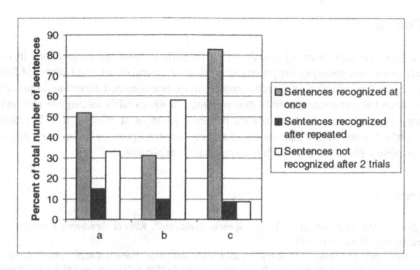

Fig. 2. Experiment results: (a) Sentences with neutral prosody features, (b) Sentences with incorrect prosody features, (c) Sentences with correct prosody features.

segmentation than the others, and have lower concatenation costs. The degree of impairment of phones is also taken into account.

The task of the synthesizer is to find a best path through a trellis which represents the sentence, that is, the path along which the least overall cost is accumulated. The chosen path determines which segments are to be used for concatenation, as shown on Figure 3.

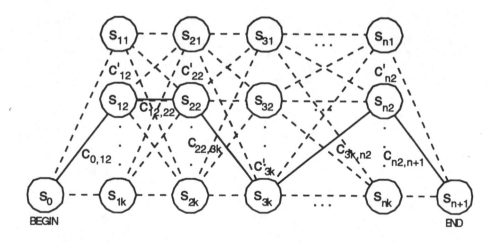

Fig. 3. Finding the best path through a trellis representing a sentence.

6 Conclusion

In this paper conception of high-quality TTS in Serbian language is described in detail. Prosody generation principles are presented, in view of several distinctive features of Serbian language. On-line selection of speech segments to be concatenated according to predefined criteria aimed at minimizing audible discontinuities leads to fairly intelligible and natural-sounding synthetic speech. After several previous attempts at creating a TTS system in Serbian which were mostly diphone-based and did not treat prosody in any way, this is the first complete TTS in Serbian which is commercially applicable.

References

1. T. Dutoit: "An Introduction to Text-to-Speech Synthesis". Kluwer Academic Publishers, Dordrecht/Boston/London (1997).
2. M. Beutnagel, M. Mohri, M. Riley: "Rapid Unit Selection from a Large Speech Corpus for Concatenative Speech Synthesis". Proceedings of EUROSPEECH '99, pp. 607–610. Budapest, Hungary (1999).
3. I. Lehiste, P. Ivić: "Word and Sentence Prosody in Serbocroatian". The Massachusetts Institute of Technology (1986).
4. Slobodan T. Jovičić: "Speech Communication, Physiology, Psychoacoustics and Perception". Izdavačko preduzeće NAUKA, Beograd, Yugoslavia (1999).
5. V. Delić, S. Krčo, D. Glavatović: "Basic Elements for ASR and TTS in Serbian Language". DOGS, pp. 32–37, Fruška Gora, Yugoslavia (1998).
6. D. Pekar, R. Obradović, V. Delić: "AlfaNumCASR – A Continuous Speech Recognition System". DOGS, Bečej, Yugoslavia (2002).
7. R. Obradović, D. Pekar: "C++ Library for Signal Processing – SLIB". DOGS, Novi Sad, Yugoslavia (2000).

Speech Features Extraction Using Cone-Shaped Kernel Distribution

Janez Žibert, France Mihelič and Nikola Pavešić

Faculty of Electrical Engineering, University of Ljubljana,
Tržaška 25, SI–1000 Ljubljana, Slovenia
E-mail: janez.zibert@fe.uni-lj.si, mihelicf@fe.uni-lj.si,
nikolap@fe.uni-lj.si
WWW: http://luks.fe.uni-lj.si/

Abstract. The paper reviews two basic time-frequency distributions, spectrogram and cone-shaped kernel distribution. We study, analyze and compare properties and performance of these quadratic representations on speech signals. Cone-shaped kernel distribution was successfully applied to speech features extraction due to several useful properties in time-frequency analysis of speech signals.

1 Introduction

Joint time-frequency signal representations characterize signals over the time-frequency plane. They combine time domain and frequency domain analyzes to yield a potentially more revealing picture of the temporal localization of signal's spectral components.

Due to varying degree of nonstationarity ranging from plosive bursts to vowel voicing speech is a complex signal and it is a tough challenge to obtain a time-frequency representation with a satisfying time and frequency resolution.

We are proposing a new modified method of speech features extracting based on mel-frequency cepstral coefficients with use of the cone-shaped kernel distribution. We are additionally studying dynamic features, which are modelled from basic parameters obtained by the new method. We are investigating several estimates of the time derivatives approximated by regression coefficients and coefficients determined by trigonometric functions.

Analyzes and tests are performed for different sets of speech features obtained from spectrogram and cone-shaped kernel distribution using speech recognition system based on hidden Markov acoustic models (HMM).

Our main goal has been to incorporate different time-frequency distributions into a speech features extraction process and potentially find an alternative way of deriving speech features based on these distributions.

2 Cone-Shaped Kernel Distribution

The cone-shaped kernel distribution (Zhao-Atlas-Marks distribution) [2] is a member of Cohen's class of time-frequency distributions [1]. The spectrogram which is almost

P. Sojka, I. Kopeček, and K. Pala (Eds.): TSD 2002, LNAI 2448, pp. 245–252, 2002.

exclusively used for the analysis of speech signals[1], is also a member of this class of the quadratic representations.

A time-frequency distribution (TFD) of Cohen's class is given by

$$C_x(t, f; \Pi) = \int_{-\infty}^{+\infty} \int_{-\infty}^{+\infty} \Pi(s - t, \xi - f)W_x(s, \xi)ds\,d\xi, \tag{1}$$

where $W_x(s, \xi)$ is a Wigener-Ville distribution [3] of the signal $x(t)$ [1,4]. The alternative definition of Cohen's class distributions can be interpreted as the two dimensional Fourier transform of the ambiguity function [3] $A_x(\xi, \tau)$ multiplied by the kernel $k(\xi, \tau)$:

$$C_x(t, f; k) = \int_{-\infty}^{+\infty} \int_{-\infty}^{+\infty} k(\xi, \tau)A_x(\xi, \tau)e^{j2\pi(f\tau+\xi t)}d\xi d\tau. \tag{2}$$

The kernel function $k(\xi, \tau)$ defines characteristics of the given distribution and provide a good way to design a representation with desired properties.

For kernel $k(\xi, \tau) = A_h^*(\xi, \tau)$, where $A_h^*(\xi, \tau)$ is a complex conjugate of ambiguity function of analysis window h, we obtain a spectrogram, which can be interpreted as a quadrat of a short-time Fourier transform:

$$S_x(t, f) = \left| \int_{-\infty}^{\infty} x(u)h^*(u - t)e^{j2\pi fu}du \right|^2. \tag{3}$$

If we impose to the distribution from the Cohen's class the condition to preserve time- and frequency-supports [4,5], one of the choices is kernel function $k(\xi, \tau) = \frac{\sin(\pi\xi\tau)}{\pi\xi\tau}$, which defines Born-Jordan distribution [4]. If we further smooth this distribution along the frequency axis, we obtain Zhao-Atlas-Marks distribution [2], defined as

$$CKD_x(t, f) = \int_{-\infty}^{+\infty} h(\tau) \cdot \left[\int_{t-|\tau|/2}^{t+|\tau|/2} x(s + \tau/2)x^*(s - \tau/2)ds \right] e^{j2\pi ft}d\tau. \tag{4}$$

Typically the smoothing window can be expressed as

$$h(\tau) = \frac{1}{\tau} \exp(-\alpha\tau^2), \tag{5}$$

which determines a cone-shaped kernel function in the ambiguity plane, hence the name the cone-shaped kernel distribution (CKD).

2.1 Comparison with Spectrogram

Spectrogram (Equation 3) and CKD (Equation 4) are members of Cohen's class of energy distributions [1]. They preserve energy of a signal over the time-frequency plane and are covariant by translations in time and in frequency [1]. All quadratic TFDs satisfy quadratic superposition principle [3] from where we get so called cross-terms which can be identified as a phenomena of interference in the time-frequency plane.

---

[1] A discrete wavelet transform and its squared modulus – scalogram are also used for the analysis of speech signals. They are members of the affine class of distributions.

The interference terms of the spectrogram are restricted to those regions of the time-frequency plane, where corresponding signal terms overlap. Hence, if two signal components are sufficiently far apart in the time-frequency plane, then their cross-terms will nearly be identical zero. This property, which is a practical advantage of the spectrogram, is in fact a consequence of the spectrogram's poor resolution, [1,3,5]. The resolution depends of the given analysis window. If we used shorter (longer) window h in (Equation 3), we would obtain better (poorer) time and poorer (better) frequency resolution [5]. This is direct consequence of the uncertainty principle [6].

In general, it could be shown that there exists a general trade-off between good time-frequency resolution and quantity of interference terms [3]. The Wigener-Ville distribution (WVD), on the other hand, has excellent time-frequency concentration owing to number of good mathematical properties, but it also possesses substantial interference terms. The main idea in of deriving other distributions from Cohen's class is to smooth WVD (ambiguity function) with a kernel (Equation 2) by preserving time-frequency resolution and reducing interference terms. If we choose for the kernel $k(\xi, \tau)$ decreasing function of product $\xi \cdot \tau$, we obtain low pass function in ambiguity plane, which reduces interference terms. Cone-shaped kernel distribution is designed from the kernel $k(\xi, \tau) = \frac{\sin(\pi\xi\tau)}{\pi\xi\tau}$, which has above mentioned characteristics.

2.2   Time-Frequency Representations of Speech Signals

Figure 1 compares a spectrogram and cone-shaped kernel distribution for a short speech segment consisting of two pitch periods of a voiced Slovene vowel /e/ spoken by a male speaker. The speech signal was sampled at a rate of 16 kHz and speech waveform represents approximately 22 ms of the sound.

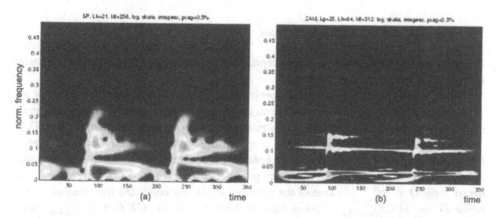

Fig. 1. Comparison of the spectrogram (a) and the cone-shaped kernel distribution (b) of a speech signal of the Slovene vowel /e/. The figures are produced using Time-frequency Toolbox [8].

Spectrogram in Figure 1(a) is everywhere nonnegative. The representation of the analyzed signal is relatively clear thanks to its excellent cross-term properties. The main disadvantage of the spectrogram is that simultaneous good resolution in time and frequency is not possible. In spectrogram in Figure 1(a) we chose shorter analysis window, so we obtained better time and poorer frequency resolution. Formant frequencies are smeared although they can be localized at every pitch period during the vowel voicing (approximately every 10 ms). There is another disadvantage of spectrogram, which can not be seen from Figure 1(a). Since spectrogram does not satisfy the marginal and the finite time support property [4], spectral content in the representation of instantaneous changes in speech signals (e.g. bursts) is smeared in time and spanning over the entire spectral domain [7].

In Figure 1(b) a representation by the CKD is shown, where the kernel function (Equation 5) with $\alpha = 1$ was used. CKD shows located formant frequencies much more precisely than the spectrogram. Note that spectral energy of formant tracks are smeared in the time direction, which is a direct consequence of using additional smoothing window (filter) in CKD to eliminate interference terms. There is another disadvantage of most of the Cohen's class distributions: they do not satisfy fundamental property of nonnegativity due to the interference terms. As a direct consequence we had to introduce additional threshold levels to suppress negative values in order to improve the representation of the analyzed signal [5].

3   Speech Features Extraction

In previous section the spectrogram and the cone-shaped kernel distribution was compared for needs of speech signal analyzes. We have shown differences and revealed some good characteristics of the CKD, which had motivated us to apply this time-frequency distribution to speech features extraction using mel-frequency cepstral coefficients.

3.1   Mel-Frequency Cepstral Coefficients

Our approach for deriving mel-frequency cepstral coefficients using CKD is similar to a basic method using spectrogram as a front-end.

Firstly some simple preprocessing operations to speech signals were applied prior to performing actual signal analysis: DC mean removal from the source waveform and pre-emphasis filtering due to physiological characteristics of the speech production system [9].

Then a time-frequency transformation of speech signal was performed. Given a discrete-time signal $s[n]$, $n = 1, \ldots, N$, we obtained time-frequency representation of dimension $N \times K$, where K is a number of frequency points. The representation can be rewritten in a matrix form $D \in \mathbf{R}^{N \times K}$. In case of the spectrogram D was computed from (Equation 3), hence $D = S[n, k]_{n=1, k=1}^{N, K}$, and in case of the CKD $D = CKD[n, k]_{n=1, k=1}^{N, K}$ was calculated from (Equation 4).

Next, a mel-filter bank analysis was performed. The bank of triangular filters equally spaced along the mel-scale frequency resolution [9] was introduced in a matrix form. If M is the matrix of filters, the filtering could be implemented as a product of matrices M and D followed by a logarithmic operation:

$$M_{TF} = \log(M \cdot D), \tag{6}$$

where $log(\cdot)$ means element-by-element log operation. Elements $m[n, q]$, $q = 1, \ldots, Q$ (Q is a number of filters) of matrix M_{TF} present log filterbank amplitudes of signal $s[N]$ in time n modelled with different time-frequency distributions.

In order to derive cepstral coefficients the discrete cosine transform (DCT) was used

$$c[i, n] = \sqrt{\frac{2}{Q}} \sum_{q=1}^{Q} m[n, q] cos\left(\frac{\pi i}{Q}(q - 0.5)\right), \qquad (7)$$

where $Q = 32$. In each frame of 10 ms length 12 cepstral coefficients were obtained appending the logarithm of the signal energy.

3.2 Modelling Dynamic Features

It is widely known that the performance of speech recognition system can be greatly enhanced by adding time derivatives to the basic static parameters [10].

According to the procedure described in previous subsection there were used different modelling approaches to estimate dynamic features from time-frequency representation of speech signals.

First approach was to perform regression analysis, where first and second order time derivatives were approximated by regression coefficients. The feature set consists from the basic cepstral parameters computed from the CKD with added the first and the second order regression coefficients is called CKD1. This is a standard approach. Derived features were used as a reference set in our further experiments.

Second approach of deriving dynamic features was estimation of coefficients of function arctan. This was performed by fitting each set i of basic features with function

$$f_{i,n}(x) = a_1^{(i,n)} \arctan(x) + a_0^{(i,n)} \qquad (8)$$

for $n \in [-N_d, N_d]$, where N_d is a number of feature vectors. We achieved this by minimizing

$$\sum_{m=-N_d}^{N_d} |c[i, m] - f_{i,n}(x_m)|^2, \qquad (9)$$

where x_m, $m = -N_d, -N_d + 1, \ldots, N_d$ were symmetrically but not equally chosen from interval $[2.5, 2.5]$. The coefficients $a_1^{(i,n)}$ were added to basic mel-frequency cepstral coefficients. This kind of features was signed as CKD2.

A similar approach was used to produce features CKD3. Here dynamic features were derived by fitting each set of basic data with function

$$g_{i,n}(x) = a_0^{(i,n)} + a_1^{(i,n)} \cos(x) + a_2^{(i,n)} \sin(x). \qquad (10)$$

This is a slightly different approach as one used in [11]. The coefficients $a_1^{(i,n)}$ and $a_2^{(i,n)}$ obtained by minimizing (Equation 9) with function $g_{i,n}(x)$, where x_m were chosen equally from interval $[0, \pi]$, were appended to basic parameters to form third set of features.

Figure 2 shows different approaches in modelling dynamic features from basic parameters based on the CKD.

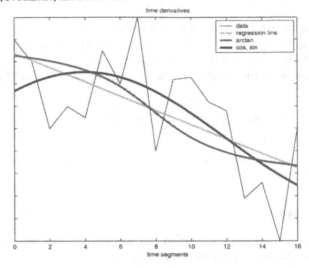

Fig. 2. Different approaches in modelling dynamic features from cone-shaped kernel distribution.

4   Speech Recognition

4.1   Phone Recognizer

A Slovene speech database K211d [12] was used for evaluation purposes. Speech database K211d is a multi-speaker isolated-word corpus designed for phonetic research studies of the Slovene spoken language. The K211d lexicon consists of 251 carefully selected words to provide a representative sample of all Slovene allophones. Ten speakers (5 female + 5 male) uttered all 251 words stored. The corpus consists of 16,947 phones derived from 32 different allophones [12]. We used speech data from 6 speakers (3 female + 3 male) for training purposes. Test part (the rest of the data) includes 8848 phones.

Phone recogniser was based on HMMs. The acoustic models were standard left-to-right HMMs consisting of three states and three output Gaussian probability functions modelled with diagonal covariance matrices. Context-independent phonetic HMMs were trained using the HTK toolkit [13].

4.2   Phone Recognition

Phone recognition was performed using identical conditions. This means that simple HMM topology for context-independent phone recognition with equal number of parameters was used through all experiments testing different kind of features.

Features named SPEC were selected as the reference set of features. The SPEC feature set included mel-frequency cepstral coefficients based on spectrogram adding first and second derivatives derived from regression analysis.

The phone recognition results for different feature sets are shown in Table 1. The phone recognition results of SPEC, CKD1 and CKD3 are almost identical. This was expected for the SPEC and CKD1 features based on similar modelling techniques only with different

Table 1. Phone recognition results with different sets of speech features.

	SPEC	CKD1	CKD2	CKD3
accuracy	78.25 %	77.97 %	70.18 %	78.19 %

time-frequency distributions. Poorer results were obtained with CKD2 features. This kind of features include just estimations of the first order derivatives modelled with coefficients of function arctan in Equation 8. There were no approximation of second order derivatives which might explain the comparable lack of accuracy.

The phone recognition results of the CKD3 features, where dynamic parameters were estimated using function (Equation 10), were comparable with SPEC and CKD1 features. In turn, we had further explored differences of the SPEC and the CKD3 feature sets in phone classification task. In Figure 3 is shown a comparison of confusion matrices of SPEC and CKD3.

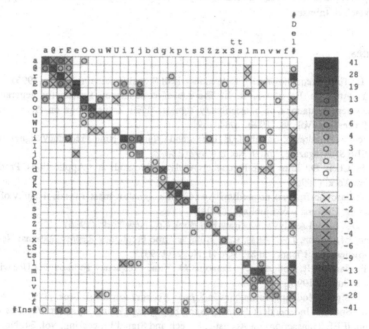

Fig. 3. Subtraction of SPEC and CKD3 confusion matrices shows differences of SPEC (circle) and CKD3 (cross) features in a phone classification task.

A modified confusion matrix [5] in Figure 3, where the CKD3 confusion matrix was subtracted from the SPEC confusion matrix, shows differences in the phone classification task for both distributions. Modified confusion matrix indicates a better recognition of vowels /i/, /0/, /o/, /@/ and phone /s/ with the CKD3 in comparison with the SPEC features. On contrary a better recognition of plosives /k/, /p/, /t/, glides /l/ and /r/ and nasal

/m/ could be seen with the SPEC. There also exists a number of substitutions of the phone /k/ by /t/ and /m/ by /n/ described with the CKD3 features. In addition, more deletions on account of insertions with the CKD3 could be noticed.

5 Conclusion

We proposed a new modified method of speech features extracting based on mel-frequency cepstral coefficients with use of different time-frequency distributions. We also investigated several estimates of the time derivatives obtained from basic measurements of the speech signals. The first and second time derivatives were approximated by regression coefficients, coefficients of function arctan, and functions sine and cosine.

Analyzes and tests are performed for different sets of speech features obtained from spectrogram and cone-shaped kernel distribution using speech recognition system build from hidden Markov models. Effectiveness of the speech features derived from CKD was demonstrated in this study. Coefficients of trigonometric functions were employed in addition to basic cepstral parameters resulting in satisfying phone recognition rate when applied to the Slovene speech database.

References

1. Cohen, L.: Time-Frequency Analysis. Prentince Hall Signal Processing Series (1995).
2. Zhao, Y., Atlas, L. E., Marks, R. J.: The use of cone-shaped kernels for generalized time-frequency representations of nonstationary signals. IEEE Transactions on Acoustics, Speech, Signal Processing, Vol. 38. (1990) 1084–1091.
3. Hlawatsch, F., Boudreaux-Bartels, G.F.: Linear and Quadratic Time-Frequency Signal Representations. IEEE SP Magazine, Vol. 9, No. 2. (1992) 21–67.
4. Quian, S., Chen, D.: Joint Time-Frequency Analysis: Methods and Applications. Prentince-Hall PTR, New York. (1996).
5. Žibert, J.: Časovno-frekvenčne predstavitve govornih signalov, master thesis. Faculty of Electrical Engineering, University of Ljubljana. (2001).
6. Papoulis, A.: Signal Analysis. McGraw-Hill Book Co., New York. (1996).
7. Loughlin, P.J., Pitton, J.W., Atlas, L.E.: Bilinear Time-Frequency Representations: New Insights and Properties. IEEE Trans. on SP, Vol. 41, No. 2. (1993).
8. Auger, F., Flandrin, P., Gonçalves, P., Lemoine, O.: Time-Frequency Toolbox: For Use with Matlab. Reference Guide. (1996).
9. Picone, J.: Signal Modeling Techniques In Speech Recognition. IEEE Proc. (1993).
10. Furui, S.: Speaker Independent Isolated Word Recogniser Using Dynamic Features of Speech Spectrum. IEEE Transactions on Acoustic, Speech and Signal Processing, Vol. 34, No. 1. (1986), pp. 52–59.
11. Dobrišek, S., Mihelič, F., Pavešić, N.: A Multiresolutionally Oriented Approach for Determination of Cepstral Features in Speech Recognition. Proceedings EUROSPEECH'97, Vol. 3. Rhodes, Greece (1997), pp. 1367–1370.
12. Mihelič, F., Gros, J., Dobrišek, S., Žibert, J., Pavešić, N.: Spoken Language Resources at LAPSC of the University of Ljubljana. Submitted for publication in International Journal of Speech Technology. (2002).
13. Young, S., Odell, J., Ollason, D., Vatchev, V., Woodland, P.: The HTK Book. Cambridge University. Entropic Cambridge Research Laboratory Ltd. (1997).

Automatic Transcription of Czech Language Oral History in the MALACH Project: Resources and Initial Experiments*

Josef Psutka[1], Pavel Ircing[1], Josef V. Psutka[1], Vlasta Radová[1], William J. Byrne[2], Jan Hajič[3], Samuel Gustman[4], and Bhuvana Ramabhadran[5]

[1] University of West Bohemia, Department of Cybernetics
Univerzitní 8, 306 14 Plzeň, Czech Republic
E-mail: psutka@kky.zcu.cz, ircing@kky.zcu.cz, psutka_j@kky.zcu.cz,
radova@kky.zcu.cz
[2] Johns Hopkins University, Center for Language and Speech Processing
309 Barton Hall, 3400 N. Charles St., Baltimore, MD 21218
E-mail: byrne@jhu.edu
[3] Charles University, Institute of Formal and Applied Linguistic
Malostranské náměstí 25, 118 00 Praha, Czech Republic
E-mail: hajic@ufal.mff.cuni.cz
[4] Survivors of the Shoah Visual History Foundation
P.O. Box 3168, Los Angeles, CA 90078-3168
E-mail: sam@vhf.org
[5] IBM T.J. Watson Research Laboratory, Human Language Technologies Group
Yorktown Heights, NY
E-mail: bhuvana@us.ibm.com

Abstract. In this paper we describe the initial stages of the ASR component of the MALACH (Multilingual Access to Large Spoken Archives) project. This project will attempt to provide improved access to the large multilingual spoken archives collected by the Survivors of the Shoah Visual History Foundation (VHF) by advancing the state of the art in automated speech recognition. In order to train the ASR system, it is neccesary to manually transcribe a large amount of speech data, identify the appropriate vocabulary, and obtain relevant text for language modeling. We give a detailed description of the speech annotation process; show the specific properties of the spontaneous speech contained in the archives; and present a baseline speech recognition results.

1 Introduction

After filming Schindler's List, Steven Spielberg established the Survivors of the Shoah Visual History Foundation (VHF) to develop archives and teaching materials based on the videotaped testimonies given by survivors of the Holocaust in order to preserve their memory and establish a basis for tolerance education around the world for generations to come.

* This work has been founded by NSF (U.S.A) under the Information Technology Research (ITR) program, NSF IIS Award No. 0122466 and by the Ministry of Education of the Czech Republic, project No. MSM234200004 and No. LN00A063

P. Sojka, I. Kopeček, and K. Pala (Eds.): TSD 2002, LNAI 2448, pp. 253–260, 2002.
© Springer-Verlag Berlin Heidelberg 2002

Today, the VHF has gathered almost 52,000 testimonies (116,000 hours of video) in 32 languages to form a 180 terabyte digital library of MPEG-1 video. Several years ago the VHF began the task of manual cataloging of the archives in order to facilitate content-based searching. 4,000 testimonies given in English (about 8 % of the entire archive) have been manually cataloged with the segment level description [1], using a domain-specific thesaurus containing 21 thousand places and concepts. Names of people have been cataloged separately (about 280,000 different items). work in addition with multilingual materials, the automation of the cataloging process is absolutely necessary if effective access to archives of such scale is required.

The MALACH (Multilingual Access to Large Spoken ArCHives) project [2] will attempt to provide improved access to this large multilingual spoken archive by advancing the state of the art in automated speech recognition. An aim of the initial phase of the project will be to develop ASR for English and Czech testimonies with subsequent extensions to French, Spanish and several Eastern European languages. This paper describes the initial work concerning the Czech part of the project.

2   Recording Conditions and Speech Collections

Testimonies were delivered for further processing divided into half-hour segments stored as MPEG-1 video files. The average duration of a testimony in the collection of the first portion of 180 Czech testimonies delivered and processed at UWB was two hours. The audio stream was extracted at 128 kb/sec in stereo, at 16 bit resolution and 44 kHz sampling rate. The speech of each interview participant – the interviewer and interviewee – was recorded via lapel microphones collected on separate channels. For annotation we chose the second part (speech contained on the second video tape) of each testimony. These segments usually do not contain any personal data of the people who provided their testimonies and are suitable for annotation. Selected parts were burned (only the channel containing voice of the survivor) on CD ROMs and were given to annotators for processing. Annotators processed the first 15 minute segments of these parts. The initial portion of these annotated testimonies consists of about 45 hours of speech.

The speech quality in individual interviews is often very poor from an ASR point of view, as it contains whispered or emotional speech with many disfluencies and non-speech events as crying, laughter etc. The speaking rate (measured as the number of words uttered per minute) varies greatly depending on the speaker, changing from 64 to 173 with the average of 113 [words/minute].

3   Speech Annotation Conventions

The audio files were divided into segments and annotated using the special annotation software Transcriber 1.4.1 which is a tool for assisting the creation of speech corpora. It makes it possible to manually segment, label and transcribe speech signals for later use in automatic speech processing. Transcriber is freely available from the Linguistic Data Consortium (LDC) web site http://www.ldc.upenn.edu/.

The rules for the annotation were as follows:

- Audio files are divided into segments; each segment corresponds roughly to a sentence.
- The beginning of a segment is marked by `<b ti>`, where the `ti` gives the time when the segment begins. The time is given in seconds.
- The instant when a speaker turn occurs is marked by `<t ti>` «spk#, n, g». The `ti` is again in seconds, `spk#` is a speaker ID according to the following table:

$$spk1 \ldots\ldots \text{interviewer}$$
$$spk2 \ldots\ldots \text{interviewee}$$
$$spk3 \ldots\ldots \text{another person}$$

n is the name and surname of the speaker (if known), and g is a letter marking the gender of the speaker:

$$m \ldots\ldots \text{male}$$
$$f \ldots\ldots \text{female}$$

- The situation, when the speakers spoke over each other is marked as follows:

`<t ti>` «spk_1, n_1, g_1 + spk_2, n_2, g_2»
SPEAKER1 : transcription of what the speaker `spk_1` said
SPEAKER2 : transcription of what the speaker `spk_2` said

If the speech from one or both speakers is completely unintelligible, it is marked as `<unintelligible>`.
- Everything said is transcribed as words, no numbers are used.
- Sentences begin with a low-case letter. Only proper names and acronyms like IBM, NATO are capitalized. If a word is spelled out, the letters are capitalized and a space is put between them.
- No punctuation is used in the transcription.
- If someone stammered and said "thir thirty", the corresponding transcription is `thir- thirty`. Note that the "-" has to be followed by a blank space. The "-" is also used in the case when a word is spoken incompletely due to some recording error. In such a case the "-" has to be preceded or followed by a blank space, depending on whether only the end or the beginning of the word was spoken. If the "-" is neither preceded nor followed by any blank space it is regarded as a part of a word.
- Sometimes a speaker uttered a word or a part of a sentence in a language other than Czech. Such parts are enclosed in `[]`.
- If human transcribers are unsure about a portion of the transcription, they enclose it in parentheses. For example, if they think a speaker said "looks like this", but are unsure, they should transcribe it as `(looks like this)`. If something is completely unintelligible, the transcription is `<unintelligible>`.
- Non-speech sounds like tongue clicks, coughing, laughter, breath noise, inhaling, and lip smacks are transcribed as `<click>`, `<cough>`, `<laugh>`, `<breath>`, `<inhale>`, and `<mouth>`, respectively.
- Background noise is marked according to the following rules: if no word overlaps with the background noise the mark `<noise>` is used; if a word or a part of an utterance overlaps with the noise, the mark `<noise_begin>` is used before the first affected word and the mark `<noise_end>` is used after the last affected word.

– Other disfluencies in the speech are marked as: <UH>, <UM>, <UH-HUH>, or <UH-HUM>.
– Distinct pauses and gaps in speech are marked with <silence>.

The complete list of all non-speech sounds used during the annotation is given in Table 1. An example of the annotated file is shown in Figure 1.

Table 1. Complete List of Non-Speech Sounds.

Non-speech sound	Transcription
Tongue click	<click>
Lip smack	<mouth>
Coughing	<cough>
Laughter	<laugh>
Breath noise	<breath>
Inhaling	<inhale>
UH	<UH>
UM	<UM>
UH-HUH	<UH-HUH>
UH-HUM	<UH-HUM>
Unintelligible	<unintelligible>
Background noise	<noise>
Start of background noise	<noise_begin>
End of background noise	<noise_end>
Silence	<silence>

```
<t 26.800> «spk2, f»
<mouth><inhale> to vám neřeknu data já si absolutně nepamatuju
<t 31.747> «spk1, f + spk2, f»
SPEAKER1: aspoň roční období
SPEAKER2: <mouth><inhale>
<t 33.372> «spk2, f»
roční tož to mohlo být v třiaštyrc- dvaaštyrycet už třiaštyrycátém roce
<b 40.838>
<noise_begin> protože to byl čas vždycky ten odstup
noise_end>
<b 45.525>
<inhale> jak ty chlapy odvedly tak sme zůstali jenom s maminkama
<b 53.172>
<inhale> v tý [Modělevi] já sem <inhale> utíkala z teho <noise> lágru
```

Fig. 1. A part of an annotated file.

4 Text Corpus Characteristics and Lexical Statistics

This section describes some features of the text corpus created by the annotation of the speech files. Several interesting lexical statistics are also presented.

Table 2 shows ten most frequent words from the Czech transcriptions and their relative occurrences (columns 1 and 2) after processing the 15 minute chunks of the first 180 testimonies. Relative occurrences of those words in the Czech TV&Radio Broadcast News corpus (UWB_B02) [3] and the Lidové Noviny corpus (LN), together with their position in the sorted frequency list, are in the columns 3 and 4, respectively.

Table 2. Ten most frequent words and their relative occurrences.

Word	Shoah	UWB_B02		LN	
a	0.044	0.021	(2)	0.025	(1)
to	0.034	0.007	(9)	0.006	(12)
se	0.022	0.018	(3)	0.017	(3)
sem	0.020	0.000	(3021)	0.000	(1326)
že	0.019	0.010	(5)	0.008	(6)
sme	0.018	-	(-)	0.000	(18432)
tam	0.017	0.001	(156)	0.000	(174)
tak	0.017	0.003	(23)	0.002	(39)
v	0.016	0.022	(1)	0.022	(2)
na	0.013	0.017	(4)	0.015	(4)

It can be seen that while the values in the columns 3 and 4 are very similar to each other, relative occurrences in this corpus are quite different. These differences are caused by the fact that the UWB_B02 and the LN corpora contain standard Czech from broadcast news and the newspaper articles whereas, this corpus consists of a transcribed spontaneous speech and therefore contains a large number of colloquial words.

A good example of the influence of colloquial Czech on the lexical statistics is the word *sem*. While in standard Czech this word means *here*, in colloquial Czech it is also used instead of the correct form *jsem ((I) am)* which naturally occurs quite frequently. Other differences between standard and colloquial Czech are very common. Some differences can even be formalized:

- Words that begin with *o* in standard Czech are prefixed by *v* in colloquial Czech *okno → vokno).*
- *ý* changes into *ej (modrý → modrej, výr → vejr).*
- *é* inside words changes to *í (plést → plíst).*
- *é* in endings changes to *ý (nové → nový).*

The rules above hold for geographical names as well. These differences will cause serious problems in language modeling and also morphological and syntactic analysis, since the text data collected so far is made up mostly of standard Czech. The available morphological analyzers, taggers and parsers were developed for the standard form of the language as well.

Personal names, geographical names and foreign words also pose a challenge for language modeling. The obvious problems that arise due to the occurence of new proper names are further compounded by the highly inflectional nature of the Czech language. The relative occurences of these problematic words in a standard LVCSR dictionary and in the corpus are given in Table 3.

Table 3. Percentages of Problematic Word Classes.

	Colloquial words	Personal names	Geographical names	Foreign words
Per_Vocab	8.27 %	3.58 %	4.76 %	2.71 %
Per_Corpus	6.55 %	0.67 %	1.63 %	0.49 %

In the table above, Per_Vocab denotes the percentage of words from the specified class as found in the LVCSR dictionary, while Per_Corpus expresses the percentage of tokens from each class as found in the corpus. The classes are described here in detail.

The class of **personal names** contains first names and last names, including dialectical variants of the first names. This class contains roughly an equal number of first and last names, however, it is to be expected that the number of the last names will grow far more rapidly than the number of the first names as the corpus increases. Thus we expect to be able to add the list of all first names in the language model dictionary, but the recognition of the last names will likely remain an issue.

The class of **geographical names** covers the names of countries, cities, rivers and other places, as well as the names of languages and nationalities, including the derived adjectives. About 1/3 of the class are words derived from the names of countries and/or nations.

The **foreign words** class contains mostly Slovak words (58 % of all foreign words) and German words (19 %). The remainder of the class is constituted by Russian words and words that are probably Hebrew or Yiddish. Some survivors also switched from Czech to Slovak during the interview.

5   Baseline Automatic Speech Recognition Results

The baseline ASR system was trained in order to check the correctness of the proposed annotation procedure and to prove the feasibility of the project task, that is, the automatic transcription of the survivor testimonies. The witnesses transcribed so far were divided into data used for the acoustic model training and for ASR performance testing.

5.1   Acoustic Models

The acoustic models were trained using the HTK, the hidden Markov model toolkit [4]. The models are based on a continuous density HMMs. The speech features parameterization employed in training are the PLP coefficients, including both delta and delta-delta sub-features. Neither speaker adaptation nor noise subtraction methods were used.

5.2   Language Models

Three language models were used in our basic experiments. All of them are standard word *n*-gram models with Katz's discounting and they were estimated using the SRILM toolkit [5]. They differ in their vocabulary and/or the training data used to estimate them.

The first model (*Shoah_closed*) uses the vocabulary from both training and test portion of the annotated data. Thus the vocabulary is artificially closed on the test set. However, only the training part of the corpus is used for the estimation of the language model parameters. This model was applied mainly because we wanted to check the correctness of the estimated acoustic models.

The second model (*Shoah_open*) is trained on the same data as the first model, but it employs the vocabulary resulting from the training data only and therefore it represents a fair language model (it does not employ any a priori knowledge about the test data).

Finally the third model (*LN_open*) uses both the vocabulary and the training data from the Lidové Noviny (LN) corpus.

5.3   ASR Results

Recognition experiments were carried out using the AT&T decoder [6] on 90 minutes of test data (from 5 male +5 female randomly selected speakers). Initial ASR results are summarized in Table 4.

Table 4. Baseline ASR results.

Language Model	Vocabulary Size	OOV rate	Recognition Accuracy		
			Zerogram	Unigram	Bigram
Shoah_closed	24 k	0 %	21.64 %	43.56 %	49.04 %
Shoah_open	23 k	8.19 %	18.92 %	37.50 %	42.08 %
LN_open	60 k	9.66 %	13.84 %	26.39 %	34.00 %

Please note that the *Shoah_open*/bigram performance is currently higher than that of the *LN_open* model. This is mainly due to the Shoah and LN corpora differences described in Section 4. Nevertheless, the LN corpus is a very valuable resource and will be used for the language modeling purposes in the future ASR experiments. However, some special approach will be necessary – for example, we will probably have to exploit the rules describing the standard-colloquial word changes (see Section 4).

For comparison, current Czech ASR results for the Broadcast News task are at the 65 % accuracy level for the 60 k vocabulary and the bigram language model and at the 70 % level accuracy for the trigram model with the same vocabulary. It shows that the survivor testimonies are really difficult to transcribe.

6   Conclusion

We have described the initial Czech language ASR development efforts in the MALACH project. We have developed a well-defined annotation procedure and have transcribed a enough speech to begin ASR development. We have observed that the language as used by the survivors differs substantially from standard Czech as contained in available text corpora and thus the language modeling in the future Czech MALACH ASR system will require specialized approaches. Finally, we have presented a baseline speech recognition results showing the difficulty that we face in developing ASR for this corpus.

References

1. http://www.clsp.jhu.edu/research/malach.
2. S. Gustman, D. Soergel, D. Oard, W. Byrne, M. Picheny, B. Ramabhadran, D. Greenberg: Supporting Access to Large Digital Oral History Archives. JCDL'02, Portland, Oregon, USA.
3. J. Psutka, V. Radová, L. Müller, J. Matoušek, P. Ircing, D. Graff: Large Broadcast News and Read Speech Corpora of Spoken Czech. EuroSpeech 2001, Aalborg, Denmark, 2001.
4. S. Young et al.: The HTK Book. Entropic Inc. 1999.
5. A. Stolcke: SRILM – The SRI Language Modeling Toolkit. http://www.speech.sri.com/projects/srilm/.
6. M. Mohri, M. Riley, F. C. N. Pereira: Weighted Finite-State Transducers in Speech Recognition. International Workshop on Automatic Speech Recognition: Challenges for the Next Millennium. 2000.

On the First Greek-TTS Based on Festival Speech Synthesis
Architecture and Components Description

P. Zervas, I. Potamitis, N. Fakotakis, and G. Kokkinakis

Wire Communications Lab., Electrical & Computer Engineering Dept.,
University of Patras, Rion-26 500, Patras, Greece
E-mail: pzervas@wcl.ee.upatras.gr, potamitis@wcl.ee.upatras.gr

Abstract. In this article we describe the first Text To Speech (TTS) system for the Greek language based on Festival architecture. We discuss practical implementation details and we capitalize on the preparation of the diphone database and on the prediction of phoneme duration module implemented with CART tree technique. Two male databases where used for two different speech synthesis engines, namely, residual LPC synthesis and Mbrola technique.

1 Introduction

The waveform speech synthesis techniques can be divided into three categories. The general-purpose concatenative synthesis, the corpus based synthesis and the phrase splicing. The general-purpose concatenative synthesis translates incoming text onto phoneme labels, stress and emphasis tags, and phrase break tags. This information is used to compute a target prosodic pattern (i.e., phoneme durations and pitch contour). Finally, signal processing methods retrieve acoustic units (fragments of speech corresponding to short phoneme sequences such as diphones) from a stored inventory, modify the units so that they match the target prosody, and glue and smooth (*concatenate*) them together to form an output utterance. Corpus based synthesis is similar to general-purpose concatenative synthesis, except that the inventory consists of a large corpus of labeled speech, and that, instead of modifying the stored speech to match the target prosody, the corpus is searched for speech phoneme sequences whose prosodic patterns match the target prosody. Last but not least, at phrase splicing technique the system units are stored prompts, sentence frames, and stored items used in the slots of these frames which are glued together.

General-purpose concatenative synthesis is able to handle any input sentence but generally produces mediocre quality due to the difference of the spectral content in the connection points. On the other hand corpus based synthesis can produce very high quality, but only if its speech corpus contains the right phoneme sequences with the right prosody for a given input sentence. Phrase splicing methods produce natural speech, but can only produce the pre-stored phrases or combinations of sentence frames and slot items. If the slot items are not carefully matched to the sentence frames in terms of prosody, naturalness is degraded. The proposed work is supported by GEMINI (IST-2001-32343) EC project.

P. Sojka, I. Kopeček, and K. Pala (Eds.): TSD 2002, LNAI 2448, pp. 261–264, 2002.

2 System Architecture

This paper describes the construction of a Greek TTS based on general-purpose concatenative synthesis architecture. In particular, two different engines have been taken into consideration, the residual LPC synthesizer and the Mbrola synthesizer.

Festival is a general multi-lingual speech synthesis system developed at Centre for Technology Research, Edinburgh, Scotland (CSTR) [1,2]. It consists off a general framework for building speech synthesis systems. It enables the construction of an operational TTS through a number APIs: from shell level, though a Scheme command interpreter, as a C++ library, and an Emacs interface. The architecture of Festival is diphone-based utilizing the Residual-Exited LPC synthesis technique. In this method, feature parameters for fundamental small units of speech such as syllables, phonemes or one-pitch-period speech, are stored and connected by rules. In our system (Figure 1), we used a database consisting of diphones.

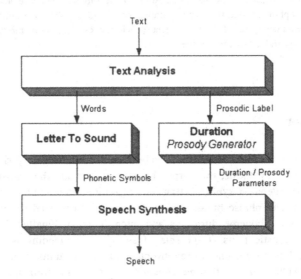

Fig. 1. TTS architecture.

Mbrola is a speech synthesizer based on the concatenation of diphones coded as Pulse Code Modulation 16 bit linear signals. It takes a list of phonemes as input, together with prosodic information (duration of phonemes and a piecewise linear description of pitch), and produces speech samples using linear coding at 16 bits, at the sampling frequency of the diphone database used. Mbrola is *not* a Text-To-Speech (TTS) synthesizer since it does not accept raw text as input [3].

3 Greek TTS Implementation

Hereafter, we describe the creation of a diphone database required from the residual LPC synthesizer provided by the Festival toolbox. Diphones are speech segments beginning in the middle of the stable state of a phone and ending in the middle of the stable state of the following one. Diphones are selected as basic speech segments as they minimize concatenation problems, since they include most of the transitions and co-articulations between phones, while requiring an affordable amount of memory, as their number remains relatively small (as opposed to other synthesis units such as half-syllables or triphones).

A 900-word phonetically balanced speech database was used for the creation of the concatenation database (Figure 2). Besides the creation of diphones and some times triphones we created and all the vowels and consonants of our language. As a result our database was consisting of 398 diphones, 24 triphones and 22 phones of the vowels and consonants. The number of the selected units and their partitioning in triphones and diphones has been chosen according to Mbrola requirements.

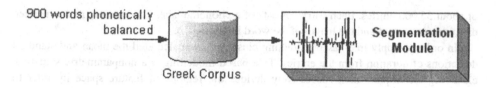

Fig. 2. Greek corpus segmentation procedure.

LPC residual synthesis requires the LPC coefficients (perceptual experiments have indicated that 16 coefficients were adequate), residual term of the various speech segments and pitch marks. Epoch-extraction technique was employed to derive the pitch periods of the signal (Figure 3a). Subsequently, we manually corrected errors in pitch-mark selection (Figure 3b).

As far as it concerns the voiced parts of the speech, the pitch-marks where placed with a synchronous rate, meaning that we first traced the periods of the signal and then the pitch-marks were placed at the max point of the period.

For the voiced parts of the signal they were placed with a constant rate.

As regards the Mbrola synthesizer we have made use of the Gr2 Greek database [4] that has been encoded in TCTS Labs [5].

4   Duration Module

The prediction of the phoneme duration in a specific phonemic and prosodic context is a crucial factor for the performance of TTS systems. For our system we used tree-based modelling and in particular the CART technique. A 500-word speech database was constructed to study the duration model of the Modern Greek language. This database covers all the Greek phonemes and their most frequent contextual combinations. It contains words of various syllabic structures in various locations. The 500 words were spoken in an isolated manner by eight Greek native adult speakers, (four male and four female). The speech database was then labelled manually. The complete database constructed contains a total

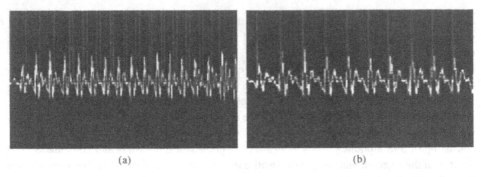

(a)   (b)

Fig. 3. a) Automatic placement of pitch-marks. b) Correction of the automatic placement of pitch-marks.

of about 35.000 entries. Each entry consists of a phoneme label, its duration, its normalized duration, its context and the length of the word it belongs to.

In order to apply tree-based modelling clustering we calculated the mean and standard deviations of duration from the entries. Tree-based modelling is a nonparametric statistical clustering technique which successively divides the regions of feature space in order to minimize the prediction error. The CART technique, a special case of tree-based modelling, can produce decision trees or regression trees with the type of duration. The advantage of the CART technique is the ease of interpreting decision and regression trees. The tree predicts *zscores* (number of standard deviations from the mean) rather than durations directly. After prediction the segmental durations are calculated by the formula:

$$Duration = mean + (zscores \times standarddeviation).$$

5   Conclusions

The work we described here was the creation of the first Greek diphone-based database for residual LPC synthesizer of Festival architecture and the application of duration derived from CART tree technique. Sample files that demonstrate the high quality of the synthesis results and a Java based web-TTS under construction are available for download [6]. Further work focuses on prosody modelling and specifically on the intonation module.

References

1. Black, A., Taylor P., (1997), "The Festival Speech Synthesis System", Technical Report HCRC/TR-83, University of Edinburgh, Scotland, UK,
    http://www.cstr.ed.ac.uk/projects/festival/.
2. Black A., Taylor, P., "The Festival Speech Synthesis System", Carnegie Mellon University, available at http://www.cstr.ed.ac.uk/projects/festival.
3. Dutoit T., "An Introduction to Text-to-Speech Synthesis". Kluwer Academic Publishers, 1997.
4. http://www.di.uoa.gr/speech/synthesis/demosthenes.
5. http://tcts.fpms.ac.be/synthesis/.
6. http://slt.wcl.ee.upatras.gr/Zervas/index.asp.

An Analysis of Limited Domains for Speech Synthesis

Robert Batůšek

Faculty of Informatics, Masaryk University, Brno, Czech Republic
E-mail: xbatusek@fi.muni.cz, WWW: http://www.fi.muni.cz/lsd/

Abstract. This paper deals with the problem of limited domain speech synthesis. Some experiments show that the segment variability is extremely large for unlimited speech synthesis. It seems that it is practically impossible to colllect the text corpus large enough to cover all combinations of even very coarse features. A natural question arises whether restricting the synthesizer to a specific domain can help to increase segment coverage. This paper provides an analysis of several limited domain text corpora and evaluates their applicability to the problem of segment selection for speech synthesis.

1 Introduction

Corpus-based synthesis has become very popular in last years. A significant progress has been reached in this field (see [4] for an overview). One of the major remaining problems is the variable quality of the speech output. Van Santen [6] has recently made an analysis that can explain the reasons of the above mentioned problem. He used a text analysis component of a speech synthesizer to generate a feature vector for each diphone detected in a large newspaper textual corpus. He used very simple feature vectors with only a few possible values of each feature. Even with these artifitially coarse vectors and a very large corpus he was not able to achieve the sufficient coverage. Making things even worse, it is not clear what is the final number of feature combinations and how large text corpus should be to ensure full coverage.

Many researches use the corpus-based approach for building speech synthesizers targeted to specific domains [3,5]. The vocabulary of these domains is typically somehow limited, although not totally closed. As van Santen's results were achieved using a general newspaper corpus, the natural question arises, whether we cannot expect better results for restricted domains. The rest of the paper provides an investigation of several limited domains.

2 Data Collection

We have collected several small corpora for experimental purposes. All of them were collected using data publicly available on the Internet. The brief characteristics of the corpora follow:

- **WEATHER** (150,000 phone-sized tokens) – brief daily weather reports from November 15, 1999 till November 15, 2001.
- **RECIPE** (594,000 phone-sized tokens) – a collection of 1,300 cooking recipes.

P. Sojka, I. Kopeček, and K. Pala (Eds.): TSD 2002, LNAI 2448, pp. 265–268, 2002.

- **ECONOMIC** (165,000 phone-sized tokens) – short daily economic reports from December 3, 2001 till April 3, 2002.
- **FAIRYTALE** (172,000 phone-sized tokens) – a children fairy tale book.

All corpora have been converted to plain text files and a structural information, e.g. distinguishing recipe names from the ingredients, was ignored. Figure 1 illustrates the vocabulary growth of the corpora. The vocabulary sizes have been normalized, i. e. the value 60 at the point 30 means that the first 30 % word tokens of the particular corpus contain 60 % phonetically distinct words occurring in the whole corpus. It seems from the chart that the most limited corpus is WEATHER. The vocabulary growth of the ECONOMIC and FAIRYTALE corpora is nearly linear and it is questionable whether they can be considered limited.

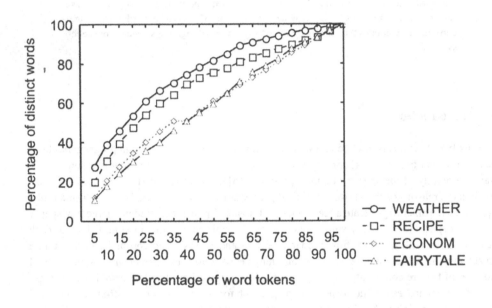

Fig. 1. The vocabulary of four inspected domains.

3   Feature Generation

All experiments have been made using the text analysis components of the Demosthenes speech synthesizer [2]. Typically, one feature vector corresponds to a phone-sized unit.

We start with a very simple feature set consisting of the phoneme label only. The elementary feature set is then refined in various ways. The newly added features may include textual features, e.g. position in the phrase, phonetic features like left and right neighbors or prosodic features, e.g. an estimated segment duration. For each feature set and each corpus, the appropriate list of feature vectors is generated. A criterion is computed for each list

Table 1. Coverage indices of several feature sets.

Feature set	WEATHER	RECIPE	ECONOM	FAIRYTALE
{phid}	1	1	1	1
{phid,previd}	0.92	0.99	0.99	0.98
{phid,previd,nextid}	0.41	0.73	0.33	0.62
{phid,inwordpos}	0.99	1	1	1
{phid,previd,inphrasepos}	0.89	0.98	0.97	0.97

determining the level of domain coverage of the given text corpus with respect to the given feature set.

The motivation behind this approach is the following. The utterances for recording the database are usually selected from the text corpus specific to the target domain. Text selection methods typically select the utterances (locally) maximizing the feature vector variability. However, it makes no sense to select utterances containing the maximum possible number of feature combinations, when the corpus **itself** does not include many combinations probably occurring in the target domain. When the corpus is recognized as insufficient for the requested feature set, it is possible to use one of the following two solutions.

First, more text data can be collected and a larger corpus built. This solution is often useful for limited domains, while it may be problematic for general purpose text corpora. The other possibility is to use a more general feature set for segment selection or a coarser values of some features.

4   Domain Coverage

So-called *coverage index* has been recently introduced as a criterion of domain coverage [6]. It is defined as a probability that all feature vectors in a randomly selected test sentence appeared in the training set. We used 90 % of each corpus for training and 10 % for evaluation. The results are summarized in Table 1. Feature types are similar to those used in [1].

Of course, the number of possible feature sets and feature values is practically infinite, and one needs to decide which set will be used for segment selection. We propose the following technique. The first step is to specify a treshold for the coverage index. All feature sets with coverage index below this treshold are considered inappropriate for segment selection. The second step is to generate some reference feature vectors containing as many details as possible. Typically, these vectors consist of the complete phonetic and prosodic specification of each unit generated by the text analysis component of a speech synthesizer. Finally, the last step is to estimate the unspecified feature vector variability for each feature set considered as a candidade set for segment selection. This variability is defined as an average distance between two undistinguishable vectors of the candidade set. The distance computation is based on the feature vectors from the detailed feature set.

We have made such an analysis for the WEATHER domain. The results are shown in Figure 2.

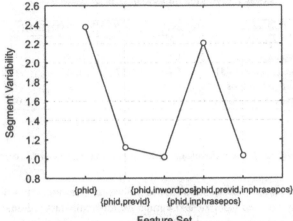

Fig. 2. An analysis of the expected variability of several feature sets for WEATHER domain. Feature sets with the coverage index less than 0.8 were not analyzed. The most suitable feature set is {phid,inwordpos} with variability 1.02.

5 Conclusions

The analysis of several restricted text corpora shows that they suffer from the extremely odd distribution of segmental features as well as the unrestricted corpora. Even the corpus of weather reports may not be considered limited, when it should be used to cover the domain with respect to a more detailed feature set. Thus, we provide here some techniques how to estimate the convenience of the particular feature set for the utterance selection.

References

1. R. Batůšek. A duration model for Czech text-to-speech synthesis. In *Proceedings of Speech Prosody 2002*, Aix-en-Provence, France, Apr. 2002.
2. R. Batůšek and J. Dvořák. Text preprocessing for Czech speech synthesis. In: *Proceedings of TSD '99*, Pilsen, Czech Republic, Sept. 1999.
3. A. W. Black and K. Lenzo. Limited domain synthesis. In *Proceedings of ICSLP*, Beijing, China, 2000.
4. B. Möbius. Corpus-based speech synthesis: methods and challenges. Technical Report 4, Stuttgart University, 2000.
5. K. Stober, T. Portele, P. Wagner, and W. Hess. Synthesis by word concatenation. In *Proceedings of the EuroSpeech '99*, pp. 619–622, Budapest, Hungary, Sept. 1999.
6. J. P. H. van Santen. Combinatorial issues in text-to-speech synthesis. In *Proceedings of EuroSpeech '99*, Budapest, Hungary, 1999.

Advances in Very Low Bit Rate Speech Coding Using Recognition and Synthesis Techniques*♣

Geneviève Baudoin[5], François Capman[2], Jan Černocký[3], Fadi El Chami[6,5],
Maurice Charbit[4], Gérard Chollet[4], and Dijana Petrovska-Delacrétaz[1]

[1] University of Fribourg, Dpt. of Informatics, E-mail: dijana.petrovski@unifr.ch
[2] Thales Communications, E-mail: francois.capman@fr.thalesgroup.com
[3] VUT Brno, Faculty of Information Technology, E-mail: cernocky@fit.vutbr.cz
[4] ENST Paris, Dpt. Signal et Images, E-mail: charbit@tsi.enst.fr, chollet@tsi.enst.fr
[5] ESIEE Paris, Dpt. Signal et Télécommunications, E-mail: baudoing@esiee.fr
[6] Université Libanaise Tripoli, E-mail: chamifadi@hotmail.com

Abstract. ALISP (Automatic Language Independent Speech Processing) units are an alternative concept to using phoneme-derived units in speech processing. This article describes advances in very low bit rate coding using ALISP units. Results of speaker-independent experiments are reported and speaker clustering using vector quantization is proposed. The improvements of speech re-synthesis using Harmonic Noise Model and dynamic selection of units are discussed.

1 Introduction

In order to achieve bit rates lower than 600 bps in speech coding, it is necessary to use recognition and synthesis techniques. By transmitting only the indexes of the recognized unit, the transmission bit rate is drastically reduced. The coder and the decoder share a dictionary of speech segments. At the decoder side speech synthesis is used in order to reconstruct the output speech, from the sequence of the transmitted symbols. The quality of the reconstructed speech data is also dependent on the choice of the synthesis method.

Current coders working at bit rates lower than 600 bps are based on segmental units related to phones (the phones being the physical realization of the corresponding phonemes). An alternative approach using automatically derived speech units based on ALISP tools was developed at ENST, ESIEE and VUT Brno [1]. These speech units are derived from a statistical analysis of a speech corpus, requiring neither phonetics nor orthographic transcriptions of the speech data. However the experiments conducted so far have only involved the speaker dependent case. In this paper we extend this technique to the speaker independent case (Section 3) and present results with VQ based speaker clustering (Section 4). We also suggest improvements using HNM synthesis and dynamic selection of synthesis units (Sections 5 and 4).

♣ The authors appear in alphabetical order.

* The research has been supported by French RNRT project SYMPATEX and by Grant Agency of Czech Republic under project No. 102/02/0124.

P. Sojka, I. Kopeče, and K. Pala (Eds.): TSD 2002, LNAI 2448, pp. 269–276, 2002.
© Springer-Verlag Berlin Heidelberg 2002

2   Principles of VLBR Speech Coding Using ALISP Units

To obtain speech units from a large speech corpus, first an *initialization* is performed. Spectrally stable zones in speech are found by temporal decomposition [2] and clustered to classes using vector quantization. This leads to initial phoneme-like transcription of the data. In the second phase, *model training*, HMMs are trained for all units. Iterations of Viterbi recognition of the training database and model re-estimations were found to be beneficial for the quality of units. A set of units, their models and transcriptions of the training data are the result of this step. The units are denoted *coding units*.

For the *synthesis* in the decoder, another type of units called *synthesis units* can be defined (see Section 6). Finally, the decoder must dispose of a certain number of *representatives* of each synthesis unit. When dealing with speech examples coming from multiple speakers, we are preserving the information about the identity of those speakers (in such a way we can select the same number of representatives per speaker). The coder must send the index of best-matching representative and information on the prosody: timing and pitch and energy contours. The decoder receives the information on coding units and derives the information on synthesis units, then it retrieves the representative from its memory. The synthesis modifies the prosody of the representative and produces output speech.

This approach was tested on American English [1], French [10] and Czech [11]. Intelligible speech was obtained for the three languages – low speech quality was attributed mainly to rudimentary LPC synthesis rather than the units themselves. The bit rate obtained is in the range of 100–200 bits/s for units encoding (without prosody information).

3   Speaker Independent Coding

In this section we address the issue of extending a speaker dependent very low bit-rate coder to a speaker independent situation based on automatically derived speech units with ALISP.

For the experiments we used the BREF database [6], a large vocabulary read-speech corpus for French. The BREF database is sampled at 16 kHz. The texts were selected from 5 million words of the French newspaper "Le monde". In total 11,000 texts were chosen, in order to maximize the number of distinct triphones. Separate text materials were selected for training and test corpora. 120 speakers have been recorded, each providing between 5,000 and 10,000 words (approximately 40–70 min of speech), from different French dialects. Different subsets of the database were used for different experiments.

As a first step a gender dependent, speaker independent coder is experimented. For the speaker independent experiments, we have taken 33 male speakers to train the ALISP recognizer. Testing was done with another set of 3 male speakers. For a baseline comparison, we generated the equivalent speaker dependent experiments. Their speech data was divided into a training set for the speaker dependent ALISP recognizer and a common set for the test coding sentences.

The speech parameterization was done by classical Linear Predictive Coding (LPC) cepstral analysis. The Linear Prediction Cepstral Coefficients (LPCC) are calculated every 10 ms, on a 20 ms window. The temporal decomposition was set up to produce 16 events per second on the average. A codebook with 64 centroids is trained on the vectors from the gravity centers of the interpolation functions, while the segmentation was performed using cumulated distances on the entire segments. With the speech segments clustered in each class, we trained a corresponding HMM model with three states through 5 successive re-estimation steps. The 8 longest segments per model were chosen from the training corpus to build the set of the synthesis units, denoted as synthesis representatives present in the dictionary. The original pitch and energy contours, as well as the optimal DTW time-warps between the original segment and the coded one were used. The index of the best matching DTW representative is also transmitted. The unit rate is evaluated assuming uniform encoding of the indexes. The encoding of the representatives increases the rate by 3 additional bits per unit.

A conventional LPC synthesizer was used in the decoder. This synthesis method in known to be responsible to a lot of artifacts and unnatural sounds of the output speech. For a test segment, a comparison of the wide-band spectrograms of an original and synthesized speech, shows that the synthesis by itself introduces a lot of degradation. The same test segment was used to evaluate the transition from the speaker dependent to the speaker independent case. The corresponding spectrograms are shown in Figure 1.

The resulting average rates for the spectral information are 140 bps for the speaker dependent case and 133 bps for the speaker independent case. Through informal listening we can conclude that the coded speech in the speaker independent mode is still intelligible. Not surprisingly, the speech quality was found to be worse in the speaker independent experiments.

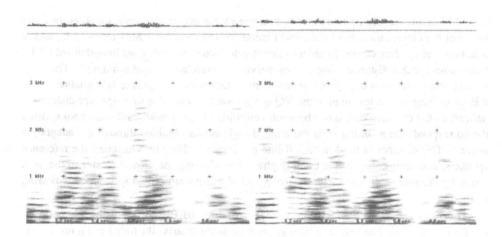

Fig. 1. Speaker dependent and speaker independent coding.

4 VQ-Based Speaker Clustering and Adaptation

Several distinct approaches are possible for handling the speaker-independent mode. One could think of training the VLBR system using a sufficient amount of representative speakers, making no distinction between the different speakers as described in the previous section. But

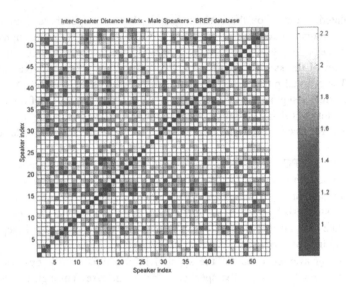

Fig. 2. Inter-speaker distance matrix for Male Speakers (54) from BREF corpus.

it could advantageously be combined with a pre-clustering of reference speakers, in order to select the closest speaker or the closest subset of speakers for HMM refinements and/or adaptation of synthesis units. In order to investigate further this idea, we have defined a VQ-based inter-speaker distance using the unsupervised hierarchical VQ algorithm [4]. The basic assumption is that training speech material from the processed speaker is available during a short training phase for running the VQ adaptation process. The inter-speaker distance is defined as the cumulated distance between centroids of the non-aligned code-books, using the correspondence resulting from the aligned code-books obtained through the adaptation process. This distance is used in the off-line pre-training phase for clustering the reference speakers, and during the on-line training phase for selecting the closest cluster to the user. From the distance matrix, sub-classes are extracted using a simplified split-based clustering method.

The proposed concept has been validated on the BREF corpus using phonetically balanced sentences. The resulting inter-speaker distance matrix illustrated in Figure 2, was derived using 16 LPC-based cepstrum features, and 64 classes. Intra-speakers distances are located on the diagonal, and should be minimal for each speaker. Illustration of the clustering process is given for the largest class, (left panel of Figure 3), a typical class (middle panel) and an isolated speaker (right panel) in terms of relative distance to the other speakers. One could note the similar positioning of speakers belonging to the same cluster. This distance is expected to be robust to channel variation, and moderate background noise, since it is based on an adaptation process, which should take into account part of the corresponding mismatch. This will be validated in future experiments using noisy data and distorted channel.

The obtained results in terms of speaker clustering using a small amount of data are encouraging. In our future works, we will study a speaker-independent VLBR structure

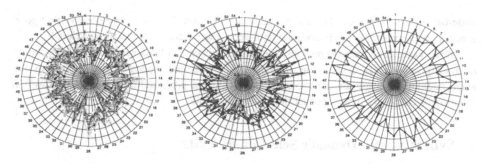

Fig. 3. Left panel: Relative distance of speakers from the largest cluster. Middle panel: Relative distance of speakers from a typical cluster (indexes 6, 14, 21, 29, 31, 43). Right panel: Relative distance of speakers from an isolated speaker (index 33).

derived from this concept, by adding HMM adaptation at the encoder, and voice conversion techniques at the decoder.

5 Harmonic-Noise Model Synthesis

On contrary to source-filter based approaches, HNM (Harmonic Noise Model) [7,9] increases the quality of speech processing by representing the speech signal by $x_t = \sum_{k=1}^{P} a_k \cos(2\pi f_k t + \phi_k) + n_t$, where the sum of cosinusoids is the harmonic part and n_t stands for the noise part. The noise part represents irregularities, as for example those produced by glottal disturbances. For speech signal, harmonic components are mainly located below 4000 Hz while noise spectral part is located above 3000 Hz. For unvoiced sound we keep the classical model, i.e. a white noise exciting an all-pole filter. For HNM, it is easy to modify speech timing. High quality speech synthesis is obtained by constraining phase continuity between successive windows.

Principal advantage of HNM is that gives a flexible method to modify voice characteristics as pitch or timbre. For this purpose, the most important features is the magnitude of the vocal tract transfer function, also called *spectral envelope*. Many works have been devoted to its estimation: The *LPC* approach, that considers that the source excitation is a white noise, performs poorly particularly for high-pitched voiced sounds. Some approaches use *interpolation techniques* between known harmonic values, but the problem has many degrees of freedom and the performed envelope may present non desirable high picks. We use an approach proposed by Galas and Rodet in [5] based on a *regularization technique with penalization*. The method is quite general and may be used with various parametrization as for example cepstral or pole envelope representations.

At first, pitch extraction is performed with sufficient accuracy to efficiently separate deterministic and noisy parts of HNM. Then we estimate spectral density η_k of noise with LPC approach. Because it is difficult to perform accurate estimation of harmonic components, particularly for high order harmonic, we restrict research of frequency harmonic to the band 0   4 kHz. The estimation procedure proposed (described in detail by Eqs. (19)–(20) p. 473 in [3]) is based on iterative computation of the penalized least-square estimator of cepstrum coefficients, with a penalization (adjusted by a smoothing parameter λ) which controls the trade-off between observed data and regularizing function. In practice we observe that good spectral envelope estimation is obtained with very few iterations, typically less than 5.

In the context of speech synthesis, spectral envelope has been used as side information to modify speech segment of the dictionary. For example, spectral envelope yields the amplitudes of harmonic components for a given value of pitch and then, using the definition equation of HNM, we may construct the modified signal.

6   Synthesis with Dynamic Selection of Units

The decoder is a speech synthesizer that operates using the information received from the coder that includes at least: ALISP coding units labels and prosody parameters. The speech synthesis is based on concatenation of synthesis units. Two types of synthesis units can be used:

Long synthesis speech units with spectrally stable extremities making concatenation easy. These long units can be constructed by aggregation of short ALISP coding units with re-segmentation in spectrally stable parts of the extremity units. The synthesizer is similar to a diphone one [8].

Short Synthesis speech units with dynamic selection of units, which is close to corpus based text speech synthesis and provided clearly better results than the first one. Here, for each ALISP class, a large number of representatives is extracted from the training corpus. These synthesis representatives are determined in order to fulfill criteria of good representation of a given segment to be coded and criteria of good concatenation of successive segments. A possible solution consists in defining representation and concatenation distance (D_R and D_C) and in choosing the representative to minimize a criterion of the form $aD_I + bD_C$. But, this solution requires to adjust the parameters a and b leading to heavy experimental trials. Therefore a different method was applied that does not requires the explicit calculation of a concatenation distance.

In the developed technique, after the training of ALISP coding units, each ALISP class is partitioned in sub-classes. Let's N_A be the number of ALISP coding classes (in practice, we used $N_A = 64$) and let's call H_j with $j \in [0, N_A \quad 1]$ the ALISP coding classes. Each H_j class contains many segments of the training corpus that were recognized as generated by the H_j HMM model. Each H_j class is partitioned in N_A sub-classes called $H_i H_j$ containing all the speech segments of class H_j that were preceded by a segment belonging to the class H_i in the training corpus. It is possible to keep as synthesis representatives all the segments of the training corpus organized in classes and sub-classes as described above or to limit the size of each sub-class to a maximal value K. If the training corpus is not large enough some of the sub-classes may be empty.

In the coding phase, the coder after recognition of ALISP units, determines for each coding unit a representative for the synthesis. The coder transmits the indexes of ALISP coding class and of synthesis representative. In the decoding phase, the synthesizer concatenates the synthesis units corresponding to the chosen representative in each ALISP class.

During coding, if a segment is recognized as belonging to class H_j and is preceded by a segment in class H_i, the representative is searched in the subclass $H_i H_j$ of class H_j. The selection of the best representative in the sub-class is done on the distance D_C of good representation of the segment. The D_C distance is based on a spectral comparison by DTW between the segment to code and the potential synthesis representatives. The distance D_C can also include a distance on prosody parameters. The index of ALISP class is transmitted on 6 bits and the index of the representative on $\log_2(K)$ bits or $\log_2(N_{max})$ bits where N_{max} is the maximum number of segments in a sub-class. It is not necessary to transmit the index of the sub-class, since the decoder has the same information as the coder concerning the preceding unit. This approach gives very good results, but it requires a large memory size at the decoder for the codebook of synthesis representatives. If no limitation is done on the number of segments in a subclass, the complete training corpus must be present in the decoder. If the size is limited to $K = 16$ segments in each subclass (small quality degradation compared to no limitation), a maximum of $16 \times 64 \times 64$ segments must be present in the decoder. If we suppose that the average segment length is 60 ms, this represents 1 hour of speech. When the number of representative segments is not limited the coder does an exhaustive search in the training corpus, but this is done efficiently (because of pre-classification by preceding segments the calculation is divided by 64).

Some of the subclasses $H_i H_j$ may be non represented in the training corpus, we developed an algorithm of substitution of the missing classes, using the fact that the ALISP classes have a numbering order that corresponds to an average spectral distance order between classes. Therefore, when a class $H_i H_j$ is missing, the algorithm searches if a class $H_{(i-1)} H_j$ or $H_{(i+1)} H_j$ exists. If not, it iterates the operation and when some class is found, it replaces the missing one.

7 Conclusions and Perspectives

This paper demonstrates that speech coding, at transmission rate lower than 400 bps, can be achieved with little degradation. In order to realize this, a speech memory is necessary at the coder and decoder sides. This memory should be identical on both sides. Only the indexes of speech segments (and some prosodic information) is transmitted between the coder and the decoder. The drawback of our proposal is the size of the memory required on both sides and the delay introduced by the maximal duration of the segments in memory (of the order of 200 msec). There are many applications which could tolerate both a large memory (let say 200 Mbytes) and the delay. Among such applications are the multimedia mobile terminal of the future (including the electronic book), the secured mobile phone, the compression of conferences (including distance education),... More work is necessary on voice transformation so that only typical voices will be kept in memory. This is an interesting topic to characterize a voice based on limited data and use this characterization to transform another voice. Applications in speaker recognition are being tested. The speech memory could also be labeled phonetically. In this manner our speech coder will be able to perform acoustic-phonetic decoding of speech, a major step toward speech recognition. In summary, we believe that speech coding by indexing is a useful step in most areas of Automatic Speech Processing.

References

1. G. Baudoin, J. Černocký, P. Gournay, and G. Chollet. Codage de la parole à bas et très bas débits. *Anales des Télécommunications*, 55(9–10):462–482, 2000.

2. F. Bimbot, G. Chollet, P. Deleglise, and C. Montacié. Temporal decomposition and acoustic-phonetic decoding of speech. In *Proc. IEEE ICASSP '88*, pp. 445–448, New York, 1988.

3. M. Campedel-Oudot, O. Cappé, and E. Moulines. Spectral envelope estimation using a penalized likelihood criterion. IEEE, Trans. on Speech and Audio Proc.:469–481, July 2001.

4. S. Furui. Unsupervised speaker adaptation method based on hierarchical spectral clustering. In *Proc. ICASSP '89*, pp. 286–289, 1989.

5. T. Galas and X. Rodet. Generalized functional approximation for source-filter system modeling. Proc. EuroSpeech, (Genova), pp. 1085–1088, 1991.

6. L. F. Lamel, J. L. Gauvin, and M. Eskanazi. BREF: a large vocabulary spoken corpus for French. In *Proc. EuroSpeech 1991*, Genova, Italy, 1991.

7. J. Laroche, E. Moulines, and Y. Stylianou. Speech modification based on harmonic + noise model. Proc. EuroSpeech. Madrid, pp. 451–454, Sept. 1993.

8. P. Motlíček. Concepts of the dissertation. Technical report, Brno University of Technology, Inst. of Radioelectronics, April 2001.

9. Y. Stylianou, J. Laroche, and E. Moulines. High quality speech modification based on harmonic + noise model. Proc. IEEE, ICASSP. Minneapolis., Apr. 1995.

10. J. Černocký, G. Baudoin, and G. Chollet. Segmental vocoder - going beyond the phonetic approach. In *Proc. IEEE ICASSP 98*, pp. 605–608, Seattle, WA, May 1998. http://www.fee.vutbr.cz/~cernocky/Icassp98.html.

11. J. Černocký, I. Kopeček, G. Baudoin, and G. Chollet. Very low bit rate speech coding: comparison of data-driven units with syllable segments. In V. Matoušek, P. Mautner, J. Ocelíková, and P. Sojka, editors, *Proc. of Workshop on Text Speech and Dialogue (TSD '99)*, number 1692 in Lecture Notes in Computer Science, pp. 262–267, Mariánské Lázně, Czech Republic, September 1999. Springer Verlag.

A Comparison of Different Approaches
to Automatic Speech Segmentation

Kris Demuynck and Tom Laureys*

K.U.Leuven ESAT/PSI
Kasteelpark Arenberg 10
B-3001 Leuven, Belgium
E-mail: {kris.demuynck,tom.laureys}@esat.kuleuven.ac.be
WWW: http://www.esat.kuleuven.ac.be/~spch

Abstract. We compare different methods for obtaining accurate speech segmentations starting from the corresponding orthography. The complete segmentation process can be decomposed into two basic steps. First, a phonetic transcription is automatically produced with the help of large vocabulary continuous speech recognition (LVCSR). Then, the phonetic information and the speech signal serve as input to a speech segmentation tool. We compare two automatic approaches to segmentation, based on the Viterbi and the Forward-Backward algorithm respectively. Further, we develop different techniques to cope with biases between automatic and manual segmentations. Experiments were performed to evaluate the generation of phonetic transcriptions as well as the different speech segmentation methods.

1 Introduction

In this paper we investigate the development of an accurate speech segmentation system for the Spoken Dutch Corpus project. Speech segmentations, on phoneme (e.g. TIMIT) or word level (e.g. Switchboard, CGN), have become a standard annotation in speech corpora. Corpus users can benefit from the fact that the segmentation couples the speech signal to the other annotation layers (orthography, phonetics) by means of time stamps, thus providing easy access to audio fragments in the corpus. For the speech technologist segmentations are indispensable for the initial training of acoustic ASR models, the development of TTS systems and speech research in general.

Some speech corpora only provide automatic segmentations, obviously requiring an accurate segmentation algorithm. In other corpora speech segmentations are checked manually. The latter case requires a high-quality automatic segmentation system as well, since a better base segmentation speeds up the manual verification procedure which is time-consuming and expensive.

Some segmentation systems are based on specific acoustic cues or features for the segmentation task [1,2,3] focusing for instance on transient behaviour or specific differences

---

* This publication was supported by the project 'Spoken Dutch Corpus' (CGN-project), which is funded by the Flemish Government and the Netherlands Organization for Scientific Research (NWO).

P. Sojka, I. Kopeček, and K. Pala (Eds.): TSD 2002, LNAI 2448, pp. 277–284, 2002.
© Springer-Verlag Berlin Heidelberg 2002

between phoneme!classes. Others use general features and acoustic modeling which are common in ASR [4,5]. The method proposed in this paper is of the latter type.

Most speech segmentation systems take as input both the speech signal and its phonetic transcription. As manual phonetic transcriptions again require a lot of time and money, they are not always available for speech corpora. Orthographic transcriptions, on the other hand, make up the speech corpus' base annotation. This is the reason why we propose a segmentation system starting from a phonetic transcription that is *automatically* generated on the basis of its orthography.

The complete segmentation process is composed of two subtasks. First, a number of alternative phonetic transcriptions is produced on the basis of a given orthographic transcription and an automatic speech recognizer is used to select the acoustically best matching phonetic representation. Then, this single phonetic transcription serves as input to a segmentation system based on either the Viterbi or the Forward-Backward algorithm.

2   From Orthography to Phonetics

The automatic conversion from an orthographic to a phonetic transcription takes two steps. First, several techniques are applied to produce a network of plausible pronunciation variants. In a second step, the single best matching phonetic string is selected by means of an ASR system. We performed the conversion on material from the Spoken Dutch Corpus, in which the orthographic annotation is enriched with codes to indicate certain spontaneous speech effects [6].

A full network of alternative phonetic transcriptions is generated on the basis of orthographic information. Lexicon lookup is a simple but efficient way to acquire phonetic word transcriptions. Yet, not every orthographic unit is a plain word. Some speech fragments contain sloppy speaking styles including broken-off words, mispronunciations and other spontaneous speech effects. Different techniques are introduced to handle these phenomena and a grapheme-to-phoneme system (g2p) was developed as a fall-back. We will first describe the g2p system. Then we focus on the other techniques and resources employed.

g2p: The g2p system is based on the Induction Decision Tree (ID3) mechanism [7] and was trained on the Flemish Fonilex pronunciation database (200 K entries) [8]. Each phoneme is predicted based on a vector of 10 variables: the grapheme under consideration, a context of 4 left and 4 right graphemes and the last decoded phoneme (feedback). Phonetic transcriptions are generated from back to front so that the last decoded phoneme corresponds to the right neighbour, which turned out to be most informative. We performed a ten-fold cross validation on Fonilex and achieved a 6.0 % error rate on the word level.

lexicon lookup: Fonilex provides (multiple) phonetic transcriptions for most of the *standard* Flemish words. Rules were developed to cover non-listed compounds, derivations and inflections formed on the basis of Fonilex entries. At this early stage, 5376 *proper nouns* (often foreign) were manually transcribed. A new g2p convertor may be trained on these transcriptions to deal with future proper noun input. Lexicon lookup is also the first option for *foreign words*. We build upon the COMLEX English database, the CELEX German database and the BRULEX French database. If a foreign word is part of more than one of these lexica, the different phonetic realizations are put in parallel since the orthography does not specify which foreign language was used.

spontaneous speech effects: For *broken-off words*, also with broken-off orthography, we first retrieve all lexicon words starting with the given orthographic string. Then, a grapheme-phoneme alignment is produced for the retrieved words which allows us to select the phoneme sequence(s) corresponding to the given orthography. *Mispronounced words* are fed to the g2p convertor. *Dialectical pronunciations*, orthographically represented by the standard Flemish word marked with a code, are dealt with by first selecting a phonetic transcription for the standard word. Dialectical pronunciation variants for the word are then generated by means of context-dependent rewrite rules. Finally, *cross-word* phonological phenomena such as assimilation, degemination and inserted linking phonemes are handled by context-dependent rewrite rules as well.

The outcome of the above techniques is a compact pronunciation network [9]. To select the transcription matching best with the speech signal, all phonetic alternatives are acoustically scored (maximum likelihood) in a single pass (Viterbi) through our speech recognition system and the most probable one is retained. The phoneme models are statistically represented as three-state left-to-right Hidden Markov Models (HMMs).

3 Speech Segmentation: Viterbi vs. Forward-Backward

Once a phonetic transcription has been selected, automatic segmentation can proceed in the following way. Sentence models are first generated by simply concatenating all relevant phoneme models. Next, the speech data are assigned (hard or soft, by respectively Viterbi or Forward-Backward) to the acoustic model of the complete phoneme sequence.

3.1 Viterbi Segmentation

The Viterbi algorithm returns the single best path through the model given the observed speech signal x_1^T (the corresponding sequence of feature vectors):

$$s_i^T = \arg \max_{s_i^T \subset S} \prod_{i=1}^{T} f(x_i \mid s_i) p(s_i \mid s_{i-1}) , \qquad (1)$$

with s_i^T a sequence of HMM states (one state for each time frame) which is consistent with the sentence model S, T being the number of time frames. Thus, the Viterbi algorithm results in the segmentation which reaches maximum likelihood for the given feature vectors.

3.2 Forward-Backward Segmentation

The Viterbi algorithm only provides us with an approximation of the quantity that is really looked for. This is illustrated in Figure 1. The Viterbi algorithm generates the boundary corresponding to (1), whereas the optimal boundary in a least squares sense matches with (2).

To find the best possible estimate of the boundary in a least squares sense the probability function of each boundary must be calculated:

$$P(b \mid S, x_1^T) = \frac{f(x_1^b \mid S_l) f(x_{b+1}^T \mid S_r)}{f(x_1^T \mid S)} , \qquad (2)$$

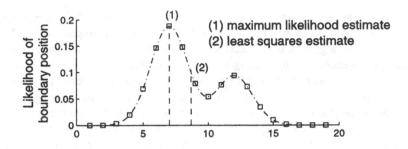

Fig. 1. Viterbi and Forward-Backward boundaries.

with

$$f(x_a^b|S_x) = \sum_{s_a^b \subset S_x} \prod_{i=a}^{b} f(x_i|s_i)^{1/\beta} p(s_i|s_{i\ 1})^{1/\beta} . \tag{3}$$

In the above equations, sentence S is divided in part S_l left and part S_r right of the boundary of interest. The extra parameter β compensates for the ill-matched assumption made by HMMs that the observations x_i are independent. The optimal value for β in our experiments was 10, but its exact value was not at all critical. The same compensation factor can be found in recognition systems [9] as well as in confidence scoring of recognized words [10] for balancing the contribution of acoustic and language model. The Forward-Backward algorithm allows for an efficient calculation of the density functions for all boundaries in a sentence. Given the probability density function of each boundary, the least squares estimate now equals:

$$E\{b\} = \sum_{b=1}^{T} P(b|S, x_1^T)\, b . \tag{4}$$

3.3 Post-processing Techniques for Segmentation

A detailed comparison of automatic and corresponding manual segmentations revealed the occurrence of biases between the respective segmentations. These biases depend on the classes of the phonemes left and right of the boundary, and can be attributed to the fact that humans use different cues than HMMs for finding the boundary between consecutive phonemes [2]. For the transition to a vowel, for example, the average deviation can be more than halved when compensating for these biases. An equally big improvement can be obtained for transitions to noise. We discerned 9 phoneme classes in total and analyzed the biases on the boundary position between each pair of classes. Those biases in the automatic segmentations are removed in a post-processing step.

In a first approach to post-processing, we shift the boundaries purely on the basis of the average biases. This simple technique is applicable to both Viterbi and Forward-Backward segmentations. A second method tries to compensate for the biases in a more advanced way by taking into account a confidence interval for the boundary. These confidence intervals are derived from the Forward-Backward method. Since the Forward-Backward algorithm calculates the probability density function for each boundary, we can regard the variance of this function as a confidence interval for the respective boundary:

$$\text{Var}(b) = \sum_{b=1}^{T} p(b \mid S, x_1^T)(b - E\{b\})^2 \,. \tag{5}$$

So we estimate the bias as a function on the boundary's confidence interval. This function is determined empirically with a polynomial fit on a train set. In Section 4.3 we will discuss results for both post-processing techniques.

4 Experiments

4.1 Description

Experiments were performed on data taken from the Spoken Dutch Corpus. Three test sets were selected, representing different degrees of difficulty for the segmentation process. Test set 1 (50 speakers) accounts for the cleanest speech in the corpus, namely the read-aloud texts. It consists of 14176 words, resulting in 17976 boundaries since pauses exceeding 50 ms were also part of the segmentation. Broadcast material (documentaries, news shows, etc.) and public speeches belong to test set 2 (23 speakers, 7135 words, 9189 boundaries). They are harder to process than the read-aloud texts as background noise might be present and the speaker's style becomes more disfluent. Finally, test set 3 (11 speakers) consists of informal interviews, discussions and school lessons for a total of 27878 words and 36698 boundaries. They pose the hardest problem for the segmentation system as they are riddled with overlapping speech, dialectical pronunciations, etc.

For the experiments we used the LVCSR system developed by the ESAT-PSI speech group at the K.U.Leuven [9,11]. The acoustic models employed in the experiments were estimated on a separate database with 7 hours of dictated speech in Flemish.

4.2 Automatic Phonetic Transcription

The automatic generation of phonetic transcriptions was evaluated by counting the number of insertions, deletions and substitutions of the automatic transcription with respect to a hand-checked reference transcription. This reference transcription was produced by a trained phonetician who corrected a baseline transcription generated by a g2p system different from the one described in this paper. The results of the comparison are summarized in Table 1. These results were obtained by using context-dependent models, which outperformed corresponding context-independent models for this task.

A detailed analysis revealed three main causes for the deviations. First, certain infrequent assimilation rules were not included in our conversion system so that the corresponding pronunciation variants did not occur in the network. Second, the acoustic models were sometimes problematic because they impose a minimal duration constraint of 30 ms (causing schwa-deletion in particular) and because train and test conditions differ (especially for test sets 2 and 3). Third, not every deviation unambiguously corresponded to an error in the automatic transcription. For example, the automatic transcription typically incorporates

Table 1. Deviations between automatic and manual phonetic transcription.

test set	ins	del	sub	total
test set 1	0.77 %	1.27 %	2.95 %	4.99 %
test set 2	1.15 %	1.59 %	3.41 %	6.15 %
test set 3	1.82 %	2.18 %	4.26 %	8.26 %

more connected speech effects than its manual counterpart. This might be due to the fact that human transcribers, having to work at a considerable speed, sometimes overlook these phenomena not present in the base transcription they were offered. For example, especially schwa and linking phonemes were inserted in the automatic transcription. In Dutch schwa can be inserted in coda position in nonhomorganic consonant clusters (e.g. /kAlm/ → /kAl@m/) [12]. Yet, this schwa-insertion is not part of the baseline phonetic word transcription provided by the g2p system. Similarly, schwa and syllable-final /n/ were often deleted in the automatic phonetic transcription. Again both phenomena are typical of Dutch connected speech.

4.3 Automatic Word Segmentation

The automatic segmentations were evaluated by counting the number of boundaries for which the deviation between automatic and manual segmentation exceeded thresholds of 35, 70 and 100 ms. Manual segmentation was performed by two persons and started from an automatic segmentation produced by the Viterbi algorithm (Section 3.1). The persons were instructed to position boundaries so that each word would sound acoustically acceptable in isolation. Shared phonemes at the boundary (e.g. he is_sad) were split in the middle, except for shared plosives (e.g. stop_please), which were isolated altogether. Noticeable pauses (> 50 ms) were segmented in the same way as words, thus producing empty chunks.

We performed experiments for both Viterbi and Forward-Backward segmentation, starting from a manual and automatic phonetic transcription. As can be seen from the post-processed results in Table 2, the forward-backward method clearly outperforms the Viterbi approach on test sets 1 and 2. The different behaviour on test set 3 is mainly due to the combined effect of using the Viterbi segmentation as a starting point for the manual verification process and the low quality of the material in test set 3, from which the human correctors quickly learned that only in few cases clear improvements could be obtained by moving boundaries. This behaviour is reflected in the number of boundaries for which alternative positions were tried by the correctors: 37.1 % and 51.7 % for test set 1 and 2 versus only 32.7 % for test set 3.

A detailed analysis showed that the majority of the remaining deviations in the automatic post-processed segmentations are transitions to and from noise and transitions to unvoiced plosives (45 %, 11 % and 15 % of the remaining 35 ms errors respectively). Since these boundaries also show large variation between the corresponding manual segmentations of different correctors, we cannot expect an automatic system to give more consistent results.

Post-processing using confidence intervals showed no improvement and hence only the results for the simplest post-processing proposed in Section 3.3 are given in Table 2. The confidence intervals can be used to predict misplaced boundaries (e.g. more than 50 %

Table 2. Results: Viterbi vs. Forward-Backward.

test set	manual phon. trans. deviations exceeding			automatic phon. trans. deviations exceeding		
	35ms	70ms	100ms	35ms	70ms	100ms
Viterbi						
test set 1	7.8 %	1.7 %	0.7 %	8.5 %	1.9 %	0.7 %
test set 2	14.4 %	6.0 %	3.4 %	15.8 %	6.3 %	3.5 %
test set 3	14.3 %	9.3 %	7.7 %	16.1 %	9.4 %	7.5 %
Viterbi post-processed						
test set 1	7.8 %	1.5 %	0.6 %	8.5 %	1.8 %	0.7 %
test set 2	14.2 %	5.5 %	3.3 %	15.0 %	5.8 %	3.4 %
test set 3	12.7 %	8.6 %	7.3 %	14.3 %	8.8 %	7.1 %
Forward-Backward						
test set 1	8.1 %	1.5 %	0.6 %	8.8 %	1.7 %	0.6 %
test set 2	14.4 %	5.6 %	3.0 %	15.6 %	5.8 %	3.1 %
test set 3	16.7 %	9.6 %	7.6 %	17.9 %	9.5 %	7.2 %
Forward-Backward post-processed						
test set 1	7.1 %	1.3 %	0.6 %	7.7 %	1.5 %	0.6 %
test set 2	13.8 %	5.0 %	2.9 %	14.7 %	5.3 %	3.0 %
test set 3	14.8 %	9.0 %	7.3 %	15.8 %	8.9 %	7.0 %

of the 75 ms deviations can be found by checking only the 10 % boundaries with the largest predicted variance) but since the sign of the deviation (shift boundary to the left or right) cannot be predicted, no better boundary positions could be produced. However, the confidence intervals may still be useful for other applications such as TTS systems for which the segments with reliable boundary positions can be selected automatically.

Finally note that using the automatically derived phonetic transcriptions results in a limited degradation in the accuracy of the boundary positions. This reflects the fact that the automatic phonetic transcription is of a high quality.

5 Conclusions and Future Research

We presented a system which first generates a phonetic transcription on the basis of orthographic information and then uses the obtained transcription to produce automatic speech segmentations. Different approaches to segmentation and bias compensation were explained and tested. The forward-backward segmentation, proposed as an alternative to the commonly used Viterbi algorithm, shows very good results, especially when considering that the Viterbi segmentation was used as starting point for the manually verified segmentation. The obtained phonetic transcriptions are also of high quality, showing the potential of ASR techniques for phonetic research. To further improve the automatic system, the following actions can (and will) be taken: (1) eliminating the mismatch between training and testing conditions by retraining of the acoustic models on the corpus that must be annotated, (2) the introduction of single state models for phonemes that tend to be pronounced very rapidly, and (3) the derivation of more assimilation rules based on what is observed in the corpus. But even without these modifications, the results obtained by the automatic system are up to state of the art.

References

1. Vorstermans, A., Martens, J.P., Van Coile, B.: Automatic segmentation and labelling of multi-lingual speech data. Speech Comm. **19** (1996) 271–293.
2. van Santen, J., Sproat, R.: High-accuracy automatic segmentation. In: Proc. EuroSpeech. Volume VI., Budapest, Hungary (1999) 2809–2812.
3. Husson, J.L.: Evaluation of a segmentation system based on multi-level lattices. In: Proc. EuroSpeech. Volume I., Budapest, Hungary (1999) 471–474.
4. Ljolje, A., Riley, M.: Automatic segmentation and labeling of speech. In: Proc. ICASSP. Volume I., Toronto, Canada (1991) 473–476.
5. Beringer, N., Schiel, F.: Independent automatic segmentation of speech by pronunciation modeling. In: Proc. ICPhS, San Francisco, U.S.A. (1999) 1653–1656.
6. Goedertier, W., Goddijn, S., Martens, J.: Orthographic transcription of the Spoken Dutch Corpus. In: Proc. LREC, Athens, Greece (2000) 909–914.
7. Pagel, V., Lenzo, K., Black, A.W.: Letter to sound rules for accented lexicon compression. In: Proc. ICSLP. Volume I., Sydney, Australia (1998) 252–255.
8. Mertens, P., Vercammen, F.: The Fonilex Manual. (1997).
9. Demuynck, K.: Extracting, Modelling and Combining Information in Speech Recognition. Ph.D. thesis, K.U.Leuven, ESAT (2001)
   Available from http://www.esat.kuleuven.ac.be/~spch.
10. Wessel, F., Ralf, S., Macherey, K., Ney, H.: Confidence measures for large vocabulary speech recognition. IEEE Trans. on SAP **9** (2001) 288–298.
11. Duchateau, J.: HMM Based Acoustic Modelling in Large Vocabulary Speech Recognition. Ph.D. thesis, K.U.Leuven, ESAT (1998)
    Available from http://www.esat.kuleuven.ac.be/~spch.
12. Booij, G.: The Phonology of Dutch. Clarendon Press, Oxford (1995).

Keyword Spotting Using Support Vector Machines

Yassine Ben Ayed[1], Dominique Fohr[1], Jean Paul Haton[1], and Gérard Chollet[2]

[1] LORIA-CNRS/ INRIA Lorraine, BP239, F54506, Vandoeuvre, France
E-mail: ybenayed@loria.fr, fohr@loria.fr, jph@loria.fr
[2] ENST, CNRS-LTCI, 46 rue Barrault, F75634 Paris cedex 13, France
E-mail: chollet@tsi.enst.fr

Abstract. Support Vector Machines is a new and promising technique in statistical learning theory. Recently, this technique produced very interesting results in pattern recognition [1,2,3].

In this paper, one of the first application of Support Vector Machines (SVM) technique for the problem of keyword spotting is presented. It classifies the correct and the incorrect keywords by using linear and Radial Basis Function kernels. This is a first work proposed to use SVM in keyword spotting, in order to improve recognition and rejection accuracy. The obtained results are very promising.

1 Introduction

Automatic speech recognition systems need to be more flexible to accept a wide range of user responses and behaviours. Unaware of technology limitations, users rightfully expect the system to work properly, even if their response includes disfluencies such as hesitation, extraneous speech and false starts. Users may also respond with utterances that do not include any of the recognizer keywords, or that include the expected keywords in a phrase or a sentence.

A recognizer must thus be able, in first time to spot a keyword embedded in speech, in second time to reject speech that does not include any valid keyword. However, word-spotting and word rejection are interrelated such that a good word-spotting capability necessarily implies a good rejection performance.

In this paper, a support vector machine based method is proposed for keyword spotting. The SVM minimizes the structural risk, i.e., the probability of misclassifying patterns for fixed but unknown probability distribution of the data. This is in contrast to traditional pattern recognition techniques of minimizing the empirical risk, i.e., of optimising the performance on the training data. This minimum structural risk principal is equivalent to minimizing an upper bound on the generalisation error [4].

The organisation of this paper is as follows: Section 2 gives a brief description of the basic principles of the SVM. The details concerning database and recognition system are given in Section 3. In Section 4, we present the way we use SVM for keyword spotting. Experimental results are described in Section 5, and conclusions are given in Section 6.

P. Sojka, I. Kopeček, and K. Pala (Eds.): TSD 2002, LNAI 2448, pp. 285–292, 2002.
© Springer-Verlag Berlin Heidelberg 2002

2 Support Vector Machines (SVM)

Support vector machines have been recently introduced as a new technique for solving pattern recognition problems [5,6]. They perform pattern recognition between two point classes by finding a decision, determined by certain points of the training set, termed support vectors. This surface, which in some feature space of possibility infinite dimension can be seen as a hyperplane. It is obtained from the solution of the problem of quadratic programming that depends on regularization parameter.

2.1 The Linear Separable Case

Consider the problem of separating the set of training vectors belonging to two separated classes,

$$D = \{(x_1, y_1), \ldots, (x_m, y_m)\},$$

where $x_i \in R^n$ is a feature vector and $y_i \in \{-1, 1\}$ a class label, with a hyperplane of equation $w.x + b = 0$.

The goal is to find the hyperplane that separates the positive from the negative examples; the one that maximizes the margin would generalise better as compared to other possible separating hyperplanes.

A separating hyperplane in canonical form must satisfy the following conditions:

$$w.x_i + b \geq 1 \quad if \quad y_i = 1$$

$$w.x_i + b \leq 1 \quad if \quad y_i = -1$$

These can be combined into one set of inequalities

$$y_i(w.x_i + b) \geq 1 \quad \forall i \in \{1, \ldots, m\}$$

The distance $d(w, b, x)$ of a point x from the hyperplane (w, b) is,

$$d(w, b, x) = \frac{|w.x + b|}{||w||}$$

The optimal separating hyperplane is given by maximizing the margin M given by the equation:

$$M = \min_{x_i | y_i = 1} d(w, b, x_i) + \max_{x_i | y_i = 1} d(w, b, x_i) = \frac{2}{||w||}$$

To maximize the margin M, one need to minimize:

$$\Phi(w) = \frac{w^2}{2}$$

The solution to the optimisation problem is given by the saddle point of the Lagrange functional (Lagrangian)

$$L(w, b, \alpha) = \frac{1}{2}w.w \sum_{i=1}^{m} \alpha_i[y_i(w.x + b) - 1]$$

Where α are the Lagrange multipliers. The Lagrangian has to be minimized with respect to w, b and with $\alpha \geq 0$. This problem can easily be transformed into the dual problem, and hence the solution is given by:

$$\alpha^0 = argmax \sum_{i=1}^{m} \alpha_i - \frac{1}{2} \sum_{i,j=1}^{m} \alpha_i \alpha_j y_i y_j (x_i.x_j)$$

with constraints,

$$\alpha_i \geq 0, \forall i \in 1, \ldots, m$$

$$\sum_{i=1}^{m} \alpha_i^0 y_i = 0$$

2.2   The Non-linear Separable Case

In this case, the set of training vectors of two classes are non-linearly separable. To solve this problem, Cortex and Vapnik [7] introduce non-negative variables, $\xi_i \geq 0$, which measure the miss-classification errors. The optimisation problem is now treated as a minimization of the classification error [8]. The separating hyperplane must satisfy the following inequality:

$$(w.x_i) + b \geq +1 - \xi_i, \quad if \quad y_i = +1$$

$$(w.x_i) + b \leq -1 + \xi_i, \quad if \quad y_i = -1$$

The generalised optimal separating hyperplane is determined by the vector w, that minimizes the functional,

$$\phi(w, \xi) = \frac{w^2}{2} + C \sum_{i=1}^{m} \xi_i$$

Where $\xi = (\xi_1, \ldots, \xi_m)$ and C are constants.
The dual problem corresponding to this case is slightly different from the linear separable case, the goal now is to maximize:

$$\sum_{i=1}^{m} \alpha_i - \frac{1}{2} \sum_{i,j=1}^{m} \alpha_i \alpha_j y_i y_j (x_i.x_j)$$

subject to

$$\sum_{i=1}^{m} \alpha_i^0 y_i = 0$$

$$0 \leq \alpha_i \leq C \quad \forall i \in \{1, \ldots, m\}$$

2.3 Kernel Support Vector Machines

In the case where a linear boundary is inappropriate, the SVM can map the input vector into a high dimensional space through function $\phi(x)$, where the SVM constructs a linear hyperplane in the high dimensional space.

Since finding the SVM solutions involve the dot products of the sample vectors $x_i.x_j$, kernel functions play a very important role in avoiding explicit producing the mappings, and avoiding the curse of dimensionality, so that

$\phi(x_i).\phi(x_j) = K(x_i.x_j)$, i.e., the dot product in that high dimensional space is equivalent to a kernel function of the current space.

In the linear and non-linear cases, the optimal separating hyperplane defined by w^0 and b^0 is determined as follows:

$$H : w^0.\phi(x) + b^0$$

where,

$$w^0 = \sum_{SV} \alpha_i \phi(x_i) y_i$$

and

$$b^0 = 1 - w^0.x_i \quad for \quad x_i \quad with \quad y_i = 1$$

The classification function is:

$$class(x) = Sign(w^0.\phi(x) + b^0)$$

$$class(x) = Sign[\sum_{SV} \alpha_i^0 y_i \phi(x_i).\phi(x) + b^0]$$

$$class(x) = Sign[\sum_{SV} \alpha_i^0 y_i K(x_i.x) + b^0]$$

Some widely used kernels are:
Linear: $K(x, y) = x.y$
Polynomial: $K(x, y) = (x.y + 1)^d$
Radial Basis Function (RBF): $K(x, y) = exp[-\frac{|x-y|^2}{2\sigma^2}]$

3 Database and Recognition System

3.1 Database

For training, we use 5300 sentences of the French BREF80 database, pronounced by 80 speakers. These sentences are recorded at 16 KHz with 16 bits. This is a general purpose database, and the sentences have no relationship with our application.

The test database contains one hour of recording speech of radio braodcast news at 16 kHz. It is segmented into fragments of duration is 20 s. This recorded speech have been pronounced by several speakers (different from the speakers of the training database). In our application we choose 10 different keywords.

3.2 Recognition System

The recognizer used in this work is a speaker independent HMM system. The modeled unit is the phone, each phone is represented by 3-state, strictly left-to-right, continuous density HMM. A word is represented by the concatenation of phone models. The number of probability density function (pdf) per state is determined during the training phase.

The parameterization is based on MFCC (Mel-Frequency Cepstral Coefficients) parameters. The user can modify this parameterization: size of the analyzing window, shift, number of triangular filters, lower and upper frequency cut-off of the filter bank, and number of the cepstral coefficients. Finally the delta (the first derivation) and acceleration coefficients (the second derivation) are added. In the following experiments, the acoustic feature vectors are built as follows: 32 ms frames with a frame shift of 10 ms, each frame is passed through a set of 24 triangular band-pass filter resulting in a vector of 35 features, namely 11 static mel-cepstral coefficients (C_0 is removed), 12 delta and 12 delta delta coefficients.

In the recognition phase, we adjust parameters in order to have no deletion keywords (as consequence we obtained a great number of insertion keywords).

4   SVM for Keyword Spotting

In this section, we describe the way we have utilised the SVM for the keyword detection. After the recognition phase, the goal is to classify a sequence of detected keywords into correct and incorrect keywords.

For each keyword, we compute the frames assigned to each phone state and extract the acoustic feature. In this work, 13 different features have been observed to provide information about the correctness of a word hypothesis were utilised. These features, as computed for each word, are:

1. The total number of frames,
2. The number of frames of the first phone,
3. The number of frames of the end phone,
4. The minimum number of frames in word phones,
5. The maximum number of frames in word phones,
6. The number of phones,
7. The average number of frames per phone,
8. The log phone posterior probability of the first phone,
9. The log phone posterior probability of the end phone,
10. The minimum log phone posterior probability,
11. The maximum log phone posterior probability,
12. The average per-frame log phone posterior probability,
13. The average duration-normalised log phone posterior probability.

For each keyword (insertion keyword, recognized correct keyword) we compute a feature vector that is used as input for the SVM.
In our work the insertion keyword belongs to the class labelled -1 and the correct keyword is assigned to the class labelled $+1$. Thus, we classify the correct and the incorrect keywords.

The SvmFu package was used for these experiments. It is available as freeware on http://www.kernel-machines.org/.

5 Experimental Results

The database used in the second phase of our experiments (after the recognition phase) is composed of 600 keywords for the training data, and 560 keywords for the test data. In this work, we use linear and Radial Basis Function (RBF) kernels.

To evalute the performances of our recognizers, we use two evaluation rates:

The False Acceptance Rate also called False Alarm Rate (FAR). It is defined by the equation:

$$FAR = \frac{Total\ \ False\ \ Acceptance}{Total\ \ False\ \ Attempts}$$

The False Rejection Rate (FRR). FRR is defined by the equation:

$$FRR = \frac{Total\ \ False\ \ Rejection}{Total\ \ True\ \ Attempts}$$

Plotting a graph of FRR versus FAR gives a Receiver Operating Characteristics (ROC) graph.

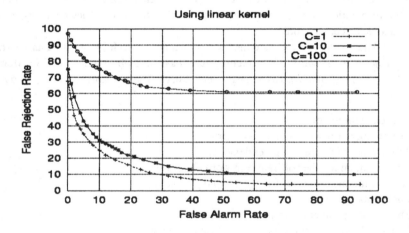

Fig. 1. ROC curves on test data using a linear kernel by varying the value of C.

The resulting ROC curves, using linear SVM by varying the value of the parameter C, $C \in \{1, 10, 100\}$ are presented in Figure 1. They show that better performances are obtained in case $C = 1$.

Figure 2 presents ROC curves corresponding to the performance obtained using RBF kernel by varying the value of the parameter σ, with $C = 1$. In our experiments, we test several values of σ and in this article, in order to alleviate the figure, we choose to present only the interesting curves for $\sigma \in \{5, 10, 70\}$. The best results are achieved for $\sigma = 70$.

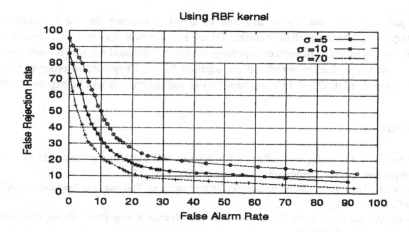

Fig. 2. ROC curves on test data using a RBF kernel by varying the value of σ.

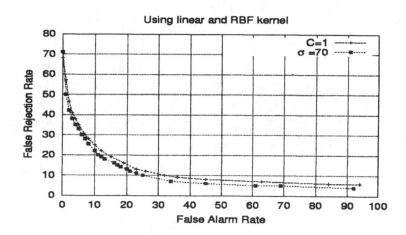

Fig. 3. ROC curves comparing the performance of the linear and the RBF kernels.

Figure 3 demonstrates that the obtained results for RBF kernel are better than results obtained for linear SVM.

6   Conclusion

This paper presents the results achieved by SVM techniques for the keyword spotting problem using linear and RBF kernels. Taking into account that is a first approach using support vector machine in keyword spotting, the results obtained seem to be very promising. In the near future, feature vector will be adjusted for each keyword in order to have more information about it. Other different kernel types and parameters will be experimented.

References

1. Kharroubi, J., Petrovska, D., Chollet, G.: Combining GMM's with Suport Vector Machines for Text-independent Speaker Verification. EuroSpeech (2001) 1761–1764.
2. Ousna, E., Freund, R., Girosi, F.: Support Vector machines: Training and Applications. A.I.Memo 1602, MIT (1997).
3. Ganapathiraju, A.: Support Vector Machines for Speech Recognition. Thesis Mississipi State University, January (2002).
4. Gunn, S.: Support Vector Machines for Classification and Regression. Technical Report ISIS-1 (1998).
5. Vapnick, V.: The Nature of Satistical Learning Theory. Springer-Verlag (1995).
6. Vapnick, V.: Satistical Learning Theory. Johon Wiley and Sons (1998).
7. Cortes, C., Vapnick, V.: Support Vector Networks. Machine Learning, Vol. 20. (1995) 273–297.
8. Burges, C.: A Tutorial on Support Vector Machines for Pattern Recognition Data Mining and Knowledge Discovery, 2(2) (1998).

Automatic Parameter Estimation
for a Context-Independent Speech Segmentation Algorithm

Guido Aversano[1,3] and Anna Esposito[2,3]

[1] Dipartimento di Fisica "E.R. Caianiello", Università di Salerno, Italy,
E-mail: guido.aversano@sa.infn.it,
[2] Department of Computer Science and Engineering, Wright State University, Dayton, Ohio, USA,
E-mail: anna@cs.wright.edu,
[3] International Institute for Advanced Scientific Studies (IIASS),
Vietri sul Mare (SA), Italy

Abstract. In the framework of a recently introduced algorithm for speech phoneme segmentation, a novel strategy has been elaborated for comparing different speech encoding methods and for finding parameters which are optimal to the algorithm. The automatic procedure that implements this strategy allows to improve previously declared performances and poses the basis for a more accurate comparison between the investigated segmentation system and other segmentation methods proposed in literature.

1 Introduction

The computational treatment of raw data, originated by real-word processes, usually requires a preliminary step in which the data has to be encoded in a form that is suitable for further processing. Ideally, the encoded data should retain only the portion of informational content which is useful to the particular task the machine is going to perform, whilst every useless information should be discarded. The choice of the encoding scheme can strongly influence the quality of the output for the overall computation. This is a well-known issue, at least from a theoretical point of view, and it is often addressed in literature as the "data preprocessing problem" (see, e.g., [1]). However, in the practice, there are frequent cases for which the most suitable encoding scheme is not known *a priori* and it becomes necessary to test several different processing methods, making a comparative choice between them (see [2] for details). But a consistent choice between encoding schemes cannot be performed without having previously defined a judging rule which is not ambiguous. This is a non-trivial task in many practical applications. An "on-the-field" instance, in which such difficulties are encountered and subsequently overcome, is presented in this paper.

The framework for what is going to be exposed is a recently introduced algorithm which performs the segmentation of speech into phonemes. A novel strategy will be used for comparing different speech encoding techniques, in order to identify which one would best fit the segmentation procedure and lead to a minimum segmentation error. Full details about the segmentation algorithm are given in the paper [3]; in the next section only a brief description of the segmentation task will be provided, in addition to a few formal definitions,

P. Sojka, I. Kopeček, and K. Pala (Eds.): TSD 2002, LNAI 2448, pp. 293–300, 2002.
© Springer-Verlag Berlin Heidelberg 2002

which serve to numerically express the performance of the whole segmentation system. This is an essential background to the discussion carried out in Sections 3 and 4, which are devoted to describe the strategy proposed to solve the ambiguities encountered in comparing performances of the segmentation algorithm.

2   The Segmentation Algorithm and Measures of Its Performance

The investigated algorithm operates on an encoded speech signal and aims to detect the exact position of the boundaries between phonemes. The only constraint imposed by the algorithm is that the encoded speech must be in the form of a time-sequence of vectors; then every "short-time" representation of the signal (i.e. any vector encoding a small time interval or "frame") can be used. The functioning of the algorithm is regulated by three parameters, namely a, b and c. The a and c parameters are integers, representing the number of speech frames which are taken into account in different phases of the algorithm implementation, whereas b takes values in the real domain. The b parameter can be pictorially described as a particular threshold level used to reject "candidates" to the role of phonemic boundary.

Shortly it will be shown that a fine tuning of the above parameters is not only desirable for granting optimal performance to the end-user, but it is also necessary for taking important decisions about the choice of the encoding technique underlying the entire segmentation process. The first step in this direction is defining some indices to quantify the quality of the performed segmentation, for given a, b and c, on a specifically encoded data set. To serve this purpose, a collection of 480 sentences was extracted from the American-English DARPA-TIMIT database. These sentences are pronounced by 48 different speakers (24 females and 24 males). Each sentence has an associated labeling file, which contains the "true segmentation", i.e. the actual positions (in samples) of the phoneme boundaries manually detected by an expert phonetician.

The sentence segmentation obtained by the algorithm is compared with the true segmentation: a phoneme boundary identified by the algorithm is defined as "correct" if it is placed within a range of ± 20 ms (± 320 samples) from a true segmentation point, as shown in Figure 1.

An index for expressing the algorithm's performance can be defined as the percentage of correctly detected phoneme boundaries:

$$P_c = 100 \cdot \frac{S_c}{S_t}, \tag{1}$$

where S_t is the total number of "true" segmentation points (S_t) contained in our database (17,930), and S_c the number of correctly detected points.

It is easy to prove that such index alone does not measure the quality of the performed segmentation. In fact, the algorithm could output a huge number of detected boundaries, incrementing, fictitiously, the probability of detecting true segmentation points, with the drawback of having introduced a large number of unwanted extra points (i.e. erroneous segmentation points). This phenomenon is known as *over-segmentation* and can be quantified by an over-segmentation rate D, defined as the difference between the total number of segmentation points detected by the algorithm (S_d) and S_t:

$$D = S_d - S_t. \tag{2}$$

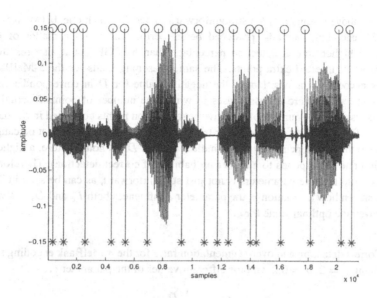

Fig. 1. Speech waveform taken from database; "true" segmentation points are indicated by *; those detected by the algorithm by o.

An alternative measure of over-segmentation expressing the percentage of extra points, $D' = 100 \cdot (S_d/S_t - 1)$, can be found in Petek *et al.* (1996) [4].

3   The Problem of Optimizing and Comparing Performances

Evidently it appears, from what has previously been stated, that an optimization procedure for the segmentation system should maximize the correct detection rate without letting the over-segmentation grow. The utility of such procedure and the necessary requirements for its functioning will become clear after having examined the following experimental results on the already mentioned data set. Values for P_c and D, found with fixed a, b, c, and adopting various encoding schemes, are reported in Table 1. References for all the tested encoding methods are given in Section 5.

Table 1. Correct detection and over-segmentation rates, found for different encoding schemes and fixed parameters $a = 2, b = 0.2, c = 6$.

Encoding	P_c	D
5-PCBF	71.4 %	459
8-PCBF	77.2 %	2577
5-MelBank	74.4 %	-606
8-MelBank	79.3 %	1581

From the above results, it is not straightforward to decide which one, between 5-PCBF[4] and 8-PCBF encoding methods, produced better performances. As a matter of fact, 8-PCBF gave a higher correct detection percentage than 5-PCBF, but it also resulted in a higher number of inserted extra-points. The same reasoning holds for the 5-MelBank and 8-MelBank encoding schemes. Notice the negative value for D in correspondence of the 5-MelBank encoding: there are also cases in which the number of points inserted by the algorithm is less than the number of effective segmentation points contained in the database. Furthermore, the optimality of a particular triple of a, b, c parameters cannot be caught at a glance, due to the interdependency of the indices P_c and D (as noted before, a higher over-segmentation rate corresponds to a higher probability of correct detection). Therefore, their dependence from the free parameters is not just straightforward, as can be seen in Table 2, where it is shown how a variation in the parameter c influences both P_c and D, in a way that does not unveil the optimal value for c.

Table 2. Correct detection and over-segmentation rates for the 8-MelBank encoding scheme, obtained fixing $a = 2$, $b = 0.2$, and for different values of the parameter c.

c	P_c	D
5	80.1 %	2048
6	79.3 %	1581
7	78.5 %	1088

4   The "Optimize-and-Compare" Procedure

It would be easier to compare the results that were reported in the above tables if all their rows had shown the same numeric value for one of the two indices P_c or D, so that the performance evaluation could be based on the other index, taking the common value as a reference level. A situation of this kind could be experimentally induced by making several trials, in which two of the three parameters are fixed and the other one is "moved around", independently until a configuration is found where D, for example, has the same value for every encoding scheme considered, and P_c remains the sole significant index for judging the performances of both the algorithm and the encoding scheme.

Such approach, however, has at least two weak points. The first is that the number of trials, which are needed to find the desired equality for D, is essentially a question of luckiness; even a skilled experimenter will be engaged in a time-consuming loop which consists in hypothesizing the value for the parameter subject to variation, waiting for the results of the relative experiment, correcting the hypothesis in the light of these results, making a new trial, and so on. What makes this process worse is that it should be repeated for every encoding scheme under testing, and for every couple of values that can be taken by the two remaining parameters. The other problem is related to the choice of the reference level: it would be better, for instance, if the common value chosen for D had some particular properties which can justify its adoption.

---

[4] PCBF stands for "Perceptual Critical Band Features". See the last section for more details.

To overcome the first of the above limitations an automatic procedure is proposed, which finds (given a particular encoding scheme) the value of the parameters a, b, and c maximizing the percentage of correct detection and satisfying the condition $D = 0$. For every fixed a and c, the procedure looks for the exact value of b for which the over-segmentation D is zero.

The choice of b as the "mobile" parameter and of $D = 0$ as the reference level can be motivated as follows. It has already been said that b plays the role of a threshold in the segmentation algorithm. Actually b, which is a real number falling within the interval $[0, 1]$, regulates almost directly the amount of segmentation points placed by the algorithm and consequently the over-segmentation D. Moreover, having fixed $a = a^*$ and $c = c^*$, D as a function of b, $D(b) = D(a^*, b, c^*)$, is decreasing monotonic;[5] when $b = 1$, D reaches its minimum value, $D = -S_t$, which is a negative number. The opposite extreme, $b = 0$, corresponds to eliminating the preliminary thresholding from the algorithm; in that point D assumes a maximum value which is not fixed but depends on a^*, c^* and on the chosen encoding. $D(0)$ is supposed to be greater or equal to zero.[6] Based on the above considerations, the choice of $D(b) = 0$ as constraint for the optimization of P_c appears the most natural one. An additional support to this choice comes from the fact that for text-dependent speech segmentation algorithms (i.e. those which rely on an externally supplied transcription for identifying phoneme boundaries) D equals 0 by definition [5].

The mentioned automatic procedure, can be schematized by the following nine steps:

1. set a and c to some integer values, a^* and c^*, using an external control mechanism (see the last step);
2. run a few experiments, on the whole data set, using different values of b belonging to the interval $[0, 1)$;
3. evaluate the indices D and P_c for such experiments obtaining a set of sampling points for the functions $D(b)$ and $P_c(b)$;
4. identify a model function $\tilde{D}(b)$ (e.g. a polynomial) which fits the obtained sampling points to approximate the behavior of the function $D(b)$ (The choice of the model function is essentially dictated by empirical considerations on the distribution of the sampling points);
5. compute the analytic zeros of $\tilde{D}(b)$; if the number of such zeros is greater than one, then the zero of interest will be the one that is found in the function's decreasing monotonic region to which the sampling points belong (e.g. if the model function $\tilde{D}(b)$ is a parabola, then only the zero associated to the descending branch should be considered, since the function we want to approximate, $D(b)$, is decreasing monotonic). The selected zero gives an estimate value for b, $\bar{b}$, for which $D(\bar{b}) \simeq 0$;
6. identify, as for D, a model function $\tilde{P}_c(b)$ to approximate the behavior of the function $P_c(b)$. This makes possible to express the estimated detection rate as $\bar{P}_c^* = \tilde{P}_c(\bar{b})$;

---

[5] More precisely, the way b is defined implies a "large-scale" monotonic behavior of the function $D(b)$. However the same definition may allow small non-monotonic fluctuations of D for little variations of the parameter b ($\Delta b \ll 10^{-4}$).

[6] Having $D(0) < 0$ would mean that the system, for every b, would always insert a number of segmentation points smaller than the number of effective segmentation points. Such a situation of "unreversible under-segmentation" would immediately suggest to change the adopted encoding scheme or the couple (a^*, c^*). Also note that $D(0) = 0$ is a very lucky circumstance, for which there would be no need to introduce thresholding in the algorithm.

7. run again the segmentation algorithm using $b = \bar{b}$ as threshold;

8. if $D(\bar{b}) \neq 0$ then go to step 4, to get a new estimate using the additional sample point represented by $D(\bar{b})$ and $P_c(\bar{b})$; otherwise $P_c^* = P_c(\bar{b})$ is assumed to be the correct detection rate corresponding to a zero over-segmentation value;

9. $P_c(a^*, c^*) = P_c^*$ is returned to the external mechanism which cares for finding the maximum of the function $P_c(a, c)$. This control routine will eventually restart the whole procedure using a new (a^*, c^*) couple.

The procedure converge to an exact zero of $D(b)$ typically after a small number (< 10) of iterations, even when a simple 2-order polynomial is used to model the over-segmentation function. However, if $D(\bar{b})$ does not vary from one iteration to the next, it is advisable to increase the order of the modeling function. In addition, it is also possible to stop the procedure at step 6; in this case the declared performance would be the estimated detection rate $\bar{P}_c^*$, with an error bounded by the two experimental P_c values that are immediately lower and higher than $\bar{P}_c^*$.

Figure 2 graphically shows how the whole presented method works: several values for the parameter c are compared, evidencing a maximum of the function $P_c(c)$ for $c = 7$.

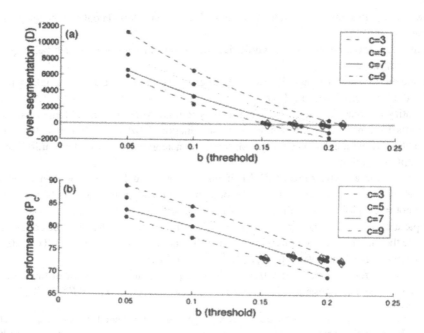

Fig. 2. A graphical representation of the "optimize-and-compare" procedure, where four values of the parameter c are compared. The maximum correct detection rate P_c is encountered for $c = 7$.

5   Preliminary Results

The above procedure was embedded in the speech segmentation algorithms and tested on several speech encoding schemes, among which Mel-frequency Cepstral Coefficients (MFCC) [6], LPC [7], PLP [8], RASTA-PLP [9], Perceptual Critical Band Features (PCBF) and Mel-frequency Bank of filters (MelBank). The optimal segmentation results were obtained using the last two cited encodings; these can be both described as the output of a bank of filters, which span the whole frequency-range or a part of it. The subdivision of the frequency axis is not uniform and tries to reproduce the particular spectral resolution of the human ear. In addition, PCBF incorporates some other perceptual-based modification of the spectrum, i.e. loudness pre-emphasis and intensity-loudness compression. Note that the MelBank analysis is preliminary to the extraction of Mel-frequency Cepstral Coefficients, so its description is included in [6]. In the same manner PCBF analysis precedes PLP analysis [8].

The proposed automatic procedure made also easier to observe how the results varied when changing the number of PCBF and MelBank filters. The number of filters is indicated by the numeral preceding the name of the encoding method (e.g. 3-PCBF, 5-MelBank). Among all the tested encoding schemes the maximum percentage of correct detection was $P_c^* = 76.53\,\%$, obtained using the 8-MelBank encoding, and $a = 2$, $b = 0.22365$, $c = 7$ as values of the free parameters. The previously declared detection rate for the algorithm was 73.6 % (using PCBF: see [3] for details), so a performance improvement of about 3 % was realized just changing the encoding scheme.

6   Conclusions

Performance evaluation for speech segmentation methods is not straightforward. The inter-dependence between the various indices, which are usually used to express the quality of a performed segmentation, must be analyzed and exploited to formulate unambiguous rules for consistently comparing different methods and architectures. The present paper tries to give an answer to this issue, introducing an original methodology for choosing the optimal speech data encoding for a particular segmentation algorithm. Optimal tuning of the parameters that regulate the algorithm is also feasible, using the fully automated procedure proposed above. Further works will include the engineering of a technique, based on the same procedure, for finding optimal parameters from a small subset of data. A detailed comparison, supported by performance evaluations, between the investigated segmentation system and other methods proposed in literature is also underway.

Acknowledgements

The authors would like to thank Prof. Maria Marinaro and Antonietta Esposito for useful suggestions and collaboration. This work has been supported by the NSF KDI program, Grant No. BCS-9980054 "Cross-modal analysis of speech signal and sense: multimedia corpora and tools for gesture, speech, and gaze research" and by NSF Grant No. 9906340 "Speech driven facial animation".

References

1. Bishop, C. M.: *Neural Networks for Pattern Recognition*. Clarendon Press (1995).
2. Esposito, A.: *The importance of data for training intelligent devices*. "From Synapses to Rules: Discovering Symbolic Rules from Neural Processed Data", proc. of 5th International School of Neural Nets "E.R. Caianiello", Apolloni B. and Kurfus K. (Eds.), Kluwer Academic Press (to appear).
3. Aversano, G., Esposito, A., Esposito, A., Marinaro, M.: *A New Text-Independent Method for Phoneme Segmentation*. Proc. of 44th IEEE Midwest Symposium on Circuits and Systems 2 (2001) 516–519.
4. Petek, B., Andersen, O., Dalsgaard, P.: *On the robust automatic segmentation of spontaneous speech*. Proc. of ICSLP'96 (1996) 913–916.
5. Pellom, B.L., Hansen, J.H.L.: *Automatic segmentation of speech recorded in unknown noisy channel characteristics*. Speech Communication 25 (1998) 97–116.
6. Duttweiler, D., Messerschmitt, D.: *Nearly instantaneous companding for nonuniformly quantized PCM*. IEEE Transactions on Communications COM-24 (1976) 864–873.
7. Rabiner, L., Juang, B.: *Fundamentals of Speech Recognition*. Prentice-Hall (1993).
8. Hermansky, H.: *Perceptual Linear Predictive (PLP) Analysis of Speech*. Jour. Acoust. Soc. Am. 87(4) (1990) 1738–1752.
9. Hermansky, H., Morgan, N.: *RASTA Processing of Speech*. IEEE Trans. On Speech and Audio Processing 2(4) (1994) 578–589.

Phoneme Lattice Based A* Search Algorithm for Speech Recognition

Pascal Nocera, Georges Linares, Dominique Massonié, and Loïc Lefort

Laboratoire Informatique d'Avignon, LIA, Avignon, France
E-mail: pascal.nocera@lia.univ-avignon.fr,
georges.linares@lia.univ-avignon.fr,
dominique.massonie@lia.univ-avignon.fr, loic.lefort@lia.univ-avignon.fr

Abstract. This paper presents the Speeral continuous speech recognition system developed in the LIA. Speeral uses a modified A* algorithm to find in the search graph the best path taking into account acoustic and linguistic constraints. Rather than words by words, the A* used in Speeral is based on a phoneme lattice previously generated. To avoid the backtraking problems, the system keeps for each frame the deepest nodes of the partially explored lexical tree starting at this frame. If a new hypothesis to explore is ended by a word and the lexicon starting where this word finishes has already been developed, then the next hypothesis will "jump" directly to the deepest nodes. Decoding performances of Speeral are evaluated on the test set of the ARC B1 campaign of AUPELF '97. The experiments on this French database show the efficiency of the search strategy described in this paper.

1   Introduction

The goal of continuous speech recognition systems is to find the best sentence (list of words) corresponding to an acoustic signal taking into account acoustic and linguistic constraints [1]. This is achieved on some systems with a stack decoder based on the A* search algorithm [2]. As the best path has to be found in the list of all possible paths, the search graph structure is a tree built by concatenation of lexical trees. Each leaf of the tree (an hypothetical word) is connected to a new full lexical tree.

The A* algorithm is a time-asynchronous algorithm. The exploration rank of node x is given by the result of the evaluation function $F(x)$ representing an estimation of the best path involving x. This means that it's possible to backtrack to an hypothesis (theory) very earlier than the deepest theory, because it has then the best evaluated score. Applied to a continuous speech recognition graph, this algorithm will explore the same word many times, with different previous paths (history).

This is why the A* algorithm is almost always used on high level graphs like word lattices. The theory progression is made word after word. It is used on multi-pass systems to find the best hypothesis from the word lattice [3], or in some single-pass systems after a fast-match algorithm to obtain a short list of candidate word extensions of a theory [4]. However, the size of the lattice for both methods has to be sufficient to obtain good results. In one-pass systems, the fast-match algorithm has to be redone each time a new theory is

P. Sojka, I. Kopeček, and K. Pala (Eds.): TSD 2002, LNAI 2448, pp. 301–308, 2002.

explored (even if another theory was already explored for that frame), because linguistic constraints changes with theory, and the list of candidates can be different.

To avoid this problem, we propose to base our search on phonemes rather than words. The progression is done phoneme after phoneme. To optimize the search when a backtrack occurs, we store for each lexical tree explored, even partially, the deepest nodes corresponding to a complete word or to a "part of word". In case of backtracking, the lexicon already computed won't be explored again. The algorithm will jump directly to the stored nodes, which will be appended to the current theory.

In the first part, we will present the standard A* algorithm and in the second part the enhanced A* algorithm for phoneme lattice. We will then present the LIA speech recognition system (Speeral) and present results obtained on AUPELF'97 evaluation campaign for French.

2   The Standard A* Algorithm

The A* algorithm is a search algorithm used to find the best path in a graph. It uses an evaluation function $F(x, y)$ for each explored node x. This estimation is computed by the sum of the cost of the path from the starting node of the graph to the node x $(g(x))$, of the current transition from node x to a next node y $(c(x, y))$, and of the estimated cost $(h(y))$ of the remaining path (from y to the final node) (Figure 1).

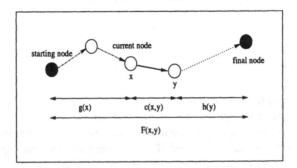

Fig. 1. The evaluation function $F(x, y)$ is the sum of the cost of the optimal path from the starting node to the current one $(g(x))$, of the current transition from current to the next node $(c(x, y))$ and of the sounding function h(y) estimating the cost of the remaining path from next node to the final node (h(y)).

The algorithm uses an ordered list called *Open* which contains all the nodes to be explored in decreasing order of their F value. For each iteration of the search algorithm, the first node x in *Open* is removed from the list and for each node y (successor of the node x in the graph) the estimation function $F(x, y) = g(x) + c(x, y) + h(y)$ is computed (Figure 1) and the new hypothesis y is added into *Open*.

The algorithm stops when the top node in the *Open* list is a goal node. It was proven that if the evaluation function F is always better than the optimal cost, this search algorithm always terminates with an optimal path from the start to a goal node. The optimality of the evaluation function is given by an optimal estimated cost function h.

3   The Phoneme Lattice Based A* Algorithm

3.1   Lexicon Coding

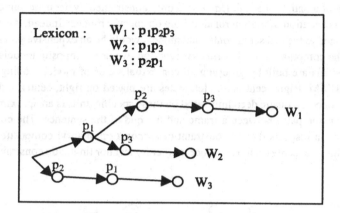

Fig. 2. The lexical tree structure.

The lexicon is expressed by the list of words in the vocabulary followed by the list of phonemes for each word. Several lists of phonemes for a same word will express different phonological variations. The shortcuts or the liaisons between words will be expressed as phonological variations. The lexicon is represented by a tree in which words share common beginning phonemes and each leaf corresponds to a word (Figure 2).

The search graph is a concatenation of lexical trees. A new lexical tree starts each time a word of a previous lexicon ends.

3.2   Linguistic Scoring

In order to have a better language model flexibility, the computation of the linguistic score is made outside the search core. Each time the algorithm needs a linguistic scoring of a theory, it calls an external function with the list of words or nodes.

Linguistic scores of new hypothesis are computed with two functions depending on current state:

- the LM_Word function is used when theory ends with a word. It processes the whole list of words of this hypothesis,
- the LM_Part function processes the whole list of words of this hypothesis including the last "pending word" (internal node n of a lexical tree). This allows a finer grained hypothesis scoring with anticipation of upcoming words through this node.

$$LM\_Part(w_1..w_k, x) = \max_{w_n} LM\_Word(w_1..w_k w_n)$$
$$\textit{where } w_n \textit{ is any leaf (i.e. word) of the sub-tree starting at } x.$$

Moreover, anticipating the linguistic constraints allows an earlier cut of paths leading to improbable words.

3.3   The Sounding Function (*Hacoust*)

The estimated cost function h retained (*Hacoust*) is an optimal probe representing for each frame the cost of a path to the end. *Hacoust* is only constrained by acoustic values computed by a backward execution of the Viterbi algorithm on specific models. Indead, the Viterbi-back algorithm applied to the full set of contextual models would be an expensive process. In order to speed-up the computation of the *Hacoust* function, we use composite models (Figure 3). Composite models are built by grouping all contextual states of models coding a phoneme into a single HMM. Right, central and left states are placed on right, center and left part of the composite ones. Acoustic decoding based on these specific units is an aproximation of the best path (phoneme path) between a frame and the end of the sentence. The corresponding sounding function respects the A* constraint of *Hacoust* optimality: composite units allow lower cost paths than contextual ones, since neither lexical nor linguistic constraints are taken into account.

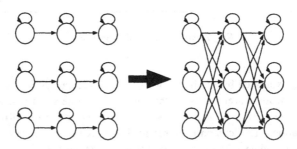

Fig. 3. Specific units used by the evaluation function: all HMMs representing a contextual unit are grouped as a larger one, composed of all contextual states.

The accuracy of the estimated cost function is very important for the searching speed so we first tried to improve this function before or during the search. However, the time saved for the search was negligible compared to the time needed to compute of a better *Hacoust* function.

3.4   A* Search Algorithm Enhancement

Outline To avoid the re-estimation of already explored parts of the search graph, the system keeps for each frame the deepest nodes of the partially explored lexical tree starting at this frame. If the currently explored hypothesis is ended by word on a frame t and there is an already developed lexical tree starting at t, then the next hypothesis will directly "jump" to the deepest nodes.

Manipulated Data

- *HypLex* represents a node in the lexical tree. Each *HypLex* contains a pointer to the node in the tree and its final frame.
- *Tab_Lex*: *Tab_Lex[t]* contains the list of the *HypLex* for the lexicon starting at the frame *t*.
- *TabEnd*: *TabEnd[t]* contains the list of word sequences already explored ending at frame *t*. These sequences constitute the different theories of "whole words" already processed.

Description As explained before, only the deepest nodes are kept in *Tab_Lex*. These nodes correspond to "pending words" or to "whole words" (i.e. leaves). If the algorithm backtracks, this storage prevents reexploring an even partially processed lexicon.

The algorithm keeps producing new hypothesis until the top of the *Open* list (i.e. current best theory) is a goal. At each iteration, the current best hypothesis *Hyp* (an *HypLex*) is taken out of the top of the *Open* list and:

- if *Hyp* is a phoneme (a node of a lexical tree), for each *New = Successor(Hyp)*:
  - if *New* is a phoneme, *New* is put in *Tab_Lex* and the best hypothesis from the start of the sentence to *New* is added to *Open*.
  - if *New* is a word, all the "whole word" hypothesis ended by *New* are stored in *TabEnd* and the best one is added to *Open* (if there was no better one before).
- if *Hyp* is a word ending at frame *t* (leaf of a lexical tree),
  - if the lexicon beginning at the end of *Hyp* was already explored, all the theories with *Hyp* followed by *Tab_Lex[t]* are generated (Figure 5).
  - otherwise, a new lexical tree is started and *Successor(Lexicon_Start)* is stored in *Tab_Lex[t]* (Figure 6).

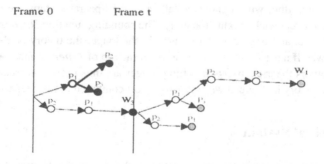

Fig. 4. Initial state of the search graph for the samples below.

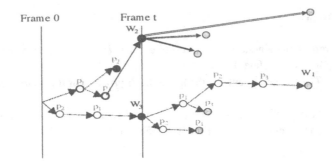

Fig. 5. The word W_2 inherits previous search buffered in $Tab\_Lex[t]$.

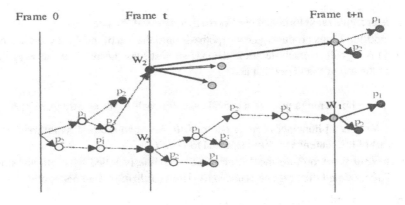

Fig. 6. The extending nodes p_1 and p_2 of the lexical tree starting at frame t are stored in $Tab\_Lex[t + n]$. Thus they will be available (without computation) to extend further hypothesis ending by a whole word at frame $t + n$.

3.5 Limiting the Open-List Size

To use the A* algorithm with a phoneme lattice in the Speeral system, we had to define a cut function to prevent backtracking too early. The sounding function *Hacoust* does not take into account lexical and linguistic constraints. So the longer the theory is, the stronger it is constrained. Even if a theory started very far from the top of *Open*, it may become the best when all the others theories in *Open* getting longer are thus more constrained. To prevent this problem, a theory is dropped when it is too short compared to the deepest one.

4 The Speeral System

The Speeral decoding process relies on the A* algorithm exposed in Section 3.4. The acoustic models are HMM models and the lattice is constituted by the n-best phonemes for each frame. This lattice is computed using an acoustico-phonetic decoding using the backward Viterbi algorithm. We also obtain at the same time the *Hacoust* function estimations needed for the

A* execution. Acoustic models are classical 3-states HMMs with Male/Female specialization and about 600 right contextual units are used for each set. States are modeled by a mixture of 32 gaussians. Acoustic models were trained on the two French databases BREF80 and BREF.

The lexicon contains 20, 000 words and we used a trigram language model computed on the text of the newspaper "Le Monde" from 1987 to 1996. For the calculus of the LM_Part function, we defined the "$Best\_Tri\_Node$" function. This function has a low memory usage.

$$LM\_Word(w_i..w_3w_2w_1) = P(w_1/w_3w_2)$$
$$LM\_Part(w_i..w_2w_1, x) = Best\_Tri\_Node(w_2w_1, x)$$
$$= \max_{w_n} P(w_n/w_2w_1)$$

where w_n is a leaf of the sub-tree starting at x.

This system was tested on the database of the evaluation campain ARC B1 of AU-PELF'97 [5]. This database constitutes the only French corpus on which several systems were tested. Table 1 shows Speeral and other systems performances. Nevertheless, Speeral results are obtained several years after the campaign and must be considered only as reference. Currently, we have obtained a word error rate of 19.0 % on the baseline system (noted Speeral in Table 1). This result is obtained with a phoneme lattice of 75 phonetical hypothesis for each frame.

Table 1. Word Error Rates of the systems for the task ARC B1 of the AUPELF'97 speech recognition system evaluation campaign. P0-1, P0-2 and P0-3 are CRIM, CRIN, LAFORIA systems. P0-3, P0-4, P0-5 are 3 alternatives of LIMSI base system. Speeral is the actual system of LIA.

System	P0-1	P0-2	P0-3	P0-4	P0-5	P0-6	Speeral
WER	39.6	32.8	39.4	12.2	11.1	13.1	19.0

It is worth noting that this system explores a very low number of word hypothesis at each frame: 200, 000 of the 300, 000 test frames generate no word hypothesis at all. The average number of word hypothesis per frame is 44 which is a very low number compared to several hundreds of generated word hypothesis per frame in classical search algorithms such as the fast-match or word lattice based ones.

5   Conclusion

We have presented an original application of the A* algorithm on a phoneme lattice rather than on a word lattice. To find a solution any speech recognition system has to over-produce hypothesis. The cost of a lattice generation is far less expensive for phonemes than for words. Exploring such a lattice would have been more time consuming without the storing process of the partially explored lexical trees allowing a large reduction of the evaluated paths. According to our first experiments, the results are encouraging. Nevertheless, better performances should be obtained by adapting acoustic models to speakers and by improving acoustic and linguistic models. Moreover, the use of such an A* algorithm allows integration of various sources of information during decoding stage by adding specific terms to the path cost evaluation function. We are working now on the exploitation of this potentiallity.

References

1. R. De Mori, "Spoken dialogues with computers," 1997.
2. J. Pearl, "Heuristics: Intelligent search strategies for computer problem solving," 1984.
3. H.-W. Hon M.-Y. Hwang K.-F. Lee R. Rosenfeld X. Huang F. Alleva, "The SPHINX II speech recognition system: An overview," *Computer Speech and Language*, Vol. 7, No. 2, pp. 137–148, 1993.
4. D.B. Paul, "Algorithms for an optimal A* search and linearizing the search in the stack decoder," *ICASSP 91*, pp. 693–696, 1991.
5. J. Dolmazon F. Bimbot G. Adda J. Caerou J. Zeiliger M. Adda-Decker, "Première campagne AUPELF d'évaluation des systèmes de Dictée Vocale," "Ressources et évaluation en ingénierie des langues,", pp. 279–307, 2000.
6. Matrouf, O. Bellot, P. Nocera, J.-F. Bonastre, G. Linares, "A posteriori and a priori transformations for speaker adaptation in large vocabulary speech recognition systems," *EuroSpeech 2001*, Aalborg.

Heuristic and Statistical Methods
for Speech/Non-speech Detector Design

Michal Prcín and Luděk Müller

University of West Bohemia in Pilsen, Department of Cybernetics,
Univerzitní 8, 306 14 Plzeň, Czech Republic
E-mail: mprcin@kky.zcu.cz, muller@kky.zcu.cz

Abstract. Speech/non-speech (S/NS) detection plays the important role for automatic speech recognition (ASR) system, especially in the case of isolated words or commands recognition. Even in continuous speech a S/NS decision can be made at the beginning and at the end of a sequence resulting in a "sleep mode" of the speech recognizer during the silence and in a reduction of computation demands. It is very difficult, however, to precisely locate the endpoints of the input utterance because of unpredictable background noise. In the proposed method in this paper, we make use of the advantages of two approaches (i.e. to try to find the best set of heuristic features and apply a statistical induction method) for the best S/NS decision.

1 Introduction

S/NS detection is an ubiquitous problem in speech processing. It consists of the classification of two clearly distinct signal conditions during speech recording: periods where the speech signal is present and pauses with background noise only. Generally, it is a very difficult task because speech waveform can be obtained in various environments (street, car, factory, office, etc.). The non-speech regions can involve sounds such as the opening or closing of a door, coughing, background music, vibrations from an engine, and so on. While significant work has been done on this problem, most efforts have attempted to extract speech frames from data containing only one specific signal type. Unfortunately, when such an algorithm is applied to separate speech from data containing different specific non-speech signals, results are generally poor.

The remainder of this paper is organized as follows. Section 2 depicts methods used in speech detection. Section 3 describes our approaches to find a set of optimal features. Section 4 includes comparative tests with a different feature set and Section 5 concludes the paper.

2 Comparison of Heuristic and Statistical Methods

Almost all algorithms of speech detection can be split into two classes. Methods of the first class are heuristic methods while methods of the second one are based on a statistical approach. The advantage of heuristic methods is their effort to find a set of optimal features

P. Sojka, I. Kopeček, and K. Pala (Eds.): TSD 2002, LNAI 2448, pp. 309–316, 2002.

for the speech/non-speech classification. Their drawback is that they use thresholds that are set heuristically (i.e. their value estimate is based on the experience of a human expert). These predefined thresholds are then used to classify a signal frame as "speech" or "non-speech". The statistical methods do not suffer from this shortcoming because their threshold setting is done more precisely by using training data and applying a statistical induction method. The disadvantage of statistical methods referred to in literature consists in the use of a feature set based on some kind of a standard speech parameterization (e.g. MFCC or PLP). We decided to use the advantages of both approaches (i.e. to try to find the best set of heuristic features and apply a statistical induction method for the speech/non-speech classifier optimal setting). The aim is to develop a classification algorithm that will best classify each audio signal frame as a speech or non-speech frame among all classifiers working with any heuristic feature set.

3 Selection of Optimal Features

First of all, features commonly used in a heuristic approach were collected creating a large basic feature set (feature vector) and then statistical speech and non-speech models were trained using EM algorithm. The training data were represented by a speech/non-speech signal transformed (i.e. parameterized) into feature vector sequences. The resulting basic feature vector comprised the following coefficients: short-time zero crossing rate (STZCR), short-time energy (STE), short-time intensity (STI), entropy (H), EE-Feature (Energy-Entropy feature), STZCR to STE ratio (ZER), product of STZCR and energy (ZEP), RMS to mean ratio (RMR), normalized correlation coefficient for lag 1 (NCC1), and periodicity of the autocorrelation functions. We also trained the classifier using a set of features commonly used in speech recognition (MFCC, PLP (+ RASTA)). Furthermore, the basic feature set was modified in several ways (for example by considering log energy instead energy, various modifications of autocorrelation functions periodicity, signal normalization, etc.).

3.1 Parameterization with Features Used in Heuristic Approach

The feature vector of this parameterization contained 11 features that describe a given frame. These features were selected from features used in [1,2,4].

Computation of individual features:

1. Short-time energy
   For each frame i, the energy E_i of the frame is obtained by the sum of squares:

$$E_i = \sum_{n=1}^{N} s_n^2 , \tag{1}$$

where s_n and N are nth signal and the total number of signals in frame i respectively. Instead the E_i also the LE_i can be used:

$$LE_i = \log E_i . \tag{2}$$

2. Entropy

For each frame i, signal within it is converted from time domain to frequency domain via the FFT equation:

$$X(\omega) = \sum_{n=\infty}^{\infty} s_n e^{-j\omega n} .$$ (3)

Then the probability density function (pdf) for spectrum can be estimated by normalizing the frequency components:

$$p_i = \frac{s(f_i)}{\sum_{k=1}^{M} s(f_k)} ,$$ (4)

where $s(f_i)$ is the spectral energy of the frequency component f_i, p_i is the corresponding probability density, and M is the total number of frequency components in FFT. Some heuristic constraints are used to improve the discriminability of the pdf between speech and non-speech signals and only the frequency from 250 Hz to 3750 Hz are considered. The limitation of the range of frequency is just because the range covers most of the frequency components of human speech signals. Therefore, we define the Equations 5 and 6 below:

$$s(f_i) = 0, \quad \text{if } f_i \leq 250\,Hz \text{ or } f_i \geq 3750\,Hz ,$$ (5)

$$p_i = 0, \quad \text{if } p_i \geq 0.9 .$$ (6)

The negative entropy H_i of frame i can be defined as:

$$H_i = -\sum_{j=1}^{M} p_j \log_2 p_j .$$ (7)

3. Energy-Entropy Feature

EE-Feature is obtained as:

$$M_i = (E_i - C_E) \cdot (H_i - C_H) ,$$ (8)

$$EE - Feature_i = \sqrt{1 + |M_i|} ,$$ (9)

where C_E a C_H denote the average energy and the entropy of the first 10 frames, respectively. Because both energy and entropy have their limitations, the blind spots in either energy or entropy, or both, can be cancelled by their multiplication. In other words, energy covers the case that was failed in entropy: babble and background music in speaker utterance; whereas the entropy covers the case that was failed in energy: non-stationary noise which belongs to mechanical sounds.

4. Short-time Intensity

For each frame i, the intensity M_i of the frame is obtained by the sum of absolute values of s_n:

$$M_i = \sum_{n=1}^{N} |s_n| ,$$ (10)

where s_n and N are nth signal and the total number of signals in frame i respectively.

5. Short-time zero crossing rate (STZCR)

The equation for computing the number of zero crossings in a block can be obtained as:

$$Z_i = \sum_{n=0}^{N-1} |\text{sgns}_n - \text{sgns}_{n-1}| w_{N-1-n} , \qquad (11)$$

where

$$\text{sgns}_n = \begin{cases} 1 & \text{for } s_n \geq 0 \\ -1 & \text{for } s_n < 0 \end{cases} \qquad (12)$$

and w_{N-1-n} is a rectangle window.

STZCR can be computed as the number of zero crossings per second, using the formula

$$STZCR_i = \frac{Z_i \cdot f_s}{N} , \qquad (13)$$

where Z_i is the number of zero crossings in a block with N samples and f_s is the sampling frequency.

6. ZER

$$ZER_i = \frac{STZCR_i}{E_i} . \qquad (14)$$

7. ZEP

$$ZEP_i = STZCR_i \cdot E_i . \qquad (15)$$

8. RMR

The ratio of the RMS to mean value is evaluated as RMR:

$$RMR_i = \sum_{n=0}^{N-1} \frac{\sqrt{\frac{1}{N} s_n^2}}{\left|\frac{1}{N} s_n\right|} . \qquad (16)$$

9. Normalized Correlation Coefficient for lag 1 (NCC1)

NCC1 is obtained by using the formula:

$$NCC1_i = \frac{\sum_{n=2}^{N} s_n \cdot s_{n-1}}{\sqrt{\sum_{n=2}^{N} s_n^2 \sum_{n=2}^{N} s_{n-1}^2}} . \qquad (17)$$

10. $M1$

The autocorrelation coefficient $R(J)$ is calculated as

$$R(J)_i = \sum_{n=J+1}^{N} s_n \cdot s_{n-J} , \qquad (18)$$

$M1$ is determined by noting the value of J for which $R(J)$ is a maximum for values of J greater than 15.

11. $M2$

Similarly, $M2$ is founded by considering $J = 15 + M1$. The same equation is used:

$$R(J)_i = \sum_{n=J+1+M1}^{N} s_n \cdot s_{n-J} . \tag{19}$$

Furthermore, the basic feature set was modified in several ways (for example by considering log energy instead energy, various modifications of autocorrelation functions periodicity, signal normalization, etc.).

In the following, presented MPP parameterizations are defined:

- MPP (ble) - the feature vector consisted of 11 coefficients mentioned in Section 3.1 For energy computing the Equation 1 was used.
- MPP_D_A (sle) - to the MPP (ble) coefficients delta and accelerations coefficients were added.
- MPP (sle) - the feature vector had 11 coefficients but the Equation 2 instead Equation 1 was applied and in others equations log energy instead energy was used.
- MPP (8p) - the feature vector was comprised 8 coefficients described in Section 3.1. The Equation 2 instead Equation 1 was employed and feature vector did not contain neither energy nor intensity. Features $M1$ and $M2$ were replaced by $|2 \cdot M1 \quad M2|$.
- MPP (jebl) - the feature vector had 1 coefficient computed according to the Equation 1.

3.2 Features Commonly Used in Speech Recognition

We also trained the classifier using a set of features commonly used in speech recognition (MFCC, PLP (+ RASTA)) [3]. Firstly, we obtained a feature vector with 27 MFCC_D_A (Mel-Frequency Cepstral Coefficients Delta Acceleration), that consisted of 9 static MFCC, 9 delta MFCC and 9 acceleration MFCC.

The next parameterization was PLP_D_A (Perceptual Linear Predictive Analysis Delta Acceleration). The feature vector also described 27 coefficients for each given frame: 8 static PLP + energy, 9 delta and 9 acceleration coefficients.

Finally, the third parameterization RASTA_D_A (RelAtive SpecTrAl Delta Acceleration) consisted of 9 RASTA coefficients, 9 delta PLP and 9 acceleration PLP. 9 RASTA coefficients were acquired from 8 static PLP coefficients and 1 energy coefficient by applying the RASTA filter with a transfer function:

$$H(z) = 0.1z^4 \cdot \frac{2 + z^{-1} \quad z^{-3} \quad 2z^{-4}}{1 - 0.98z^{-1}} . \tag{20}$$

Furthermore, we decided to join all presented features in the subsection 3.2 into a total vector of parameterization TOGETHER (MPP+MFCC+PLP+RASTA_D_A). This total vector had 53 coefficients for each frame (8 MPP, 9 static MFCC, 9 static PLP and 27 RASTA_D_A coefficients).

4   S/NS Detection Experiments

In order to find the best parameterization technique (the best feature set) we had to perform many experiments for various modifications of the basic feature set. The experiments were accomplished on a set of waveforms (files) that were cut out from speech utterances (μ law format, $8\,kHz$ sample rate) obtained from phone calls about information on train connections. The waveforms were divided into two classes. The first class contained non-speech (low-level noise) files. 379 waveforms were used for training and 22 files for testing. The second class consisted of waveforms containing only speech (1324 for training and 100 for testing).

Two statistical models were trained for each kind of parameterization. The first model was a model of speech (S_CH), which was trained with waveforms containing only speech. The second one (i.e. model of non-speech (N_S)) was trained on non-speech (low-level noise) waveforms. This pair of model represents one speech/non-speech detector and was trained for various number of components of Gaussian mixture. Each feature vector is evaluated by S_CH model and N_S model. If the probability assigned by the S_CH model is greater than the probability assigned by the N_S model, given frame is detected as speech and vice versa.

The accuracy of each proposed speech/non-speech detector was then investigated. The tests accomplished so far were done on waveforms containing only clean speech or only low-level noise (silence). As can be seen from Figure 1, the decision whether given frame is speech or non-speech, is performed by using S/NS detection network.

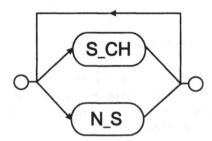

Fig. 1. Recognition network of the S/NS detection.

Many tests were carried out for various parameterizations (feature set). Table 1 lists the S/NS detection accuracy on 5 speech utterances with quiet, (low-level) volume. Each parameterization (e.g. PLP_D_A) was trained for various number of components of Gaussian mixture. Such number of components was selected from each parameterization (e.g. from all PLP_D_A parameterizations) that best classified all tested waveforms. The PLP_D_A parameterization had the best results for the number components of Gaussian mixture 26. As mentioned earlier, the tests were accomplished only on waveforms with clean speech or low-level noise (without speech) and each pair of model representing one speech/non-speech detector were used for the S/NS decision.

For example, row 10 in Table 1 describes PLP_D_A mix 26. It means that the feature vector with PLP coefficients (8 static PLP + energy + 9 delta PLP + 9 acceleration PLP)

Table 1. A comparison of the best selected parameterizations on 5 speech waveforms.

SPEECH WAVEFORMS:	X0054	X0436	X0552	X0681	X0686	SPEECH	NOISE
Number of frames:	109	34	104	84	34	365	0
Parameterizations							
MPP (ble) mix 22	78/31	0/34	3/101	23/61	0/34	104	261
MPP_D_A (sle) mix 18	21/88	0/34	0/104	22/62	0/34	43	322
MPP (sle) mix 8	109/0	0/34	104/0	79/5	6/28	298	67
MPP (8p) mix 20	109/0	0/34	104/0	29/55	8/26	213	152
MPP (jebl) mix 32	72/37	0/34	23/81	30/54	11/23	173	192
MFCC_D_A mix 10	109/0	2/32	101/3	48/36	9/25	269	96
PLP_D_A mix 26	109/0	4/30	91/13	50/34	34/0	288	77
RASTA_D_A mix 22	109/0	29/5	104/0	47/37	34/0	323	42
TOGETHER mix 10	109/0	5/29	104/0	46/38	32/2	296	69

was used for the S/NS detection. The number components of Gaussian mixture is 26. The testing speech waveform X0552 consists of 104 frames. 91 frames were detected as speech and 13 frames as non-speech. The column "SPEECH" describes the sum of frames that were detected as speech (a maximum value is 365). It can be seen from Table 1 that RASTA_D_A mix 12, PLP_D_A mix 26 and MPP (sle) mix 8 are the best parameterizations for S/NS detection. Since the results are very similar and PLP coefficients for speech recognition are used in our ASR system, we decided to apply the feature vector with PLP coefficients to the S/NS decision too. The advantage of this choice is, that the same feature vector is first introduced to the S/NS detector and then for speech recognition.

5 Conclusions

This paper has shown a statistical approach to S/NS detection together with an investigation of several (heuristic) feature sets. The parameters of the models (speech and non-speech) were set by applying the statistical induction method. The various parameterizations were tested for finding the best features set for the speech/non-speech decision in the utterance. When the speech waveforms were louder or waveforms were normalized, each of the proposed and presented parameterizations successfully detected waveforms as speech. However, all parameterizations had problems on waveforms with low-level speech (see in Table 1). All parameterizations infallibly detected the noise in low-level noise utterances.

Acknowledgment

This work was supported by the Grant Agency of the Czech Republic, project No. 102/02/0124.

References

1. Yang, C-H., Hsieh, M-S.: Robust Endpoint Detection for In-Car Speech Recognition, ICSLP 2000, Beijing, Paper Number 251.
2. Zhu, J., Chen, F.: The Analysis and application of a New Endpoint Detection Method Base on Distance of Autocorrelated Similarity, ESCA, EuroSpeech'99, Budapest, Hungary. ISSN 1018-4074, pp. 105–108.
3. Karray, L., Monné, J.: Robust Speech/non-speech Detection in Adverse Conditions Based on Noise and Speech Statistics, ICSLP'98, Sydney, Paper Number 430.
4. Tessama, T.: New Methods for the Detection of Voiced, Unvoiced, Silent, Transition Regions in Speech Signals, Advances in Modelling & Analysis, B, AMSE Press (France), Vol. 31, No. 3, 1994, pp. 1–10, 1993.

An Analysis of Conditional Responses in Dialogue*

Elena Karagjosova and Ivana Kruijff-Korbayová

Saarland University, Saarbrücken, Germany,
E-mail: elka@coli.uni-sb.de, korbay@coli.uni-sb.de
WWW page: http://www.coli.uni-sb.de/

Abstract. We analyze naturally occurring collaborative responses of the form "Not (if) c/Yes if c". We distinguish two cases: when c is established in the context, the conditional response indicates a possible need to revise c, and thus opens negotiation; otherwise, the conditional response raises the question whether c. We discuss the contexts where such responses are used and the dialogue acts they realize. We propose a uniform approach to their generation and interpretation.

1 Introduction

The goal of this paper is to provide a basic account of *conditional responses* (CRs) in collaborative dialogues in terms of their appropriateness conditions and the dialogue moves they perform. This work originates from our interest in collaborative turns in task-oriented dialogue; for example, responses which contain more than just the response particles *yes, no* or *ok*. As instances of such collaborative responses we encountered the CRs in (1:9) and (2:4), where the positive or negative polarity of the response is *contingent* upon some *attribute value* (A/V). In addition, a CR seems to suggest that for another A/V the response would have the opposite polarity. Consider (1).[1]

(1) 1.A: uh, let's see what would get you there then leaving probabl- the seventh. from San Jose or San Francisco?

2.C San Francisco. actually Oakland would be good too on that

3.A: I don't know if there are any red eyes from there let's see

4.C: ok

5.A: there is one on United that leaves Oakland at eleven thirty p.m. and arrives Chicago five twenty five a.m.

6.C: so that's a two hour hold there

7.A: yes

8.C: waiting for that flight ok any others?

9.A: uh not from Oakland.

10.A: departing from San Francisco it's about the same

---

* Work on this paper was supported by SIRIDUS (Specification, Interaction and Reconfiguration in Dialogue Understanding Systems), EC Project IST-1999-10516. We would like to thank Geert-Jan Kruijff for extensive comments on our work.

[1] We looked at the Verbmobil appointment-scheduling corpus [1] and the SRI's American Express travel agency data [2]. The examples in this paper are from [2]. A and C mean "agent" and "customer", respectively.

P. Sojka, I. Kopeček, and K. Pala (Eds.): TSD 2002, LNAI 2448, pp. 317–320, 2002.

(1:9) gives a negative CR to the question (1:8); there are no other flights from Oakland. This answer is contingent on the A/V of departing from Oakland, and leaves open, or even seems to suggest, the possibility of a flight from another departure city, namely the previously mentioned San Francisco. This possibility is addressed and refuted in (1:10).

(2:4) gives a positive CR as a confirmation of the assertion (2:3). But this CR is contingent on the A/V "rate": only if the going rate is higher, the customer has to pay both a penalty and the going rate. The CR implies that for the same or lower rate, the customer only has to pay the penalty. (2:5) re-confirms that the rate is going to be higher.

(2)   1.C: there's a hundred dollar fine
       2.A: okay
       3.C: and p- penalty plus ahh we pay for the going rate
       4.A: yeah if ther- if it's going to be a higher rate
       5.C: it's going to be a higher rate, ok now [...]

Following on our proposal in [3], we consider the suggestion implicit in (1:9) and (2:4) that for another A/V the response would have the opposite polarity, as an *implicature* rather than part of the assertion, since it is cancellable (cf. (1:10)). The assertions and implicatures corresponding to CRs are summarized in Figure 1. The utterance to which the CR replies may be either a yes/no question (whether q holds) as in (1:8), or an assertion proposing q for acceptance or rejection, like (2:3). In the approach to dialogue modelling we are using, q is represented as the current *question under discussion* (QUD, [4]).

QUD	q	q
Response	Not (if) c	Yes if c
Assertion	If c, not-q	If c, then q
Implicature	Possibly, if not-c, then q	Possibly, if not-c, then not-q

Fig. 1. Patterns of conditional responses.

Even though CRs are not very frequent in the two corpora we studied, they are efficient means for collaboration, which enable to hint at alternatives in solving a task. Our goal therefore is to provide the basis for understanding and generation of CRs in a dialogue system designed to handle collaborative dialogues in the travel domain.

Overview. The rest of the paper is organized as follows. In Section 2 we discuss the interpretation and appropriateness conditions of CRs. In Section 3 we discuss the dialogue moves corresponding to CRs. We end the paper with conclusions, where we briefly address issues of future interest.

2   Uses of Conditional Responses

[5] characterize CRs in terms of the speaker's motivation to provide information "about conditions that could affect the veracity of the response". However, they only consider cases like (2) in which the A/V on which the CR is contingent has not yet been determined in the preceding context. Cases like (1) are left unnoticed. In the present section we briefly address

the two cases we distinguish.The distinction turns out to be important for the *dialogue move* that such responses perform (cf. Section 3).

CR with not-determined A/V (NDCR). A CR can be contingent on an A/V c which has not yet been determined in the preceding context, as in (2).

The interpretation of an NDCR as a response to a QUD q is that (i) it is still not determined whether q, because (ii) the answer is contingent on c (Figure 1), and thus (iii) the question whether c holds is implicitly raised. Consider (2:4) which raises the question whether "higher rate" holds. This question is resolved in the next turn (2:5).

From the production point of view, we observe that it is appropriate to produce NDCR when (i) responding to a QUD q, where (ii) the response is either q or *not-q*, depending on some additional A/V c which has not yet been established in the context.

CR with contextually-determined A/V (CDCR). Another context in which a CR is appropriate is when a response to a QUD q is contingent on an A/V c that has already been established in the preceding context, as in (1).

The interpretation of a CDCR is that (i) it is determined whether q or *not-q* holds, because (ii) the answer (specified in Figure 1) is contingent on c and c is established. Moreover, (iii) the CDCR indicates the reason for the answer. There is an additional aspect of a CDCR which distinguishes it from NDCR. Namely, by reminding of the A/V on which the response is contingent, a CDCR (iv) proposes to reconsider the earlier made decision by implicitly re-raising the question whether c should hold. Thus, a negotiation phase is opened in which either the conflicting A/V is revised, or is confirmed. In the latter case a different solution to the overall goal needs to be sought.

Re-raising c differs from raising a "new" question at least in two aspects: c must be *negotiable*, and the re-raised c requires not only a positive or negative reply but also some kind of acknowledgment whether or not the A/V is to be revised (and how).

From the production point of view, we observe that it is appropriate to produce a CDCR when (i) responding to a QUD q, where (ii) the response is either q or *not-q*, depending on an A/V c which has been established in the preceding context and is negotiable.

For both NDCR and CDCR, the choice between a positive or a negative one depends on which one is more cooperative in the context. This in turn depends on what the preferred answer to the question whether q is assumed to be.

3   Conditional Response Dialogue Moves

As we have seen, the two different kinds of CRs provide a response contingent on an A/V where a CDCR makes a proposal for revising the contextually determined A/V (1:9), and a NDCR raises the question whether the A/V holds (2:4). This suggests that CDCR and NDCR perform different dialogue moves. We now briefly consider how CRs could be characterized in terms of the DAMSL standard for dialogue annotation [6].

Forward looking function. We assign CDCRs the forward looking function of *open option*, and NDCRs the one of *info-request* (although the other participant is not always obliged to provide an answer to it, as we argue in [3]).

Backward looking function. We assign CRs multiple backward looking functions. Both CDCRs and NDCRs are assigned the function *answer* (if preceded by a question) or *non-answer* otherwise. In addition, CDCRs are assigned the function *partial reject/accept* (depending on polarity), and NDCRs the function *hold*.

4 Conclusions

In this paper we proposed an analysis of *conditional responses*, which arise naturally in dialogues allowing for mixed initiative and negotiation. We proposed two types of conditional responses: One type describes the case where the answer is contingent on an A/V that has not yet been determined in the context (NDCRs). The other type deals with an A/V that has already been set in the context, and which now needs to reconsidered (CDCRs). The distinction properly clarifies the different effects on dialogue context conditional responses may have. We also tried to characterize the differences in the dialogue moves performed by CDCRs and NDCRs.

We are developing an implementation of CRs in the GoDiS system [7]. GoDiS is an experimental system based on the information-state update approach to dialogue as proposed in the TRINDI and SIRIDUS projects [8,9]. It was initially designed to handle information-seeking dialogues in the travel domain.

The distinction of two types of CDCRs seems relevant for the appropriate prosodic realization of this kind of responses in English. For example, NDCR is appropriate with a neutral prosodic pattern, whereas the CDCR seems to require prosodically marked contrast. We plan to investigate the prosodic properties of CRs with respect to context. Another future objective is to investigate how various other surface form realizations of CRs we found in the corpora, such as *only (if)*, *but only (if)*, *unless*, relate to each other and how they fit the pattern in Figure 1.

References

1. Verbmobil-Corpus: Data Collection for a Speech to Speech Translation System in the Scheduling Domain. Institut für Phonetik, München (1995).
2. SRI: Amex Travel Agent Data. http://www.ai.sri.com/~communic/amex/amex.html (1989).
3. Karagjosova, E., Kruijff-Korbayová, I.: Conditional Responses in Information Seeking Dialogues. In: Proceedings of the 3rd SIGdial Workshop on Discourse and Dialogue, Philadelphia, Pennsylvania, USA (2002) Forthcoming.
4. Ginzburg, J.: Interrogatives: Questions, Facts and Dialogue. In: Lappin, S., ed.: The Handbook of Contemporary Semantic Theory. Blackwell, Oxford, UK/Cambridge, USA (1996), pp. 385–422.
5. Green, N., Carberry, S.: A Computational Mechanism for Initiative in Answer Generation. User Modeling and User-Adapted Interaction 9 (1999), pp. 93–132.
6. Allen, J., Core, M.: Draft of DAMSL: Dialogue Act Markup in Several Layers. http://www.cs.rochester.edu/research/cisd/resources/damsl (1997).
7. Kruijff-Korbayová, I., Karagjosova, E., Larsson, S.: Enhancing collaboration with conditional responses in information seeking dialogues. (2002) Under review.
8. Cooper, R., Larsson, S., Matheson, C., Poesio, M., Traum, D.: Coding Instructional Dialogue for Information States. http://www.ling.gu.se/projekt/trindi/ (1999).
9. Lewin, I., Rupp, C.J., Hieronymus, J., Milward, D., Larsson, S., Berman, A.: Siridus System Architecture and Interface Report (Baseline). http://www.ling.gu.se/projekt/siridus/ (2000).

Some Like It Gaussian … *

Pavel Matějka[1], Petr Schwarz[2], Martin Karafiát[2], and Jan Černocký[2]

[1] VUT Brno, Faculty of Elec. Eng. and Communication, E-mail: matejkap@feec.vutbr.cz
[2] VUT Brno, Fac. of Inf. Technology, E-mail: schwarzp@fit.vutbr.cz,
karafiat@fit.vutbr.cz, cernocky@fit.vutbr.cz

Abstract. In Hidden Markov models, speech features are modeled by Gaussian distributions. In this paper, we propose to gaussianize the features to better fit to this modeling. A distribution of the data is estimated and a transform function is derived. We have tested two methods of the transform estimation (global and speaker based). The results are reported on recognition of isolated Czech words (SpeechDat-E) with CI and CD models and on medium vocabulary continuous speech recognition task (SPINE). Gaussianized data provided in all three cases results superior to standard MFC coefficients proving, that the gaussianization is a cheap way to increase the recognition accuracy

1   Introduction

Gaussianization is a process, where the data are transformed to data with Gaussian distribution. This idea was inspired by data distribution modeling in HMMs [1,5]. Here the distributions are modeled by Gaussian mixtures. In ideal situation, the data should have Gaussian distribution per class (for example phonemes). Unfortunately, we do not know a-priori to which class a given feature vector belongs. Therefore our approach will be the global gaussianization of the data. Gaussianization was already tested on the speaker verification task [2]. This work presents its results while applied to standard MFC coefficients for speech recognition.

2   Gaussianization of Data

The goal of gaussianization is to transform data, which has non Gaussian distribution denoted $p(x)$ to data, which has Gaussian distribution $\mathcal{N}(y, \mu, \sigma)$. It is feasible if we find the transform function $y = f(x)$. First it is necessary to estimate the distribution of original data $\hat{p}(x)$ using histogram and define the target Gaussian distribution – for simplicity, we choose zero mean and unity variance: $\mathcal{N}(y, 0, 1)$. Cumulative distribution functions $\hat{P}(x)$ and $P_{\mathcal{N}}(y)$ are computed from distributions. It is then easy to find, for each value of $\hat{P}(x)$ the corresponding value of $P_{\mathcal{N}}(y)$ which leads directly to the transform function $y = f(x)$. Care must be taken at the edges of this function, as the edge values of histograms are not reliably estimated.

There are several approaches to the estimation of transform function. It is possible to compute it over the *whole database, per speaker, per utterance* or only for some *time section*

---

* Supported by Grant Agency of Czech Republic under project No. 102/02/0124.

P. Sojka, I. Kopeček, and K. Pala (Eds.): TSD 2002, LNAI 2448, pp. 321–324, 2002.

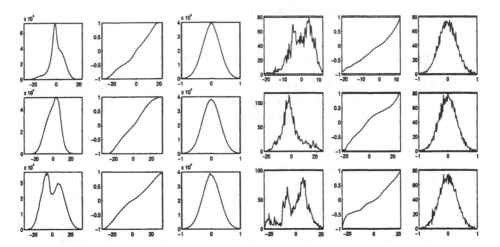

Fig. 1. Examples of distributions and transformation functions with global and per-speaker gaussianization. c_1, c_2, and c_0 are shown.

around the destination frame. We may expect better results if we use smaller unit, because the method can adapt better to data. But it is true only to some extent – the unit is too small, the recognition becomes worse, because there are not enough data for reliable estimation of the transform function. In this paper, results for the first two cases are presented.

3   Experiments and Results

SpeechDat – Context Independent Models   Czech SpeechDat-E database [4] was used in the first experiments to assess the gaussianization. The database consists of 1052 sessions containing various items, 700 sessions were used for training and 352 for tests.

Phoneme-based recognizer of isolated words was *trained* on phonetically balanced words from the training data (W∗ items), after discarding of some corrupted ones, 2777 words were used. For *tests*, 1394 words were used. The size of context-independent (CI) phoneme set was 42. Phoneme models had standard architecture, 3 emitting states with no state skip. The number of Gaussian components was a parameter in experiments (see the tables).

The feature extraction was done using 13 MFC coefficients, including c_0 (similar to log energy, but not the same, as we are summing the *log* energies of frequency bands). Velocity and acceleration features were added. No normalization was applied. The recognizer with those features (MFCC_0_D_A in HTK notation) was the *baseline*.

The gaussianization was first done globally for all the speech data. The histogram in the $\hat{p}(x)$ estimation had 50 points. The results are denoted *glob gauss* and some distributions and transform functions are shown in left panel of Figure 1. Next, the data were gaussianized per speaker. Again, histograms had 50 points. This time, they were less reliably estimated (right panel of Figure 1). In tables, the result is denoted *spk gauss*.

The results summarized in Table 1 show clearly the power of gaussianization: even the global one helps the recognizer to gain several percent for low number of Gaussians. Per-

Table 1. Recognition accuracy in SpeechDat-E experiments with CI and CD models.

#mixture components	SpeechDat-E CI models			
	1	2	4	8
baseline	80.92	85.58	88.59	90.24
glob gauss	82.42	86.44	89.45	90.39
spk gauss	88.88	91.68	93.47	95.05
#mixture components	SpeechDat-E CD models			
	1	2	4	8
baseline	94.98	96.27	96.63	96.77
glob gauss	94.40	95.12	95.98	96.27
spk gauss	96.48	96.56	97.06	97.13

Table 2. Word error rates on SPINE.

#mixture components	1	2	4	8
baseline	65.7	55.7	47.3	44.6
glob gauss	60.9	49.5	45.4	43.5
spk gauss	44.2	39.0	36.0	34.4

speaker gaussianization increases the accuracy with 8 Gaussians by almost 5 percent and makes the CI recognizer comparable to the baseline CD one.

SpeechDat – Context Dependent Models In this experiment, context-dependent triphones were created using a set of phonetic questions. The models were initialized on phonetically balanced words (2777), but then re-trained on the entire training part (36330 items). The number of logical triphones was 77662, the numbers of physical triphones and tied states varied from one experiment to another, but were around 7500 and 2400. The same feature extraction (MFCC_0_D_A) was used and data gaussianization was performed exactly in the same way as above.

The results in the Table 1 show that in this case, the global gaussianization hits the recognition accuracy. We have however gained 0.36 % in case of speaker-based processing, which is not a negligible improvement for accuracies around 96–97 %.

SPINE Third set of experiments was run on SPINE data. SPINE (Speech in Noisy Environments) is an evaluation run by the Naval Research Laboratory. The task a medium-sized vocabulary recognition on several military environments. The training and evaluation data from 2000 were used to assess performances of our features. We disposed of data pre-segmented at CMU (Carnegie Mellon University) into speech and silence regions [3]. The recognizer used – SPHINX – came also from CMU. The *training data* consists of 140 conversation (each has 2 channels) completed with 18 directories with DRT (Diagnostic Rhyme Test) words with added noises. There are 15847 files in the training set. The *evaluation data* consists of 120 conversations (each with 2 channels). There are 13265 files in the evaluation set. 12 first conversations were selected as the short evaluation set, including 1353 files. Every of the results reported here were obtained on this short set.

The same features as for SpeechDat (MFCC_0_D_A) were used as the baseline. Then, data were gaussianized globally and per speaker, again with histograms estimated on 50 points. Table 2 presents the word-error rates (WER)[3] of the system.

The improvement of 10 % can be attributed to non-optimal baseline, but it clearly shows the power of gaussianization. On contrary to some feature extraction techniques, helping the CI models but hurting CD ones, our method integrates smoothly with CD models.

4   Conclusion

The paper demonstrates the possibility to decrease WER only with a "cheap" transform in feature extractor. Moreover, the decreasing of number of Gaussian components in models has less effect on gaussianized data than on the original ones. It means less CPU power for training models and faster recognition.

References

1. B. Gold and N. Morgan. *Speech and audio signal processing*. John Wiley & Sons, 2000.
2. J. Pelecanos and S. Sridharan. Feature warping for robust speaker verification. In: *Proc. Speaker Odyssey 2001 conference*, June 2001.
3. R. Singh, M. L. Seltzer, B. Raj, and R. M. Stern. Speech in noisy environments: robust automatic segmentation, feature extraction, and hypothesis combination. In: *Proc. ICASSP 2001*, Salt Lake City, Utah, USA, May 2001.
4. H. van den Heuvel et al. Speechdat-east: Five multilingual speech databases for voice-operated teleservices completed. In: *EuroSpeech 2001*, Aalborg, Denmark, September 2001.
5. S. Young, J. Jansen, J. Odell, D. Ollason, and P. Woodland. *The HTK book*. Entropics Cambridge Research Lab., Cambridge, UK, 1996.

---

[3] WER is used in the SPINE community rather than accuracy.

Kernel Springy Discriminant Analysis and Its Application to a Phonological Awareness Teaching System

András Kocsor[1] and Kornél Kovács[2]

Research Group on Artificial Intelligence
of the Hungarian Academy of Sciences
and University of Szeged*
H-6720 Szeged, Aradi vértanúk tere 1., Hungary
E-mail: kocsor@inf.u-szeged.hu, kkornel@inf.u-szeged.hu

Abstract. Making use of the ubiquitous kernel notion, we present a new nonlinear supervised feature extraction technique called Kernel Springy Discriminant Analysis. We demonstrate that this method can efficiently reduce the number of features and increase classification performance. The improvements obtained admittedly arise from the nonlinear nature of the extraction technique developed here. Since phonological awareness is a great importance in learning to read, a computer-aided training system could be most beneficial in teaching young learners. Naturally, our system employs an effective automatic phoneme recognizer based on the proposed feature extraction technique.

1 A Phonological Awareness Teaching System

The most important clue to the process of learning to read is the ability to separate and identify consecutive sounds that make words and to associate these sounds with its corresponding written form. To learn to read in a fruitful way young learners must, of course, also be aware of the phonemes and be able to manipulate them. Many children with learning disabilities have problems in their ability to process phonological information. So we decided to construct a computer-aided training software package which makes use of a very effective automatic phoneme recognizer in the background and provides visual feedback, on a frame-by-frame basis, in the form of flickering letters (see Figure 1a). So as to make the sound to grapheme association easier a unique picture is attached to each letter. In addition, the transparency of letters is proportional to the output of the speech recognizer. Our experiments and general observations show that young people are more willing to practice with the computer than with traditional drills. To reinforce this point we found we could make impressive progress in a very short training period.

Since a highly efficient automatic phoneme recognizer can make the teaching system reliable, we decided to develop a novel feature extraction technique which proved to be suitable for this task. In the next section we describe this method, followed by results and concluding remarks.

* This work was supported under the contract IKTA No. 2001/055 from the Hungarian Ministry of Education.

P. Sojka, I. Kopeček, and K. Pala (Eds.): TSD 2002, LNAI 2448, pp. 325–328, 2002.

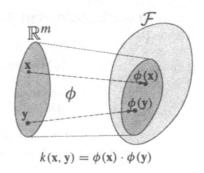

Fig. 1. (a) A phonological awareness teaching system. (b) The kernel idea. $\mathcal{F}$ is the closure of the linear span of the mapped data. The dot product in the kernel feature space $\mathcal{F}$ is implicitly defined. The dot product of $\sum_{i=1}^{n} \alpha_i \phi(\mathbf{x_i})$ and $\sum_{i=1}^{n} \beta_i \phi(\mathbf{x_i})$ is $\sum_{i,j} \alpha_i \beta_j k(\mathbf{x_i}, \mathbf{x_j})$.

2   Kernel Springy Discriminant Analysis

The approach of feature extraction could be either linear or nonlinear, but it seems there is a technique (which is most topical nowadays) that is, in some sense, breaking down the barrier between the two types. The key idea was originally presented in [1] and was again applied in connection with the general purpose Support Vector Machine [2,3]. In the following this notion is also used to derive a novel nonlinear feature extractor.

Without loss of generality we shall assume that, as a realization of multivariate random variables, there are m-dimensional real attribute vectors in a compact set $\mathcal{X}$ over $\mathbb{R}^m$ describing objects in a certain domain, and that we have a finite $n \times m$ sample matrix $X = [\mathbf{x_1}, \cdots, \mathbf{x_n}]^\top$ containing n random observations. Let us assume as well that we have k classes and an indicator function $\mathcal{L} : \{1, \ldots, n\} \rightarrow \{1, \ldots, k\}$, where $\mathcal{L}(i)$ gives the class label of the sample $\mathbf{x_i}$.

Now let the dot product be implicitly defined (see Figure 1b) by the kernel function k in some finite or infinite dimensional feature space $\mathcal{F}$ with associated transformation ϕ:

$$k(\mathbf{x}, \mathbf{y}) = \phi(\mathbf{x}) \cdot \phi(\mathbf{y}). \tag{1}$$

Kernel Springy Discriminant Analysis (KSDA) searches for a linear transformation in $\mathcal{F}$ having the form $Q\dot{X}$, where Q is a real n by n orthogonal matrix containing variational parameter values obtained by the method, while $\dot{X}$ is a short-hand notation for the image matrix $[\phi(\mathbf{x_1}), \cdots, \phi(\mathbf{x_n})]^\top$. If we have a new attribute vector $\mathbf{y}$, the transformation can be employed by $Q\dot{X}\phi(\mathbf{y}) = Qk(X, \mathbf{y})$, where the column vector $k(X, \mathbf{y})$ is $[k(\mathbf{x_1}, \mathbf{y}), \cdots, k(\mathbf{x_n}, \mathbf{y})]^\top$. Thus in the kernel feature space $\mathcal{F}$ this type of linear transformation can be expressed only by dot products, which requires only kernel function evaluations. Moreover, since ϕ is generally nonlinear the resultant transformation is a nonlinear transformation of the original sample data. Knowing ϕ explicitly – and, consequently, knowing $\mathcal{F}$ – is not necessary. We need only define the kernel function, which then ensures an implicit evaluation. The construction of an appropriate kernel function (i.e. when such a function ϕ exists) is a non-trivial problem, but there are many good suggestions about the sorts of kernel functions which might be adopted along with some background theory [2,3]. From the functions available, the two most popular are[1]:

Polynomial kernel: $\qquad k_1(\mathbf{x}, \mathbf{y}) = \left(\mathbf{x}^{\mathsf{T}}\mathbf{y}\right)^d, \qquad\qquad d \in \mathbb{N},$ (2)

Gaussian RBF kernel: $\qquad k_2(\mathbf{x}, \mathbf{y}) = \exp- \|\mathbf{x} - \mathbf{y}\|^2/r), \qquad r \in \mathbb{R}_+.$ (3)

The stationary points of the Rayleigh quotient formula will furnish the row vectors of the orthogonal matrix $\mathbf{Q}$ of the KSDA transformation[2]:

$$\gamma(\boldsymbol{\alpha}) = \boldsymbol{\alpha}^{\mathsf{T}} \dot{X} A \dot{X}^{\mathsf{T}} \boldsymbol{\alpha}/\boldsymbol{\alpha}^{\mathsf{T}}\boldsymbol{\alpha},$$ (4)

where

$$A = \sum_{i,j=1}^{n} \left(\Phi(\mathbf{x_i}) - \Phi(\mathbf{x_j})\right)\left(\Phi(\mathbf{x_i}) - \Phi(\mathbf{x_j})\right)^{\mathsf{T}} \Theta_{ij}$$ (5)

and

$$\Theta_{ij} = \begin{cases} -1, & \text{if } \mathcal{L}(i) = \mathcal{L}(j) \\ 1, & \text{otherwise} \end{cases} \qquad i, j = 1, \ldots, n.$$ (6)

It is straightforward to prove that (4) takes the following form:

$$\gamma(\boldsymbol{\alpha}) = \boldsymbol{\alpha}^{\mathsf{T}} \left(K\tilde{\Theta}K^{\mathsf{T}} - K\Theta K^{\mathsf{T}}\right)\boldsymbol{\alpha}/\boldsymbol{\alpha}^{\mathsf{T}}\boldsymbol{\alpha},$$ (7)

where $K = \dot{X}\dot{X}^{\mathsf{T}} = [k(\mathbf{x_i}, \mathbf{x_j})]$ and $\tilde{\Theta}$ is a diagonal matrix with the sum of each row of Θ in the diagonal. After taking the derivative of (4) we readily see that the stationary points of $\gamma(\boldsymbol{\alpha})$ can be obtained via an eigenanalysis of the following symmetric eigenproblem:[3] $(K\tilde{\Theta}K^{\mathsf{T}} - K\Theta K^{\mathsf{T}})\boldsymbol{\alpha} = \lambda\boldsymbol{\alpha}$. If we assume that the eigenvectors are $\boldsymbol{\alpha}_1, \cdots, \boldsymbol{\alpha}_n$ then the orthogonal matrix Q is defined by $[\boldsymbol{\alpha}_1 c_1, \cdots, \boldsymbol{\alpha}_n c_n]^{\mathsf{T}}$, where the normalization parameter c_i is equal to $(\boldsymbol{\alpha}_i^{\mathsf{T}} K \boldsymbol{\alpha}_i)^{-1/2}$. This normalization factor ensures that the two-norm of row vectors of the transformation matrix $Q\dot{X}$ is unity.

---

[1] For a given kernel function ϕ is not always unique as the kernel k_1, the dimension of the feature space $\mathcal{F}$, is at least $\binom{m+d-1}{d}$ while with k_2 we get infinite dimension feature spaces.

[2] The name of this method stems from the utilization of a spring & antispring model, which involves searching for directions with optimal potential energy using attractive and repulsive forces. In our case sample pairs in each class are connected by springs, while those of different classes are connected by antisprings. New features can be easily extracted by taking the projection of a new point in those directions where a small spread in each class is attained, while different classes are spaced out as much as possible. Let $\delta(\mathbf{v})$ be defined by $\sum_{i,j=1}^{n}((\Phi(\mathbf{x_i}) - \Phi(\mathbf{x_j}))^{\mathsf{T}}\mathbf{v})^2\Theta_{ij}$. Using this term, which in $\mathcal{F}$ defines the potential of the spring model along the direction $\mathbf{v}$, we find that $\gamma(\boldsymbol{\alpha})$ is equal to $\delta(\dot{X}^{\mathsf{T}}\boldsymbol{\alpha})/\boldsymbol{\alpha}^{\mathsf{T}}\boldsymbol{\alpha}$. Technically speaking, KSDA searches for those directions $\mathbf{v}$ of the form $\dot{X}^{\mathsf{T}}\boldsymbol{\alpha}$ along which a large potential is obtained. Intuitively, if larger values of γ indicate better directions and the chosen directions need to provide independent feature information, then choosing stationary points that have large values is a reasonable strategy.

[3] In contrast to [4], KSDA can be performed by solving a symmetric eigenproblem rather than an unsymmetrical one.

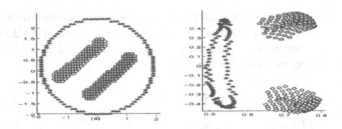

Fig. 2. KSDA transformation of artificial data. (a) is the initial data, and (b) is the result.

3   Results

In Figure 2 we can see the result of a KSDA transformation using a Gaussian RBF kernel on artificial data with three different class labels. Without a doubt, the classes are well separated. For training and testing purposes we also recorded samples from 120 speakers (children of age 6–7) at a sampling rate of 22050 Hz in 16-bit quality. Each speakers uttered all the Hungarian vowels, one after the other, separated by a short pause. Since we decided not to discriminate their long and short versions, we worked with 9 vowels altogether. Initially, the signals were processed in 10 ms frames, from which the log-energies of 24 critical-bands were extracted using FFT and triangular weighting. In our tests we used the filter-bank log-energies from the centremost frame of the steady-state part of each vowel and smoothed the feature trajectories to remove the effect of brief noises and disturbances ("FBLE Smooth" set, 24 features). Afterwards, in a second set of features we extended the smoothed log-energies with the gravity centers of four frequency bands, approximately corresponding to the possible values of the formants ("FBLE+Grav" set, 24+4 features). These gravity centers are supposed to give a crude approximation of the formants. Naturally, both initial feature sets were transformed by KSDA using the third-order polynomial kernel. Since Q was defined by only those eigenvectors with the largest 16 eigenvalues we also performed a dimension reduction when applying the KSDA transformation. Then, as a classifier the well-known Support Vector Machine [2,3] was employed using the same kernel as before. In the trials 80 speakers were used for training and 40 for testing. For the sets "FBLE Smooth" and "FBLE+Grav" the recognition errors were 6.08 % and 5.27 %, respectively, while after a KSDA transformation they were 3.24 % and 2.8 %, respectively.

References

1. AIZERMAN, M. A., BRAVERMAN, E. M. AND ROZONOER L. I., Theoretical foundation of the potential function method in pattern recognition learning, *Auttomat. Remote Cont.*, Vol. 25, pp. 821–837, 1964.
2. VAPNIK, V. N., *Statistical Learning Theory*, John Wiley & Sons Inc., 1998.
3. CRISTIANINI, N. AND SHAWE-TAYLOR, J. *An Introduction to Support Vector Machines and other kernel-based learning methods* Cambridge University Press, 2000.
4. KOCSOR, A., TÓTH, L. AND PACZOLAY, D., A Nonlinearized Discriminant Analysis and its Application to Speech Impediment Therapy, *in V. Matoušek et al. (Eds.): Proc. of the 4th Int. Conf. on Text, Speech and Dialogue*, LNAI 2166, pp. 249–257, Springer Verlag, 2001.

Large Vocabulary Speech Recognition of Slovenian Language Using Data-Driven Morphological Models

Tomaž Rotovnik, Mirjam Sepesy Maučec, Bogomir Horvat, and Zdravko Kačič

Faculty of Electrical Engineering and Computer Science, University of Maribor
Smetanova 17, 2000 Maribor, Slovenia
E-mail: `tomaz.rotovnik@uni-mb.si`, `mirjam.sepesy@uni-mb.si`,
`bogo.horvat@uni-mb.si`, `kacic@uni-mb.si`
WWW: `http://www.dsplab.uni-mb.si`

Abstract. A system for large vocabulary continuous speech recognition of the Slovenian language is described. Two types of modelling units are examined: words and subwords. A data-driven algorithm is used to automatically obtain word decompositions. The performances of one-pass and two-pass decoding strategies were compared. The new models gave promising results. Recognition accuracy was improved by 3.41 % absolute at approx. the same recognition time. On the other hand we achieved 30 % increase in real time performance at the same recognition error.

1 Introduction

The Slovenian language is a highly inflected language, like other languages in the Slavic family. It possesses significant properties, which make it stand out as a potentially problematic language for automatic speech recognition. Slavic languages have complex morphological structures. It is possible to produce many different word forms from the same root using suffixes. This experiment has shown that the Slovenian corpus requires a vocabulary of 600 K words in order to achieve a 99 % training-set coverage. The vocabulary size for the Slovenian language must, therefore, be of an order of magnitude larger than the English language. Currently the most advanced speech recognition systems can handle vocabularies of 20 K up to 60 K words. In view of this we need to restrict vocabulary size, in the case of Slovenian language. This would result in a high Out Of Vocabulary (OOV) rate. To solve this problem we propose the use of smaller lexical units.

2 Vocabulary, Pronunciation Dictionary, and Language Models

Two different types of language models were built: word-based models and models at a sub-word level (named morphological models). A corpus of 60 M words obtained from the archives of a Slovenian newspaper VEČER, spanning the period from 1998 through 2000 was used for training them.

A vocabulary of word-based models was chosen to be the most frequent 20 K words from the training corpus.

P. Sojka, I. Kopeček, and K. Pala (Eds.): TSD 2002, LNAI 2448, pp. 329–332, 2002.

The inflectional change of a word mostly affects word ending, whereas the stem remains unchanged. In view of this words were split into two smaller lexical units: stems and endings. Some words (non-inflectional) cannot be decomposed and so they are left unchanged. Decomposition is determined automatically using the longest-match principle (scanning the list of endings). The list of endings was defined by an iterative algorithm, which searches for the minimum number of different units in a training-set. Decomposing vocabulary words resulted in 8497 different basic units. Vocabulary size was reduced by 58 %.

Phonetic transcriptions of words were made automatically under basic grammatical principles using 30 phones. The number of phones was smaller than usual, because no differentiation was made between long and short vowels, and some rare phones were excluded. The sub-word vocabulary contained 134 homographs from stems and 31 homographs from endings (see Table 1). Homographs are words or parts of words that have the same orthographic transcription but different phonetic transcription.

Table 1. Vocabulary of stems and endings.

	Unique	Homographs	Σ
Stems	6836	134	6970
Endings	1661	31	1692
Σ	8497	165	8662

Some examples of word decomposition are shown in Table 2. The first two words in the table have the same orthographic and phonetic transcriptions but different meanings (homographs). They differ in the accentuation of vowels during pronunciation. The third word has the same ending as the first two words. The last four words have the same stem and different endings, except the fourth and fifth words which do not have endings at all.

Table 2. Examples of word decomposition into stem-ending.

Word	Decomposition		Transcription	Translation	Possible new biphon
	stem	ending			
kamen	kam	-en	kam - En	Stony	a-m
kamen	kam	-en	kam - @n	Stone	a-m
česen	čes	-en	CEs - @n	Garlic	E-s
pol	pol	-0	pOL	pole(celestial)	/
pol	pol	-0	pOw	Half	/
poleg	pol	-eg	pOl - Eg	Beside	O-l
polčas	pol	-čas	pOw - Cas	half-time	O-l

Bigram, trigram and fourgram backoff language models were built [4]. The trigram and fourgram models were only used for rescoring, whereas the bigram language model was used for generating word graphs.

3 Acoustic Models

Word internal triphone models with 16 Gaussians mixtures for each state and for each model were built as acoustic models. The basic models had to be expanded using all unseen biphones for the sub-word based models. When decomposing words into stems and endings, and using word internal triphones (biphones and monophones included) from word-based vocabulary, it is possible to get new biphones as shown in Table 2. Thus all the missing biphones were created and added to the basic triphone models. The total number of models was 5983. The number of states was reduced from 10 K to 3 K after performing tree-based state tying. 4090 tied-state triphone models were obtained.

Acoustic models were trained on SNABI speech database [1]. It contains the speech of 52 speakers where each speaker read, on average, more than 200 sentences and 21 speakers also read the text passage. The total database consists of approx. 14 hours of speech.

4 LVCS Recognition

Two different decoding strategies were used. The first strategy included a standard time-synchronous Viterbi beam search decoder [2]. The second strategy is called two-pass decoding and includes two recognition stages [3]. A word graph is achieved as a result of keeping more than 1-best hypothesis. It defines possible word strings which can be used as grammar constraints in the second pass decoding. Although the process of word graph generation is very time-consuming, more complex acoustic and language models are used in order to obtain better overall performance regarding accuracy.

5 Results

The results were evaluated on the SNABI test-set. It consisted of 779 pronunciations spoken by 7 speakers and contained phonetically rich sentences.

A baseline system using words as basic units, Viterbi beam search decoder and bigram language models were used. Results are shown in Table 3. A recognition accuracy of only 41.6 % was obtained. Using words as basic units provide an OOV rate of 22.26 %. A 2-pass decoder with the same vocabulary and trigram language model was used for the second baseline system. Better recognition accuracy was achieved against real time degradation (57 % increase).

Morphological models were used in the next experiments. The OOV rate was improved by 70 %. Recognition accuracy was slightly better, (0.5 % absolute) by using a one-pass decoder, but real time performance increased by 29 % because of a smaller search space. The second experiment included a two-pass decoder with trigram language models for rescoring. Comparing recognition accuracy with the second baseline system, it can be seen that slightly worse results were obtained (about 2 % absolute), while real time performance increased by 32 %. The best results were obtained in the last experiment, when a four-gram language model was used. A four-gram language model attempts to capture the correlation between the stems and endings of two neighbouring words. It can be seen as a counterpart to the word-based bigram model. Comparing the results of the two-pass decoder using four-grams of stems and endings with those of the one pass decoder using word bigrams, recognition accuracy improved by 3.41 % absolute.

Table 3. Results of experiments.

Basic units	words			stems and endings		
Vocabulary size	20,000			8,662		
OOV [%]	22.26			6.51		
Decoding Strategy	ACC [%]	Mem [MB]	Speed [RT]	ACC [%]	Mem [MB]	Speed [RT]
1. Pass (bigram)	41.62	70	9.66	42.05	45	6.90
2. Pass (trigram)	44.16	200	15.18	42.24	155	10.26
2. Pass (four-gram)	-	-	-	45.03	530	10.40

6 Conclusion

Recognition accuracy at sub-word level is as good as word based recognition, while real time recognition performance increases. The greatest benefit of modelling inflected languages at sub-word level is OOV rate improvement. This proposed technique for word decomposition is language-independent and can easily be applied to other Slavic languages.

References

1. Kačič, Z., Horvat, B., Zögling, A.: Isues in design and collection of large telephone speech corpus for Slovenian language, LREC 2000.
2. Young, S., Odell, J., Ollason, D., Kershaw, D., Valtcheva, V., Woodland, P.: The HTK Book, Entropic Inc., 2000.
3. Zhao, J., Hamaker, J., Deshmukh, N., Ganapathiraju, A., Picone, J.: Fast Recognition Techniques for Large Vocabulary Speech Recognition, Texas Instruments Incorporated, August 15, 1999.
4. P. Clarkson, R. Rosenfeld: Statistical language modeling using the CMU-Cambridge toolkit. In: *Proceedings of EuroSpeech*, 1997.

Uniform Speech Recognition Platform
for Evaluation of New Algorithms

Andrej Žgank, Tomaž Rotovnik, Zdravko Kačič, and Bogomir Horvat

Institute for Electronics, Faculty of EE & CS, University of Maribor,
Smetanova 17, SI-2000 Maribor, Slovenia
E-mail: andrej.zgank@uni-mb.si

Abstract. This paper presents the development of a speech recognition platform. Its main area of use would be the evaluation of different new and improved algorithms for speech recognition (noise reduction, feature extraction, language model generation, training of acoustic models, ...). To enable wide usage of the platform, different test configurations were added – from alphabet spelling to large vocabulary continuous speech recognition. At the moment, this speech recognition platform is implemented and evaluated using a studio (SNABI) and a fixed telephone (SpeechDat(II)) speech database.

1 Introduction

The evaluation and comparison of new results with those of the standard approach is very important during the process of developing a new algorithm or method for speech processing. We decided to build a uniform speech recognition platform in order to simplify and standardize this step in the development procedure.

This system is based on the similar "COST 249 refrec" project [1] with several new and different features. There have also been other similar projects in the past (e.g. SAM [2]), but none of them were designed for a broad spectrum of tests using different database types. This speech recognition platform consists of perl scripts and programs in C language, and is implemented for Unix (tested on Linux and HP-UX). Port to the Windows platform is planned in the future. The scripts use the public domain HTK toolkit [3] for the designing and testing of acoustical models.

2 Architecture Overview

2.1 Training Part

This speech recognition platform is divided into three parts in order to achieve a uniform operation using different databases. The first part is the interface between the database and the data format of speech material needed in the second part. The user must prepare the data for the second part manually in those cases when the data preparation part cannot be completed using the platform. The second part can be universal for all databases and

P. Sojka, I. Kopeček, and K. Pala (Eds.): TSD 2002, LNAI 2448, pp. 333–336, 2002.

present the core training procedure of the platform because the interface handles the data processing. The last part consists of different speech recognition test configurations. The currently presented implementation of uniform speech recognition platform is developed for two different acoustic environments: for studio (Slovenian SNABI-studio database [4], 13779 utterances in the training set) environment and for fixed telephone lines (Slovenian FDB 1000 SpeechDat(II) [5], 28938 utterances in the training set).

In database interface, audio signal is converted into features with the use of 12 mel cepstral coefficients and energy. The size of the feature vector is 39 with the first and second derivatives. The user can simply add his own different frontend to the interface, as it is expected that different feature extraction methods will be tested in the future.

In the second part, the speech recognition system is constructed with speaker independent HMM acoustic models. Ordinary acoustic models for phonemes are generated with 3 state left-right topology, while there are additional models for acoustic events (silence, noise, cough, ...) with different, more complex topology. The user can choose between the training of context independent or context dependent models. The best models generated by the speech recognition platform are context dependent models with 8 Gaussian mixtures per state.

2.2 Testing Part

Different language models are used due to the extensive spectrum of testing configurations (from small vocabulary isolated words to large vocabulary continuous speech). The simplest one is the word-loop model and the most complex are the bigram and trigram back-off language models [6]. The large vocabulary continuous speech recognition with trigram language model is performed using the two pass decoder. New unseen triphones can occur when testing different language models or recognition vocabularies with context dependent acoustic models. This problem is solved in such a way, that unseen triphones are added to the acoustic models, without re-training the whole system. The n-gram language models, used in the SNABI implementation of the platform, are trained on a 50M words text corpus from the Slovenian newspaper "Večer".

Table 1. Number of utterances and word error rates (WER) for different SpeechDat(II) test sets.

	A1-6	I1	B1,C1	Q1-2	O2	W1-4
Num. of utter.	1070	193	380	346	194	749
Monophones	21.59	11.92	13.40	8.67	40.72	52.87
Triphones	7.57	7.25	7.96	1.45	13.02	23.29

3 Evaluation of Implementation

The first part of the platform evaluation was performed on a SpeechDat(II) database [5]. The same test set (A – words, I – isol. digits, BC – conn. digits, Q – yes/no, O – city names,

W – phon. rich words [7]) was used as in the "COST 249 refrec" project [1] to enable a comparison of the results. The results are presented in Table 1. The best performance for both types of acoustical models: monophones (8.67 % WER) and triphones (1.45 % WER), was achieved with the yes/no (Q1-2) test set. This test configuration was the easiest, due to there only being 2 words in the recognition vocabulary [7]. The worst speech recognition result was for the W1-4 (phonetically rich words) test set with 52.87 % WER for monophones and 23.29 % WER for triphones. The number of words in this recognition vocabulary was 1500, which also represents the hardest recognition task for the SpeechDat(II) database. If these results are compared with the results from the "COST 249 refrec" project [1], it can be seen that WER for some test sets are similar or equal. The I1 test set in the "COST 249 refrec" project also achieved 7.25 % WER and the Q1-2 test set 1.16 % WER. The greatest difference is observable with the W1-4 test set, where the COST 249 refrec project achieved WER of 34.31 % for monophones. The main reason for this distinction in word error rate is the fact that the training procedure in our platform is currently much simpler than in the "COST 249 refrec" project.

Table 2. Number of utterances and word error rates (WER) for SNABI test sets with word-loop language model.

	ABC	Connected dig.	Isolated dig.	Words
Num. of utter.	52	100	48	271
Monophones	65.38	10.33	2.08	2.95
Triphones	19.23	4.00	2.08	0.74

Table 3. Number of utterances and word error rates (WER) for SNABI test sets with 2-gram and 3-gram language model.

	MMC	Lingua 1	Lingua 2
Num. of utter.	1092	518	671
Monophones, 2-gram	28.08	42.04	65.05
Monophones, 3-gram	22.24	32.62	62.59
Triphones, 2-gram	9.87	18.32	45.53
Triphones, 3-gram	6.69	12.09	42.85

The second part of the platform evaluation was performed on SNABI models and database. The first sub-part of the tests (Table 2) was completed using the word-loop language model. The word error rate (WER) for comparable test configurations (isolated digits, connected digits, words) was significantly better than in the case of SpeechDat(II) database, due to the studio quality of speech in the SNABI database. The hardest task with the word-loop language model was the alphabet spelling test set with 65.38 % WER for monophones and 19.23 % for triphones. The second sub-part of the tests (Table 3) with the

SNABI database was performed with the use of n-gram language models. The Lingua 1 test set is only acoustically independent of the training set, whilst the Lingua 2 test set is both acoustically and textually independent of the training set. The improvement in results when the triphone acoustic models or 3-gram language model were used is obvious for all test sets in the second sub-part. The best performance (6.69 % WER) was achieved with the MMC test set. The average number of words in a sentence for this test set was 5.9. The average number of words in the Lingua 1 test set was 10.2 – this fact is reflected in an increase of WER to 12.09 % in comparison with the MMC test set. The 42.85 % WER for the Lingua 2 test set is mainly caused by the different topics of speech and text corpus used.

4 Conclusion

This paper describes the design and evaluation of a uniform speech recognition platform its main area of use will be the evaluation of new algorithms. Implementation with Speechdat(II) and SNABI database was presented. The results were compared to previous published results using the same database. In the future, a part for database segmentation will be added to this platform. The platform and the results of these implementations using different databases will be available on our home page.

References

1. Lindberg, B., Johansen, F.T., Warakagoda, N., Lehtinen, G., Kačič, Z., Žgank, A., Elenius, K., Salvi, G.: A noise robust multilingual reference recogniser based on SpeechDat(II). ICSLP 2000, Beijing, China, 2000.
2. Pols, L.C.W.: Evaluating the performance of speech input/output systems. A report of the ESPRIT-SAM project. Proc. DAGA '91, 139–150, Bochum, Germany, 1991.
3. Young, S.: The HTK Book (for HTK version 3.1). Cambridge University, 2001.
4. Kačič, Z., Horvat, B., Zögling A.: Issues in Design and Collection of Large Telephone Speech Corpus for Slovenian Language. Proc. LREC-2000, Athens, 2000.
5. Kaiser, J., Kačič, Z.: Development of the Slovenian SpeechDat database. Proc. LREC-1998, Granada, Spain, 1998.
6. Clarkson, P.R., Rosenfeld, R.: Statistical Language Modeling Using the CMU-Cambridge Toolkit. Proc. of the EuroSpeech '97, Rhodes, Greece, 1997.
7. van den Heuvel, H., Boves, L., Moreno, A., Omologo, M., Richard, G., Sanders, E.: 2001. Annotation in the SpeechDat Projects. International Journal of Speech Technology, 4(2):127–143.

Speech Enhancement Using Mixtures of Gaussians for Speech and Noise

Ilyas Potamitis, Nikos Fakotakis, Nikos Liolios, and George Kokkinakis

Wire Communications Lab., Electrical & Computer Engineering Department
University of Patras, Rion-26 500, Patras, Greece
E-mail: potamitis@wcl.ee.upatras.gr

Abstract. In this article we approximate the clean speech spectral magnitude as well as noise spectral magnitude with a mixture of Gaussians pdfs using the Expectation-Maximization algorithm (EM). Subsequently, we apply the Bayesian!inference framework to the degraded spectral coefficients and by employing Minimum Mean Square Error Estimation (MMSE), we derive a closed form solution for the spectral magnitude estimation task adapted to the spectral characteristics and noise variance of each band. We evaluate our algorithm using true, coloured, slowly and quickly varying noise types (Factory and aircraft noise) and demonstrate its robustness at very low SNRs.

1 Introduction

In spite of key contributions on the subject of *Short-Time Spectral Attenuation* algorithms (STSA) as applied to speech enhancement [1,2,3], there is still need for further work primarily on the problem of balancing the trade-off between noise reduction and speech distortion. The STSA family of algorithms attempts to uncover the underlying spectral magnitude of speech by applying a gain function to the observed, noisy short-time spectra, where the gain function is related to the noise power spectrum.

In this work we propose a novel STSA algorithm that incorporates into a Bayesian formulation the long term pdf of each spectral band of an ensemble of clean recordings resulting in a better treatment of low energy spectral regions, while the spectral magnitude of noise is modelled by a mixture of Gaussians that allows for compensating the effect of time-varying noise types. A mixture of Gaussians is employed to account for the representation of the the magnitude of each spectral band of an ensemble of high quality speech (three minutes of phonetically balanced speech from speakers of both genders were found sufficient). The descriptive parameters of each mixture are derived from the observed spectral bands of the clean data by employing the EM algorithm. Assuming the availability of noisy data, we incorporate a Gaussian mixture model for the background noise and derive the descriptive statistics of the mixtures using the EM algorithm.

Objective as well as subjective evaluation of signals degraded with additive Factory noise, and DC-3 aircraft noise at low SNRs confirm the benefit of our approach. The proposed work is supported by GEMINI (IST-2001-32343) EC project.

P. Sojka, I. Kopeček, and K. Pala (Eds.): TSD 2002, LNAI 2448, pp. 337–340, 2002.
© Springer-Verlag Berlin Heidelberg 2002

2 Description of the Algorithm

Let $s(m)$ denote the clean time-domain signal corrupted by noise $n(m)$ where (m) is the discrete-time index. The observed signal $x(m)$ is given by: $x(m) = s(m) + n(m)$ and is subjected to Short Time Fourier Transform (STFT). Based on the generalized spectral subtraction framework [3], we can derive a linear-spectral representation of a clean speech signal corrupted by additive noise using a $2N$ point FFT as:

$$x_{\kappa,l}^{\alpha} = s_{\kappa,l}^{\alpha} + n_{\kappa,l}^{\alpha} \quad \kappa = 0, \dots, N. \tag{1}$$

where x_{κ} denotes the spectral magnitude of the degraded sub-band κ, n_{κ} the noise spectral magnitude, l the frame index and $1 \leq \alpha \leq 2$. Prior knowledge about the time frequency distribution of s_{κ} is provided by a mixture of Gaussians that model the undegraded spectral bands of the available clean speech corpora (Eq. 2). Practically, 2–3 minutes of clean speech, unrelated to the signals to be enhanced, were found sufficient to tune the free parameters of the algorithm.

For notational convenience we set $x = x^{\alpha}$, $s = s^{\alpha}$, $n = n^{\alpha}$ and we drop subscript κ, l implying that the subsequent analysis holds for every time-trajectory of spectral sub-band κ independently, in the linear spectral domain. We have found that setting $\alpha = 3/2$ optimises performance, though, the subsequent analysis holds for every α.

$$f(s) = \sum_{m=1}^{M} p_m G\left(s; \mu_m, \sigma_m^2\right), \qquad \sum_{m=1}^{M} p_m = 1 \tag{2}$$

The pdf of the spectral magnitude of noise is modeled by a mixture of Gaussian as:

$$f(n) = \sum_{\kappa=1}^{K} p_{\kappa} G\left(n; \mu_{\kappa}, \sigma_{\kappa}^2\right), \qquad \sum_{\kappa=1}^{K} p_{\kappa} = 1 \tag{3}$$

where, M is the total number of mixture components, p_m, μ_m and σ_m are the prior probability, mean and standard deviation of the mth Gaussian speech mixture, while p_{κ}, μ_{κ} and σ_{κ} are the prior probability, mean and standard deviation of the κth Gaussian noise mixture. The descriptive statistics of the Gaussian mixture i.e p_m, μ_m, σ_m, p_{κ}, μ_{κ} and σ_{κ} are computed by the EM algorithm. Means are initialized uniformly over the interval of each spectral band magnitude, while weights are set to equal values and variance is lower-bounded to avoid picking narrow spectral peaks. Subsequently we proceed in deriving the MMSE estimation of the underlying spectral coefficients $\{s\}$ as $S_{\mathrm{MMSE}}=E\{s|x\}=\int s f(s|x)ds$. The pdf of $\{s\}$ given the observation $\{x\}$ is derived by the Bayesian formula $f(s|x)=f(x|s)f(s)/f(x)$. Combining $f(s|x)$ and S_{MMSE} results in:

$$S_{\mathrm{MMSE}} = \frac{\int s f(x|s) f(s)ds}{\int f(x|s) f(s)ds} \tag{4}$$

Substituting Eq. 2 and Eq. 3 into Eq. 4 and by carrying out some simple algebra, we derive the underlying spectral magnitude in terms of an integral which is expressed in closed form through parabolic cylinder functions. (See Appendix for details in the definition and evaluation of the integrals I_1, I_2). Based on the Gaussian assumption for the spectral magnitude pdf of noise the MMSE estimation of the underlying clean spectral magnitude is

$$S_{MMSE} = \frac{\sum\limits_{\kappa=1}^{K} \sum\limits_{m=1}^{M} \frac{p_\kappa}{\sigma_\kappa} \frac{p_m}{\sigma_m} I_2(b_{m,\kappa}, c_{m,\kappa}, d_{m,\kappa})}{\sum\limits_{\kappa=1}^{K} \sum\limits_{m=1}^{M} \frac{p_\kappa}{\sigma_\kappa} \frac{p_m}{\sigma_m} I_1(b_{m,\kappa}, c_{m,\kappa}, d_{m,\kappa})}. \tag{5}$$

Based on the fact that the information of the speech signal is encoded in the frequency domain and that human hearing is relatively insensitive to phase information, we focus on the short-time amplitude of the speech signal leaving the noisy phase unprocessed. After the enhancement procedure has been applied, noisy phase is added back and the time-domain signal is subsequently reconstructed using inverse FFT and the weighted overlap and add method.

3   Simulation and Results

We performed speech enhancement experiments using real factory noise taken from the NOISEX-92 database as well as aircraft noise. Each noise type was added to 10 clean speech files of 5 sec. mean duration so that the corrupted waveform ranges from   10 to 10 SNRdB. The number of Gaussian mixtures is set to nine for noise and six for speech as the objective measures indicated marginal gain by augmenting the number of mixtures. The SNR and the IS measures of the enhancement obtained by our technique are shown in Figure 1a and Figure 1b respectively. The IS distortion measure is based on the spectral distance between AR coefficient sets of the clean and enhanced speech waveforms over synchronous frames of 15ms duration and is heavily influenced due to mismatch in formant locations. As indicated in Figures 1a, 1b, our method consistently effected a strong enhancement over all SNRs while the low energy parts of the spectrum are preserved even at 0 dB SNR. We attribute this fact to the *a-priori* modelling of clean spectral bands and to the mixture modelling of noise that permits a variable weighting for the generalized magnitude of noise for each spectral band and each frame. Parallel listening tests are well correlated with the objective measures and indicate that periodic components are strongly suppressed.

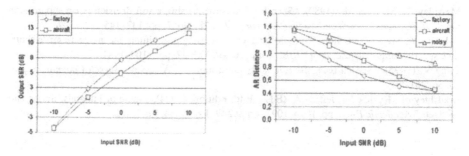

Fig. 1. a) SNR measurements, **b)** Itakura-Saito AR-distance measurements. Noise is Factory noise (NOISEX-92) and of an approaching DC-3 aircraft noise.

4 Conclusions

The application of SNR and Itakura-Saito (IS) measures confirmed the benefit of modeling clean spectral bands and the spectral bands of noise with a mixture of Gaussians. The key idea of independent modeling of the multimodal, heavy tail pdf of the magnitude of spectral bands with a mixture of Gaussians combined with MMSE formulation, can supply an efficient solution to a series of spectral estimation problems. We demonstrated the benefit of this enhancement technique at very low SNRs with true, slowly and quickly varying noise types. We suggest that the incorporation of the long term pdf of each band as a-priori information leads to estimators adapted to the spectral characteristics and noise variance of each band leading to better treatment of low energy time-frequency regions. Future work focuses on the incorporation of different techniques for the adaptive estimation of the variance of noise and the adaptive estimation of the descriptive statistics of the Gaussian mixture of noise as well as combining soft decision rules for estimating speech presence uncertainty.

Appendix

$$I_\nu = \int_0^{+\infty} s^{\nu-1} \exp\left(-b_m s^2 - c_m s - d_m\right) ds =$$

$$= \exp(-d_m)(2b_m)^{-\frac{\nu}{2}} \Gamma(\nu) \exp\left(\frac{c_m^2}{8b_m}\right) D_{-\nu}\left(\frac{c_m}{\sqrt{2b_m}}\right)$$

$$D_{\nu+1} - z D_\nu(z) + \nu D_{\nu-1}(z) = 0, \text{ (Eq. 3.462, [4])}$$

$$D_{-1}(z) = \exp\left(\frac{z^2}{4}\right)\sqrt{\frac{\pi}{2}}\left\{1 - erf\left(\frac{z}{\sqrt{2}}\right)\right\} D_{-2}(z) =$$

$$= \exp\left(\frac{z^2}{4}\right)\sqrt{\frac{\pi}{2}}\left\{\sqrt{\frac{\pi}{2}}\exp\left(\frac{z^2}{4}\right) - z\left[1 - erf\left(\frac{z}{\sqrt{2}}\right)\right]\right\}$$

$$b_{m,\kappa} = \frac{1}{2}\left(\frac{1}{\sigma_m^2} + \frac{1}{\sigma_\kappa^2}\right), \quad c_{m,\kappa} = -\left(\frac{\mu_m}{\sigma_m} + \frac{x-\mu_\kappa}{\sigma^2\kappa}\right), \quad d_{m,\kappa} = \frac{1}{2}\left(\frac{(x-\mu_\kappa)^2}{\sigma_\kappa^2} + \frac{\mu_m^2}{\sigma_m^2}\right)$$

References

1. McAulay R., Malpass M., (1980), "Speech enhancement using a soft decision noise suppression filter," *IEEE Trans. Speech and Audio Processing*, Vol. 28, No. 2, pp. 137–145.
2. Ephraim Y., Malah D., (1984), "Speech Enhancement using a minimum mean-square error short-time spectral amplitude estimator," *IEEE Trans. ASSP*, Vol. 32, pp. 1109–1121.
3. Gong Y., (1995), "Speech recognition in noisy environments: A survey," *Speech Communication*, 16, pp. 261–291.
4. Gradshteyn I., Ryzhik M., Jeffrey A. (Eds.), Fifth edition, (1994), "Table of Integrals, Series and Products," *Academic Press*, pp. 1094–1095, Eq. 9.247, Eq. 9.254, Eq. 3.462.

Fitting German into N-Gram Language Models

Robert Hecht, Jürgen Riedler, and Gerhard Backfried

Speech, Artificial Intelligence, and Language Laboratories
Operngasse 20B, A-1040 Vienna, Austria
E-mail: {robert,juergen,gerhard}@sail-technology.com

Abstract. We report on a series of experiments addressing the fact that German is less suited than English for word-based n-gram language models. Several systems were trained at different vocabulary sizes using various sets of lexical units. They were evaluated against a newly created corpus of German and Austrian broadcast news.

1 Introduction

The performance of an ASR system is to a large extent determined by how well the language model and vocabulary fit the speech to be recognized. The recognition lexicon should contain most of the words likely to appear, i.e. a minimum out-of-vocabulary (OOV) rate should be achieved, as low lexical coverage leads to high word error rates (WER). State-of-the-art ASR systems typically utilize full form word lexica and language models (LM). However, languages like German exhibit a large variety of distinct lexical forms. Thus, a morphological decomposition of orthographic words could improve OOV rates trading-off with larger WER due to neglection of coarticulatory effects regarding pronunciation and shorter span of language model contexts.

Amongst the main mechanisms for creating new words in German are such diverse elements as inflection, derivation, and compounding. Inflections and derivations are typically formed with a limited number of short affixes. Compounding is a very productive process in which the tendency to convey information in a compressed form leads to accumulation of more and more components [1]. New words are formed spontaneously and frequently occasionalisms emerge which will not be seen in any texts used to train language models. German orthography requires their constituents to be written as one word, thus resulting in a potentially unlimited set of compounds.

Remedies for strongly inflecting and compounding languages roughly divide into two branches: morphology-based [2,3] and data-driven [4] compound word splitting, both often accompanied by grammar models other than simple n-grams (e.g. class-based or long-distance models).

In the broadcast news domain, [2] focussed on identifying and processing the statistically most relevant sources of lexical variety. A set of about 450 decomposition rules, derived using statistics from a large text corpus together with partial inflection stripping reduced OOV rates from 4.5 % to 2.9 %.

The study described in [3] is based on the Verbmobil database consisting of over 400 human-to-human dialogues. Decomposition along phonological lines reduced vocabulary size as well as perplexity, which in turn lead to a more robust language model. In a further step, suppression of decomposition of very frequent compounds yielded lowest WERs.

P. Sojka, I. Kopeček, and K. Pala (Eds.): TSD 2002, LNAI 2448, pp. 341–346, 2002.

In [4] it is claimed that splitting of compounds according to morphological rules into linguistically meaningful sub-units does not ensure relevance of these constituents for the speech recognition task (in this case for German parliamentary speeches). Inspired from statistically-based methods of word identification in Asian languages, where orthographic convention does not dictate word boundaries, a data-driven approach to word splitting was examined. Splitting junctures within words were determined by counting the words in the corpus that start and end with the letter sequence under consideration. A 35 % reduction in OOV rates was achieved. However, the recombined models trail the baseline system in performance.

2 Corpora

2.1 Acoustic Model

Our training (test) set consists of 175 (9) TV news broadcasts from six German and one Austrian channel, recorded between November 1999 and March 2000. They comprise 60:54 (4:22) hours of raw data and 47:42 (3:36) hours of speech. Transcription was done using the Transcriber tool [5] whose output is a textual version of the transcripts with markup for speaker turns, speaker names, genders, and non-speech events, etc.

2.2 Language Model

The language model (LM) consists of the audio transcripts (490 k words) and texts from newspapers and journals from 1994 through 1999 (300 M words). In the LM training, the audio transcripts were emphasized by a weighting factor.

The normalization performed on the LM texts included:

- Slang and dialect words were replaced by their Standard German correspondent (if it was possible to find one). Their pronunciations were kept.
- Cardinals were spelled out and split into the "smallest possible" parts, e.g. 324 was transcribed as *drei hundert vier und zwanzig*.
- Ordinals: in German, ordinals are marked by a period after the number, e.g. 324. meaning 324th. This is problematic because, due to case endings and syntactic context, German ordinals can be spelled out in six different forms, e.g. *dritter, dritte, drittes, drittem, dritten, drittens* (third). Since there is no way to find the correct ending without syntactical analysis, we chose to spell out the non-terminal parts, but to write the last component (which carries the ending) as a number followed by a period, e.g. 324. → *drei hundert vier und 20.* In the decoding dictionary, we listed all possible pronunciations for the entries 1., 2. etc.
- Words containing both numbers and letters were split, e.g. *16jähriger* → *sechzehn jähriger* (16 year-old).
- Case Normalization was applied, since nouns and nominalized words are capitalized in German.
- Abbreviations were expanded where possible.
- In 1998 the official German orthography was re-standardized. Part of our language model texts still followed the old German orthography and thus had to be converted to be consistent with the rest of the system.

3 Experiments

3.1 ASR System

A speaker-independent, large-vocabulary speech recognizer based on BBN's Rough'n'Ready suite of technologies [6,7,8] is used in our experiments. It employs continuous density Hidden Markov Models (HMM) for acoustic modeling and word-form n-grams for language modeling. The recognition process is implemented as follows: at first a cepstral analysis of the acoustic waveforms is performed to extract a feature vector for each frame of speech. These feature vectors serve as input for three decoder passes. The first (fast-match) pass uses a phonetically tied-mixture (PTM) model based on within-word triphones and a bigram language model. The second (backward) pass employs a state-clustered tied-mixture (SCTM) model depending on within-word quinphones and a trigram language model to produce a set of N-best hypotheses. Then a third, more detailed analysis using a cross-word SCTM model is used to rescore the N-best list to select the final answer.

3.2 Specifics of German

German has a number of peculiarities that make it less suited for n-gram modeling than e.g. English. Among these are:

- compound words (see Section 3.3),
- highly inflective nature: leads to bigger vocabularies and to difficulties to resolve word forms that sound similar,
- flexible word order,
- dialects: German has a large number of local varieties, making it difficult to build a system which can cope with speech from different regions.

3.3 Compound Words

German is a compounding language, capable of expressing complex concepts in a single word. A compound word consists of one terminal component which is qualified by one or several non-terminal components, e.g. in *Baumstamm* (tree trunk) the terminal component *Stamm* is qualified by the word *Baum*. The non-terminal components often end in suffixes, the most common ones being *-s*, *-es*, *-n*, and *-en*. Sometimes the non-terminal components are truncated, as in *Sachkenntnis* (expertise), where the first part is derived from the word *Sache* (matter). Compounding can be applied to several classes of words: mostly nouns, but also verbs, adjectives and adverbs.

The abundance of compound words means that for any fixed dictionary size, the OOV rate is much higher than on comparable systems in English (where typically for the BN domain and vocabularies of 65 k words this number is less than a percent). On the other hand, it is not advisable to arbitrarily inflate the dictionary to improve the coverage, because too many entries will lead to higher WER because of confusion of similar sounding (rare) words.

We used the following simple approach to decompose them into their constituents: a decomposition of a word in the corpus was considered valid if

- all constituents were in the dictionary,

- all constituents were at least four letters and four phonemes in length,
- the case of the last constituent matched the case of the compound,
- at least one combination of the pronunciations of the constituents matched a pronunciation of the compound.

The first rule was necessary to check if the fourth was fulfilled. The second rule is motivated by the fact that too short fragments lead to poor recognition results. The third rule has a grammatical background: since in German all nouns are capitalized, the rule essentially demands that if the compound is a noun, the terminal component also has to be a noun and vice versa. This is an attempt to filter out splittings which violate basic word-forming rules. The last rule was introduced to guard against parts with identical spelling but different pronunciations.

This procedure splits compound words mostly in accordance with morphological rules. However, the non-terminal components of identical spelling and pronunciation were sometimes "mixed-up", e.g. *Anfangspunkt* (starting point) was split into *anfangs Punkt*, using the word *anfangs* (initially) instead of the correct decomposition *Anfang* + suffix *-s*.

Because of their abundance, non-terminal constituents with suffix *-s* were treated separately. If a word could not be split, we checked if there was an allowed split of the form $(w_1 + s + w_2)$, where (w_1) and (w_2) were in the dictionary. If this split was successful (according to our rules), the word $(w_1 s)$ was added to the dictionary.

This procedure was able to decompose approximately 231 k of the 559 k entries of our dictionary. Figure 1 shows a reduction of OOV rates for vocabulary sizes ranging from 50 k to 300 k entries. For a 50 k-word vocabulary we obtain an improvement of almost 32 %, for 100 k words we still gain 28 %. Of course, the improvement becomes smaller with increasing vocab size, so the effect is particularly noticable when the vocabulary size is limited.

In the audio and language model training texts, all compounds were replaced by the constituents into which the above procedure had split them. The language model was retrained and the vocabulary adjusted to the newly decomposed words. Following recognition, all sequences of words that could be the result of a split compound word were recombined into one word. This procedure is somewhat simplistic, but it gave good results for vocabularies with approximately 50 k words.

We also investigated an alternative approach in which all non-terminal components of a compound word were marked. Following the recognition step, the word following a marked word was appended to it and the casing adjusted. This procedure has the advantage that it is capable of generalization: it can recognize compound words that were never seen in the training material, if all components are in the recognition lexicon.

As Figure 2 depicts, decompounding improves the recognition rate mainly at moderate vocab sizes. At 50 k words, the simple (list-based) approach gave an improvement of almost 1 %, while the approach with the marked non-terminal components leads to an improvement of 1.6 %.

4 Summary

We created a corpus of German broadcast news of a variety and size which supercedes existing material in this domain [2,9]. From this corpus several BN transcription systems were trained and evaluated at different vocabulary sizes. Various schemes of decomposition

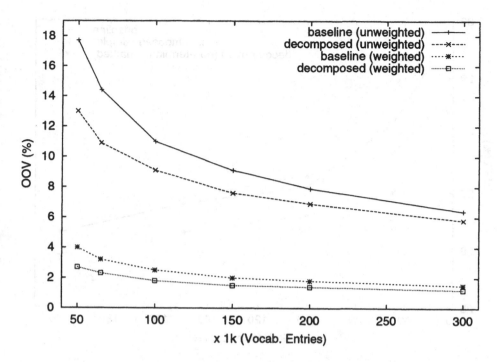

Fig. 1. OOV rates versus vocabulary size for the baseline and the decomposed system. Unweighted percentages take only unique words into account whereas the weighted numbers are calculated using total word counts.

were implemented to account for inflection and *ad hoc* formation of compound words in German. The benefit in word error rate we gained by decomposition of vocabularies of up to 65 k entries seems to be annihilated at larger vocabulary sizes (200 k). This may be due to lack of language model context and training and increased acoustic confusability. For the future we would like to examine the observed trends for even larger vocabulary sizes. We will measure the impact on run-time as the resulting models are meant to be used within the Sail Labs real-time BN indexing environment [10].

References

1. Stedje, A.: Deutsche Sprache gestern und heute. UTB für Wissenschaft, München (1999).
2. Adda-Decker, M., Adda, G., Lamel, L.: Investigating Text Normalization and Pronunciation Variants for German Broadcast Transcription. Proceedings of the 6th International Conference of Spoken Language Processing, ICSLP 2000 (Beijing, China).
3. Larson, M., Willett, D., Köhler, J., Rigoll, G.: Compound Splitting and Lexical Unit Recombination for Improved Performance of a Speech Recognition System for German Parliamentary Speeches. Proceedings of the 6th International Conference of Spoken Language Processing, ICSLP 2000 (Beijing, China).

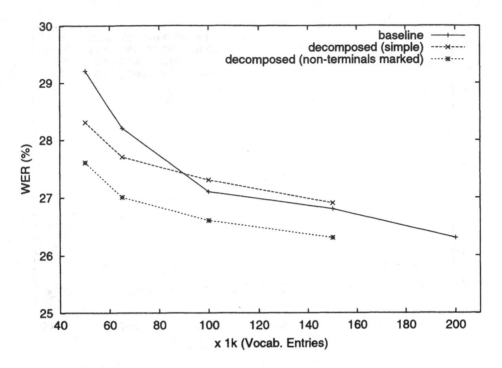

Fig. 2. WER rates for the baseline and the various decomposed systems.

4. Berton, A., P. Fetter, P., Regel-Brietzmann, P.: Compound Words in Large-Vocabulary German Speech Recognition Systems. Proceedings of the 4th International Conference of Spoken Language Processing, ICSLP 1996 (Philadelphia, Pennsylvania, USA).

5. Barras, C., Geoffrois, E., Wu, Z., M. Liberman, M.: Transcriber: Free Tool for Segmenting, Labeling and Transcribing Speech. Proceedings of the 1st International Conference on LREC (1998).

6. Kubala, F., Jin, H., Nguyen, L., Schwartz, R., Matsoukas, S.: Broadcast News Transcription. Proceedings of the IEEE International Conference on Acoustics, Speech, and Signal Processing, ICASSP 1997 (Munich, Germany).

7. Nguyen, L., Matsoukas, S., Davenport, J., Liu, D., Billa, J., Kubala, F., Makhoul, J.: Further Advances in Transcription of Broadcast News. Proceedings of the 6th European Conference on Speech Communication and Technology, EuroSpeech 1999 (Budapest, Hungary).

8. Colthurst, T., Kimball, O., Richurdson, F., Han, S., Wooters, C., Iyer, R., Gish, H.: The 2000 BBN Byblos LVCSR System. Proceedings of the 6th International Conference of Spoken Language Processing, ICSLP 2000 (Beijing, China).

9. Kemp, T., Geutner, P., Schmidt, M., Tomaz, B., Weber, M., Westphal, M., Waibel, A.: The Interactive Systems Labs View4You Video Indexing System. Proceedings of the 5th International Conference of Spoken Language Processing, ICSLP'98 (Sydney, Australia).

10. Backfried, G., Hecht, R., Loots, S., Pfannerer, N., Riedler, J., Schiefer, C.: Creating a European English Broadcast News Transcription Corpus and System. Proceedings of the 7th European Conference on Speech Communication and Technology, EuroSpeech 2001 (Aalborg, Denmark).

Audio Collections of Endangered Arctic Languages in the Russian Federation

Marina Lublinskaya[1] and Tatiana Sherstinova[2]

[1] Institute of Linguistic Research, Russian Academy of Science
Tuchkov per. 9, St. Petersburg, 199053, Russia
E-mail: lublin@ling.ras.spb.ru
[2] St. Petersburg State University
Department of Phonetics
Universitetskaya nab. 11, 199034, St. Petersburg, Russia
E-mail: tanya@ts4306.spb.edu

Abstract. In the Russian Federation 63 minority languages are mentioned in the "Red Book of the Languages of Russia". This means that they are practically dying out and it is highly important to make and preserve original recordings of these languages and to prepare their documentation. Arctic peoples of Russia are demographically small and the number of speakers using their languages is decreasing dramatically. The paper describes three projects related to two Northern Languages – Nenets and Nganasan: the Nenets Audio Dictionary, the Nganasan Audio Dictionary and the Russian-Nenets Online Multimedia Phrase-book.

1 Introduction. Maintaining Endangered Languages – The Importance of the Problem

The dramatic process of social degradation and dying out of many minority languages is a serious problem of the world community. This problem "demands an urgent solution as in 10–20 years there may be nothing left to save" [2]. In the Russian Federation there are more than 200 languages spoken by the native population, and "there is no need to prove the thesis that a significant number of languages on the territory of Russia are now under threat of total extinction" [2]. Thus in Russia 63 minority languages are mentioned in the "Red Book of the Languages of Russia" (1994), which means that they are practically dying out [10].

In order to preserve the information about these languages for the future generations and to maintain the knowledge of these languages by the young people, it is necessary "to document as much material on these languages as possible and to use this for language descriptions, grammars, compilation of dictionaries and edited collections of oral and written literature" [3]. It is very important to make and preserve original recordings of these languages, and the less the number of native speakers of some language, the more necessary it is to record and describe it as quickly as possible [7].

It is also important to develop teaching methods, in particular for younger members of certain ethnic groups, who have no sufficient knowledge of their native language and to make them aware of the value of their heritage. In those cases where language revival is impossible,

P. Sojka, I. Kopeček, and K. Pala (Eds.): TSD 2002, LNAI 2448, pp. 347–353, 2002.

it is very important for linguists and ethnologists to organize a collection of acoustic data and documents on endangered languages [3].

Arctic peoples of Russia are demographically small and the number of speakers using them is decreasing dramatically. This paper describes three projects related with two Northern Languages – Nenets and Nganasan.

2   Concise Description of Nenets and Nganasan

The Nenets are a small people living along the Arctic Ocean between the Kola Peninsula and the mouth of the river Yenisey. In spite of the huge territory, its original population counted to 35000 persons in 1989. Nenets is the native language for 77.1 % of them. Comparing to other small Northern languages of Russia the Nenets one is rather safe. In spite of its comparative safeness no general description of Nenets phonetics, prosody and grammar has been made up to present.

Nganasan is another northern population in Eurasia, inhabiting the Taymyr Peninsula in Siberia. It seems that the size of this population never exceeded 1000–1,500 persons. According to the date of the last All-Union Census (1989), the number of Nganasans was 1278 persons. The majority lives in three villages - Volochanka, Ustj-Avam and Novaya. The administrative center is the town of Dudinka. According to recent field data, only ca. 50 % of the entire population (in the younger generation – not more than 10–15 %) continues to use Nganasan [10]. It is mostly the Russian and Dolgan languages which replace the native language. Nowadays only about one hundred ethnic Nganasans continue to lead a semi-nomadic life of hunters and fishermen, preserving the native language in their everyday life as well.

Both Nenets and Nganasan languages belong (together with Enets, which is now practically extinct) to the Northern-Samoyedic subgroup of the Samoyedic Group of the Uralic language family.

The main danger to both these languages hides in Russian bilingualism of most of the native speakers. "Pure" Nenets and Nganasan speakers are mainly nomadic (reindeer herdsmen). The parents usually want their children to have better life conditions in the future, and try to send them to towns for study. In towns the national speech ability is being gradually replaced by the Russian practice. The young generation prefers to use Russian as a language of communication in most cases.

Moreover, as reported in [13], "there are obvious danger signs in both the physical and the national and cultural existence of the Nenets people. Government industrial and military officials determine which settlement areas, positions, rights and privileges are available to them. Nuclear experiments have been carried out unobstructed in Novaya Zemlya. The Norilsknikel concern alone has polluted 5 million hectares of Nenets grazing-lands and almost 1 million hectares of forests. The pollution of heavy metals has been transferred to the humans through mosses and reindeer meat. The average life expectancy of Nenets is 45–50 years, the suicide rate is unusually high. Only 41 % of Nenets are employed and usually in jobs which require low qualification". Practically, the same may be said about the Nganasans.

Both Nenets and Nganasan languages are registered in the UNESCO Red Book on Endangered Languages and in the Red Book of the Peoples of the Russian Federation [11,10].

3   How New Information Technologies May Help to Save and Popularize the Endangered Languages

Modern information techniques, especially speech databases, represent convenient tools to preserve acoustic data of different kind. Besides, they allow to combine in a single application both written information about the language and its actual audio recordings. In addition to reading a written text, at the same moment a scientist can now listen to its recording. That makes linguistic databases and similar computer systems the proper instrument for preserving and studying small and disappearing languages.

The impetuous development of the Internet allows to extend applications of speech databases. Until recently they could be accessible only in large archives or libraries. Nowadays there are many examples of representative speech databases in the Web. We consider both speech and Internet technologies to be a basis for actual maintenance of the endangered languages, as the publication of any linguistic database in the Web will allow access to its textual and audio data to all users of the Internet.

A special program has been proposed and started by the Department of Phonetics of St. Petersburg State University, which aim at the creation of Phonetic Funds and Multimedia Dictionaries for the minority languages of Russia. The Department of Phonetics has always been characterized by its interest in minority languages of Russia: here not only the phonetics of the languages of the peoples of the North and the Far East are studied, but earlier in the last century also the necessary recommendations for creating written languages were given [3].

In addition, there are several joint projects of the Department of Phonetics of St. Petersburg State University, the Institute of Linguistic Research of the Russian Academy of Science, and the Department of Linguistics of Groningen University, The Netherlands: "Writing and Teaching of Samoyedic" (a phonetic project, related to the peoples and languages of Russian North) and "Nenets Speech Varieties on the Internet" (a Web-publication of the Russian-Nenets Phrasebook).

First of all, it was considered important to make an inventory of the existing record-ings, which are currently preserved in collections of state archives. The work started with making a digital catalogue for collections of the Sound Archive of the Insti-tute for Russian Literature of the Russian Academy of Sciences – the Pushkinsky Dom, which is the richest audio collection of speech and folklore of the peoples of the Russian Federation. The finished part of this catalogue is available in the Web: http://www.speech.nw.ru/phonetics/homepage.html. Fragments of the spoken language, folksongs and fairy tales preserved in the Phonogrammarchive may also be found on this site. As the quality of the old archival recordings usually is far from perfect, many of the archival collections deserve serious reconstruction, decoding and digitization.

In order to make new recordings of the minority languages it is necessary to organize scientific expeditions, which imply field recordings with portable good sound recording equipment. The other way is to invite native speakers of the language to the main research centers in St. Petersburg or elsewhere and to make professional recordings using studio facilities. Fieldwork expeditions and studio recordings allowed us to collect substantial sound data in Nenets and Nganasan.

4   The Nenets Audio Dictionary

The Nenets Audio Dictionary was created in the St. Petersburg Institute of Linguistic Research of the Russian Academy of Science in cooperation with the Department of Phonetics of St. Petersburg State University. Its main aim is to preserve the specialties of Nenets phonetics.

The structure of the Audio Dictionary is based on the Nenets-Russian Dictionary composed by N.M.Tereshchenko, from which it borrows the completeness of translation, text examples, linguistic remarks and comments. It was elaborated in the form of the database created by means of DBMS Access 97/2000 utilities. Audio data are stored in the database in raw-format, which allows their processing and analysis in Windows-compatible applications. The number of words in the core database is limited to 4000 (as presented in the School Nenets Dictionary for Tundra Nenets dialect composed by N. M. Tereshchenko). Variants of pronunciation are given for word likewise in the Yurak-Samojedisches Worterbuch, composed by T. Lehtisalo [5]. Along with the recording of standard word pronunciation, another variants of pronunciation in subdialects of Nenets Tundra dialect may be presented. Supplementary phonetic information concerns word accent and number of syllables.

Native Nenets speakers from different region – Kanin tundra, Bolshaya Zemlya, Yamal Peninsula and Taymyr – recorded all the words and phrase examples. At present dictionary articles consist of the following parts (database forms): "Concise article form", "Complete article form", "Phonetic form", "Russian meanings of the word", and "Phrase and phraseo-logical examples in Nenets". The user may choose one of the main four forms to work with the Dictionary. They are mutually connected and allow the data search. A detailed description of the Nenets Audio Dictionary may be found in [7].

The most interesting part of the Dictionary is the "Phonetic form", which consists of: sound button for standard pronunciation of the word; speaker's name; transcription of the word (in present version this field is left to be filled in by the user himself, using Nenets transcription symbols); number of syllables; accent detachment of syllable (meaning 0/1 for every syllable); word accent information; sound buttons for another variants of pronunciation and corresponding speaker names. The variants of pronunciation vary in different regions. Because of that the Dictionary may be completed by other speakers, as well as by new words, new phrase examples, and texts of different types. The Audio Dictionary may be used to represent and study all aspects of Nenets phonetics and grammar.

5   The Nganasan Audio Dictionary

The necessity to create the Nganasan Audio Dictionary was determined by the fact that at present no representative collections of Nganasan audio data exist (neither in Russian institutes nor libraries or abroad). The oral tradition plays a central role in the Nganasan culture, because the first alphabet for the language was proposed just in the last ten years. Now only few aged persons speak Nganasan really perfectly. Young teachers with native knowledge of Nganasan live far from the larger educational centers in St. Petersburg or Moscow. Even at the Taymyr Regional Center for Advanced Education there are no Nganasan speaking persons younger than forty.

It is only in the last years that certain steps were made to support the Nganasan language and culture: several textbooks for children and adults as well as folklore materials have been published, mostly in Dudinka. The less becomes the number of qualified native speakers of Nganasan, the more important and urgent becomes the recording and documentation of this language – before the native competence diminishes and ultimately disappears.

The Nganasan Audio Dictionary should fill a gap in accessible audible data on this language. The text basis for the dictionary is the Nganasan-Russian dictionary, which is now in print. It was compiled by two speakers of Nganasan – Nadezhda Kosterkina and Alexander Momde, and edited by T. Zhdanova and V.Gusev. The records were made by several Nganasan speakers, including Nadezhda Kosterkina herself and the wife of Alexander Momde – Anna. Alexander himself couldn't articulate when the recordings were made because of his serious disease; he died in the winter of 2000.

The speech corpus for Nganasan Audio Dictionary consists of recordings of the Nganasan Dictionary made by two Nganasan speakers. The whole number of words is about 4000. Many of them are accompanied by phrase examples or by idiomatic expressions.

The supporting database proposes the following parameters of description: Nganasan word, grammatical characteristics of the word, word inflections, Russian translation, Nganasan phrase examples and Nganasan idiomatic expressions with their translations into Russian, sound file names for each Nganasan word or phrase. Working with the Dictionary, the user has the possibility to listen to each Nganasan word/phrase by means of simple clicking on the corresponding button.

6 The Nenets Online Multimedia Phrase-Book

The Nenets Multimedia Phrase-book was prepared for the Web-publication within the framework of a joint project "Writing and teaching Samoyedic" by the Research Group on Phonetics and Ethnolinguistics, University of Groningen, The Netherland, and the Department of Phonetics of St. Petersburg State University, Russia.

The Russian-Nenets phrase-book embraces 21 general topics. These topics and the majority of Russian expressions were borrowed from the Nganasan-Russian phrase-book [1]. This approach is justified by the fact that the Nenets and Nganasan people being geographical neighbors have much in common. The phrase-book was recorded by three native Nenets speakers, who represent three main dialects of the Nenets language: central (Bolshezemelsky), eastern (Yamalsky), and western (Kaninsky). All of them were born in the tundra, and from their childhood they took part in nomadic reindeer grazing. Now they are students of St. Petersburg State Pedagogical University named after A.A.Herzen, and perfectly speak Russian. It should be mentioned here that now it is impossible to find a Nenets speaker, younger than 70 years old, who does not know Russian rather well. The speakers were asked to make translations of each phrase of the phrase-book and then to record the whole phrase-book. Creating the database we tried to preserve the original spelling made by the speakers, though frequently one and the same word might be spelt in different ways, because there is not yet any normative spelling for Nenets. Moreover, Nenets is mostly used as a spoken language. In the following two phrases one and the same underlined word "hour" is spelt in two quite different ways:

Сян часна маня ядабтагунь'? . . . . *When (at what hour) we shall meet?*

Сидя сяс ваерамад обт' тэвгунь. · *Let's meet in two hours.*

The speakers could not translate into Nenets some phrases, describing atypical phenomena for the language. Thus, no speaker could translate "*At 5:15 p.m., Moscow time*". It turned out that the speakers from Yamal better know the deer-raising, and identify local birds and animals. However, it was interesting to find that in the speech of these young girls the animals are called by the ancient allegorical names. For example, the following expressions have the meaning "*wolf*":

ӈэсында хэвхана пивна [ядерта] · *wolf* (Yamalsky dialect)

пиня'мэна эсыд хэвхана · *wolf* (Kaninsky dialect)

яхӑнанда тёняны · *wolf* (Bolshezemelsky dialect)

The two first phrases may be word-by-word translated as "*who [goes] around the settlement*". The speaker of Bolshezemelsky subdialect called the wolf "*the neighbor of our land*". The bears are called "*spring earth inhabitant*", the eagles are named "*big birds*":

нара ям' мядота · *bear* (Yamalsky dialect)

аркаюм' тиртя · *eagle* (Kaninsky dialect).

The Nenets borrowed many words from Russian. For example, they did not have welcome greetings and borrowed them from Russian, as well as a number of "polite" expressions (e.g., see topics "Agreement/Disagreement", "Farewell", "Surprise", "Gratitude", "Approval").

The presented topics describes both the traditional Nenets life and housekeeping (e.g., topics "Family. Family relations. Age", "Hunting. Fishing. Deer-raising", "Flora and Fauna") and the new phenomena for the tundra life ("Shop", "Post. Telegraph. Telephone").

The audio phrase-book was created in the form of a speech database, and then this database was adapted to the Internet and published on the site: http://www.speech.nw.ru/Nenets/.

This phrase-book represents a good manual to get acquainted with the Nenets language. Our further steps will be the translation of the phrase-book into English so that it may become accessible to more scientists and other users of the Web.

7   Conclusion

In the process of development of audio collections for endangered languages we have faced a number of challenges, which complicate the process of data collection and processing. First, there is no accepted norm both in pronunciation and spelling in most of the minority languages. Because of that it is difficult to select a unique spelling. Without uniform spelling it is impossible to carry out an automatic search for words in the databases. The other problem is a large difference between generations of the minority people. The younger the speaker – the less is his (her) native language practice. Besides, there are some technical problems (e.g., national fonts representations for the Internet), which deserves further development and standardization.

The developments presented in the paper may be considered as a model for the creation of sound collections and speech databases for other minority languages of the Russian Federation.

Acknowledgments

The project "Nenets Audio Dictionary" and expeditions to Taymyr in 1996 and 2000 were supported by Russian Humanitarian Scientific Fund. The development of the Nganasan Audio Dictionary is supported by the Endangered Language Fund (project "Collection of Audio Material in The Nganasan Language"). The creation of the Nenets online Multimedia Phrase-book is supported by Groningen University, the Netherlands within the framework of the project "Writing and teaching Samoyedic" – "Nenets Speech Varieties on the Internet" and the project "Voices of Tundra and Taiga" of the Netherlands Organization of Scientific Research (NWO).

References

1. Aaron, T., Momde, A.: Nganasan-Russian phrase-book. Dudinka (1985).
2. Berkov, V.P.: How to save the disappearing languages of Russia? In: Archives of the Languages of Russia. Groningen-St. Petersburg (1996) 39–44.
3. Bondarko, L.V., de Graaf, T.: Archives of the Languages of Russia. Introduction. Groningen-St. Petersburg (1996) 5–12.
4. Janhunen, J., Salminen, T.: UNESCO Red Book on Endangered Languages: Northeast Asia
   http://www.helsinki.fi/~tasalmin/nasia_report.html#TNenets.
5. Lehtisalo, T.: Jurak-Samojedisches Worterbuch. Helsinki (1956).
6. Lublinskaya, M.D.: Audio dictionary as a mean for saving and studying endangered languages. In: The Proc. of the IX-th International Finno-Ugric Congress in Tartu. Materials of the Congressus Nonus Internationalis Finno-Ugrisrarum. 7–13.8.2000. Tartu (2000) 344–345.
7. Lublinskaya, M.D., Sherstinova, T.Y., Kuznetsova, E.Y.: Multimedia Dictionary of Nenets. In: Proceedings of International Workshop on Computational Lexicography and Audio Dictionaries "COMLEX 2000", September 22–23, 2000, Patras, Greece (2000) 105–107.
8. Nenets-Russian Dictionary: Moscow. "Sovetskaja Encyclopedia" (1965).
9. Nenets-Russian, Russian-Nenets Dictionary: Leningrad, "Prosveshchenije" (1982).
10. "Red Book of the Languages of Russia": Moscow, "Academia" (1994).
11. "Red Book of the Peoples of the Russian Empire":
    http://www.eki.ee/books/redbook/nenets.shtml.
12. Skrelin, P., Sherstinova, T.: Models of Russian Text / Speech Interactive Databases for Supporting of Scientific, Practical and Cultural Researches. In: Proceedings of II International Scientific Conference LREC 2000 (Language Resources and Evaluation), Athens (2000) 185–189.
13. Vaba, L., Viikberg, J.: The Endangered Uralic Peoples. Short Reference Guide. Editor Andres Heinapuu. http://www.suri.ee/eup/nenets.html.

Part III

Dialogue

"**Dialogue**: a discussion between two or more people or groups,
especially one directed towards exploration of a particular subject
or resolution of a problem: *interfaith dialogue*."

NODE (New, Oxford Dictionary of English), Oxford, OUP, 1998, page 509.

Prosodic Classification of Offtalk: First Experiments

Anton Batliner, Viktor Zeißler, Elmar Nöth, and Heinrich Niemann

Lehrstuhl für Mustererkennung, Universität Erlangen-Nürnberg, Martensstr. 3
91058 Erlangen, Germany
E-mail: batliner@informatik.uni-erlangen.de
http://www5.informatik.uni-erlangen.de

Abstract. SmartKom is a multi-modal dialogue system which combines speech with gesture and facial expression. In this paper, we want to deal with one of those phenomena which can be observed in such elaborated systems that we want to call 'offtalk', i.e., speech that is not directed to the system (speaking to oneself, speaking aside). We report the classification results of first experiments which use a large prosodic feature vector in combination with part-of-speech information.

1 Introduction

1.1 The SmartKom System

SmartKom is a multi-modal dialogue system which combines speech with gesture and facial expression. The speech data investigated in this paper are obtained in large-scaled Wizard-of-Oz-experiments [7] within the SmartKom public scenario: in a multi-modal communication telephone booth, the users can get information on specific points of interest, as, e.g., hotels, restaurants, cinemas. The user delegates a task, for instance, finding a film, a cinema, and reserving the tickets, to a virtual agent which is visible on the graphical display. This agent is called 'Smartakus' or 'Aladdin'. The user gets the necessary information via synthesized speech produced by the agent, and on the graphical display, via presentations of lists of hotels, restaurants, cinemas, etc., and maps of the inner city, etc. The dialogue between the system and the user is recorded with several microphones and digital cameras. Subsequently, several annotations are carried out. The recorded speech represents thus a special variety of non-prompted, spontaneous speech typical for man-machine-communication in general and for such a multi-modal setting in particular. More details on the system can be found in [13], more details on the recordings and annotations in [10,11].

1.2 Offtalk

The more elaborate an automatic dialogue system is, the less restricted is the behaviour of the users. In the early days, the users were confined to a very restricted vocabulary (prompted numbers etc.). In conversations with more elaborate automatic!dialogue systems like SmartKom, users behave more natural; thus, phenomena can be observed and have to be coped with that could not be observed in communications with very simple dialogue systems.

P. Sojka, I. Kopeček, and K. Pala (Eds.): TSD 2002, LNAI 2448, pp. 357–364, 2002.

In this paper, we want to deal with one of these phenomena that we call 'offtalk'. Offtalk is defined in [10] as comprising 'every utterance that is not directed to the system as a question, a feedback utterance or as an instruction'. This comprises reading aloud from the display. Other terms are 'speaking to oneself', 'speaking aside', 'thinking aloud'. In most cases, the system should not react to these utterances, or it should process them in a special way, for instance, on a meta level, as remarks about the (mal-) functioning of the system, and not on an object level, as communication with the system.

In the annotation, two different types of offtalk are labelled: read offtalk (ROT) and other offtalk (OOT); every other word is via default annotated with the label NOT as 'no offtalk'. If the user reads aloud words presented on the display, this is labelled as ROT; it was decided not to tell apart all other types of offtalk, e.g., speaking aside to another person or speaking to oneself, because these decisions are often not easy to make. Moreover, such a detailed labelling system would end up with a small number of tokens for each sub-type which anyhow had to be mapped onto higher classes in order to process them automatically. Offtalk as a special dialogue act has not yet been the object of much investigation [1,6] most likely because it could not be observed in human-human communication. (In a normal human-human dialogue setting, offtalk might really be rather self-contradictory, because of the "Impossibility of Not Communicating" [14]. We can, however, easily imagine the use of offtalk if someone is speaking in a low voice not *to* but *about* a third person present who is very hard of hearing.)

In the following example, a user wants to reserve two tickets for the cinema; first, the German original is presented, then an English translation. In the German example, <P> denotes pauses, +/ and /+, respectively, beginning and end of a repair, and <hm> a filled pause. Offtalk is labelled adjacent to the pertinent word, without blanks. Most of the annotated phenomena are, however, filtered out of the German example; the English translation contains only the wording; here, ROT is given in capitals, and OOT boldface and recte.

system: *in diesem Kino können Sie nur telefonisch reservieren*
user: *kannst du mich dahin verbinden <P> Aladdin*
system: *diese Funktion ist momentan leider nicht verfügbar <P> kann ich Ihnen auch anders helfen*
user: *<hm> <P> das<OOT> is'<OOT> doof<OOT> <hm> <P> <A> geh doch noch mal zurück <P> Aladdin <P> zurückgehen*
system: *einen Augenblick bitte*
user: *ja <P> +/wie sieht d=/+ wie sieht das aus mit dem Kino Schloß <P> dreiundzwanzig fünfundvierzig Armageddon <P> zwei Karten Aladdin <P> hoffentlich<OOT> nich'<OOT> wieder<OOT> telefonisch<OOT> doch<OOT>*
system: *in diesem Kino können Sie nur telefonisch reservieren*
user: *<hm> das<OOT> is'<OOT> natürlich<OOT> auch<OOT> doof<OOT> <P> gibt es noch eine andere Möglichkeit <P> sicher<OOT> nicht<OOT> <P> zurück*
system: *Reservierungen können nur im Kino StudioEuropa durchgeführt werden*

user: *aha na dann <P> gib mir doch mal das <P> Kino Europa <P> Kino Europa ah das sieht doch schon gut aus gut dann nehmen wir mal <P> <hm> <P> AmericanHistoryX zwoundzwanzig fünfundvierzig <P> aha<OOT> Reservierung<ROT> bestätigen<ROT> da<OOT> kommen<OOT> wir<OOT> doch<OOT> schon<OOT> der<OOT> Sache<OOT> näher<OOT>*

system: *For this cinema, only reservation by phone is possible.*

user: *Can you connect me, Aladdin?*

system: *I'm afraid, at the moment, this is not possible.*

user: **That's bad** *– well – please go back, Aladdin – go back!*

system: *One moment please!*

user: *Well, what about, what about the Castle Cinema, 10.45 pm, Armageddon – two tickets, Aladdin –* **I hope it's not again reservation by phone.**

system: *For this cinema, only reservation by phone is available.*

user: **Again, that's bad.** *Is there another possibility?* **I guess not!** *Go back!*

system: *Reservations are only possible for the Studio Europe.*

user: *Well, okay, Studio Europe, Studio Europe, that's fine, well, then let's take – uh – AmericanHistory, 10.45 pm,* **okay, CONFIRM RESERVATION, now we are coming to the point.**

At least in this specific scenario, ROT is fairly easy to annotate: the labeller knows what is given on the display, and knows the dialogue history. OOT, however, as a sort of wast-paper-basket category for all other types of offtalk, is more problematic; for a discussion we want to refer to [11]. Note, however, that the labellers listen to the dialogues while annotating; thus, they can use acoustic information, e.g., whether some words are spoken in a very low voice or not. This is of course not possible if only the transliteration is available.

2   Material and Features Used

The material used for the classification task consists of 81 dialogues, 1172 turns, 10775 words, and 132 minutes of speech. 2.6 % of the words were labelled as ROT, and 4.9 % as OOT. Note that the recording is, at the moment, not finished yet; thus, this material represents only a part of the data that will eventually be available.

It is still an open question which prosodic features are relevant for different classification problems, and how the different features are interrelated. We try therefore to be as exhaustive as possible, and we use a highly redundant feature set leaving it to the statistical classifier to find out the relevant features and the optimal weighting of them. For the computation of the prosodic features, a fixed reference point has to be chosen. We decided in favor of the end of a word because the word is a well-defined unit in word recognition, and because this point can be more easily defined than, for example, the middle of the syllable nucleus in word accent position. Many relevant prosodic features are extracted from different context windows with the size of two words before, that is, contexts 2 and 1, and two words after, i.e. contexts 1 and 2 in Table 1, around the final syllable of a word or a word hypothesis, namely context 0 in Table 1; by that, we use so to speak a 'prosodic 5-gram'. A full account of the strategy for the feature selection is beyond the scope of this paper; details and further references are given in [2]. Table 1 shows the 95 prosodic features used and their context. The mean values DurTauLoc, EnTauLoc, and F0MeanGlob are computed for a window of 15 words (or less, if the utterance is shorter); thus they are identical for each word in the context of five words, and only context 0 is necessary. Note that these features do not necessarily represent *the* optimal feature set; this could only be obtained by reducing a much larger set to those features which prove to be relevant for the actual task, but in our experience, the effort needed to find the optimal set normally does not pay off in terms of classification performance [3,4]. The abbreviations can be explained as follows:

duration features 'Dur': absolute (Abs) and normalized (Norm); the normalization is described in [2]; the global value DurTauLoc is used to scale the mean duration values, absolute duration divided by number of syllables AbsSyl represents another sort of normalization;

energy features 'En': regression coefficient (RegCoeff) with its mean square error (MseReg); mean (Mean), maximum (Max) with its position on the time axis (MaxPos), absolute (Abs) and normalized (Norm) values; the normalization is described in [2]; the global value EnTauLoc is used to scale the mean energy values, absolute energy divided by number of syllables AbsSyl represents another sort of normalization;

F0 features 'F0': regression coefficient (RegCoeff) with its mean square error (MseReg); mean (Mean), maximum (Max), minimum (Min), onset (On), and offset (Off) values as well as the position of Max (MaxPos), Min (MinPos), On (OnPos), and Off (OffPos) on the time axis; all F0 features are logarithmized and normalized as to the mean value F0MeanGlob;

length of pauses 'Pause': silent pause before (Pause-before) and after (Pause-after), and filled pause before (PauseFill-before) and after (PauseFill-after).

A Part of Speech (PoS) flag is assigned to each word in the lexicon, cf. [5]. Six cover classes are used: AUX (auxiliaries), PAJ (particles, articles, and interjections), VERB (verbs), APN (adjectives and participles, not inflected), API (adjectives and participles, inflected), and NOUN (nouns, proper nouns). For the context of +/- two words, this sums up to 6×5, i.e., 30 PoS features, cf. the last line in Table 1.

Table 1. Ninety-five prosodic and 30 PoS features and their context.

features	context size				
	−2	−1	0	1	2
DurTauLoc; EnTauLoc; F0MeanGlob			•		
Dur: Norm,Abs,AbsSyl		•	•	•	
En: RegCoeff,MseReg,Norm,Abs,Mean,Max,MaxPos		•	•	•	
F0: RegCoeff,MseReg,Mean,Max,MaxPos,Min,MinPos		•	•	•	
Pause-before, PauseFill-before; F0: Off,Offpos		•	•		
Pause-after, PauseFill-after; F0: On,Onpos			•	•	
Dur: Norm,Abs,AbsSyl	•			•	
En: RegCoeff,MseReg,Norm,Abs,Mean	•			•	
F0: RegCoeff,MseReg	•			•	
F0: RegCoeff,MseReg; En: RegCoeff,MseReg; Dur: Norm		•			
API,APN,AUX,NOUN,PAJ,VERB	•	•	•	•	•

Table 2. Recognition rates in percent for different constellations; leave-one-out, offtalk vs. no-offtalk; best results are emphasized.

constellation	predictors	offtalk	no-offtalk	CL	RR
	# of tokens	806	9969	10775	
5-gram	95 pros.	67.6	77.8	72.7	77.1
raw feat. values	95 pros./30 PoS	67.7	79.7	**73.7**	**78.8**
5-gram, only PoS	30 PoS	50.6	72.4	61.5	70.8
uni-gram	28 pros. 0	68.4	73.4	70.9	73.0
raw feat. values	28 pros. 0/6 PoS 0	68.6	74.5	71.6	74.0
uni-gram, only PoS	6 PoS	40.9	71.4	56.2	69.1
5-gram, PCs	24 pros. PC	69.2	75.2	72.2	74.8
uni-gram, PCs	9 pros. PC 0	66.0	71.4	68.7	71.0

3   Classification

We computed a Linear Discriminant classification: a linear combination of the independent variables (the predictors) is formed; a case is classified, based on its discriminant score, in the group for which the posterior probability is largest [8]. We simply took an a priori probability of 0.5 for the two classes and did not try to optimize, for instance, performance for the marked classes. For classification, we used the jackknife (leave-one-out) method. The computation of the features was done with the spoken word chain ('cheating'). Tables 2 and 3 show the recognition rates for the two-class problem offtalk vs. no-offtalk and for the three-class problem ROT, OOT, and NOT, resp. Besides recall for each class, the *CL*ass-wise computed mean classification rate (mean of all classes) CL and the overall classification (*R*ecognition) *R*ate RR, i.e., all correctly classified cases, are given in percent. We display results for the 95 prosodic features with and without the 30 PoS features, and for the 30 PoS features alone – as a sort of 5-gram modelling a context of 2 words to the left and two words to the right, together with the pertaining word 0. Then, the same combinations are given for a sort of uni-gram modelling only the pertaining word 0. For the last two lines in Tables 2 and 3, we first computed a principal component analysis for the 5-gram- and for the uni-gram constellation, and used the resulting principal components PC with an eigenvalue > 1.0 as predictors in a subsequent classification.

4   Interpretation

Best classification results could be obtained by using both all 95 prosodic features and all 30 PoS features together, both for the two-class problem (CL: 73.7%, RR: 78.8%) and for the three-class problem (CL: 70.5%, RR: 72.6%). These results are emphasized in Tables 2 and 3. Most information is of course encoded in the features of the pertinent word 0; thus, classifications which use only these 28 prosodic and 6 PoS features are of course worse, but not to a large extent: for the two-class problem, CL is 71.6%, RR 74.0%; for the three-class problem, CL is 65.9%, RR 62.0%. If we use PCs as predictors, again, classification performance goes down, but not drastically. This corroborates our results obtained for the

Table 3. Recognition rates in percent for different constellations; leave-one-out, ROT vs. OOT vs. NOT; best results are emphasized.

constellation	predictors	ROT	OOT	NOT	CL	RR
	# of tokens	277	529	9969	10775	
5-gram	95 pros.	54.9	65.2	71.5	63.9	70.8
raw feat. values	95 pros./30 PoS	71.5	67.1	73.0	**70.5**	**72.6**
5-gram, only PoS	30 PoS	73.3	52.9	54.7	60.3	55.1
uni-gram	28 pros. 0	53.1	67.7	64.0	61.6	63.9
raw feat. values	28 pros. 0/6 PoS 0	69.0	67.1	61.5	65.9	62.0
uni-gram, only PoS	6 PoS	80.1	64.7	18.2	54.3	22.1
5-gram, PCs	24 pros. PC	49.5	67.7	65.3	60.8	65.0
uni-gram, PCs	9 pros. PC 0	45.8	62.6	60.0	56.1	59.8

classification of boundaries and accents, that more predictors – ceteris paribus – yield better classification rates, cf. [3,4].

Now, we want to have a closer look at the nine PCs that model a sort of uni-gram and can be interpreted easier than 28 or 95 raw feature values. If we look at the functions at group centroid, and at the standardized canonical discriminant function coefficients, we can get an impression, which feature values are typical for ROT, OOT, and NOT. Most important is energy, which is lower for ROT and OOT than for NOT, and higher for ROT than for OOT. (Especially absolute) duration is longer for ROT than for OOT – we'll come back to this result if we interpret Table 4. Energy regression is higher for ROT than for OOT, and F0 is lower for ROT and OOT than for NOT, and lower for ROT than for OOT. This result mirrors, of course, the strategies of the labellers and the characteristics of the phenomenon 'offtalk': if people speak aside or to themselves, they do this normally in lower voice and pitch. The most important difference between ROT and OOT is, however, not a prosodic, but a lexical one. This can be illustrated nicely by Table 4 where percent occurrences of PoS is given for the three classes ROT, OOT, and NOT. There are more content words CW in ROT than in OOT and NOT, especially NOUNs: 54.9 % compared to 7.2 % in OOT and 18.9 % in NOT. It is the other way round, if we look at the function words FWs, especially at PAJ (particles, articles, and interjections): very few for ROT (15.2 %), and most for OOT (64.7 %). The explanation is straightforward: the user only reads words that are presented on the screen, and these are mostly CWs – names of restaurants, cinemas, etc., which of course are longer than other word classes.

Table 4. PoS classes, percent occurrences for ROT, OOT, and NOT.

PoS	# of tokens	NOUN	API	APN	VERB	AUX	PAJ
ROT	277	54.9	8.3	17.0	1.8	2.9	15.2
OOT	529	7.2	2.5	10.8	9.3	5.7	64.7
NOT	9969	18.9	1.9	7.8	9.5	8.7	53.2

5 Concluding Remarks

Offtalk is certainly a phenomenon whose successful treatment is getting more and more important, if the performance of automatic dialogue systems allows unrestricted speech, and if the tasks performed by such systems approximate those tasks that are performed within these Wizard-of-Oz experiments. We have seen that a prosodic classification, based on a large feature vector – actually the very same that had been successfully used for the classification of accents and boundaries within the Verbmobil project, cf. [2] – yields good but not excellent classification rates. With additional lexical information entailed in the PoS features, classification rates went up. However, the frequency of ROT and OOT is rather low and thus, their precision is not yet very satisfactory; if we tried to obtain a very high recall for the marked classes ROT and OOT, precision would go down even more. Still, we believe that already with the used feature vector, we could use a strategy which had been used successfully for the treatment of speech repairs within the Verbmobil project, cf. [12]: there, we tuned the classification in such a way that we obtained a high recall at the expense of a very low precision for speech repairs. This classification could then be used as a sort of preprocessing step that reduced the search space for subsequent analyses considerably, from some 50.000 to some 25.000 instances. Another possibility would be an integrated processing with the A* algorithm along the lines described in [9], using other indicators that most likely will contribute to classification performance as, e.g., syntactic structure, the lexicon (use of swear words), the use of idiomatic phrases, out-of-sequence dialogue acts, etc. Eventually, experiments will have to be conducted that use word hypotheses graphs instead of the spoken word chain.

Acknowledgments

This work was funded by the German Federal Ministry of Education, Science, Research and Technology (*BMBF*) in the framework of the SmartKom project under Grant 01 IL 905 K7. The responsibility for the contents of this study lies with the authors.

References

1. J. Alexandersson, B. Buschbeck-Wolf, T. Fujinami, M. Kipp, S. Koch, E. Maier, N. Reithinger, B. Schmitz, and M. Siegel. Dialogue Acts in VERBMOBIL-2 – Second Edition. Verbmobil Report 226, Juli 1998.
2. A. Batliner, A. Buckow, H. Niemann, E. Nöth, and V. Warnke. The Prosody Module. In W. Wahlster, editor, *Verbmobil: Foundations of Speech-to-Speech Translations*, pages 106–121. Springer, Berlin, 2000.
3. A. Batliner, J. Buckow, R. Huber, V. Warnke, E. Nöth, and H. Niemann. Prosodic Feature Evaluation: Brute Force or Well Designed? In *Proc. 14th Int. Congress of Phonetic Sciences*, volume 3, pages 2315–2318, San Francisco, August 1999.
4. A. Batliner, J. Buckow, R. Huber, V. Warnke, E. Nöth, and H. Niemann. Boiling down Prosody for the Classification of Boundaries and Accents in German and English. In *Proc. European Conf. on Speech Communication and Technology*, volume 4, pages 2781–2784, Aalborg, September 2001.
5. A. Batliner, M. Nutt, V. Warnke, E. Nöth, J. Buckow, R. Huber, and H. Niemann. Automatic Annotation and Classification of Phrase Accents in Spontaneous Speech. In *Proc. European Conf. on Speech Communication and Technology*, volume 1, pages 519–522, Budapest, September 1999.

6. J. Carletta, N. Dahlbäck, N. Reithinger, and M. Walker. Standards for Dialogue Coding in Natural Language Processing. Dagstuhl-Seminar-Report 167, 1997.
7. N.M. Fraser and G.N. Gilbert. Simulating Speech Systems. *Computer Speech & Language*, 5(1):81–99, 1991.
8. W.R. Klecka. *Discriminant Analysis*. SAGE PUBLICATIONS Inc., Beverly Hills, 9 edition, 1988.
9. E. Nöth, A. Batliner, V. Warnke, J. Haas, M. Boros, J. Buckow, R. Huber, F. Gallwitz, M. Nutt, and H. Niemann. On the Use of Prosody in Automatic Dialogue Understanding. *Speech Communication*, 36(1–2), January 2002.
10. D. Oppermann, F. Schiel, S. Steininger, and N. Behringer. Off-Talk – a Problem for Human-Machine-Interaction? In *Proc. European Conf. on Speech Communication and Technology*, volume 3, pages 2197–2200, Aalborg, September 2001.
11. R. Siepmann, A. Batliner, and D. Oppermann. Using Prosodic Features to Characterize Off-Talk in Human-Computer-Interaction. In *Proc. of the Workshop on Prosody and Speech Recognition 2001*, 2001, pages 147–150, Red Bank, October 2001.
12. J. Spilker, A. Batliner, and E. Nöth. How to Repair Speech Repairs in an End-to-End System. In R. Lickley and L. Shriberg, editors, *Proc. ISCA Workshop on Disfluency in Spontaneous Speech*, pages 73–76, Edinburgh, September 2001.
13. W. Wahlster, N. Reithinger, and A. Blocher. SmartKom: Multimodal Communication with a Life-like Character. In *Proc. European Conf. on Speech Communication and Technology*, volume 3, pages 1547–1550, Aalborg, September 2001.
14. P. Watzlawick, J.H. Beavin, and Don D. Jackson. *Pragmatics of Human Communications*. W.W. Norton & Company, New York, 1967.

Statistical Decision Making from Text and Dialogue Corpora for Effective Plan Recognition*

Manolis Maragoudakis, Aristomenis Thanopoulos, and Nikos Fakotakis

Wire Communications Laboratory
Department of Electrical and Computer Engineering
University of Patras
Rion-26 500, Patras, Greece
E-mail: mmarag@wcl.ee.upatras.gr, aristom@wcl.ee.upatras.gr,
fakotaki@wcl.ee.upatras.gr

Abstract. In this paper, we introduce an architecture designed to achieve effective plan recognition using Bayesian Networks which encode the semantic representation of the user's utterances. The structure of the networks is determined from dialogue corpora, thus eliminating the high cost process of hand-coding domain knowledge. The conditional probability distributions are learned during a training phase in which data are obtained by the same set of dialogue acts. Furthermore, we have incorporated a module that learns semantic similarities of words from raw text corpora and uses the extracted knowledge to resolve the issue of the unknown terms, thus enhancing plan recognition accuracy, and improves the quality of the discourse. We present experimental results of an implementation of our platform for a weather information system and compare its performance against a similar, commercial one. Results depict significant improvement in the context of identifying the goals of the user. Moreover, we claim that our framework could straightforwardly be updated with new elements from the same domain or adapted to other domains as well.

1 Introduction

The majority of the dialogue systems that provide informational services such as news broadcasting, stock market briefing, route information and weather forecasting are system driven, meaning that the computer controls the process of interaction, expecting standardized, pre-defined queries from the user. By following this approach, the quality of the dialogue deteriorates and is circumscribed in narrow semantic limits, lacking any mixed-initiative notion. In such systems, domain knowledge is handcrafted by an expert who should pay prominent attention during the design phase, in order to create a representation that would be as robust as possible to the potential user's utterances variations. Such handcrafting of knowledge bases is infeasible for grappling with update or modification problems, since their structure is complex and domain specific. In addition, one should also consider that

---

* This work was supported by the "Generic Environment for Multilingual Interactive Natural Interfaces" GEMINI project (IST-2001-32343).

P. Sojka, I. Kopeček, and K. Pala (Eds.): TSD 2002, LNAI 2448, pp. 365–372, 2002.

particularly for those interactions that occur via the telephony networks, direct and effective understanding of the intentions of a user is of great importance.

The term that has been introduced to describe the process of inferring intentions for actions from utterances is called "*plan recognition*" [3,11]. Deriving the underlying aims can be assistive for a plethora of purposes such as predicting the agent's future behaviour, interpreting its past attitude creating a user model or narrowing the search space of a database query. Previous AI researchers have studied plan recognition for several types of tasks, such as discourse analysis [8], collaborative planning [10], adversarial planning [1], and story understanding [4].

For the present work, we propose a bayesian networks approach to modeling domain knowledge obtained from past dialogue acts and using it for interpreting the aims that lie beneath user's expressions. The structure as well as the conditional probability distributions of the networks are learned from manually annotated data derived from past dialogues. Furthermore, in order to effectively cope with unknown terms that may be found in a query, thus enhancing plan recognition accuracy, we estimate their semantic role from similar words of the system's vocabulary. The semantic similarities are obtained by applying a statistical algorithm, namely information theoretic similarity measure [12] to raw text corpora.

We have applied the proposed method to a meteorological information system for the territory of Greece, which we call MeteoBayes and evaluated both its internal design issues and its performance against another, already operating system called METEONEWS[1] that can be accessed through the telephone. METEONEWS was designed and implemented using hand-coded domain knowledge and did not incorporate any plan recognition algorithm while in our system, MeteoBayes, we obtain domain knowledge from manually annotated dialogue parts and encode it into a group of bayesian networks for the inference of a user's plan. Our experimental results depict significant improvement in the discourse quality, meaning the ability to quickly identify the user's aims. Moreover, we compare the complexity of each system's architecture and their potential ability either to be updated with new semantic elements or to be adapted to different domains.

2   Domain Description

Our bayesian framework for plan recognition and dialogue managing for a weather information application, which from now on shall be referred as MeteoBayes, centers on conversations about goals typically handled by people located at the help desks of the weather information centers. We conducted an observational study of the weather forecast domain by recording 180 dialogue acts using the Wizard of Oz technique and by studying the log files of the METEONEWS telephone interactions. Through the reviewing process, we were able to identify a primal set of user goals as well as a key set of linguistic characteristics, relevant to the problem of detecting a user's demand. Observations revealed a group of 320 goals, with 48 of them mutually exclusive and exhaustive. One critical parameter that came into light during the reviewing process and needed to be taken into consideration is that users who interacted with the telephone service tended to clarify their goals from their initial utterances, while those who participated in the Wizard of Oz experiments in the laboratory were more

---

[1] Developed by Knowledge S.A. and Mediatel S.A

abstract and haze in their plans. This phenomenon is caused from the telephone charging factor, which subconsciously forces the user to be more self-inclusive.

Upon completion of the domain analysis, five different semantic features were identified:

- Forecast: the concept of weather prognosis, including all possible variations such as general forecast, weather conditions in a specific area, wind bulletin, sea conditions, etc.
- Temperature: includes temperature and humidity report, heat or freeze alerts, etc.
- Time period: whether the weather forecast refers to today, tomorrow, from 3–6 days or for the whole week.
- Area: includes 10 big cities, 30 towns and 5 pelages in the Greek region.
- Land/Sea: whether the user is interested in a continental or thalassic area of a given place.

In addition to those features, we discovered considerable linguistic variability concerning the interactions. At times, users employed conventional phrases such as *"I would like to learn the temperature of Athens on Monday"* or *"Is tomorrow a sunny day in Rhodos?"*. However, there was a significant number of abbreviated, more telegraphic queries such as *"Weather in Crete"* or *"Temperature today?"*. Furthermore, there were cases where the goal was implied rather than stated. For example, the question *"Is the canal of Rion-Antirion accessible?"* implies the user's intention to be informed about the sea conditions in the thalassic area of the Gulf of the city of Patras.

3   Architecture

The proposed structure aims at the development of a dialogue system that would be independent of manual-coded domain knowledge and capable of easy adaptation to a different task. To achieve this, we have incorporated three separate modules, two off-line training systems and an on-line dialogue manager. The schematic representation that depicts their interconnection is shown in Figure 1.

3.1   Learning Domain Knowledge from Dialogue Acts

The off-line module that is responsible for the automatic acquisition of domain knowledge from the dialogue corpus operates as follows: Initially, we identify the primal set of semantic features that describe the task from the entire set of the past dialogue acts. This is actually the only phase where a domain expert is required. We have developed a parametric annotation tool in which such a specialist could dynamically define the input and output variables that enclose all the information which is suitable in order to perform an interaction. Regarding the annotation phase, note that not only nouns are used but linguistic elements that define a user's plan, such as temporal adverbs, present participles and adjectives, are annotated as well.

Upon completion of this procedure, a parser modifies the annotated dialogue corpus into a training set of lexical-semantic vectors that correspond to the mapping of the lexical parts of a user's utterance with the implied output semantic representation of his intentions. This training set will be used for the construction of the Bayesian networks that will encode the domain knowledge. These networks are learned using the following approach. Given

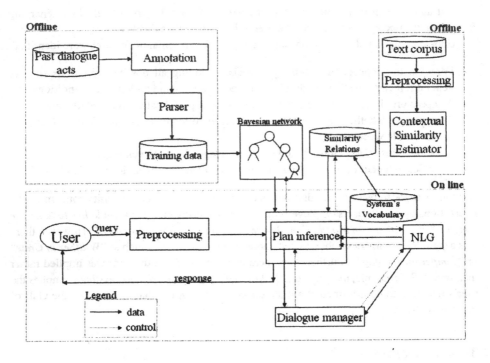

Fig. 1. Architecture of the proposed framework.

a training set D that contains n different variables, the probability $P(B|D)$ that a candidate network B is describing the data is estimated using the Equation [7].

$$P(D|B) = \prod_{i=1}^{n} \prod_{j=1}^{qi} \frac{\Gamma\left(\frac{\Xi}{q_i}\right)}{\Gamma\left(\frac{\Xi}{q_i} + N_{ij}\right)} \prod_{k=1}^{ri} \frac{\Gamma\left(\frac{\Xi}{r_i q_i} + N_{ijk}\right)}{\Gamma\left(\frac{\Xi}{r_i q_i}\right)} \qquad (1)$$

Γ is the gamma function, n equals to the number of variables and r_i denotes the number of values in $i{:}th$ variable. q_i denotes the number of possible different data value combinations the parent variables can take, N_{ij} depicts the number of rows in data that have $j{:}th$ data value combinations for parents of $i{:}th$ variable, N_{ijk} corresponds to the number of rows that have $k{:}th$ value for the $i{:}th$ variable and which also have $j{:}th$ data value combinations for the parents of $i{:}th$ variable and Ξ is the equivalent sample size, a parameter that determines how readily we change our beliefs about the quantitative nature of dependencies when we see the data. In our study, Ξ equals to the average number of values variables have, divided by 2.

3.2   Learning Semantic Similarities of Words from Text Corpora

The purpose of the additional off-line module is to estimate the semantic role of words not appearing in our dialogue corpus from similar words, using a database of semantic similarity relations, constructed from raw text corpora on the basis of contextual similarity.

Obtaining this information is very important in situations where an unseen term occurs in a user's phrase, permitting the flow of the interaction without having to ask the user for query reformulation.

Corpus-based automatic extraction of word similarities employs a central notion of contextual lexical semantics, denoting that semantic properties of words can be defined "by their actual and potential context" [6] and therefore words that are found to share similar contexts along text corpora have certain semantic properties in common as well. Several measures for contextual similarity have been employed, such as the cosine [13], the minimal loss of mutual information [2], a weighted Jaccard similarity metric [9] and an information theoretic similarity measure [12]. [9] and [12] applied their measures on sets of syntactic dependencies from an analyzed corpus (i.e. $<word_1, syntactic\_relation, word_2>$), which presupposes that a reliable syntactic parser will be available for the language of interest. Since our goal was to apply a generic and easily portable technique for the identification of similar concepts from raw text corpora, bypassing the need of sophisticated linguistic analysis tools, we considered a single contextual relation: Plain adjacency in text. Specifically, we considered as adjacent the words which are not separated by more than five content words nor by sentence boundaries. We used Lin's metric [12], which assigns a similarity value in the interval [0, 1] and, considering a single relation, is simplified to:

$$\text{sim}(w_1, w_2) = \frac{\sum_{(w) \in T(w_1) \cap T(w_2)} \left(I(w_1, w) + I(w_2, w) \right)}{\sum_{(w) \in T(w_1)} I(w_1, w) + \sum_{(w) \in T(w_2)} I(w_2, w)} \tag{2}$$

where $T(w)$ is the set of words such that the mutual information $I(w, w') > 0^2$, with

$$I(w, w') = \log \left(\frac{c_{12} \cdot N}{c_1 \cdot c_2} \right) \tag{3}$$

where c_{12} is the frequency of the co-occurrence of w_1 and w_2, c_i the number of times w_i appears in the set of relations and N the number of the extracted relations from the corpus. From the obtained set of similarity relations we maintained only the N-best relations for every word of the system's vocabulary (we set $N = 100$).

For this task we used the balanced ILSP/ELEYTHEROTYPIA corpus (1.6 million words), including news and articles obtained from a Greek daily newspaper.

The process so far is time-consuming but it is executed off-line and produces a set of relations of a rather small size. The on-line part is triggered by the occurrence of an out-of-vocabulary word, which is classified to the most plausible category using K-nearest neighbour classification (we set $K = 5$).

In both learning processes the training text (i.e. the dialogue and newswire text corpora respectively) is pre-processed using a two-level morphological analyser that outputs the lemma of the word, in order to gather denser statistical data. Consequently, lemmatisation is also applied to the input query during the on-line process.

Additionally, we have included a date module that interprets any date format into the temporal periods we described in the domain description section. The purpose of the pre-processing stage is to identify parts of the input and match them to the domain lexicon items.

---

[2] We actually used $I(w, w') > 1$ in order to reduce the size of $T(w)$ and thus computational cost and because values of I (mutual information) near zero indicate rather uncorrelated pairs.

3.3   The Dialogue Manager

The dialogue manager takes control after this stage and queries the appropriate Bayesian network in order to identify a plan. The response is guided to the plan inference module where it is interpreted and, according to the degree of certainty about a user's plan, the NLG component replies either with the direct database answer or with verification and supplementary information sentences. In case an unknown word appears, the plan inference module consults the similarity relations database providing the system's vocabulary as a filter. The system's vocabulary term that mostly matches the unknown word (if any) is then considered to be the correct and the inference procedure is resumed.

4   Experimental Results

The evaluation of MeteoBayes focused on two different aspects. The former is the plan recognition performance with and without the semantic similarities knowledge base and the latter is to compare its architecture complexity with that of METEONEWS platform. Our approach was based on a set of 50 dialogue acts, provided by 10 users who were previously informed about the task and the possibility to imply their intentions than explicitly declaring them. This set was augmented by another set of 50 questions obtained by the log files of METEONEWS' past interactions. The total number of questions was 415. We separated this number into those questions where the goal was clearly defined and to those where it was not. Let us denote the former set as Q_c ($|Q_c|=295$) and the latter set as Q_i ($|Q_i|=120$). As previously mentioned, the system was capable of identifying 48 mutually exclusive goals. Tables 1 and 2 tabulate the performance in terms of plan recognition accuracy without and with the semantic similarities module for both sets respectively. We manually set an empirical lower bound of certainty about the aim of a user to 60%. In case where the system could not meet this threshold, the plan inference module asked for a reformulated user question.

As can be observed in Table 1, 12 queries needed reformulation by the user, thus corresponding to 96 % accuracy. From these queries, only 1 was unable to be understood even after reformulation, which corresponds to an error rate of 8 %. On the contrary, in the Q_i set, the number of incorrectly identified queries is 41 (66 %) and 7 items of this set could not be recognized even after the reformulation, resulting to an error rate almost 2 times greater than that of the Q_c set. This performance is expected, since the intentions were implied by the users and not straightforwardly expressed. The reformulation stage did not necessarily involve the complete syntactic/semantic rephrasing of the question, but included spelling error checking as well.

The results obtained by incorporation of the semantic similarity database for unknown words (Table 2), indicate that there is actually little effect in the case that the user's goal is clearly defined while, in the opposite case, a significant improvement is accomplished. In the Q_i set particularly, the error rate after the reformulation stage drops by almost 45 %.

Concerning the evaluation of the architecture complexity, we examine the number and structure of the resource files needed, along with their flexibility to be updated since we cannot perform a straightforward comparison between the hardware and human-month effort required for both the METEONEWS and MeteoBayes development. From the METEONEWS point of view, there are 61 grammar files that interconnect in order to cover

Table 1. Plan recognition performance without the word similarities.

Category	Amount	Accuracy
Q_c	295	
Reformulation of a Q_c question	12	96%
Unidentified object	1	92%
Q_i	120	
Reformulation of a Q_i question	41	66%
Unidentified object	7	83%

Table 2. Plan recognition performance using the database of similarity relations.

Category	Amount	Accuracy
Q_c	295	
Reformulation of a Q_c question	13	95.5%
Unidentified object	0	100.0%
Q_i	120	
Reformulation of a Q_i question	21	82.5%
Unidentified object	2	90.5%

the weather forecast domain. These grammars are written in JavaScript grammar format and they utilize a template oriented approach. The parsing is performed by Philips Speech PERL 2000© platform. As regards to MeteoBayes, the total number of lexical resource files is only 5, corresponding to the semantic features described in Section 2. They contain the stem of the words that indicate each category. The average number of semantic relations we maintain for resolving unknown terms is 70 times the number of the system's vocabulary words. In case that new lexical elements should be included, the only step would be a simple addition in the corresponding lexical resource file while with METEONEWS, the same procedure would require the construction of a new grammar with potentially additional modifications to old ones, plus a new compilation of all.

In addition to its ability to be easily updated, we claim that the proposed framework can effortlessly be adapted to another domain. Once obtaining the dialogue acts and defining the semantic entities, the procedure of incorporating this knowledge into a dialogue system is uncomplicated. Only the Bayesian networks and the NLG responses will vary from task to task. The plan inference engine will remain the same.

5 Conclusion

The identification of a user's plan could contribute to the significant improvement of natural language human-computer interaction systems, since they enrich the dialogue quality, which is a very significant factor, particularly for telephone applications. Given the obvious high cost of manually encoding domain knowledge, this paper has presented a novel, Bayesian framework that aims to achieve plan inference ability without the need for hand-coded knowledge. In particular, we have introduced a platform that employs manually annotated past dialogue acts in order to obtain domain knowledge. This information is encoded into a group of Bayesian networks and is used for the user's goals identification procedure by a discourse manager module. Moreover, in order to cope with the complicated issue of unknown terms, an off-line system that learns semantic similarities from raw text was incorporated. The generated relations were used to replace the unknown word with a system's vocabulary term that had the most similar meaning. We have implemented the proposed approach by developing a weather information dialogue system, called MeteoBayes and compared it against another, hand-coded weather information system, named METEONEWS. Experimental results have depicted significant plan recognition accuracy. Moreover, the framework could straightforwardly be updated with new elements. Concluding, we argue that our method can be adapted to different domains with slight modifications.

References

1. Azarewicz, J., Fala, G., Heithecker, C.: Template-based multi agent plan recognition for tactical situation assessment. In: Proceedings of the Sixth Conference on Artificial Intelligence Applications (1989), 247–254.
2. Brown P. F., DellaPietra V. J., DeSouza P. V., Lai J. C., Mercer R. L.: "Class-Based n-gram Models of Natural Language", Computational Linguistics, Vol. 18 (4), (1992). 467–479.
3. Carberry L.: Incorporating default inferences into plan recognition. In Proc. 8th Nat. Conf. AI 1 (1990), 471–478.
4. Charniak E., Goldman, R. P.: A Bayesian model of plan recognition. Artificial Intelligence, 64 (1), (1993), 53–79.
5. Clark H. H.: Using Language. Cambridge University Press (1996).
6. Cruse D. A.: Lexical Semantics. Cambridge University Press, Great Britain (1986).
7. Glymour C. and Cooper G. (Eds.): Computation, Causation & Discovery. AAAI Press/The MIT Press, Menlo Park (1999).
8. Grosz B. J. and Sidner C. L.: Plans for discourse. In: Cohen P. R., Morgan J. L., and Pollack M. E., (Eds.): Intentions and Communication. Cambridge, MA: MIT Press. (1990) 417–444.
9. Grefenstette G.: Explorations in Automatic Thesaurus Discovery, Kluwer Academic Publishers, Boston (1994).
10. Huber M. J., Durfee E. H.: Observational uncertainty in plan recognition among interacting robots. In: Working Notes of Workshop on Dynamically Interacting Robots, Chambery, France (1993) 68–75.
11. Kautz H. A., Allen J. F.: Generalized plan recognition. In Proceedings of AAAI (1986) 32–37.
12. Lin D.: Automatic retrieval and clustering of similar words. In Proceedings of the COLING-ACL, (1998), Montreal, Canada.
13. Schütze H.: Dimensions of Meaning, Supercomputing '92 (1992) 787–796.

Natural Language Guided Dialogues for Accessing the Web

Marta Gatius and Horacio Rodríguez

Software Department*, Technical University of Catalonia

Abstract. This paper proposes the use of ontologies representing domain and linguistic knowledge for guiding natural language (NL) communication on the Web contents. This proposal deals with the problem of obtaining and processing the Web data required to answer users queries. Concepts and communication acts are represented in a conceptual ontology (CO). Domain-restricted linguistic resources are obtained automatically by adapting the general linguistic knowledge to cover the communication acts for a particular domain. The use of domain-restricted grammars and lexicons has proved to be efficient, especially when the user is guided in introducing the sentences. To answer users queries the system fires the appropriate wrappers to extract the data from the Web. The CO provides a unifying framework to represent and process the knowledge obtained from the Web. Following this proposal, a dialogue-system for accessing a set of Web sites on the travelling domain in Spanish has been implemented.

1   Introduction

The Web is a huge repository of text, images and services. Although the Web was designed primarily for human use, a user faces different problems when accessing a specific Web site: locating the relevant Web sites, accessing different protocols and facilities, executing services, etc. A lot of browsers, meta-browsers and information agents have been built to address the problem of locating Web sites where useful information is placed (see for instance [13]). However, there are not many Web query systems supporting friendly and intelligent interaction. There are NL interfaces (NLIs) to different types of applications (i.e. databases), however they cannot easily be adapted to support communication about information on the Web. The main reason is that Web sources are not designed to be processed automatically, besides they are hetergeneous and change rapidly.

Although the NLI systems to several Web sites gather information from various Web sources, this problem differs from the Information Extraction [7,17], Information Integration [11,15] and the Question Answering [3,20] paradigms. In NLI systems, tasks are well defined and users can be guided to express their information needs. Additionally, many NLI systems use domain knowledge to respond to users requests in an intelligent manner [16].

In this paper we discuss GIWeb, a NLI system designed to support communication on the contents of a collection of domain-restricted Web sites. The system uses a CO representing domain concepts and communication tasks and a linguistic ontology (LO) representing general linguistic knowledge. GIWeb generates domain-restricted linguistic resources by

* Grup de recerca consolidat 2001 SGR 00254, supported by DURSI

P. Sojka, I. Kopeček, and K. Pala (Eds.): TSD 2002, LNAI 2448, pp. 373–380, 2002.

adapting the general linguistic knowledge in the LO to cover the communication tasks for a particular domain. The use of domain-restricted grammars and lexicons has provedto be efficient especially when the user is guided about the conceptual/linguistic coverage of the system. The system guides the user by displaying on the screen the NL options acceptable at each state of the communication. Once the query has been processed, the dialogue component controls the obtaining and processing the information on the Web required to answer. The system is capable of responding properly to a variety of requests involving knowledge in a collection of domain-restricted Web sites. The current implementation of the system has been applied to provide access to several Web sites containing information on trains and buses.

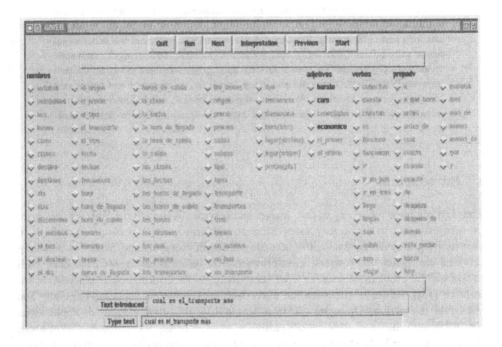

Fig. 1. Guiding the user to introduce the NL sentences.

An overview of the system is given in Section 2. The Section 3 describes the tuning of domain-restricted linguistic resources. Section 4 describes the flow of communication. Finally, specific details of the representation of the information extracted from the Web in the CO are given in Section 5.

2 An Overview of the System

The NL components of the system were adapted from those of GISE [9,10], a system using a CO to support NL communication with Knowledge Based Systems. GISE components were adapted to support NL queries on information on the Web. The tasks of communication in NL query systems mainly consist of operations consulting particular knowledge on the domain. In those systems, user interventions cover a rich variety of linguistic phenomena. The system must support direct, concise and ungrammatical utterances to achieve a natural interaction. Additionally, tackling consults about information on the Web involves extracting and processing the data from various Web sources.

In the system GIWeb, the knowledge involved in NL communication is represented in separate, reusable knowledge bases: the CO, representing the conceptual knowledge, the Linguistic Ontology (LO), representing general linguistic knowledge, and a set of control rules (CRs), in charge of generating the domain-restricted grammars and lexicons by adapting the general linguistic resources to those required for a specific domain. A wrapper system was incorporated for accessing the information in the Web.

CO is the skeleton for anchoring the description of the concepts of a particular domain. The CO is organized in three independent taxonomies, representing domain concepts, attributes describing these concepts and operations to be performed on the domain concepts. The CO provides a framework for integrating and processing the information from several Web sources.

The attributes describing concepts were classified according to a syntactic-semantic taxonomy in order to favour the generation of the domain-restricted grammars. The basic classes are associated with the different grammar roles appearing in the sublanguage used in communication with several types of applications (i.e. query systems). The syntactic-semantic classification of attributes allows a variety of different linguistic coverages for each class of attribute. Nineteen basic classes of attributes have been defined. Although the classification of attributes is based on Spanish linguistic distinctions, it is easily portable to other languages.

The taxonomy of operations describes the communication tasks. Operations are classified as simple or complex. Simple operations involve only one conceptual instance and complex operations involve several instances. Complex operations provide inferential and reasoning capabilities to answer complex questions.

The general linguistic knowledge needed to cover the expression in Spanish of the operations the system performs is represented in the LO. Following the Nigel grammar [19], the linguistic knowledge was organized in three main classes: the class *clause* (having a subject and a finite verb), the class *group* (having a head and a variable number of modifiers) and the class *word* (representing verbs, nouns, articles, etc.). Objects representing linguistic classes are assumed to be domain independent. Objects representing the specific aspects of the information to be expressed for each domain are represented as instances of the linguistic classes. LO includes 130 subclasses of the class *clause*, 53 subclasses of the class *group* and 93 subclasses of the class *word*.

The linguistic structures necessary for a particular domain are generated by the CRs. Rules are of the form: *conditions* → *actions*. Conditions basically consist of descriptions of objects. Rules are applied over objects in the CO and the LO satisfying conditions. The actions performed by the rules are operations consulting and modifying the objects in the CO and LO. Rules are grouped into rulesets. Each ruleset performs a different action and each rule in the ruleset considers a different object class. The basic set of control rules consists of 46 rules grouped into 9 rulesets.

The information from the dynamic heterogeneous sources in the Web is obtained by wrappers. In the Web environment, a wrapper can be defined as a processor that converts information stored as in a HTML document into information explicitly stored as a data structure for further processing. The primary advantage of building wrappers to extract information from the Web is that they provide an integrated access to several sources. GIWeb incorporates a wrapper system providing a special language for describing Web pages. Although a description must be given for each page organization, frequently there are Web pages sharing a common organization, such as those generated by a Web service. GIWeb uses two families of wrappers.

3   Obtaining Domain-Restricted Grammars and Lexicon

Obtaining the domain-restricted linguistic resources consists of adapting the CO and the LO to a specific domain. Representing the domain knowledge in the CO consists of describing the concepts involved in the communication for a particular domain as subclasses of the general concepts. Each domain concept is described by an identifier, a primitive relation (*isa*) relating it to the taxonomy of concepts and a set of attributes. All attributes describing concepts have to be incorporated into the taxonomy of attributes. Concepts and attributes appearing in the communication are linked to one or more lexical entries in the domain lexicon. These lexical entries include all the forms associated with the expressions of the concepts and attributes in the operations (names, verbs, adjectives). The addresses of the Web sites containing information about a concept are also included in the concept description.

Once domain knowledge has been incorporated, CRs generate the grammar and lexicon representing the operations on the domain concepts. The process is performed in three steps:

1. Generating instances of the CO operations for the domain concepts. Different operations are generated considering the classes of the attributes.
2. Generating LO instances supporting the expression of the operations generated in the first step.
3. Representing the LO instances created in the second step as DCG rules and lexical entries.

Most of the CO operations are based on the attributes describing the domain concepts. The linguistic structures required to express these operations are obtained considering the syntactic-semantic classes of the conceptual attributes. To illustrate this process, we will consider the CO operation *minimum_attribute_value_o*, obtaining the conceptual instance-having the minimum value of a specific attribute. This operation is based on the attributes in the class *of_quantity*, expressing a quantity (and associated with a unit). The expression of this operation depends on the subclass of the attribute. For example, in the travelling domain three attributes belonging to subclasses of the *of_quantity* class were used to describe the concept *transport:price, arrivaltime* and *departuretime*. The attribute *price* belongs to the class *of_cost*. The attributes *arrivaltime* and *departuretime* belong to the class *of_time*. For the attributes in the class *of_cost*, the operation could be expressed using the form: *¿Cuál es <concept name> más económico? (Which is the cheapest <concept name>?)*.

If the attribute belongs to the class *of_time*, the patterns to express this operation would be: *¿Cuál es el primer <concept name>? (Which is the first <concept name>?)* and *¿Qué <concept name> <attribute verb> antes?(Which <concept name> <attribute verb> first?)*.

In case of the concept name *tren* (*the train*) and the attribute verb *salir* (*departure*) the resulting question would be: *Cuál es el primer tren?* (*Which is the first tren?*) and *Qué tren sale antes?* (*Which train leaves first?*).

In the grammars and lexicons generated, categories are augmented with syntactic and semantic features. Rules and lexical entries are associated with semantic interpretation based on lambda calculus. The semantic features associated with the categories correspond to identifiers of concepts and attributes. The semantic interpretations associated with the lexical entries consist of lambda values and functions representing CO operations, concepts, attributes and values. Each grammar rule expressing an operation includes the operation identifier and its preconditions. The incorportaion of the conceptual knowledge from the CO into the rules and lexical entries facilitates the processing of user interventions.

4   The Dialogue System

GIWeb guides the user in introducing the NL utterances by displaying the NL options acceptable on the screen. The user can type the complete query or, alternatively, build a sentence by selecting the active options on the screen. As can be observed in Figure 1, only valid continuations of the fragment already uttered are active. Once the user has selected an option, it is passed to an incremental parser. When the parser returns all items that can be recognized in the next step, the interface updates the NL options that must be active. Once a whole sentence has been recognized and interpreted by the parser, it is passed to the dialogue controller (DC). The information passed to the DC consists of a set of possible semantic interpretations. Each interpretation includes the operation identifier, the concept identifier and the operation parameters expressed in the user intervention. If necessary, the DC completes this information using history of the dialogue and the conceptual knowledge represented in the CO. A simple attentional structure is used to record the focus of attention. The concept over which an operation is performed and the rest of parameters expressed are considered the focus of attention.

The DC consults the definition of the operation in the CO to obtain its mandatory arguments and their default values. The values of the mandatory arguments not expressed in the user intervention are obtained from the focus of previous sentences. If these values are not expressed in previous sentences, the default values are used. The DC attempts to disambiguate ambiguous semantic interpretations by considering the operation definition and the context. In case there is more than one correct interpretation then the one referring to the focus of attention of previous sentences is selected.

The DC has been designed with the assumption that the user would introduce sentences by using the NL options the system displays. Assuming the options introduced are those acceptable to the grammar generated for a specific domain simplifies the DC. Dealing with the sentences introduced by the user directly would require an increase in the DC complexity. In this case, users can introduce sentences that do not express correct operations, or even ones that do not express any operation at all. To deal with these problems, the functionality of the DC would necessarily have to include new tasks, such as those reformulating or confirming user interventions, opening or/and closing the dialogue, etc.

Once a complete operation is obtained, it is executed over the instances of the domain concepts represented in the CO. If no satisfactory answer is obtained, then the DC is in

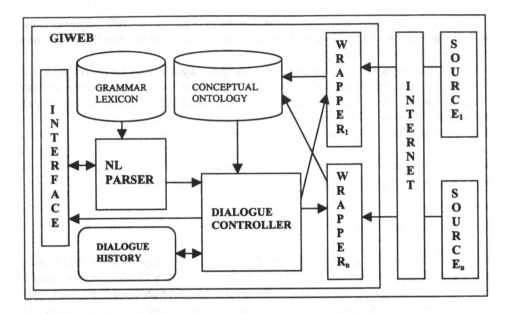

Fig. 2. The components of the dialogue system.

charge of activating the corresponding wrappers to extract the information from the Web. The addresses of the Web pages containing particular information about a concept are obtained from the concept description. An address can also represent a request to a URL Web service. In this case, the parameters required for the service must be specified. Each Web address is associated with the description of the HTML source and a class of wrapper. The DC calls the corresponding wrapper classes and passes them the Web addresses, the page descriptions and, in case of requests to Web services, the information the services require. The wrappers represent the information extracted from the Web as instances of the CO domain concepts. Then, the user consult is executed again over the CO. Finally, the answer, if existing, is passed to the interface.

5   Obtaining the Information from the Web

Currently, only semi-structured and structured Web pages have been considered. The information in these pages is usually represented as lists of attributes (tuples) delimited by HTML-tags. Extraction patterns for those pages are often based on tokens and HTML-tags. The Web pages are accessed by wrappers. Several approaches are being proposed to reduce the cost of implementing a specific wrapper for each Web source: special languages for writing wrappers [4], semi-automated tools [1], automatic generation of wrappers [5,6,12,14,18].

For GIWeb, we have designed and implemented a simple wrapper system allowing an easy interaction with the CO. This system uses an explicit description of the HTML source to be analyzed. When adapting the system to a domain the set of Web sources that would be consulted during communication are selected and described. The description of a Web page consists of three parts: the organization of the page, the textual processing to be done over the data extracted and the representation of the resulting data in the CO. The first part describes the tags delimiting the tuples and the attributes in the tuples in the HTML source. This description includes information about possible nested structures (attributes represented as tuples) and about the different types of information stored in an attribute (text, internet addresses, images or codes). In the second part of the page description, the textual processing required is indicated using a set of predefined types: text, integer, brackets, list, time, data, weekday,... There is a default presentation for these types. For example, by default the text will be written in lower case letter, without accents and without spaces. The third part of a Web page description contains the information necessary to represent the data extracted as instances of a particular domain concept in the CO. The description of the page must indicate the name of the concept described as well as the correspondence between the attributes of the tuples in the page and the attributes describing each conceptual instance. Information about a particular instance can appear in more than one page.

6 Conclusions

In this paper a NL dialogue system for accessing the Web has been presented. The main issue in the design of the system is the reusable and efficient representation of the conceptual and linguistic knowledge involved in communication. The organization proposed favours the obtaining of domain-restricted grammars and lexicons. The use of domain-restricted linguistic resources and guiding the user about the conceptual/linguistic coverage of the system improves the communication process. The taxonomy of concepts in the CO provides a unifying framework for integrating information from differentWeb sources. The taxonomy of operations allows the system to answer complex queries. The modular organization of the relevant knowledge into separate data structures provides great flexibility for adapting the system to different domains and languages. The proposed architecture could be applied to other types of dialogue systems, such as those providing access to e-commerce applications.

References

1. Ashish, N., Knoblock, C.A.: Wrapper generation for semistructured Internet sources. ACM SIGMOD Workshop on Managment of Semi-structured Data (1997).
2. Bateman, J.A., Kasper, R.T., Moore, J. D., Whitney, R. A.: A General Organization of Knowledge for Natural Language Processing: the Penman Upper Model. Technical report. USC/Information Sciences Institute (1990).
3. Cardie, C., Ng, V., Pierce, D., Buckley, C.: Examining the Role of Statistical and Linguistic Knowledge Sources in a General-Knowledge Question-Answering System. The Sixth Applied Natural Language Processing Conference (2000).
4. Cohen, W.: Recognizing Structure in Web Pages using Similarity Queries. AAAI (1999) 59–66.
5. Cohen, W.: Whirl: A word-based information representation language. Artificial Intelligence, 118, (2000) 163–196.
6. Cohen, W., Jensen, L.S.: A structured wrapper induction system for extracting information from semi-structured documents. IJCAI Workshop on Adaptive Text Extraction and Mining (2001).

7. Eikvil, L.: Information Extraction from World Wide Web – A Survey. Report 945 (1999). ISBN 82-539-0429-0. Available at:
   http://www.nr.no/documents/samba/researchareas/BAMG/Publications/webIE/rep945.ps.
8. Garcia-Molina, H., Papakonstantinou, D., Quass, A., Rajaraman, Y., Sagiv, Y., Ullman, J., Vassalos, V., Widom, J.: The TSIMMIS approach to mediation: Data models and languages. The journal of Intelligent Information Systems (1997).
9. Gatius, M., Rodríguez, H.: Adapting general linguistic knowledge to applications in order to obtain friendly and efficient NL interfaces. VEXTAL Conference (1999).
10. Gatius, M.: Using an ontology for guiding natural language interaction with knowledge based systems. Ph.D. thesis. Technical University of Catalonia (2001).
11. Hearst, M.A.: Information Integration Trends and Controversies. Column IEEE Intelligent Systems, 13 (1998) 17–20.
12. Hsu, C., Dung, M.: Generating finite-state transducers for semistructured data extraction from the WEB. Journal of Information Systems, 23 (1998) 521–538.
13. Kobayashi, M., Takeda, K.: Information Retrieval on the Web. Computing Surveys, 32 (2000).
14. Kushmerick, N.: Wrapper induction: Efficiency and expressiveness. Artificial Intelligence, 118 (2000) 15–68.
15. Levy, A.Y.: Combining Artificial Intelligence and Databases for Data Integration. Special issue of LNAI: Artificial Intelligence Today; Recent Trends and Developments (1999).
16. Maybury, M.: Intelligent Multimedia Interfaces. AAAI Press & Cambridge MA: The MIT Press, Menlo Park, CA (1993).
17. Muslea, I.: Extraction Patterns for Information Extraction Tasks: A Survey. AAAI Workshop on Machine Learning for Information Extraction (1999).
18. Muslea, I., Minton, S., Knoblock, C.: Hierarchical Wrapper Induction for Semistructured, Web-based Information Sources. Conference on Automated Learning and Discovery(CONALD) (1999).
19. The Penman NL Generation Group. The Nigel Manual. Information Sciences Institute of the University of Southern California. Draft (1988).
20. Voorhees, E. Overview of the TREC 2001 Question Answering Track. Presentation to the Text Retrieval Conference, USA (2001).

Evaluating a Probabilistic Dialogue Model
for a Railway Information Task*

Carlos D. Martínez-Hinarejos and Francisco Casacuberta

Institut Tecnològic d'Informàtica, Departament de Sistemes Informàtics i Computació
Universitat Politècnica de València, Camí de Vera, s/n, 46022, València, Spain
E-mail: cmartine@iti.upv.es, fcn@iti.upv.es

Abstract. Dialogue modelling attempts to determine the way in which a dialogue is developed. The dialogue strategy (i.e., the system behaviour) of an automatic dialogue system is determined by the dialogue model. Most dialogue systems use rule-based dialogue strategies, but recently, the probabilistic models have become very promising. We present probabilistic models based on the dialogue act concept, which uses user turns, dialogue history and semantic information. These models are evaluated as dialogue act labelers. The evaluation is carried out on a railway information task.

1 Introduction

The Computational Linguistics field covers a lot of natural language applications which have been developed over the past few years. Most of these applications are based on extracting rules from real data and, afterwards, include them in a computer system to develop the task. In contrast, viewpoint, probabilistic modelling attempts to automatically extract these rules from real data by using statistical inference techniques [1].

Dialogue systems are one of the most recent natural language processing applications. In these systems, a machine tries to emulate a human being in a dialogue with a person in order to achieve a final objective. The way the system behaves (i.e., the kind of answers and questions the system makes) is known as dialogue strategy [2]. This dialogue strategy is determined by the dialogue model. As we mentioned above, the dialogue model has usually been a rule-based model which is obtained from analyzing real dialogues from the task that the system is developed for [3]. However, recent efforts have been made in probabilistic models for dialogue systems [4]. The main advantage of these models is that they are easy to build, while the rule-based models are more difficult to build. However, the probabilistic models require annotated corpus.

This corpus annotation is based on the fact that dialogue models should only take into account essential information to determine the dialogue strategy. Therefore, the corpus should be annotated with labels which determine the essential information for each turn. One of the most popular options in dialogue labelling is the use of dialogue acts [5,6] to annotate the corpus. A dialogue act is a semantic label which takes into account the user's intention and

---

* This work was partially supported by Spanish CICYT under project TIC 2000-1599-C02-01 and Programa de Incentivo a la Investigación de la Universidad Politécnica de Valencia.

P. Sojka, I. Kopeček, and K. Pala (Eds.): TSD 2002, LNAI 2448, pp. 381–388, 2002.

the basic data given in a segment (a segment is a sub-utterance in the turn with isolated semantic meaning). This definition could be easily extended to system turns. Within this framework, the dialogue model should determine the next dialogue act(s) the system should perform.

In this work, we present two probabilistic dialogue models which are based on dialogue acts. Section 2 describes the basic model which is only based on the user's words. Section 3 extends this model by using semantic information provided by a semantic module. Section 4 describes the corpus and the experiments carried out with both models and the results obtained. Finally, Section 5 presents some conclusions about the results.

2   The Initial Probabilistic Dialogue Model

The general problem of dialogue could be viewed as a process of searching for the most correct (or most likely) action that the system could perform. This decision could be based on several factors, but the most common ones are last user turn and the previous history of the dialog. Using these two factors, our model should be able to determine the next dialogue act(s) to be performed.

From this perspective, the dialogue problem can be formulated as a search for the optimal system dialogue act that can be carried out (according to the last user turn and the dialogue history). Therefore, given the last user-turn word sequence ω and the dialogue history d (dialogue acts sequence), the system dialogue act $\hat{\mathcal{D}}$ that the model should determine is:

$$\hat{\mathcal{D}} = \underset{\mathcal{D}}{\operatorname{argmax}} \operatorname{Pr}(\mathcal{D} \mid \omega, d) = \underset{\mathcal{D}}{\operatorname{argmax}} \operatorname{Pr}(\mathcal{D}, \omega, d) \qquad (1)$$

For the sake of simplicity, in the presentation of the model, and without a loss of generality, we assume that ω is divided into *segments*. Therefore, we can rewrite the probability term as:

$$\operatorname{Pr}(\mathcal{D}, \omega, d) = \sum_{D} \operatorname{Pr}(\mathcal{D}, D, \Omega, d)$$

where $D = D_1 D_2 \ldots D_l$ is the sequence of dialogue acts of the last user turn (each of which corresponds to a segment) and where $\Omega = \Omega_1 \Omega_2 \ldots \Omega_l$ is the sequence of segments (each of which are a word sequence). The sum can be approached with a max operator, which is:

$$\operatorname{Pr}(\mathcal{D}, \omega, d) \approx \max_{D} \operatorname{Pr}(\mathcal{D}, D, \Omega, d)$$

Now, we can make the following breakdown:

$$\operatorname{Pr}(\mathcal{D}, D, \Omega, d) = \operatorname{Pr}(d) \operatorname{Pr}(\mathcal{D}, D, \Omega \mid d)$$

$$\operatorname{Pr}(\mathcal{D}, D, \Omega \mid d) = \operatorname{Pr}(D, \Omega \mid d) \operatorname{Pr}(\mathcal{D} \mid d, D, \Omega) \qquad (2)$$

Now, the first factor on the righthand side of (2) can be broken down into:

$$\operatorname{Pr}(D, \Omega \mid d) = \prod_{i=1}^{l} \operatorname{Pr}(D_i, \Omega_i \mid D_1^{i-1}, \Omega_1^{i-1}, d) \qquad (3)$$

Each term of the product of (3) can be rewritten as:

$$\Pr(D_i, \Omega_i \mid D_1^{i-1}, \Omega_1^{i-1}, d) = \Pr(D_i \mid D_1^{i-1}, \Omega_1^{i-1}, d) \Pr(\Omega_i \mid D_1^i, \Omega_1^{i-1}, d)$$

Where $D_k^m = D_k D_{k+1} \ldots D_m$ and $\Omega_k^m = \Omega_k \Omega_{k+1} \ldots \Omega_m$, with $k \leq m$.

Several approximations can be adopted to reduce the model complexity. For this term, we make the following assumption:

$$\Pr(D_i, \Omega_i \mid D_1^{i-1}, \Omega_1^{i-1}, d) \approx \Pr(D_i \mid D_{i+1-n}^{i-1}) \Pr(\Omega_i \mid D_i) \qquad n \geq 2 \qquad (4)$$

That is, we assume that a dialogue act only depends on the last n dialogue acts (not on the whole dialogue history), and that the words of a segment depend only on the corresponding dialogue act of the segment. The first term can be easily approached by a n-gram (i.e., a n 1 length history) and the second term can be approached using Hidden Markov Models (HMM).

Now we deal with the second term on the righthand side of (2). It can be assumed that:

$$\Pr(\mathcal{D} \mid d, D, \Omega) \approx \Pr(\mathcal{D} \mid d'^s_{s+2-m}) \qquad m \geq 2 \qquad (5)$$

Where s is the number of dialogue acts in the history d', which is equal to concatenating D to d. This assignation of the new dialogue act can be performed using a m-gram language model (i.e., a $m - 1$ length history). Obviously, other (more realistic and more expensive) assumptions can be adopted.

Eventually, the simplified and approximated model obtained is:

$$\operatorname*{argmax}_{D} \left[\max_{D} \Pr(\mathcal{D} \mid d'^s_{s+2-m}) \prod_{i=1}^{l} \Pr(D_i \mid D'^{i-1}_{i+1-n}) \Pr(\Omega_i \mid D_i) \right] \qquad (6)$$

where D' is equal to $d \cdot D_1 \cdots D_{i-1}$. In other words, it is necessary to extend the current user history to the previous dialogue acts in the dialogue in order to get enough history for the used n-gram. Therefore, the argument $\mathcal{D}$ which maximizes the previous formula is the next dialogue act that the system should perform. This model was previously presented by the authors in [7].

The meaning of the basic parts of the model are:

- $\Pr(D_i \mid D_{i+1-n}^{i-1})$: this is the N-gram used for assigning the user's dialogue acts; note that the used history is not only limited to the dialogue acts of the current turn (it can be extended to previous dialogue acts and even to system dialogue acts).
- $\Pr(\Omega_i \mid D_i)$: this is the model that assigns a dialogue act based on the words of the segment, i.e., an emitting model (such as a HMM) [1].
- $\Pr(\mathcal{D} \mid d^s_{s+2-m})$: this is the N-gram which assigns the most likely dialogue act based on the dialogue history (which is limited to $m - 1$ previous dialogue acts).

All these probability distributions could be automatically estimated using a labeled corpus of dialogues. However, more information sources can be added to this simple model. In the following section, we explain how to add semantic information to this basic model in order to obtain a more powerful model.

---

[1] Note that in practice the segments are not given.

3   Including Semantic Information: The Extended Dialogue Model

The model presented in (6) is quite simple, but this simplicity makes it weak in certain situations. More information sources can be added to strengthen this model. Most dialogue systems use an understanding module which assigns a sequence of semantic units to a word sequence. This feature can be easily incorporated into our dialogue model, which can assign dialogue acts using only the semantic unit sequence or combining it with the word sequence.

Therefore, the initial optimization problem can now be formulated by:

$$\hat{\mathcal{D}} = \operatorname*{argmax}_{\mathcal{D}} \Pr(\mathcal{D} \mid u, \omega, d) \tag{7}$$

where u is the semantic units sequence which is given by the understanding module.

If we develop (7) in the same way as we did (1), the following simplified model (which was also presented in [7]) can be obtained:

$$\operatorname*{argmax}_{\mathcal{D}} \left[\max_{\mathcal{D}} \Pr(\mathcal{D} \mid d'^{s}_{s+2-m}) \prod_{i=1}^{l} \Pr(D_i \mid D'^{i-1}_{i+1-n}) \Pr(U_i \mid D_i) \Pr(\Omega_i \mid D_i) \right] \tag{8}$$

where U_i represents the semantic unit sequence of the segment i (as Ω_i represents the word sequence of the segment i). In this model, $\Pr(U_i \mid D_i)$ can be modeled as $\Pr(\Omega_i \mid D_i)$, i.e, using an emitting model such as a HMM.

The usefulness of the models presented in (6) and (8) when implementing a complete dialogue system was presented in [7]. However, a specific evaluation of the models to compare their quality with other models was not carried out in that work. In the following section, we describe the experiments carried out in order to make the evaluation of the models as labellers [4].

4   Evaluation Experiments and Results

In this section, we will describe the dialogue corpus used in the evaluation, the implementation results and the results obtained with the presented models.

4.1   Corpus Details

The corpus used in our evaluation is known as *Basurde* [8]. *Basurde* is a project about building a telephone dialogue system for spontaneous speech in Spanish for a railway information task. In this task, the user can ask about timetables and fares for the nation-wide trains. This corpus contains a total of 226 spoken dialogues in Spanish which were obtained using the Wizard of Oz technique [9]. These dialogues ask for typical information about railways, such as departure and arrival times, cost of the trip, train types, extra services, etc.

These 226 dialogues were transcribed and semantically annotated. The semantical annotations were made at two levels: at the *frame* level, which provides the information of the current turn, and at the *understanding* level, which provides the adequate understanding labels for the subsegments of the current turn. Only 194 dialogues were fully semantically

Original user turn: *I want to go to Madrid on the Alaris.*

Semantically annotated turn: *I want*:consult *to go*:< dept_hour> *to*:dest_marker *Madrid*:dest_town *on the Alaris*:train_type.

Semantically annotated and categorized turn: *I want*:consult *to go*:< dept_hour> *to*:dest_marker INSTANCE:dest_town *on the* INSTANCE:train_type.

Fig. 1. User turn and its semantic final form.

annotated; 19 were partially annotated due to their complexity and the rest were not annotated due to special complications (they were mainly nonsense or out-of-task dialogues).

The entire 226 dialogues were also annotated at dialogue level using the set of labels defined in [10]. These labels are composed by three levels; the first level expresses the *speech act*, i.e., the intention of the user in the segment; the second level provides the *frames* (collections of data) used in the segment; the third level provides the *cases*, i.e., the specific data given in the segment. A total of 565 dialogue acts (labels) were defined (391 for the user and 174 for the system), which were applied to 1,656 user turns and to 2,546 system turns.

This corpus was divided into training and test subsets. The training subsets were different for each model (because of the different availability of data for each model). However, the test subset was formed by the same 75 dialogues. These test dialogues were also annotated, and this annotation is the reference for the comparision of the transcriptions that the model provided.

4.2 Experimental Issues

A categorization was defined for the model defined by (6) in order to reduce data sparseness. This categorization included names of cities, hours, days, fares, services and train types among others. The total number of dialogue acts included in the training dialogues was 432 (137 for the system and 295 for the user), and the total number of training segments (for the user) was 1197.

The model defined by (8) was implemented using one more assumption. In this implementation, $Pr(U_i | D_i) \cdot Pr(\Omega_i | D_i)$ was implemented by $Pr(\Omega_i, U_i | D_i)$. Ω_i, U_i is considered as a unique sequence. Therefore, the input for this model is different from the input for the previous model; this input must contain the words and the understanding labels. In our implementation, the understanding labels were obtained from an understanding module which is fully described in [11]. The obtained sequence can also be categorized in a way similar to the one for the previous model. An example of this process is shown in Figure 1.

The total number of dialogue acts included in the training dialogues for this model was 394 (137 for the system and 257 for the user), and the total number of training segments (for the user) was 1060.

For both models, HMM with a two-state, left-to-right topology with loops were used as emitting model, using the available data for each model to estimate their parameters. A non-smoothed 3-gram, which was estimated from the 151 training dialogues, was used as a dialogue history model. The evaluation was carried out assuming the correct history previous to the current user turn and using the model to obtain these user turn dialogue acts (i.e., only the user assignment models, $\Pr(D_i \mid D_{i+1-n}^{i-1})$ and $\Pr(\Omega_i \mid D_i)$ or $\Pr(\Omega_i, U_i \mid D_i)$ were used).

4.3   Results

Each model was applied to the 75 test dialogues in order to obtain a labelling of the user turns. This labelling was compared to the reference labels in the original annotated dialogue using the *accuracy* measure [4], which in our case was computed as $acc = 100 \cdot \frac{corr}{corr+sub+ins+del}$, where $corr$ is the number of matching dialogue acts, sub the incorrect substitutions, ins the number of insertions and del the number of deletions. In order to obtain results with a more reasonable number of labels, we can reduce our evaluation to the first and second levels only, or to a more reduced set of labels using the similarities among these labels.

We also have to take into consideration the number of test dialogue acts that are not present in the training set, i.e., the segments which are labelled with a dialogue act which is not present in the training set. We call the proportion of these segments in the test set the *forced error rate*. Therefore, these segments are disregarded when computing the real accuracy, which is defined as $acc_{real} = 100 \cdot \frac{acc}{100-forced}$, where acc is the accuracy calculated with the previous formula and *forced* is the forced error rate.

All the evaluation results (for the different sets of labels) are presented in Table 1. These results indicate a very low accuracy rate for the whole set of labels. The rate becomes higher when the set of labels is reduced. Accuracy also improves when semantic information is used. A brief comparation with other models is shown in Table 2.

Table 1. Accuracy results for dialogue models defined by (6) and (8).

Model	Number of labels	Accuracy	Forced errors	Real accuracy
Defined by (6)	391	17.9 %	16.1 %	21.3 %
Defined by (8)	391	23.6 %	17.5 %	28.6 %
Defined by (6)	101	33.6 %	3.4 %	34.8 %
Defined by (8)	101	38.8 %	6.7 %	41.6 %
Defined by (6)	35	54.9 %	0.8 %	55.3 %
Defined by (8)	35	55.3 %	3.8 %	57.4 %

As Table 2 indicates, our results using all the labels are worse than the results obtained using other models. However, when restricting the comparison, our results improve dramatically and are closer to other systems' results. Nevertheless, these results are not really comparable, because of the variability of the tasks involved, the different label sets used and the different training set size.

5   Conclusions and Future Work

In this work, we have presented a new probabilistic dialogue model. This dialogue model basically uses a Hidden Markov Model based on words to assign the dialogue act(s) to the user turn. It also uses a N-gram as language model when assigning these dialogue acts. This

Table 2. Accuracy results for different models, with different number of labels and different size in the training sets.

Model (Authors)	Task	Nr. of labels	Training size	Accuracy
Our best model (361 lab.)	Basurde,2002	391	1060	28.6 %
Our best model (101 lab.)	Basurde,2002	101	1060	40.4 %
Our best model (35 lab.)	Basurde,2002	35	1060	57.4 %
Samuel	Verbmobil,1998	18	2701	75.1 %
Wright	MapTask,1998	12	3276	64.0 %
Fukada	Jap. C-Star, 1998	26	3584	81.2 %
Nagata	ATR, 1994	15	2450	39.7 %
Stolcke	SwitchBoard, 2000	42	198000	65.0 %

model can be easily extended to use semantic sequences. The evaluation of the model is carried out by using it as labeller for the user turns.

However, the results obtained are not comparable to other tasks, and no conclusions about performance can be obtained. Furthermore, details on the evaluation of the other models are not available (accuracy definition, test set details, evaluation process, etc.) and, therefore, it is not clear whether the evaluation process is adequate to compare results.

In our opinion, this independent evaluation of the model is not precise enough to evaluate a complete dialogue system, which depends on more factors. A more complete evaluation of the dialogue system (using the EAGLES metrics [12], for example) is necessary, although it would be more costly. In spite of this, we also conclude that the proposed model might be a good starting point for developing more complicated and correct models which may improve the results obtained.

Future work on the proposed model is channeled in two main directions. The first is to improve the basic models on which the model is based; for example, the use of a 4-gram or 5-gram instead of the current 3-gram may improve the accuracy of the model. The second is to add more information sources to the current model; for example, the frame state (the data provided the past dialogue turns) could be an appropriate source of information. It would be interesting to model the influence of the frame state on the probabilistic model we have proposed.

References

1. Ch. Manning, H. Schütze 2001. *Foundations of statistical natural language processing*. MIT Press.
2. A. Zampolli G.B. Varile. 1996. *Survey of the state of the art in human language technology*. Cambridge University Press, Giardini Editori.
3. M. Araki and S. Doshita. 1998. A robust dialogue model for spoken dialogue processing. In *Proc. Int. Conf. on Spoken Language Processing*, Volume 4, pp. 1171–1174.
4. A. Stolcke, N. Coccaro, R. Bates, P. Taylor, C. van Ess-Dykema, K. Ries, E. Shriberg, D. Jurafsky, R. Martin, and M. Meteer. 2000. Dialogue act modelling for automatic tagging and recognition of conversational speech. *Computational Linguistics*, 26(3):1–34.
5. J. R. Searle, 1969. *Speech acts*. Cambridge University Press.

6. T. Fukada, D. Koll, A. Waibel, and K. Tanigaki. 1998. Probabilistic dialogue act extraction for concept based multilingual translation systems. In *Proc. Int. Conf. on Spoken Language Processing*, volume 6, pages 2771–2774.

7. C. D. Martínez-Hinarejos, F. Casacuberta. 2002. Probabilistic dialogue modelling Submitted to *40th. Aniversary Meeting of Association for Computational Linguistics*.

8. A. Bonafonte, P. Aibar, N. Castell, E. Lleida, J. B. Mariño, E. Sanchis, M. I. Torres 2000. Desarrollo de un sistema de diálogo oral en dominios restringidos. I Meeting on Language Engineering, Sevilla, Spain, 6th-10th November 2000.

9. M. Fraser and G. Gilbert. 1991. Simulating speech systems. *Computer Speech and Language*, 5:81–99.

10. C. Martínez, E. Sanchis, F. García, P. Aiba: 2002. A labelling proposal to annotate dialogues Third International Conference on Language Resources and Evaluation, Las Palmas de Gran Canaria, 29–31 May, 2002, to appear.

11. E. Segarra, E. Sanchis, M. Galiano, F. García, and L. Hurtado. to appear. Extracting semantic information through automatic learning techniques. *Pattern Recognition Letters*.

12. N. Fraser, 1997. *Assessment of interactive systems*, pages 564–614. Mouton de Gruyter.

Applying Dialogue Constraints to the Understanding Process in a Dialogue System[*]

Emilio Sanchis, Fernando García, Isabel Galiano, Encarna Segarra

Departamento de Sistemas Informáticos y Computación (DSIC),
Universidad Politécnica de Valencia (UPV),
Camino de Vera s/n, 46022 Valencia, Spain
E-mail: esanchis@dsic.upv.es, fgarcia@dsic.upv.es, mgaliano@dsic.upv.es,
esegarra@dsic.upv.es

Abstract. In this paper, we present an approach to the estimation of a dialogue-dependent understanding component of a dialogue system. This work is developed in the framework of the Basurde Spanish dialogue system, which answers queries about train timetables by telephone in Spanish. A modelization which is specific to each dialogue state is proposed to improve the behaviour of the understanding process. Some experimental results are presented.

1 Introduction

The construction of dialogue systems applied to limited domain information systems is an important objective in the area of Human Language Technologies. The advance in the design and analysis of the different knowledge sources involved in a spoken dialogue system, such as speech processing, language modeling, language understanding, or speech synthesis, has led to the development of dialogue system prototypes. Some characteristics of these systems are: telephone access, limited semantic domains and mixed initiative [6,4,1].

The work that we present in this paper is an approach to the construction of the understanding module of the Basurde dialogue system [2]. The system's task consists in answering telephone queries about railway timetables in Spanish. In this system, the output of the speech recognizer is the input of the understanding module, which in turn supplies its output to the dialogue manager.

The representation of the meaning of the user utterances is made through the semantic frames. The frame determines the type of communication of the user turn as well as the data supplied in the utterance.

There are two kinds of classical approaches to the problem of language understanding: the first is based on the use of rules to detect markers and keywords to obtain the frame type and its attributes; the second one is based on the use of models which are automatically learnt from samples. Some of these are based on stochastic models (HMM and Stochastic Regular Grammars) that can be automatically learnt by means of Grammatical Inference techniques [3,10,8].

---

[*] Work partially funded by *CICYT* under project 2000-0664-C02, Spain.

P. Sojka, I. Kopeček, and K. Pala (Eds.): TSD 2002, LNAI 2448, pp. 389–395, 2002.

One advantage of using models and learning techniques of this kind, is that it allows us to adapt to new tasks and situations, such as reestimation with new data, context changes, new tasks or different languages. However, one drawback is that it is necessary to have a large amount of training data, which is especially difficult to obtain in the case of dialogues.

In the Basurde system the representation of the dialogue structure is done by means of a stochastic network of dialogue acts. One advantage of this structure is that it gives a prediction of the next dialogue acts expected from the user. In this work, this information is used in the understanding process. In particular, different understanding models are used depending on the last dialogue act of the system. Other approaches of dialogue-dependent understanding models have been recently investigated [5].

2   The Basurde Task

The Basurde task [2] consists of telephone queries about the Spanish train timetables. The kind of queries (semantic restrictions) are: questions about timetables, prices, and services, for long distance trains. A corpus of 200 person-to-person dialogues corresponding to a real information system were recorded and analyzed. Then, four types of scenarios were defined (departure/arrival time for a one-way trip, a two-way trip, the prices and services, and one free scenario). A total of 215 dialogues were acquired using the Wizard of Oz technique. The total number of user turns was 1460 (14.902 words).

3   Dialogue Act Labels

The structure of a dialogue can be represented through dialogue acts. To do this, a set of labels of dialogue acts must be defined. The number of labels must be large enough to show the different intentions of the turns and to cover all the situations. If the number is too high the models will be underestimated because there aren't enough training samples. On the other hand, if we define a small set of just a few labels, only general purposes of the turn can be modeled. In the Basurde system a three-level label set was proposed [7]. The first level of each dialogue act describes the dialogue behavior. These labels are generic for any task. The second level is related to the semantic representation of a sentence and is specific to that task. The third level takes into account the data given in the utterance.

A stochastic network of dialogue acts can be learnt from training samples by using these labels. This network represents the dialogue structure and strategy and can be used by the Dialogue Manager to generate the dialogue acts of the system. It can also help in the recognition and the understanding process by means of the generation of hypotheses of the expected acts of the user.

We will center our interest on the first-level, which is used to direct the understanding process. The first level can take the following values:*Opening, Closing, Undefined, Not_understood, Waiting, New_query, Acceptance, Rejection, Question, Confirmation* and *Answer.*

An example of some turns annotated with the first-level labels is shown in Figure 1. Note that each turn can have more than one label associated to it.

S1: Bienvenido al sistema automático de información de trenes regionales y de largo recorrido, qué desea? (S:*Opening*)
    (*Welcome to the information system for train timetables. What information would you like?*)
U1: Puede decirme a qué hora salen los trenes de Valencia a Barcelona? (U:*Question*)
    (*Can you tell me what time the trains from Valencia to Barcelona leave?*)
S2: De Valencia a Barcelona,(S:*Confirmation*) qué dia quiere salir? (S:*Question*)
    (*From Valencia to Barcelona, what day do you want to leave?*)
U2: El próximo jueves (U:*Answer*)
    (*Next Thursday*)

Fig. 1. Example of a labelled dialogue.

4   Semantic Representation

In our system, the representation of the meaning of user turns is done using semantic frames; that is, each frame represents a semantic concept and it can have some attributes and values associated to it. The set of frames defined for this task is the following: *Departure_time, Return_departure_time, Arrival_time, Return_arrival_time, Price, Return_price, Length_of_trip, Train_type, Services, Confirmation, Not_Understood, Affirmation, Rejection* and *Closing*.

As we have mentioned above, a set of attributes can be associated to each frame. For example, the sentence:

> Cuál es el precio de un billete de Valencia a Barcelona?
> (*How much is a ticket from Valencia to Barcelona?*)

is represented as follows:

> (PRICE)
>   Destination: Barcelona
>   Origen: Valencia

5   Categorization

As the number of instances of some attributes can be very low, problems of coverage and lack of training samples can occur when learning stochastic models from a corpus. Therefore, we had to reduce the number of words in our lexicon by using lemmas and categories. Due to the complex conjugation of Spanish verbs we had to substitute any conjugated form of a verb with its corresponding infinitive form. We also had to substitute any instance of a city name with the category City-Name; any instance of day of the week with the category Day-Name; and the same with numbers, months, etc. We defined seven categories in the lexicon. This way, we reduced the size of our lexicon from 637 to 370 different words.

6   The Understanding Process

The understanding process is done in two phases. The first phase consists of a transduction of the input sentence in terms of an intermediate semantic language. As this intermediate semantic language that we defined is sequential with the input, some sequential transduction techniques can be used. In the second phase, a set of rules transduces this intermediate representation in terms of frames. As the intermediate language is close to the frame representation, this phase only requires a small set of rules in order to construct the frame. An example of the actions in this second phase is the conversion of relative dates and hours into absolute values. For example "next Monday" into "mm/dd/yr" or "in the morning" into "interval hours (from 5 to 12)".

The first phase of the understanding process is based on automatically learnt stochastic models. We have defined a set of 53 semantic units, which are a kind of semantic categorization. Each semantic unit represents the meaning of words (or sequences of words) in the sentences. For example, the semantic unit "consult" can be associated to "can you tell me", "please tell me", "what is", etc. This way, an input sentence (sequence of words) has a semantic sentence (sequence of semantic units) associated to it, and there is an inherent segmentation. An example is shown:

Spanish

w_1: por favor v_1: consulta
w_2: a que hora salen los trenes? v_2: <hora_salida>
w_3: hacia v_3: marcador_destino
w_4: Alicante v_4: ciudad_destino

English

w_1: please v_1: query
w_2: what is the railway timetable? v_2: <Departure_time>
w_3: to v_3: destination_marker
w_4: Alicante v_4: destination_city

The semantic sentence V for the semantic model training is:

$$consulta\ <hora\_salida>\ marcador\_destino\ ciudad\_destino$$
$$(query\ <Departure\_time>\ destination\_marker\ destination\_city)$$

The stochastic modelization is divided into two levels. The higher level (semantic model) represents the sequences of semantic units allowed. In the lower level (semantic unit models) the language (sequences of words) associated to each semantic unit is modelled. An annotated training corpus is used to obtain the stochastic models. Each sentence of the training set consists of the sequence of words, the sequence of semantic units and the associated segmentation.

Let T be a training set of pairs (W, V) of sequences of words and semantic units. We learn a model A_s for the semantic language $L_s \subseteq \mathcal{V}^*$, and a set of models (one for each semantic unit $v_i \in \mathcal{V}$, where $\mathcal{V}$ is the set of semantic units). The model A_s for the semantic language L_s is estimated from the semantic sentences $V \in \mathcal{V}^*$ of the training sample. The model A_{v_i} for each semantic unit $v_i \in \mathcal{V}$ is estimated from the set of segments, w_i, of the training sample associated to the semantic unit v_i. These estimations are made through automatic learning techniques.

In this work, a classical bigram model was estimated for the semantic model A_s, and the models for the semantic units, A_{v_i}, were also estimated as classical bigrams. However, other

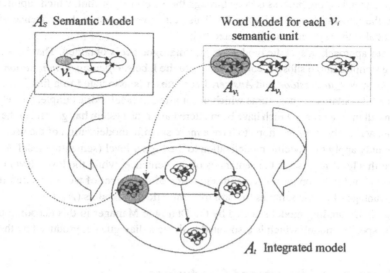

Fig. 2. Scheme of the two-level approach.

techniques can be used for the estimation of both models. This is the case of grammatical inference techniques such as the ECGI or MGGI [9,10].

In our approach the understanding process is as follows: Given the sequence of words of the input sequence $W = w_1 w_2 \ldots w_n$, the process consists of finding the sequence of semantic units $V = v_1 v_2 \ldots v_k$ which maximizes the probability:

$$\widehat{V} = \underset{V}{\operatorname{argmax}} \, P(W|V) P(V)$$

The term $P(W|V)$ is the probability of the sequence of words W given the sequence of semantic units V. We approach this probability, following the Viterbi criterium, as the maximum for all posible segmentations of W in $|V|$ segments.

$$P(W|V) =$$
$$= \underset{\forall l_1, l_2, \ldots l_{k-1}}{\max} \{ P(w_1, \ldots, w_{l_1} | v_1) \cdot P(w_{l_1+1}, \ldots, w_{l_2} | v_2) \cdot \ldots \cdot P(w_{l_{k-1}+1}, \ldots, w_n | v_k) \}$$

where the probability of each segment is done by means of bigram probabilities of words given the associated semantic unit:

$$P(w_i, \ldots, w_j | v_s) = P(w_i | v_s) \prod_{k=i+1}^{j} P(w_k | w_{k-1}, v_s)$$

The term $P(V)$ is the bigram probability of the sequence V.

$$P(V) = P(v_1) \prod_{i=2}^{k} P(v_i | v_{i-1})$$

The understanding process is done through the Viterbi algorithm, which supplies the best path in the integrated model (Figure 2.). This path gives not only the sequence of sematic units but also the segmentation associated to it.

In our approach, a specific model for each dialogue act is obtained. That is, we split the training samples into 6 subsets, corresponding to the labels: *Opening, Confirmation, Waiting, New_query, Not_understood* and *Answer*. Each subset is associated to a first-level dialogue label, and it contains the user turns which occur after its label. For example, the set *Opening* contains all the user turns which have been uttered after the system has generated the *Opening* dialogue act. In this way, we hope to have a more specific modelization of the user turns.

We only apply the specific modelization to the higher level (semantic model A_s). This is because this level represents the semantics of the sentence, while the lower level represents the specific instantiation of this semantics in terms of sequences of words. Therefore, we can take advantage of all the samples to learn the semantic unit models (A_{v_i}).

The understanding model selected by the Dialogue Manager in this decoding process is only the specific model, which is associated to the last dialogue act produced by the system.

7   Experimental Results and Conclusions

In order to study the appropriateness of Specific Language Understanding models (SLU), a preliminary experimentation on the Basurde task was conducted. The obtained results were then compared with the results for the same task but using a unique Language Understanding model (LU). In this section, we present the results of these two types of models for the same task. At the light of these results, some conclusions will be drawn.

The corpus consisted of the orthographic transcription of a set of 215 dialogues, which were obtained using the Wizard of Oz technique. These dialogues contained 1,460 user turns which were our experimental set. For this set, a cross-validation procedure was used to evaluate the performance of our models. The experimental set was randomly split into five subsets of 292 turns. One of our experiments then consisted of five trials, each of which had a different combination of one subset taken from the five subsets as the test set, with the remaining 1,168 turns being used as the training set.

We defined four measures to evaluate the accuracy of the models:

- the percentage of correct sequences of semantic units (%cssu).
- the percentage of correct semantic units (%csu).
- the percentage of correct frames (%cf); i.e., the percentage of resulting frames that are exactly the same as the corresponding reference frame.
- the percentage of correct frame slots (frame name and its attributes) (%cfs).

The experimental results (%cssu, %csu, %cf and %cfs) obtained by using LU and SLU models are shown in Table 1.

From Table 1, it can be concluded that using SLU models helps to slightly improve the understanding process.

In the light of the results obtained, we can conclude that using Specific Language Understanding Models is a good way to implement the required feedback between the dialogue manager and understanding modules.

Table 1. Experimental Results.

	%cssu	%csu	%cf	%cfs
LU	68.1	87.6	80.84	89.1
SLU	69.6	88.1	81.9	89.3

More works should be done to improve feedback. For instance, SLU and LU model can be interpolated in order to avoid the lack of coverage of specific models. It can also be defined new sets of specific models.

References

1. Cmu communicator spoken dialog toolkit (csdtk).
   http://www.speech.cs.cmu.edu/communicator/.
2. A. Bonafonte, P. Aibar, N. Castell, E. Lleida, J.B. Mariño, E. Sanchis, and M.I. Torres. Desarrollo de un sistema de diálogo oral en dominios restringidos. In: *I Jornadas en Tecnología del Habla, Sevilla (Spain)*, 2000.
3. H. Bonneau-Maynard and F. Lefèvre. Investigating stochastic speech understanding. In: *Proc. of IEEE Automatic Speech Recognition and Understanding Workshop (ASRU)*, 2001.
4. J. Glass and E. Weinstein. Speech builder: facilitating spoken dialogue system development. In: *Proc. in EuroSpeech*, Volume 1, pp. 1335–1338, 2001.
5. K Hacioglu and W. Ward. Dialog-context dependent language modeling combining n-grams and stochastic context-free grammars. In: *Proc. of ICASSP*, 2001.
6. L. Lamel, S. Rosset, J.L. Gauvain, S. Bennacef, M. Garnier-Rizet, and B. Prouts. The limsi arise system. *Speech Communication*, (31):339–353, 2000.
7. C. Martinez, E. Sanchis, F. García, and P. Aibar. A labeling proposal to annotate dialogues. In: *Proc. of third International Conference on Language Resources and Evaluation (LREC))*, 2002.
8. F. Pla, A. Molina, E. Sanchís, E. Segarra, and F. García. Language understanding using two-level stochastic models with pos and semantic units. In: Lecture Notes in Artificial Intelligence 2166, *Proc. of 4th International Conference TSD*, pages 403–409, 2001.
9. E. Segarra and L. Hurtado. Construction of Language Models using Morfic Generator Grammatical Inference MGGI Methodology. In: *Proc. of EuroSpeech*, pages 2695–2698, 1997.
10. E. Segarra, E. Sanchis, I. Galiano, F. García, and L.F. Hurtado. Extracting semantic information through automatic learning. In: *Proc. of IX Spanish Symposium on Pattern Recognition and Image Analysis (AERFAI)*, pages 177–182, 2001.

Evaluation of Prediction Methods
Applied to an Inflected Language

Nestor Garay-Vitoria, Julio Abascal, Luis Gardeazabal

Laboratory of Human-Computer Interaction for Special Needs
University of the Basque Country
Manuel Lardizabal 1; E-20018 Donostia
Phone: +34 943 018000; Fax: +34 943 219306
E-mail: nestor@si.ehu.es, julio@si.ehu.es, luisg@si.ehu.es

Abstract. Prediction is one of the techniques that has been applied to Augmentative and Alternative Communication to help people enhance the quality and quantity of the composed text in a time unit. Most of the literature has focused on word prediction methods that may easily be applied to non-inflected languages. However, for inflected languages, other approaches that mainly distinguish roots and suffixes may enhance the results (in terms of keystroke savings and hit ratio) of predictive systems. In this paper, we present the approaches we have applied to the Basque language (highly inflected) and the results they achieve with a particular text (that was not used while creating the initial lexicons the systems use for prediction). Starting from this evaluation, one of the presented approaches is suggested as being the best.

1 Introduction

People with severe motor and oral disabilities that use Augmentative and Alternative Communication systems in order to write messages need a long time to compose them. The communication speed they achieve is very low (estimated at 2–10 words/minute) in comparison to the speed achieved in spoken conversations (estimated at 120–180 words/minute) [3].

This situation may be alleviated if the required time to compose messages is reduced. One of the techniques to do this is anticipation or prediction, which consists in trying to guess what a person is going to say or write immediately after what has been said or written [7]. In this way, apart from enhancing the communication speed, the physical effort required to compose messages may be reduced because the same information quantity can be composed with fewer keystrokes.

Even the study of prediction techniques was initially devoted to alleviate some of the needs of people with disabilities, people without disabilities may take advantage of them if they are adequately integrated in applications and have an appropriate interface[1] [6].

However, there is no unique valid approach to all languages. Most of the references in the literature are related to the case of non-inflected languages (such as English, French

---

[1] These applications try to minimise the user's effort when using the computer. For example, enhancing the quality and/or the quantity of the composed text, as the correction of the spelling.

P. Sojka, I. Kopeček, and K. Pala (Eds.): TSD 2002, LNAI 2448, pp. 397–403, 2002.
© Springer-Verlag Berlin Heidelberg 2002

or Spanish), where roots have a small amount of variations (for example, in the number: spy/spies). In this case, as the number of different forms of a root is small, it is possible to include all of them in the dictionary the system requires to work. In these languages, the block that is normally treated by the system is the word itself (they are word prediction methods) [5,10,11,12,13,14]. Unfortunately, in inflected languages (such as Basque, German or Swedish) roots have a huge amount of variations and it is nearly impossible to store all of them in the dictionary[2]. Therefore, the prediction of a word is carried out in various steps; typically, roots and suffixes are distinguished and then a word is completed in a two-step process (one step for the root and another for the suffix) [4]. A complete revision of the problem may be found in [8,9]. Then, in inflected languages the prediction treats morphemes and they are morpheme prediction methods.

In the next sections, we are going to present the methods that we have studied in order to apply to the Basque language. Their main characteristics are expressed and the results they achieve are presented and compared, trying to determine which method is the most suitable.

2   Prediction Techniques Studied for the Basque Language

In this section we briefly present the prediction methods that we have applied in the case of Basque. For a more detailed description see [9].

2.1   Prediction by Frequencies

The first methods that we have studied are based on purely statistical information in order to determine the blocks the systems offer to the user as proposals.

Word Prediction. As a starting point, we consider the word as the block to be treated by the predictor. The system has a lexicon where the words and their frequencies are stored. This system offers the most frequent words that start with the string the user has written so far, in the same way they are stored in the lexicon. This operational way can be used for any language, if a lexicon of the required characteristics is included in the system. All the required adaptations are automatically made by updating the frequencies.

The main objectives of this first approach are to distinguish the involved knowledge in the problem environment and to make comparisons with the rest of the approaches.

Morpheme Prediction. In this approach, there are two lexicons: one for roots and another for the suffixes, each containing the frequency of the associated morphemes. From this approach onwards, both the system and the user have to clearly distinguish roots and suffixes. One way to clearly distinguish if the system is working with roots is including some dots in the interface at the end of the lemmas (for example, "know..."); in the same way, the system will be working with suffixes if the proposals are preceded by dots (for instance, "...ing"). The cognitive interface has also to offer the feature of explicitly changing from root prediction to

---

[2] For example, in the case of the Basque language a noun may have 62 basic declensions, but as it is an agglutinative language, suffixes may be recursively concatenated. Then, with two levels of recursion it has been estimated that a noun may have 458,683 forms [1].

suffix prediction. This change is implicitly made when the proposals are accepted or when the user stops composing the treated unit (root or suffix), with perhaps a final space or a similar character.

This system starts proposing the most frequent roots that begin with the string the user has written so far until the root is guessed or entirely written; it then proposes the suffixes until the word is guessed or completed. Next, it starts once more with the roots and so on. The adaptations are made by updating the frequencies.

As the case of the verbs is special in the Basque language (their most probable suffixes are very different in relation to those of nouns), new approaches that take syntactic information into account are tried.

2.2 Morpheme Prediction Using Probability Tables Taking Categories into Account

Still distinguishing roots and suffixes, syntactical information is added to the lexicons. Moreover, there are a number of bidimensional tables that store the relative probabilities of the categories of the suffixes to appear after the categories of the roots and *vice versa* for making predictions.

In this system, the most probable roots, starting with the written string and whose categories are the most probable after the last composed suffix, are then proposed. After composing the root, the suffixes are then treated, and so on. Adaptation is performed by updating the frequencies of the lexicons and the entries of the used tables.

However, there are various problems to solve, as there are ambiguous morphemes and new roots and suffixes that may appear if adapted to the user's vocabulary. Possible ways to solve these problems may be found in the literature: systems that typically try to guess the category, others that directly ask the user for the missed information, or some systems that give a special category (related to the new roots or suffixes) in order for the information to be completed when the user is ready to do so (perhaps by a specific user or in a specific session).

2.3 Prediction Using Syntactic Grammars

In these cases, some grammars are defined using rules that show how some composed categories may be decomposed in a succession of categories (that can be simple or composed). Each rule has a weight that refers its probability of apparition. There is also a table that stores the probability a syntactic category of a root that has to start a sentence. The sentences are parsed using the *chart* bottom-up method [2].

Morpheme Prediction. In this system, the dictionaries continue storing syntactic information. The system offers the most probable roots with the appropriate start whose categories are most likely to appear after the categories at the beginning of the sentence; then, the suffixes are proposed in a similar way and the process is repeated again and again. With the first word of a sentence, the most probable roots are proposed taking the probability table into account. As seen, the entire start of the sentence is considered. Therefore, the computational complexity of this approach is higher than the previous ones.

In the adaptation, there is a need to update the frequencies of the dictionaries, the weights of the rules and the entries of the probability table.

Morpheme-Based Prediction with Acceptation of Entire Words. In our studies, we have found it is very usual in Basque that a root acts as an entire word (that is to say, no suffix is added to a root very frequently). This approach is based in this feature in order to enhance the results the previous approaches achieve.

The lexicons, the rules and the probability table are the same as the last previous approach. It tries to guess the entire word if possible; if not, the roots are tried and then the suffixes as in the case of the previous approach. Thus, as seen, the entire beginning of the sentence is taken into account again.

The adaptation is also done in the same way as in the last previous approach.

In order to distinguish if a root is accepted as a word or a mere root, the acceptation protocol is changed to make the total and partial acceptations possible, respectively.

3   Achieved Results

These five presented approaches have been evaluated by programs that emulate the user's behaviour. In every approach, the results that are achieved when the system offers from 1 to 10 proposals to the user are studied. We have limited the study up to 10 proposals because of the difficulties in managing more than 10 proposals in the physical interface; it is complicated, very exhausting and time consuming to read them and select one.

Atal hau aipatutako zerbitzuak mantendu eta antolatzeaz arduratuko da, baita erabiltzaile interesatuei beren informazioa unibertsitateko intranet sarean eta interneten eskueran izateko aholkatzeaz ere.
Atal^ hau^ aipa^tutako zerbitzu^ak manten^du eta^ antola^tzeaz ardura^tuko da^, baita^ erabiltza-ile^ interesatu^ei beraiek^en informazio^a unibertsitate^ko intranet^ sare^an eta^ internet^en es-kuera^n izan^teko aholkatze^az ere^.

Fig. 1. Example of a Basque sentence without delimiters of morphemes (above) and with them (below), being "^" the delimiter.

The word prediction approach is associated with a lexicon that has been created starting from some Basque corpora. This lexicon has 8,969 entries, each composed by a word and its frequency. The lexicon of the rest of the approaches is also taken from those corpora decomposing words in their roots and suffixes. Concretely, they have 4,771 roots and 233 suffixes (44.21 % items less than in the first approach).

The study of the performance of the techniques has been done by using texts that have not been used while creating the lexicons, to prevent favourable tendencies. In this paper, we show the results achieved with the most representative text. As there is a need to distinguish roots and suffixes in four of the approaches (while this is not necessary in the first), we have two versions of the text: one with delimiters of roots and suffixes (for the last four approaches) and another without the delimiters (for the first), as shown in Figure 1. Thus, depending on the used version, the text has 2,691 or 2,974 characters. The text is a technical report related to computer science and Internet.

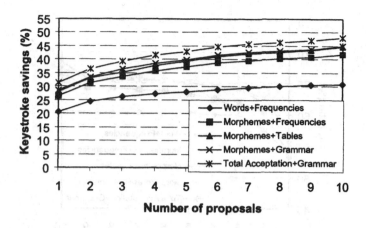

Fig. 2. Keystroke savings with the different approaches.

In Figure 2, we show the keystroke savings in percentiles that have been obtained in the different approaches with the mentioned text. Keystroke savings (KS) are defined in (1).

$$KS = \frac{total\ \#\ of\ keystrokes\ -\ \#\ of\ written\ keystrokes}{total\ \#\ of\ keystrokes} \tag{1}$$

The main qualitative enhancements appear when the morphemes are separately treated (instead of treating the words) and when a root may be accepted as a whole word (instead of not giving this possibility). The second approach enhances the results of the first between 5.83 % and 11.08 % in absolute values (28.24 %-35.89 % in relative values). The third presented approach enhances 1.55 %-2.66 % in absolute values (4.80 %-6.50 % in relative values) the results of the second. The fourth is better than the third in 0.27 %-1.11 % absolute (0.62 %-3.15 % relative) and the last enhances 2.63 %-3.13 % the fourth in an absolute way (6.87 %-9.16 % relative enhancement).

In Figure 3, the hit ratios that have been achieved are shown. The hit ratio (HR) in word prediction is as (2). When distinguishing roots and suffixes hit ratio is calculated as (3), being HRR the hit ratio for roots and HRS the hit ratio for suffixes. In the last approach, if HRW is the hit ratio for roots that work as words, P the probability that there is no suffix added to a root (1>=P>=0) and HR, HRR and HRS are previously defined, we define HR as in (4).

$$HR = \frac{\#\ of\ times\ a\ word\ is\ guessed}{\#\ of\ written\ words} \tag{2}$$

$$HR = \frac{HRR + HRS}{2} \tag{3}$$

$$HR = HRW \times P + \left(\frac{HRR + HRS}{2}\right) \times (1 - P) \tag{4}$$

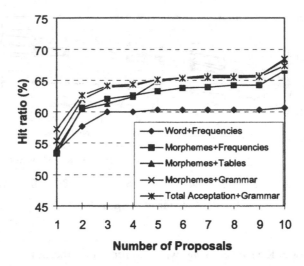

Fig. 3. Achieved hit ratios in percentiles.

In general, the last presented approach achieves the best hit ratios, with an increase in absolute terms that vary between 12.75 % and 15.23 % the following in absolute values (generally the fourth). This enhancement with respect to the rest is mainly due to the fact that when accepting a root as a word, there is an implicit acceptation of its null suffix, and this type of suffix is otherwise impossible to guess (at least in the approaches that distinguish roots and suffixes). The approaches that work with morphemes are all similar to the rest. With one proposal, the word prediction presents a similar hit ratio; however, in the rest of the cases it is the worst.

4   Conclusions

Five approaches to make predictions in an inflected language such as Basque have been presented. The second, third and fourth approaches are very similar, but the savings are enhanced in the order they have been presented. The last presented method is similar to the fourth with the possibility of accepting roots as words, due to the special characteristics of Basque (where this fact has a high probability). This last approach is the one that achieves the best results. Therefore, it is expected that the same strategy of accepting roots as entire words may be applied to the second and the third presented approaches in order to enhance their results.

We suggest the last presented approach (morpheme-based prediction using syntactic grammars with acceptation of entire words) as the most appropriate in order to obtain the best results. It is worth concluding by saying that the word prediction by frequencies is language-independent while the rest depend on the characteristics of the analysed language (in our case, Basque).

Acknowledgements

This paper is part of the Ph.D. thesis memory presented by the first author in the University of the Basque Country. The involved work has been partially financed by contracts and projects.

The authors would like express their gratitude for all the help provided in this work. A special thanks also goes for the people from the Laboratory of Human-Computer Interaction for Special Needs, in the Computer Science Faculty of the University of the Basque Country.

References

1. Agirre E., Alegria I., Arregi X., Artola X., Díaz de Ilarraza A., Maritxalar M., Sarasola K., and Urkia M. 1992. XUXEN: A Spelling Checker/Corrector for Basque Based on Two-Level Morphology. *Proceedings of the 3rd Conference on Applied Natural Language Processing Association for Computational Linguistics.* 119–125.
2. Allen J. 1995. Natural Language Understanding. *Benjamin Cummings Publishing Company.* 2nd Edition.
3. Alm N., Arnott J.L. and Newell A.F. 1992. Prediction and Conversational Momentum in an Augmentative Communication System. *Communications of the ACM 35, Number 5.* 46–57.
4. Bertenstam J. and Hunnicutt S. 1995. Adding Morphology to a Word Predictor. *The European Context for Assistive Technology (Proceedings of the 2nd TIDE Congress).* IOS Press/Ohmsa, Bruselas. 312–315.
5. Carlberger J. 1997. Design and Implementation of a Probabilistic Word Prediction Program. *Master's Thesis in Computer Science,* NADA, KTH, Stockholm (Sweden). Taken from http://www.speech.kth.se/~johanc/thesis/thesis.doc.
6. Darragh J. J., Witten I. H. and James M. L. 1990. The Reactive Keyboard: A Predictive Typing Aid. *Computer,* 23 (Number 11 November). 41–49.
7. Garay-Vitoria N. and González-Abascal J. 1997. Intelligent Word-Prediction to Enhance Text Input Rate. *Proceedings of the Intelligent User Interfaces 97 Congress.* ACM Press, New York (USA). 241–244.
8. Garay-Vitoria N. and Abascal J. G. 1997. Word Prediction for Inflected Languages. Application to Basque Language. *Proceedings of the Natural Language Processing for Communication Aids Workshop Sponsored by the Association for Computational Linguistics.* Association for Computational Linguistics. 29–36.
9. Garay-Vitoria, N. 2001. Sistemas de Predicción Lingüística. Aplicación a Idiomas con Alto y Bajo Grado de Flexión, en el Ámbito de la Comunicación Alternativa y Aumentativa. *Servicio Editorial de la UPV-EHU, Leioa (Bizkaia).* ISBN: 84-8373-355-2.
10. Heinisch B. and Hecht J. 1993. Word Prediction: A Comparison of Six Programs. *TAM Newsletter,* 4–9. Taken from http://www.edc.org./FSC/NCIP/.
11. Higginbotham D. 1992. Evaluation of Keystroke Savings Across Five Assistive Communication Technologies. *Augmentative and Alternative Communication,* 8. 258–272.
12. Koester H.H. and Levine S.P. 1998. Model Simulations of User Performance with Word Prediction. *Augmentative and Alternative Communication* 14, 25–35.
13. Van Dyke J. A. 1991. Word Prediction for Disabled Users: Applying Natural Language Processing to Enhance Communication. *Thesis submitted for the degree of Honors Bachelor of Arts in Cognitive Studies.* University of Delaware.
14. Venkatagiri H.S. 1993. Efficiency of Lexical Prediction as a Communication Acceleration Technique. *Augmentative and Alternative Communication,* 9. 161–167.

Knowledge Based Speech Interfacing for Handhelds

C.K. Yang and L.J.M. Rothkrantz

Data and Knowledge Engineering
Delft University of Technology
Mekelweg 4, 2628 CD Delft, The Netherlands
E-mail: L.J.M.Rothkrantz@cs.tudelft.nl

Abstract. Speech technology is rapidly developing and has improved a lot over the last few years. Nevertheless, speech-enabled applications have not yet become mainstream software. Furthermore, there is a lack of proven design methods and methodologies specifically concerning speech applications. So far the application of speech technology has only been a limited success. This Paper describes a project done at CMG Trade Transport & Industry BV. It is called SWAMP and is an example of the application of speech technology in human-computer interaction. The reasoning model behind the speech interface is based on the Belief Desire Intention (BDI) model for rational agents. Other important tools that were used to build the speech user interface are the Microsoft Speech API 5 and CLIPS.

1 Introduction

Speech is the most common mode of communication between people. Although speech communication is not a perfect process, we are able to understand each other with a very high success rate. Research has shown that the use of speech enhances the quality of communication between humans, as reflected in shorter problem solving times and general user satisfaction [1]. Furthermore, speaking to humans subjectively seems to be a relatively effortless task [2]. The benefits mentioned above are some reasons that have moved researchers to study speech interaction systems between humans and computers.

In September 1999 CMG Trade, Transport & Industry BV started the Wireless Automotive Messaging (WAM) project. Its purpose was to develop new wireless services in the field of traffic and transport. The WAM application is based on the Client-Server model. The server is stationary while the client travels with the user in his car. Because the clients are mobile, communication is based on wireless techniques.

This paper discusses the SWAMP (Speech Interfacing in the Wireless Automotive Messaging Pilot) project started in October of the following year. The purpose of the SWAMP project was to analyse if a speech interface is better suited for the WAM pilot. Therefore the WAM client is extended with a speech interface: the SWAMP client. This offers a way for the driver to interact with the system while his hands and eyes remain free, ideal for car driving situations.

P. Sojka, I. Kopeček, and K. Pala (Eds.): TSD 2002, LNAI 2448, pp. 405–412, 2002.

2   The SWAMP Client

Speech interaction between the user and the SWAMP application is based on dialogues. Generally, the user starts a speech interaction by indicating (via speech) what his desires are. The system then leads the user through a dialogue in which it tries to retrieve information regarding these desires. If eventually all the necessary information is collected, the application takes the appropriate actions to realise the user's desires. The general assumption behind the speech interface is that the user wants to accomplish something with his utterances, i.e. he has a certain goal in mind. The set of all services the SWAMP application has to offer is just a subset of all the goals the user can possibly have. Goals that don't correspond to a service, however are beyond the domain of the speech interface and are ignored. The speech interface is divided into 3 components.

1. The speech recognition or ASR component: Its function is to recognise the user's utterance and transform it into a format that can be processed.
2. The dialogue management component: Its function is to process the input from the speech recognition component to figure out what the user wanted to accomplish and take the appropriate actions to realise the user's wishes. This component is the main focus in this paper.
3. The speech synthesis or TTS component: Its function is to generate speech output to the user.

Figure 1 gives a graphical overview of how the speech interface is implemented. The main application is the original WAM client modified in such a way that it can communicate with the dialogue manager.

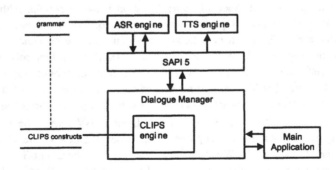

Fig. 1. Overview of SWAMP implementation.

The SWAMP client is implemented in C++ (Microsoft Visual C++ 6.0 enterprise edition). Initially it was the intention to build the speech interface to run on Windows CE but due to limitations in software and hardware of handheld computers, Windows NT was ultimately chosen.

The Microsoft Speech Application Programming Interface 5.0 (SAPI5) is used as middleware between the engines and the SWAMP application. SAPI5 acts as a communication layer between the dialogue manager and the speech resources (ASR and TTS engine). It takes care of hardware specific issues such as audio device management and removes implementation details such as multi-threading. This reduces the amount of code overhead required for an application to use speech recognition and synthesis. Another advantage of using middleware is that the choice of the final ASR and TTS engine can be postponed till a later stadium (e.g. until there is more budget for better engines). The CLIPS expert system tool is designed to facilitate the development of software to model human knowledge or expertise. CLIPS is embedded in the SWAMP client. It can be viewed as the knowledge processing and management unit of the dialogue manager.

3 Dialogue Design

With each initial utterance from the user, the speech interface tries to find the corresponding service involved. Once the goals of the user are clear it tries to accomplish the service by checking whether all the information needed is available. If this is not the case, the speech interface must initiate a dialogue to retrieve the required information from the user until the task can be performed. All possible dialogues that the speech interface can be involved in must be designed beforehand. This includes speech prompts for each situation, and all possible user responses on those prompts. Furthermore design involves the definition of a grammar that captures the syntax of whole conversations into a few simple grammar rules.

3.1 Design Approach

The goal of the speech interface is to give a user access to the SWAMP services by means of simple speech interaction. To achieve this, one can choose between two different approaches: 1) demand a longer learning time for the speech interface and require the user to adapt his speaking style or 2) make it easy for the user by allowing an extensive grammar and modelling more and more complex dialogues so that the user can speak to the system as with another human.

Speech User Interface (SUI) designers have learned that humans are extraordinarily flexible in their speech and readily adapt to the speaking style of their conversational partners. This is not a new finding: think about how easily we adjust our speech depending on whether we are speaking to children or other adults. This flexibility has useful implications for designing the speech interface: after extensive use of the speech interface (as the user gets acquainted with the grammar and has more experience) some dialogues become less and less common. Since the user will adapt his style of interacting and refrain to only those dialogues that were successful in the past. Because of this finding and the choice of our typical user ("he is familiar with current computer technology") the first approach was chosen: only model the most common utterances and let the user adapt to it.

3.2 Dialogue Representation

Without a proper representation technique, the dialogues can quickly become very complex and unmanageable. In this project dialogues are represented by flow diagrams containing nodes representing start/begin points of a dialogue, boxes representing actions (e.g. an utterance from a user or an action from the system), diamonds representing decisions point and arcs to connect the nodes, boxes and diamonds. A dialogue always begins with a start node and ends with an end node. Within these nodes, the dialogue travels from box to box along the arcs and branching at the decision diamonds. A successful dialogue corresponds to a path in the flow diagram from the start node to the end node. Speech dialogues are context sensitive. In our representation, the context is defined by the positions within the dialogue flow. Each box represents a certain state or context. The arcs branching from a box indicate the options available within that context and the branches leading to a box define how that context can be achieved.

The power of above dialogue representation technique lies in the fact that dialogues are represented in a generic way. E.g. the (user action) boxes define what the user can say at that moment in the dialogue, but not how it must be said (this is defined in the grammar). In this way, a single path in the dialogue flow diagram can represent whole categories of similar dialogues.

A well-modelled dialogue flow diagram is one where each possible dialogue flow can fit in. This implicates that common communication errors, such as misunderstandings, should be modelled as well as mechanisms for correcting and preventing these errors, such as requests for confirmation and roll back. Table 1 shows an example dialogue for the kilometre registration (KM registration) service. The flow of this dialogue fits into the flow diagram in Figure 2 (accentuated).

Table 1. Example dialog.

U: Change trip type
S: Is it a business or a private trip?
U: It's a business trip?
S: OK, what's the project ID for this business trip?
U: Project ID is SWAMP
S: Do you want to set the project ID to SWAMP?
U: Yes
S: OK, trip type is set.

In practice the dialogues can become so complex and the dialogue flow diagrams so large that it is best to split them up into one main dialogue and several smaller sub dialogues. For each sub dialogue a separate dialogue flow diagram is designed and referred to in the main dialogue flow diagram (by means of sub dialogue nodes). Another use for the dialogue flow diagrams occurs during the testing phase. Since each path from the start node to the end node corresponds to a successful dialogue. The correctness of the implementation of the dialogues can easily be verified if all the paths in the dialogue flow diagrams can be traversed

3.3 Grammar

The SAPI5 design specification requires the grammar of an application must be a context-free grammar (CFG) written in a format specified in the SAPI5 grammar schema. This schema describes the SAPI 5.0 speech recognition grammar format and is based on the XML framework. The ASR engine uses the CFG to constrain the words contained in the user's utterance that it will recognise. Basically the grammar file consists of a set of grammar rules in the grammar schema syntax. The complete specification of the schema can be found in the SAPI5 online help. Grammar rules can have an activation state, which can be set to active of inactive. SAPI5 recognises active rules and conversely does not recognise deactivated ones. The application may change the state of the rules during execution. So if a rule is no longer needed, it may be deactivated.

In order to indicate the functional parts of a sentence i.e. the parts that actually contain relevant information, the CFG can be extended with semantic information declared inside the grammar. This enables the ASR engine to associate certain. Recognised word strings with name/value-meaning representations. The dialogue manager then applies these meaning representation associations to understand and control the dialogue with the user.

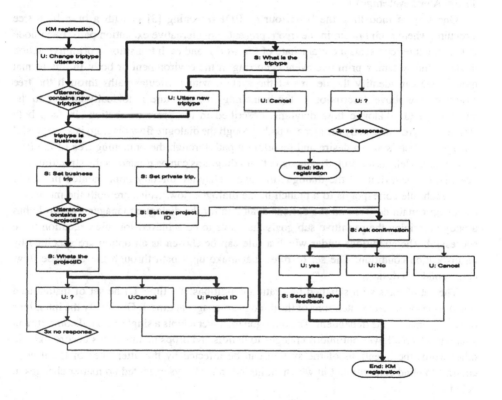

Fig. 2. Dialogue flow diagram for the KM registration service.

The grammar rules are derived from a corpus of utterances by hand. Crucial in this process is the determination where the relevant information is located within an utterance. Once this is accomplished, the derivation process is straightforward.

4 The Reasoning Model

In the search for a suitable reasoning model for the dialogue manager: one that is capable of adequately describing the reasoning behaviour of the dialogue manager, the Belief-Desire-Intention (BDI) model [4] was chosen. In an implementation of a dialogue manager according to this model, the dialogue manager continuously executes a cycle of observing the world and updating its beliefs, deciding what intention to achieve next, determining a plan of some kind to achieve this intention, and then executing the plan.

There exist a correspondence between concrete CLIPS data structures and the attitudes in the BDI model. Beliefs in the BDI model are implemented as facts and rules in CLIPS. Facts are used to construct the dialogue manager's internal representation of the world. Facts can be seen as propositions and thus can only consist of a set of literals without disjunction or implication. Therefore special rules (belief rules) are used to complete the representation of beliefs. Belief rules represent the general relationship between facts (e.g. IF utterance=help THEN AlertLevel=high).

One way of modelling the behaviour of BDI reasoning [3] is with a branching tree structure, where each branch in the tree represents an alternative execution path. Each node in the structure represents a certain state of the world, and each transition a primitive action made by the system, a primitive event occurring in the environment or both. In this formal model, one can identify the desires of the system with particular paths through the tree structure. The above description of the branching tree structure is logically similar to the structure of the dialogue flow diagrams described in the previous section. In fact, both structures represent exactly the same: a path through the dialogue flow diagram is a successful dialogue, which is also a desire and therefore a path through the branching tree of the BDI reasoning model. As a result, the dialogue flows diagrams can be treated as the structures that describe the behaviour of the dialogue manager. They are directly implemented in CLIPS rules; each rule corresponds to a branch in the dialogue flow. Rules are both the means for achieving certain desires and the options available for the dialogue manager. Each rule has a body describing the primitive sub goals that have to be achieved for rule execution to be successful. The conditions under which a rule can be chosen as an option are specified by an invocation condition. The set of rules that make up a path through the dialogue flow, correspond to a desire.

The set of rules with satisfied invocation conditions at a time T (the set of instantiated rules) correspond to the intentions of the dialogue manager at time T. Obviously the intentions of the system are time dependent. The dialogue manager adopts a single-minded commitment strategy, which allows continuous changes to beliefs and drops its intentions accordingly. In other words the intentions of the system can be affected by the utterances of the user in contrast to blind commitment in which an intention is always executed no matter changes in beliefs.

5 An Example

In the previous section it was shown that the desires of the dialogue manager can be represented by dialogue flow diagrams. The flow diagrams are systematically translated into an executable system formulated in CLIPS rules. This section discusses the implementation of the desires. In particular the heuristics used for the translation from dialogue flow diagrams to CLIPS rules.

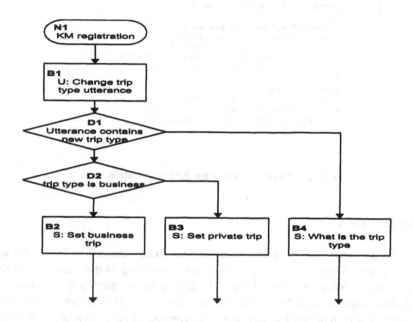

Fig. 3. Part of the dialogue flow diagram for KM registration service.

Suppose we must transform a dialogue flow diagram as in Figure 3. This dialogue is initialised when the user utters a phrase that matches the grammar for a change trip type utterance (box B1). Notice that box B1 has 3 branches (to the boxes B2, B3 and B4), furthermore we see that the action in B1 is a speech action from the user. From this we conclude that the dialogue flow should be implemented using 3 speech rules. The invocation conditions for each rule are the evaluated values of the expressions in the decision diamonds D1 and D2. The body of each rule contains the actions specified in the corresponding destination boxes. Furthermore, the body of the rules also contain actions to anticipate what follows after the action e.g. after box B4 the user must supply the new trip type so the grammar rules for trip type utterances should be activated.

The CLIPS rule in Figure 4 corresponds to the branch from box B1 to B2 (Figure 3). The keyword RECOGNISED in line 2 indicates that a user's utterance is recognised. The grammar rule that matched the utterance is *VID_KMREG_TRIPTYPE*. Furthermore, the property name TripType with value business satisfies condition D1 and D2. The actions taken satisfy B2 (between the < *SAY* > tags in line 5) and anticipate future utterances of the user by activating the *VID_YES_NO* grammar rule and de-activating all other main grammar rules. Thereby limiting the user's input to only boolean values. The other actions in the rule body are used to update the internal representation of the world.

```
1    (defrule KM_Registration_Business
2       ?in<-(RECOGNISED 161 VID_
                KMREG_TRIPTYPE 50 TripType
                business)
3       ?pos<-(POSITION MAIN RUNNING)
4       =>
5       (printout t "<SAY>Do you want set
          the triptype to business?</SAY>
6                   <ACT>VID_YESNO</ACT>
7                   <DEACT>"?*Mainrules*"</DEACT>
9                   <REACT></REACT>" crlf)
10      (retract ?in)
11      (retract ?pos)
        (assert (POSITION MAIN KMREG))
        (assert (WANT CONFIRM))
        (assert (QUESTION KMREG business))
    )
```

Fig. 4. CLIPS rule – part of the KM registration service.

6 Conclusions

The model presented here allows for man-machine speech interaction. Indeed the speech interface of the SWAMP application implemented according to this model is capable of handling simple dialogues with the user. The dialogues are described and visualised as generic flow diagrams resembling branching tree structures [3]. The chosen representation technique has also contributed greatly to the containment of the complexity in the dialogue models. Furthermore it allows an easy translation to executable CLIPS rules.

References

1. Chapanis, A. "Interactive Human Communication: Some lessons learned from laboratory experiments", In: Shackel, B. (Eds.) "Man-Computer Interaction: Human Factor Aspects of Computers and people", Rockville, MD: Sijthoff and Noordhoff, page. 65, 1981.
2. Nusbaum, H., et al., "Using Speech recognition systems: Issues in cognitive Engineering", In: Syrdal A. et al. (Eds.), Applied Speech Technology, Boca Raton, CRC press, page 127, 1995.
3. Rao, A. and Georgeff, M., "BDI Agents: From Theory to Practice", in Proceedings of the First International Conference on Multi-Agent Systems (ICMAS-95), 1995.
4. Wooldridge, M., "Reasoning about Rational Agents", The MIT Press, Cambridge, Massachusetts, 2000.

Different Approaches to Build
Multilingual Conversational Systems

Marion Mast[1], Thomas Roß[1], Henrik Schulz[1], and Heli Harrikari[2]

[1] IBM European Voice Technology Development
Vangerowstr. 18, 69115 Heidelberg, Germany
E-mail: tross@de.ibm.com, mmast@de.ibm.com, henriks@de.ibm.com
[2] NOKIA Research Center, Itämerenkatu 11–13
FIN-00045 Nokia Group
E-mail: Heli.Harrikari@nokia.com

Abstract. The paper describes developments and results of the work being carried out during the European research project CATCH-2004 (Converse in AThens Cologne and Helsinki)[3]. The objective of the project is multi-modal, multi-lingual conversational access to information systems. This paper concentrates on issues of the multilingual telephony-based speech and natural language understanding components.

1 Introduction

CATCH-2004 aims to develop a multilingual, conversational system providing access to multiple applications. The system is designed to support multiple client devices such as kiosks, telephones and smart wireless devices. It will also allow users to interact with multiple input modalities. The architecture is composed of two major frameworks: a server-side Multi-Modal Portal providing a flexible middleware technology for interacting with multiple clients in multiple modalities and languages, and a telephony-based conversational Natural Language Understanding (NLU) system. The common core application in CATCH-2004 is so-called 'City Event Information' (CEI) that provides information about cultural events in the three cities involved in the project. This paper however concentrates on the further developments, namely 'Sports Application' (SPA) developed for English, German, and Greek as well as 'Program Guide Information Service' (PGIS), which is available in English and Finnish. The SPA application covers sport events of the Olympic Games in Athens in 2004, including information such as olympic and world records, the history of sports and the venues. PGIS is an electronic program guide where users can obtain information about TV programs based on various search parameters, such as channel, date, program type, and performer. Additional information about programs is also available, for example, description, restrictions, and duration.

This paper discusses architectural aspects of the telephony-based multilingual conversational NLU system. In Section 2, different approaches to build multilingual conversational

---

[3] The project is co-funded by the European Union in the scope of the IST programme (IST 1999-11103). The paper represents the view of the authors.

P. Sojka, I. Kopeček, and K. Pala (Eds.): TSD 2002, LNAI 2448, pp. 413–420, 2002.

systems and specific multilingual aspects of the components are discussed. Section 3 gives more details about the specific components. The initial results comparing the performance of different architectures are shown in Section 4. Finally we present some ideas for further work.

2   Approaches for Multi-lingual Conversational Systems

The conversational systems and overall system architecture is based on the IBM ViaVoice Telephony toolkit and the IBM ViaVoice Telephony Natural Language Tools. It is shown in Figure 1.

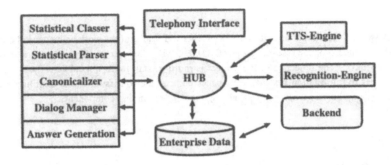

Fig. 1. General System Architecture.

Communication between the components is executed via a hub which works as a dispatcher that calls and routes information between involved modules. The telephony interface handles basic telephony functions, such as accepting and disconnecting calls, detection of hang-ups, recording and playing back audio material, and DTMF tone detection. After recording an utterance, the speech recognition module is invoked. The decoded text is delivered to the statistical classer, where simple application-specific concepts are identified. The canonicalizer then extracts canonical values for these basic concepts, followed by the statistical parser that computes the semantic parse from the classed sentence. The dialogue manager interprets the parser result in the dialogue context, requests backend information, and produces the system reaction for the user utterance, which is then passed to the TTS engine.

2.1   Multilingual Architecture

The scale of multilinguality for a conversational system can reach from parallel monolingual systems towards completely multilingual systems. We have implemented the two extreme architectural solutions, which we will describe here. In our first approach two parallel monolingual modules are maintained for the classer and parser in the NLU, and similarly for language modelling (LM) and vocabularies in the speech recognition. By maintaining all modules for all languages continuously active, the language can be determined separately for each utterance. The switch of the language is possible at any stage of the conversation. Both monolingual classers provide the preferred output for the utterance, after which confidence measures are compared, and consequently the language of the utterance is determined. Alternatively, the language might be determined by comparing both monolingual classers and parsers, and then selecting the best scored parses. Furthermore, if a monolingual backend database is given, a translation mechanism must be implemented. First, the translation executed in the canonicalizer guarantees that the relevant parts of the database query will be in the correct language, whereas the translation in the answer generation leads to the answer in the same language as the original query was uttered. The advantage of this approach is that the maintenance of the system is easier: incorporating various monolingual components into the system requires only slight modifications. Furthermore, having separate modules for separate languages might also result in better accuracy (see Section 4 for evaluation).

It is a conversational system where all components are fully multilingual. NLU continues to determine the language here as well, but now we have implemented two alternative ways of language identification. The decision can be made by the classer based on specific language tags attached to the sentences, or alternatively during the parsing with similar tags. This architectural solution allows the language switch between utterances and even within an utterance. Accuracy issues could be an argument against fully multilingual components. Maintenance issues also support solutions with at least certain components separate for different languages. The same applies to adding new languages into the system: as long as the monolingual application is available, incorporating its components into the parallel approach is relatively easy. Another aspect is the environment in which such a system will be deployed. In the case of a telephony system, which provides communication in the users' mother tongue, it's rather unlikely that a user will switch between languages in an utterance or even between utterances. When deploying a kiosk system (e.g. at a train station or airport), the demands might be quite different. It may be difficult for the system to determine the end of a dialogue with one user, and the beginning of the next one. Thus, a system that allows switching of languages between utterances might be preferable.

3   Components

3.1   Acoustic Model

The speech recognition engine used here is the IBM ViaVoice decoder. It is described in some detail e.g. in [1]. The training of the 8 kHz system is a bootstrap procedure based on an initial acoustic model built from downsampled 22 kHz data only. In a first step, cepstral features and their first and second order derivatives are computed. With the bootstrap system, the training data is viterbi aligned against its transcription. Based on this alignment, a decision tree is constructed for subphonetic HMMs by querying phone context. The data corresponding to a subphone (leaf) is clustered and consequently modeled by a mixture of Gaussians with diagonal covariance matrices. The so created models are refined by running a few iterations of the forward-backward training algorithm, see e.g. [2].

The main purpose for a multilingual acoustic model in this scenario is to enable decoding of utterances from more than one language. But benefits can also be expected when decoding monolingual data: decoding non native speakers as well as decoding words foreign to the respective language might profit from a multilingual acoustic model. An important step in building a multilingual acoustic model is the definition of a phonology common to the languages covered. All models compared here are based on a phonology described in [6]. The main difference between models considered here is the number of utterances per language in the training set. Other parameters, e.g. the number of HMM states or Gaussian mixture components are similar but not identical due to stochastic aspects in the training procedure. In the initial lexeme selection step, spellings are tagged with language specific identifiers to avoid erroneous cross language selections. The four acoustic models compared are different with respect to the training data as follows: Model m_{uk} is trained on UK English data only, model m_{gr} on German data only. Model m_{ml_1} is trained on 30 k utterances of each of the languages US English, UK English, German and Finnish, 10 k utterances of French, Italian and Spanish and 3 k utterances of Greek. Model m_{ml_2} has the same data as model m_{ml_1} plus additional 20 k for Spanish, French and Italian and additional 60 k for German. The selection of model m_{ml_1} is based on positive results on tests against non native English test data, model m_{ml_2} was selected to have comparable amounts of German and English in the training.

3.2   Language Model

Here, widely used 3-gram language models are used, both word- and class-based. Given that conversational NLU systems are based on relatively small training corpora, class-based LMs show advantages [4]. During the recognition each speech frame is labeled and passed to the acoustic fast match which uses continuous density Hidden-Markov-Models (HMM). For all words with a high fast match score (the fast match list) a LM score is computed based on the sequences of words decoded so far. This reduces the number of words for which the computationally more expensive so-called detailed match has to be computed in the next processing step. A heuristic search algorithm determines at each step, which paths to expand. The best path covering all input data is selected as the decoder output [1]. For constructing a multilingual LM two potential methodologies exist. In the first approach, statistics are computed for all corpora separately, as is the case in our first approach. In the second approach, the corpora for each language are merged and statistics as well as the vocabulary are based on it. Here, an utterance is decoded within the respective LM between two firm up points. A firm up point, determined by e.g. the end of an utterance, silence, or noise, also depends on optimization criteria for the decoding process. Once a firm up point has been determined, the best decoding path across the separate models is selected. This will favour language-consistent decoding. A common vocabulary and language model may suffer from unigram probabilities that occur for words with spellings in more than one language. For both Finnish and English, the PGIS application contains a multilanguage vocabulary (movie names, actors etc.). Apart from a potential overlap of unigram probabilities, this leads to a number of bi- and trigrams across these names that may enable language switches between firm up points. Furthermore, the idea of incrementally adding new languages to a system would benefit from the aspect of having separate vocabularies and language models.

3.3   NLU

For NLU we use a two-level parsing strategy. On the first level, the classer identifies simple semantic concepts (usually to set up a backend request). The classing is done with a statistical parser trained from a corpus of annotated sentences [3]. Each word within a sentence has to be tagged with its appropriate class tag. Tagged words are combined to labelled constituents if they can be assigned to the same semantic concept. On the second level, the parser extracts semantic concepts as well as the focus and intention of the utterance. It is also trained from annotated sentences, whereby the partial expressions assigned to simple semantic concepts identified by the classer are replaced by identifiers of the respective concept. The parser follows the same statistical parsing methodology as the classer, but more layers of labels may be necessary to assign detailed semantic concepts. The tags and labels are used by the dialogue manager to identify the current task and decide the next step. Tags and labels used for an application are the same across all languages. Only the values of the simple semantic concepts, e.g. names or numbers, may differ. A detailed description of the monolingual conversational systems developed during CATCH2004 is provided in [5].

3.4 Dialogue Management

The Form-based Dialogue Manager (FDM) is a framework for free-flow dialogue management [7]. It allows a task oriented, mixed initiative dialogue with a user. The framework can handle various types of dialogue features e.g. asking for missing information, clarifying ambiguities, and inheriting information from the dialogue context. Each task is modelled as a form that has the knowledge of the information needed to perform this task, e.g. calling the backend, selecting the answer according to the reply from the backend. For each user utterance canonicalized attribute-value pairs created from the class- and parse-tree are fed into the slots of the respective form. Furthermore, the FDM scores the forms and selects the one most suitable for the information provided with these attribute-value pairs. Since the classer and parser use the same tags and labels across languages, the dialogue manager is language-independent. The FDM triggers system responses to the user by composing textual messages from templates. The selection of the appropriate template is dependent on the dialogue situation. Usually a template is designed to concatenate valuable slots of the respective form with pre-defined expressions. For the multilingual approach the answer templates are provided for each language and the system selects the template according to the language used in the actual utterance.

4   Evaluation of Multi-lingual Components and User Tests

4.1   Speech Recognition

Table 1 and Table 2 give recognition results on four different test sets: set T_{gr} is a sample of spontaneous German utterances taken from a running application with queries about sport events. Set T_{en_1} is a similar test set in English. While T_{gr} utterances are taken from native speakers only, T_{en_1} contains approx. 45 % UK English utterances and 55 % utterances from non native English speakers. Set T_{fi} consists of Finnish utterances (native) taken from the Finnish and set T_{en2} is taken from the English PGIS dialogues. In T_{en2}, we *only* have non native English speakers in the test set. This comparison shows both the influence of multilingual data in the training set as well as the effect of multilingual vocabularies and language models. As can be seen in Table 1, for both English and German, the models trained on monolingual data perform best. For both German and English, adding additional 60 k

German utterances to the training set has an expected effect: While the German word error rate is reduced by approx 10 % relative (8 %, if the multilingual task is used), the English word error rate goes up approx. 8 % (both cases). Decoding against a multilingual LM shows for German less (relative) degradation than for English and Finnish.

Table 1. Decoding Results (word error rates) for English (T_{en_1}) and German(T_{gr}) against mono- and multilingual acoustic models and tasks.

	m_{uk}	m_{gr}	m_{ml_1}	m_{ml_2}
T_{gr} - mono. LM	-	18.2 %	24.4 %	22.0 %
T_{gr} - multi. LM	-	-	24.6 %	22.6 %
T_{en_1} - mono. LM	17.1 %	-	20.2 %	21.9 %
T_{en_1} - multi. LM	-	-	23.8 %	25.7 %

For the PGIS test sets, a comparison of monolingual, parallel and combined multilingual LMs and vocabularies were conducted with acoustic model m_{ml_1}. Note that all speakers in T_{en_2} are non native. The results support initial considerations that the accuracy might profit from separated LMs.

Table 2. Comparsion of decoding Results (word error rates) for English (T_{en_2}) and Finnish(T_{fi}) against mono- and multilingual acoustic models and tasks.

	monolingual	parallel (2 LMs)	combined (1 LM)
T_{en_2}	19.2 %	27.0 %	29.7 %
T_{fi}	5.6 %	6.4 %	7.9 %
Total	-	16.7 %	18.8 %

4.2 NLU

The data we used to test the performance of the NLU components in the different architectures were collected during user tests with the English and German monolingual SPA telephony system. Each test set contains around 340 sentences. The English test persons were mainly non native English speakers. The data were tested with the respective monolingual classer and parser, and a multilingual classer and parser for German and English. The multilingual components were built by simply merging the monolingual training corpora without further tuning of the classer or parser. Additionally, we evaluated the parallel approach by testing the data with both monolingual classers and parsers and choosing the best scored parse (see Table 3). The accuracy is calculated on a sentence level, only if each tag and label for each word in the sentence is correct, the sentence is rated as correct. The number of errors which really influenced the system behaviour negatively was much smaller, e.g. for the German data 3 % for the classer and parser. For the classer the parallel approach seems to work better than the multilingual one. On the parser side the numbers are close together.

Table 3. Classer and parser accuracy for English and German data.

	Monolingual	Parallel	Multilingual
German Classer data	96 %	96 %	93 %
English Classer data	94 %	93 %	92 %
German Parser data	83 %	83 %	82 %
English Parser data	82 %	81 %	82 %

4.3 User Tests

With the PGIS system we did initial user tests with a multilingual Finnish - English system, based on the parallel approach described in Section 2.1 8 testers conducted 82 dialogues with the system. On average, there were 7.7 utterances and 2.9 tasks per dialogue. 7 testers were native Finnish speakers and 1 neither Finnish nor English native speaker. 50 % of the user utterances were Finnish and English respectively. The results are given in Table 4. The word error rate is between the error rate of the Finnish and English system. The multilingual classer is slightly worse than the monolingual one, but the multilingual parser is comparable or better than the monolingual components, so is the task completion rate. Of course the

Table 4. Results from user tests with a Finnish-English system.

	English	Finnish	Multilingual
Word Error Rate	29 %	27 %	28 %
Classer	1 %	3 %	5 %
Parser	5 %	2 %	2 %
Task completion rate	75 %	78 %	78 %

results presented are only initial and need to be confirmed by further tests e.g. with more languages and more user tests.

5 Conclusion and Future Work

In this paper we have presented different architectural approaches to multilingual conversational systems, initial results from the component evaluation of the different solutions as well as results from initial user tests with a Finnish-English system. In many respects, the results show the superiority of the multilingual architecture with parallel language-specific components. First of all, the evaluation demonstrates better or equal accuracy of the parallel system.

Furthermore, the maintenance of this approach has turned out to be relatively easy: the system can be constructed from monolingual systems, and adding new languages requires only slight modifications in the overall system. However, the parallel approach is more expensive when it comes to processing power for all parallel components. First results from user tests with the parallel approach are promising and show, that multilingual systems can be built with rather small performance degradation. Various issues require further investigation. First, the effects of the different architectures on the performance accuracy and speed must be looked into in more detail, and incorporating additional languages is also an issue in the near future. Secondly, the influen e of non-native s; eakers on the performance of the system has to be taken into consideration more thoroughly usability issues also require attention in order to properly decide, which approach is the most suitable one for the various needs for multilingual conversational systems in the future.

References

1. P. Gopalakrishnan, D. Nahamoo, L. Bahl, P. de Souza and M. Picheny. Context-dependent vector quantization for continuous speech recognition. In: *Proc. of the IEEE Int. Conference on Acoustics Speech, and Signalprocessing*, Minneapolis, 1993.
2. F. Jelinek. *Statistical Methods for Speech Recognition*. The MIT Press, Cambridge, Ma., 1997.
3. F. Jelinek, J. Lafferty, D. Magerman, R. Mercer, A. Ratnaparkhi, and S. Roukos. Decision tree parsing using a hidden derivational model. In: *Proc. of the ARPA Human Language Technology Workshop*, 1994.
4. G. Maltese, P. Bravetti, H. Crèpy, B. Grainger, M. Herzog, and F. Palou. Combining word and class-based language models: a comparative study in several languages using automatic and manual word-clustering techniques. In: *EuroSpeech*, Aalborg, Denmark, 2001.
5. M. Mast, Th. Ross, H. Schulz, H. Harrikari, V. Demesticha, Y. Vamvakoulas, and J. Stadermann. A conversational natural language understanding information system for multiple languages. In: *NLDB*, Madrid, Spain, 2001.
6. F. Palou, P. Bravetti, O. Emam, V. Fischer, and E. Janke. Towards a common phone alphabet for multilingual speech recognition. In: *ICSLP*, 1999.
7. K. A. Papineni, S. Roukos, and R. T. Ward. Free-flow dialogue management using forms. In: *EuroSpeech, Budapest*, 1999.

Strategies to Overcome Problematic Input in a Spanish Dialogue System

Victoria Arranz, Núria Castell, and Montserrat Civit

TALP Research Center, Universitat Politècnica de Catalunya
Campus Nord - C6, Jordi Girona, 1-3, 08034 Barcelona, Spain
E-mail: varranz@talp.upc.es, castell@talp.upc.es, civit@talp.upc.es

Abstract. This paper focuses on the strategies adopted to tackle problematic input and ease communication between modules in a Spanish railway information dialogue system for spontaneous speech. The paper describes the design and tuning considerations followed by the understanding module, both from a language processing and semantic information extraction point of view. Such strategies aim to handle the problematic input received from the speech recogniser, which is due to spontaneous speech as well as recognition errors.

1 Introduction

The nineties witnessed a boosting in spoken dialogue system development. The need for machines offering more natural and efficient ways to communicate reinforced the importance of such systems. Demand for "intelligent" and "human-like" applications has led researchers and developers in the field of Human Language Technologies to attain products such as *TRAINS* [1], *LIMSI ARISE* [2] and *Philips TABA* [3], in the train timetable information domain. Our system goes further than train scheduling and allows the user obtain a wide range of information about a trip (e.g., prices, duration, on-board services) while providing a relatively user-friendly mixed-initiative communication. In addition, this system has been developed for Spanish, a language with barely any such tools.

A very important issue in such systems, and a main concern for the current work, is poor speech recognition and its side-effects on the system modules to handle it. [4] claims to deal with them in the framework of unification grammar. Litman's [5] spoken dialogue system, *TOOT*, adopts a rather pragmatics-oriented approach: it automatically adapts its dialogue strategies so as to predict and respond to problematic input. [6], on the other hand, emphasises a more semantic-driven approach, as it is a more robust strategy. Our system follows this latter strategy and uses a semantic extractor that performs robust and flexible searches based on partial parsing, phrase structures, lexical key-words and morphological information (cf. Section 4). Further, our system has also implemented a number of pragmatics-oriented strategies for the dialogue manager to overcome communication difficulties generated by poor input [7].

The starting point of our system was the study of real data (a human-human corpus and a human-machine, *Wizard-of-Oz* technique-based [8], dialogue corpus collected) whose results

P. Sojka, I. Kopeček, and K. Pala (Eds.): TSD 2002, LNAI 2448, pp. 421–428, 2002.
© Springer-Verlag Berlin Heidelberg 2002

were used for the development and training of the system modules and which represent a very valuable resource for further research as such in Spanish language.

The architecture of the system follows that of other such dialogue systems [7,9]. The speech recogniser [10] makes use of an acoustic and a language model, the former being language-specific and the latter domain-specific and thus built for our task. As expected when dealing with spontaneous speech, the recogniser needs to incorporate the treatment of extra-linguistic phenomena. Yet, there remains a certain amount of noise and problematic input that will go on to the next module. The way the understanding module deals with these problems (cf. Section 2), which makes the system more robust, is the main issue in this paper.

The understanding module starts with a linguistic processing of the transcription of the spoken utterance (cf. Section 3) so as to extract its semantic content and formalise it inside *frames* that summarise the intervention (cf. Section 5.1). These *frames* are sent to the dialogue manager [7] that also generates *frames* to transmit the necessary information to the natural language generator. Such *frames* are converted into sentences that the synthesiser outputs as a spoken response to the user's query.

2   Problems to Be Tackled

The understanding module receives the transcription of the spoken utterance generated by the recogniser. Unfortunately, as it is well known in spontaneous speech, erroneous transcriptions take place. On the one hand, the recogniser is not perfect and it generates transcription errors itself. On the other, dealing with spontaneous speech implies having to face problems such as disfluencies.

Three different types or recognition errors must be considered: the first one is **excess of information**, i.e., the recogniser adds words that do not belong to the user's utterance. The second one is **erroneous recognition**, i.e, words detected by the recogniser do not match those really uttered by the user. The third error type is **grammar errors**, i.e., orthographic transcriptions can produce grammatical errors, including changes in grammatical categories.

These three error types can be handled at two different levels. At the recognition level, the tool should be tuned for the task domain. Also, the strategy of closing the entry channel, when necessary, should be considered. At a language processing level, our semantic information extractor can handle noisy input by focusing its extraction on specific syntactic phrases, lexical entries (word forms and lemmas), and even PoS labels (cf. Section 4).

Syntactic disfluencies have also been considered when designing the semantic informa-tion extractor. Most cases are sorted out at this stage (cf. Section 4). Other disfluencies, such as lexical variations, pauses, noises,..., must be tackled by tuning the speech recogniser. Yet, the result of semantic extraction from the received input will also be confirmed by the dia-logue manager when this is considered necessary for the query. This is a further attempt to get round any misrecognitions.

3   Tuning NLP Tools

This section describes briefly the tuning of the morphological analyser *MACO+* (*Morpho-logical Analyzer Corpus Oriented*) [11] and the shallow parser *TACAT* [11] to our dialogue system. Both are robust and wide-coverage tools.

3.1 Morphological Analysis

The study of the corpora developed and the railway company DB has lead us to refine the task lexicon: it has provided us with all necessary city and station proper names (which have been labelled in a specific manner so as to ease their recognition), as well as guided us in the reduction of the lexicon to the most-frequent domain words. All tests carried out with the task lexicon have given the expected results, i.e., all forms have been assigned the correct label.

Besides reducing the number of forms, we have also reduced ambiguity in agreement with the specificity of the domain. *MACO+* assigns lemma/PoS-tag pairs for each word form and then, the statistical tool *RELAX (Relaxation Labelling Based Tagger)* [11] disambiguates any remaining ambiguous words.

3.2 Syntactic Analyser

The syntactic analysis is performed with *TACAT*, a chart-based analyser making use of a chunk grammar that does not express any dependency relation between the constituents [11]. The grammar is context-free since it was originally designed for non-restricted domain language and later adapted for the present application. This adaptation has consisted in a) taking certain analysis rules out, such as those for verbal periphrases, and mostly b) adding domain-specific rules, in particular those to detect days of the week, dates, hours and minutes.

This analyser takes as input the output of the morphological tagger. Then it generates syntactic trees where the non-terminal nodes are syntactic labels such as NP, PP, VP and the terminal ones contain the word form, lemma and PoS tag. These trees become the input for the semantic information extractor.

4   Information Extraction and the PRE+ Environment

The semantic information to be generated for the dialogue manager is based on the concept of *frame* [12], which can be easily translated into a DB query. A *frame* can convey two different types of information: *concepts*, which are the specific information the user is enquiring about, and *cases*, which are the restrictions to be applied to the *concepts*. For instance, *DepartureTime* is a *concept* which can have different *cases*, such as *DepartureCity*, *DestinationCity*, etc.

Information extraction is performed by means of the production rule environment *PRE+* [13]. *PRE+* works with rules whose model is: *condition ==> action. Conditions* establish the morphosyntactic context to be satisfied for *actions* to be applied. For instance, in Spanish, *DepartureCity* is always preceded by prepositions *de, desde* (from). Thus, as expressed in this rule, any city name preceded by *de, desde* can (and must) be interpreted as the value for this *case*:

```
(rule DepartureCity1
  ruleset DepartureCity
  priority 10
  score [0,_,1,0]
  control forever
  ending Postrule
```

```
(InputSentence ^tree <+a>tree_matching(
 [{pos=>grup-sp} [{lema=> de|desde}]
 [{pos=> np000c0, forma=>?forma}]]))
(consulta ^attributes +attr)
 ->  (?_ := Print(DepartureCity,?forma))
     (?_ := REM(DepartureCity,X,+a))
     (+attrfi := NRPush(DepartureCity,?forma,+attr))
     (delete 2)
     (create consulta ^attributes +attrfi))
```

The main condition in this rule is the one starting with *InputSentence*. This condition specifies the type of syntactic element, *grup-sp* (PP), to be searched for by the rule. This element must be a node of the syntactic tree and must have two daughters: the first one must have one of the prepositions *de, desde* as lemma; its sister must be a city proper name (must have tag *np000c0*[1]). Since this is the name providing the necessary information, *DepartureCity*, this form must be kept (as indicated in *forma=>?forma*) to be later used in the action of the rule.

The last five lines of the previous rule express the actions of the rule. Leaving aside internal elements related to the functioning of *PRE+*, the third line in this block is the main action, which extracts the information and creates the *case+value* that will be sent to the dialogue manager in the next *frame*.

The main advantage of this formalism is that it allows to search for semantic information in a very flexible variety of ways: searching for word forms, lemmas and PoS tags. Regarding syntax, phrase structure can be specified as much as required, if relevant, but it can be left unspecified otherwise. This makes the system considerably robust when facing problematic input received from recognition. For instance, the condition can be more restricted to specify either the type of sister nodes our initial *grup-sp* must have, or how many daughter (and/or granddaughter) nodes it can have, etc.

Below follows a rule that holds a more complex condition. In this case, the specification of syntactic structure starts at sentence level (*S*). *S* must have two daughters, a PP and an NP. The daughters of the PP must be exactly *con, salida* (with, departure), while its sister NP must have as nucleus a city name:

```
[{pos=>S}
 [{pos=>grup-sp} [{lema=> con}] [{lema=> salida}]]
 [{pos=>sn} [{pos=> np000c0, forma=>?forma}]]])
```

4.1   Rule Organization

Rules are structured according to a hierarchy that is established *a priori* and that determines their application conditions. The mother ruleset is called **top** and its daughters are mostly domain-specific **rulesets**. The dependency relation between rulesets is always expressed with an *isa* relation. Each defined **rule** belongs to a unique ruleset, relation expressed with the *ruleset* property. Given these relations, rules inherit their properties from the rulesets they belong to.

---

[1] Digit #6, for semantic case, contains **c**, meaning *city* name (while **e** means *station*).

4.2 Ruleset and Rule Control

Rulesets have several control properties associated which direct the way to apply rulesets. There is a global (top-level) control at an inter-ruleset level that manages the order of ruleset application and allows to handle complex or ambiguous situations, such as, potential rule overlapping at an inter-ruleset level.

The strategy of ruleset application has been established following the studied corpora. The first rule applied when the semantic information extractor starts is rule **top1** (shown below), which belongs to ruleset **top** and it has high priority. The action of this rule creates an ordered *concept* list that determines the order of evaluation for the rulesets. This is due to the fact that each *concept* is associated to one ruleset.

```
(rule top1
  ruleset top
  priority 1
  control one
  -> (create concepts ^list
     [CS_DepartureTime DepartureCity,
      DestinationCity, DepartureDestinationCity, [...], Fi])
     (create consulta ^attributes [])
     (?_ := Tacat2WM()))
```

At a rule level, there are also some control properties. The initial part of the left-hand side of one *DepartureCity* rule is shown here:

```
(rule DepartureCity1
  ruleset DepartureCity
  priority 10
  score [0,_,1,0]
  control forever
  ending Postrule
  (InputSentence ...
```

The priority of a rule inside the ruleset is expressed by means of the **priority** property. Despite the fact that the **control** property is already established at a ruleset level, it is also possible to restrict the application of individual rules using the same property.

The most important rule property is that of **score**. Combining the values of its four parameters a large number of syntactic analysis problems can be tackled, problems that are due to the use of spontaneous speech (such as the example below) or misrecognition (cf. Section 2). These parameters permit to express a) the use of tree permutations, b) the maximum depth of the search level, c) the maximum number of leaves allowed in between terminal elements, and d) the maximum number of leaves allowed inside each element. For example, parameter (c) will have value 0 in user turns like: "Can I have the timetables for the Barcelona Bilbao trains?", allowing us to extract the *DepartureDestinationCity* value, despite not having the usual prepositions ("*from* Barcelona *to* Bilbao") next to the city names.

5   Semantic and Pragmatic Frame Tuning

Although our system is based on a detailed study of the domain-specific corpora, there are pragmatic issues that need to be taken into account. *Frames* have been tuned to the needs of the information exchange protocols and the limitations of the modules in order to achieve a more robust communication between the user and the system, as well as between the modules themselves. This tuning has helped simplify the existing structure and has been carried out bearing in mind the speech acts considered for this particular task. On the one hand, we have the **User Speech Acts** (*Query, Incomplete, Return Trip, Affirmation, Negation* and *Closing*) which have been resumed to four different frames (cf. Section 5.1). On the other, there are the **System Speech Acts** (*Query to the User, Explicit Confirmation, Implicit Confirmation, Answer to Query, Lack of Understanding, Opening, Closing, Offer* and *Web Stalled*) which have been summarised in seven different *frames*. Thus, the system only needs to handle 11 main *frames*, which contain a very rich variety of information in a very limited number of structures.

5.1   *Frames* in the Understanding Module

To start with, given that semantic extraction is performed by means of a set of rules written in *PRE+* (cf. Section 4) and that this environment is based on lexico-syntactic patterns, all reasoning behind the content of a *frame* and its corresponding labelling is carried out by the dialogue manager. This entails some implementation constraints for the understanding module:

- This module will only generate a set of *frames* carrying one of the following: a) precise queries to the system; b) *case* information that cannot be allocated by this module in any *frame* and that can only be tagged as *incomplete*, and c) answers to system queries that only hold an affirmation or negation.
- *Query frames* are marked with **Q** and those containing incomplete information with **I**. *Affirmation* and *negation* are labelled **A** and N^2, respectively.
- *Frames* will contain either a generic label or a non-generic one, where the former has one information field and only refers to the type of *frame*. The latter allows to include further information fields and thus provide further specifications on a particular *frame*. For instance, **I** opens a generic-label *frame*, while **Q** initiates a non-generic one. A *query frame*[3] does always specify what particular information the user is enquiring about:

```
((Q_DepartureTime
    (DepartureCity Barcelona)
    (DestinationCity Bilbao)))
```

---

[2] *Closing* is covered by *Negation* since the former is always preceded by a negation and the dialogue manager is aware of the type of question such negation replies to.

[3] The list of query labels considered for the current domain task is: *Q_DepartureTime, Q_DepartureTime-R, Q_ArrivalTime, Q_ArrivalTime-R, Q_Price, Q_DepartureStation, Q_DestinationStation, Q_TripDuration, Q_TrainType, Q_Services, Q_DepartureDate, Q_DepartureDate-R, Q_ArrivalDate* and *Q_ArrivalDate-R*. Labels ending in **R** refer to the return trip, avoiding to create a specific *frame* for this speech act.

while a generic *incomplete frame* providing information about two attributes for a query looks as follows:

((I
    (DepartureDate 10-05-2001)
    (DepartureInterval 13.00–21.00)))

The complete *frame* is encapsulated as an information pack by means of brackets. There are three different levels of brackets: a first one containing each *case/attribute* and its value; a second one enclosing all *cases* with their *frame* label, thus building up simple *frames*, and a third one enclosing all information relevant to that dialogue turn. The latter can contain a single *frame* or allow for the building of *frame sets*, as it happens in the query below:

((Q_DepartureTime
    (DepartureCity Barcelona)
    (DestinationCity Bilbao))
(Q_Price
    (DepartureCity Barcelona)
    (DestinationCity Bilbao)))

This frame encapsulation makes the communication exchange easier for the awaiting modules since it establishes the whole information structure and thus informs the coming module whether it should be waiting for any further simple *frames* within a structure or not.

6 Conclusions

This paper describes the strategies adopted to handle problematic input and ease communication between modules in a Spanish railway information dialogue system for spontaneous speech. The strategies here presented are those concerning the understanding module and have allowed the development of a considerably robust system.

On the one hand, the tuning of NLP tools has helped reduce morphosyntactic ambiguity, thus lending a hand to our semantic information extraction environment, *PRE+*. This environment is highly flexible, allowing to perform searches as restricted or general as necessary, and by means of syntactic structures, lexical items and morphological elements (such as lemmas or PoS tags).

On the other, the semantic *frames* have been designed so as to avoid ambiguity and store semantic information in a clear and easy-to-exchange manner.

Finally, both system and speech corpora developed constitute important resources for future research in Spanish language.

References

1. Allen, J.F., Miller, B.W., Ringger, E.K., Sikorski, T.: A Robust System for Natural Spoken Dialogue. *Proc. of ACL '96* (1996).
2. Lamel, L., Rosset, S., Gauvain, J.L., Bennacef, S. The Limsi Arise System for Train Travel Information. *Proc. of ICASSP '99* (1999).

3. Souvignier, V., Kellner, A., Rueber, B., Schramm, H., Seide, F. The Thoughtful Elephant: Strategies for Spoken Dialogue Systems. *IEEE Trans. Speech Audio Processing* **8** (2000).
4. Nakano, M., Miyazaki, N., Yasuda, N., Sugiyama, A., Hirasawa, J., Dohsaka, K., Aikawa, K. WIT: A Toolkit for Building Robust and Real-Time Spoken Spoken Dialogue Systems. *Proc. of 1st SIGdial Workshop on Discourse and Dialogue*, Hong Kong (2000).
5. Litman, D.J., Pan, S. Predicting and Adapting to Poor Speech Recognition in a Spoken Dialogue System. *Proc. of 7th National Conference on AI (AAAI-2000)*, Austin, Texas (2000).
6. Zue, V.W., Glass, J.R. Conversational Interfaces: Advances and Challenges. *Proc. of the IEEE. Special Issue on Spoken Language Processing* **88(8)** (2000).
7. Álvarez, J., Arranz, V., Castell, N., Civit M. Linguistic and Logical Tools for an Advanced Interactive Speech System in Spanish. *Engineering of Intelligent Systems (LNAI 2070)*, Springer Verlag (2001).
8. Fraser, N.M., Gilbert, G.N. Simulating Speech Systems. *Computer Speech and Language* **5(1)** (1991).
9. Giachin, E., McGlashan, S. Spoken Language Dialogue Systems. *Corpus-Based Methods in Language and Speech Processing*, ed. by Young, S. and Bloothooft, G., Kluwer Academic Publishers, Dordrecht (1997).
10. Bonafonte, A., Mariño, J.B., Nogueiras, A., Rodríguez, J.A. RAMSES: El Sistema de Reconocimiento del Habla Continua y Gran Vocabulario Desarrollado por la UPC. *Proc. of VIII Jornadas de I+D en Telecomunicaciones*, Madrid (1998).
11. http://www.lsi.upc.es/~nlp/tools.html.
12. Minker, W., Bennacef, S., Gauvain, J.L. A Stochastic Case Frame for Natural Language Understanding. *Proc. of ICSLP'97* (1997).
13. Turmo, J. PRE+: A Production Rule Environment. Tech. report LSI-99-5-T (1999).

Dialogue Systems and Planning

Guy Camilleri

IRIT, CCI-CSC, Université Paul Sabatier,
118 route de Narbonne, 31062 Toulouse Cedex 4 France

Abstract. Planning processes are often used in dialogue systems to recognize the intentions conveyed in dialogue. The generation of utterances can also be achieved by a planning/execution mechanism. Some advantages of this kind of mechanism are: knowledge sharing, modular design, declarative description, etc.
In this paper, we present some planning mechanisms and the related models enabling the dialogue management (generation and understanding).

Introduction

In many works, a plan-based framework is used to represent goals (intentions) conveyed in dialogue. The philosophical studies of natural language proposed by Austin [1], Searle [2], Grice [3] and Bratman [4] constitute the theoretical bases of intentional plan based approaches of dialogue. These studies regard utterances as actions carried out by an agent (or speaker) in a particular environment. This association unifies the representation of actions to utterances, and consequently their handling mechanisms. Hence, utterances can be a part of a plan containing other utterances and/or actions. In this way, the dialogue can be modeled by an action plan. This kind of pragmatic context provides some agents goals hierarchically organized.

In this paper, we propose to describe the dialogue utterances generation and interpretation through plan-based models. In the earlier approaches, the interpretation mechanism builds a model (in the form of plans) describing the participant's intentions in dialogue. The generation process is rarely described. The intentions plan (built during interpretation) seems to be used as an input (data) by a utterances generator. Like Wilensky [5] we think, it is interesting to manage utterances generation through a plan-based model. Such approaches propose a plan model to guide the generation process. The main advantages of this modeling are:

- The relations between tasks (responsible of utterances generation), and tasks motivating their achievement, are described in an explicit way.
- The generation process is more modular (a declarative specification is used).
- This kind of description unifies the knowledge representations used by the interpretation and generation mechanisms. Hence, these mechanisms can share some models (knowledge) and processes.

The first section of this paper presents the main plan-based models used to manage dialogue. We discuss then the problems arising from the use of these models in utterances

P. Sojka, I. Kopeček, and K. Pala (Eds.): TSD 2002, LNAI 2448, pp. 429–436, 2002.

generation and we present new models enabling the integration of an exclusive plan management[1] of dialogue. We briefly discuss the advantages of such kind of modeling framework. Finally, this framework is illustrated by an example.

1 Plan-Based Models Used in Dialogue

Grosz and Kraus [6] have developed a formal model that specifies the beliefs and intentions that must be held by collaborative agents engaged in a collective activity. This model called Shared Plan (SP) is applied in a dialogue understanding context. The essential idea is that agents participating in a dialogue (discourse) have a collaborative behavior. The SP specifies all needed features to achieve a collective or individual goal. Agents produce utterances to reach a goal that is, they intend to satisfy all features expressed in the SP for this goal.

Lochbaum [7] has defined her interpretation process with the SP concept. The outcome of this process is represented by a graph structure, her Rgraph (or Recipe Graph). This graph represents all recognized goals participating to more abstract ones. In fact, this structure is a hierarchical tree of goals. Rgraph is a multi-agent plan containing detected goals of the dialogue participants.

Carberry, Lambert [8], Ardissono [9] use a Discourse Model (DM), Litman and Allen [10] a Plans Stack (PS), to capture the intentions of the dialogue participants. DM and PS are very similar to Lochbaum's Rgraph.

For the modeled agent (system), these dialogue representations seem to describe the system beliefs on user's intentions, and some local intentions of the system. The system has a description of the common activity (as Rgraph, DM, PS, etc.). The part of the representation describing the system beliefs on the users intentions is often used as data (input) for utterances generation. The relations between interventions (actions) of the system agent and its partners are modeled through multi-agents plans.

2 Generating Dialogue through Plan-Based Models

We think that the understanding of intentions is not the recognition of some "common" plan, but in particular the understanding of the fact that the other partner may/must have a complementary view.

The use of Rgraph or DM or ... plan-based models in generation process poses some problems. These models describe the intentions (goals) of discourse participants. At least two agents interact in discourse, therefore these plan-based models are multi-agent plans. Unfortunately, multi-agent plans can not be performed. Generally, some tasks miss in multi-agent plans to be carried out by agents. For example, the multi-agent plan: Obtain-Info--Ref(A,B,...) by achieving Ask-Ref(A,B,...) and Answer-Ref(B,A,...) can not be performed in this form by A. To achieve his part of this plan, the A agent must wait the B's answer. This waiting task is not described in this multi-agent plan. However, this task is required to the Obtain-Info-Ref(A,B,...) achievement.

---

[1] Interpretation and generation.

More generally, an agent only achieves his actions[2]. Plans performed by an agent are thus mono-agent plans. Therefore, an executable plan-based model must be mono-agent. The interaction modeling in these mono-agent plans requires the utilization of synchronization tasks (as wait, etc.). The previous multi-agent plan can be translated for A agent as follow: Obtain-Info-Ref(A,B,...) by Ask-Ref(A,B,...) and Wait--Answer(A,B,...). The synchronization task Wait-Answer(A,B,...) replaces the task Answer-Ref(B,A,...) ascribed to B agent. This Obtain-Info-Ref(A,B,...) plan version is now achievable by A agent.

3   Modeling Principle for Dialogue Generation and Understanding

The key point of our modeling principle is: each knowledge is described from the point of view of the modeled agent. As discussed above, dialogue generation requires mono-agent plans.

3.1   Modeling Primitives

The primitives proposed here are conceived to be handled by some classical mechanisms of planning, plan-based approaches of discourse and knowledge systems research areas. A task/method paradigm is chosen to describe our hierarchical models.

Task.   A task is an action represented as follows:

NAME	Task name
PAR	List of handled typed parameters
OBJECTIVE	Task goal expressed in state form
METHODS	list of methods achieving the task

The parameter list specifies the set of world objects handled by the task. All defined methods (or way to achieve) during the modeling phase are recorded in the method list of the considered task.

Method.   A method describes a way (at only one level of abstraction) to achieve a task.

HEADER	Task carried out
COND-APP	Applicability conditions
PREC	Preconditions set
EFFECTS	Effects set
CONTROL	Subtasks performance order
SUBTASKS	Subtask set

The action carried out by a method is indicated by the heading. Applicability conditions[3] are used to constrain the method instantiation. Preconditions and effects sets are handled in

---

[2] Ascribed to him.

[3] as action parameters.

the usual way. The order of subtasks performance is described in the control field; subtasks are recorded in the subtasks set.

Terminal Task. A terminal task is directly executable. Its execution does not require the description of its decomposition.

Handling Mechanisms. Mechanisms applied in our plan-based models are planning (plan recognition[4]) processes and execution engines. Cond-app, Prec, Effects and Subtasks are used for planning and plan recognition purpose (see Camilleri [11,12]).

Execution engines commonly used in task/method models can roughly be sketched by the following steps:

1. If the current task is a terminal task then execute it, else
2. Select an applicable method (by checking Cond-app and Prec) to the current task.
3. Apply the selected method by performing the control field, which determinates the new task to be executed, and so on.

These execution engines can be applied on a task/method model to generate dialogue. The production of utterances results from the discourse tasks achievement (as `Ask-ref(...)` task of Figure 1), that is the application of an execution engine on discourse tasks.

3.2 Agent Plan Libraries

In plan-based approaches of discourse understanding, two kinds of knowledge play a crucial role: plan library, which enumerates the set of possible domain plans and user model describing agent's preferences. The former represents the knowledge allowing the achievement of domain goals, usually the latter describes the methods more likely employed by a particular agent (or group of agents).

The domain plan library appears in the majority of approaches as common ground knowledge. However, some possible differences of knowledge between agents are modeled through the methods and the goals preferences in user model. User model can also contain some plans, which are specific to a user. Usually, these particular plans correspond to erroneous (flawed) plans. In fact, all possible plans (methods) allowing the domain tasks achievement are described in domain plans. This library is filtered by user's preferences.

The plan recognition process interprets utterances from the plans contained in the common ground knowledge. The understanding process is guided by the user model, which possibly adapts plans to the modeled user.

In our plan-based framework, plans are used to generate and understand dialogues. Models are described in the task/method paradigm previously presented.

In our framework, the following categories of plan libraries are used:

- The *Domain plan library* represents all agent's goals (tasks) and methods typical to the application domain. This library specifies all way used by the agent to achieve the domain tasks.

---

[4] Plan recognition is the process of infering (in term of plans) an agent's intention from his observed behavior.

– The *Agent plan library* describes the agent's behavior. The agent's behavior library is composed of discourse, activity, extension/execution and cooperative sub-libraries. These sub-libraries are independent of the application domain, and thus more generic. Discourse plans describe the different ways to communicate with others. The activity library represents agent life cycle. Extension/execution plans specify the planning/execution process. The cooperative plans define the distribution[5] and adapt plans to the current cooperative context.

– The *User plan library* describes the system's (or modeled agent) beliefs on its users. This library consists of two categories of plans: The system's beliefs on the methods employed by users to carry out tasks, and the system's beliefs on the system representation owned by users (image of oneself). The later category describes the methods whose users think the system uses.

4   Dialogue Example

In this part, we illustrate our plan-based framework by the following dialogue adapted from Ardissono et al. [9]. Agents participating to this dialogue are a system (noted S) and a user (U). The dialogue domain is the exam university registration. Students use this system to register themselves for exams.

U: Could you register me for the m10
    exam?
S: What's your name?
U: Mario Rossi.
S: Ok, you are registered.

A part of S's plan-based models used in this example are mentioned in Figure 1. The system goal is to register the user Register(S,U,ex) by obtaining the user name (tasks Request-ref(...) and Perceive-ref(...)), checking the user situation (Check--student(...)) and registering him/her (Register-student(...)). The system also knows the user registration way (cf. user plan library). Only, the discourse and activity plan libraries are partly exposed, for brevity reasons the problem solving level (composed of extension/execution and cooperative plan libraries) is not presented here.

All plan libraries are mono-agent.

The plans in Figure 2 represent the various goals recognized and achieved by the agent S (system) during the proposed dialogue. The plan in the left side (boxed with wide dotted line) describes user's task recognized from his utterances and model. The plan sketched in the right side (boxed with small doted line) represents the system tasks plan recognized by user corresponding in this application to the system plan.

The utterance "Could you register me for the m10 exam?" is translated by the surface act Utterance-act(...). The plan recognition is applied to interpret (explain) this task from the Register(...) task. This process builds the plan in the top left corner (Figure 2) by accomplishing the following reasoning: The user has performed the Utterance-act(...) to achieve Locutionary-act(...), because the former task is only a subtask of the

---
[5] The agents which perform tasks.

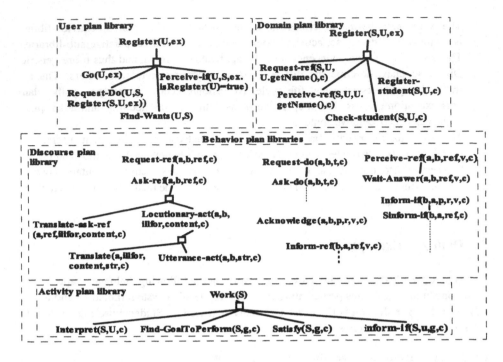

Fig. 1. Agent models.

latter. The `Locutionary-act(...)` is a subtask of several methods, but the utterance form analysis indicates that this utterance is an `Ask-do(...)` act. The `Ask-do(...)` belongs to the `Request-do(...)` method which is a subtask of `Register(u1,m10)` task.

The generation of the "What's your name?" utterance is provoked by the top right plan execution. The system performs the `Work(s)` task by choosing and executing the method { `Interpret(...)`, `Find-GoalToPerform(...)`, ...}, and so on. Utterance production is accomplished by the `Utterance-act(...)` achievement.

In Figure 2, the boxed plan corresponds to the path responsible of a speak turn. Subtask/task links mean that the bound tasks are either a subtask or the same task as the upper task. Goal edges specify that an effect of the original task indicates to the hearer that the speaker wants something, and the task in the target side describes the way whose the agent considers the goal[6].

All built plans are mono-agent plans. A direct link between a question (as "What's your name?") and an answer ("Mario Rossi") does not exist. This link is accomplished through a goal adoption task `Find-GoalToPerform(...)`. We do not try to model the dialogue for itself but we describe the agent behavior, which entails the dialogue generation.

---

[6] In this example, the agent adopts the goal.

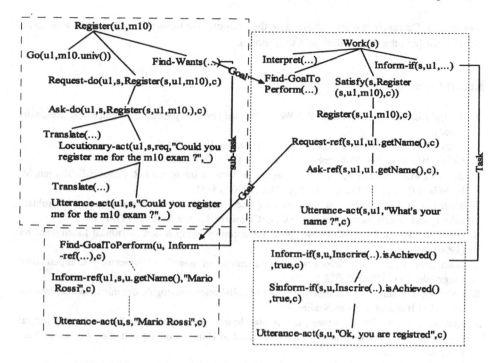

Fig. 2. Dialogue Plans.

Conclusion and Future Work

Using plan-based model to generate utterances in dialogue enables an incremental system modeling. It is difficult in practice to completely model all behaviors of an intelligent system and its users in one step. We think that plan-based models appear to be a good way to represent agent's behavior. These models are expressed in a declarative way, which improve the model readability, modularity; they also facilitate the system maintenance, evolution, etc. and enable an incremental design.

The dialogue generation and understanding is a huge problem, however we think that the representation of agent's behavior seems to be a good approach to manage dialogue[7]. The knowledge of the others points of view appears to be important to design agents. Of course, all the knowledge constituting an agent is built (and inferred) from the agent's point of view. However, the agent can have some knowledge about points of view of the others. The key point of our modeling principle is that we represent the knowledge of an agent participating to (inside) the collective activity. We do not try to represent the dialogue, neither to describe the knowledge of all agents engaged in the activity. Only the necessary knowledge to the goals achievement of the modeled agent is regarded and established.

The agent plan library seems to be generic and reusable in several applications. Our aim is to design a set of agent plan libraries representing the potential agent behavior. This library set can constitute a knowledge base from which an agent library (for an application) can be

---

[7] Enabling to handle a great number of dialogues.

constructed. Currently, we are focalized on the cooperation library and the features required to represent (and the way to design) a user model.

References

1. Austin, J.L.: How To Do Things With Words. Havard University Press, Cambridge Massachussetts (1962).
2. Searle, J.S.: Les Actes de Langage. Editions Hermann Paris (1972).
3. Grice, P.H.: Meaning. Philosophical Review 56 (1957) 377–388.
4. Bratman, M.E.: Intentions in Communication. In: What is Intention? P.R. Cohen, J.L. Morgan, M. E. Pollack (Eds.) MIT Press, Cambridge MA (1990) 15–31.
5. Wilensky, R.: Meta-planning: Representing and using knowledge about planning in problem solving and natural language understanding. Cognitive Science 5 (1981) 197–233.
6. Grosz, B., Kraus, S.: Collaborative plans for complex group action. Artificial Intelligence 86 (1996) 269–357.
7. Lochbaum, K.E.: A collaborative planning model of intentional structure. Computational Linguistics 24 (1998) 525–572.
8. Carberry, S., Lambert, L.: A tripartite model of collaborative dialogue. Submitted to International Journal of Human-Computer Studies.
9. Ardissono, L., Boella, G., Lesmo, L.: A plan based agent architecture for interpreting natural language dialogue. appear in International Journal of Human Computer Studies, Academic Press 52 (2000) 583–635.
10. Litman, D., Allen, J.: A plan recognition model for subdialogues in conversations. Cognitive Science 11 (1987) 163–200.
11. Camilleri, G.: A generic formal plan recognition theory. In: IEEE International Conference on Information, Intelligence and Systems ICIIS 1999. (1999) 540–547.
12. Camilleri, G.: Une approche, basée sur les plans, de la communication dans les systèmes à base de connaissances coopératifs. Ph.D. thesis, Université Paul Sabatier, IRIT (Institut de Recherche en Informatique de Toulouse) (2000).

A Flexible Framework for Evaluation of New Algorithms for Dialogue Systems

Pavel Cenek

Department of Information Technology, Faculty of Informatics
Masaryk University Brno, Czech Republic
E-mail: xcenek@fi.muni.cz
Currently affiliated with Norut Information Technology Ltd,
Tromsø, Norway
E-mail: pavel.cenek@itek.norut.no

Abstract. Research in the field of dialogue systems often involves building a dialogue system used for evaluation of algorithms, collection of data and various experiments. A significant amount of time is needed to create such a system. In order to facilitate this task, we created a flexible, extensible and easy to use framework which can be used as a base for experimenting with dialogue systems. Major features of the framework are introduced in the paper together with possible ways of their practical use.

1 Introduction

Research in the field of dialogue systems often involves building an experimental dialogue system which is used for statistical data collection, various measurements, performance tests, etc. A significant amount of time is spent on creation of such a system before the scientific work itself can start.

This paper introduces Elvira – a flexible, extensible and easy to use framework for building, evaluating and experimenting with dialogue systems. The framework makes it possible to concentrate on the scientific problem itself and can be easily used for a wide range of research tasks and experiments, e.g. discourse analysis, research in the field of dialogue strategies, statistical processing of dialogues, testing methods of natural language understanding and robust speech recognition, modeling of prosody and other human language technologies related to dialogue systems [1,2,3].

2 Dialogue Flow Description

A flexible dialogue framework should support an easy to use method of the dialogue flow description with possibilities for easy modifications of the dialogue. In this aspect Elvira relies on VoiceXML [4,5], which is generally accepted as a standard for the dialogue flow description. It is designed for description of information retrieval dialogues [6] and in addition to that the dialogue model used in VoiceXML allows to very simply distinguish each dialogue step and its phases.

P. Sojka, I. Kopeček, and K. Pala (Eds.): TSD 2002, LNAI 2448, pp. 437–440, 2002.
© Springer-Verlag Berlin Heidelberg 2002

The VoiceXML specification describes required and optional features of each VoiceXML interpreter, but says very little about ways of their implementation. Elvira offers an implementation which fulfills requirements of the VoiceXML specification and adds many features VoiceXML is not primarily designed for. This is achieved by the use of a sophisticated architecture rather than use of proprietary extensions of VoiceXML. Elvira features include: running of the dialogue using various sources of user's input including speech recognition, various kinds of output including speech synthesis and various grammars for defining expected user's input, broad logging possibilities and more.

Major features are described in the following section.

3   Elvira's Features and Possible Ways of Their Use

3.1   Extensibility and Modularity

Extensibility and modularity of the framework is achieved by the use of a component based architecture.

Elvira consists of several components. Each of them provides a set of precisely defined interfaces for communication with other components. The rest of the component is private and invisible for the rest of the world. Therefore it is very simple to replace one component by another with a different implementation as long as the other component implements the same interfaces.

Components can be linked to the core of the framework (also called *Elvira core*) dynamically, therefore a component can be replaced by another without touching the rest of the system.

Components have to implement only some "mandatory" interfaces which are essential for successful run of the system. By implementing other interfaces they can provide an extended functionality if it is useful for the current application. The situation when an interface is not implemented can be easily detected and Elvira core can avoid the use of such non-implemented interface. This principle allows researchers to deal only with things relevant for their current experiment.

Every component is characterized by its unique name and by its category. It ensures the great flexibility of Elvira. The names are typically used in the configuration files to specify which component should be used for a specific task in the system. Thus the composition and features of your current dialogue system can be determined just by changing a configuration file. In the configuration file, one can specify, among other characteristics, the input source, output destination and what kind of events should be logged and which components should be used for logging.

A component can also be picked based on its category. It is for instance used for the automatic support of new grammar analyzers. Each component ensuring grammar analysis defines its category so that it contains mime-type of the supported grammar format and every grammar used in a VoiceXML document specifies its mime-type. When Elvira core needs a specific grammar analyzer, it simply uses a component with the right category. Thus everything what we need to support a new grammar type is to copy the proper component into a location where Elvira core can find it.

3.2 Output

As described above, output destination and features are dependent on the currently used output component. The most common types are textual output and speech output.

The textual output component is very simple to implement and the output itself is faster then speech output. It can save time in the debug and test phase and it can be easily replaced by a speech output in the final version of the system.

The output component is a good example of a component with an optional interface. Every output component can optionally implement an interface for processing the speech prosody. If the interface is available, Elvira core uses this interface for passing prosodic information from VoiceXML to the output component. A component which uses its own mechanism for prosody modeling or generates no prosody at all simply does not implement this interface.

3.3 Input and Grammars

Input source and capabilities depend on the currently used input component. Possible source types include, but are not limited to, keyboard, microphone, phone or text file.

Keyboard input is very simple and unlike speech recognition does not suffer from input recognition errors. It can be very well used for example for testing of some methods of natural language understanding. Input from a text file can be used for simulations without need of a human operator.

A microphone or a phone is typically used as input for real dialogue applications. Every input component has access to the list of currently active grammars. The grammar components can optionally provide interfaces for collaboration with the input component. Based on information from the grammars, a model of the expected user's input can be built for the speech recognizer. Communication between the input component and the active grammars is in no way influenced or restricted by the Elvira core. It opens large space for testing various kinds of algorithms of robust speech recognition.

The recognized utterance is analyzed using active grammars, and semantic information is returned. The semantic information is assigned into slots and then processed by the dialogue logic described by means of VoiceXML. The complexity of the semantic information is not limited by Elvira, it is the responsibility of the dialogue logic to deal with it. Since a true scripting language is a part of VoiceXML, the possibilities for the representation of semantics and its processing are very broad.

Also grammar analyzers can be of various kind. They can be very simple and recognize only semantics of words from a predefined list, or they can be much more complex using sophisticated language models extracting semantics from free form speech. Elvira can serve as a good framework for both cases.

3.4 Logging

Many research activities related to dialogue systems are based on statistical methods. Elvira can be used for collecting statistical data in various formats. Every interesting event in the Elvira core or another component can be logged. Of course Elvira uses components for this purpose.

An application can define which events should be logged and can assign different components for the logging of different events. It allows the creation of several separated logs containing only information which should be kept and processed together.

4 Conclusion

Elvira is a flexible framework for the work with dialogue systems. Only the basic characteristics were introduced in this paper. Also only very simple ways of their use were described here. Description of more sophisticated techniques is beyond the scope of this paper.

The utility of the framework also depends on the availability of various components. The basic distribution of Elvira offers some simple input, output and grammar components, so that it can be tested without any programming. Source codes of some components are also available and can serve as a base for development of other components. The repository of available components for Elvira will probably grow in time, making its utility higher and higher.

Elvira is available at `http://www.fi.muni.cz/lsd/elvira`.

References

1. De Mori, Renato: Spoken Dialogues with Computers. Academic Press, London, 1997.
2. Smith, R. V., Hipp, D. R.: Spoken Natural Language Dialogue Systems – A Practical Approach. Oxford University Press, 1994.
3. Cole, Ronald, et al., eds: Survey of the State of the Art in Human Language Technology, 21. November 1995. `http://cslu.cse.ogi.edu/HLTsurvey/HLTsurvey.html` last visited 30. March 2002.
4. VoiceXML Forum: Voice Extensible Markup Language (VoiceXML) Version 1.0. 7. March 2000. `http://www.voicexml.org/specs/VoiceXML-100.pdf` last visited 30. March 2002.
5. McGlashan, Scott, et al., eds: Voice Extensible Markup Language (VoiceXML) Version 2.0; W3C Working Draft, 23. October 2001. `http://www.w3.org/TR/2001/WD-voicexml20-20011023/` last visited 30. March 2002.
6. Kopeček, I.: Modeling of the Information Retrieval Dialogue Systems; in Proceedings of the Workshop on Text, Speech and Dialogue – TSD '99, Lectures Notes in Artificial Intelligence 1692, Springer-Verlag, 1999, pp. 302–307.

From HTML to VoiceXML: A First Approach

César González Ferreras, David Escudero Mancebo, and Valentín Cardeñoso Payo

Departamento de Informática, Universidad de Valladolid, 47011 Valladolid, Spain
E-mail: cesargf@infor.uva.es, descuder@infor.uva.es, valen@infor.uva.es

Abstract. In this work, we discuss the construction process of the voice portal counterpart of a departmental web site. VoiceXML has been used as the dialogue modelling language. A prototypical system has been built using our own VoiceXML interpreter, which easily integrates different implementation platforms. A general discussion of VoiceXML advantages and disadvantages is reported and a simple startup procedure is proposed as a means to build voice portals starting from legacy web sites.

1 Introduction

Internet is our biggest information repository nowadays and web browsing the natural access mechanism to it. However, network browsing is not the most used way to access information in everyday life. Mobile devices cope the market and voice is the prominent communication channel in this environment.

Nevertheless, not enough attention has been paid yet to methodological approaches to spoken dialogue systems design and scarcely any reference can be found to ways of exploiting all the legacy information systems that companies are developing and maintaining using generic web technology.

Since spoken dialogue based interaction is essentially affected by sequential mode of operation, complemented in best cases with some form of asynchronous reaction from the user side, the careful design of spoken dialogue systems starting from their counterparts in web environments is still an open question.

In this work, we present our first efforts towards the definition of a integration methodology of web contents navigation and spoken driven information accessing. To this end, we present a first case of study in which a simple web site has been analyzed and rebuilt as a voice portal, using a VoiceXML platform developed at our site.

2 Description of the Problem

The goal of our application is to access information through the telephone line: a voice portal version of the Computer Science Department web site at *Universidad de Valladolid*.

The system started from HTML material, from the web pages of the Department, where you can find general information, information of the teaching activities, a description of the research teams and members contact information.

All this information has to be provided through a voice interface, so we have to be aware of the characteristics of the voice compared to GUI: voice interaction must be sequential, while visual interaction can show all the information at once [3]. This implies that an explicit navigation model is needed, and a technique or language for modelling applications.

P. Sojka, I. Kopeček, and K. Pala (Eds.): TSD 2002, LNAI 2448, pp. 441–444, 2002.

3   Solution

Finite State Diagrams (FSD) have been used to model the dialogue. Using this formalism, we can specify dialogue states and transitions between them [2]. In each state there is a system message, which will be send to the user, and a language model (LM) to describe the expected user input. Each transition has a condition which is used to select the next state.

This is the easiest approach, where the system has the initiative and guides the user through the contents of the portal. There are some limitations of flexibility, although this model is really suitable for navigation, because it resembles the web one.

To map web contents to a FSD, representing the way the system makes the navigation, we have proposed a set of rules to automatize that transformation:

1. The structure of the web site must be captured using a graph. This graph can be used as our first FSD, which has to be improved to achieve an user-friendly interaction.
2. Each state in the FSD with large amount of information to be send to the user has to be changed: navigation through its contents must be allowed. There are two ways of doing this:
   (a) Split that state into several ones, adding the proper transitions between them.
   (b) Enable a search mechanism through the contents of that state.

Eventually, LM must be associated to each state:

1. A grammar made up of all literal strings found in all associated conditions that go out from that state.
2. In search states, we have to build a grammar that can cope with all possible queries we can expect from the user.

The finite state diagram associated to our application is shown in Figure 2, which evolved from the web structure in Figure 1.

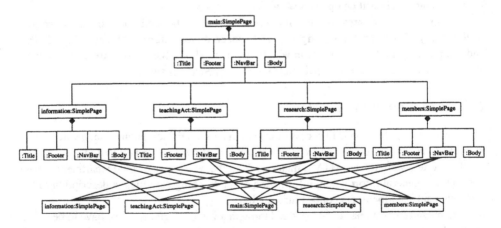

Fig. 1. Departmental Web Site Structure.

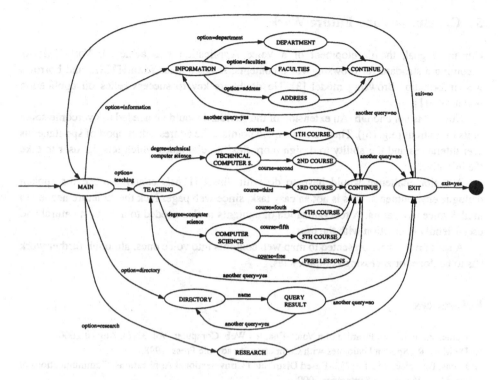

Fig. 2. Finite State Diagram of the Application.

By now, the construction of the FSD is made manually, following the proposed set of transformation rules, although we are working in the automatization. This will involve the parsing of the HTML code and the identification of the relevant elements of each page. Having in mind that each web site has its own style, an initial configuration would be required from the user, to enable the system parsing web pages properly. This avoids the need of a special design of the web pages and enables the reuse of legacy systems.

4 Underlying Platform

Once the application is modelled, the next step is designing the underlying platform to implement the whole system.

VoiceXML was chosen to modelling dialogues. It is one of the emerging voice-telephone technology, and is a standard that allows layered independence between the application and the technological platform at hand. As a result, developed applications can be executed in different platforms.

Taking the architectural model described in the standard as reference [4,5], the system has three main components: the *Document Server*, the *VoiceXML Interpreter* and the *Implementation Platform*. The system developed by our group implements the version 1.0 of the standard [4], but we are expecting to adapt to the newer version 2.0 [5], at the moment under development.

5   Conclusions and Future Work

Our main goal, the development of a Voice Application was achieved. VoiceXML is becoming a standard for browsing voice contents. It takes ideas from HTML, and borrows web information browsing model [3]. No doubt its key to success relies on application portability [1].

But that is not enough. An extension of the standard would be needed to overcome some of its limitations (e.g. [6]). There are two main points to be addressed: support of spontaneous user utterances and the ability to design more flexible dialogues which lets the user to take the initiative.

A major challenge would have to do with direct HTML contents reuse for spoken dialogue environments. This is not an easy task, since web pages lack the structure needed to model voice navigation. A reorganization of contents is also needed to achieve a natural and user-friendly interaction with the user.

A set of rules were presented to map web contents into voice ones, although further work has to be done for accessing complex sites.

References

1. Danielsen, P. J.: The Promise of a Voice-Enabled Web. Computer. Vol. 33(8), August 2000.
2. De Mori, R.: Spoken Dialogues with Computers. Academic Press. 1998.
3. Lucas, B.: VoiceXML for Web-Based Distributed Conversational Applications. Communications of the ACM. Vol. 43(9), September 2000.
4. VoiceXML Forum: Voice eXtensible Markup Language (VoiceXML) Version 1.0. March 2000. http://www.voicexml.org/specs/VoiceXML-100.pdf.
5. W3C: Voice eXtensible Markup Language (VoiceXML) Version 2.0. October 2001. http://www.w3.org/TR/2001/WD-voicexml20-20011023/.
6. Tsai, A., Pargellis, A.N., Lee, C., Olive, J.P.: Dialogue Session Management Using VoiceXML. Proceedings of the European Conference on Speech Technology, EuroSpeech. 2001.

Voice Chat with a Virtual Character:
The Good Soldier Švejk Case Project*

Jan Nouza, Petr Kolář and Josef Chaloupka

SpeechLab, Technical University of Liberec
Hálkova 6, 461 17 Liberec, Czechia
E-mail: Jan.Nouza@vslib.cz, Petr.Kolar@vslib.cz, Josef.Chaloupka@vslib.cz

Abstract. In this paper we present our initial attempt to link speech processing technology, namely continuous speech recognition, text-to-speech synthesis and artificial talking head, with text processing techniques in order to design a Czech demonstration system that allows for informal voice chatting with virtual characters. Legendary novel figure Švejk is the first personality who can be interviewed in the recently implemented version.

1 Introduction

It is good for any research if its state-of-the-art can be demonstrated on applications that are attractive not only for a small scientific community but also for wider public.

A nice example of an interesting show-product demonstrating capabilities of the recent speech technology was presented on the IVVTA workshop in 1998 [1]. It showed a naturally looking voice dialogue with a virtual character. The designers of the system chose Albert Einstein as the target person to whom one could address questions about his life and work. The system employed a continuous speech recognition engine that was able to accept spoken questions and translate them into a sequence of semantic symbols. According to the list of given key-words the computer selected a (more or less) appropriate response and replayed it to the human interviewer. The Einstein's reactions had form of video sequences prerecorded by an actor. The primary aim of that demonstration was to show the current advances of the speech research, yet various applications in education and entertainment offered themselves.

Being inspired by that idea we decided to develop a similar system that integrates the results of our research in speech and text processing. Recently we have been able to build up such a demo product using our middle-size vocabulary speech recognition engine applicable for continuously spoken Czech utterances [2], a TTS module developed in the Institute of Radioengineering in Prague [3] and a virtual animated face that can be synchronized with synthesized or natural speech signal [4]. We put these modules together and linked them by a simple 'chat manager'.

---

* The project was supported by the Grant Agency of the Czech Republic (grant no.102/02/0124) and through research goal project MSM 242200001.

P. Sojka, I. Kopeček, and K. Pala (Eds.): TSD 2002, LNAI 2448, pp. 445–448, 2002.

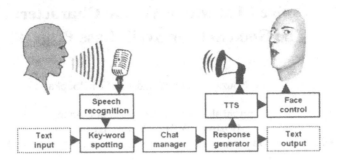

Fig. 1. Schematic diagram of the interaction between human and virtual character.

2 Design of Voice Chatting System

The system is depicted in Figure 1. Let us note its two operation modes. The simpler one uses text input and output. In this mode the user types his or her questions and receives answers again in printed form. Optionally, the virtual character's responses can be generated by an artificial face producing synthesized speech. This mode is very helpful especially during the development and debugging phase. In the second mode the system accepts spoken input and translate it into the text form. The main components of the system are briefly described in the following subsections.

2.1 Speech Input Module

The module provides the speech recognition of the human user's questions. These are supposed to be fluently spoken utterances. Two options for translating them into a sequence of text symbols are available now. The first one employs a real-time key-word spotting technique [5]. It can identify about 1,000 key-words while the rest of the utterance is covered by filler models. No language modeling is applied except of controlling the performance through a word/filler insertion penalty. The second type of the speech input module employs our own speech recognition engine developed for Czech language [2]. Here the speech decoding is supported by a bigram language model. In general, the latter approach outperforms the former in case the input utterances remain inside the given vocabulary and keep the rules of standard Czech.

2.2 Talking Head Module

This module was built up with the use of the Baldi engine [6]. We have modified and complemented the original software so that it can be applied for Czech. Moreover, it is capable of animated talking both in synthesized as well as in 'natural' mode. In the latter case it employs phoneme recognition to generate an appropriate sequence of visual patterns (visemes). The head can take on a mask (a texture) of any person.

2.3   Chat Manager Module

Within this particular project this is the most crucial part. In ideal case it should provide natural language (analysis and synthesis) processing capabilities. In practice our goal is more modest. The recent version supports a simplified analysis of the text string coming out from the recognition module. The string is decomposed into lexical tokens by applying a lemmatization scheme [7] and mapped onto a semantic model prepared for the given application. No disambiguation procedures neither syntactic analysis are applied at the moment. The major reason for this simplification consists in the fact that the speech recognition module is not perfect and produces errors of different kind: mainly substitutions of similarly sounding words, confusions in suffixes, false word insertions, deletions, etc. We must also except the fact that the voice interaction has form of chit-chat rather than a meaningful dialogue.

3   The Good Soldier Švejk Project

The personality we have chosen for the initial case project is the legendary Czech literature character Švejk. Our choice had several pragmatic reasons. First, Švejk is so famous that its role in the project must attract both specialists as well as wide public. Second, Švejk is a true prototype of a chatting person ready to response with pleasure to any topic. His rather strange and off-topic reactions are well-known and typical for his behavior. This gives our system an exceptional chance to hide – or at least to excuse – most confusions caused by erroneous functions of the speech and language processing modules. Third, we have the complete Hašek's novel in electronic form, which allows us to make a detailed analysis of the novel text, both on lexical as well as on linguistic level. (The text contains 198,976 words, from which 33,218 are different. If we omit all words that occurred less than three-times we can reduce the working lexicon to some 8,000 words and simplify thus the recognition task.)

The chat strategy implemented so far has the following scheme: The dialogue is launched by a short introductory part, usually an exchange of greetings. After that an 'open conversation' starts. Here, the system tries to extract from the input utterance the key-words that identify any of the pre-selected themes. Some topics are covered by a single Švejk's response or comment, other cause a move into a 'target-oriented' dialogue. In the latter case Švejk starts to chat with his human partner. Within a series of questions the system tries to fill some slots in an internal form in order to select an appropriate response or story to be told by Švejk. The slots can be filled in a random order and they can handle also situations like "don't know" or "not identified". Explicit confirmation at some instants helps in recovering from unintentional detours in the chat caused by speech recognition or text analysis errors. Švejk's replies are generated from a list of prepared sentences, phrases and stories that can be partly modified according to the current context. At any dialogue turn the system checks if the user still remains in the target oriented branch or whether he or she wants to change the topic or even quit the chat. In case the system does not understand the questions or if it become confused about the themes it lets Švejk tell one of his famous stories.

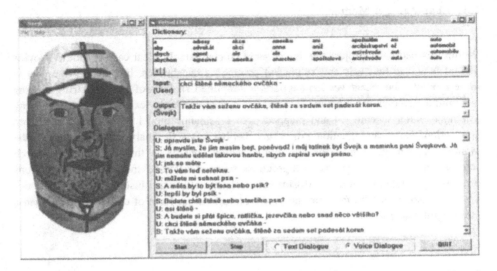

Fig. 2. Chatting with Švejk who is represented by animated talking face.

4   Conclusions

The main goal of this project is to study possibilities of linking speech and text processing techniques and present them in the way that is attractive even for wider public.

References

1. Furness, T. A: Interactive Voice Technology in Virtual Environments. Invited talk at IVVTA (Interactive Voice Technology for Telecom. Applications) Workshop. Torino, 1998.
2. Nouza J.: Strategies for Developing a Real-Time Continuous Speech Recognition System for Czech Language. In: Sojka P. et al. (Eds.): *Text, Speech and Dialogue*, Proceedings of the Fifth International Conference, Brno, Czech Republic, September 9–12, 2002, pp. 189–196.
3. Přibil, J.: Czech and Slovak TTS System Based on the Cepstral Speech Model. In: Proc. of the 3th Int. Conference DSP '97, Herľany (Slovakia), September 3–4, 1997, pp. 23–26.
4. Chaloupka, J., Nouza, J., Přibil, J.: Czech-Speaking Artificial Face. In Proc. of Biosignal Conference. Brno, June 2002 (in print).
5. Nouza, J.: A Scheme for Improved Key-Phrase Detection and Recognition in the InfoCity System. Proc. of 5th ECM2S workshop. Toulouse, May 2001, pp. 237–241.
6. Cole et al.: Intelligent Animated Agents for Interactive Language Training. Proc. of STiLL'98, Stockholm, 1998, pp. 163–166.
7. Hajič, J.: Unification Morphology Grammar. Ph.D. Thesis. Charles University, Faculty of Mathematics and Physics, Prague, 1994.

Application of Spoken Dialogue Technology in a Medical Domain

I. Azzini[1], T. Giorgino[1], D. Falavigna[2], R. Gretter[2]

[1] Dept. of Computers and Systems Science - University of Pavia, 27100 Pavia, Italy
E-mail: ivano@aim.unipv.it, toni@aim.unipv.it
[2] Istituto per la Ricerca Scientifica e Tecnologica, ITC-irst - Via Sommarive 1,
38050 Povo, Trento, Italy,
E-mail: falavi@itc.it, gretter@itc.it

Abstract. The paper describes the ITC-irst approach for handling spoken dialogue interactions over the telephone. In particular, we have used the technology to develop a telemedicine prototype system that provides health-care to chronic patients. First, the system architecture will be summarized, then we will describe an automatic service for home monitoring of patients affected by hypertension pathology. Patients must periodically introduce data into a database containing their personal medical records. The collected data are managed, according to well established medical guidelines, by a software agent connected to a relational database, which contains the detailed history of each patient.

1 Introduction

The spoken dialogue system developed in ITC-irst can handle mixed initiative interactions over the telephone for information access in restricted domains. In the past some prototype services were developed and tested for train timetable inquiry and tourism information access [1,2]. Since last year the system has been used for developing a tele-medicine service that will provide health assistance to chronic patients[3]. In this system, the patients periodically call a dedicated telephone number and engage a spoken dialogue with the system, which interacts with them to acquire clinical data, monitors their style of life and asks about the presence of side effects. We tried to keep the dialogue as close as possible to the interaction between a physician and a patient; the service also gives advice, by issuing alerts and prompts as appropriate, to keep the patient in a low risk class. For doing this, the system is connected to a database that records the detailed medical histories of the patients being followed. We have chosen a group of patients, affected by hypertension, in care at the "San Matteo Hospital" in Pavia, Italy; they would normally have to meet their physician approximately every 2–4 weeks. The goal of the periodical examination is to monitor blood pressure values, heart rate, weight, habits and other variables used to estimate certain standard risk indicators. As suggested in [3], we have extracted the domain knowledge from a set of world-widely accepted guidelines for the hypertension and dyslipidemia pathologies.

---

[3] This work has been partially done within the framework of the "Homey" project (Home Monitoring by Intelligent Dialogue Systems), funded by European Union.

P. Sojka, I. Kopeček, and K. Pala (Eds.): TSD 2002, LNAI 2448, pp. 449–452, 2002.
© Springer-Verlag Berlin Heidelberg 2002

2   The Dialogue System

The basic idea underlying the dialogue engine lies on the definition of a set of "contexts", containing "concepts" associated to subgrammars. Therefore, a direct relation between concepts and grammars, activated during the various dialogue turns, has to be established.

Our approach for language modeling makes use of recursive transition networks [4]. These are finite state networks whose arcs allow linking other grammars in a recursive way. The resulting language is context free. Since the decoding step of a speech utterance can backtrack both the grammars and the words along the best path of the language graph, the recognized string consists of a mix of words and structured information. Semantic tags are included in the recognized string as reported below:

```
Hi, my name is (NAME(Ivano Azzini)NAME) and I have a (PRESSURE( pressure
of (VALUE(2 hundred and 10)VALUE) )PRESSURE) and today I (WEIGHT(weigh
(VALUE( one hundred )VALUE) kilos)WEIGHT).
```

In the string above the semantic tags NAME, PRESSURE and WEIGHT identify the related variables to collect. Note that the string above can be seen as a parse tree.

The development of the understanding part of an application basically consists in designing a set of grammars for each elementary information (concept) to collect, hence each basic concept has associated one or more grammars. In the example above, a possible grammar for the concept NAME can be a list of the names and surnames linked in several ways (i.e. name-surname, surname-name, surname); for the concept PRESSURE the grammar could be a list of numbers ranging within a predefined interval, and so on.

On the other hand, part of sentences that do not convey useful information (such as: "my weight is," "I weigh," "the weight today is," etc.) can be efficiently represented with stochastic language models (i.e. n-gram language models). In our approach we arrange grammars into two separate levels. A bigram grammar is at the top level, and includes links to regular grammars at a lower level; each of the latter is associated to a concept. Initially, bigrams are trained on a small set of hand-written sentences representing (in the designer's intention) what the users will say. Once a prototype is built, field data can be recorded from user interactions. Then, the collected data are transcribed and used to update bigram probabilities. In previous experiments we demonstrated that the approach was effective for handling a domain such as access to tourism information. Refer to [1] for more details.

3   Patient Monitoring Service

Two actors are allowed to enter data into a clinical database. The physician uses a conventional (graphics, keyboard and mouse) interface to store and update data. The patient is allowed to enter the data that she/he can acquire at home by using the telephone. One dedicated server with adequate hardware is connected to the telephone network and runs a commercial "call center" software, which answers phone calls and routes them to the ASR and TTS. When one call arrives, the dialogue engine is started. After authenticating the user, it reads from a "state vector" a set of discrete variables encoding a patient specific "target function". This last one determines which data must be acquired coherently with the evolution of the pathology on the basis of the knowledge related to the patient clinical history. In general, some fields of the basic concepts in the dialogue description could not be filled according to patient habits (e.g. if the patient is not a smoker the system will not ask if she/he smokes, if the patient is not subjected to a pharmacological therapy the system will not ask for it, and so on). Hence, the state vector tell us which fields of the dialogue description have to be acquired (mandatory) or not. Typically the target function has the following form:

Field	Value
Sport	(mandatory|optional)
Smokes	(mandatory|optional)
Blood Pressure	(mandatory|optional)
Weight	(mandatory|optional)
Heart Rate	(mandatory|optional)
. . . .	. . . .

The target function is updated according to information contained in the database. This task is accomplished by a software agent ("adaptivity agent") connected to a relational database, which holds the detailed medical records of each patient. As previously seen, the issues considered by the agent include habits, e.g. whether she/he is a smoker; history of prescribed drugs, because one wants to check for the presence of relevant side effects; whether she is on diet, etc. Exceptional events like hang-up, multiple recognition errors and missing values ("I don't know") are also handled by the agent; this allows the relevant state information to be carried on between calls, so that the missing information can be asked the next time the patient calls, if it is appropriate. The whole system therefore exhibits the *long-term* adaptation behavior described in [3]. This long-term adaptation for each patient takes place *after* she/he has completed the conversation with the system. The system is therefore able to adapt itself to the evolution of the disease, new patient habits or features, new physician directions, etc.

We also consider a different kind of adaptation strategy, which we have called *short-term* (or punctual) adaptation. This kind of adaptation takes place *during* the course of a dialogue; it can handle a range of user's behaviors, as it is shown in the example below, that reports a piece of patient-system interaction for heart rate checking.

Sys: Tell me your heart rate, please.
Pat: I have not measured it but today my weight is almost 85
Sys: So your heart rate is missing and your weight is 85
Pat: My weight is 84
Sys: So your heart rate is missing and your weight is 84
Pat: Yes.
Sys: I remind you that your physician prescribed a diet. Your weight has increased by 2 kilograms since last call

The system short-term adaptation can be seen, for example, in the following case. The dialogue system assumes that the calling patients are healthy; if this happens the dialogue is "short", i.e. in few turns the system can obtain all the necessary medical information from the patient and the call is ended. Nevertheless, the patient could be subjected to a pharmacology therapy, which could have serious side effects. In this case the system has to manage the unexpected event "The patient is not well" by activating a more complex dialogue with her/him. More specifically, after certain significant questions, a special set of grammars is activated in the background. One of them is triggered when the name of a malaise is possibly uttered. If this happens, the system reads the field "prescribed drugs" from the patient records and activates an investigation on the possible side effects for those drugs. This investigation is conducted with different levels of detail, in relation to the severity of the side effect. If the discovered malaise presents a certain gravity, the system urges the patient to immediately contact a physician.

4   Data Collection

Up to now, the described patient monitoring system parameters (essentially the language models) have been tuned only by means of trials carried out in the Laboratory. A further refinement of the system is going to be carried out by collecting data from a small selected set of users (about 50 people), not necessarily patients affected by hypertension.

Each participant to the experiment will be assigned a specific profile with respect to hypertension; he will be then instructed to call the service and provide answers according to the given profile. The personal profile will specify whether he is affected by slight hypertension, whether he has to follow a diet or a pharmacological therapy, etc. Furthermore, each participant will be given a form containing the clinical data to provide to the system, according to his profile (e.g. minimum pressure, maximum pressure, cardiac frequency, prescribed drugs, etc.). The participants will have to call the service and answer to the questions of the system. All the interactions will be recorded and trascribed in order to measure the performance of the present system and for improving the language models and the dialogue strategy as well.

References

1. D. Falavigna, R. Gretter, M. Orlandi: Mixed Language Model for a Dialogue System over the Telephone. *Proc. of ICSLP*, Beijing, Vol. 1, pp. 585–588, October 2000.
2. C. Barbero, D. Falavigna, R. Gretter, M. Orlandi, E. Pianta: Some Improvements on the IRST Mixed Initiative Dialogue Technology. In P. Sojka et al.(Eds.): *Proc. of TSD 2000 Workshop*, Brno (Czech Republic), pp. 351–356, September 2000.
3. I. Azzini, D. Falavigna, R. Gretter, G. Lanzola, M. Orlandi: First steps toward an adaptive dialogue system in medical domain. In: *Proc. of EuroSpeech*, Aalborg (Denmark), September 2001.
4. F. Brugnara, M. Federico: Dynamic Language Models for Interactive Speech Analysis. In: *Proc. of EuroSpeech*, pp. 1827–1830, Rhodes, Greece, 1997.

A Voice-Driven Web Browser for Blind People

Simon Dobrišek, Jerneja Gros, Boštjan Vesnicer, France Mihelič, and Nikola Pavešić

University of Ljubljana, Faculty of Electrical Engineering,
Laboratory of Artificial Perception, Systems and Cybernetics,
Ljubljana, Slovenia,
WWW: simond@fe.uni-lj.si,
WWW home page: http://luks.fe.uni-lj.si/~simond

Abstract. A specialised small Web browser with a voice-driven dialogue manager and a text-to-speech screen reader is presented. The Web browser was built from the GTK Web browser Dillo, which is a free software project in the terms of the GNU general public license. The new built-in screen reader is now triggered by pointing the mouse and uses the text-to-speech module for its output. A dialogue module together with a spoken-command input was also introduced into the browser. It can be used for navigation through a structure of common Web pages. The developed browser is primarily intended to be used with the new Web portal, exclusively dedicated to blind and visually impaired users. All the Web pages at the portal or at sites that are linked from this portal are expected to be arranged as common HTML/XML pages, which complies with the basic recommendations set by the Web Access Initiative.

1 Introduction

Modern information-technology facilities are often not suitable for blind and visually impaired people. Such problems in communication are well known to many disabled persons. If they are unable to use their hands, read or speak, they are forced to use technical aids to overcome their problems. For blind or visually impaired persons the Braille coding of texts is a common aid. This type of coding requires special editions of written corpora or special additional hardware components when used with computers. The solution is relatively costly and requires special skills from the user.

Over the past ten years a considerable advance has been made in the development of automatic text-to-speech and speech recognition systems. Such systems offer a more natural and user-friendly way of communication for the blind or visually impaired persons; the communication goal can be achieved faster and they offer access to large text corpora via modern technical equipment (over computer networks, scanners, etc.) and have a relatively low price [11].

However, these new technologies are very language dependent and general solutions for all languages cannot be applied directly [8]. If speech technologies are to be used with the Slovene language the language-dependent parts of the systems must be developed for this purpose using knowledge of Slovene-language phonology, syntax and semantics.

Spoken-language technologies have been one of our main research activities for more than twenty years. Our prime interest is to develop a core technology for the Slovene

P. Sojka, I. Kopeček, and K. Pala (Eds.): TSD 2002, LNAI 2448, pp. 453–459, 2002.

spoken language that could be customised for different kinds of applications. We found the development of a voice-driven Web browser for Slovene-speaking blind people important to our research for several technical and non-technical reasons, among them is the possibility to help the disabled people.

A voice-driven Web browser called Homer was developed for reading Slovenian texts obtained from the Internet site of the Association of Slovenian Blind and Visually Impaired Persons Societies. The Homer Web browser demonstrates how the ways of accessing daily news and other useful information can be improved for disabled users.

1.1   The Kalliope Web Portal

The World Wide Web server called Kalliope has a long-term ambition to become a specialised Web portal for blind and visually impaired people in Slovenia. The Kalliope Web portal is planned to retrieve the Electronic Information System [4] (EIS) of the Association of Slovenian Blind and Visually Impaired Persons Societies (ZDSSS). All the Web pages at Kalliope will comply with the basic recommendations set by the Web Access Initiative [10] and will be tagged with a few additional XML tags, which will enable user-friendly navigation using the presented dialogue module. The portal will also serve as a site that links to other Web sites in Slovenia that are important to the blind and visually impaired community and are accessible via the presented Homer Web browser. The portal will have its access restricted to ZDSSS members since many texts from the EIS database fall under copyright restrictions.

Our first task was to reformat the EIS text corpora and to transfer them to the new portal. The majority of the text files at the EIS database are stored in a plain, non-tagged text format and so a special HTML/XML tagger is needed to convert these texts into a structure of common HTML/XML pages. Virtually all of the available text files at the EIS require a unique tagger function for this conversion as the texts are provided from different sources. Presently, scripting programs for such conversions are being developed.

Initially, we concentrated on Slovenian daily newspapers which are probably the most interesting and the most frequently accessed texts at the EIS. The scripting programs automatically retrieve the original compressed newspaper-text archives from the EIS. These programs are symbolically shown in Figure 1 as a retriever module. A tagger function, specially designed for each of the newspapers, then forms the structure of the HTML/XML pages. The HTML/XML structure is formed and refreshed at the Kalliope server every few hours. The first page contains links to issues for all weekdays and a link to the most recent issue. The sub-pages contain links to the newspaper heading pages with links to the individual article pages. All the pages contain hidden XML tags, which are required for the dialogue module to make a distinction between different parts of Web pages.

2   The Homer Web Browser

The Homer Web browser was not built from scratch. New modules were just introduced into the source code of one of the publicly available Web browsers, which is now considered to be yet another module of the whole Homer system.

When seeking the appropriate Web browser we considered the following criteria:

- The source code has to be written entirely in C.
- It has to be a multiplatform browser.
- It has to be small, stable, developer-friendly, usable, fast, and extensible.
- It has to be a free software project in the terms of the GNU general public license.

We found that the GTK Web browser Dillo [1] was perfect for our needs.

2.1   The Homer System Structure

The whole system consists of four main modules. The system structure is shown in Figure 1

Input to the system is performed via a keyboard, with some specially selected keys or by using the speaker-independent spoken command recognition module that runs in parallel with the other modules. The voice control of the system additionally facilitates working with the system as there is no need to use mechanical interfaces. The dialogue module manages dialogues with users and performs access to the Web pages via the Web browser.

The most important part of the system is the first fully developed Slovenian text-to-speech system [5], which is essential for blind users. It enables automatic generation of Slovene speech from an arbitrary Slovenian text written in a non-tagged plain-text format using one of the standard character encodings, like the Slovenian version of the 7–bit ASCII coding or the WIN-1250 and the ISO-8859-2 codings.

The Homer browser was designed to run on a standard PC with a minimum of 64 MB of RAM with a built-in standard 16–bit sound card and a standard headset with a close-talking microphone. Initially it was developed for Linux platform and later ported to the Microsoft Windows 9x/ME/NT/2000/XP operating systems. For the best performance it uses multi-threading and other advantages of the 32–bit environment. It requires approximately 15 MB of disk space for the program code and for the text-to-speech and speech recogniser module inventory.

2.2   Screen Reader Module

Our first step was to add a screen-reader function to the existing Dillo source code. The built-in screen reader is now triggered by pointing the mouse and uses the text-to-speech module for its output. When a user stays for a moment at a certain position on the Web page the text beneath the pointer is sent to the output text-to-speech module. The output module works in a separated thread with a time-out function that prevents the user from overfilling the synthesis buffer with a fast pointer motion when browsing through the Web page.

An important feature of the screen reader is that it generates special distinctive non-speech sounds which inform users about changes to the current positions of the mouse pointer. Such sounds are generated when users leave or enter a particular area of the displayed Web page.

The screen-reader function supports not only text parts of common Web pages but some basic graphic objects as well, such as non-animated images, lines, bullets, buttons and input text fields. When a user stays for a moment with a mouse pointer pointing at such graphic objects then the system sends a short description of the object to the text-to-speech module. An example of such a description would be: *"Button labelled 'send', sized 60×20 pixels."*.

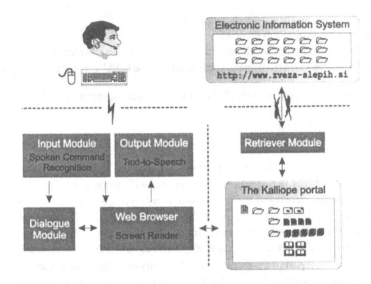

Fig. 1. The structure of the Homer Web browser.

The screen reader works in several different modes. It can read individual words, sentences, lines and paragraphs of the displayed Web page. It can read page headings and the whole page as well. The reading mode can be changed by using the function keys on a standard PC keyboard.

2.3 Input Module

The input interface manages the keyboard entry and/or spoken-command recognition. Each of the spoken control commands is associated with its accelerator key on a standard PC keyboard.

The speaker-independent spoken commands recognition module is based on tied-mixture continuous HMMs of fundamental phone transition-like units [3]. These models are used as the fundamental models in a silence / commands / silence HMM graph. A number of improvements to the acoustic modelling were introduced. Variable HMMs structures were implemented and a unique initialisation of the model parameters using a Slovene diphone speech database was used. The parameters of the fundamental models were estimated from the Gopolis spoken-language database [2], which contains several hours of speech from 50 speakers. Using this large database the fundamental HMMs were made speaker-independent.

The whole speech recognition module is designed in an open manner, enabling fast adaptation to different applications with isolated spoken-command recognition input, and also for larger vocabularies of up to several hundred words. The recognition procedure also offers the unrecognised spoken-command category classification, which activates a request for repetition of the command. The current version of the speech recognition module allows use of a spoken command grammar which is translated into an HMM graph.

A preliminary off-line evaluation of the spoken-command recognition accuracy, using a clean speech database of ten test speakers, yielded an average recognition error rate lower than 2 %. However, the actual recognition rate is strongly dependent on the spoken-command grammar and the user's behaviour while interacting with the system. In practise, the online recognition error rate increases, but remains below 5 %.

2.4 Dialogue Module

The dialogue module manages dialogues with users, accesses Web pages via the Web browser module and performs the system-control function. Its design is based on our experiences with the design of a similar dialogue module in another speech recognition system [7].

Since a structure of common Web pages can always be presented as a tree structure, the dialogue module enables transitions between all the tree nodes at any stage of the processing and navigating through a list of sub-nodes at each of the tree nodes as well. There are only three main actions that the dialogue module takes or offers to user. These actions are: opening of a Web page tree node, navigating through a list of sub-nodes, and closing a Web page tree node. Each of the tree nodes represents a link, a page itself, or a part of a page.

All the actions can either be just offered to the user or are taken immediately after the dialogue module successfully interprets a recognised spoken command or a keyboard entry, even though the dialogue is still in the process of describing the current position in the Web page tree or is in the process of reading/describing a part of the Web page. As a result, these two different dialogue strategies were implemented. When an action is explicitly offered then a *yes/no* answer is expected from the user. This dialogue strategy is called *passive-user behaviour*. On the other hand, an *active-user behaviour* strategy means that the dialogue module expects the user to interrupt the dialogue process with spoken commands.

The first strategy is more suitable for beginners; the second is more suitable for expert users since it enables faster navigation. Both strategies have to be combined when the dialogue is in the process of reading a selected text. In this case the user is allowed to occasionally interrupt the reading process with commands. As an example a typical *passive-user* dialogue with the system would be something like:

system: *"Welcome to the Kalliope Web portal!"*
system: *"Would you like to open the ZDSSS messages ... "*
user: *"Skip!"*
system: *"Would you like to open the daily newspaper section?"*
user: *"Yes."*
system: *"Would you like to open The Independent?"*
user: *"Yes."*
system: *"Would you like to open the News ... "*
user: *"Next!"*
system: *"Would you like to open the Sports page?"*
user: *"Yes."*
system: *"Would you like to read the article: 'Mika won again'?"*
user: *"Yes!"*
system: *"The selected article has 456 word. The subtitle is ... "*
user: *"Skip!"*
system: *"Mika had a brilliant race and succeeded to burst ... "*
user: *"Close!"*
system: *"Would you like to read the article: 'Keep the gold coming'?"*
...

The dominantly *passive* dialogue strategy requires only *yes/no* answers and a small number of easy-to-remember navigation commands. We found that this dialogue strategy provides a very comfortable interaction with the system, even though it has proved to be rather time consuming and even annoying to expert users.

The *active* dialogue strategy requires some additional navigation commands. In the best case we could use a dynamic spoken-command grammar instead of using just a static list of commands. The current version of the speech recognition input module did not allow us to use the dynamic spoken-command grammar, thus we carefully selected a small number of navigation commands. We found that the navigation speed is very comfortable when using eight basic commands. Their English translations are: *"Open!"*, *"Close!"*, *"Skip!"*, *"Previous!"*, *"Repeat!"*, *"Restart!"*, *"Pause!"*, and *"Resume!"*. With these commands a user can open and close Web page tree nodes and navigate through a list of sub-nodes at any position in the tree.

A typical *active-user* dialogue would be now something like:

system: *"Welcome to the Kalliope Web portal!"*
system: *"I have the ZDSSS messages – daily newspapers – ..."*
user: *"Open!"*
system: *"I have The Daily Star – The Independent – ..."*
user: *"Open!"*
system: *"I have the News – the Sports – ..."*
user: *"Open!"*
system: *"I have the articles: 'Mika won again' – .."*
user: *"Open!"*
system: *"The selected article has 456 word. The subtitle is ..."*
user: *"Skip!"*
system: *"Mika had a brilliant race and succeeded to burst ..."*
user: *"Repeat!"*
system: *"Mika had a brilliant race and succeeded to burst ..."*
user: *"Close!"*
system: *"I have the articles: 'Keep the gold coming' – 'Hughes Takes Gold' – ..."*
user: *"Restart!"*
system: *"I have the articles: 'Mika won again' – 'Keep the gold coming' – ..."*
user: *"Open!"*
...

Please note that the newspaper titles in the above examples do not really exist in the EIS database. The Slovenian newspapers are *Delo, Dnevnik, Večer*, etc.

The current version of the dialogue module supports only the two described dialogue strategies. The presented list of basic navigation commands was extended with the names of the most frequently accessed sections at the Kalliope portal. Thus, the navigation commands: "Open daily newspapers!", "Open The Daily Star!", and similar, are now supported. By using of these commands the speed of navigation is increased even more.

2.5   Output Module

For the automatic conversion of the output text into its spoken form the first Slovenian text-to-speech system called S5 [5] based on diphone concatenation was applied. The non-tagged plain text is transformed into its spoken equivalent by several modules. A grapheme-to-allophone module produces strings of phonetic symbols based on information in the written text. A prosodic generator assigns pitch and duration values to individual phones. The final speech synthesis is based on diphone concatenation using TD-PSOLA [9].

3   Conclusions and Future Work

The development of the Homer system and the Kalliope portal is still in progress. We expect the system to evolve towards a specialised Web browser with a mouse-driven Text-to-speech screen reader and a voice-driven dialogue manager that handles all the Web pages arranged at the Kalliope portal or at sites that are linked from this portal.

Improvements in the sense of more accurate and robust speech recognition and a user-friendly system to control high-quality speech synthesis are planned for the future. Work on speech recognition that incorporates a larger dynamic spoken-command grammar is already under way. We are expecting further suggestions from the blind and visually impaired community, especially with regards to the design of the strategy for communication with the system and, of course, remarks on the Slovene speech synthesis quality. Many measurements and research in the field of micro and macro prosody modelling of Slovene speech should be done as well as recordings of new diphone databases with different speakers.

References

1. The Dillo Web browser. (2002). http://dillo.sourceforge.net/.
2. Dobrišek, S., Gros, J., Mihelič, F., Pavešić, N. (1998). 'Recording and Labelling of the GOPOLIS Slovenian Speech Database'. *Proceedings ot the First International Conference on Language Resources and Evaluation*. Granada, Spain. 2: pp. 1089–1096.
3. Dobrišek, S. (2001). *Analysis and Recognition of Phones in Speech Signal*. Ph.D. Thesis (in Slovene), University of Ljubljana.
4. EIS - the Electronic Information System. (2002).
   http://www.zveza.slepih.si/zdsss/eis/.
5. Gros, J., Pavešić, N. and Mihelič, F. (1997). 'Text-to-speech synthesis: A complete system for the Slovenian language'. *Journal of Computing and Information Technology*. **CIT-5**, 1:11–19.
6. Huang, X.D., Ariki, Y. and Jack, M.A. (1990). *Hidden Markov Models for Speech Recognition*. Edinburg Information Technology Series. Redwood Press Limited, London.
7. Ipšić, I., Mihelič, F., Dobrišek, S., Gros, J. and Pavešć, N. (1995). 'Overview of the Spoken Queries in European Languages Project: The Slovenian Spoken Dialogue System'. *Proceedings of the Scientific Conference on Artificial Intelligence in Industry*. High Tatras, Slovakia. pp. 431–438.
8. Jelinek, F. (1998). *Statistical Methods for Speech Recognition*. The MIT Press. Cambridge, Massachusetts.
9. Moulines, E. and Charpentier F. (1990). 'Pitch-Synchronous Waveform Processing Techniques for Text-to-Speech Synthesis Using Diphones'. *Proceedings of the National Academy of Sciences of the United States of America*. **92. 22**:, pp. 9999–10006.
10. WAI – Web Access Initiative. (2002). http://www.w3.org/TR/WAI-WEBCONTENT.
11. Zajicek, M., Powell, C. and Reeves, C. (1999). 'Ergonomic factors for a speaking computer interface'. In M. A. Hanson, E. J. Lovesey and S. A. Robertson (Eds.), *Contemporary Ergonomics - The proceedings of the 50th Ergonomics Society Conference, Leicester University*. Taylor and Francis, London, pp. 484–488.

Enhancing Best Analysis Selection and Parser Comparison

Aleš Horák, Vladimír Kadlec, and Pavel Smrž

Faculty of Informatics, Masaryk University Brno
Botanická 68a, 602 00 Brno, Czech Republic
E-mail: hales@fi.muni.cz, xkadlec@fi.muni.cz, smrz@fi.muni.cz

Abstract. This paper discusses methods enhancing the selection of a "best" parsing tree from the output of natural language syntactic analysis. It presents a method for cutting away redundant parse trees based on the information obtained from a dependency tree-bank corpus.

The effectivity of the enhanced parser is demonstrated by results of inter-system parser comparison. The test were run on the standard evaluation grammars (ATIS, CT and PT), our system outperforms the referential implementations.

1 Introduction

The total number of atoms in the Universe is estimated to be 10^{90}. The average number of parsing trees per input sentence strongly depends on the background grammar and thence on the language. There are natural language grammars producing at most hundreds or thousands of parsing trees but also highly ambiguous grammar systems producing enormous number of results.

Ambiguity on all levels of representation is an inherent property of natural languages and it also forms a central problem of natural language parsing. A consequence of the natural language ambiguity is a high number of possible outputs of a parser that are represented by labeled trees.

For example, a grammar extracted from the Penn Treebank and tested on a set of sentences randomly generated from a probabilistic version of the grammar has on average 7.2×10^{27} parses per sentence according to Moore's work [1]. Such a mammoth extent of result is also no exception in parsing of Czech [2] due to free word order and rich morphology of word forms whose grammatical case cannot often be unambiguously determined.

A traditional solution for these problems is presented by probabilistic parsing techniques [3] aiming at finding the most probable parse of a given input sentence. This methodology is usually based on the relative frequencies of occurrences of the possible relations in a representative corpus.

In the following text, we present an acquisition of training data for the best analysis selection. The underlying mechanism is based on the pruning constraints that automate the process of transformation of a dependency tree-bank corpus.

The results are then compared to running times of a referential parsing system. The comparison indicates that our system is fully able to compete with the best current parsers.

P. Sojka, I. Kopeček, and K. Pala (Eds.): TSD 2002, LNAI 2448, pp. 461–466, 2002.
© Springer-Verlag Berlin Heidelberg 2002

2 Best Analysis Selection

First, in order to be able to exploit the data from PDTB, we have supplemented our grammar with the dependency specification for constituents. Thus the output of the analysis can be presented in the form of pure dependency tree. In the same time we unify classes of derivation trees that correspond to one dependency structure. We then define a canonical form of the derivation to select one representative of the class that is used for assigning the edge probabilities.

This technique enables us to relate the output of our parser to the PDTB data. However, the profit of exploitation of the information from the dependency structures can be higher than that and can run in an automatically controlled environment. For this purpose, we use the mechanism of *pruning constraints*. A set of strict limitations is given to the syntactic analyser, which passes on just the compliant parses. The constraints can be either supplied manually for particular sentence by linguists, or obtained from the transformed dependency tree in PDTB.

The transformation is driven by guidelines specified by linguists. These guidelines relate the following information:

- *afun* – analytical function attribute from PDTB 1.0,
- *term* – corresponding nonterminal or preterminal from the metagrammar,
- *mtag* – morphological tag constraint,
- *lexit* – lexical item constraint.

The automatic procedure for generating the pruning constraints then successively tries to match the analytical function attribute in the input sentence with the records in the transformation guidelines. Each match found is then checked for agreement in the particular morphological tag and lexical item according to the given criteria (currently a pattern matching based on text regular expressions). If all required fields comport with the guidelines, the corresponding subtree is chosen as the specified nonterminal or preterminal from the metagrammar. The syntactic analysis with the pruning constraints applied then prunes those parsing trees from the resulting chart that do not contain the requested nonterminal or preterminal in that position.

Table 1. Simplified example of transformation guidelines.

#	afun	term	mtag	lexit
	Sb	np	k1	
	Sb_Ap	np		
	Obj	np		
	Atr	modif	k2	
	AuxP	pn		

If more than one records in the guidelines match, the first match is applied. This mechanism allows to prefer the most specific records to the general ones, which differ in the lexical item constraint or the morphological tag constraint only, used e.g. in the differentiation of various adverbial types:

#	afun	term	mtag	lexit
	Adv	np	k1	
	Adv	adv		

The process of transformation guidelines preparation is divided into several steps to assure the consistency of acquired pruning constraints. After every change, the results are checked against a testing set of input sentences and the differences are reported to the user for arbitration.

The integration of the pruning constraints obtained automatically through the mechanism of transformation guidelines has shown to be very efficient. The tedious work of the training data acquisition for the best analysis selection algorithm has been substantially facilitated. Examples of the reduction are displayed in the following table:

sentence #	# words	# analyses	# pruned analyses	reduced to (%)
00214	30	3112504044	2146560	0.07
00217	3	2	2	100
00287	12	56	4	7
00308	7	10	6	60
00486	6	1	1	100
00599	35	44660	4872	11
00612	25	2369063760	1048896	0.04
00842	17	409920	6336	1.5

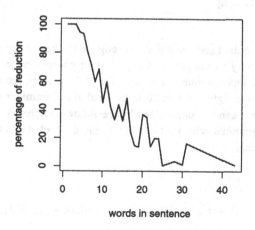

Fig. 1. The dependency of the reduction (%) of the number of resulting analyses on the number of words in the input sentence.

The table presents examples of sentences which were randomly chosen from the set of 1000 sentences analysed first without pruning constraints and then with automatically generated pruning constraints.

The average percentage of reduction on all the tested sentences has achieved 30 % (see Figure 1). The future work on the refinement of transformation guidelines will be concentrated on further reduction of the number of automatically pruned analysis trees.

3 Parser Comparison

The effectivity comparison of different parsers and parsing techniques brings a strong impulse to improving the actual implementations. Since there is no other generally applicable and available NL parser for Czech, we have compared the running times of our syntactic analyser on the data provided at

　　　http://www.cogs.susx.ac.uk/lab/nlp/carroll/cfg-resources/.

These web pages resulted from discussions at the Efficiency in Large Scale Parsing Systems Workshop at COLING 2000, where one of the main conclusions was the need for a bank of data for standardization of parser benchmarking.

3.1 HDddm Parsing Technique

The parsing technique of our system is based on the head driven approach with improvements regarding the process of confirmation of viable hypotheses. The HDddm (head driven with dependent dot move) parsing technique refers to the fact that the move of one "dot" in the head driven parsing step is dependent on the opposite move of the other one.

The head of a grammar rule is a symbol from the right hand side. For example, the second nonterminal (np) is denoted as the head symbol in the following grammar rule

```
np -> left_modif np
    head($2)
```

The epsilon rule has a special head symbol ϵ. The edge in the head driven parser is a triplet $[A \rightarrow \alpha_\bullet \beta_\bullet \gamma, i, j]$, where i, j are integers, $0 \leq i \leq j \leq n$ for n words in the input sentence and $A \rightarrow \alpha \beta \gamma$ is a rule in the input grammar. The direction of the parsing process does not move unidirectionally from left to right, but it starts at the head of the grammar rule.

The parsing algorithm can be summarized by the following schema, where the symbol G stands for the input grammar with a set of rules P and the root symbol S, $a_1, \ldots, a_n$ are input words (preterminals):

Initialisation phase

1. for each $p \in P \mid p = A \rightarrow \epsilon$ add edges $[A \rightarrow {}_{\bullet\bullet}, 0, 0], [A \rightarrow {}_{\bullet\bullet}, 1, 1], \ldots, [A \rightarrow {}_{\bullet\bullet}, n, n]$ to the chart.
2. for each $p \in P \mid p = A \rightarrow \alpha \underline{a_i} \beta$ (a_i is the head of the rule) add edge $[A \rightarrow \alpha_\bullet a_i{}_\bullet \beta$, i-1, i] to the chart.

Iteration phase

1. if edge E in the chart is in the form $[A \rightarrow \,_\bullet\alpha_\bullet, j, k]$, then for each edge:
   $[B \rightarrow \beta_\bullet\gamma_\bullet A\delta, i, j]$ in the chart, create edge $[B \rightarrow \beta_\bullet\gamma A_\bullet\delta, i, k]$.
   $[B \rightarrow \beta A_\bullet\gamma_\bullet, k, l]$ in the chart, create edge $[B \rightarrow \beta_\bullet A\gamma_\bullet, j, l]$.
2. if E is in the form $[B \rightarrow \beta_\bullet\gamma_\bullet A\delta, i, j]$, then for each edge $[A \rightarrow \,_\bullet\alpha_\bullet, j, k]$ in the chart, create edge $[B \rightarrow \beta_\bullet\gamma A_\bullet\delta, i, k]$.
3. if E is in the form $[B \rightarrow \beta A_\bullet\gamma_\bullet, k, l]$, then for each edge $[A \rightarrow \,_\bullet\alpha_\bullet, j, k]$ in the chart, create edge $[B \rightarrow \beta_\bullet A\gamma_\bullet, j, l]$.
4. if E is in the form $[A \rightarrow \beta_\bullet\gamma_\bullet a_{j+1}\delta, i, j]$, then create edge $[A \rightarrow \beta_\bullet\gamma a_{j+1}\delta, i, j+1]$.
5. if E is in the form $[A \rightarrow \beta a_{i\bullet}\gamma_\bullet, i, j]$, then create edge $[A \rightarrow \beta_\bullet a_i\gamma_\bullet, i\text{-}1, j]$.
6. if E is in the form $[A \rightarrow \,_\bullet\alpha_\bullet, i, j]$, then for each rule $B \rightarrow \beta\,\underline{A}\,\gamma$ in the input grammar, create edge $[B \rightarrow \beta_\bullet A_\bullet\gamma, i, j]$ (symbol A is the head of the rule).

N.B., that the left dot in the edge cannot move leftwards until the right dot moves to the right. The parser never creates edges like $[A \rightarrow \alpha_\bullet\beta A\gamma_\bullet\delta, i, j]$ for non empty β. This approach avoids the redundant analysis of such edges. On the other hand, the parser does not use any top-down filtering or "follow check" technique.

The efficiency of the parser depends to a considerable extent on the choice of grammar rule heads. The current positions of heads in our grammar have been chosen experimentally and they accords with the conception of the leading constituent in the traditional Czech grammars.

3.2 Running Time Comparison

The best results reported on standard data sets (ATIS, CT and PT grammars) until today are the comparison data by Robert C. Moore [1]. In the package, only the testing grammars with input sentences are at the disposal, the release of referential implementation of the parser is currently being prepared (Moore, personal communication).

Table 2. Test grammars and test sentences.

Grammar	CT	Atis	PT
Rules	24,456	4,592	15,039
Nonterminals	3,946	192	38
Terminals	1,032	357	47
Test sentences	162	98	30
Average Parses	5.4	940	more than 2^{64}
Grammar	CT	Atis	PT

The basic characteristics of the testing grammars are presented in Table 2. A detailed description of these grammars is given in the [4].

The results of the parser comparison appear in Table 3. The values in the table give the total CPU times in seconds required by the parser to completely process the test set associated with the grammar.

Table 3. Running times comparison (in seconds).

ATIS grammar, Moore's LC_3 + UTF	11.6
ATIS grammar, our system	4.19
CT grammar, Moore's LC_3 + UTF	3.1
CT grammar, our system	4.19
PT grammar, Moore's LC_3 + UTF	41.8
PT grammar, our system	17.75

Since we could not run the referential implementation of Moore's parser on the same machine, the above mentioned times are not fully comparable (we assume that our tests were run on a slightly faster machine than that of Moore's tests). We prepare a detailed comparison, which will try to explain the differences of results when parsing with grammars of varying ambiguity level.

The longer running times on the data of the CT grammar are caused by little ambiguity of the grammar, so that our parsing technique optimized for highly ambiguous grammars cannot display its strong suits.

4 Conclusions

The methods of the best analysis selection algorithm show that the parsing of inflectional languages calls for sensitive approaches to the evaluation of the appropriate figures of merit. The acquisition of these output arranging quantities is based on a representative training data set. The method of pruning constraints described in this paper enables to automate the process of treebank corpus transformation.

The integration of the presented methods to the parsing system has no destructive impact on the efficiency of the parser. This is documented by the comparison of the running times. Our system outperforms the results of the best referential parsing system on highly ambiguous grammars, for which it is optimized.

Future directions of our research lead to improvements of the quality of training data set so that it would cover all the most frequent language phenomena. The overall efficiency of the parser will be guaranteed by supplementary filtering techniques, which are going to be implemented.

References

1. R. C. Moore. Improved left-corner chart parsing for large context-free grammars. In: *Proceedings of the 6th IWPT*, pp. 171–182, Trento, Italy, 2000.
2. Pavel Smrž and Aleš Horák. Large scale parsing of Czech. In *Proceedings of Efficiency in Large-Scale Parsing Systems Workshop, COLING 2000*, pp. 43–50, Saarbrücken: Universität des Saarlandes, 2000.
3. H. Bunt and A. Nijholt, editors. *Advances in Probabilistic and Other Parsing Technologies*. Kluwer Academic Publishers, 2000.
4. R. C. Moore. Time as a measure of parsing efficiency. In *Proceedings of Efficiency in Large-Scale Parsing Systems Workshop, COLING 2000*, pp. 23–28, Saarbrücken: Universität des Saarlandes, 2000.

Author Index

Subject Index

Lecture Notes in Artificial Intelligence (LNAI)

Lecture Notes in Computer Science